THE HASIDIC ANTHOLOGY

Tales and Teachings of the Hasidim

THE
HASIDIC ANTHOLOGY

Tales and Teachings of the Hasidim

Translated from the Hebrew, Yiddish, and German
Selected, Compiled and Arranged by

LOUIS I. NEWMAN

IN COLLABORATION WITH
SAMUEL SPITZ

SCHOCKEN BOOKS · NEW YORK

First Schocken Paperback edition, 1963

Second Printing, 1968

TABLE OF CONTENTS

TABLE OF CONTENTS

TABLE OF CONTENTS ix

INTRODUCTION

THE HASIDIM: THEIR HISTORY, LITERATURE AND DOCTRINES

By Louis I. Newman

This Anthology of Hasidic lore and wisdom derives its material from the utterances attributed to the leaders and sages of the religious movement of Hasidism which originated during the middle of the 18th century in Podolia, with the appearance of Israel ben Eliezer (1700-1760), the "Master of the Good Name," the "Baal Shem Tov" or the "Besht," as he came to be known. The parables, tales, aphorisms, epigrams, fables, anecdotes, exegetical comments and interpretations ascribed to the Besht formed the foundation for the sayings and writings of his contemporary Disciples and their descendants, and for the succeeding generations of their descendants who carried forward his legacy. The leaders of the movement came to be known as "Zaddikim" or "Righteous Ones" and their adherents as "Hasidim" or "Pious Ones." An oral tradition incorporated first in manuscripts and later printed in book form, arose among the millions of the followers of Hasidism, remaining fluid until today, ever broadening and deepening among the Jewish masses, mainly of Eastern Europe, and in other centers of populous Jewish settlement throughout the world as well.

The movement of Hasidism is one of the most remarkable manifestations of the religious spirit in modern times. Humble in origin, it has won for itself the increasing attention and appreciation of scholars and the general public, and it is today the subject of enthusiastic study and comment in rationalistic circles of Western countries. Its chief emphasis has been upon a sense of mystical ecstasy in the communion of God and man; upon the joyful affirmation of life; upon compassion, charity and love; upon democracy and brotherhood between the rich and the poor; and upon the moral values of the religious system. Hasidism is Judaism with particular points of interest, emphasis and practice; it is a free and intensely emotional expression of Judaism adapted to the common people. Out of the experience of multitudes of Masters and Disciples for nearly two centuries has emerged a vast, many-sided and fascinating literature, from which it is possible to cull masterpieces of spiritual and ethical insight. Hasidism is more than a cult; it is a culture.

The career of Hasidism may be divided into two major eras: the first, the period of the 18th and early 19th century until 1815; the second, the period embracing most of the 19th century when the movement reached the height of its outward success, and later entered into the phase of general spiritual retrogression. (Dubnow, i, 69-70.)* These two epochs may be subdivided into the following four periods: first, the period of the rise of Hasidism (1740-81), covering the activity of the Founder, the Besht, as well as of his first Disciples, the Great Maggid, Dov Baer of Mezeritz and Rabbi Jacob Joseph ha-Kohen of Polennoye (the Pulnoer); it includes also the first years of the struggle between the leaders of Rabbinism and Hasidism; second: the period of growth and dissemination (1782-1815) during which Hasidism captured the masses of the folk with amazing rapidity; at the same time, the dynasties of the Zaddikim branch out among the communities of Eastern Europe; Hasidic centers increase, and Hasidic doctrines undergo many variations and refinements; the struggle between the Hasidim and their Opponents, the "Mithnagedim" reaches its height during this period, and the religious schism is definitely established; third, the period of the strengthening of Zaddikism, the phase of the movement which centered about the personality of the Zaddikim, the Saints and Perfect or Righteous Ones of the cult; the advocates of Haskalah, or "Enlightenment" enlist in the battle against certain aspects of the movement (1815-1870); Hasidic doctrine is absorbed more and more by the cult of the Zaddikim who oftentimes tend to subordinate the rationalistic principle, so fundamental in Judaism, to superstition and thaumaturgy; a fanatical zeal is directed against the independent thought of the Maskilim by the apologists of Hasidism; fourth, the period of Hasidism's decline (from 1870 to the present time); European secular culture makes profound inroads into Hasidic civilization; the new Hebrew literature undermines the Hasidic philosophy of life among the younger generation. Nevertheless the common people remain under the spell of the movement and its Zaddikim, and though few distinguished personalities arise among them, certain of the leaders maintain their sway over hundreds of thousands of faithful followers. The literary creative power of Hasidism is weakened in its "old age," and the current of Jewish interest sweeps into new channels. Side by side with Rabbinism, Hasidism remains one of the major pillars supporting traditional Judaism in contemporary life.

ISRAEL BAAL SHEM TOV, THE BESHT

The beginnings of Hasidism can be understood chiefly through the personality of Israel Baal Shem Tov, the Besht, who looms with

*Dubnow references are to *Geschichte des Chassidismus* by Simon Dubnow, 2 vols., Berlin, 1931.

titanic size in the history of modern religions. A simple villager, born in Okop (Tlust), Podolia, on the old Polish-Turkish border, he demonstrated himself to be a man of striking magnetism, intense religious fervor and sage human insight. He became renowned first as a traditional miracle-worker, a "Baal Shem," or "Master of the Name," the Magic Name of God, wherewith he was reputed to perform wonders. He drew to himself many followers (see 97:9, p. 242), who added the adjective "Tov" or "Good" to his appellation, thereby indicating the reverence and confidence he enjoyed among the folk. The Rabbis of the regions where he resided or visited soon came to oppose him because of his supposed lack of Talmudic scholarship and his magical practices, but he rapidly gained in authority and fame. The group about him attained the dimensions of a sect, and then broadened out into a movement of far-flung influence and power.

The Besht brought his message into a Jewish world torn by the contrasts of the mysticism of Isaac Luria of Safed (1534-1572), the Talmudic legalism which for centuries had been the dominant force in Jewish life, and the aftermath of the Pseudo-Messianic movement of Sabbatai Zevi which had continued to win allegiance among multitudes even after its central hero in 1666 had abandoned Judaism for Islam. During the early eighteenth century the social and economic circumstances of Polish Jewry were deplorable (Dubnow, i, 29 ff.). The people were the target of religious incitement by the Catholic ecclesiastical group, the secular authorities imposed onerous taxes, pogroms were frequent, the ritual murder charge was promoted to arouse the peasantry against Jewish communities, opportunity for general education was almost non-existent, and the morale of Polish Jewry was at its lowest ebb. To offset the gloom and hardships of the Jewish masses, the Besht began a ministry, seeking to underscore the joyful affirmation of life. He counselled against asceticism and self-affliction, preaching instead the hallowing of all passions and delight in the service of God. He condemned retirement from the world and recommended active participation in human experiences, accepting life with gratitude, enthusiasm and resolution.

Though the activity of the Besht covers a period of more than twenty-five years, his literary "reliquiae" consist of only a few letters. The Master did not write down his doctrines, but communicated them by word of mouth to his pupils, or Disciples, and friends. Two of the Besht's letters severely criticize fasting and self-castigation as iniquitous inventions of Satan who desires to alienate man from God. To his Disciple and literary legatee, Rabbi Jacob Joseph, the Pulnoer, the Besht wrote in admonition against the extreme asceticism to which for the moment his Disciple had submitted.

To understand the manner in which the Besht transmitted his teachings, it is necessary to describe the procedure by which the oral tradition of the Hasidim came into being. The Besht's pupils listened to him in conversations; in public addresses; at the discourse on the occasion of the Third Sabbath Meal; in the synagogue, when he expounded portions of the Law, and on other relevant occasions, in the circle of his adherents. Sometimes his Disciples made annotations directly from his spoken words; sometimes these notes were on the basis of hearsay and reports of other persons who had been present, or who had received an account of the Besht's utterances at second-hand; sometimes an imaginative record of his statements would be written down. These notes necessarily, therefore, were incomplete and frequently incorrect, inasmuch as students rarely reproduce with accuracy the opinions of their instructors. Emendations, alterations, additions, and individual interpretations entered into the body of authentic material for which the Master himself was responsible. It is not surprising to read that the Besht once exclaimed, at the sight of a written record of his oral teaching: "I have not spoken a single word of this" (Spiegel, i, 153).* When the sayings and stories of the Besht and the Disciples who followed him in succeeding generations were disseminated among the people, they received even more embellishment and change.

JESUS AND THE BESHT; HASIDISM AND CHRISTIANITY

Like Jesus, the Besht appreciated that he could secure the allegiance of the common people only if he permitted them to disseminate stories about his powers of healing, his miracles as a wonder-worker and the like. History is filled with such examples. Hasidism commenced with the thaumaturgy of a Baal Shem, but it eventuated in a religion and cult for millions; Christianity, likewise, began with the wonder-deeds of a young Rabbi, and through the multiplicity of forces playing upon it, became a faith for vast multitudes. Though originally a Jewish movement, Christianity moved outside the circle of the national life of Israel; Hasidism, however, persisted as a Jewish movement, influencing in modern times more and more non-Jews, but remaining dominantly a message to the Jewish folk. It gives an inkling of what the preachment of Jesus, the Master and his Disciples might have become, if Hellenic, Roman and other alien elements had not been synchronized with it, in order to form the basis for the new faith of Pauline Christianity. Jesus was an "artist in parable and a master of morality" as Joseph Klausner has

*Spiegel references are to *Hebrew Reborn* by Shalom Spiegel, New York, 1930.

called him; the Besht also was supremely effective as a teacher of ethics through the medium of parables, folk-tales, aphorisms, fables, epigrams and sermons. Both men were mystics, with an intense sense of the Immediacy and Omnipresence of God, the Loving Father. Both men gathered about themselves bands of Disciples, with whom they stood in the classic relationship of Rabbi (Master) and Pupil (Disciple). Jesus developed his system upon the foundation of traditional Jewish teaching, and gave to it at the same time a personal direction and content; the Besht, also, accepted the fundamentals of the inheritance of Israel, but emphasized those features which appealed to his own individuality and temperament, thereby creating a new group in Jewry with its own creed and practices.

The chief difference between early Christianity and Hasidism lies in the absence among the Hasidim of a political interest: the ideal of the Messiah plays a role in its teaching, but no single personality was selected to whom adoring Disciples attributed the title of Redeemer. The career of Jesus in this respect must be compared in Jewish history to the activities of the Pseudo-Messiahs, such as Moses of Crete, Abraham Abulafia, David Alroy, Sabbatai Zevi in the 17th and Jacob Frank in the 18th century. The Hasidim had many points of association with the governments of the countries wherein they were active, and oftentimes the secular authorities intervened in their affairs. Moreover, the tribulations and sufferings of Israel weighed heavily upon them, and they prayed and worked for the ingathering of scattered Israel, and the restoration of Palestine. But the Hasidim did not focus these interests in a Neo-Messianic effort, nor was this the motive force in their ethical, religious and social system. The political environment wherein Jesus and his Disciples found themselves, brought about the special circumstances which resulted in the tragic death of the Master at the hands of the Roman overlords. Among the Hasidim, however, the Messianic ideal remained what it undoubtedly would have remained among the followers of Jesus, namely, the hope for an era of perfection when the highest aspirations of man, created in the image of God, would be realized. The Besht lived for sixty years, was subjected to no known persecution by the non-Jewish rulers of the Ukraine and Poland, and died in peace. During the last four years of his life, the Besht witnessed the influence of the Frankist movement in his vicinity, a Pseudo-Messianic movement, based on the Sabbataian "heresy," which resulted in the conversion of its adherents to the Christian faith. There are legends regarding the appearance of the "Turkish Messiah," Sabbatai Zevi, to the Besht, but, it is recounted, the Besht when subjected to temptation, thrust him away so mightily that Zevi fell into the regions where he beheld him in the same plane as Jesus. The Besht declared that in Zevi there had been a holy spark, but the Satan had caught him in his net.

LEADING DISCIPLES OF THE BESHT AND
THEIR WORKS

We may turn now to a consideration of a few of the leading Disciples of the Besht and their writings, in an endeavor to trace the continuing channel of Hasidic literature. Though the Pulnoer is the first inheritor of the Besht's tradition, it obtained an even finer expression through the "Great Maggid," Rabbi Dov Baer of Mezeritz (1710-1772). This Disciple of the Master was eager to give permanence to his philosophy in book form, but he was too gifted a teacher to be able to write, and his time was dedicated to the protection of the youthful Hasidic movement from the onslaughts of its adversaries. The Maggid's own formulations have been brought down to posterity in the unreliable records of his pupils, although independent Zaddikim of note carried forward his doctrines with clarity, power and literary skill. Rabbi Solomon of Luck in 1784 issued at Koretz a selection of the Sabbath sermons which he had heard his Master preach, under the title: *Maggid Devarav Le-Yaakov* or *Likkutei Amarim,* which went through several editions and became the foundation for other collections, some of which were issued without the name of the Disciples responsible.

Rabbi Menachem Mendel of Vitebsk (d. 1788), like the "Great Maggid" continued the concept of the Omnipresence of God, to be found in the soul of all things; and in 1814, Israel Joffe, at Kopyss, issued his *Peri ha-Aretz (Fruit of the Earth),* the Sabbath sermons of the Vitebsker, together with utterances of Rabbi Abraham, the son of the "Great Maggid." Rabbi Menachem Mendel occupies a unique place in Hasidic history because of his migration to Palestine and the encouragement he thereby gave to Hasidic interest in the rebirth of Zion.

Rabbi Schneur Zalman of Ladi (d. 1813) is regarded as the founder of the important system of "Habad" Hasidism, laying emphasis upon Wisdom, Reason and Knowledge, the initials of these words in Hebrew forming the descriptive phrase. Lithuanian rationalism, the desire to restore to Rabbinic study its authority as a pathway to God, and an affection for the mystical lore of the Kabbalah combined to make the "Habad" School a vital force in the extension of the movement. Rabbi Schneur Zalman issued in 1796 a re-working of the *Shulchan Arukh,* and in the same year, the *Tanya,* his vigorous portrayal of Hasidic doctrine was printed . Rabbi Schneur oftentimes echoes words of his old friend, the Vitebsker, and though the Berditschever, the Medzibozer and other colleagues did not hesitate to offer critical comment upon the Ladier's viewpoint, the author of the *Tanya* won the widest esteem and reverence.

Rabbi Nachman of Bratzlav (1772-1810), great-grandson of the Besht, is without doubt the foremost narrator of Tales which Hasidism has produced, and is considered by many as the "greatest story-teller" of the Jewish people. The narratives of the Bratzlaver are quaint, filled with visions, supernatural events and personalities, fables of complex, but vivid imagery, "convincing in their concrete-ness, most audacious in their fantasy, and ennobled by a profound symbolism." The Bratzlaver's tales were intended not only to relieve the distress of the people, as the Besht had wished through the medium of his instruction, but chiefly to serve as a "vestment for his doctrines. Although his motive was to teach, his stories grew beyond their purpose, losing themselves in an overflowing abundance of vivid invention and fanciful detail that causes both author and hearer to forget their didactic aim" (Spiegel, p. 158).

MAJOR FOUNDATIONS OF HASIDIC WRITINGS

The foundations of Hasidic literature are the classic writings of the Jewish literary heritage, and there is scarcely a feature of the movement which is not discernible in previous aspects of Jewish life. The Besht himself was a combination of the Rabbi, the Maggid, or Preacher, and the Seer, or Prophet. His followers, the Zaddikim, received not only their name from Hebraic literature, but their per-sonality and outlook represented certain phases of Judaism raised to an intense and oftentimes extreme degree. The adherents of the Zaddikim adopted a Biblical name, applied many centuries before to the "Hasidim" who formed the spearhead of the heroic defense against the Hellenizers in pre-Maccabean Palestine, and who became the precursors of the Pharisees, from whose midst Jesus himself emerged.

When the Hasidim turned to the Torah, it was with an appre-ciation of its contribution to the evolution of Israel and its faith, but they constantly stressed the gentle and amiable features of the Law. They were great lovers of the Psalms, the verses of which they delighted to paraphrase, in order to elicit the message of toler-ance, kindliness, forbearance and good-will, uppermost in their own system of belief. They rejoiced in the fervor and ecstasy of the Psalmists, and amply quoted those Psalms which underscored their own deep yearning for communion with the Universal God, the Omnipresent Being Whose chief attributes in their eyes were Love, Forgiveness and Grace. They found the Prophets a source of stimulating instruction, but the larger political and international preachment of an Isaiah, an Amos and a Jeremiah, seemed less mean-ingful to them than their utterances regarding inner faith, charity, sincere religion of the heart, and the good life. The Song of Songs was particularly appealing to the Hasidim because its imagery was useful not only in describing Israel as the Bride of God, but also to voice their own sense of immediate association with the Loving Being in the Heavens. The exegetical comments of the Hasidim, which formed so substantial a part of their literature, are in direct line of descent with the works of the great commentators of Jewish history, but it was inevitable that the Hasidic writers should turn their interpretation of Holy Writ to their own doctrinal interests. As a result the Hasidic exegetes and preachers took considerable liberty with Biblical texts, and paraphrased Biblical verses according to their special ethical or mystical inclination. Included within the Hasidic commentaries are expressions of moral principles, tales, and epigrams of extraordinary beauty, which patient readers and investigators have sought to cull and oftentimes re-work. Nothing is so revelatory of Hasidic psychology as its Biblical commentaries, wherein the teachings of love, joy, pity, humility and inwardness are reinforced by the appeal to sacred authorities.

The *Pirkei Avoth,* or the *Ethics of the Fathers,* the classic compilation of Rabbinic ethical maxims uttered before and during the Talmudic era, naturally became a favorite source for Hasidic quotation and discussion. Many of the moral judgments of the Hasidim constitute in themselves a "New Ethics of the Fathers," and in some instances, tend to surpass the ancient model, in their pungency, insight and literary power. Unlike the Karaites who had combatted the Rabbis eight centuries before, the Hasidim did not turn aside from the Talmud. Depending largely upon the temperament and outlook of individual Zaddikim, they allowed individual leaders great freedom in their approach to Rabbinic literature. Many Zaddikim found stimulus in a discussion of the Halakhah, or Talmudic jurisprudence, and several selections of this Anthology deal with moot questions of Jewish law. Other Zaddikim were not interested primarily in Jewish legalism. All, however, occupied themselves with the Midrash, which, by and large, may be said to have proved the chief inspiration of Hasidic teaching. The Midrash contains imaginative fiction of ethical import, folk-tales, parables, legends, biographies, bits of human experience narrated in graphic form with a moral message, either by implication or directly expressed; fables, transmitted from the literature of other peoples, or originating in Jewish life; aphorisms, epigrams, and sayings of wisdom. It was therefore upon the Midrash that the great preachers of Israel drew for their chief illustrative material.

Another foundation-element in the making of Hasidism was the Kabbalah, or the tradition of Jewish esoteric lore. The Besht and his followers emphasized the essentials of Kabbalistic cosmology, but once more the temperament and individuality of the various Zaddikim determined the use to which the mystical literature of Israel should be placed. The *Zohar,* the writings of the "Ari" or Rabbi Isaac Luria of Safed and other Kabbalists profoundly influenced Hasidism, particularly at its inception, but the movement went far beyond the Kabbalah in its application of a doctrine adapted to reality, and in its preachment of a new morality.

HASIDIC TALES AND SAYINGS

The tales of the Hasidim are marked by terseness, brevity and directness. They are models of simplicity and compactness. These stylistic qualities grew out of the importance which the Zaddikim attached to the instruction of the untutored and humble folk among their adherents.

The message of the Hasidic tales and teachings can be best understood when it is remembered that the Besht spoke in sublime similes, like all primary religious figures, wherewith to convince the learned; but he also possessed the power to fascinate the masses with his tales. "Tradition adds that these tales were such that everyone heard in them a personal message which was to shape his entire life, although they addressed themselves to all. These tales which have come down in his name are, indeed, charming in their simplicity and marvelous in their fantasy" (Spiegel, p. 157). The Lizensker once contrasted himself with Rabbi Schmelke, saying that whereas the latter cured the spirit by means of delicate medicines, he was but a "horse doctor," and he could give treatment only with plain and homely medicines, such as the Ten Commandments (135:4; p. 346). The message of the Zaddikim depended upon the particular viewpoint of the individual teacher. Rabbi Dov Baer, the Great Maggid, was interested in communal organization; the Berditschever stressed "the higher fear" which led to the higher enjoyment and the "higher love"; the Ladier, as we have seen, stressed the study of the Torah, and Wisdom, Reason, and Knowledge; the Karliner believed that the "Zaddik should carry the flock" as a father carries his child; the Ropshitzer was a man of great wit and insight; Rabbi Bunam was a rationalist par excellence. Each outstanding Zaddik had his own special points of emphasis.

Nevertheless the very factors in the environment which gave birth to Hasidism, and the severities to which the Jews of Eastern Europe were subjected, left its imprint upon the substance and tendencies of the movement. Its constant reiteration of the message of pity, love and forgiveness may have arisen because the daily experience of the Hasidim at the hands of others lacked these qualities so sadly; their interest in joy, laughter, gaiety, the song, the dance and the cup of cheer may have been a compensation for the gloom and rigor of much of life as they witnessed it round about; their insistence upon enthusiasm and enkindlement in worship, and upon sincerity in conduct and observance may have been a foil for the tepid and formalistic traits of much of Jewish observance in their neighborhood; their preachment of humility, modesty, democracy and brotherhood may have been offered as a curative for unwarranted distinctions between the learned and the ignorant, the rich and the poor, the powerful and the weak.

The stories and sayings of this Anthology portray the message

of Hasidism more eloquently than any commentary regarding them.
The most indifferent reader cannot but be impressed by the intrinsic
mood of Hasidic lore. The utterances of the Hasidim are replete
with wisdom; they breathe loving kindness and mercy; they exalt
the inwardness of faith far above mere ceremonial piety. They display a moving relationship between the Master and the Disciple;
they commend the virtue of charity, and the duty to practice it; they
endeavour to illustrate the vanity of human possessions, and the
importance of spiritual and moral values. They enjoin the rich to
abstain from pride of wealth and the powerful not to vaunt themselves in their might. They link the individual with the community,
with the people of Israel, with humanity and with God. They preach
sincerity and fervor in worship; they stress compassion for the sinner
and forgiveness of his transgressions; they describe God as a Merciful and Compassionate Being, against Whom mortals can render
judgment if He afflicts them heartlessly. Hasidic theology at moments
is pantheistic; at others Humanistic, in the sense in which the term
has gained currency today; at still other moments, it is traditionally
in line with pristine Jewish concepts of God, the Soul, and their
communion. Hasidism has all the contradictions inevitable in a
movement which affected millions of believers, and it is possible to
find statements on opposite sides of almost every theme of this Anthology. Nevertheless Hasidism remains basically Judaism in its
particularistic and universalistic aspects, but its peculiar flavor lies
in its elevation into prominence of the more tender, sympathetic and
humane elements of Jewish thought and practice.

1. THE AFTER-LIFE

1. What Is Paradise?

The Oheler Rabbi dreamed that he was in Paradise and was conducted to the Room of the Tannaim. He beheld a Tanna studying the Talmud. "Is this, then, all there is to Paradise?" the Rabbi exclaimed. He heard a voice answer him: "Moses, you believe the Tannaim are in Paradise. You are wrong. Paradise is in the Tannaim."

P. v. K., p. 12a.

2. Charity to the Departed

The Apter Rabbi invited the Lizensker to abide with him when he came to Apt. In the morning he entered his guest's room and heard the Lizensker say to himself: "Melech, Melech, how sinful you are! You deserve no share in the World-to-Come by any act of yours! But we are taught that God Himself observes His own Torah. Therefore, it follows that God dispenses charity. And what is God's charity to departed souls? He donates a share in the World-to-Come to those who are poor in good deeds. Hence, I am emboldened to hope I may receive a portion of His charity."

E. Tz., p. 30.

3. The Wedding Ring

Said Rabbi Bunam: "The Talmud compares this world to a wedding.[1] It is as if a man laboriously makes every preparation for his marriage, but forgets to purchase a wedding ring; hence, the ceremony cannot proceed. In the same way, a man may labor his entire life, but forget to sanctify himself through the Torah and the Mitzwoth. When he comes to the Eternal World he cannot enter, and his whole life is for naught."

S. I., p. 60.

[1] Erubin, 54.

4. Creating Paradise

Said the Mezeritzer Maggid: "A man's kind deeds are utilized by the Lord as seed for the planting of trees in the Garden of Eden; thus, each man creates his own Paradise. The reverse is true when he commits transgressions."

E. O., p. 32.

I

5. Neighbors in the After-Life

The Ropshitzer said: "I would rather sit near a man of intelligence in Purgatory than near a man of folly in Paradise."

M. D., p. 243.

When Rabbi Simeon Yaraslaver heard the Ropshitzer's remark, he exclaimed: "I vow that no man of folly ever enters Paradise."

Ohel N., p. 114.

6. His Reward

The Koznitzer Maggid said: "God is my witness that my chief enjoyment is a fervent prayer. God grants me this pleasure as a reward for the few good deeds which I have performed. I truly fear that I shall have no further compensation left for my 'future life.' "

N. H. K., p. 15.

7. The After-World

Said the Koretzer: "All Israel shall have a share in the World-to-Come, but not an equal share.

"We are commanded to fast on Yom Kippur [1] as a symbol of reminder that the pleasures of the After-Life do not include either food or drink. Maimonides teaches that there is neither fire nor water, nor any other material substance in the World of the Spirit."

Nof. Tz., p. 21.

[1] Lev. 23:27.

8. Enjoyments in Paradise

Said the Koretzer: "All pleasures, even a witty saying, come to you from your share in Paradise. The more you enjoy in this world, the less will be left over to you in the World-to-Come. Be wise, therefore, and restrain yourself in the pursuit of pleasures. Leave a portion for your enjoyment in the After-Life which is everlasting."

M. P., p. 12.

9. The Foolish Rebbe

Said the Ropshitzer: "We are told by our Sages [1] that the wicked rest on the Sabbath in Purgatory. It stands to reason that if a man was accustomed during his lifetime to spend his Sabbath at a Rebbe's, and that the Rebbe is now in Paradise, he should be granted permission to visit his Rabbi there. And what a foolish person the Rebbe would be if he allowed his adherent to be returned to Purgatory!"

E. Tz., p. 92.

[1] Zohar, in the Preface.

10. Master and Disciple

Rabbi Bunam asked his disciple, the Kotzker Rabbi: "If, after death, I am ordered to go to Gehenna, what shall I do?"
The Kotzker made no reply.
"I will tell you what I shall do," continued Rabbi Bunam. "I shall quote the phrase from the Talmud: [1] 'If a disciple is banished, his teacher is banished with him,' and I shall demand that my teachers, the 'Yud' and the 'Seer' of Lublin be ordered to follow me."
The Kotzker Rabbi remarked: "For you, Rabbi, this supposition is merely theoretical, but for me it will prove valuable."

S. S. K., ii, 16.

[1] Makkoth, 10.

11. Purgatory for the Wicked

Said the Pulnoer: "No Purgatory can be worse for the wicked than permission to enter the Garden of Eden. They find there no pleasure to which they were addicted in life: no eating or drinking or any other pleasures of the body. They see merely Zaddikim, deriving great joy from the nearness of the Lord. And who are these Zaddikim, who occupy places of prominence in Paradise? They are the very persons upon whom the wicked poured out their scorn in life, and whose learning they thoroughly despised. What, then, can these wicked persons feel in Paradise but bitterness? Can they know the joy of the Shekinah's nearness, inasmuch as they never trained themselves in their lifetime for the enjoyments of the spirit?"

Kahana, p. 134.

12. The Two Palaces

Said the Besht: "Frequently we observe a Zaddik lamenting unto the Lord because of his poverty, yet failing to gain any improvement of his position. This should not be construed to mean that the Lord does not concern himself for the Zaddik. Nay, it is rather a sign of God's great love for him. A parable will illustrate this: 'A prince of tender age built himself a little house of toy boards. A careless servant inadvertently struck it with his foot, and the fragile structure fell to pieces. The weeping child complained to the king and besought him to punish the servant. The king, however, had secretly intended to surprise his beloved son by building for him a miniature palace of solid and beautiful materials. Therefore, knowing of the rare gift in store for the prince, he did not act upon the lad's complaint.'
"It is the same with the Zaddik, God's cherished son. The Lord has made ready for him a splendid abode in Paradise. He, therefore, gives slight attention to the Zaddik's complaints of temporary discomforts in this insignificant world below."

K. S. T., p. 16a.

13. The Purpose of Martyrdom

Said the Besht: "We are told in the Talmud [1] that when Moses ascended to Heaven to receive the Law, he found God occupied with forming the ornaments to the letters of the Torah. He was told that Rabbi Akiba would find a meaning in each ornament. Moses declared: 'I see his knowledge; may I be privileged to behold his reward?' He was, thereupon, shown the sight of Rabbi Akiba undergoing cruel torture at the hands of the Romans. Moses asked: 'Is this then the reward of the Torah?' God replied: 'Be silent; thus has it come to Me in Thought.'

"The explanation is, as follows: A Zaddik's soul does not at first ascend to the upper regions of Paradise. In the beginning he resides in a lower Eden, where he is still in incomplete bliss; only by degrees is he conducted to higher and higher realms. If he has left a son or a daughter or a fund of money for charity, and is remembered through the offering of a prayer and charity on the anniversary of his death, this memorial serves as an aid in the ascension of the Zaddik in Paradise.

"Rabbi Akiba, however, was so perfect a Zaddik and labored so industriously in learning and teaching the Holy Torah, that God wished to lead his soul immediately to the highest region of Paradise. This is the region known as 'Thought.' And He subjected Rabbi Akiba to a cruel death in order to cleanse his soul of any slight impurities which may have contaminated it."

K. S. T., p. 26a.

[1] Menachoth, 29b.

14. The Penitent's Privilege

Our Sages teach that a penitent may gain access to a place in Heaven which is barred even to the perfect Zaddik.[1] Rabbi Israel Isaac of Alexander explained this in a parable:

"A man visited the King's palace, and was informed he might not open any doors marked 'private.' A day later, however, he was pursued by a band of brigands, and as he passed the palace entrance, he found sanctuary in a private room. He explained his action, saying that he feared being slain in the crowded public chambers, as the brigands might be lost in the crowd. No penalty was, therefore, visited upon him.

"In the same way, the penitent, escaping the Evil Angels created by his sins, is permitted to enter the secret chambers of Heaven, closed to others, even to the Zaddikim."

M. H. H., p. 4.

[1] Sanhedrin, 99; Berakhoth, 34.

15. The Goodness of Life

Said Rabbi Bunam: "Life is good, for it may bring to a man the joys of the World-to-Come. Hence, if one shows contempt for life by self-destruction, he is deprived of his share in the World-to-Come."

R. T., p. 164.

16. With the Twelve Loaves

It was the custom of Hasidic leaders to place upon their Sabbath table twelve loaves of white bread in imitation of the Holy Temple.[1] The Gerer Rabbi once remarked that a Rebbe who becomes a leader in order to gain fame or fortune will be dragged into Gehenna by his twelve loaves.

[1] Levit. 24: 5, 6, 8.

M. E. H., ii, 56.

17. The Paradise of the Unlearned

The Gerer Rabbi in a discussion of life after death remarked that it is impossible for an unlearned man truly to enjoy Paradise even though he may honestly deserve it. He illustrated his point by relating the following tale:

A Zaddik was traveling in the early spring in a wagon. The roads were in terrible condition; the axles of the wheels broke several times, and the horses plowed with difficulty through the slush and mire. Friday morning came and a great distance was yet to be covered before the Zaddik could reach his destination. He turned to the teamster and said: "It is important I arrive at my goal before the advent of the Sabbath." The teamster promised to do his very best. A horse fell dead from exhaustion, but the teamster continued with the second horse, and succeeded in reaching the Zaddik's destination before the Sabbath.

On Sunday the Zaddik heard that the second horse had also died from exhaustion, and that the teamster's grief was so great that he was stricken with illness. The Zaddik ordered the best medical attention for him, but in vain; the man died. When his soul came before the Heavenly Tribunal, the counsel for the defense won the case, and Paradise was ordained for the poor teamster. His soul arrived there, but it found no pleasure whatsoever in the spiritual and cultural atmosphere of even the lowest region. He was then sent into an imaginary world where he was presented with a beautiful carriage harnessed to four magnificent horses, and where the roads stretched before him, always dry and always level. The teamster was able to enjoy only an imaginary Paradise, not the true one.[1]

M. E. H., i, 81-2.

[1] Compare the story of Elmer Rice's "The Adding Machine" when Mr. Zero's soul enters the Elysian Fields; also the scene in Heaven as portrayed in Molnar's "Liliom"; see also 53: 3.

18. The Torah and Paradise

Said the Medzibozer: "After my death I anticipate being in Paradise. For even if admittance should be denied me, I shall loudly begin to recite and discuss new Torah, and all the Zaddikim in Paradise will assemble to hear me. The place where I will stand will become Paradise."

M. E. H., i, 85.

2. THE AGED

1. The Bratzlaver Concerning "the Aged"

Said the Bratzlaver: "Old men bring stability to Israel and give good counsel to the people.

"The prosperity of a country is in accordance with its treatment of the aged.

"Elderly men who are popular with young women are usually without wisdom."

Sef. Ham., p. 66.

2. Self-Forgiveness in Old Age

Said the Lizensker: "We often see an old man who has spent his life in excesses, imitating in his declining years the works of the pious. He does not indulge himself in food; he rises early to pray and to recite the Psalms. He imagines he has become a pious man by the performance of acts which simulate piety. But he forgets that his abstinence from food and sleep is due chiefly to his weakened desires. He becomes so self-satisfied that he 'forgives himself his own sins.' The result, however, is that he dies without true repentance. May the Lord preserve us from such a fate!"

O. E., p. 58.

3. Signs of Old Age

When Rabbi Schmelke came to Nikolsburg to commence his rabbinical duties there, he was once visited by a crowd of young men. They carried canes and wore eyeglasses, but their faces were beardless. The Rabbi said to them: "In former times when a man felt the need of a cane and eyeglasses, and when he discovered graying hairs in his beard, he knew that he was growing old. He, therefore, began to devote more time to repentance and to deeds of piety. The Satan, however, found this procedure unfavorable to his interests, and he proceeded to persuade the young men to carry canes, wear eyeglasses, but no beards. Thus they might be unaware that old age was approaching and they would not be prompted to turn to repentance and piety."

O. E., p. 137.

4. Free-Will and Habit

Said the Koretzer: "If the desires of an old man are weakened with the decline of his body, what becomes, then, of his free-will? It may be argued that the reason he sins less frequently is that he has a weaker impulse to sin. This is not so. His impulse, while weaker by virtue of the weakening of his body, is still strong through the force of habit. Moreover, is not also his power of resistance to evil weakened?"

Nof. Tz., p. 58.

5. *The Old Man's Experience*

An old man was met by Rabbi Ber of Radeshitz, and, recognizing in him a boyhood friend, the Rabbi asked: "How are you doing?"

The old man answered: "Berel, Berel, I will tell you. What a man does not work out for himself, he does not have."

The Rabbi was struck by the response, and thereafter repeated it frequently to his Hasidim.

S. S. K.. ii, 112.

6. *Venerable Listeners*

The Alexanderer Rabbi was informed that so large a crowd assembled to hear his sermons that many were compelled to remain in the synagogue court; moreover, many aged persons had fallen asleep because of the heat. The Rabbi was pleased to hear of these large assemblies, and paraphrased Psalm 92:14 and 15: "Planted in the house of the Lord, they shall flourish in the courts of our God; they shall still bring forth fruit in old age; they shall be full of sap and richness." His version was: "Those who are seated in the House of the Lord, those who stand in the Courts of our God, and those who are asleep because of their high old age, shall all of them be vigorous in body and youthful in spirit."

S. S. K., p. 79.

3. ANGER

1. *Delay Your Wrath*

The Gastininer Rabbi made it a rule for himself never to express his displeasure with any one on the same day when he was offended by that person. On the morrow he would say to the man: "I was displeased with you yesterday."

S. S. K., iii, 29.

2. *Without Anger*

The Ropshitzer told the following story: "A wealthy Jew of Wilna purchased an Ethrog for a thousand zloties. When he had finished reciting the blessing over it,[1] a man near by asked the loan of it so that he might also pronounce the blessing. The owner complied with the request. But the borrower unfortunately dropped the Ethrog to the ground and it was damaged. The wealthy man bethought himself of the large sum he had spent on the Ethrog in the hope of pleasing the Lord by this evidence of his adherence to the

[1] Singer, p. 218.

divine command. He reminded himself, however, that should he feel anger against the borrower who had dropped the Ethrog, this would be displeasing to the Lord. He therefore took back the spoiled Ethrog without a word of reproach and in complete calmness of spirit."

O. N., p. 38.

3. Doubling a Loss

The Lubliner asked his wife to arrange for the preparation of his evening meal earlier than usual, inasmuch as he wished to have more time for the performance of a certain good deed. It chanced that supper was laid later instead of earlier than usual. The Lubliner said: "It would be natural for me to scold the people of my household for disobeying me. But I wished to gain time to please the Lord. Shall I displease Him by becoming angry, and thereby double my loss?"

N. H. L., p. 21.

4. The Example of Self-Restraint

Rabbi Leib Saras said: "Of what avail is mere study of the Torah when he who learns is contaminated by pride and temper? The good man should himself be the Torah, and people should be able to learn good conduct from observing him."

Dubnow, H. of Ch., p. 180.

5. The Covenant

The disciples of Rabbi Menachem Mendel of Rimanov entered into a covenant and signed a scroll wherein they made avowal: "This is a Covenant of Fellowship in a search for the truth and an everlasting striving after righteousness and humble bearing. We who signed it, essay with all our might to return to God, that a wall may separate us no more from His holiness and His law." Whatever they decreed, they entered upon that scroll—as for example: "Resolved to abstain from words of scolding and denunciation, which our Holy Rabbi has barred as transgressing the law against murder."[1]

Em. L., p. 53.

[1] Baba Metzia, 58.

6. Silence Under Provocation

Said the Kotzker Rabbi: "The verse in Psalms 81:8: 'I answered thee in the secret place of thunder; I proved thee at the waters of Meribah'[1] teaches us that the Lord will answer the prayer of the man who keeps his anger secret, though highly provoked by the other man's quarrelsomeness."

S. S. K., i, 67.

[1] Meribah = Quarrelsomeness.

7. *More Pleasing Than Fast-Days*

The Sassover said: "If thy neighbor offend thee, refrain from wrath, and it will be more pleasing in the sight of God than a thousand fast-days; listen to revilings without retort, and it will stand you in stead of a thousand self-inflictions." [1]

[1] See also 21: Conduct and Its Rules.

Bl., Gem., p. 69.

8. *Abuse and Forbearance*

The Kobriner Rabbi related that in his boyhood a year of famine had occurred, and the poor wandered from village to village to beg food from the Jewish residents. A number of them came to his mother's home, and she prepared the oven to bake for them. Some of the beggars, growing impatient, began to abuse her with their words, and the distressed woman started to weep. Her small son, the future Rabbi, said to his mother:

"Why should you be troubled by their abuse? Does not this help you to aid them with a pure heart, and to perform a good deed in perfection of spirit? On the other hand, had the poor praised and blessed you, the good deed would be less praiseworthy, since you might have performed it to gain their praises, and not entirely in obedience to the Lord's command and for the sake of His service."

O. Y., p. 50.

9. *Patience under Annoyance*

The Vorker Rabbi said: "The truly humble man is unable to feel anger. Even if he is interrupted when busy, he will show no annoyance. He always believes the other man to be more important than himself. He is like a woodchopper addressed by the King. Is it conceivable that the woodman should feel irritation against the King for being bothered when occupied with his labors? An excellent example of such a humble man is Hillel. The well-known story relates that two persons made a wager that Hillel could be brought to show anger. Though the questioner harassed Hillel with vain queries while he was preparing for the Sabbath, Hillel retained his calm." [1]

[1] Sabbath, 31.

S. S. K., ii, p. 82.

10. *Charity Without Anger*

The author of "Turei Zahav," [1] Rabbi David, was asked by a poor man for the loan of a gold piece. He did not have the money in his possession and gave the man his silver beaker to pawn. On Friday he went to the pawnshop to redeem the beaker and was informed that the man had received two gold pieces on it from the pawnbroker. Rabbi David, however, showed no sign of displeasure,

[1] Comments on the Codes, or the "Taz."

and quietly remarked: "I am glad I did not have the money at hand when I was asked to loan a gold piece, since the borrower evidently was in need of two gold pieces. By giving him my beaker to pawn, I enabled him to secure what he required without being compelled to implore a second man for the loan of the other gold piece."

O. Y., p. 217.

11. Atonement for Anger

The Stanislaver Rabbi was accustomed to be awakened every morning by the Warden, in order to be punctual at divine worship. One morning the Warden failed to call the Rabbi and he came late to synagogue. The Rabbi, who was quick-tempered, struck the Warden twice on the cheek. Immediately he regretted his hasty act, and resolved to make atonement by leaving the town and wandering about as a beggar for a year. When the year had ended, he returned to Stanislav, but his ragged garments and uncut hair and beard made him unrecognizable. He came to the synagogue and stood near the door among other poor tramps. At the conclusion of the Services he was invited to the President's home for the Sabbath meal. His behavior pleased the host, and he was invited to remain for the night. The disguised beggar awoke early, and after his ablutions, began quietly to recite Psalms.

Soon after the Warden came to awaken the President, and finding him still asleep, stole the silver candlesticks from the dining room table. Hiding them beneath his cloak, the Warden knocked at the President's bedroom door. When the latter emerged, he noted at once that the candlesticks were missing, and asked the Warden if he had seen any stranger about. The Warden expressed the opinion that the tramp had stolen the candlesticks. The Rabbi thereupon asked the Warden: "Will you take an oath that I stole them?" This query so enraged the Warden that he slapped the Rabbi's face twice. When he was about to do so a third time, the Rabbi exclaimed: "You owe me two blows only, and I wish no interest. Return the candlesticks to their place, and announce to the congregation that their Rabbi has returned."

T. M., p. 24.

12. The Control of Wrath

The Koretzer said: "Long ago I conquered my anger and placed it in my pocket. When I have need of it, I take it out."

M. D., p. 214.

13. Smoking Mellows Anger

A Hasid asked the Lubliner for a remedy to maintain control of his temper.

"Smoke a pipe," replied the Rabbi. "Smoking mellows a man."

N. H. L., p. 29.

14. *Master of His Words*

Rabbi Wolf Zitomirer said: "The angry man fills his mouth with live coals and with needles, sharp and hard. For each angry word he utters, he deserves to be banished from holiness in shame and disgrace, and to suffer grievously until his soul is purified from its blemishes. Every man must be master of his mouth."

D. E. M. R., p. 31.

15. *Is Anger Permissible?*

Rabbi Mendel Libavitzer was accustomed to restrain an angry rebuke until he had investigated the Codes to learn whether anger is permissible in the particular instance. But how much genuine anger could he feel after searching for the authority of the Shulchan Arukh?

Ohel N., p. 56.

16. *Boaz and Ruth*

Said the Ropshitzer: "Anger is to be avoided in all circumstances. Had Boaz become angry at Ruth when she sought him out, he would never have married her, and King David would not have been born."

Ohel N., p. 57.

17. *The Bratzlaver on "Anger"*

"1. Break your anger by compassion for the one with whom you are angry.

2. Anger and cruelty arise from a deficiency of understanding. Study the Torah to improve your understanding.

3. He who is obsessed by anger loses his image of God.

4. Abstinence from food is oftentimes a corrective of anger.

5. Anger prevents God's abundance from descending to us.

6. He who subdues his anger achieves a good name.

7. Anger causes a man to be far from truth.

8. An angry man cannot pray properly.

9. An angry man cannot attain the goal to which he aspires.

10. The holiness of Palestine aids a man to break off anger, indolence and melancholy.

L. E. H., pp. 48-9.

11. He who restrains his anger will not see his enemies rule over him.

12. Anger leads to contempt and to sin.

13. The angry man's wisdom and prominence cannot endure.

14. God loves the man who forgives his offenders and shows them not an angry face.

15. The man who is habitually obsessed by anger fails to enjoy his life and feels all the tortures of Purgatory.

16. The angry man has no respect for the Shekinah. He forgets his learning and increases folly within himself.

17. The sins of the angry man will surely outweigh his merits.

18. Anger after meals is dangerous to life.

19. Anger is injurious to health and to eyesight.

20. A well-prepared meal is an antidote to anger.

21. He who is not in the habit of complaining about people is well-beloved.

22. Falsehood and jealousy cause anger.

23. Through anger one brings upon himself trials in courts-of-law.

24. Anger shortens the days of one's life.

25. The man without anger is able to humble the arrogant.

26. If one is angry it is a sign that all his good works are for the purpose of obtaining honors.

27. One who becomes angry at a respectable poor man angers God.

28. Anger comes to the man who must bear too heavy a burden.

29. Melancholy follows anger.

30. Strictness leads to quarrels.

31 Charity prevents anger."

Sef. Ham., p. 77.

4. ANIMALS AND HOW TO TREAT THEM

1. The Cow That Ascended to Heaven

Before Rabbi Meyer Premislaner became known as a "Rebbe," he was exceedingly poor, and his livelihood was obtained from a cow, whose milk he sold among the neighbors. It was the Rabbi's unvarying custom to save some money each week, and to distribute it for Sabbath among the poor.

Once he was unable to save anything. Without hesitation, he slaughtered the cow, and gave away the meat to the poor. His wife arose in the morning, and could not find the cow. She ran to Rabbi Meyer, crying bitterly that the cow was missing.

Rabbi Meyer answered: "The cow is not missing; she has gone up to Heaven."

S. M., p. 4.

2. Address Them Properly

When Rabbi Wolf Zbarazer was on a journey, he would not permit the driver to beat his horses, saying to him: "You have no need even to scold them, if you understand how to address them properly."

S. H. H., chapter 4.
Reflex, May, 1929, p. 67.

3. Man's Bidding and God's

The Sassover was accustomed to attend county fairs, and there to do good offices to those in need. Once it befell that some cattle-breeders had left their animals standing in the market-place with their thirst unslaked, while their owners attended to their affairs elsewhere. The Sassover, perceiving this, made the rounds with a bucket and gave the calves their drink. A dealer, returning from an errand and seeing a stranger thus employed, mistook him for a hired man, and commanded him to give drink to his cattle. The Rabbi obeyed, and, after having performed his chore, was offered a coin. He laughingly refused, saying: "Get thee hence, man; I did not do thy bidding, but God's, Who commands us to be merciful to His creatures."

Bl., Gem., p. 188.

4. Watching the Horses

One wintry day, Rabbi Wolf Zbarazer traveled in a coach to a Circumcision Feast. After a time, he left the warm room, went out to the coachman who stood guarding the horses, and said:

"I will watch the horses; go in and warm yourself."

Soon after, the guests noted the absence of the Rabbi, and they discovered him outside trembling from the cold.

T. H., p. 322.

5. A Lesson to Malcontents

On a frosty winter-night a man reached the little town of Lekhivitz, where Rabbi Phineas (later of Frankfort) presided over the community. The traveler, frost-bitten and disconsolate, looked about him for a house of rest and comfort. He saw from afar a little dwelling and a room alight within—the house of the Rabbi. He knocked at the window and begged for leave to warm himself before the fire. Rabbi Phineas opened the door for the unknown guest, gave him food and drink and agreeable lodging. The man secretly thought: "What a world of good and evil fortunes—the Rabbi dwells in peace and security, while I must journey weary lengths in quest of bread!" The next morning he inquired of the Rabbi: "Since I am a poor laborer and suffer hardships in this world, am I certain of a share in the World-to-Come?"

The Rabbi replied: "Your horse has the better title than yourself to share in the World-to-Come, if we follow your way of thinking. At this moment you are taking your ease before a comfortable fire, whereas your horse, God's creature like yourself, and even harder-worked than you, stands out-of-doors in the cold, ready to carry you wherever you choose, without complaining."

Bl., Gem., p. 136.

6. The Killer of Cattle

Several Hasidim of Kolomeya complained to the Sadagurer that the Shochet in their community was a miserly and inhospitable man. The Rabbi exclaimed: "And do you eat the meat from his Shechitah?" This question was equivalent to a prohibition, and henceforth no one purchased meat.

The Shochet came to the Rabbi, and said: "Where do you find that a Shochet must be hospitable?"

The Rabbi replied: "We find in the Talmud that some persons are born with a passion for shedding blood. One becomes a murderer, a second, a soldier, and a third, a Shochet.[1] The question arises: why do we make use of meat from an animal killed by a man who is like a murderer? The whole Shechitah legislation has been formulated in order to prevent brutal treatment of the animal, and what is more brutal than to let it perish at the hands of a near-murderer?

"The answer is that a Shochet should have a good heart, notwithstanding his love for the shedding of animals' blood; he then may be trusted to avoid brutality in shedding this blood.

"Thus if a Shochet is kind to his fellow-men, he may be trusted to slaughter animals in a mild manner. But, if he is unkind, he is in truth a near-murderer, who cannot be trusted to observe the kind methods of slaying animals prescribed by the Law."[2]

F. R. H., E., p. 113.

[1] Sabbath, 156a; paraphrase.
[2] See "Without Credentials," 81:4, for another story regarding a Shochet.

7. The Animals and Their Qualities

A great Rabbi said: "The Creator turned to the animals and said: 'Cooperate with Me in forming a higher being, to whom each of you shall donate a desirable characteristic. The cat will contribute modesty; the ant, honesty; the tiger, courage; the lion, bravery; the eagle, diligence, and so forth. Thus will man not only be akin to you, but will also represent the finest in you.' "

F. U. A. O., i, 8.

5. APHORISMS [1]

1. Aphorisms Collected by Rabbi Lazerov

"1. Luxury feeds more poor than philanthropy.

2. Woe to him whom nobody likes; but beware of him whom everybody likes.

3. One half of the word: 'Freethinkers' is true; they are free, but no thinkers.

[1] This material, while non-Hasidic, is included as a basis of comparison with the Hasidic items. There are many parallels, and many direct influences from Hasidic sources.

4. In accordance with your friends, I measure your wealth. In accordance with your enemies, I measure your greatness.

5. Man should be master of his will and slave of his conscience.

6. Fear only two: God and the man who has no fear of God.

7. To be contrite means to add no fresh sins to the old.

8. One who looks for a friend without faults, will have none.

9. Fear the one who fears you.

10. One who has confidence in himself gains the confidence of others.

11. The most humble man thinks himself greater than his best friend thinks he is.

12. Gold is the blood of society. Too little or too much is unhealthy for its possessor.

13. One who cannot survive bad times cannot see good times.

14. False friends are like migratory birds; they fly away in cold weather.

15. One who thinks he can live without others is mistaken. One who thinks others cannot live without him is more mistaken.

16. One who believes that anything can be accomplished by money is likely to do anything for money.

17. While pursuing happiness we escape from contentment.

18. It is easier to abandon evil traits to-day than to-morrow.

19. Want makes people better; luck makes them worse.

20. For the unlearned, old age is winter; for the learned, it is the season of the harvest.

21. Fear of a misfortune is worse than the misfortune.

22. Teach your children in youth, and they will not teach you in your old age."

E. J. W., pp. 174-189.

6. APOSTATES

1. *"He Bringeth Down the Proud and Raiseth Up the Lowly"*

A wealthy Jew was reciting in the Prayer the sentence: "He bringeth down the proud and raiseth up the lowly." [1] The thought occurred to him that the Lord could not demean him, inasmuch as his wealth was so vast and secure. Thereupon he resolved to renounce his ancestral faith since it propounded so obvious an untruth. He went to the local bishop with his plan, and the latter enjoined him to sign an agreement that he could not alter his decision under penalty of surrendering all his property to the church. The Jew signed the agreement without hesitation, and in celebration of his forthcoming conversion, joined the bishop in a drinking bout.

The Jew fell asleep in the bishop's room, and on awaking, remembered his villainous plan. He ran out of the bishop's house in great distress, feeling that in truth he had been brought low by the

[1] Singer, p. 43.

possible loss of his property and the imminent discovery of his hasty
agreement to become an apostate.   He was ashamed to return to his
home and roamed the city in despair.   Seeing a light burning in a
hut, he entered and sought to gain lodging.

There he found the Besht reciting the midnight Services, which
are Memorial Elegies for the destruction of Jerusalem.   At the conclusion of the recital, the Besht invited him to relate his trouble.   The
Jew revealed his experience, concealing no detail.   The Besht said:
"Now are you convinced that the Lord is able to bring down the
proud to the earth?   Do you also believe now that he can exalt the
lowly?"

"Yes, truly I do," answered the man.

The next moment they heard the church bells tolling, and a cry
went forth to send rescuers to the home of the bishop which was
afire.   All efforts to save the building were in vain, and the bishop
himself was near suffocation when they dragged him out.

There being no agreement now in existence, no change had taken
place in the Jew's position, and he remained wealthy and respected.

But henceforth he never again doubted the ability of the Lord
to do His will.

O. Y., p. 124.

2. *Convenient Conversion*

A Jewish farmer came to the Belzer for his blessing.   The Rabbi
inquired whether he was faithful in his observance of the Sabbath.
The farmer confessed that he worked in the field on the Sabbath
if necessary.   The Rabbi persuaded him to abandon this practice,
but the farmer besought him for permission to continue this Sabbath labor until after the harvest.   The Rabbi thereupon recounted
to him the following narrative:

"A Jewish villager was very loyal to the nobleman who owned
the village.   At a banquet the nobleman boasted to his friends of
the Jew's allegiance.   'He will do anything for me,' he exclaimed.

" 'If this Jew will become a Catholic at your request,' commented
one of the company, 'then I will believe your assertion as to his
loyalty.'

"The nobleman summoned the Jew and his wife, who, after consultation, decided to accede to the village-owner's command.

"Soon after, the nobleman summoned them again, and said:
'You may return to your former faith, inasmuch as it is more
convenient for me in many matters to deal with a Jew than with a
Christian.'

"Again there was a consultation, and the former Jew replied:
'Gladly will I return to the faith of Israel, but as it is near to Passover, and much strenuous labor is required in preparation for the
Holyday, we petition you to permit us to delay our re-conversion
until after Passover.' "

The farmer, hearing this tale, appreciated the absurdity of his

stipulation, and promised henceforth to observe the Sabbath un-
conditionally.[1]

D. S., p. 24.

[1] This is one of the best-known tales. See "The Half-Hearted Proselyte,"
138: 3.

7. ASCETICISM AND ITS UNWISDOM

1. *The Snare*

An old Hasid came to the Ropshitzer and described the chastisements to which he subjected himself, showing his sackcloth attire
for the mortification of his body.

"How powerful is the Satan," exclaimed the Rabbi. "An old
man like yourself he has succeeded in capturing in his snare."

M. D., p. 249.

2. *The White Horse*

A young man came to the Riziner and asked to be ordained as a
Rav. The Riziner inquired regarding his daily conduct, and the
candidate replied: "I always dress in white; I drink only water; I
place tacks in my shoes for self-mortification; I roll naked in the
snow; and I order the synagogue caretaker to give me forty stripes
daily on my bare back."

Just then a white horse entered the courtyard, drank water, and
began rolling in the snow.

"Observe," said the Riziner. "This creature is white; it drinks
only water; it has nails in its shoes; it rolls in the snow, and receives
more than forty stripes a day. Still it is nothing but a horse."

M. D., p. 250.

3. *Mortification is Unnecessary*

Said the Besht: "I received the letter indited by your unsullied
hand, and saw from its first lines that Your Worship believes mortification necessary. This shocked me to my innermost soul. By the
counsel of God and His Shekinah, I order you to abandon such
dangerous practices, which are but the outcome of melancholia and
depression. The Glory of God reposes not where there is mourning, but only where joy in His dictates prevails. For it has been
explicitly commanded: 'Thou shalt not hide thyself from thine own
flesh.' "[1]

Shivchei ha-Besht, p. 30.
Spiegel, p. 144.

[1] Isaiah 58:7, read on Yom Kippur. This excerpt is taken from a letter
addressed to the Pulnoer.

4. *The Boundaries of Asceticism*

Said the Besht: "Asceticism should be practiced only at the commencement of a man's self-discipline, until his evil inclinations are

subdued. Later he should conduct himself in a normal way and be in communication with his comrades. Otherwise he will fall into pride."

M. P. T., ii, 75.

5. Not Fasting, But Joy

The Hasidim hold with Rabbi Eleazar Hakapar, that a man whose life is replete with fastings and self-inflictions, does not deserve the name of a Zaddik [1]; and with Abayi, that sack-cloth and ashes are of no avail, only true repentance and good deeds [2]; also, with the Talmud Jerushalmi, that he who enjoyeth not what his eyes have seen will have to answer for it on High [3]; and, finally, with Samuel, that "Whoever fasts is called a sinner." [4]

Once a Jew in great tribulation of heart came to the Besht, inquiring: "How many days have I to fast, to make atonement for a grievous sin?" The Besht replied: "Not through fasting is the ire of God averted, but through joy of which the Psalms are harbingers. Say the Psalms with inward rejoicing, and you will be quit of your sin."

Men learned in the Law came to the Besht on an errand of dispute. "In times gone by," they protested, "there were pious men aplenty, fasting from Sabbath to Sabbath, and inflicting their own bodies with self-devised torments. And now your Disciples proclaim it to all who care to listen that much fasting is unlawful and self-torment a crime."

The Besht made answer: "It is the aim and essence of my pilgrimage on earth to show my brethren by living demonstration, how one may serve God with merriment and rejoicing. For he who is full of joy is full of love for men and all fellow-creatures." [5]

Bl., Pr., p. 36 ff.

[1] Taanith, 11a, paraphrased.
[2] Ibid., 16a.
[3] Kiddushin, 4: 12.
[4] Taanith, 11a.
[5] Compare, however, Rabbi Eleazar says: "One who is able to fast and fasts, is called a holy man." Rabbi Levi says: "One who fasts is called a Hasid." (Taanith, 11.)

8. ASPIRATION

1. The Ladder and the Board

The Gerer Rabbi said: "Two men ascended a roof, one by a ladder, the other by a board. The difference lay in the fact that the one who climbed the ladder was able to count the rungs already ascended, and those yet to climb; the one who used the board could not estimate the space to climb until he was on the roof.

"The Lord commands us: 'Thou shalt not go up by steps upon my altar.' (Exodus 20:26). This means: Do not estimate that you have already performed most of your duties towards the Lord and that you have earned the privilege of slowing down. You cannot determine till the end of the effort whether you have reached the summit."

S. S. K., ii, 38.

2. Discovery and Recovery

Said Rabbi Bunam: "Solomon counsels us (Prov. 2:4): 'Seek her (wisdom) as silver, and search for her as for treasures.' There are two kinds of seeking. A man may look for a treasure which he has heard may be in the vicinity. Or, a man may search for something which he has lost. The first seeker does not fatigue himself in the quest, but, if he does find the treasure, he is overjoyed. The second man labors diligently to find the object of his search, but, when he discovers it, he experiences but little joy, since he has only regained that which he had already possessed. In seeking holy wisdom we should do both: labor diligently, as if we had lost it, and be overjoyed on attaining it, as if he had uncovered a great treasure."

S. I., p. 81.

3. Well-Directed Strength

Said the Besht: "The strength thou wert willing to lose through fasting, devote to the Torah and to worship. Thereby wilt thou ascend to a higher state."

K. S. T., 16b.

4. Heavens Ever Higher

Said Rabbi Yerachmiel: "Let no one be hesitant to serve the Lord because the way seems too high for him. At first every way is as high as the heavens above; yet, after laboring to achieve thy aspiration, it will become near to thee. Then thou wilt be shown new ways high beyond the skies thou hast attained, to which thou again shouldest aspire. Begin in a modest way; maintain an earnest effort to attain higher and higher realms, and before thy demise thou shalt have attained undreamed-of heights of perfection."

Tif. B., p. 8-9.

9. ATONEMENT

1. His Atonement

A wealthy Jew could not find a large sum of money in his household and he suspected his maid-servant had stolen it. He ordered her arrest. The gendarmerie subjected her to grievous hardships, and, after being released from custody, she fell sick and died.

The householder became conscience-stricken and went to the Dzikover Rabbi for counsel. The Rabbi told him to leave his home and business, and to wander about as a beggar for two years. He further instructed him to beg no food or clothing, and to take it only when it was offered him; moreover, he was to accept no ride.

The man adhered to these stipulations, and after two years, he returned home with his conscience relieved.

K. E., pp. 9-13.

10. BLESSINGS

1. Blessing Over Drink

Rabbi Wolf Zitomirer was an innkeeper in a village. A Jewish teamster entered and asked for a glass of brandy. As he was about to drink it without reciting a blessing, the Rabbi stopped him and said: "Do you realize by what miraculous laws God has produced the fruit of the soil before it became the drink which you enjoy? Yet you forget to offer Him a brief blessing."

The teamster promptly recited the blessing, and the Rabbi answered: "Amen."

M. G., ii, 26a.

2. Blessing for Unlawful Enterprises

Said the Magelnitzer Rabbi: "There are people who come to me seeking a blessing for their enterprise though it is unlawful. They believe I need not concern myself whether my blessing is acceptable to the Lord. This is absurd. My blessing may be of aid if the supplicant is deserving, and the enterprise or thing desired is lawful. Then I implore the Lord to have compassion upon the supplicant, and to grant his or her desire. But my blessing on behalf of an undeserving person or for an illegal purpose must necessarily prove futile, since the Lord will refuse my petition."

S. Ch., p. 64.

3. Torah and Life

In the Morning Services there are two blessings, one on the restoration of the soul after its night-rest,[1] and one on the teaching to us of the Torah by the Lord.[2] Rabbi Bunam declared that we should first say the Blessing on the Restoration of Life Consciousness. We entrusted our Life Soul unto God and have received it back refreshed by repose; it is fit that the first thing we should do is to thank the Guardian on High who has shielded our Soul.

The Gerer Rabbi, however, declared that the Blessing: the Teaching of the Torah should first be recited, inasmuch as Life without Torah is merely earthly and worthless.

S. S. K., ii, 13.

[1] Singer, p. 4.
[2] Singer, p. 5.

4. Forgetting Worldly Desires

Rabbi Bunam said: "In Genesis 48:18-19 we find a controversy between Jacob and Joseph. Joseph insists that Menasseh shall have preference in Jacob's blessing, inasmuch as he is the first-born, whereas Jacob maintains that Ephraim should take precedence.

"Allegorically this can be explained, as follows: Joseph, the Zaddik, believed that one should first forget this world of toil, and should despise all the vanities of the earth (Menasseh,—forget); then his spirit will become fruitful (Ephraim,—fruitful). Jacob, however, felt that this is impossible, at least for most people, and he, therefore, wished that after a man has become fruitful in worldly goods, sufficient for his needs, he may forget his material desires, and turn to spiritual concerns."

S. S. K., iii, 51.

5. The Blessing of the Males

The daughter of Rabbi Yokel Gluger was very learned in Hebrew. Once she heard a teamster recite the benediction: "Blessed art Thou, Who hast not made me a woman." [1] She asked her father: "Do I not know more than he does?" Her father replied: "Every man when he recites this blessing has in mind his own wife."

A Bishop once asked a Rabbi: "Why does the Jew bless God for not making him a Gentile? [2] Does not this show hatred?"

"Not at all," answered the Rabbi. "We love our womenfolk, and yet we recite a similar blessing concerning them. The reason for the blessings is that a woman and a non-Jew have fewer Mitzwoth to perform."

Ohel N., pp. 87-8.

[1] Singer, p. 6.
[2] Singer, p. 5.

6. Even Sinners Are Blessed

The Sassover Rabbi said: "It was by the will of God that Jacob received the blessing from Isaac when he disguised himself as Esau. For had Isaac knowingly given his blessing to Jacob, it would be effective only when Jacob's descendants conduct themselves with the perfection of Jacob; whereas now the Israelites enjoy the blessing even when they sin, since Isaac intended to bless the sinful Esau."

F. U. A. O., i, 65.

7. The Man of God

Said the Lentzner Rabbi: " 'And this is the blessing wherewith Moses, the man of God, blessed the children of Israel' (Deut. 33:1). Moses blessed the children of Israel that each one of them might become 'the man of God.' "

E. A., p. 30.

8. Good in Evil

Said the "Yud": "We read (Deut. 11:26): 'Behold I set before you this day "Berakhah" (a blessing) "Wekelalah" (and a curse).' God says: 'I propose unto you Mitzwoth as an investment, whereby you may enjoy during this life "Berakhah," the accrued interest, "Wekelalah," and the principal will remain for you in the World-to-Come.' 'Wekelalah' contains the initials of the words: 'Wehakeren Kayemeth Lakhem Laolam ha-Baha' ('And the Fund will be established for you in the World-to-Come')." [1]

Tif. Yeh., p. 27.

[1] Mishnah, Peah chapter 1. See Morning Service, Singer, p. 5.

9. Singular and Plural

Said Rabbi Yerachmiel: "It is written (Exodus 23:25): 'And ye shall serve the Lord your God, and He will bless thy bread.' It may be asked why the verse begins in the plural and ends in the singular. The answer is this: Each one who labors that another person may likewise serve the Lord, shall be blessed."

Tif. B., p. 3.

The Kotzker remarked on the same verse: "We serve the Lord as members of the congregation of Israel, but we eat our food as individuals."

R. T., ii, 38.

11. BOOKS

1. A Holy Work

When the Berditschever received a copy of the small book, "Tanya," by Rabbi Schneur Zalman Ladier, he exclaimed:
"This is a miracle! To bring so great a God into the compass of so small a book." [1]

S. ha-Has., p. 200.

[1] "A Book is life beyond life"; see elsewhere.

2. The Book-Case

Rabbi Bunam said: "One who devotes himself to the study of the Torah but neglects the service of the Lord, is like a book-case filled with good books. The book-case stands by itself and the books stand by themselves, entirely without connection. A zealous reader is required."

S. S. K., i, 13.

3. The Two Readers

There are two kinds of readers of serious books. One is like the man who squeezes wine grapes with his finger tips. He secures only the watery juice from the ends of the grapes, and, inasmuch as it does not ferment, he complains that the grapes are defective. This type of reader glances hurriedly at the pages of a volume and finds no merit in the writings.

The other kind of reader is like the man who squeezes out the full juice from the grapes. It ferments and turns into pleasing wine. This type of reader delves deeply into the words he is reading, and finds delight in the thoughts they convey.[1]

[1] From the "Seder ha-Yom" quoted in *Midrash Ribesh Tov*, p. 8.

4. *The Seraph's Worship*

Rabbi Uri of Strelisk asked a Hasid who was a gifted artist to fashion an illustrated frontispiece for a manuscript by the Karliner Rabbi. It was early in the morning before the commencement of Services.

The Hasid said: "But Rabbi, it requires time to do satisfactory work. Why may I not undertake it after Services?"

The Rabbi replied: "When I enter a House of Worship, I give all of myself to God. I can never be sure whether I will return home alive. If my soul should thus depart from me, people will imagine that this is my manuscript, rather than the Karliner's."

O. O., pp. 31-2.

5. *Proving Authorship*

The Belzer was seated at a Sabbath meal with his Disciples, singing the prescribed hymns. When they had finished the hymn: "It is the holy Sabbath day," the Rabbi remarked:

"Do you not find the last verse odd? It runs as follows: 'All voices should cease when my songs are lifted up; for they drip like dew; they shall not trespass upon my domain: in the path of poetry, my lot has fallen; become upright and make no use of the beauty of the song that was made pleasant by me.'

"I learned that the author of this hymn had departed on a journey, and, when he returned, was surprised to hear that another man had claimed that he had written it. The poet complained to the community leaders, and both claimants were invited to add a verse. Both submitted their compositions, and the work of the true author harmonized with the entire hymn."

D. S., p. 169.

6. *When the Learned and Unlearned Grow Old*

An unmannerly man said to the Slonimer Rabbi: "The books of your younger days were superior to your present writings; yet the Talmud says that a learned man becomes wiser with age."[1]

The Rabbi replied: "The Talmud adds that unlearned persons be-

[1] Sabbath, 152; Mishnah Kinnim, 3:6.

come more stupid with age. It requires intelligence to appreciate my later writings."

O. I. H., p. 183.

7. The Ignorant Finder

Rabbi Mendel Vitebsker was asked why he believed himself sufficiently versed in the Kabbalah to write a book on the subject. He replied with the following parable:

"A king lost his signet ring and worried lest the finder might forge the royal signature to illegal documents. The princes and ministers dispersed throughout the royal parks to search for it. It was a farmer, however, who chanced to pick up the ring. He did not know its value, but, since it was lying near the palace grounds, he returned it to the Chamberlain.

"I am like the farmer," said the Rabbi, "ignorant of the true possibilities of the science of Kabbalah, but, nevertheless, able to discover and compile wisdom in it."

M. R. T., p. 13.

8. Dangerous Books

The Hasidim came to Rabbi Phineas of Frankfort with this question: "Master, who, if anyone, is to study the 'Guide to the Perplexed'?"

The Master replied: "Know that the 'Guide' is like an apothecary's shop. The chemist dwelling within prepares many useful remedies, for many ills, being licensed as a man of skill. But he who has no learning of remedies and diseases,—let him beware how he meddles with the contents of the shop. The smallest error may kill a man; the least want of precaution may involve grievous punishment, and any mistake entails loss of reputation."

Bl., Gem., p. 150.

9. Discipline from a Book

Rabbi Bunam said: "I was once grossly insulted and wept from indignation. I went over and kissed my adversary." The Rabbi was asked by his Hasidim to tell who dared abuse their holy leader. He took out the book, "Shevet Musar," a work on admonition and discipline, and said: "Here is the guilty one. Read it yourselves with earnestness, and it will demonstrate to you your faults and offenses, until you, also, will weep."

S. I., p. 29.

10. Charity or Books

The Tzanzer could never spare the money for the purchase of a new book. He used to say: "I must use this money to supply the poor who depend upon me for aid."

E. Tz., p. 129.

11. The Bratzlaver on "Books"

"1. He who is able to write a book and does not write it, is as one who has lost a child.

2. Every author should weigh his work to determine whether it has any connection with the 'Book of Humanity,' namely, whether humanity will receive any benefit from it.

3. It is oftentimes easy for the man of culture to discover whether an author has originated the ideas included in his book, or whether they are merely copied by him.

4. We should not regret overmuch the loss of many of the holy writings of our forefathers; for had it been possible to preserve these books, we would today be in possession of many heretical works as well." [1]

Sef. Ham., pp. 112-113.

[1] It is clear from this statement that the Rabbis appreciated the fact that Jewish literature in all centuries has embraced works of piety and impiety. Even in the Bible itself, Ecclesiastes and Job are to be found.

12. A Companion in Slumber

The Dzikover in his testament commanded that his sermons be not printed. He added an explanation: "If my manuscripts are printed, what will happen? My Disciples will eat and drink over-much on the Sabbath, take my book, lie down on a couch, open my book and fall immediately asleep. I do not care to be their companion in slumber."

D. D., p. 327.

12. BORROWING AND LENDING

1. Each to His Own Verse

The Radziminer Rabbi said: "We find in the Bible injunctions applicable to every one. Thus, the lender should apply to himself the commandment to be patient with the borrower.[1] The borrower must be cognizant of the statement that it is despicable to borrow and not repay as soon as possible.[2] It is, however, wrong for one to keep in mind the adjuration directed at the other. For instance, the borrower should not remind the lender that the latter is commanded to be patient. That is not his verse. On the other hand, the lender should not remind the borrower that it is evil not to repay promptly. He must stick to his particular verse."

S. S. K., iv, 101.

[1] Exodus 22:24.
[2] Psalms 37:21.

2. Master and Slave

The Seer was very fond of Rabbi Hirsch of Ziditzov, one of his Disciples, and loved to have conversation with him. Once, after a long sojourn, Rabbi Hirsch borrowed of the Master a few florins to defray the cost of his homeward journey. The Seer, after giving him the money, said: "Little Hirsch, thou art my bondsman now, as it is said in King Solomon's words: the borrower is slave to the lender." (Proverbs 22:7)

"Nay," rejoined Rabbi Hirsch. "It is you, Master, who are my bondsman now. Our Sages have taught: he who buys himself a Jewish slave, sets a master over himself." (Kiddushin, 22a)

Bl., Gem., p. 233.

3. The Reward of Frugality

The Karliner told the following parable: "A wealthy man took pity on two poor men and advanced them money to enable them to earn a living. The wiser man opened a small store, and, living very frugally, saved enough money to return the loan; at the same time, he had money left over wherewith to maintain his business. The benefactor was delighted and made him a gift of the original sum.

"The other borrower began to live expensively, and could not meet his obligation. The lender was angered, and foreclosed upon him. The point is obvious: he who plans his life to fit his circumstances oftentimes meets with pleasant surprises. The reverse is true in the case of the unthinking and improvident."

S. S. K., iv, 137.

4. Usury

The Kotzker Rabbi said to a money-lender: "In Leviticus (25:37) we read: 'Thy money shalt thou not give him upon interest (for biting).'[1] This means that you should not make your money earn the food you eat, and that the borrower should work for you. Earn your living by the work of your own hands."

Kotzker Maasioth, p. 52.

[1] Neshekh = usury or biting.

5. Erasing Debts and Sins

Said the "Yud": "We read (Deut. 15:9): 'Beware that there be not a base thought in thy heart, saying: the seventh year, the year of release is at hand, and thy eye be evil against thy needy brother, and thou give him naught, and he cry unto the Lord against thee, and it be a sin in thee. Why does the Torah specify here that 'it be a sin'? Is it not obvious that one who refuses to aid the needy commits a sin? The answer is, that on each Yom Kippur the Satan complains bitterly that he labors earnestly the entire year to induce people to sin, and now all sins are erased automatically. The Heavenly Judge replied: 'The Jews release the poor of their debts to them; hence, it is fitting that I release them of their obligations to me.' But, if a Jew refuses to loan money to a needy brother-Jew because he will be compelled to cancel the debt, then his sins shall also not be erased, and they shall remain sins."

Tif. Yeh., pp. 32-33.

6. *A Curse to Israel*

A Hasid asked the Rimanover to pray in his behalf so that he might secure a needed loan from a non-Jew. The Rabbi declined, saying: "How can I pray for that which is included among the things which are a curse to Israel?" [1]

Em. L., p. 47.

[1] Deut. 28:44. "[The Stranger] shall lend to thee, and thou shalt not lend to him; he shall be the head, and thou shalt be the tail."

13. BUSINESS AND LIVELIHOOD

1. *Torah and Business*

A man came to the Kozmirer Rabbi to ask his blessing in a financial enterprise. The Rabbi turned away his face, and refused to listen to the petitioner. A few moments later another Hasid spoke with the Rabbi regarding a business matter, and received his blessing. The first one felt piqued, and asked the Rabbi why he refused to listen to him, whereas he gave his blessing to the second. The Rabbi answered:

"I shall explain my attitude by a parable: A merchant came to a market-town, and entered a wholesale place to make the necessary purchases. He became so interested in the stock that he remained there until late in the evening. When he wished to leave, he noticed that the axle of his wagon was broken. It was too late to secure one, and he told the wholesaler his trouble. The latter offered him an extra axle reserved for his own wagon.

"Another man, whose axle was broken, asked the wholesaler to sell him one also. But the wholesaler replied: 'Do you think that I deal in axles? The other man purchased various materials from me; hence, I give him my help, but you are not my customer.'

"In the same fashion," continued the Kozmirer Rabbi, "the Hasid to whom I gave my blessing learns from me Torah and ethics; hence, I aid him in business affairs as well. But you have never come to me for instruction in any matter. Why should I aid you in purely worldly affairs?"

N. H. L., p. 81.

2. *Buying the Wind*

A villager told the Kotzker Rabbi that the owner of the village demanded his rent, but that he lacked the money required. The Rabbi advised him to buy anything offered for sale, except stolen goods. The villager then went to the landlord to inquire if he had anything to sell. The nobleman was surrounded by a crowd of friends, and, desiring to amuse them, he proposed to the Jew that he buy the wind from him. Obedient to the Rabbi's advice, the Jew accepted the offer, and asked the village-owner to draw up a contract for ten years to the effect that he sold him the wind for one hundred thalers a year. The formal contract was signed, and the Jew gave a sum of money as the first payment. There were several wind-mills on the land belonging to the nobleman which he leased out. The Jew showed the contract to each miller, and asked them to pay him for the privilege of using the wind. The Jew was soon able to pay the nobleman the rent due him.

Kotzker Maasioth, p. 121.

3. Crossing the Red Sea

Said Rabbi Bunam: "We read in the Talmud that sustenance is as the crossing of the Red Sea.[1] Why is this comparison made? When the children of Israel saw Egyptians in the rear of them, and the Red Sea in front of them, they could not comprehend in what manner God would come to their aid. One believed in this way, another in that; but no one actually believed they would be able to cross the Red Sea. In the same fashion, when a man must make a livelihood, he devises various plans, but God brings it to him in His own way."

[1] Pesachim, 118.

S. I., p. 110.

4. Aids to a Livelihood

Said the Koretzer: "Five things can help us to achieve a livelihood: first, regular and earnest study; second, strict honesty; third, regular prayers for sustenance; fourth, devotion of a tithe to charity; fifth, not to be extravagant or a reckless spender."

Nof. Tz., p. 12.

5. The Bee and Its Sting

Said the Ropshitzer: "To obtain a livelihood from a man is oftentimes like obtaining honey from a bee: it is accompanied by a sting."

F. U. A. O., i, 21.

14. CHARACTER

1. Like Snow

Said the Riziner: "I dislike the man who is like snow: at first white and pure; later, muddy and soiled."

M. D., p. 223.

2. Three Characters

Said the Kotzker: "Three characters can be found in a man about to perform a good deed: if he says: 'I shall do it soon,' his character is poor. If he says: 'I am ready to do it now,' his character is of average quality. If he says: 'I am doing it,' his character is praiseworthy."

M. D., p. 223.

3. The Blanket

Said the Riziner: "Various types of people come to me, but not all are influenced by my counsel to improve themselves. If a man is covered by a blanket, his inner warmth is increased. But if a stone is covered in this way, it receives no warmth." [1]

B. P., p. 60.

[1] See 107:6.

4. The Seraph

The Lubliner Rabbi told a visiting Hasid from Strelisk that Rabbi Uri of his city had "two faces." When the Hasid repeated this to Rabbi Uri, the latter smilingly remarked: "If he knew me better, he would have said that I have 'four faces'; [1] it is thus the Seraphim are described." Henceforth he became known as the Seraph. It was explained that these several faces represented the changes on his countenance during his various occupations: when praying, when learning, when eating, and when receiving visitors.

S. B., pp. 40-41.

[1] Ezekiel 1:6.

5. The Chess Game

Rabbi Bunam said: "We should learn to be careful of every move we make in life, just as the chess player takes care before making a move. Before we take any action, we should think in advance if we will have cause to regret it."

S. S. K., v, 58.

6. Strength of Character

Said the Gerer Rabbi: "We find that Joshua, the faithful servant of Moses, who 'was full with the spirit of wisdom,' [1] was required by the admonition of the Lord to be strong and unbending in his observance of the Torah.[2] How much the more must we, who lack wisdom and strength of character, be constantly on the alert against weakening in our piety, lest we succumb to vices and temptations."

S. S. K., iii, 39.

[1] Deut. 34:9.
[2] Joshua 1:7.

7. The Maggid's Shoe-Laces

Rabbi Leib Saras, speaking metaphorically, was wont to say: "I did not journey to Rabbi Dov Baer of Mezeritz to learn from him interpretations of the Torah, but to note his way of tying his shoe-laces and doffing his shoes. For of what worth are the meanings given to the Torah, after all? In his actions, in his speech, in his bearing, and in his fealty to the Lord, man must make manifest the Torah."

Bl., Gem., p. 64.

8. Undesirable Traits

The Maggid of Koznitz said: "There is an eternal lesson to be found in every tale of the Torah. For example: the story of Cain and Abel teaches us the consequences of jealousy; the story of the Flood: the result of lust; and the story of the Tower of Babel: the outcome of lacking a knowledge of our limitations. In every one of us can be found some of these undesirable traits, and the fate of those who allowed themselves to be overpowered by them, should be a warning to us."

S. S. K., iii, 58.

9. Self-Analysis

Said the Gerer Rabbi: "Every Jew possesses some good trait, pleasing unto the Lord, but no one of us is able to diagnose himself adequately to discover which trait it is. You may be sure that the qualities which bring you self-satisfaction are not those which the Lord approves in you."

S. S. K., ii, 52.

10. The Chief Trait

After the death of Rabbi Uri Strelisker, one of his Hasidim came to Rabbi Bunam. The latter welcomed him and asked him what particular trait of character it was Rabbi Uri's main purpose to instill in his Hasidim. The Hasid replied: "I believe Rabbi Uri sought to make his Hasidim very humble. The Rabbi would order a rich Hasid to draw water at the pump, and to bring in the pail on his shoulder—a thing the man would never have done at home."

Rabbi Bunam remarked: "My way is different; I will explain it to you by a parable: 'Three men were convicted of a crime, and were lodged in a dark dungeon. Two of them were men of intelligence, but the third was a witless person. When food was lowered in the dark, the witless one did not know how to take his share, and would break the plate, or cut himself with the knife. One of his fellow-prisoners sought to aid him by rehearsing with him the necessary behaviour, but the next day, a different arrangement of the food would baffle him again. One of the prisoners then remarked: 'Why waste time teaching this fellow every time? Help me to bore a hole in the wall to admit light, and then he will know how to eat un-aided.' Likewise, I attempt to admit into the soul of a man the fear and the love of God. This is a light whereby a man can learn wise conduct in its entirety, and not trait by trait."

N. R. B., ii, 36-8.

11. The Tailor's Duty

A distinguished Rabbi visited the Mezeritzer for the first time and was received with marked coldness. The Mezeritzer paid little heed to his visitor and even did not hesitate to ridicule him. After the Sabbath, however, the Mezeritzer turned to the Rabbi and said to him: "Let me explain my treatment of you by narrating this story: 'A tailor completed a garment for Rabbi Ezekiel Landau of Prague and brought it to the Rabbi to fit it. He was compelled to pull the garment this way and that, and to take numerous measurements, to the great discomfort of the Rabbi. After the fitting, the tailor begged Rabbi Ezekiel's pardon for the necessity of causing him discomfort.' Now, my friend, you may understand that my treatment of you was necessary to enable me to discern how by your personality and traits of character you may fit into our company."

Sh. Z., p. 14.

12. Finding Our Own Character

Said the Koretzer: " 'Of four sons does the Torah speak,' are the words of the Passover Haggadah. Each one of us can discover his own character in the Torah."

Nof. Tz., p. 33.

13. Self-Praise

Said the Besht: "A man ought to be generous in his praise of a good man. But when he wishes to praise himself and remarks: 'Reuben is very wise, and no one has succeeded in outwitting him except myself,' such praise is unworthy. In this trait, as in others, we must practice discrimination. In love, we must love good and not evil; in fear, we must fear God and not poverty; in praise, we must praise God and not ourselves; in thirst for learning, we must learn Torah and not futile subjects."

K. S. T., p. 11b.

14. Every Human Trait

Said the Besht: "Man should learn pride, and not be proud; he should learn anger, but not feel angry. For man should be a complete personality, possessing all human traits. Does not the Torah picture God as possessing both justice and mercy?"

K. S. T., p. 16b.

15. The Unfriendly World

A Rabbi once said: "Formerly it was true that a man succeeded in the world by devoting himself to the study of the Torah, by service to God, and by kindness to his fellow-creatures, in accordance with the teachings of Simon, the Just (Ethics 1:2; Singer, p. 184). And the man who indulged in envy, cupidity and ambition would be unwelcomed by the world, as Rabbi Eleazar Hakapar remarked. (Ethics 4:28; Singer, p. 198)

"Nowadays, however, the reverse is true. The man who spends his life in devotion to the Torah, and in kind deeds is oftentimes unknown to the world, whereas the man who labors to satisfy his selfish ambitions through envy or cupidity is oftentimes revered by the world."

Rev. H. Masliansky, J. M. J., Dec. 2, 1932.

16. The Title: "Yehudi"

The Gerer Rabbi said: "The Talmud asks with reference to Mordecai, why he is called 'Yehudi' (a Jew) thought he was a Benjaminite. It answers that one who abstains from idolatry is called 'Yehudi.' [1]

"The Talmud also teaches that pride,[2] anger,[3] evil speech,[4] flattery[5] and the like, are comparable to idolatry. My master, the 'Yud' who avoided these traits as much as it is possible for a human being to do, is, therefore, fittingly called 'Yehudi' or 'Yud.' "

Tif. Yeh., p. 6.

[1] Megillah, 13.
[2] Sotah, 5.
[3] Sabbath, 105.
[4] Erkin, 15.
[5] Sotah, 42, paraphrased.

17. Three Types of Character

Said the "Yud": "There are three types of character among servants of God. The servant of the Lord who labors the entire day and yet believes he has as yet accomplished nothing, stands at the summit of merit.

"The servant who has done nothing worth-while in his service unto the Lord and is aware of this, is a character of average merit. He may yet commence to labor in the service of the Lord.

"The servant who is a Zaddik and is proud of this knowledge, is the least commendable character. He deceives himself all his days, and his devotion to the Torah and the Mitzwoth is wasted."

Tif. Yeh., p. 45.

15. CHARITY

1. A Half-Successful Prayer

The wife of a Ropshitzer said to him: "Your prayer was lengthy today. Have you succeeded in bringing it about that the rich should be more generous in their gifts to the poor?"

The Rabbi replied: "Half of my prayer I have accomplished. The poor are willing to accept them."

O. N., p. 29.

2. *Bread Upon the Waters*

Rabbi Itzikel of Kalish was known for his kindness to every one. Once a non-Jewish beggar asked the Rabbi's wife for some bread. At the moment she had only a full loaf, newly-baked, and she disliked cutting it lest it become dry. But the Rabbi enjoined her to give the beggar a portion of this bread.

A few years later, the Rabbi was traveling through the Carpathian mountains towards Hungary. On the way brigands captured him and his companions, and brought them to their chieftain. The latter recognized the Rabbi as his benefactor when he came begging at his door. He freed Rabbi Itzikel and restored to him his possessions.[1]

O. H., p. 15.

[1] Title is suggested by Ecclesiastes, 11:1.

3. *The Safest Investment*

The Ladier disliked spendthrifts intensely, and the members of his family used to hide from him anything costly which they had purchased. Once his grandson, Mendel (later of Libavitz) forgot to remove his expensive silk belt when he entered the room to answer the Rabbi's summons. The Rabbi noticed it and said: "Are you so rich that you can afford so costly a belt? Tell me, what are you doing with your dowry?"

"I gave it to a rich merchant," answered Mendel, "to invest for me."

"And what will you do if he fails? Obey me, and donate your money to charity. It is the safest investment."

Naturally this advice was not followed, and soon after the money was lost in the collapse of the merchant's enterprises.

S. ha-Has., p. 203.

4. *The Rabbi's Decision*

A woman and a man came to Rabbi Phineas Hurwitz of Frankfort with complaints. The woman's lament was that her husband was over-generous in his charities, and the man's complaint was that his rich brother refused to give him any assistance whatsoever. Both defendants were summoned into the presence of the Rabbi.

The husband offered as his defense the fact that he feared an early death, and wished to acquire a great store of good deeds for the profit of his soul.

The brother defended himself by saying that he feared to give away any portion of his wealth lest he have insufficient for his old age.

The Rabbi rendered his decision as follows: "May the Lord protect you both from that which you fear."

This decision was deemed just by the Lord. The philanthropist who feared a short life, lived until a ripe old age, and the miser who was afraid of living too long, was soon summoned by death.

S. ha-Tov, p. 88.

5. Charity Versus Psalm-Singing

The Kaminker related the following story:

"Once I resolved to devote a whole day to the recitation of the entire Book of Psalms. When towards evening, I was approaching the end, the Warden of my Rabbi, the Tzidnover Maggid, came over to me, and said that the Maggid wished to speak with me. I requested him to inform the Rabbi that I would see him as soon as I had finished.

But the Warden returned and bade me come immediately. The Maggid asked me: "Why did you not obey my first summons?" I explained the reason.

The Maggid replied: "I called you to make a collection for an indigent Jew. Psalms can be chanted by the Angels as well, but mortal men are needed to aid the destitute. Charity is a greater duty than the chanting of Psalms, inasmuch as the Angels cannot perform charity."

Beth Phineas, pp. 31-2.

6. Returning Our Gifts

Said the Bratzlaver: "Be not afraid to spend for charity and holy purposes; have confidence that God will return your gifts manifold."

L. E. H., pp. 17-19.

7. A Warning

The Khelmer Maggid reproved some wealthy men for being niggardly to the poor. He said: "We read (Deut. 15:11): 'For the poor shall never cease out of the land.' It follows, therefore, that if the poor should starve to death, some of you will grow poor in order to justify God's statement."

E. J. W., p. 59.

8. Candlesticks

The Punideler Rabbi sold all his belongings in a year of famine in order to aid the poor. His wife hid the Sabbath candlesticks and waited until better times came before she took them out of their place of concealment. When the Rabbi saw them, he fainted. On being revived, he said with a sigh: "How many of the poor could have been fed with the money these candlesticks would have brought!"

M. D., pp. 296-7.

9. Without Ceremony

A Hasid asked Rabbi Bunam: "Why do we not say a blessing when giving charity, as we do when performing other Mitzwoth?"

The Rabbi replied: "Were a blessing required before giving charity, one could give an excuse that he is not clean enough to pronounce the prayer. Hence the Torah has freed him from reciting the 'Berakhah' and expects him to aid the indigent without delay."

S. S. K., i, 150.

10. The Extra Donation

Said Rabbi Bunam: "When members of a community are invited to contribute to a fund, each an allotted amount, some insist upon giving more than their quota. This extra donation is of special delight to the Lord. When the Tabernacle was completed, relates the Midrash, a surplus of gold was discovered. Moses inquired of the Lord what use should be made of it. The Lord instructed him to use it for the making of the receptacle for the Two Tables of the Covenant—the most sacred objects in the Tabernacle." [1]

S. S. K., p. 6.

[1] Shemoth Rabba, 51:1.

11. The Gullible Innkeeper

The Ropshitzer narrated the following experience of his youth:

"I was once walking with other Hasidim to our Rabbi. We discovered we had no money left for the remainder of the long journey to Lublin, where the Rabbi resided. I saw ahead of us on the road, a Jewish inn, the owner of which was known to be hostile to all wanderers and averse to giving them food without payment. He was also known to give charity only to the Charity Chest of Rabbi Meyer Baal ha-Nes. At the same time he mistrusted everyone and expected that Rabbi Meyer Baal ha-Nes would himself at some time come for the money. It was his impression that the Rabbi was still alive, though it was generally known he had been dead for many years. I ordered my comrades to walk ahead of me, and to inform the innkeeper that the son-in-law of Rabbi Meyer Baal ha-Nes would soon arrive. An excellent meal was prepared; I was heartily welcomed, and the Charity Chest was emptied for me. When we reached Lublin, I handed over the contents of the Chest to the Rabbi, to be sent to the Land of Israel."

O. N., p. 46.

12. The Hopeful Thief

The Berditschever traveled from town to town seeking to gather money for a worthy cause, but he met with only moderate success. He regretted the waste of time, and resolved not to undertake a similar enterprise in the future. On returning home he witnessed a gendarme beating a thief who had been caught red-handed. The Rabbi paid the thief's fine, and upon his release inquired if he had not been taught a lesson to abstain from thievery henceforth.

The thief replied: "What if I were beaten! This time my luck was poor, but next time it will be better."

"I must bear this reply in mind," thought the Berditschever. "My own success this time was meager, but I must not abandon a good deed because of setbacks. Next time I may have better fortune."

Kahana, p. 253.

13. The Pawned Beaker

A Rabbi noticed a golden goblet on the Tzanzer's table, and took it in his hand to examine it. The Tzanzer said: "A childless man willed this cup to me, so that I might remember his soul when I use it for Kiddush, Havdalah and Grace after Meals." [1] The next year, the same Rabbi visited the Tzanzer again, and beheld on the table an old silver goblet instead of the golden one. He asked the Tzanzer's son regarding it, and the Tzanzer, who overheard the question, answered: "I was compelled to pawn the golden beaker in order to perform a deed of charity. The soul of the departed donor appears to me in my dreams, and requests me to make use of his goblet, but what can I do? I have not the means to redeem it."

E. Tz., p. 126.

[1] Prayers usually recited over a cup of wine.

14. The Substitutes

Rabbi Shalom Kaminker came to the Belzer on a Sabbath during Hanukah. He turned to the Hasidim and said: "At the home of my late Master, the Ropshitzer, I observed that the Hanukah light was only a substitute, but here I see that even the Sabbath light is merely a substitute." He was asked to explain himself, and he said: "The Ropshitzer kept his silver Hanukah candlesticks in pawn and used the money for charity. But he kept the silver Sabbath candlesticks at home. Here the Belzer Master has but iron candlesticks, even for the Sabbath."

Ohel N., p. 135.

15. Charity More Powerful Than the Zaddik

Rabbi Eliezer Itinga of Dukla asked the Tzanzer to pray for the recovery of his ill son, Joseph. The Tzanzer asked him for a "ransom" of 160 coins (the numerical value of "Joseph") which the father brought over promptly. The Tzanzer thereupon divided the money among the poor, and instructed them to implore God to send a cure to the son of Eliezer. Charity is more powerful than the Zaddik himself.

E. Tz., p. 129.

16. Creating Angels

Said the Koretzer: "He who assists another person creates the Angel Azriel (Divine Helper). He who gives money for charity creates the Angel Zadkiel (Divine Philanthropist)."

"He who is in need of charity and knows he cannot survive without assistance, should not accept it with a wry face and a sense of dislike. Why show hatred to the Angel of Charity newly created by the act of charity?"

Nof. Tz., p. 15.

17. Near to God

The Premislaner commented on the verse: "'The master of the house shall come near unto God, to see whether he has not put his hand unto his neighbor's goods.'"[1] He said: "One who puts his hand unto his own goods to aid his neighbor is near to God."

E. A., p. 47.

[1] Exodus 22:7.

18. Hearts Are Trumps

The Poznaner Rabbi received a letter from a poor woman, a mother of six small children, in which she stated that she had no money to feed her large family, inasmuch as her husband was ill. She added that undoubtedly more money changed hands at one card game at the club of merchants than her husband earned in an entire year.

The Rabbi, thereupon, went to the club and asked permission to join the game. As soon as he sat at the table, and the cards were distributed, the Rabbi threw the woman's letter on the table, and exclaimed: "Hearts are trumps."

The merchants read the letter, and gave to the Rabbi all the money in the bank of the game, so that he might present it to the destitute woman.

L. H. F., p. 92.

19. Rabbi Schmelke and the Beggar

Rabbi Schmelke once had no money to give to a beggar. He ransacked his wife's drawer, took from it a ring and gave it to the destitute man. His wife returned, saw that the drawer was open and that her ring was missing. She raised a hue and cry, and when her husband explained his action, she asked him to run after the beggar, since the ring was worth fifty thalers.

The Rabbi ran swiftly in pursuit, and catching up with the beggar, said: "I have just learned that the ring is worth fifty thalers. Let no one cheat you by giving you less than its value."

J. Margoshes in the Jewish Morning Journal, Nov. 18, 1932.

20. The Charitable and the Uncharitable

The Besht commented on the passage: "As to almsgiving, there are four dispositions: he who desires to give, but not that others should give; he who desires others to give, but not himself; he who gives and wishes others to give; he who gives not himself and wishes

not others to give.[1] The last person seems to have no connection
with almsgiving; hence there may be only three dispositions. Why
are four, however, mentioned? Light is known to exist because
there is darkness; wisdom because of folly; righteousness because of
wickedness; pleasure because of pain; memory because of forgetfulness. One is the chair upon which the other sits; one is like the
man who holds an object in his upraised hand, and the other is like
the object thus held. In the same way, the uncharitable man is the
chair on which the charitable sits; or the hand which raises up the
uncharitable."

K. S. T., p. 14a.

[1] Ethics 5: 16; Singer, p. 202.

21. Breaking Off Sins

The "Yud" was accustomed to give away all his possessions to
charity. A Hasid asked him: "Are we not taught by our Sages not
to give away more than a fifth-part of our wealth?"[1]
The "Yud" replied: "A fifth part is sufficient to fulfil the duty of
giving alms. But when a man wishes to 'break off his sins by almsgiving' (Daniel 4:24), he may give his all, for 'all that a man hath
will he give for his soul (his life).'" (Job 2: 4).

Tif. Yeh., p. 3.

[1] Kethubhoth, 50a.

22. Food for God

Said the Trisker Maggid: "It is written: 'My food which is
presented unto me for offerings.' (Numbers 28:2). This means:
'Your offerings to charity constitute My food which you should
present unto Me.'"

V. S., p. 44.

23. The Reward of Charity

The Ropshitzer was told that his Master, the Rimanover, blessed
a man, and that the latter was becoming richer every day. He inquired why this man deserved to receive a blessing of such magnitude. The Rimanover replied: "I merely blessed him that he might
enjoy a comfortable living. But the man gives away so much to
charity that his fortune must be increased abundantly by Heaven, so
that he may have sufficient for his personal comforts."

Ohel N., p. 35.

24. An Avenue of Salvation

Said the Bratzlaver: "Aiding the deserving saves a man from
melancholy, indolence, vanity of speech and pride."

K. L. H., p. 5.

25. A Perfect Zaddik

Said the Kossover: "We are told by our Sages that one who donates a coin in order that his son may live is a perfect Zaddik.[1]

[1] Pesachim, 8.

Why is this so? I will explain by relating an episode in my experience. Among my adherents was a man of affluence who was always ready with a sizable donation when solicited. Once he came to me imploring that I offer a prayer for his son who was dangerously ill. I was greatly surprised, however, that he did not offer to make a donation to charity for the sake of his son's recovery. I then understood the Talmudical saying. A man may donate when appealed to, because he possesses a clement heart, but he may be unconvinced it will benefit him as well as the poor. He is a plain Zaddik. Another, however, donates because he will receive greater profit than the indigent; he may even be inclined to miserliness and possess a stubborn heart. Yet because of his belief he chooses to break his natural inclination. He is a perfect Zaddik."

E. Tz., p. 67.

26. It Is Too Late

The Bialystoker Maggid narrated the following story:

"A wealthy man died and his soul was being taken to the Heavenly Tribunal. On the way the soul of the magnate passed through a palatial room where many spirits seemed to be in bliss. The rich man's soul begged permission to remain there. 'You may remain,' answered the escorting Angel, 'provided you have in your possession the price of entrance.'

'To be sure I have,' retorted the soul. 'I have brought an abundance of money with me.'

'It is not money that is acceptable here,' was the answer. 'Do you see these charity receipts? It is these that are necessary for entrance to this palace in Eden.'

'Let me return to earth,' petitioned the spirit, 'and I shall convert my wealth into receipts from institutions of charity. Then I will return here.'

'It is too late now,' was the Angel's answer."

Told to Samuel Spitz by Mrs. Miriam Tetove.

27. Contrary to Man's Nature

Said the Kossover: "If you give a donation to a poor man, and the latter returns it, asking for a still larger gift, your acquiescence to his request will bring you a boundless reward, since it is contrary to the nature of man."

E. Tz., p. 66.

28. The Bratzlaver on "Charity"

A.

"1. Before the recital of prayers, a man should give to charity. Thus will he avoid alien thoughts.

"2. Through charity a man is rescued from poverty and made the possessor of wealth.

"3. Charity draws mercies down from Heaven.

"4. Through charity man's mind is clarified, and he attains the fear and love of God.

"5. Charity awakens within a man compassion for his soul; it prompts him to repent, and to strive for holiness.

"6. Charity brings perfection to every financial enterprise. A man should always bear in mind that his desire for profit is for the purpose of being able to donate to charity.

"7. Through charity and kindness a man attains to godliness.

"8. Upon charity the universe is founded.

"9. Give charity before departing on a journey, and you will be saved from delays and irritations.

"10. Through charity you may subdue the body to the soul, and folly to reason. Thus you will go forth from darkness to light, from death to life; from animality to humanity. You will lose forgetfulness and gain memory.

"11. Charity for Palestine is greater than charity for other lands. Through it you include yourself within its holy atmosphere.

"12. When you give aid to scholars, you gain a share in their sacred learning.

"13. He who gives no charity and performs no deeds of kindness is no true human being.

"14. Charity transforms a man's impulse to cruelty into kindness of heart. This is the chief service of charity.

"15. Charity is a cure for every heartache.

"16. Imitate God by being compassionate and forgiving. He will in turn have compassion upon you, and pardon your offenses."

L. E. H., pp. 89-91.

B.

"1. Charity and kind deeds are the best mediators between Israel and their Father in Heaven.

"2. Charity brings Redemption nearer; it saves from death, and causes the Shekinah to approach.

"3. He who gives to charity places the Lord in his debt. He is called a 'perfect Zaddik' and he finds it easy to turn away from evil.

"4. While it is commendable to aid students of the Torah more than commoners, the Jewish law knows no such distinction. The latter also must be aided.

"5. He who restores to its owner a stolen object is like one who gives to charity.

"6. Arbitration is justice blended with charity.

"7. Express your thankfulness to him who aids you, and say not he has made no gift of his own.

"8. Charity has the weight of all Mitzwoth together.

"9. Greater is he who makes the appeal for charity than the giver himself.

"10. A penny here and a penny there add up to a great sum.

"11. Greater than Moses is he who gives charity anonymously.

"12. He who gives a penny to a poor man receives six blessings: he who shows his sympathy with the poor man receives eleven blessings.

"13. He who practices charity is endowed by God with means, and he shall have rich, wise, and learned sons.

"14. On Rosh ha-Shanah it is decreed how much a man shall lose throughout the year. If he is sensible he will take this loss in the form of gifts to charity.

"15. Jerusalem will be ransomed through charity.

"16. Great is hospitality for it unites those who are far apart.

"17. When people do not give to charity, the government takes away their money through new forms of taxation.

"18. Give charity with both hands, and your prayer will be heard.

"19. Faith, truth, and family peace come to the man of charity.

"20. The produce of the field grows well on the land of the charitable farmer.

"21. In times of tribulation your charities are remembered in Heaven.

"22. The king and his lords are the friends of the philanthropist.

"23. Terrors cannot dwell in the abode of the charitable man.

"24. He who appeals for charity brings salvation.

"25. A home that supports no charity will be the prey of flames.

"26. By the virtue of charity a man is preserved from pride, and he attains the merit of humility.

"27. Generosity brings in its train the love of Zaddikim.

"28. Jews who give to charity are not expelled from the land.

"29. Charity brings prosperity and peace.

"30. Charity shields a man's children from misfortunes.

"31. He who feels resentment when he beholds a man prospering who formerly was poor, is a partner of Satan.

"32. A Mitzwah that costs money is worth more than one that costs nothing.

"33. He who gives charity with a smile is truly a whole-hearted man.

"34. Give charity while thou hast the means; while the opportunity is thine, and while thou art thine own master.

"35. He who provides a suitable livelihood for a learned man shall sit in the Heavenly Academy.

"36. Charity is greater than the sacrifices brought to the altar; yet kindness is greater than charity.

"37. Deserving causes and the deserving poor are scarce. Miss not your opportunity to give wisely.

"38. Even a poor man must give some charity. He may then be saved from the poverty which afflicts him.

"39. Philanthropists prevent plagues in their towns.

"40. Charity is of great use on the Judgment Day.

"41. Kind-hearted folk should be watchful lest their kindness does not result in more evil than good.

"42. Kindhearted people live long.

"43. The money a man gives to Palestine preserves his wealth.

"44. The giving of a tithe to charity turns maledictions into blessings."

Sef. Ham., pp. 123-127.[1]

[1] The sources of these aphorisms, many of them quoted directly from the Talmud, are found in the *Sef. Ham.*, Ed. 1912, etc.

29. With All Thy Possessions

Rabbi Nahum Tzernobiler asked a wealthy man to contribute a large sum to a charitable cause. The man refused. Rabbi Nahum thereupon sold his share in the World-to-Come and used the money for the cause. His Hasidim inquired how he could bring himself to make such a sale. The Rabbi answered: "I say twice daily in the 'Sh'ma': 'Love thy God with all thy heart, with all thy soul and with all thy possessions.'[1] What beside my share in the World-to-Come does a poor man like myself possess? Shall I prove to be a falsifier and refuse to give to God that which I do in truth possess?"

D. D., p. 97.

[1] Talmudical translation of "Meodekha"; Berakhoth, 54. The verse is in Deut. 6:5.

16. CHILDREN

1. Learning from the Child

Rabbi Bunam said: "We may learn three things from the child in serving the Lord. First, the child is always happy at being alive. Second, the child is always active. Third, the child always cries for anything he wishes. In the same fashion, we should serve the Lord in a joyful mood; we should always be zealous to perform the Lord's commands; we should tearfully implore the Lord to fulfil our aspirations."[1]

S. S. K., i, 53.

[1] "The Great Maggid" is said to have remarked to his disciple, Rabbi Sussya: "The tenfold doctrine I cannot teach you, but you may learn it as an apprentice from an infant and a thief. Three things you may learn from an infant: first, to be cheerful without special cause; second, not to lie inert, even for a moment; third, to demand with all thy strength, whereof thou mayest have need." See Fuchs, James, "From a Chassidic Treasure Trove," *Jewish Tribune,* Dec. 19, 1930, p. 5; translated from "Der Grosse Maggid" of Martin Buber. See 65:4.

2. Delight in Children

Rabbi Meyer Hurwitz of Tiktin heard that a dozen distinguished Rabbis, all of them his grandsons, planned to pay him honor by attending a family gathering in celebration of his birthday. The aged Rabbi immediately sent a messenger to halt their plans, and enjoined him to deliver the following word: "From the children that the Lord has granted me, I expect delight in the World-to-Come, not in This-World."

S. ha-Tov, p. 112.

3. The Beloved Child

Said the Besht: "The Lord does not object even if one misunderstands what a man learns, provided he only strives to understand out of his love of learning. It is like a father whose beloved child petitions him in stumbling words, yet the father takes delight in hearing him."

Dubnow, T. ha-Has., p. 55.

4. The Lord Understands His Children

The Berditschever overheard a young man mumbling his prayers. He called him into his presence on the plea of asking a question. When the youth stood before him, the Rabbi began to mumble his words, and the young man could not understand him. He said this to the Rabbi, who remarked: "Is it not exactly in this manner that you have prayed to God?"

"Yes," answered the youth. "I was in a hurry, and therefore did not recite distinctly. Yet it is my hope that God understood me as a father always understands the mumblings of his little child."

This explanation pleased the Rabbi and he made use of it on numerous occasions.[1]

Kahana, p. 265.

[1] Spiegel, S., *Hebrew Reborn*, p. 149 has the following: "God loves not so much the man of learning and intelligence as the man of simple mind who artlessly and confidently puts all his faith in Heaven. Rabbi Nachman of Bratzlav used this simile: "As a father rejoices when his son makes his first halting steps and finds delight in him although he cannot walk, so the Holy One, Blessed be He, finds delight in everyone in Israel who endeavours to fulfil a commandment."

5. Refrain from Indulging Children

Said the Bratzlaver: "Children will be healthy and well-bred, if parents do not play with them overmuch and do not indulge them too generously."

L. E. H., p. 17.

6. The Heights of Love

Schmelke's pupil, Moshe Leib Sassover, sat at the bedside of all the sick boys of his city, nursing and tending them. Once he said: "He who cannot suck the matter from the boils of a child sick with the plague has not yet gone halfway up the height of love for his fellow-men."

E. Tz., p.45 (Spiegel, p. 147).

7. For Outsiders

The Ropshitzer Rabbi chanced to pass through a village in which ten male Jewish adults resided. They owned a small house of worship and a tiny cemetery. The Rabbi met a Jewish child and said to him: "Tell me, my boy, since the community has only ten males over thirteen, if one of them should die, what good will the synagogue be? Or, if no one should die, of what use is the cemetery?"

The child promptly answered: "The cemetery is intended for strangers passing through the village."

This sagacious reply won the Rabbi's praise.

Shivchei Naftali, p. 18.

8. Children's Sport

The Radiner Rabbi, author of "Hafetz Hayyim" heard that children were playing a trick on the water-carrier. They would fill his pails at the town-pump with water at night, during the winter, so that the poor man would be compelled to break the ice in the pails the following morning. He made it a habit, therefore, to empty the pails at midnight when he left the synagogue.

M. D., p. 296.

9. Impious Children of Pious Parents

Said the Rimanover: "Children of excellent religious upbringing oftentimes become impious. Why is this so? Is it not taught that if a lad receives good breeding, it will become habitual with him, and he will not forsake it in maturity?[1] The reason for the impiety of children is that oftentimes they are reared on money dishonestly gained. When they grow up, they imitate their parents."

Em. L., p. 48.

[1] Proverbs, 22:6.

10. Learning As a Child

Said the Koretzer: "In the 'Ethics of the Fathers' (4:25),[1] it is said: 'If one learns as a child, what is it like? Like ink written on clean paper. If one learns as an old man, what is it like? Like ink written on blotted paper.' It may be asked: 'Why discourage the older man?' But the sentence may be understood thus: 'One who learns as a child, namely as one who concentrates his thoughts on that which he is learning, and has no foreign thoughts at the time, is like ink written on clean paper; his learning will be engraved upon his mind, and in his heart.' Thus, even an old man may learn as a child, if he displays the necessary concentration."

Nof. Tz., p. 58.

[1] Singer, p. 198.

11. *The Bratzlaver on "Children"*

"1. When your children grow up, their ability to gain a livelihood grows accordingly. Have no anxiety regarding them.

2. A modest woman has good children.

3. A well-nourished mother has healthy children.

4. We have the kind of children we deserve.

5. It is like unto murder to chop down a fruit-bearing tree.

6. One who adopts an orphan is like unto him who begot him.

7. One who teaches a fatherless child is like unto him who begot him.

8. One who marries for money shall have unworthy children, and shall lose the dowry within a short time.

9. One who competes unfairly with another is as one who commits adultery.

10. Good children are a source of cure and healing for their parents.

11. One should show no favoritism among his children.

12. One should teach his children good manners from babyhood.

13. One who longs to perform a Mitzwah but finds no opportunity to do so, will see his son perform the righteous deed.

14. If husband and wife quarrel, they cannot raise good children.

15. The strict leader will not have understanding sons.

16. One who displeases his parents will have disobedient sons.

17. When the father is quick-tempered, his sons are fools.

18. One is immortal if his descendants study the Torah."

Sef. Ham., pp. 26-33.

12. *What Hast Thou Brought?*

The Sassover was persuaded by his wife's father to try his hand at business. When the merchants of the little town left for the market in the larger city, the future Rebbe joined them. On his arrival, the Sassover repaired to the synagogue, became engrossed in his studies, and was forced to return home empty-handed. On his arrival, his children, like those of his comrades, began to cry out: "Father, what hast thou brought us?"

The Rabbi fell to the ground unconscious, and when he was revived, his father-in-law anxiously inquired: "Have you lost the money?"

"No," replied the Sassover; "the money is intact. But the cries of my children reminded me that when I return to my Source, I shall be asked the same question: 'What hast thou brought?' And I shall be unable to show anything whatsoever."

No more persuasion was attempted to initiate him in the ways of business.

D. D., p. 244.

13. A "True Jew"

A hard frost covered the ground; the cold penetrated the garments and chilled the body. Nevertheless, the Gerer, as was his custom, arranged that his two grandchildren, still in their tender childhood, should accompany him, seated on the sled, as he journeyed to visit the Kotzker. A friend of the Rabbi protested, and said: "Can they not wait to acquire a knowledge of Hasidism until they are older? Why risk their health in this cold?" The Rabbi smiled and answered: "Be not anxious; it is worth every hardship for these youngsters to look upon a 'true Jew.'"

M. E. H., i, 69.

17. CHRISTIANITY AND JUDAISM

1. Moses and Balaam

Said Rabbi Bunam: "The Midrash tells us that Balaam was sent to the non-Jews as a Prophet so that the non-Jews might have no excuse for rejecting monotheism.[1] But the non-Jews can say: 'Why did the Jews receive a saintly Prophet, whereas ours is one of poor repute and character?'

"The answer is as follows: Moses wished to teach the Egyptians and others also the true conception of God. But their wise men refused to believe in him because they doubted his miracles. Yet when Balaam came to them, they had faith in his superstitious assertions. Hence, on the Day of Judgment, the non-Jewish nations will be asked: 'Since you did believe in some supernatural acts, why did you not believe in Moses and his teachings?'"

N. R. B., ii, 46-7.

[1] Bemidbar Rabba, 20:1.

2. Jesus, the Jew

The Pulnoer Rabbi in one of his works relates this parable regarding Jesus: "A Christian king once invited the ambassadors of several countries to a banquet. Among the guests was a Jew. In the theological discussion which ensued, the king invited a Mohammedan guest to state his opinion regarding Jesus. The Moslem asserted that Jesus was not the Son of God, but merely a distinguished Prophet.

"The Jew, when called upon, stated his belief that Jesus was merely a Jew. Wishing to soften his answer, he thereupon received permission to relate the following story:

"'A dealer in gems discovered that one of his jewels possessed a flaw which rendered it of lesser value. He departed for another city, where he was unknown, dressed himself in peasant garb, and went to a jeweler with the tale that he owned a gem which he would sell, cheaply, since he was no expert. The jeweler bought it for a few coins, and, in his eagerness to drive a bargain, neglected to examine it. He re-sold it to a customer, who in turn re-sold it, until it came at last to the king. The king asked the judgment of his expert jewelers, and they, not wishing to inform him he had been deceived, pronounced it genuine. The king then asked the gem-dealer who had originally sold it, and he pronounced it valueless. The king was greatly angered, but the jeweler said: 'How can I testify that it is genuine, when it was I who by donning peasant garb persuaded a jeweler to purchase it?'

"Thus it is with us Jews. Jesus was one of us. Who, therefore, knows better than ourselves his true nature?"

Kahana, S. ha-Hasiduth, p. 90.

18. CIRCUMCISION

1. *A Lesson in Manners*

Said the Belzer: "Circumcision is performed on the eighth day in order to teach us the following lesson: when we pay a visit we should first greet the matron of the home, and then give our attention to the master. The infant is given an opportunity first to welcome the Sabbath Bride before he is initiated into the company of the Master." [1]

D. S., p. 81.

[1] Tanchuma, Ed. Buber; Lev. 22:27; ii, 94.

2. *Elijah's Punishment*

A Warsaw Jew, who cared little for religion, invited the Gerer Rabbi to the circumcision of his son, which was to be performed on the Sabbath. On his arrival, several of the guests threw away their cigars. The Rabbi noticed this desecration of the Sabbath, and spoke as follows:

"There is a Midrash [1] to the effect that the Prophet Elijah was punished for complaining that Israel had forgotten God's Covenant,[2] and, as a penalty, he was ordered to be present in spirit at every circumcision. For this reason, the chair, on which the person who holds the child sits during the circumcision, is named 'Elijah's Chair.' I have never understood why being present at the sacred ceremony should be deemed a punishment. But now I perceive that it is a grave annoyance to be present at some ceremonies of our faith."

S. S. K., iv, 102.

[1] Pirkei d'Rabbi Eliezer, 29.
[2] Circumcision is called a "covenant" in Genesis 17:10.

3. *The Informer's Invitation*

A man known as an informer against his fellow-Jews, came to the Radomsker and said: "Rabbi, I have come to invite you to accept the Mitzwah of holding my son at his circumcision."

The Rabbi replied: "You are continually committing offenses, yet you expect to honor others by extending to them Mitzwahs."

"But Rabbi," countered the informer. "If you should shame me by refusing, you will have committed an offense."

"Look here, my man," answered the Rabbi. "You permit yourself serious offenses, yet you are unwilling to permit me to commit even a minor one."

Then he spoke at length to the informer, and the latter promised to offend no longer against his brethren.

O. S., p. 57.

4. Without Thought of Reward

Said the Premislaner: "We read the words: 'Even as he has entered into the covenant, so may he enter into the Torah, the nuptial canopy, and into good deeds,' [1] Even as the boy enters through circumcision into the covenant of the Sons of Abraham without any thought of pride or self-benefit, so may he enter into the Torah, marriage and good deeds in the same spirit of service without reward."

E. A., p. 55.

[1] Singer, p. 365.

5. Circumcision of the Heart

Said the Gerer: "Since we are commanded to call the Sabbath a day of delight,[1] how may we listen to a sermon which prompts us to thoughts which sadden our soul since they show to us all our shortcomings? And is not work for the improvement of our soul a difficult labor which should be forbidden on the Sabbath?

"The answer is that the improvement of our soul is called in Deuteronomy (10:16): 'Circumcision of the obduracy (foreskin) of our heart,' and we are taught that 'circumcision overcomes the sanctity of the Sabbath.' " [2]

R. T., ii, 80.

[1] Isaiah 58:13.
[2] Sabbath 132. "Obduracy" is in Isaac Leeser's Translation of the Bible.

6. The Future of the Child

At a Circumcision Feast, the Berditschever said: "We read (Psalms 119:162): 'I rejoice at Thy word as one that findeth great spoil.' We are now present at the performance of God's Covenant with the seed of Abraham, and we should rejoice. Some may think: 'Why this joy?' How can we tell whether the new member of our people will grow into a man of righteousness?' The Talmud [1] answers this question by teaching us to bless God as the Lord of Goodness who doeth good unto others, even when we receive a doubtful blessing. For example, if a man should find a treasure, he should bless the Lord, even though he fears that his discovery will be confiscated by the government, and he will be punished for keeping it. In the same fashion, when a new baby is a blessing to us

[1] Berakhoth, 60.

in the present, it is not our function to look into the probable future. This is the message the Psalmist would convey to us in his words."

E. O., p. 60.

19. COMFORT AND CONSOLATION

1. *Remembering Another's Sorrow*

Rabbi Isaac Meyer of Ger lost every one of his thirteen sons. When the youngest died, the mother refused to be comforted. Her husband said to her:

"Our sons have not died in vain. If a misfortune like ours should happen to another man, he will remember that Isaac Meyer [1] lost thirteen holy sons, and he will not feel angry against the Lord."

S. S. K., p. 78.

[1] His successor was his grandson, Aryeh Leb Alter.

2. *The Mourner's Kaddish*

Rabbi Bunam said: "A king selected out of his armies a regiment of royal guards of whom he was extremely proud. When a member of the royal regiment died, the loss was deeply felt by him.

"Likewise, when a Jew dies, a member of God's Chosen People, the Lord takes the loss to heart, there being one less to glorify and sanctify His Name. We, therefore, pray: 'May His Great Name regain Its Greatness and Its Sanctity' [1] since the son of the departed takes his father's place."

S. S. K., v, 69.

[1] See Singer, p. 77.

3. *"My People"*

The Medzibozer said, in comment on the words: "Comfort ye, comfort ye, My people, saith your God" (Isaiah 40:1): "When God calls you 'My People,' be comforted by this."

Butz. D., p. 16.

4. *Earth's Obedience*

The Lubliner said to Rabbi Mordecai of Tzernobil: "When I reflect upon my continuous misdeeds, I fall into despair. The only comfort I derive is from the knowledge that I shall soon return unto earth, and earth does not disobey God."

Tif. Yeh., p. 23.

20. COMPASSION FOR SINNERS

1. *Aware of Their Quality*

The Lubliner said: "I love more the wicked man who is aware of his wickedness, than the good man who is aware of his goodness."

M. D., p. 221.

2. *Tolerating the Sinner*

Rabbi Sussya was seated in the reception room of the Mezeritzer Maggid. A man known for his evil ways, entered the room to seek the Maggid's presence. He came over to the Maggid and with characteristic brazen-facedness stated his wish. Rabbi Sussya could not restrain himself, and shouted at the sinner:

"How dare you approach this Holy Rabbi without a sense of shame for your transgressions?"

When the man had left, Rabbi Sussya besought the Maggid's forgiveness for his interference. The Maggid said:

"Learn from me, Rabbi Sussya, to tolerate the sinner. Ignore the wickedness in him, and endeavor to elicit the good."

This became Rabbi Sussya's habit, and when he would encounter a sinner, he would blame himself for being a sinner, and tearfully implore the Lord for pardon. This self-accusation always moved the real sinner to repentance, and he would beg the Rabbi to instruct him in the ways of self-betterment.

T. H. A., p. 42.

3. *Forbidden Food*

The Gerer Rabbi visited a wealthy Jew on behalf of a communal cause. He found him eating his dinner and wished him a good appetite. The host laughingly remarked: "If the Rabbi knew that I am eating forbidden food, he would forbear from wishing me a good appetite."

The Rabbi replied: "Indeed, mine host, it is particularly to you that my wish applies. If you were partaking of forbidden food, not because you are hungry, but because you do not concern yourself with a disregard for the Law, your transgression would be more serious." [1]

S. S. K., p. 74.

[1] Abodah Zarah, 26b.

4. *Transgression With Knowledge*

Said the Riziner: "We read in Isaiah (26:10): 'May the wicked be spared, who never learned righteousness.' This shows that it is better not to learn the duties of piety if one does not intend to observe them. One who transgresses knowingly cannot hope for mercy without repentance." [1]

N. I., p. 29.

[1] The text is translated in J. Translation, as "Let favour be shown to the wicked, yet will he not learn righteousness."

5. *Rabbi Levi Isaac, the "Compassionate"*

The surname of Rabbi Levi Isaac, as carried in the registers of the authorities, was "The Compassionate," a name not borne by his father before him. This name came to him in the following fashion:

When the Imperial decree bade every one add a surname to his given name, and the Jews were tardy in fulfilling this behest, the Warden of Berditschev went from house to house, to enforce registration. When he came to the Zaddik's house, speaking his errand by rote, the Zaddik looked above and beyond him, and said, not heeding him: "Follow in the footsteps of the Lord, and as He is compassionate, be thou compassionate." [1] But the Warden, catching hold of the word, took out his list and entered: Rabbi Levi Isaac; surname, the Compassionate.

I. L. B., p. 144.

[1] Based on Sotah, 140.

6. Put Off Your Na'al

The Dinover offended the Ropshitzer and paid him a visit to placate him. Seeing the Dinover tremble from fear, the Ropshitzer said: "It is true that it lies within my power to punish you for your disrespect. Fear not, however, for I shall not use this power. The Lord said to Moses: 'Put off thy shoes from off thy feet' (Exodus 3:5). This word 'Na'al' (shoe) contains the initials for the words: 'Nesicha' (Bite); 'Akitzah' (Sting); and 'Lechisha' (Hiss). In the 'Ethics of the Fathers' (2:15),[1] we are told that these are the three means by which the Sages inflict punishment for disrespect. But the Lord instructed Moses, the first of the Sages, not to use these powers of punishment if the sinner regretted his offense."

E. Tz., p. 112.

[1] Singer, p. 189.

7. Standing Before the Lord

The Koretzer commented on the verse: "But Abraham stood yet before the Lord" (Gen. 18:22). Abraham and his successors, the Zaddikim in each generation, still stand before the Lord to implore compassion for sinners, as Abraham did on behalf of the Sodomites."

Nof. Tz., p. 53.

8. The Bratzlaver on "Compassion"

"1. Where there is no compassion, famine breaks out.

2. Where there is no compassion, crime increases.

3. He who feels no compassion will become insane.

4. He who repays good for evil will live many years.

5. Evil desires depart from the compassionate.

6. If we do not aid another in his tribulation, it is as if we caused him the tribulation.

7. Toothache comes to a man who has no compassion for animals."

Sef. Ham., p. 147.

21. CONDUCT AND ITS RULES

1. Sayings of Rabbi Moshe Leib Sassover

A. Gate of the Fear of God

"1. A man cannot attain fear of God except through meekness and through disdain of worldliness.

2. Picture to yourself the vastness of the Universe, and you will feel awe towards its Creator.

3. A man can obtain nothing from God, except through prayer offered in a spirit of awe and with love for Him.

4. A man cannot serve the Lord with awe and in love, one hour of the day and forget Him the remainder of the day."

B. Gate of Prayer

"1. If you have accepted the Kingdom of God during your prayer and then have disobeyed His commands later, you have mocked your King.

2. How can you serve God in awe and love, if you do not know why you should fear and love Him?

3. To subdue your anger is worthier than fasting.

4. To hear yourself insulted and not to make reply is worthier than self-chastisement."

C. Joy in Service

"1. If you are of small account in your own eyes, you have ascended to a position of holiness.

2. The joy of your service demonstrates the strength of your belief in God.

3. If melancholy overpowers you, it will be easy for you to transgress against the entire Torah.

4. If you are convinced that This-World serves you as an avenue to Eternal Rest, how can you be melancholy?

5. If you are convinced that you are a trusted servant of the Supreme King, you have true cause for rejoicing.

6. Bitter is death to the wicked, but sweet is death to the pious, since it brings to them Eternal Rest.

7. This-World is the world of deeds. Proper deeds and contentment bring to a man immortality and eternal life.

8. No tribulation is worthy of attention unless it interferes with the performance of proper deeds."

D. Good Traits of Character

"1. Remove anger from your heart, 'for anger rests in the lap of fools.' (Eccl. 7:9.)

2. The Bible says: 'A soft answer turneth away wrath.' (Proverbs 15:1.)

3. Whether evil or good events betide, let it be the same to you, since you are a stranger and a sojourner on this earth.

4. A sigh breaks the body of a man. (Berakhoth, 58.)

5. Wherefore shouldst thou have anxiety over a world that is not thine?

6. If peace is absent, everything else is lacking.

7. Be patient in the enduring of insults, for what art thou and what is thy life?

8. Insult comes to thee in place of misfortunes.

9. Close thine eyes that thou mayest not behold evil and impurity.

10. Silence is a fence around wisdom. (*Avoth*, 3:17; Singer, p. 193.)

11. Be deliberate and thou wilt have no regrets.

12. Do not reprove another unless thine own actions are correct.

13. If thou art not a loyal friend of Israel, thou hast not tasted fear of the Lord.

14. The soul of another Jew is as much a part of Godhead as thine own soul, and thou art his brother.

15. A man may be an upright servant of the Lord until temptation comes to him. It is only the one who has withstood temptation who is truly righteous.

16. If opposition causes a man to turn away from the Lord, it is a sign that he was far from Him before.

17. If you are convinced that good and evil occurrences are the handiwork of the Lord, you will not be distressed if anything transpires in your own life which is not in accordance with your desires."

E. Belief

"1. If you cannot comprehend a mortal man's thoughts, how much the less can you hope to comprehend God's reasons. All that is possible is merely to have faith.

2. If passion burns within you, remember who endowed you with this passion, and you will not make use of it for evil purposes.

3. A holy man was healed by the use of many drugs. He said: 'Now I have received proof that the contents of the universe were created for the benefit of man.'"

H. G., p. i-v.

F. Miscellaneous

"1. Be not offended by one who harms thee. Some of the goodness resident within him may be lacking in thee.

2. It is not permissible to petition God by prayer to change natural laws for your own sake.

3. The main superiority of man over animals is in his power of speech. But if we speak vanity and folly, we are no better than animals.

4. In material pleasures, we feel gladness for the moment only. But in divine pleasures, our feeling of gladness never ceases."

E. Tz., pp. 58-9.

2. The Lightning Flashes

The Riziner declared that Hasiduth demands not only nobility of spirit, but also nobility of dress and manners. He wished to emphasize not only the duties of man to God, but also the duties of man to man. He cited the following parable: "A man walked on a country road one moonless night. From time to time flashes of lightning illumined the path. Once when he looked towards the sky to observe how the flash split the heavens, he fell into a pit. He climbed out with difficulty, and henceforth resolved to avail himself of the light from the flashes in order to see the road clearly.

"Hasidism," added the Riziner, "is a flash of lightning in a dark universe. Avail yourself of it in order to walk through this world without disaster."

D. D., p. 307.

3. The Two Tablets

The Ropshitzer declared that previous to his birth, an Angel showed him a tablet divided into two columns.

On the right he read: "In order to know the Torah, a man must have no compassion on his wife and children. If he works to satisfy their needs, he will have no time to study the Torah" (Erubin, 22). On the left, opposite, he read: "He who pities people, is pitied in Heaven. A man must care for his family even beyond his strength, for their lives are dependent upon his" (Hullin, 84).

On the right: "The learned man should be like unto a fiery flame" (Taanith, 4). On the left: "Who will inherit the World-to-Come? The meek and lowly one, who bows when entering and leaving" (Sanhedrin, 88).

On the right: "A man should be wise in his fear of the Lord" (Berakhoth, 17). On the left: "You shall be simple-hearted before your God.[1] If you are simple-hearted, your lot is with your God" (Yalkut Shofetim).

On the right: "Be satisfied with a minimum, like Rabbi Chanina ben Dosa" (Taanith, 24). On the left: "'He who pledges himself not to drink wine, and thus afflicts his body, is called a sinner" (Taanith, 11).

He continued in this strain for a while, and then said: "I was engrossed in the thought of how difficult it is to find a way of behavior which will reconcile these antinomies. Suddenly I heard the words: 'Mazal Tov,[2] a male child is born.' I remained wondering, and since then I still labor to find the way to follow both rules, however contradictory."

D. D., pp. 237-8.

[1] Deut. 18:13, paraphrase.
[2] "Good Luck."

22. CONTENTMENT

1. *Contentment of Spirit*

Rabbi Bunam commented on Genesis 49:15: "For he saw a resting-place that it was good, and the land that it was pleasant, and [1] he bowed his shoulder to bear, and became a servant under task-work." He said:

"One who desires release from worries may obtain it by bending his shoulder to bear complacently anything which may befall him, and by being satisfied of spirit no matter what its outcome."

S. S. K., i, 13.

[1] The substitution of "when" for "and" turns the verse into an ethical statement.

2. *"Dort Wo Du Nicht Bist"*

A Hasid asked Rabbi Bunam's advice on the wisdom of moving to another village. He reminded him of the Talmudic counsel, that if a man cannot prosper in one community, he should journey to another.[1] The Rabbi replied: "The Talmud may mean that, if he is dissatisfied in his home community, he may take up his residence in another. There, however, he may discover that conditions are even worse."

S. S. K., ii, 93.

[1] Baba Metzia, 75.

3. *Aphorisms on Contentment*

Said the Kobriner:

"1. If I were but certain that I have really aided one man to serve God better, I would be contented.

"2. If I knew that I have answered a single 'Amen' as it ought be uttered, I would be contented.

"3. If I knew that when my soul arrives in Heaven, it will be announced that a 'Jew' has been brought in, I would be contented."

O. Y., p. 164.

4. *Do Not Complain*

The Turbiner Rabbi narrated the following tale: "Two Hasidim were traveling to the Besht by horse and wagon. On a narrow road, they were compelled to slacken their pace because a nobleman's carriage ahead had developed a defect in one of the wheels. One Hasid complained that with such slow going they would be unable to reach Medziboz for the Sabbath. The other Hasid replied: 'What God brings to pass, is for good.' They soon came to a still narrower pass, and found it blocked by a milk wagon which had broken down. The nobleman ordered the milk cans to be transferred to another wagon, and the broken wagon to be pushed aside. Later the nobleman took a branch road, and the Hasidim were able to drive ahead quickly. 'You see, now, that I was right,' said the Hasid who had not complained. 'Had the nobleman not been ahead of us, we should have been forced to wait until the milk wagon had been repaired. The owner would never have bothered to transfer the milk cans for our sake.' "

Nif. Haz., p. 9.

23. CONTROVERSY WITH GOD

1. A Judgment for the Rabbi

A terrible famine once occurred in Ukraine and the poor could buy no bread. Ten Rabbis assembled at the home of the "Spoler Grandfather" for a session of the Rabbinical Court. The Spoler said to them:

"I have a case in judgment against the Lord. According to Rabbinical law, a master who buys a Jewish serf for a designated time (six years or up to the Jubilee year) must support not only him but also his family.[1] Now the Lord bought us in Egypt as his serfs, since He says: 'For to Me are the sons of Israel serfs,'[2] and the Prophet Ezekiel declared that even in Exile, Israel is the slave of God. Therefore, O Lord, I ask that Thou abide by the Law and support Thy serfs with their families."

The ten judges rendered judgment in favor of the Spoler Rabbi. In a few days a large shipment of grain arrived from Siberia, and bread could be bought by the poor.[3]

Tifereth Maharal, p. 158.

[1] Kiddushin, 22.
[2] Leviticus 25:55.
[3] This is a particularly fine story, and lends itself to treatment in a drama. It is an expression of the idea in Micah 6:3: "O My people, what have I done unto Thee? And wherein have I wearied Thee? Testify against Me." See also the Book of Job. The phrase in the Hebrew is: "Din Mishpat Be-Kadosh Baruch Hu."

2. Let Israel Triumph

Said the Koznitzer Maggid: "There is a controversy between Israel and the Lord. The Lord says to us: 'Return unto Me . . . and I will return unto you' (Zechariah 1:3). Israel answers: 'Turn Thou us unto Thee, O Lord, and we shall be returned' (Lamentations 5:21). Therefore Jeremiah pleads: 'Wherefore wilt Thou forget us because of Thy wish to win the controversy?[1] Say, O Lord: 'My sons have triumphed over me'[2] and 'Cause us to return, etc.' "

E. O., p. 82.

[1] In Lamentations 5:20; the word "La-Netzach" means "forever" or "to triumph."
[2] This expression is found in the Talmud; Baba Metzia, 59.

3. Dispute With the Lord

A poor man came to the Radviller Rabbi and complained of his poverty. The Radviller had no money to give him, but, in lieu of a donation, he comforted him with the words of the verse (Proverbs 3:12): "For whom the Lord loveth He correcteth." [1]

His father, the Zlotzover Maggid, witnessed this and said to his son: "Truly this is an unworthy way to aid the indigent. The verse should be understood thus: 'For he that loveth the Lord shall argue with Him.' He should plead: 'Why shouldst Thou cause a man to put himself to shame by begging aid, when it is in Thy power, O Lord, to vouchsafe him his necessities in an honorable fashion?'"

A. H., p. 18-19.

[1] The Hebrew verb "Yokiach" means "correcting, arguing, punishing, admonishing."

4. Accusing God of Wrong-Doing

Said the Karliner: "We are told to judge all men in the scale of merit.[1] If this applies even to men, how much the more, then, does it apply to God?"

M. D., p. 238.

[1] "Ethics of the Fathers" 1:6; Singer, p. 185.

5. Letting God Off Easily

After Yom Kippur the Berditschever called over a tailor and asked him to relate his argument with God on the day before. The tailor said:

"I declared to God: You wish me to repent of my sins, but I have committed only minor offenses: I may have kept left-over cloth, or I may have eaten in a non-Jewish home, where I worked, without washing my hands.

"But Thou, O Lord, hast committed grievous sins: Thou hast taken away babies from their mothers, and mothers from their babies. Let us be quits: mayest Thou forgive me, and I will forgive Thee."

Said the Berditschever: "Why did you let God off so easily? You might have forced Him to redeem all of Israel."

O. I. H., p. 20.

6. A Justified Complaint

In the vicinity of Rabbi Moshe Leib of Sassov there lived a poor woman who was pursued by misfortune, since one child after another was taken from her in the first year of its life. She wept long for her little ones. Once she poured forth her anguish to the Rabbi's wife, and spoke in her bitterness a word against the injustice which God had inflicted upon her. The wife of the Rabbi interrupted her, saying: "A Jewess must not speak thus. She must accept patiently whatever transpires, and say: 'What God does, is just and righteous in my eyes.'"

But the poor woman wept still more pitifully; she was terrified lest she had sinned against God.

Rabbi Moshe Leib heard the loud lamentations, and stepped outside in order to learn the cause. His wife related to him the whole situation, and mentioned the blasphemous words which had fallen from the lips of her neighbor.

"The poor woman is justified," exclaimed the Rabbi. "Through what cause has she earned so harsh a punishment? Why should her children die in their infancy? Were they not received into the Covenant of Abraham? Why does the Holy One, Blessed be He, chastise her so cruelly and incessantly?"

And Rabbi Moshe Leib turned his countenance to the bereaved woman, and said: "You will soon bear a son, and, with the help of God, he will live long, and I will even be at his wedding."

And it happened, just as the Rabbi had said.

Bl., Pr., p. 170.

7. God's Crown

While reciting the Selichoth prayers, the Sassover Rabbi exclaimed: "O Lord, consider that Thou perforce must need that Israel should sin for the fulfilment of Thy thirteen attributes which are like thirteen gems in 'Thy Crown.' Otherwise Thou wouldst lack some of Thy most precious gems: 'Long-suffering and Forgiving Iniquity' (Exodus 34:7), and Thy Crown would lose much of its glory. Thus, even by their sins the children of Israel contribute to Thy glory, and they deserve to be treated with clemency."

F. R. H.-E., pp. 246-7.

8. Without Sight

Said the Sassover: "As we believe in Thee, O Lord, though we see Thee not, so aid us, though Thou seest no good within us."

E. Tz., p. 58.

9. Give Us Our Needs

Said the Savraner: "Rabbi Obadiah Bertinoro, the famous commentator on the Mishnah, says: 'Even when we turn to transgressions, have mercy upon us, and let our needs be open before Thee' (Berakhoth, chapter 4, Mishnah 4). The meaning of these words is, as follows: 'Even when we transgress, Thou shouldst pity us, O Lord, for it is known to Thee that we do so because of our needs. Were we supplied with our necessities, we would not transgress in our dealings.'"

E. A., p. 36.

10. A Trial With God

The Emperor of Austria promulgated a law that a tax of 400 guldens be levied on every Jewish marriage. A poor man came to the Lizensker and complained: "I have a case in judgment against God. He commanded that men multiply, and yet he permitted a decree which makes marriage impossible for most Jews. My daughter is betrothed, but neither I nor the bridegroom can pay so enormous a tax."

The Lizensker pondered a moment, and then exclaimed: "Let the Dayyanim sit in judgment." In his argument he said: "It is the law that if a man is half-serf and half-free, his master must give him his freedom in order that he may be able to marry, since a Jew may not wed a female serf, and a Jewess may not be given in marriage to a male serf.[1] We are partly serfs of God, and partly freemen because of our free-will. It is because we are serfs that the decree has been directed against us Jews only. Let God, Our Master, either free us from this decree, or else give us freedom from our service to Him, so that we may marry as other nations may."

Soon after a messenger arrived with the joyful tidings that the harsh decree had been abolished.

Hith. Z., pp. 49-50.

[1] Gittin, 41.

24. COURAGE (PHYSICAL)

1. The Rabbi and the Bear

Rabbi Uri Strelisker in company with several Hasidim traveled by stagecoach through a forest. Suddenly the horses halted, and the driver saw a bear coming towards them. The Rabbi walked up to the bear and gazed steadily into his eyes. Thereupon the bear turned and walked away.

"This is not a miracle," explained the Rabbi. "The Lord blessed men, and said to them: 'And the fear of you and the dread of you shall be upon every beast of the earth' (Gen. 9:2). No unspoiled man need fear any beast."

Or Olam, pp. 29-30.

2. The Fiery Trial

Rabbi Sussya, to place his powers of endurance to the trial, once thrust his hand into the fire. When he winced and withdrew his hand, he marveled not a little, saying: "What a gross clod must Sussya's body be, to be afraid of the fire."

B., p. 439b.

3. The Savage Dogs

The Sassover once heard that a Jew who was unable to pay his rent had been imprisoned by the village-owner. He went to the latter and petitioned him to have pity on the poor man. The landowner became enraged and drove him from the house. The Rabbi returned to renew his entreaties. Then the angry owner turned loose his savage dogs. The Sassover calmly bared his arms and said: "If it is decreed in Heaven that these dogs shall harm me, let it be so." The dogs halted in their tracks and refused to touch the Rabbi. The landowner was overwhelmed with remorse, and he released the imprisoned debtor.

D. D., p. 245.

25. COURTESY AND MANNERS

1. *Never Eject the Poor*

Said the Slonimer: "Beware of discourtesy to the poor. If you turn them out of your home, you have been guilty of ejecting the Lord Himself, for 'He standeth at the right hand of the needy' (Psalm 109:31)."

O. Y., p. 208.

2. *Table Etiquette*

Said the Bratzlaver: "A man should eat slowly and with etiquette even if alone at the table."

L. E. H., p. 8.

3. *Holiness in Courtesy*

Rabbi Jacob Joseph Pulnoe, author of "Toledoth Jacob Joseph," a famous Hasidic book, was by nature a man of hasty temper. The Besht desired to teach him a lesson in calmness. He sent a man to the synagogue where the Rabbi was seated studying, and ordered him to interrupt him. The man did so, and said: "May I know who you are?"

"I am the Rabbi of Pulnoe," was the reply.

"Do you make a comfortable living from your position?" continued the questioner.

The Rabbi became angry at the interruption, and failed to make a reply. The man then said: "You are guilty of dispossessing the Lord from His abode."

"How is this?" queried the Rabbi.

"I will explain it to you," said the man. "We say in our prayers: 'But Thou art holy, O Thou that dwellest amid the praises of Israel.'[1] Hence, when a Jew accosts another and inquires concerning his livelihood, and the one questioned gives the customary answer: 'God be praised,' the Lord dwelleth within this praise. But, since you have refused to make a reply, the Divinity which approached with expectation to take residence within your words of praise, was compelled to depart."

The Pulnoer admitted the truth of this reasoning, and resolved to be more courteous in the future.

P. I., p. 21.

[1] Psalms 22:4; Singer, p. 73.

4. *Children or Builders?*

Rabbi Isaac of Lentzner related the following story: "In my youth I was accustomed to study all night in the synagogue, and to snatch a little sleep after sunrise. Once I became so engrossed in a subject that I did not lie down for rest until a short time before Services. I awoke but had not time to change from my sleeping robe. A worshiper came, and admonished me for appearing at Services in so unseemly a garment. I replied as follows: 'We read in the Evening Service for Sabbath (Singer, p. 122): "Read not here 'Banayich,' 'Thy children,' but 'Bonayich,' 'Thy builders,' namely 'Thy students.' " When the general public call at a palace, they must be garbed in fitting dress, but when builders enter to make repairs, they enter in their working clothes.' The man smiled, and walked away satisfied."

Nif. Haz., p. 26.

5. Manners in Drinking

Said Rabbi Bunam: "One should not gulp down his glass of water, but should drink slowly, even as he should eat slowly. Understand that we are not mere animals, and, even though we must feed our body, we must do so in a mannerly way, in order that we may display our superiority over the animals. This discipline will aid your soul. Especially in drinking water we are in danger of imitating the animals, since we drink it as we find it in its natural state, without preparing it for human use."

R. T., p. 184.

26. CREATION AND EVOLUTION

1. God is the Creator

Said the Sassover: "The Torah begins with the words: 'In the beginning God created.'[1] This means: the first thing to know is that God is the sole Creator of everything."

M. Hat., p. 60.

[1] Gen. 1:1.

2. Offering the First Part

Said the Lekhivitzer: "The Torah begins with the word: 'Bereshith'[1] which may be translated: 'for the sake of the first' the Lord hath created the world. All that the Creator demands is that a man make a beginning in the right direction; thereafter He will aid him to continue in the right path. To symbolize this He ordained that we should devote to the Lord the first fruits; the first stalks of grain; the first-born cattle; and the Law of Tradition commands us to devote the first part of every day to prayer."

O. Y., p. 14.

[1] Gen. 1:1.

3. The Unfinished Vessel

Rabbi Bunam said: "The Lord created the world in a state of beginning. The universe is always in an uncompleted state, in the form of its beginning. It is not like a vessel at which the master works and he finishes it; it requires continuous labor and unceasing renewal by creative forces. Were there a second's pause by these forces, the universe would return to primeval chaos."

S. S. K., ii, 17.

4. The Re-Creation of the World

Said the Besht: "It is written (Lamentations 3:23): 'They are new every morning: great is thy faith.' A man should believe that each day the world is re-created, and that he is reborn each morning. His faith will then be increased, and he will take a fresh interest daily in his service to the Lord."

M. R. T., ii, 24.

5. "For My Sake"

The Bratzlaver said: "Declare at all times: 'The world was created for my sake.' Do not declare: 'Of what concern is this to me?' But do your share to add some improvement, to supply something that is missing, and to leave the world a little better for your sojourn in it."

K. L. M., p. 6.

6. Infinite Understanding

Said Rabbi Bunam: "We read (Psalms 147:5): 'Great is our Lord and mighty in power; His understanding is infinite.' Let me explain this: God causes an insignificant fact to occur in order that it may bring in its train another occurrence; the second causes a third, and this is continued a myriad of times. All the events have been caused directly by the first insignificant occurrence. When God caused the first thing to happen, he understood every least thing to the end of time, and knew what the impulse of the first thing would cause to transpire. This is what we have in mind when we offer praise that God's understanding is infinite."

R. T., p. 233.

7. Hints from Genesis

Rabbi Wolf Strikover finds these hints in the first verse of the Bible (Gen. 1:1): "Bereshith" has the initial letters of 1) "Bitachon," or trust; 2) "Ratson," or will; 3) "Ahavah," or love; 4) "Shetikah," or silence; 5) "Yir'ah," or fear; 6) "Torah," or learning. These are the most important essentials in the character of a man of goodness.

"Bara" reminds us of the three most important and fundamental material needs: 1) "Bara," suggests children from "Bar," a son; 2) "Bara," health, from "Bari," healthy; 3) "Bara," food, from "Bar," grain.

"Bara Elohim Eth." The last letters of these words spell "Emeth," truth. The creation can rest only upon truth.

F. U. A. O., i, 7.

27. CURES, PHYSICAL AND MENTAL

1. *Tranquillity of Spirit*

Said the Sassover: "We read (Psalm 29:11): 'The Lord will grant strength unto His people; the Lord will bless His people with peace.' It is customary for sick people to be quarrelsome and irritable. Hence, we implore the Lord to give us health and bodily strength so that we may be blessed with peace and tranquillity of spirit."

M. Hat., p. 62.

2. *Cheerfulness Cures*

A youth came to the Radomsker Rabbi and complained that he suffered from a nervous ailment which brought him evil dreams in the night.

"It is your melancholy that is responsible," said the Rabbi. "Always be cheerful and you will be cured."

Beth Shelomo, pp. 31-44.

3. *"Charity Saves From Death"*

The "Yud's" child became dangerously ill, and the mother implored the Rabbi to pray for him. The "Yud" ordered her to sell everything in the house and to distribute the money to the poor. His wife did so, but no improvement was noted in the condition of the child. The weeping mother asked her husband what she should now do.

"Sell the windows of the house for charity," said the Rabbi. When this was done, the child became well.[1]

N. H., p. 6.

[1] Title suggested by Proverbs 10:2; 11:4.

4. *Spiritual Healing*

The Medzibozer Rabbi said: "The Psalmist declares: 'O Lord, my God, I cried loudly unto Thee and Thou didst heal me.'[1] This signifies that the act of crying unto God is in itself a source of healing for spiritual ailments."

The Kobriner finds this idea in the words: "For I am the Lord that healeth Thee" (Exodus 15:26); "The knowledge that God is the Lord is a cure for maladies of the mind and heart."

O. Y., p. 74.

[1] Psalm 30:3.

5. *Prayer for the Sick*

A Hasid once importuned the Gastininer Rabbi to promise a cure for his sick wife. The Rabbi replied: "Were I able to accomplish cures, I would have visited the sick of my own accord and effected their healing. All I am able to do is to pray for the sick person; you can and should do the same."

S. S. K., iii, 100.

6. The Most Earnest Prayer

The "Yud" became dangerously ill, and the inhabitants of his town proclaimed a fast and universal prayer for the Rabbi's speedy convalescence. A villager chanced to come to town, and went to the tavern for a drink of brandy. Several townsfolk overheard him, and informed him that drinking was prohibited for the day.

The villager at once went to the synagogue and prayed: "O Lord, please cure the Holy Rabbi, so that I may have my drink."

Soon after the Rabbi began to recover his strength, and said: "The prayer of the villager was more acceptable than any of yours. His expressed the greatest longing and the most earnest supplication for my prompt recovery."

S. S. K., ii, 81.

7. The Lord and Strict Justice

Rabbi Joshua, son of Rabbi Shalom of Belz, had occasion to pray for the recovery of an impious Jew who was dangerously sick. He said: "It may be true that the patient deserves to die if judged by the rules of strict justice. But it is only the judges of the lower tribunals who have no choice under the law and must sentence the offender according to his acts. The king, however, the chief magistrate of the country, may issue a pardon in disregard of the law.

"Thou, O Lord, art like the king, the Judge of all the earth, and mayest grant a pardon. I implore Thee to exercise Thy right of mercy, as Abraham said (Genesis 18:25): 'The Judge of all the earth need not exercise justice.' " [1]

D. S., p. 174.

[1] The usual translation is: "Shall not the Judge of the earth do justly?" Rabbi Joshua drops the question mark.

8. Psalms and Their Curative Value

A Gentile physician believed that his wife was hopelessly ill, and in order not to witness her death agonies, he left the town. When he returned a month later, he found his wife much improved, and on the way to complete recovery. He was told that a "Rebbe" had advised his family to arrange for the chanting of Psalms on behalf of her recovery—a Jewish custom of long-standing. As soon as this was done, an improvement in the sick woman's condition was noted.

Later the Gentile physician wrote a medical work concerning the ailment of his wife, and remarked at its conclusion: "If all the remedies enumerated here are of no avail, Psalms should be chanted in Hebrew."

L. H. F., p. 113.

9. Music as a Cure

When the "Yud" heard that the Koznitzer Maggid was very weak, he summoned two of his Disciples and said: "Go to Koznitz and sing before the Maggid." They arrived on a Friday, and, on representing themselves as men with good voices, they were invited to sing the Sabbath hymns. With every song the Maggid felt better and better. He finally exclaimed: "The 'Yud' knew that I have walked in all worlds except in the world of music. He sent me his singers to demonstrate to me that I still have a task in this life: to explore the 'world of song.'"

Nif. Yeh., p. 59.

10. An Overdose of Words

Said Rabbi Bunam: "We are taught that the words of wisdom are 'health to all their flesh' (Proverbs 4:22). This is why Abtalyon said: 'Ye sages, be heedful of your words' (Ethics of the Fathers, 1:11; Singer, p. 185). Since words are as medicine, they must be carefully measured, and precautions taken against an overdose."

S. I., p. 87.

11. The Healing of the Poor

The Dzikover said: "It is written: 'And ye shall serve the Lord your God, and He will bless thy bread and thy water; and I will remove sickness from the midst of thee' (Exodus 23:25). How shall we understand the connection between bread and water, and the cure of sickness? It is thus: when a malady overtakes a person, he may obtain medicine for it, or take the cure at mineral springs with healing properties. But what shall the poor do, since they can afford neither? It is to them that the Lord speaks in this verse: 'Serve Me, and I shall cause your bread and your water to contain the healing powers of medicines and mineral waters, necessary for the cure of your ailment.'"

E. Tz., p. 100.

12. "For Thy Name"

The Medzibozer commented on the words: "Heal us, O Lord, and we shall be healed." [1] He said: "Heal for us Thy name and Thy Throne, and we shall be healed as a consequence."

Butz. D., p. 31.

[1] Singer, p. 47.

13. The Healing of Souls

Said the "Yud": "All commentators on the Torah ask: 'Why is it written: "For I am the Lord that healeth thee" (Exodus 15:26), when it is said before this: "I will put none of the diseases upon thee"? Since there will be no diseases, what need is there of healing?'

"The answer is, as follows: previously, the plagues of Egypt served to heal the souls of Israel through their fear of a punishment similar to the trials of the Egyptians. Now, after the Exodus, if Israel obeys the Lord, He need no longer enforce their obedience and loyalty through fear of penalties, but He will heal their souls by demonstrating through His Providence that He is the Lord."

Tif. Yeh., p. 34.

28. DANCING

1. Why the Rabbi Learned to Dance

The Spoler Grandfather told the following experience of his youth:

Once he arrived in a small town and heard that the nearby Polish Count had jailed a Jew for debt. He learned also that it was the Count's custom to compel his victims to dance at a ball he held on his birthday. If the prisoner danced satisfactorily, he was freed; otherwise, he was returned to the dungeon. The Rabbi resolved to free the Jew, secured a dancing instructor, and soon became very proficient. On the night of the ball, he crept to the dungeon and succeeded in entering the basement. Soon he heard the groans of the poor Jew, and prevailed upon him to change clothes when the opportunity came. The Rabbi carefully enlarged the hole through which food was passed to the prisoner, and thus the exchange was made. When the Count's servants arrived to take the prisoner to the ball, the real victim walked out into the basement, and the Rabbi stepped forward. The deception was unnoticed in the dim light. The Rabbi was brought to the ball, where he was ordered to don a dried bearskin, and to dance opposite the village overseer in imitation of a bear. He was told that if he failed to perform the correct steps, the overseer was privileged to beat him, but if the overseer danced incorrectly, he would be beaten. The Rabbi danced masterfully, and was released after punishing the cruel overseer, who had asked permission to imprison the debtor instead of granting him an extension of time.[1]

The Spoler remained an excellent dancer his whole life.

T. Mah., p. 147.

[1] For other stories on Ransoming Debtors, see Debtors and Their Release, Rubric 32.

29. DEATH

1. On Death

"Hasidim are not curious inquirers into first things and last— both life and death to them are fulfillment. What is the destiny of the plant that springs forth from the soil? To grow and to wither. It is the law and the will of God. And therewith Man must

likewise rest content, without inquiry into the Why and the Wherefore. Let him rejoice at being called into life, and return to the
fountainhead of his being when the call to him goes forth."

Bl., Pr., p. 23.

2. For the Eternal World

Rabbi Moshe Sopher said: "Many people complain that they have
nothing with which to live. Would it not be more sensible for them
to complain that they have nothing with which to die?"[1]

M. D., p. 243.

[1] Non-Hasidic, but in Hasidic mood.

3. The Angel of Death in the Synagogue

Said a Rabbi: "There is a Talmudical saying that the Angel of
Death conceals his tools in the synagogue.[1] I would paraphrase this
as follows: the Angel of Death supports the synagogue. Were it
not for those who recite Kaddish and the Yizkor Services,[2] the
synagogues would undoubtedly be empty at all times."[3]

O. I. H., p. 187.

[1] Baba Kama, 60.
[2] Memorial Services.
[3] Non-Hasidic, but in Hasidic mood.

4. The Happy Dead

After Rabbi Moses Ladmirer had departed from Lekhivitz, another pretender arrived on the scene in the person of Rabbi Mordecai,
a disciple of Rabbi Asher of Stalin. He endeavored to gain the
approval of the Lekhivitzer Hasidim by recalling to them the holiness
and greatness of his late Master. Rabbi Noah thereupon related the
following tale:

"An old woman visited the cemetery, and gazing at the peaceful
graves, she commented: 'Holy souls! Pure souls! How happy is your
lot! How soothing is your sleep! And yet I have no wish to be with
you!' "

O. Y., p. 45.

5. With a Clear Conscience

Said the Slonimer: "Happy is he who ends his days in repentance
and holy service, and dies with a clear conscience."

O. Y., p. 202.

30. DEATH: COURAGE IN FACING IT

1: "My Father's Mansion"

Rabbi Schmelke and Rabbi Moshe Leib of Sassov were traveling
on a ship. A dangerous storm threatened to destroy the vessel.
Rabbi Schmelke went over to the Sassover and perceived that he
was engaged in a joyful dance.

"Why are you dancing?" inquired Rabbi Schmelke.

"I am overjoyed at the thought that I shall soon arrive in the mansion of my Father," [1] replied the Sassover.

"I shall join you, then," said Rabbi Schmelke.

But the storm spent its force, and the ship reached port in safety.

M. Hat., p. 49.

[1] The phrase "My Father's House hath many mansions" in the New Testament was doubtless unknown to the Rabbi, but Jesus used it knowing the Jewish sources in the same way as Rabbi Moshe Leib.

2. The Lord Is Now King

Said Rabbi Schmelke: "In the Evening Prayer we say: 'The Lord is King; the Lord was King; the Lord will be King, for ever and ever.' [1]   This order appears to be incorrect.   It should be: 'The Lord was King,' then, 'the Lord is King.'   The reason for saying it in this order is as follows: a man may be suddenly summoned by death, and if the order of recital were first: 'He was King,' he would not have acknowledged that the Lord is King at the time that he died."

S. ha-Tov, p. 43.

[1] Singer, p. 101.

31. DEATH: HOW THE HASIDIM DIED

1. The Purpose of Creation

In the hour of his death the Baal Shem said: "Now I know the purpose for which I was created."

B., p. 330.

2. The End of Rabbi Sussya

Rabbi Sussya lived to a great age.   For seven years before his death, he was bedridden and in pain, in atonement, it was said, for the sins of Israel.   His gravestone is inscribed: "Here lieth he who served God in love, rejoiced in pain, and turned many away from guilt."

B., p. 441b.

3. The Divine Nothing

Just before he died, Rabbi Schneur Zalman of Ladi asked his grandson: "Dost thou see aught?"

The grandson looked at the Rabbi in surprise.   Thereupon the dying man said: "I see as yet only the Divine Nothing that gives life to the universe."

B., p. 471.
Reflex, May, 1929, p. 66.

4. In His Last Year

As the Maggid of Koznitz, sick unto death in the last year before his death, on the eve of Yom Kippur, stood and prayed before the Ark, he was silent before he spoke the words: "He said: 'I forgive';" then he addressed God, saying: "Lord of the Universe, Thou alone knowest how great is Thy glory; and Thou alone knowest how great is the weakness of my body. And Thou knowest this as well, that I have stood before the Ark in prayer, this entire month, day after day, not on my behalf, but for Thy People, Israel. Therefore I beseech Thee: if it has been easy for me to take upon myself the yoke of Thy people, and to perform this service with my suffering body, how can it be burdensome for Thee, unto Whom is Omnipotence, to speak two words?" Thereupon in a moment his countenance was overwhelmed with joy, and he cried in a mighty voice: "He spoke: 'I forgive!' "

B., pp. 490-1.

5. In the Moment of Death

In the moment of death the Apter cried out: "Why does the Son of Jesse delay?" He wept and said: "The Rabbi of Berditschev promised before his death he would disturb the peace of all the Saints and not cease until the Messiah would come. But they have so overwhelmed him with delights in mansion after mansion, that he has forgotten. But I will not forget."

B., p. 507.
Bl., Gem., p. 230.

6. The Departure

One of the Disciples of Rabbi Moshe Leib of Sassov was Rabbi Mendel of Kossov. Once Rabb Moshe Leib said to him: "Mendele, I yearn to be united with you in this world; you have a little son, I a little daughter." Nothing further did he say. Rabbi Mendel answered: "I will journey home and return to you with my little son."

On the first day of the month Shebat he entered Sassov again, accompanied by his little David. Rabbi Moshe Leib rejoiced greatly and ordered a solemn meal in honor of the Festival of the New Moon. At the table much Torah was discussed, and the countenance of Rabbi Moshe Leib glowed with great happiness.

Later the betrothal was celebrated and they remained in festive mood until the early morning hours.

On the following morning Rabbi Mendel prepared for his departure, and betook himself to the Study of Rabbi Moshe Leib in order to say farewell. . "Father-in-law," said Rabbi Moshe Leib, "I desire that you and the bridegroom shall be present in the hour of my death."

Rabbi Mendel shrank back and cried: "Do you wish to disturb the joy of the betrothal?"

"No demurring will help any longer," said Rabbi Moshe Leib. "I set little store at tarrying in this world-below, and must depart." On the fourth day in the month of Shebat Rabbi Moshe Leib died, and Rabbi Mendel was present to see him depart.

Bl., Pr., pp. 172-3.

7. Learning to Die

When Rabbi Bunam was lying on his deathbed, his wife wept bitterly. Thereupon he said: "Why dost thou weep? All my life has been given me merely that I might learn to die."

M. D., p. 244.

8. Optimism and Faith

When Rabbi Elimelech of Lizensk perceived that his end was approaching, he made himself master of an extraordinary cheerfulness. One of his Disciples inquired the reason for his unusual mood. The Rabbi thereupon took the hand of his faithful disciple into his own, and said: "Why should I not rejoice, seeing that I am about to leave this world below, and enter into the higher worlds of eternity? Do you not recall the words of the Psalmist: (23:4) 'Yea, though I walk through the valley of the shadow of death, I will fear no evil, for Thou art with me.' Thus does the grace of God display itself."

Bl., Gem., p. 145.

9. The Battle

On a day of the Festival of Simchath Torah the Ropshitzer stood at the window, and saw how the Hasidim celebrated and danced in the courtyard. He was in an exalted mood and his countenance was illumined with great joy. Suddenly he moved his hand as a signal that they should cease. They saw that his face had become pale and they were stricken with great fright. Gradually he recovered himself and cried out with great enthusiasm: "And, if a commanding officer of the army falls, is the battle broken off? Friends, continue your dance."

At that very moment his friend, Rabbi Abraham, had breathed forth his soul in Ulanov.

E. Tz., p. 89 (Bl., Pr., p. 196).

10. The Command

During his illness the physicians ordered a medicine for Rabbi Eisig of Kalev. When he refused to take it, his friend Rabbi Isaiah Aaron said to him: "You must, you must. It is a matter of the 'rescue of the soul.' It is a matter of life and death."

Thereupon Rabbi Eisig cried out: "Hear! Hear! The knave says: I must."

He raised his eyes to Heaven and continued: "Lord of the Universe! It is clear to Thee that I have never moved a single finger without consecration and reflection, yet he dares to say to me: I must."

E. Tz., p. 73 (Bl., Pr., p. 189).

11. *The Lamentation of the Shekinah*

Rabbi Pinchas of Koretz passed away suddenly while in Spitovka, on a journey to the Holy Land. On the same day—the 10th of Elul, 5551 (1791), Rabbi Jacob Samson of Spitovka, who already resided in the Holy Land, saw a vision: The Shekinah, God's Majesty, appeared to him in the form of a woman in lamentation; he perceived that her lamentation was for a friend of her youth who had died. Thereupon he awoke and cried with grief: "Rabbi Pinchas of Koretz has died!"

He was asked how he knew this.

"Outside of him," he replied, "there exists in this day no Zaddik, for whom the Shekinah would lament." He stood up, made the rent in his garment according to tradition as a sign of his grief, and spoke the blessing of God's righteousness. For many days he mourned his passing.

After a long time the news came to the Holy Land: Rabbi Pinchas is no more.

Bl., Pr., p. 86.

12. *To The End of His Days*

On the second of Iyar, 5538 (1778), Rabbi Schmelke, sitting erect in his chair, with face serene and vision undimmed, convoked his Disciples around him and said: "Know, all of you, that this is my dying day." They burst into tears, but he continued, reproving them: "Know that the soul of the Prophet Samuel dwells within me. Of this I am assured by three tokens: I am called Samuel; I am, like the Prophet, of the tribe of Levi; and, like his life, mine has lasted fifty-two years. But his name was pronounced: Samuel, and mine: Schmelke, and so I remained Schmelke to the end of my days."

With this he bade his weeping Disciples depart, leaned back in his chair, and died.

M. Hat., p. 48 (B., p. 430).

13. *The Two Homes*

The Kotzker Rabbi said: "Death is merely moving from one home to another. If we are wise, we will make the latter the more beautiful home."

S. S. K., ii, 94.

14. *The Time of Confession*

When Rabbi Zalman Hasid was nigh unto death, his friends came to his bedside, and asked him to recite the "Confession," enjoined for the occasion. The Rabbi smiled and said: "Friends, do you really believe a death-bed confession contains much merit? No, friends! A man should 'confess' when he is seated at his dining-table, and eating the good food thereon."

Sh. Z., p. 33.

15. God's Partner

Rabbi David Leikes lived more than a hundred years. He was esteemed as an authority in the civil law of the Rabbis, and his decisions were admired by all the Dayyanim. Once a very complicated case arose, when the aged Rabbi was on his death-bed. His demise was expected hourly. The Dayyanim hoped that the ancient Rabbi's mind might still be sufficiently clear to aid them, perhaps for the last time. They visited his home and stated their request. The Rabbi's children protested vigorously, and argued against troubling him, lest thereby his end be hastened. Suddenly the door opened, and the dying Rabbi entered. "Do you know," he said, "that we are taught by the Talmud [1] that one who judges a case correctly becomes thereby God's partner? Yet you wish to deprive me of this opportunity."

He gave his decision in the difficult case in a manner so remarkable that it left no doubt of its correctness; he returned to his bed with the help of his children, and a moment later he died.

F. R. H.-M. i, 163-5.

[1] Sabbath, 10.

16. The Remaining Hours

Said the Koretzer: "My teacher, the Besht, realizing the imminence of his death, exclaimed: 'Lord of the Universe, I make Thee a gift of the remaining hours of my life.' This is true martyrdom for the sake of the Lord."

Nof. Tz., p. 11.

17. "My Work is Done"

When Rabbi Yekuthiel Teitelbaum, grandson of the Oheler, became dangerously ill in his old age, he declined an opportunity to call in a physician of great renown. He explained his refusal by relating the following story: "The famous Rabbi, Joel Sirkis, wished to publish his authoritative work on rabbinic law. Another Rabbi sought to dissuade him, saying: 'My dear friend, follow my counsel, and do not publish this work during your lifetime. As long as it remains unprinted, you may add to it, and revise it. Thus your life's mission will be uncompleted and God will lengthen your days to permit you to accomplish your life-work. But, if you give evidence that you have already completed your task, you may be summoned by death much earlier.'

"Rabbi Sirkis answered: 'My work is finished, and I desire to give students the benefit of it, even though I may die.' It is the same in my case," continued Rabbi Yekuthiel. "My work is ended, and no physician can help me." He never recovered.

P. v. K., p. 17a.

18. In Terror of Death

The Gerer was traveling a difficult road with his nephew, the Piltzer.[1] The horses found themselves on a steep hill, and became terror-stricken. The Piltzer cried out in fright, but his uncle remained undisturbed.

"Why cry out?" asked the Gerer. "A man ought feel terror and premonition of mortal danger always, for he may die at any moment. King David was conscious of the imminence of death all the days of his life, and while under this emotion, he composed his greatest Psalms."

M. E. H., i, 103.

[1] The Piltzer was Pinchas Elijah Rotenberg, son of Jacob Joseph Rotenberg, brother of the Gerer Rabbi, who changed his name to Alter.

19. The Loss of a Mitzwah

When Abraham Mordecai, the last remaining son of the Gerer Rabbi, died, a Hasid sought to comfort him with the traditional words from Job:[1] "The Lord hath given and the Lord hath taken." The Gerer responded: "My grief comes not because I have lost my son to everlasting life, since this was God's will. My sorrow arises from the knowledge that I shall now lack the opportunity to perform the Mitzwah: 'Ye shall teach them diligently unto your sons.'"[2]

M. E. H., ii, 10.

[1] 1:21.
[2] Deut. 6:7.

20. Why We Fear to Die

The Gerer Rabbi said: "Why does a man fear to die? Is he not returning to his Father in Heaven? The reason lies in this: in the World-to-Come, a man obtains a clear retrospect of all his deeds upon earth. When he perceives the senseless errors he has committed, he cannot abide himself. Therein lies his Purgatory."

M. E. H., ii, 78.

21. Death-bed Repentance

During the last year of his life, the Gerer said: "According to Maimonides, in the second chapter of the Rules of Repentance,[1] penitence is perfect only when the Omniscient One can testify that the sinner will never repeat the offense. I am uncertain, however, in my own mind, whether death-bed repentance is perfect, even though it is obvious that the dying man will never again be guilty of the same transgression."

M. E. H., ii, 82.

[1] Second Paragraph.

22. Strength for a Jew

When the Gerer was undergoing his last illness, the physician who attended him advised him to gain a little strength by more sleep. The Rabbi replied: "Does not the wise physician know that it is Torah and Tefillah (prayer), not sleep, which grants strength unto a Jew?"

M. E. H., ii, 85.

32. DEBTORS AND THEIR RELEASE

1. Ransoming the Imprisoned

Rabbi Eleazar Lippe, the father of Rabbi Elimelech and Rabbi Sussya, learned that a certain grower had a large quantity of flax for sale. He came to the village, and was told that the Jewish inn-keeper and his family had been imprisoned by the grower for non-payment of their rent. He immediately used the money he had brought with him in order to pay the debt of the poor Jew, and began to reprove the grower for his cruelty. The latter was moved by the words of chastisement; he returned the ransom money, and Rabbi Eleazar purchased the flax at a low price.

T. H. A., pp. 10-11.

2. Two-fold Mercy to Prisoners

Rabbi Sussya came to a man of wealth to ask for a donation to ransom a family about to be imprisoned for debt. The man was not at home, and the Rabbi sat down to wait for him. Looking about the room he noticed a bird beating its wings against the wall of a cage. The Rabbi said to himself: "It is fitting that I should ransom this imprisoned creature, since I am on a mission of mercy to ransom human beings about to be imprisoned." He opened the cage and the bird flew out. When the owner returned, he said to him: "The Lord is good to all; and His tender mercies are over all His works." (Psalm 145:9). The owner heeded Rabbi Sussya's message, and he gave him a goodly donation, with which Rabbi Sussya gained freedom for the unfortunate family.

T. H. A., pp. 32-34.

3. Typical Kindness

Rabbi Mendel of Kossov once stopped at an inn on his way to visit Rabbi Wolf of Tzarny Austry. He heard the landlord sighing and weeping during the night, and inquired the reason for his anxiety. The innkeeper informed him that he was deeply in debt, and was threatened with dispossession. The kind-hearted Rabbi comforted him, collected the needed money from some wealthy men, and paid the innkeeper's debts.

In later years when he had become a renowned Rabbi, a Jew

came to him weeping. A large sum of money had been entrusted to him with which to purchase supplies, and it had been stolen, threatening him with expulsion from his home, in the village. The Kossover halted the Services in the synagogue, and announced that no Services would be held until the money required was collected. This was done and the Jew's livelihood was safeguarded for him.[1]

N. Haz., pp. 39-41.

[1] This story is included to illustrate the typical acts of kindness which the Hasidic Rabbis performed. Halting the Services was a common method, used also by non-Hasidim.

4. *The Perfect Deed of Kindness*

The Besht related this tale:

"A Jew together with his wife and children were brought in chains to a city, and the guard called out in a loud voice: 'Unless three hundred thalers are paid for the ransom of these prisoners, they will be cast into prison for life, since they have not paid their rent to the owner of the inn.' No one was able to furnish the ransom money, though compassion for the unfortunates was universal.

"A young serving-man had saved up the sum of one hundred and fifty thalers over many years of service; he took pity on the pathetic victims, and resolved to ransom them. He went to a serving-girl who had saved up the same amount, and proposed that they should join in performing the great 'Mitzwah'. She consented, and both gave their money to the guard, who released the prisoners immediately. The lad and the maiden had fallen in love, and they determined to marry; together they went to a kinsman of the boy in another town to invite his aid. On the way, they heard the groan of a child underneath a bridge. He had fallen into the deep mud and was unable to extricate himself. The serving-lad rescued the child and restored him to his distracted parents. The father, a rich landlord, amply rewarded the young couple, by presenting to them a dairy and a stable; he also leased to them the nearby inn. The child's mother made generous gifts to the bride for her marriage, and the young couple began their life together under happy auguries.

"It pays to perform a 'Mitzwah' in a perfect manner," said the Besht.

B. Z., pp. 36-42.

5. *Ransom Through a Ruse*

The Ziditzover followed his Rabbi, the Sassover, out of town. He saw him halt an Hungarian nobleman and engage him in friendly conversation. The Rabbi asked the nobleman: "Who is this driver of yours? He appears to me to be a Jew."

"You are right," replied the nobleman. "He owed me money and I took him into my service."

"But he does not seem to be an efficient teamster. A great man like yourself should have a capable servant. Give him to me, I beg of you, as a servant."

The nobleman refused. Thereupon, the driver, who had overheard the conversation, overturned the carriage as if by a mishap, and imperiled the safety of the owner and his family. The nobleman became enraged, and drove away the teamster with the exclamation: "Begone! Let me not see your face again."

The Sassover took the driver to his home, instructed him in the religious laws of Judaism which he had almost forgotten, and aided him to establish himself as a householder.

E. Tz., pp. 48-9.

6. The Bratzlaver On "Freeing the Imprisoned"

Said the Bratzlaver:

"1. Pride of heart casts a man into prison.

2. He who ransoms prisoners will have no outcasts in his family.

3. He who never leaves his home is as if he sojourned in prison.

4. He who invites the Zaddik's counsel, but acts to the contrary, is oftentimes cast into prison.

5. He who feeds the hungry is never imprisoned.

6. A student who graduates prematurely from his school of Rabbinic law and issues immature decisions, falls into prison.

7. A slanderer is often cast into prison."

Sef. Ham., pp. 121-2.

7. Ransoming With Kisses

The Sassover, while on a Friday afternoon walk, beheld a horrid sight: a nobleman with his wife and child were seated in a carriage to which a Jew and his family were harnessed. The nobleman was lashing his victims with a whip, and forcing them to pull the carriage. The Rabbi, a man of dignified mien and known to non-Jews as a holy man, halted the carriage, took the nobleman's child in his arms, expressed admiration for its beauty, and kissed it. The nobleman, thereupon, requested the Rabbi to bless the child, and he did so. He then explained to the parents that the cries of the Jewish family had an injurious effect upon the child's nerves, and besought the nobleman to release his victims. The nobleman cut the ropes and freed the unfortunates.

On his arrival at the synagogue, the Sassover mused: "How can I offer prayer, after I have kissed a child of cruel parents? Did not my mouth become unclean? But in the 'Perek Shirah,'[1] we find that even unclean animals praise the Lord. Is, then, my mouth more unclean than theirs?"

After this meditation, he commenced to pray with fervor.

E. Tz., p. 52.

[1] "Perek Shirah" is an odd composition, printed in many Prayer Books, stating what verse each animal employs in offering songs unto God. It is understood to be allegorical.

33. DECEIT AND DISHONESTY

1. Do Not Deceive

Said the Lekhivitzer: "We read (Leviticus 25:17): 'And ye shall not wrong one another; but thou shalt fear thy God; for I am the Lord your God.' This means: 'Do not deceive [1] one another by asserting that you are truly God-fearing persons.' "

O. Y., p. 41.

[1] "Thonu" means "to deceive or wrong."

2. Cheating The Soul

Rabbi Bunam asked one of his adherents: "What is a Hasid?" The man replied that a Hasid is one who does more than he is required to do by the Law.

"Correct," said the Rabbi. "The Law tells us: 'Do not wrong one another,'[1] and the Hasid takes care not to wrong his own soul as well."

S. S. K., iii, 5.

[1] Lev. 25:17.

3. Abstaining from Misrepresentations

A young Hasid, who was accustomed to devote much time to the study of the Talmud and the tenets of Hasidism, became so involved in his business, that he was compelled to forego his studies. On a holiday visit to the Kotzker Rabbi, he bitterly complained of this.

The Rabbi answered: "I will explain to you the passage which is recited at the conclusion of each chapter of the 'Pirkei Avoth': Rabbi Hananiah ben Akashia said: 'The Holy One wished to benefit Israel; therefore He gave them a multitude of commandments.' We may ask: where is the benefit of being in duty bound to observe many commandments? This is a great hardship. Would it not have been preferable to receive merely a limited number of precepts which we could fulfil correctly? The answer is: the great variety of precepts makes it possible for a Jew in every occupation to obey some of the divine injunctions. The farmer, the planter, the builder of houses, and others—each has his particular commandments to fulfil, and, thereby, gain favor in the eyes of the Lord.

"The Merchant, also, by abstaining from misrepresentations, overcharge, and other business deceptions, will please the Creator." [1]

S. S. K., p. 74.

[1] See Philo, quoted in Hertz, "The Book of Jewish Thoughts," p. 289.

4. The Adulterated Honey

A village dealer, accustomed to visit the Kotzker Rabbi frequently, suddenly ceased to come. An acquaintance, who met him on the street, informed him that the Rabbi had inquired for him.

The dealer replied that he would come next week. When he came, the Rabbi welcomed him and asked the reason for his absence. The dealer replied that he had been ashamed to visit the Rabbi because he had begun to deal in adulterated honey, selling it to purchasers as pure.

The Rabbi said: "I cannot stop you in this deception at one stroke, inasmuch as you need your business for a livelihood. But I will help you out of the situation. Promise me that when you are able to secure only six cents of profit on the pound, you will not handle the honey, but for seven cents you will make the transaction." The dealer promised to do so. The next time he came, the Rabbi exacted a promise not to handle the false honey under ten cents profit per pound. This was increased from time to time. To be able to sell his goods at higher prices, the dealer was compelled to offer purer honey, until at last he sold only pure and unadulterated honey. His customers found that the higher the price they paid, the finer the honey, and they proved themselves willing to pay. Gaining the confidence of his customers, he soon acquired a monopoly of pure honey, and became prosperous.

The dealer thanked the Rabbi with heartiness, for showing him the pathway towards integrity, and for demonstrating to him the truth of the axiom: "Honesty is the best policy."

Kotzker Maasioth, p. 4.

5. Stealing and Cheating

Said the Koretzer: "One who does not cheat will suffer no loss through larceny, as it is written: 'Steal not and cheat not.' [1] This demonstrates a connection between stealing and cheating."

Nof. Tz., p. 9.

[1] "Ye shall not steal; neither shall ye deal falsely." (Leviticus 19:11.)

6. The Cheat

Said the Vorker: "He who cheats in even a single matter is far from all righteousness. He who is truthful is near to all goodness."

Em. K., p. 61.

34. DEMOCRACY

1. Conversation with the Everyday Man

A man asked the Ladier Rabbi: "Wherein does the Rabbi's greatness over other people display itself?"

The Rabbi replied: "You may recognize the truly great man by observing how he talks to various ordinary people. It requires sagacity for the learned man to be able to converse with an everyday man and hold his attention."

S. S. K., iv, 135.

2. Welcome for Commoners

Said the Berditschever: "I have learned to welcome even the ignorant and untutored to my home. Does not the Lord do likewise? When the time of the Resurrection comes, and the Lord prepares a Banquet for the righteous, I shall be privileged to mingle with the guests. If it is asked: 'How did this uncultured person find entrance among us?' I shall reply: 'I deserve to be here because I also gave hospitality at my banquets to men more ignorant than myself.' "

E. O., p. 61.

3. Sharing in Devoted Service

When Rabbi Elimelech of Lizensk returned home from a town that he had visited, his Hasidim accompanied him for a long distance. As the wagon wherein he journeyed passed out of the towngate, the Rabbi alighted, and instructed the driver to go on; then he walked among those who accompanied him. The Hasidim asked him in surprise why he did this, and he answered: "When I saw how devotedly you were performing your generous task of accompanying me, I could not refrain from sharing in it."

E. Tz., p. 19 (B., p. 442.) (Refl., p. 65).

4. All Are Equal

Rabbi Menachem Mendel of Vitebsk said: "Before the Endlessness of God, the highest saint and the lowliest commoner are equal."

M. R. T., p. 49.

5. No One Is Superior

The "Yud" related the following: "When I was a child my father showed me in the Prayer Book the Hebrew letter 'Yud.' He then told me that when two 'Yuds' stand together, they form a word by themselves. This word is the Holy Name of the Lord.

"I asked: 'Suppose one letter 'Yud' stands just above another 'Yud', does this also form a Holy Name?'

" 'No,' replied my father.

"Then and there I learned a lesson: 'When two Jews (Yuden) associate on an equal footing and discuss a subject of Torah, the Indwelling Presence of God is with them. But when one of them holds himself superior to the other, God is not there." [1]

[1] See 187:5.

N. H., p. 64.

6. Each Man to His Task

Said the Belzer: "We read in the 'Ethics of the Fathers' (1:2): 'Upon three things the world rests: upon Torah, upon divine service and upon the performance of kind deeds' (Singer, p. 184).

"Every good Jew should adopt one of these injunctions as his major obligation. The Rav should concentrate upon the Torah; the Rebbe should devote himself to the service of the Lord; and the plain Jew should strive to perform deeds of kindness. Then in truth will the world enjoy stability."

D. S., p. 25.

7. The Zaddik Must Lower Himself

The Pulnoer Rabbi said: "When the Zaddik is on the high rungs of the ladder of righteousness, he has no communication with ordinary folk. He must descend to a lower rung if he is to prevail in elevating every-day people to a higher level. This is illustrated by the story of Jacob's Ladder, which stood on the ground though it reached to the Heavens."

Dubnow, T. ha-Has., p. 99.

8. Coarse Trades

Said the Riziner: "Coarse trades are held in contempt. A tinsmith is little esteemed, and a bricklayer less, for they handle lowly substances. How do matters stand with me? What is coarser than a clod averse to spiritual elevation? And yet do I not work with this material, for the greater glory of God?"

Bl., Gem., p. 289.

9. The Rank and File

At a Hasidic convocation, the Gerer Rabbi said: "We are assembled here to accomplish a worthy purpose by united strength. We should not forget, however, that, though at this gathering, we, the leaders, play the important rôle, it is the rank and file of the people from whom we derive this importance. Without them we are helpless. We should be unmindful of ourselves, and should strive to uplift the humblest of our adherents. Every Jew we aid spiritually and culturally adds to the strength of our position as leaders."

S. S. K., iii, 39.

10. Red Blood

Said Rabbi Bunam: "No Jew, however learned and pious, may consider himself an iota better than a fellow-Jew, however ignorant or irreligious the latter may be. This is confirmed by the law that if a learned and pious Jew were commanded to slay the ignorant and impious one, or be himself slain, he must accept death rather than kill the other. No one can tell whose blood is redder [1] and whose life is more important in the eyes of God. If a man in this crucial moment has no right to deem himself superior to another, what right can he possibly have to do so on less critical occasions?"

S. I., p. 46.

[1] Pesachim, 25.

11. The Teamster Who Became a Rabbi

There lived in Lemberg a teamster, named Elkanah. Every Friday at noontime he would put away his horse and wagon, and commence to prepare for the Sabbath. He would don his Sabbath raiment and traverse the neighborhood to collect food for the needy. His little house would soon be crowded with the unfortunate and the homeless who always found a welcome there. In a sweet voice Elkanah would recite the Sabbath Services and later expound the weekly portion of the Torah. A meal would then be provided for all guests at which hymns would be chanted with great enthusiasm. People residing in the neighborhood began to frequent the Services at Elkanah's home. In time he was accepted as a Rabbi by many adherents, and they secured for him a large and goodly residence. Multitudes of Jews, who in the eyes of the Wardens of the great Rabbis were considered lowly and insignificant, preferred the former teamster as their Rabbi. They understood him well, and they appreciated his respect for them and his interest in their welfare. Other good men of little learning and humble status became Rabbis in other poverty-stricken localities. One was an ex-soldier, another an ex-baker. These local Rabbis gained wide followings among the poor Jews of Lemberg, and their influence for good among their disciples was considerable. They also endeavored to provide for the material wants of their adherents, and were in many ways the prototype for political and labor leaders in our day.

F. R. H.-M., ii, 238.

12. The Hermit

Said the Medzibozer, commenting upon the utterance: "And be not wicked in thine own esteem (or by thyself)" (Ethics 2:18):[1] "A man has been given his life to contribute his share in the improvement of the world. If thou art a hermit, avoiding the society of thy fellows, thou art inclined to wickedness."

Butz. D., p. 7.

[1] Singer, p. 190.

13. The Stimulus to Sociability

At a Circumcision Feast there were present the Lubliner Rav, Rabbi Azriel Hurwitz, who was a Mithnaged, and the "Yud." The Rav said to the "Yud": "Pray explain to me why Hasidim seek sociability through drink, while the Mithnagedim do so through a discussion of a subject of the Torah. Is not our method preferable?"

"Why, no," retorted the "Yud." "We find that after Rabbi Elisha ben Abuyah became an apostate, Rabbi Meir deemed it proper to discuss Torah with him but would drink no wine with him. The reason why the Sages have forbidden Jews to drink non-Jewish wine is to guard against any intimacy leading to intermarriage.[1] Since, however, there is no prohibition against discussing

[1] Sabbath, 17b.

Torah with a non-Jew, it stands to reason that drink creates more sociability than discussion of the Torah."

Nif. Yeh., p. 44.

35. DILIGENCE

1. Laziness and Deliberation

Said the Kotzker Rabbi: "The lazy man and the deliberate one are both unhurried in action. The difference between them is that he who deliberates uses the interval for thinking over the merits of the action required; whereas, he who delays the action because of indolence, is found to act at last when it becomes imperative without having given the matter due thought."

S. S. K., iv, 21.

2. The Diligence of Satan

Said the Besht: "When you perceive the Satan diligently seeking to persuade you to commit an evil deed, understand that he is endeavoring to fulfil his duty as he conceives it. Learn from him diligence in performing your bounden duty—namely, to battle and overcome his persuasion."

K. S. T., p. 10a.

3. The Diligence of Haman

Said the Besht: "From the diligence of Haman learn to perform with enthusiasm the will of Mordecai."

K. S. T., p. 31a.

4. Jacob and Pharaoh

Said the Premislaner: "We read: 'And Jacob awaked out of his sleep, and he said: "Surely the Lord is in this place"' (Gen. 28: 16). As soon as the pious Jacob awoke, he proceeded to serve the Lord. But concerning Pharaoh, the man of common clay, we read: 'So Pharaoh awoke. And he slept.' [1] When Pharaoh awoke, he merely turned on his side and continued to sleep. Herein lies the difference between the diligent man of God and the indolent man of the world."

[1] Genesis 41: 4-5.

E. A., p. 48.

36. DIVINITY WITHIN MAN

1. Divinity in Man

Said the Tzernobiler:

"1. Divinity within a man is limited because a man is limited in his ability to receive it.

"2. Divinity has no limit, but finite man cannot comprehend this.

"3. Divinity created matter so that man, composed of matter and soul, may have a conception of it. It follows, therefore, that all matter may be likened to a parable by means of which Divinity can be understood."

F. R. H., M. i, p. 33.

2. The Indwelling Shekinah

The Medzibozer commented on the verse: "I will not give sleep to mine eyes, nor slumber to mine eyelids; until I find out a place for the Lord, a dwelling place for the Mighty One of Jacob" (Psalms 132:4). He said: "I will not rest until I create a dwelling-place for God within me; until I make myself ready and worthy for the residence of the Shekinah within my being."

Butz. D., p. 7.

3. In the Form of a Son

The Medzibozer commented upon the verse: "And he said: 'I will certainly return unto thee when the season cometh round; and lo, Sarah, thy wife, shall have a son' (Gen. 18:10). The Angel promised to return, yet it is not written that he did so. It may therefore be understood that the Angel intended to say: 'I shall return unto thee in the form of a son.'"

Butz. D., p. 7.

4. The Nature of Man

Said the Koretzer: "'Aleph' means the 'Source, the Leader.' The word: 'Ish' (Man) is composed of the 'Aleph,' and the word 'Yesh' (There Is). This signifies that there is in Man the Source, that Divinity abides in Man. 'Aleph,' read backwards, is 'Peleh,' a 'miracle.' Thus we may also state: a miracle there is in man."

Nof. Tz., p. 51.

37. DRINK AND DRUNKARDS

1. His Only Failing

An ailing man came to the "Yud" and asked him to pray for his health. The "Yud" told him to make the request of a man by the name of Shalom, in an adjacent town. There the only Shalom was a drunkard who lived on the outskirts of the town in a miserable hut. The man waited until he became sober, and then made his request. The drunkard asked for a gallon of brandy, and, after receiving it, advised the man to bathe in the river, and he would be cured. This proved to be correct.

When meeting the "Yud" later, the man asked the Rabbi why he had sent him to a drunkard. The Rabbi replied:

"Shalom, my friend, has an exceedingly kind nature, and he oftentimes helps people when he is able to do so. His only fault is a love of strong drink, but this craving saves him from every other sin."

N. H., p. 41.

2. The Difference

The Riziner was asked by a Mithnaged: "Why is it that after Services we Mithnagedim learn the Mishnah, and you Hasidim drink brandy?"

The Rabbi replied: "Your prayers are lifeless, and it is customary to learn the Mishnah for the sake of the souls of the dead. The prayers of the Hasidim, however, are alive and vital, and a drink of excellent brandy is beneficial to the living."

M. D., p. 47.

3. The Drunkard and the Sober Man

The Pulnoer Rabbi related the following parable:

"In a forest there lived a company of bandits who preyed upon travelers. A drunkard and a sober man, journeying through the woods, were attacked and robbed. A merchant asked the drunkard later: 'Can I pass safely through the forest?' The drunkard replied: 'Yes, there is no danger.' When attention was called to his bruises and his torn clothing, he had nothing to reply.

"The merchant turned to the sober man with his question and received a warning to travel armed and in company with guards.

"While passing through this world," remarked the Pulnoer, "we encounter two kinds of advisers. One, like the drunkard, informs us that life is full of enjoyments and no dangers are in its path. If we follow this counsel, we suffer vain regrets in this life and in the After-World. The other adviser cautions us against pitfalls and urges us to prepare ourselves with good deeds for the World-to-Come."

Kahana, Sef. ha-Has., p. 88.

4. The Craving

A man who had been reformed under the guidance of the Lekhivitzer Rabbi, complained to him that at times he was strongly attracted to his former habits. The Rabbi said: "I know of a barkeeper who wearied of the disorder and violence indulged in by his drunken customers, and therefore transformed his saloon into a peaceful food store. One night a semi-intoxicated man came to his door and knocked for admittance, as he had formerly done oftentimes. Was the erstwhile barkeeper surprised at this? He understood that it was natural for the caller to forget his change of business while under the influence of strong drink. All he had to do was to remind the visitor of this fact, and the latter left promptly.

"It is the same with you. It is natural for you to crave your former habits of evil. But merely remind yourself that you have definitely altered your manner of living, and the craving will depart from you."

O. Y., p. 31.

5. *Wine in Moderation*

Said the Koretzer: "The Talmud [1] declares that wine taken in moderation unfolds the brain of a man. He who is a total abstainer is rarely possessed of wisdom."

Nof. Tz., p. 13.

[1] Erubin, 58; Yoma, 76; Baba Bathra, 12.

6. *The Bratzlaver on "Drink"*

"1. Drunkenness causes a man to fall from his high estate, to accept bribes, to deny truth and to rely upon untruths.

"2. God has no love for the drunkard.

"3. The drunkard cannot plead his case.

"4. Drunkenness exiles a man from his home.

"5. It is impossible for a drunkard to avoid harm to someone."

Sef. Ham., pp. 150-1.

7. *The Bearskin*

The Rimanover found some Hasidim heavily immersed in drink. They did not recognize him as a famed Zaddik, and believed him to be an ordinary Hasid. He inquired: "Why do you drink so much? You will be unable to offer prayers properly." The Hasidim answered: "Our Zaddik will gain forgiveness for us even if we mumble our prayers."

The Rimanover then revealed his identity, and said: "Let me recount to you a parable which I am accustomed to narrate at the Seder. A bear was seen in the woods near a village. The woodsman was notified. He went first to the tavern for a drink, and not having money, he asked that the cost of the drinks he charged against his account. 'When I shoot the bear, his skin will bring me a substantial sum, and I will then pay you,' boasted the forester. Being intoxicated, however, he missed his aim, and the bear turned on him. The woodsman lay down on the ground and feigned death. The bear sniffed at his face and finally walked away.

"When the inn-keeper had an opportunity to speak to the forester, he inquired: 'What did the bear whisper in your ear?' The woodsman answered: 'He told me not to charge up drinks against his skin before I had slain him.'

"I say the same thing to you," continued the Rimanover to the Hasidim. "Do not charge up your drinks against the Zaddik, before you are assured that he will intercede for you."

D. D., pp. 217-8.

38. EATING

1. The Bratzlaver on "Etiquette for Eating"

"1. One who eats more than he needs is worse than an animal.

"2. Overeating is the cause of many maladies.

"3. When one eats with the motive of gaining bodily strength to serve the Lord, his food becomes incense before him.

"4. Unripe fruit is dangerous. There is a prohibition against breaking off unripe fruit from the tree, just as there is a prohibition against chopping down a fruit-bearing tree until it dies.[1]

"5. A man should eat slowly and with etiquette even if alone at the table."

L. E. H., p. 8.

[1] Deut. 20 : 19.

2. The Bratzlaver on "Food"

"1. He who eats no forbidden food shall be saved from illness.

"2. Where there is justice and observance of the law, an abundance of food will be found.

"3. He whose food is tasteless in his mouth can know thereby that God is displeased with him."

Sef. Ham., p. 24.

3. Food from the Lord

Said the Besht: "When you eat and take pleasure in the taste and sweetness of the food, bear in mind that it is the Lord who has placed into the food its taste and sweetness. You will, then, truly serve Him by your eating."

M. R. T., p. 20.

4. Eat Sparingly

Said the Koretzer: "It is best to eat sparingly. Thereby a man tends to lengthen his life. We find among animals and reptiles that those which eat the least, live the longest."

Nof. Tz., p. 21.

5. Food for Health

Said the Mikolayever: "Eat and drink because you are commanded to safeguard your health.[1] Such eating is a pious deed. But to eat merely to satisfy a craving is a form of transgression."

E. A., p. 58.

[1] Deut. 4 : 15. "Take ye therefore good heed of yourselves."

6. Hurried Eating

The "Yud" and his son, Yerachmiel, lost their way on the road to Rimanov. After many hours of wandering, they discovered the road once more, and soon after halted at an inn. The innkeeper gave them some baked potatoes to appease their hunger while awaiting the meal. The son snatched the potatoes from the man's hand. The "Yud" rebuked him, saying: "My son, your hunger does not excuse your lack of good manners. No one ought ever show undue craving for food." As a penalty, he ordered Yerachmiel to sit with the driver instead of inside the coach.

Tif. Yeh., p. 14.

7. The Zaddik's Meals

Rabbi Moses Przevorsker declared that the sumptuous meals served at the tables of the Zaddikim helped to bring down an abundance of sustenance for Israel. We find mention of such meals at the table of Rabbi Judah ha-Nassi.[1]

Rabbi Zevi Elimelech Dinover visited the Ziditzover. When potatoes, then a new vegetable recently imported from America, were placed on the table, the Dinover declined to eat them. But the Ziditzover persuaded him to partake of them, thereby bringing down an abundance of this "fruit of the earth" in its new home.

P. v. K., p. 43a.

[1] Abodah Zara, 11, and Tossafoth.

39: ENEMIES: FORBEARANCE TOWARDS THEM

1. Do Not Hate

Said the Kotzker Rabbi: "Do not hate the Jew who has wronged you. He has offended you through the evil elements within him, but it may be that his good elements are greater than the goodness within yourself."

S. S. K., iv, 109.

2. The Loyal Hasid

The Talner Rabbi came to a town which was in the "sphere of influence" of the Rezistzover Rabbi. The latter's Hasidim were angry at his "trespassing" upon their Rabbi's "territory." One of them was unable to restrain himself, and he threw a stone into the Talner's coach. The Talner picked it up and said to his companions: "I shall keep this stone as a symbol of the self-sacrifice (Mesirath Nefesh)[1] of a loyal Hasid." He placed it later among his treasures.

M. D., p. 52.

[1] "Mesirath Nefesh" means readiness to give up one's life or happiness for an idea. A Hasid believes that one who displeases a Zaddik courts death.

3. Slandering the Besht

Before Isaac Horowitz was called to Hamburg as Chief Rabbi, he held this position in Brody. He was a zealous opponent of the Besht, and spoke of him habitually in unfavorable terms.

Once the Besht said to his Disciples: "Go to the Holy Gaon, Rabbi Isaac, and speak ill of me to him."

The Disciples looked at him in amazement.

Then he said: "Do this, in order that the great man may find satisfaction and his heart may rejoice."

Bl., Pr., p. 66.

4. Why Lessen Their Joy?

Several Hasidim came to the Besht and said: "Our opponents, the sages of Brody, persecute us continually, and accuse us, Heaven forbid, of disobedience to the Law and irreverence towards the traditions of our forefathers. We can endure it no longer, and we must answer them."

"Our adversaries," replied the Besht, "do this certainly out of pious zeal. They believe they are performing a good deed, and they take joy in oppressing us. Why should we seek to deprive them of their joy?"

Bl., Pr., p. 64.

5. The Patient Rabbi

The Rozdoler Rabbi was accustomed to aid his opponents, and to forbear with those who abused him. Once his wife asked him why he did not take steps to punish them in order to halt their calumny. He replied:

"You have seen the crowds which come to me with their donations. The reason why multitudes go to the Zaddik is because he is the foundation of the world,[1] and they endeavour to strengthen the foundation. But I am not a Zaddik. Why, then, do they come to me? The reason is that when there is no Zaddik to uphold the world, another will suffice, namely the one who hears abuse and remains silent. In this wise the Talmud[2] explains the words (Job 26:7): 'He suspended the earth on no word.'[3] Because of this, I am entitled to receive the approval and support of the people."

E. K., p. 61.

[1] Proverbs 10:25.
[2] Hullin 89a.
[3] Another translation is: "He hangeth the earth over nothing": "Tolah erets al-belimah."

6. Forbear From Revenge

When a war broke out between the Hasidim and their opponents, Rabbi Elijah of Wilna did not resort to argument; he fulminated against those who upheld Hasidism a decree of expulsion from the community, placing them under the great ban.

When Rabbi Dov Baer heard of this, he turned to his disciples, expounding the Law: "Our adversaries hold with this commandment: you shall remove the evil from your midst.[1] Be it our part to hold with another: 'Thou shalt not avenge nor bear malice.'"[2]

[1] Deut. 21:21.
[2] Levit. 19:18.

Rabbi Dov Baer encompassed all Hasidism in the two ideas: Love of God and Love of Men.

Rabbi Dov Baer forbade his followers to withstand the enemy in angry dispute. When in their despair, they turned against their persecutors, placing them under the ban, the Rabbi took it so heavily to heart that he fell into a sore distemper.[3] He did not live to watch the struggle; he died long before it reached its height.

Bl., Gem., p. 44.

[3] The Maggid said to his Disciples: "By this action you have caused the loss of your leader, but your gain is that henceforth you will triumph over your adversaries in every controversy." Nine of the Maggid's close Disciples agreed upon the issuance of the ban. They wished the Ladier to complete the Minyan, but were uncertain of his attitude. When the Ladier, the profoundest Talmudist among them, appeared, they asked him for a legal opinion on the case. He replied that according to the Law, those who abuse a "Disciple of the Sages" should be excommunicated. Then they told him of their decision, and he was unable to refuse to abide by his own legal opinion (Maimonides, Rules of Talmud Torah, 4:12, based on Berakhoth, 19a).

7. Imitating Our Enemies

Said the Belzer: "Oftentimes we observe the thoroughness with which an evil man plans a deed, and the untiring effort with which he executes it. Should we not imitate him when we endeavor to perform a good deed? We read in Psalm 119:98: 'From mine enemies shalt Thou teach me wisdom in doing Thy commandments.'"[1]

D. S., p. 80.

[1] The J. T. gives this verse as: "Thy commandments make me wiser than mine enemies, for they are ever with me." Apparently the Belzer played upon the verse which in the Hebrew reads: "Meloyevai tehackmeni mitswosekha."

8. The Flask of Wine

An opponent of Rabbi Schmelke wished to shame him in public. He sent him a flask of very old and strong wine on the day before Yom Kippur in the hope that he would become drunk from it. The Rabbi tasted a little and perceived the sender's intention. When he was reciting Psalms after the Services, he repeated several times the verse (Psalm 41:12): "By this I know that Thou delightest in me, that mine enemy doth not triumph over me," and translated it thus: "By this I shall know that Thou art pleased with me, that those who wished to disgrace me receive no harm because of me."[1]

Rabbi Schmelke's adversary was moved by the Rabbi's prayer for his enemies, and begged him for forgiveness. Rabbi Schmelke remarked: "You would not have done me injury, but only good, if your plan had succeeded. The disgrace would have washed away many of my sins. I regret truly that awe of the Holy Day sobered me."

[1] The verb "Yaria" in this verse may be derived from "Teruah," "blowing the bugle of victory," or from "Ra" which means "harm," or evil.

The erstwhile adversary became one of Rabbi Schmelke's most loyal adherents.

M. Hat., p. 27.

40. ENTHUSIASM

1. *Warmth of Service*

Said the Riziner: "I will illustrate to you the necessity of warmth in the service of the Lord. The Torah [1] bids us when we become unclean to immerse ourselves in water and thereby be purified. But if the water is frozen, can we immerse ourselves in it? A frozen heart cannot purify an unclean life."

[1] Lev. 15:13.

Beth Phineas, p. 52.

2. *The Enthusiastic Philanthropist*

The late Brisker Rav remarked concerning a certain philanthropist who was known as an enthusiastic contributor to every charity: "He is a most admirable man, but he possesses one fault; he enjoys almsgiving so much that he desires people should always be needy, in order that he may aid them." [1]

Rabbi Meyer Berlin in the J. M. J., June 12, 1931.

[1] Non-Hasidic in origin, but Hasidic in mood.

3. *Growing Cold*

Rabbi Moses Sopher used to say: "On a day when I read no book of moral instruction, I feel my reverence for the Lord growing cold." [1]

[1] Non-Hasidic.

D. Z., p. 6.

4. *A Drowning Man*

Said the Besht: "Laugh not at the motions of a man who prays with fervor. He makes these motions in order to save himself from foreign thoughts which intrude upon him and threaten to engulf his prayer. Would you laugh at a drowning man who makes motions in the water in order to rescue himself?"

K. S. T., p. 16a.

5. *Live Coals and Ashes*

Rabbi Mordecai Tzernobiler and the Riziner established themselves in great splendor, in direct contradiction to the custom of their parents. The Riziner gave the following explanation: "Formerly Hasidism was burning like live coals, and therefore was in danger of speedy extinction. Now, however, we have placed ashes upon these coals, and it is our hope that they will endure for many generations."

F. R. H.-M., i, 110.

6. The Mezeritzer on "Cleaving and Ecstasy"

"1. A man should have his mind constantly occupied with holy thoughts. If he has occasion to meditate upon worldly things, let it be as if he had left his permanent abode temporarily, with the complete intention of returning thereto as quickly as possible.

"2. Every man should retain some holy thought in his greatest lapse from grace. When a coal still retains a spark, it may be rekindled into a flame. If the spark has departed, it can no longer be restored. In the same fashion, if a man ceases to cleave to holiness in his thoughts even to the smallest degree, his soul may be extinct.

"3. Thought may be utilized for holy or unholy purposes. Should not a man's intellect elevate his thoughts to the Supreme Mind, rather than degrade them to materialism? Is it not natural for mind to cleave to mind?

"4. Man is called 'Adam' when he unites himself with the 'Aleph' or the Source. Otherwise, he is merely 'Dam,' a maker of blood.

"5. In Exile, it is easier to find divine inspiration than in the days of the Temple. When a king is at home, it is difficult to obtain an audience with him. But when he is traveling, he may be easily approached.

"6. Fire-fighters often combat fire with fire. In the same fashion, a man may battle the fires of evil within him, by kindling his ecstasy for holiness into flame.

"7. A man's ecstasy for the Lord is not genuine unless he takes joy in it.

"8. When a man has attained ecstasy in serving the Lord, it abides with him whatever Mitzwah he performs.

"9. Ecstasy is the pleasure derived from doing God's will. The Mitzwah is its garment."

T. M. M., pp. 153-164.

7. "Abraham, Isaac and Jacob"

The Apter once was awakened by three knocks on his window. It was the Beadle who thus summoned worshipers in the early morning to Services. The Rabbi felt an unusual enthusiasm and buoyancy; he dressed rapidly and strode over to the synagogue. There he asked the Beadle: "When you knocked at my window, did you have in mind an idea of especial holiness?"

"Nay," answered the Beadle. "I am unlearned in ideas of holiness,[1] but there is a tradition in my family which I have inherited from my father, that I recite the names of Abraham, Isaac and Jacob when I knock thrice."

These words, pronounced with simple sincerity, sufficed to bring down enthusiasm wherewith to serve the Lord.

D. D., p. 230.

[1] Kavvanoth.

41. ENVY AND COVETOUSNESS

1. *"Thou Shalt Not Covet"*

Said the Radviller: "The commandment: 'Thou Shalt Not Covet' [1] is placed at the end of the Decalogue because he who has observed this commandment is certain to have observed all those which precede. But he who has not sufficient self-discipline to fulfil this prohibition against coveting must commence anew with the first commandment: belief in the justice of God. For had he sincerely believed in God, he would not be covetous of that which God had allotted as the share of others."

E. O., p. 66.

[1] Exodus 20:17.

2. *The Peasant's Shanty*

The Alexanderer Rabbi discussed Ibn Ezra's comment on the commandment: "Thou Shalt Not Covet" [1] which runs as follows: "Thou shalt not think of coveting the property of another in the same way that a peasant does not think of coveting the royal palace." The Rabbi added: "If you are a distinguished person, do not covet the possessions of a poor worker, in the same way that a king does not think of coveting a peasant's shanty."

S. S. K., i, 107.

[1] Exodus 20:17.

3. *Envying The Wrongly-Placed*

The Besht once journeyed with his little son Hirsch to Medziboz to visit the ailing Rabbi of the town. The Rabbi was a man of means, and in his house there stood a cabinet of silverware which Hirsch admired greatly.

"My son," said the Besht. "Thou thinkest in thy heart that this silverware standeth in the wrong place and that it should be in thy father's house. You are right by half and wrong by half. The silver truly stands in the wrong place, but not because it is not ours. It should rather be given away as charity, instead of glittering here as futile ornaments."

Bl., Pr., p. 53.

4. *The Wine-Goblet*

Once Rabbi Isaac, the Radviller, came to Zbaraz on a visit to his brother. As the two Rabbis sat down at the table, the wine-goblet of Rabbi Wolf caught the favorable attention of Rabbi Isaac who was a very rich man. He took it in his hand and examined it closely.

When Rabbi Wolf observed this, he said: "My dear brother, in order that you may not disobey the commandment: 'Thou shalt not covet,' [1] I give you as a present this wine-goblet."

Bl., Gem., p. 261.

[1] Exodus 20:17.

5. Envy of Greatness

A Rabbi who disliked the Kotzker Rabbi asked him to name the greatest Zaddik living. The Kotzker answered:

"If the person who you surmise may be the greatest Zaddik is like a spider in your eye, how much sharper will be your dislike for the person who you are sure is the greatest Zaddik."

S. S. K., v, 46.

6. Is It Good to be a Rebbe?

When the government built a road near Kobrin, a Jew, who was employed by the contractor in the supply division, visited the Kobriner Rabbi on a Sabbath. He arrived at the Rabbi's home at mealtime. Observing the excellent food and the well-heated room, he thought in his heart: "How fine it is to be a Rebbe and to live in comfort, instead of being compelled oftentimes to work out-of-doors in the cold and stormy weather!"

Just then a woman entered, crying bitterly that her son was dangerously ill, and imploring the Rabbi to pray for his recovery. Every one present was deeply distressed by the poor woman's desperation.

The Rabbi who had surmised the workman's thoughts by observing the expression of his face, turned to him, and said:

"Well, do you still think it is good to be a Rebbe?" [1]

O. Y., p. 146.

[1] See under "Fellow-Feeling in the Rabbi."

7. The Poor Man's Sacrifice

The Kozmirer Rabbi commented upon the law in Leviticus enjoining a wealthy man to bring one lamb for his sin offering, whereas the poor man must bring two doves, one as a burnt offering, and one as a sin offering (Leviticus 5:7).

"Why," asked the Rabbi, "should the poor man be required to bring two?"

"The reason is," he said, "that when a poor man brings his dove, he is thinking: 'O, why am I so neglected by the Lord, that I cannot afford to bring Him more than a little dove.' And the Midrash [1] tells us that the burnt offering was brought to gain forgiveness for evil thoughts. Therefore, the poor man who is envious and complains against the Lord's ways, is required to bring the second sacrifice."

Ha-Beer, vii, part i, p. 46.

[1] Wayyikra Rabba, 7:3.

8. An Unsatisfactory Distribution

Rabbi Hirsch Rimanover was overjoyed when his second wife bore him a son, all the sons by his first wife having died. At the

Feast of Circumcision he issued an order that the poor of Rimanov should receive all the viands they could consume. Everyone was happy and satisfied.

The Rabbi then compiled a list, in accordance with which he instructed that sums of money should be distributed. His Warden reported to him that this plan caused grievous dissensions and quarrels since some were envious of those who received more.

The Rabbi, thereupon, remarked: "The Lord Himself is unable to satisfy every person with His distribution of wealth. How can I be expected to succeed where He does not?"

M. T., p. 30.

9. Envying the Newcomer

Said Rabbi Asher Ropshitzer: "We find that when a new Rabbi comes to a town, his advent is greatly resented by the resident Rabbi, who fears the newcomer's competition. It was different in the case of Moses. When Joshua wished to prevent Eldad and Medad from unfolding their prophecies to the people,[1] Moses exclaimed: 'Art thou jealous for my sake? And, oh, that one might render all the people of the Lord prophets, that the Lord would put His spirit upon them.' This is the reason for the Bible's judgment regarding Moses: 'And there arose not a prophet since then in Israel like unto Moses' " (Deut. 34: 10).

E. Tz., p. 104.

[1] Num. 11: 28-9.

10. The Bratzlaver on "Envy"

"1. When envy will cease, Redemption will come.

"2. Envy is oftentimes the cause of destruction and murder.

"3. Envy of another man's property may cause derangement of mind."

Sef. Ham., p. 143.

11. Not Even for Temporary Use

Rabbi Bunam once came to Tortzin where a room was prepared for him in the residence of a wealthy man. As soon as he entered the vestibule, he turned and departed from the house. Another room was found for him in the dwelling of a poor man. Later he explained his action.

"I did not leave the rich house because I found anything evil there, but because I did not desire to transgress against the commandment: 'Thou shalt not covet thy neighbor's house,' even for temporary use" (Exodus 20: 17; Deut. 5: 18).

S. I., pp. 30-1.

42. EVIL AND GOOD

1. Evil and Good

The Besht said: "Absolute evil does not exist. When the good man perceives evil-doers, he rejoices in goodness."

Dubnow, T. ha-Has., p. 54.

2. Adam's Sin

The question was propounded to Rabbi Isaac of Vorki: "What was Adam's true sin?" He answered: "His true transgression was that he took care of the morrow. The serpent deluded him, saying: thou art an unprofitable servant, being unable to distinguish between good and evil. Eat of this fruit, and thou wilt be of service, choosing the good and receiving high reward. And Adam, concerned about the morrow, listened and did evil. He would not have done so, if he had cared only for the duty of the hour: namely, to obey God's commandments, and to resist the serpent."

B., p. 584m.

3. Evil From On High

"Out of the mouth of the Most High proceedeth not evil and good?" On this sentence (Lamentations 3:38) Rabbi Sussya made comment: "Nothing is evil, for whatever is so in man's estimation, is also good." In Midrash Tanchuma to Genesis, we read: "Nothing that is evil comes from on High." Even wickedness may serve a man to bring about conversion. While the strands of cause and effect are being unravelled, we grope about, calling things good and evil. What first appears as evil fortune, may discover itself, years later, as the best of events and a cause for rejoicing. Says the Zohar:[1] "Man does not know the taste of sweets, until after the bitter."

Bl., Pr., p. 21.

[1] To Sedrah "Tazria."

4. The Tree of Life

The Lizensker interpreted thus, Genesis 3:22-24: "And the Lord God said: 'Behold the man is become as one of us, to know good and evil.' He acquired the power to think and to desire both good and evil, just as in the world of divinity there are holy and unholy spirits. 'And now, lest he put forth his hand, and take also of the tree of life, and eat, and live forever.' He became endowed with the ability to do evil, and thereby to die; on the other hand he is able to do good and gain immortality for his soul, by partaking of the tree of life, namely, by obedience to the Lord's instruction. 'Therefore the Lord God sent him forth from the Garden of Eden, to till the ground whence he was taken.' Since good deeds cannot be performed, and self-improvement cannot be achieved in Paradise where there are no evil impulses, the Lord sent him forth from the state of primitive happiness to labor in the world of strife and impulse.

"So He drove out the man; and He placed at the east of the Garden of Eden the Cherubim, and the flaming sword which turned every way, to keep the way of the tree of life.' Therefore, the Lord placed within man the quest for pleasure and the evil desire that revolves continuously in his brain, inflaming his heart with its intensity and its urgent power. They guard the way and force man to battle them. Over them he must gain victory before he can perform the will of the Lord, and thereby gain the right to immortality."

Noam E., p. 16.

5. Breaking Up the Evil Nature

The Berditschever strove always to interpret beneficently those verses which relate to evil or punishment for Israel. On the text (Exodus 32:34): "Nevertheless in the day when I visit,[1] I will visit their sin upon them," the Rabbi said.

"This phrase does not mean that the Lord will consider further sins as second offenses, and punish them more severely on that account. Quite the contrary is to be understood.

"Who would you say deserves more approbation for his good behavior: the member of an excellent family or the son of a common family? The latter, to be sure. He has conquered the evil habits implanted within him by heredity and upbringing, and has become a well-mannered gentleman.

"Hence, when Israel accepted with alacrity the Commandments, the Lord deemed it a characteristic action of a well-born people, in whom obedience had become second nature. No special commendation was, therefore, vouchsafed to them for this prompt acquiescence.

"But, when almost immediately, they transgressed by worshipping the Golden Calf, it became clear that submission to authority was not a mere habit with them; that, therefore, their previous acceptance of the Torah was a deliberate action, dictated by their heart and mind. As to their noble origin, any inheritance of good conduct due to it had been lost long before by reason of their serfdom.

"Hence, now, God appreciated the greatness of their act in accepting the Torah. It demonstrated that they had broken through the evil inclinations they had acquired in Egypt, at least on that occasion. And God promised to remember this fact always, and to be lenient towards them in His judgments."

E. O., p. 63.

[1] or "Remember."

6. The Nature of Good and Evil

Said the Koretzer: "A man cannot be consciously good unless he knows evil. No one can appreciate pleasure unless he has tasted bitterness.

"Good is only the reverse of evil, and pleasure is merely the opposite of anxiety.

"And the Lord said: 'It is not good that a man should be alone; I will make him a help-meet for him' (Gen. 2:18). And God said: 'There can be no goodness in man while he is alone without an evil impulse within him. I will endow him with the ability to do evil, and it will be as a help-meet to him to enable him to do good, if he masters the evil nature within him.'

"Without the evil impulse, man could do no evil; but neither could he do good."

Nof. Tz., p. 52.

7. Good in the Evil Man

The Medzibozer commented upon the verse: "And yet a while, and the wicked is no more; yea, thou shalt look well at his place and he is not" (Psalms 37:10). He said: "Even the evil man is not thoroughly bad; there is yet a little [1] in him that is not wicked. Look well for the goodness within him, and you will discover he is not truly evil."

Butz. D., p. 20.

[1] "Me'at" is "a while" or "a little."

8. Living in Paradise

The Bratzlaver said: "The knowledge that whatsoever occurs to you is for your good, raises you to the heights of living in Paradise."

K. L. M., p. 5.

9. God Does the Rest

Said the Bershider: "A man should not think contemptuously of his ability to do good. Let him but choose and God does the rest. Is there any limit to God's ability?"

M. P., p. 44.

43. EXILE AND REDEMPTION

1. Fruit in the Seed

The Gerer Rabbi said: "Exile contains redemption within itself, as seed contains the fruit. Right work and real diligence will bring out the hidden reward."

S. S. K., i, 13.

2. In a Strange Land

Commenting on Psalms 137:4, the Riziner said: "The words 'How can we sing the Lord's song in a strange land' mean: 'How can we sing songs when the Shekinah is in a strange land.'"

E. O., p. 137.

3. The Shekinah's Exile

Said Rabbi Schmelke: "We read in Psalms 42:4: 'My tears have been my food day and night; while they say unto me all the day: where is thy God?' Because we cry day and night only for food, therefore we remain in exile. The Lord saith: Would that they cried unto Me: 'Why is our God not in His Holy City? Why is the Shekinah still in exile?' Then Redemption would speedily come."

S. ha-Tov, p. 44.

4. The Length of Our Exile

Said the Radomsker: "It is often asked why the present exile lasts so long. One reason may be that the Shekinah is impatient to return to Palestine and desires that the good Jews be redeemed, even if the impious ones assimilate and become non-Jews. But the Zaddikim have compassion on the irreligious also, and petition the Lord to allot them a longer time wherein to strive for the repentance of the impious, so that they also may be redeemed."

O. S., p. 47.

5. Travail of Redemption

Rabbi Abraham Jacob of Sadigura once faced the following dilemma. During a merciless persecution of the Jews in Russia, he stayed his prayer for divine intercession, saying: "This, I am told and am inclined to believe, indicates that the labors giving birth to Redemption are upon us. But the travails are so terrible that the Jews cry unto heaven, protesting their inability to sustain them. Then God in His mercy abates the pains and Redemption is delayed. Whether I pray, then, or stay my prayer, I have reason, either way, to be heavy of heart."

Bl., Gem., p. 325.

6. The Hindrance

Once in a certain year Rabbi Jacob Yitzchak Lubliner was confident of the advent of the Redeemer before the end of the year. But the twelvemonth came to an end and Redemption was still far to seek. The Rabbi said to his favored disciple, the "Yud": "The common people have turned from their evil ways, and on their part there is no hindrance to Redemption. It is the scholars that bar the way; they cannot attain to humility, and therefore, not to repentance."

B., p. 480.

7. Sheep That Wait

In his comments on the Torah, Rabbi Aryeh Leib Gerer wrote the following discussion of Genesis 29:7: "Israel says to the Lord: 'If the day of redemption is to be long awaited; if the time that Thy sheep should be assembled to be taken home, has not yet arrived, I implore Thee, O Lord, do not leave them to perish during the long interim; water the sheep and go and feed them so that they may have the strength to wait.'"[1]

S.S.K., ii, 33.

[1] The verse reads: "And he said: 'Lo, it is yet high day, neither is it time that the cattle should be gathered together; water ye the sheep and go and feed them.'"

8. Submission to Exile

The well-known Rabbi Samuel of Posen illustrated the verse in Isaiah 51:13 by the following parable:

"A nobleman's son was guilty of grave disobedience towards his father. As a punishment he was exiled to work as a farmhand for one of the nobleman's tenants. The father expected that his son would feel the ignominy of so lowly a position and would beg for forgiveness. The son, however, became accustomed to his work and seemed to have forgotten his former estate.

"The nobleman instructed his vassal to treat his son roughly. The son, thereupon, begged his father to instruct his employer to treat him kindly. The father replied in anger: 'Does the cruelty of the farmer's treatment of you constitute all that matters? Have you fallen so low in your self-esteem that with benevolent treatment your condition as a farmer's servant would be acceptable to you?'

"The Prophet exclaims: 'And hast forgotten the Lord thy Maker . . . because of the fury of the oppressor?' (in exile). And where is the fury of the oppressor? The vital thing is your state of exile and your contentedness to remain in exile."[1]

Shaar Bath Rabim, Exodus, p. 16.

[1] See below No. 18. "The Foolish Request."

9. The Real Exile

Rabbi Henoch of Alexander once said: "The real exile of Israel in Egypt was that they had learned to endure it."

S. S. K., iii, 130 (in name of Rabbi Bunam). (B., p. 650).

10. God's Sabbath

Many unfortunates came to the Belzer Rabbi with their tribulations and complaints. The Belzer remarked:

"We say in the Grace after meals on the Sabbath: 'May the All-Merciful give us a share in the day which shall be wholly Sabbath and a rest to the Everlasting.'[1] At present in our Exile we give no rest to the Almighty from our complaints. We therefore implore that the millenium shall come near when every dissatisfaction will disappear because all men will understand God's ways. Then will He enjoy rest."

D. S., p. 34.

[1] "May the All-Merciful let us inherit the day which shall be wholly a Sabbath and rest in the life everlasting." "U-menuchah le-chayei ha-olamim." There is frequent play upon the meaning of words in Hasidic lore, which allow themselves to be translated in at least two different ways. (See Singer, p. 284.)

11. The Three Exiles

Said the Belzer: "There are three kinds of exile: exile among the nations; exile among Jews; and exile among one's own desires. The first is the easiest to bear. The nations may be influenced by gifts and good will, and respite may thereby be gained.

"Harder is the exile of a Jew among Jews. His Jewish adversary knows every wile used by Jews, and will oppress his fellow-Jew in distress until he has gained everything the latter can give and borrow.

"The worst exile is the exile from peace of mind. It is suffered by one who is overpowered by his evil desires at the same time that he is aware of their wickedness. The last-named needs redemption most urgently, as it is said (Psalms 130:7): 'With Him is plenteous redemption. And He will redeem Israel from all his iniquities.' "[1]

D. S. p 74

[1] The spiritualization of the Exile concept, as is done also with respect to Palestine.

12. The Three Struggles

The Belzer expounded the thought of the Three Exiles on another occasion in a different version:

"Every person must undergo three types of struggle in order to defeat the evil impulse:

"First, when he is among fellow-Jews, who endeavor to persuade him to follow evil.

"Second, when he is among non-Jews, who seek to allure him to their ways.

"Third, when he is filled with evil desires in his own heart. This last is the severest struggle to bear."

D. S., p. 100.

13. Service in Exile

Said the Lizensker: "In his palace a king demands regularity and perfection of service. When he travels, however, he is satisfied with the accommodations available. Likewise, in the Holy Land, the

Lord demanded perfect service from Israel, but in Exile, He is satisfied with the poorer service we render Him."

Tif. Yeh., p. 10.

14. On Guard

Said the Koretzer: "The most severe birthpains occur just before delivery. Likewise, the gravest tribulations will immediately precede the Redemption.

"Our redemption from Egypt was the only complete one, inasmuch as no one Jew remained behind. The Shekinah abides in Exile in order to protect the Jews who remain there."

Nof. Tz., p. 24.

15. The Shepherd's Voice

The Medzibozer commented on the verse: "I have gone astray like a lost sheep; seek Thy servant; for I have not forgotten Thy commandments" (Psalms 119:176). He said: "When a sheep is lost, the shepherd hunts for it at once, and calls out to it without delay, lest the sheep forget the sound of his voice. The Psalmist says: 'O Lord, seek us out without delay while we have not as yet forgotten Thy commandments. If Thou delayest, we may forget Thy voice and fail to heed it.'"

Butz. D., p. 16.

16. Joy in God's Victory

Commenting on the verse: "We will shout for joy in Thy victory" (Psalms 20:6), the Medzibozer said: "When Thou shalt come out of Thy exile, we shall shout for joy."

Butz. D., p. 24.

17. Prayers for Redemption

The Ropshitzer said: "No prayer for the coming of the Redemption is wasted. Each one of us causes Redemption to approach nearer to its culmination. When Redemption is at hand, it shall become known in what manner every prayer was useful."

Ohel N., p. 21.

18. The Foolish Request

Rabbi Bunam reproved the congregation for imploring from the Lord only a livelihood in Exile, instead of praying for the advent of the Messiah when a livelihood will be granted as a matter of course. He told the following parable:

"A king banished his erring son to a farm to perform there hard labor. Soon after the king received a letter from the prince, and opened it, prepared for reconciliation with him if the youth petitioned for it. But the son merely asked his father to instruct the farmer to feed and clothe him better. 'How foolish of him!' thought the king. 'Had he been restored to residence in the royal palace, his problems of food and attire would have been solved as a matter of course, and in a manner more agreeable to him.' " [1]

S. ha-Tov., p. 142.

[1] See above No. 8. "Submission to Exile."

19. Grainstalks or Pearls?

Rabbi Judah Zevi of Stretin declared: "We say: 'And mayest Thou assemble the dispersed as one assembles grainstalks.' Why do we not say: 'as one assembles pearls'? The reason is this: when we gather assembled pearls, we cleanse them of all impurities and select only those that are pure. Had we, therefore, said: 'Assemble us as pearls out of the Dispersion,' it would imply that we asked only for the Redemption of the pure Zaddikim. But he who gathers grainstalks does so with hay clinging to them. We likewise petition that we may all be redeemed—the grain ears with the hay-stalks, the Zaddikim with the ordinary Jews."

E. Tz., p. 141.

20. In His Separate Corner

Rabbi Mendel Rimanover said: "If ten Jews come together and converse regardings subjects of the Torah, they feel none of the hardships of the Exile. But when they separate, each in his own corner, every individual among them begins to feel the rigor of the Exile."

D. D., p. 216.

44. FAITH AND TRUST

1. In God

The Kotzker Rabbi explained the verse in Psalm 37:3: "Dwell in the land, and cherish faithfulness." He said: "This should be interpreted: 'sleep on the bare ground but grow in belief.' " [1]

S. S. K., i, 69.

[1] Or "Dwell on earth and feed thyself with belief."

2. The Essence of Faith

The Lekhivitzer explained thus the verse (I Kings 18:21): "How long do ye pass over the two paragraphs?" [1] He said "There are two paragraphs in the Jewish Code which constitute the essence of religion. Chapter I in 'Orach Hayyim,' paragraph 7, reads: 'I shall set the Lord always before me'; [2] and chapter 231, paragraph 2, reads: 'In all thy ways know God.' " [3]

O. Y., p. 39.

[1] Or "How long halt ye between two opinions?" "Seiphim" is also the name for Paragraphs in the Code.
[2] Psalms 16:8.
[3] Proverbs 3:6.

3. *The Bratzlaver on "Trust"*

"1. Trust in the Lord for your sustenance, and He will justify your confidence.

2. Be not afraid to spend for charity and holy purposes; have confidence that God will return your gifts manifold.

3. Even if you are unconvinced that you merit God's blessing, remember that He is merciful.

4. False trust is a belief that God will bless dishonest deeds and protect the transgressor from discovery.

5. False trust is to believe that God will grant a man success, even if he engages in a large enterprise and borrows heedlessly from other people."

L. E. H., pp. 17-19.

4. *Trust Not Man*

A poor man implored the Kotzker Rabbi to give him a letter, requesting one of his rich adherents to present him with a sizable donation, so that he might be able to marry off his grown-up daughter. The letter was given, and after a long journey on foot, the indigent Hasid reached the home of the wealthy one. The rich man read the letter from the Rabbi, and handed the poor man a single Thaler.

The unfortunate petitioner walked away sadly, his hopes shattered. An hour or so later, he was hailed by the magnate, who sat in a carriage, filled with fine foods and wedding garments. To his astonishment, the poor Hasid was informed that these had been prepared for his daughter's wedding.

"Since you intended from the first to accede to the Rabbi's request," said the delighted man, "why did you cause me anxiety?"

"My reason was," replied the rich man, "to teach you not to put your trust in any man, even if it be the great Rabbi. You seem to have forgotten there is a God in Israel."

S. S. K., iv, 22.

5. *The Bratzlaver on "Faith and Belief"*

A.

"1. Redemption depends upon faith; lack of faith was the cause of our Exile.

2. Faith, prayer, miracles and Palestine are interdependent.

3. To attain faith concentrate the full power of the mind upon the words of your prayers.

4. Those who deny all miracles lengthen our Exile.

5. When our faith is weak, the Lord denies us a true leader.

6. When we break in upon our anger with mercy, the Lord does likewise.

7. Oftentimes a man believes he ought be a leader because he desires to benefit his fellows; this is untrue; he is in reality seeking self-honor, and hides his true intention under a mask of kindness.

8. All virtues rest on the foundation of faith in God.

9. A man must not rely upon pure reason; he must mix faith with it.

10. Unworthy teachings bring unbelief and enmity to religion.

11. Belief and faith work for perfection; knowledge is imperfect without faith.

12. When faith is weakened, opportunities for a peaceful livelihood are missing; men do not aid each other, but wander about to find bread.

13. Faith is the portal to holiness.

14. The man of perfect faith feels the thing in which he believes as if it were in truth matter, subject to the perception of his senses.

15. Those of imperfect faith often mistake the intermediary thing for the essential. The business man, for example, believes that his bread is earned through trading; those who are of ill health believe that medicine achieves a cure. They forget the Cause of Causes.

16. He whose faith is strong may be granted understanding, whereby he can know by reason what he has believed without reason.

17. Faith expands within a man, and gives him patience, joy and diligence. Such faith is easiest to acquire in Palestine.

18. Believe that God stands above you and hears every word of prayer you utter; then, in truth, will your worship be fitting.

19. Faith should not only rest in the heart; it should also be expressed by word of mouth. The utterance of words of faith strengthens a man's faith.

20. Better is the superstitious believer than the rationalistic unbeliever.

21. True faith needs neither evidence nor research.

22. The life of a man of faith may alone be called true living. A man of faith has confidence and never descends to despair.

23. The unbeliever has nothing to comfort him in adversity." [1]

L. E. H., pp. 3-7.

[1] See under "Truth and Falsehood," the Aphorisms of the Bratzlaver. See also "Seeking Communion with God."

B.

"1. A man should believe in God by virtue of faith rather than miracles.

2. Lowliness and study of the Torah lead to faith.

3. Believe that every change you observe is not by chance, but by the will of God.

4. When doubt of the Lord's decrees comes to your mind, keep silence. Your own thoughts will then answer you.

5. When you have great men as your adversaries, know that you have fallen from faith.

6. Faith is of importance equal with charity.

7. Faith comes through silence and through charity.

8. Envy, anger and pride cause loss of faith.

9. Through faith a man is able to comprehend God and to have faith in Him.

10. Faith will bring you forgiveness and blessings.

11. He who lacks faith will receive no benefit from admonition and reproof.

12. Faith, humility and peace in Israel are requisite for the Redemption.

13. If we fail to fulfill our duty to proclaim our faith in the Lord among the nations, they are thereby prompted to compel us to accept non-Jewish culture.

14. Faith rests in the mind, and it makes us willing to suffer martyrdom if need be."

Sef. Ham., pp. 18-23.

"15. He who trusts in the Lord feels no fear.

16. Trust in the Lord leads to peace.

17. Faith and the fear of Heaven lead to trust in God.

18. He who lacks the feeling of trust will speak untruths.

19. Trust saves from worries, tribulations and shame.

20. Trust saves us from the necessity of asking the help of man.

21. Flattery causes the loss of trust.

22. Trust causes man to approach nearer to God."

Sef. Ham., p. 38.

6. The True Believer

Said the Mezeritzer:

"1. Who is the true believer in God? The man who believes
That the Shekinah is within him always and guards him;
That he is in the Creator and the Creator is in him;
That he looks upon the Creator, and the Creator looks upon him;
That the Creator may accomplish His will; He may create worlds and destroy them in a moment;
That in Him is the source of all good, and of all misfortune;
That His influence and His Living Power are present in everything;
That only God is to be feared and trusted.

2. Love and fear descend from God, who endowed all living nature with a spark thereof. Therefore why love or fear the spark when you may love and fear the Whole Source whence it came?

3. Belief is the foundation of everything. There can be service of the Lord from tradition without learning. But there cannot be service of the Lord without belief."

T. M. M., pp. 101-3.

7. When Punishment is Decreed

Said the Besht: "When it is decreed in Heaven that punishment is to be meted out to a sinner, the power of trust in the Lord is taken away from him."

K. S. T., p. 9a.

8. The Lack of Faith

Said the Bratzlaver: "Lack of faith is the cause of our Exile. When faith will take the place of rationalism, the Messiah will come. A man may gain faith only through truth. He knows the truth only through intimacy with great leaders."

K. L. M., p. 12.

9. A Consequence of Faith

The Besht told this story: "I once stopped at an inn for the Sabbath. Suddenly a peasant went over to the table and knocked on it thrice. The innkeeper explained that this was a signal agreed upon by the village-owner and himself that the rent for the inn must be paid, or heavy penalties would be inflicted. I inquired if he had the money and he replied that he was penniless; nevertheless he had no anxiety and observed the Sabbath with a joyful spirit. In the evening he departed to confer with the village-owner. I saw, as I watched, that a merchant halted at the door, and after a short conversation gave a roll of money to the innkeeper. The merchant entered, and in reply to my query, informed me that he had purchased from the innkeeper next season's produce, and had paid him in advance to assure delivery. I then saw that perfect trust in the Lord receives its timely reward."

N. Besht, p. 11.

10. The Lord as Partner

The Apter Rabbi told this story: "I chanced to sojourn once at a village inn, and noticed that the innkeeper owned two boxes for cash; whatever money he received, he divided equally between the two receptacles. I was curious as to the meaning of this, and, making known my identity, I asked him the reason for his odd action. The innkeeper replied as follows: 'Once I lost all my money in an unlucky venture, and was unable to keep my inn. My wife advised me to look for a partner, and I went to the city to do so. Passing through the forest, I suddenly conceived the idea to implore the Lord to enter into partnership with me, and I promised to devote to charity His half share. I prayed to the Lord, and suddenly I found some money on the ground. I regarded this as a sign that my prayer was accepted, and since then I have faithfully observed the oral contract, and I am prospering.' I praised the innkeeper's simple trust in the Lord, and pronounced a blessing over him."

N. Besht, p. 45.

11. *The Means of Providence*

Said the Besht: "There are two kinds of men who have confidence in Providence. The first look for the manner by which God will vouchsafe them His abundance, and they are anxious when it seems to them they have not found His means for answering their needs. This type of trust and confidence is unworthy.

"The second men of trust have full confidence in the Lord. They believe He will sustain them in return for their loyal service; and they seek not the means utilized by Providence. Theirs is genuine trust.

"The first believe they must aid God to provide for them and that they must seek out the opportunity. The second believe that God will provide for their wants without assistance, and that He will send them the opportunity for livelihood, since He is the Cause of Causes."

M. R. T., ii, 31.

12. *The Fiftieth Door*

Said the Besht: "We read in the Talmud [1] that forty-nine doors of understanding out of fifty were opened to Moses. But since man aspires always to know more, how did Moses continue? The answer is that when he found the fiftieth door closed to him as unapproachable to the human mind, he substituted faith and meditated again upon those phases of knowledge open to him.

"It is thus that every man should discipline his mind. He should study and reflect to the utmost of his ability. When he has reached a point where he is unable to comprehend further, he may substitute faith, and return to the learning within his grasp. Beyond a certain degree of research, both the sage and the ignorant man are alike. It may be that some will apply to you the verse: 'The simpleton [2] believeth every word,' [3] but you may remind the scoffers of another verse: 'The Lord preserveth the simple.' " [4]

Tif. Yeh., p. 22.

[1] Rosh Hashanah, 21.
[2] Or "thoughtless."
[3] Proverbs 14:15.
[4] Psalms 116:6.

13. *The Merchant and the Rabbi*

Said the Sassover: "We read in the Talmud: The Rabbis knew not the meaning of the verse: 'Cast thy burden upon the Lord, and He will sustain thee' [1] until a traveling merchant told them. [2]

"The Rabbis who obtain an annual salary do not well understand the true meaning of trust in the Lord. It is the merchant whose livelihood is unsafe, and who must await God's help continually, who truly appreciates the meaning of dependence upon Him.

[1] Psalm 55:23.
[2] Megillah 18.

"Another explanation is: The Rabbis did not know whether the verse permits a man in need of a helping hand to combine his trust in the Lord with a request for help from the people. Without being asked for the favor the merchant said: 'Throw your burden on my camel,' at the very moment they were discussing the verse. They received it as an omen that the verse implies that man should not ask for the favors of mortals, but petition for God's alone."

P. v. K., p. 45b.

14. A Tale of Trust in the Rebbe

A poor villager was accustomed to visit the town on Friday to chop wood and to buy goods for the Sabbath with his earnings. Once he earned only six kreutzers which he divided into three parts: two for white bread; two for wine; and two for candles. Before he could spend it, however, the Sassover, still unknown to fame, encountered him, and said: "Young man, buy me two kreutzers' worth of tea, and you will have a goodly share in the World-to-Come."

The youth said to himself: "The Sabbath is only a miniature of the 'Olam ha-Bah' (World-to-Come); I may as well purchase the reality for myself." He bought the tea for the Rabbi. The latter drank it and said: "Buy me tea for two kreutzers more, and you will be blessed with all good." The man consented. But when the Rabbi asked him for tea a third time, promising blessing for all his descendants, the villager refused, inasmuch as he wished at least candles for the Sabbath.

The Rabbi then inquired from the youth what property he owned. When informed that he possessed a cow, the Sassover told him to sell it to the first bidder, bring the money to the town, and seek to find him. When a bidder arrived, the villager asked thrice the worth of the cow in order to test the efficacy of the Rabbi's blessing, and to his surprise, the price was acceptable.

When the youth came to town, he saw a large crowd in attendance at the auction of an estate. He resolved to place the Rabbi's blessing to a further test and entered a bid. The other bidders sought to persuade him to desist, but when he refused, they decided to punish him by withdrawing from the auction, thereby forcing him to buy the estate or lose his deposit. Thus the estate was sold to the villager for a very low price. On the street he met a priest who stopped him and invited him to come to his home. There the priest said he wished to be a partner in the transaction inasmuch as he understood the villager would be unable to settle the purchase price himself. He also asked that the affair be kept secret inasmuch as a priest might not engage in business. The priest gave him the money for the estate and the villager made a secret assignment to him of part of it. A few days later the priest died unexpectedly of an infectious disease, and was buried in his clothes. The agreement which the priest had kept in a secret pocket was buried with him, and the young man became the sole owner of the estate.

When the now wealthy man located the Sassover, the Rabbi said to him: "Had you given me the last two kreutzers and thus shown your implicit trust, you would have been saved the situation with the priest." [1]

E. Tz., pp. 46-8.

[1] The Hasidim narrated these stories in order to glorify the Rebbe of their allegiance. A few are included in this Anthology in order to give the full flavor of Hasidic literature.

45. THE FAITH OF ISRAEL

1. An Unwearying Faith

The Kotzker was reading in Isaiah (43:22) "Yet Thou hast not called upon Me, O Jacob, Neither hast thou wearied thyself about Me, O Israel."

"There is a fine parable illustrating this verse in the works of the Dubner Maggid," said the Rabbi. "It runs as follows:

'Two men, one a jeweler and the other an ironmonger, brought their wares to a certain town. A porter who had delivered their goods at the inn, came later to ask for his pay. He made the error, however, of believing the jeweler to be the owner of the heavier case, and he refused the small coin offered to him as inadequate.

'Your case of goods was very fatiguing,' said the porter. 'I am entitled to more money.'

'You are mistaken,' answered the jeweler. 'My wares, though precious in value, are an easy burden to bear; they tire no one.'

"In the same fashion," said the Rabbi, "the Prophet speaks to Israel: 'My faith wearies no one; you must have taken up with another by error.'" [1]

S. S. K., ii, 23.

[1] See my poem "Once an Abbe Asked a Rabbi," in *Joyful Jeremiads*, p. 5. This is built upon an item in Joseph the Zealot's polemical treatise, "Answers to the Unbelievers"; see *Revue des Etudes Juives*, i, 240. In this colloquy, the Rabbi shows the Abbe two fishmarkets, one with commonplace goods patronized by many; the other with precious goods, patronized by a few; this is by way of answer to the Abbe's inquiry why synagogues have no bells to summon their worshipers to prayer.

2. Cure in Reverse

Said Rabbi Bunam: "Each plague that God brought upon Egypt became a cure for Israel. The blood plague cured them of the diseases of the blood; the boil plague cured them of diseases of the skin. The hardening of Pharaoh's heart caused Israel to believe in the Lord."

S. I., p. 75.

3. A True Confession

A Rabbi told the following story: "When the early Reform Rabbi, Dr. Holdheim, became old, he suffered from an ailment of the foot. He was asked how he had contracted the malady. 'I went too far,' was the reply."

Lustiger Haus Freund, p. 28.

4. The Weaponless Leader

Said the Besht: "A hero promised to defend his city, and showed to the inhabitants his many weapons. He was met by the foe unexpectedly, however, when he had no weapons on his person; he was captured, and the undefended city fell. In the same way, people depend upon their Rabbi to protect them against irreligion. But, if Satan succeeds in deceiving the Rabbi, all of them fall into error. Each man should learn his duties for himself, and he should be able to prevent wrong deeds by indicating their falsity, if the leader should happen to be weaponless."

K. S. T., p. 10a.

5. Tradition and Reason

The Besht commented on the phrase: "Our God and God of our Fathers."[1] He said: "Some persons have faith because their fathers taught them to believe. In one sense, this is satisfactory: no philosophical axioms will break their belief; in another, it is unsatisfactory, since their belief does not come from personal knowledge.

"Others come to belief through conviction after research. This is satisfactory in one sense: they know God from inner conviction; in another, it is unsatisfactory: if other students demonstrate to them the fallacy of their reasoning, they may become unbelievers.

"The best believers are those whose beliefs are satisfactory in every way: they believe because of tradition and also through their own reasoning. This is what we mean when we say: 'Our God and the God of our Fathers.' The Lord is our Master, both because we know He is our God, and because our fathers have taught us that He is God."

K. S. T., p. 15b.

[1] Singer, p. 44.

6. The Feeble and the Strong

The Kobriner Rabbi said: "We read: 'So the feebler were Laban's, and the stronger Jacob's' (Gen. 30:42). Those who waver in their beliefs and whose attachment to their God and His Torah is feeble, belong to Laban, the insincere. But those who are strong in their faith and firm in their adherence to the Lord and his teachings, belong to Israel."

F. U. A. O., i, 74.

46. FAMILY RELATIONSHIPS

1. Find the Good

Rabbi Bunam said: "Jacob ordered Joseph to go and see whether it was well with his brothers. (Genesis 37:14.) Jacob used to hear from Joseph 'evil reports of his brothers,' and he, therefore, instructed him not to persist in looking for their misconduct, but rather to find the good in them."

S. S. K., i, 9.

2. God as a "Near Relation"

Said the Sachatzover Rabbi: "When a man is in dire need and has a rich relative, he usually receives aid a few times; after that, the relative is no longer ready to be of assistance. But if he has many relatives, he may obtain succor a long time. The Torah tells us (Deut. 4:7): 'For what great nation is there, that hath God so nigh unto them,[1] as the Lord our God is whensoever we call upon Him?' The Lord is not described as a near relation, but as near relations, and 'whensoever we call upon Him,' he treats us as a near relative, from whom we ask aid for the first time."

S. S. K., iv, 90.

[1] In Hebrew, Kerovim = Relations or Near Ones.

3. Mere Talk

The Vorker Rabbi discussed the saying in the Ethics (5:13)[1] which reads: "He who says, What is mine is mine . . . , his is a neutral character:—some say, this is a character like that of Sodom."

He said: "A man is asked to give charity. He answers: 'What is mine is for mine. I prefer to assist members of my own family.' This is a sign of a mediocre personality; one of a higher character assists strangers as well. Some other men when asked to make a donation to charity, 'say' they will do so later, but they actually give nothing. They are comparable to the inhabitants of Sodom."

S. S. K., ii, 113.

[1] Singer, p. 201.

47. FASTING

1. The Wrestling Match

"The custom of self-infliction," said the Berditschever, "is nought but a ruse of the Satan, to darken man's brains, and has nothing in common with true piety. It is as if two men were wrestling with each other. Thinks one: If I thump his chest or twist his arms, he may yet get the better of me, but if I numb his head with a hard blow, he will be like one dead. In the same manner, the Evil One lures on and persuades his man to fast on days when fasting is not ordained, and thereby causes darkness and confusion in the brain of the man, and prompts him to fall into sin."

Bl., Gem., p. 69.

2. Greater Than Fasting

Tradition credits Rabbi Elimelech with having said: "If it stood within my power, I would abolish all fast-days, with the exception of Atonement Day, because of the dark humors of the age." And the Sassover said: "If thy neighbor offend thee, refrain from wrath, and it will be more pleasing in the sight of God than a thousand fast-days; listen to revilings without retort, and it will stand you in stead of a thousand self-inflictions." [1]

Another Zaddik, Rabbi Hayyim of Kossov, said: "A Jew, perchance, may recite a psalm with such fervor as to incline heaven much farther than if he spent all his life in fasting."

[1] See Conduct 21: B, 3 and 4.

Bl., Gem., p. 69.

3. Fasting and Talking

The author of the book "Rosh ha-Givah," writes: "It is more desirable to abstain from talking than to abstain from eating, since this will injure neither the body nor the soul."

O. Y., p. 90.

4. The Wounded Soul

Said the Koznitzer Maggid: "He who is guilty of many transgressions and desires to repent should not halt to repair the defects of his soul, but should immediately commence to perform deeds of kindness, pray fervently, and avoid further transgressions. When his strength in goodness is established, then he should labor for the atonement of his former sins. Should he, however, disregard this counsel, and, from the start, indulge in fasting and mortifying his body in atonement for his sins, he is liable to weaken in resolution, and abandon his effort at reformation. It is like the wounded soldier who seeks to escape the enemy in pursuit. If he halts to dress his wounds, he is certain to be captured."

E. O., p. 81.

5. The Student May Not Fast

The Lizensker visited Rabbi Schmelke at Nikolsburg. Passing a house, he heard through the open window, a student, by name Mordecai Bennet (later Rabbi of Nikolsburg), devoting himself to the Torah with great zeal. He went over to him and said: "Repent, my Brother, repent!"

Rabbi Bennet met Rabbi Schmelke and told him of the Lizensker's mysterious injunction. Rabbi Schmelke looked hard at his companion and said: "You look as if you indulged in severe fasting. This is a grave sin for a man blessed with so remarkable an intelligence for the study of the Torah. The fasting weakens you, and forms a serious obstacle to your study."

S. ha-Tov, p. 74.

6. The Inconsiderate Peasant

The Lekhivitzer related the following parable: "A peasant was on his way home from market one winter day. He stopped at an inn, tied his horse to the post, and proceeded to enjoy himself merrily. In the meantime his poor horse stood outside in the deep snow, without food or drink, trembling from the cold.

"By the same token, there are men who fast often, thereby torturing their bodies, at the same time that their thoughts—which are an index to the true personality of men—turn to worldly affairs. These men are like the peasant and his horse."

O. Y., p. 33.

7. Why Did He Fast?

The Ropshitzer wished to test whether a certain man, reputed to fast from Sabbath to Sabbath, and to spend all day in synagogue, was truly pious or merely a hypocrite. He ordered some boys to annoy him, and then went to the synagogue and called out to them: "Why do you harass a man who fasts on Mondays and Thursdays?"

The man turned to him and said: "Have you not heard that I fast from Sabbath to Sabbath?"

The Ropshitzer then recognized the true nature of the pseudo-Zaddik.

O. N., p. 57.

8. A Deception to Himself

Once upon a time there came to the Maggid of Koznitz a man who wore sackcloth next to his body by way of penance, and who always fasted from Sabbath to Sabbath. The Maggid said to him:

"Dost thou think that evil temptations will go out of thy way? They nest like vermin in thy sackcloth. He is a better man who pretends to fast from Sabbath to Sabbath and secretly takes a couple of bites of food each day; for he merely deceives others. But thou art to thyself a deception and a lie."

Reflex, May, 1929, p. 67.

9. The Dwelling-Place of God

Said the Lentzner: "A man may fast only at the time when he is so engrossed in the Torah and in piety that he feels no hunger. But he who suffers from the lack of food may not afflict his body, since God dwells therein."

E. A., p. 31.

10. Why Fast?

Commenting on fasting, the Ziditzover said: "Why fast? If a man fasts with the idea of gaining a favor from Heaven thereby, it is a futile self-affliction, and it will be of no avail. If a man fasts for the sake of Heaven, is it not better to devote himself to learning for the sake of Heaven?"

P. v. K., p. 43b.

48. FATHER'S INFLUENCE AND DUTY

1. *Helping a Needy Son*

A young man came to the Gerer Rabbi with a complaint that his father refused to give him material assistance. The Rabbi summoned the father and inquired the reason. The father pleaded poverty.

The Rabbi remarked: "Do you remember what Moses said when the Sons of Israel demanded meat? 'Have I conceived all this people? have I brought them forth, that Thou shouldest say unto me: Carry them in thy bosom? . . . Whence should I have flesh to give unto all this people?' (Numbers 11:12-13.) Does this not demonstrate to you clearly, that had Moses been asked for meat by those he had conceived, he would not have given the excuse that he did not have it? A father must endeavor with all his ability to aid his needy son."

S. S. K., ii, 59.

2. *The Dream*

Rabbi Bunam was told by a Hasid that the latter's father had appeared in a dream and had counseled his son to become a Rabbi.

Rabbi Bunam remarked: "The next time your father comes to you, ask him to appear in a dream to the Hasidim, and persuade them to become your adherents."

S. S. K., iv, 45.

3. *The Voice*

The Besht told the following parable: "A father and his young son were walking through a wood. The boy begged his father for permission to hunt for berries, and promised to answer his father's call. When the father perceived that his son had gone a considerable distance, he called out to him, but the boy, busy with his search for berries, failed to reply. The father overtook him and said: 'If you do not heed my voice, you will lose your way.' It is the same with us. If we do not give heed to the voice of our spiritual leader when we seek for the fruits of life, we too shall lose our way."

S. S. K., i, 122. (See also E. Tz., p. 34, as told by the Lizensker.)

4. *Wild Oats*

Said the Gerer Rabbi: "Some parents believe it is permissible for their sons to sow their wild oats, so that vice may lose its allurement and they may be convinced that the experience is not worth the effort. This policy is incorrect and should be avoided. We learn this from Moses. According to the Midrash Mekhilta (to Exodus

18: 3), the father-in-law of Moses, Jethro, persuaded Moses to allow his eldest son, Gershom, to visit the pagan temples, and attend the pagan schools, in order that he might be convinced of their worthlessness. Then, said Jethro, he will turn to the worship of the Lord out of conviction rather than tradition.

"The outcome, however, was that there remained in Gershom's family a tradition of the ways and allurements of paganism, and when Jonathan, his son, was in want, he readily consented to make use of this knowledge, and become a priest in the pagan temple." [1]

S. S. K., ii, 36.

[1] Judges 18: 30 and footnote "a" in J. T.

5. The Examination

A visitor, desiring to please his host, proposed to examine the latter's son in a certain field of studies. The son did not know the subjects, but his father assisted him in preparation. When the guest held the examination, the son answered the questions accurately. Observing the father's pleasure at his son's skill, the guest extended the test to include more difficult questions, and the son successfully replied, to the abounding satisfaction of his father.

"The guest," said the Sudilkover, "is the Evil Inclination, which visits a man in order to test his powers of self-mastery. Our Father in Heaven aids us through His Torah and Commandments; yet He takes delight in us if we can withstand temptations. Still more is He glad if we are able to conquer evil desires when circumstances afford us ample opportunity to indulge them."

Kahana, p. 88.

6. The Son Corrects His Father's Faults

Rabbi Schmelke explained the phrase: "Visiting the iniquity of the fathers upon the children" (Deut. 5:9) as follows: "When one has committed a sin which he did not expiate in his life-time, the Lord in His Mercy causes this very sin to visit the son. If the son does not succumb to it, his father's sin is forgiven."

S. ha-Tov, p. 23.

7. The Highest Example

Said the Koretzer: "We recite in the Sh'ma: 'And these words . . . shall be upon thy heart, and thou shalt teach them diligently unto thy children.' [1] When these words go forth from your heart, they will truly influence your children for good."

Nof. Tz., p. 49.

[1] Deut. 6: 6-7.

8. The Unlearned Father

The Koretzer counseled a certain Jew not to live in a village. He said in explanation to inquirers: "This Jew has not a learned father from whom to acquire strength of character and holy thoughts

wherewith to combat the non-Jewish environment. He should, therefore, reside in town among Jews."

M. P., p. 19.

9. *Let Us Not Be Children*

Said the Mezeritzer: "A father lifted up his little son who had
fallen, and, noting a splinter in the boy's foot, he extracted it, unmindful of the lad's cries of pain. He then said: 'If you are not
more careful in your play, you will suffer again the pain you felt a
moment ago.' Both were in fear: the father, that infection would
attack his son's foot; the boy, that he might again undergo the pain
of having a splinter extracted. The father feared the wound, the
son the cure. Likewise, God punishes us in order to cure us of our
sins. He fears the harm to our souls, but we fear the punishment
which is a cure. Let us no longer be children, but let us understand
that which ought truly inspire fear within us."

T. M. M., pp. 232-3.

49. FATHER'S LOVE FOR SON

1. *The Delinquent Son*

A father complained to the Besht that his son had forsaken God.
"What, Rabbi, shall I do?"

"Love him more than ever," was the Besht's reply.

S. S. K., iii, 147.

2. *The Lord's Happiness*

Rabbi Phineas Hurwitz of Frankfort explained the verse (Psalm
42:3): "My soul thirsteth for God, for the Living God; when shall
I come and appear before God?"

"A nobleman banished his son for misbehavior. The son mused:
'O how I yearn to behold my father once more! How I suffer at
being absent from him. But I know well that my father also suffers
greatly by reason of our separation. Would that he but ordered me
to return, and both of us would be happy!'

"We know that the Lord yearns to redeem his eldest son, Israel,
the moment Israel desires redemption in all sincerity. And the
Psalmist says: 'My soul thirsteth to be reunited with Thee, and to
make Thee happy by my nearness to Thee.'"

S. ha-Tov, p. 33.

3. *Loving God with Our Whole Heart*

Rabbi Bunam said: "We find that when Jacob came to Egypt and
saw Joseph, Joseph fell on his father's neck.[1] It does not say, however, that Jacob fell on Joseph's neck. Rashi explains that Jacob
was reciting the 'Sh'ma,' namely, Jacob was occupied with the idea

[1] Gen. 46:29.

of loving God with all his heart, as we are later commanded to do in the 'Sh'ma.'

"Upon beholding Joseph alive, after mourning him for twenty-two years, Jacob was filled with great love for his son. He decided, however, to devote this deep emotion to God, so that his love for a human being might not be greater than his love of God. It is in the matter of love, rather than of fear, that we are asked to give our whole heart."

S. S. K., iii, 53.

4. Fatherly Pity

The Magelnitzer commented on the prayer (Singer, p. 59), which reads as follows: "As a father hath mercy upon his children, so, O Lord, have mercy upon us, and save us for Thy name's sake."

The Rabbi said: "A father forgives his offending son, when the latter appeals to him, even if he is not sure that the son's contrition is sincere, since he cannot read his son's heart.

"Likewise we petition the Lord to forgive us when we pray for pardon, even if our repentance is not complete. In this respect we imitate a mortal father. We entreat that God, also, deal with us as if He did not know our heart."

S. Hay., p. 71.

5. Seeking Out Our Father

Said the Mezeritzer: "A father was playing with his little son. He hid himself for sport, and the boy, after looking for him, finally found him. This increased his father's affection for him. Likewise, God sometimes hides Himself, and when we, seeking Him out, eventually find Him, He loves us all the more."

T. M. M., p. 232.

6. Forgiving God

Said the Koretzer: "There is a saying which declares that God asks the forgiveness of Israel for commanding them to bring a donation of a half-shekel. He asks pardon inasmuch as some Israelites who possess a miserly nature, may resent the necessity of a gift. It is like a father who orders his son to perform a distasteful chore to learn whether the son will overcome his distaste through a sense of obedience. Though the son may perform the chore, the father feels a sense of guilt at subjecting his son to this irritation."

Nof. Tz., p. 57.

50. FATHERS AND SONS

Parental Example

1. "My Father's God"

Said the Belzer: "Every Jew should so conduct himself that his sons will rejoice to say: 'The God of my Father.'" (Gen. 32:10.)

D. S., p. 51.

2. Believers Inspire Belief

The Belzer Rabbi commented on the verse Exodus 10:2: "And that thou mayest tell in the ears of thy son, and of thy son's son, what I have wrought upon Egypt, and My signs which I have done among them; that ye may know that I am the Lord." "It may be remarked that the end of the verse would have seemed more correct if it had been expressed thus: 'that they shall know that I am the Lord.'

"But the verse was intentionally worded 'ye' instead of 'they' in order to furnish us a lesson. Recount to your sons the wonders of the Lord, but remember that this will have a beneficent influence upon them only if you yourselves recognize that He is the Lord."

D. S., p. 176.

3. Not Prayer, but Example

A man asked the Kotzker Rabbi to pray for him in order that his sons might study the Torah diligently. The Rabbi replied: "If your sons will see that you are a diligent student, they will imitate you. But if you neglect your own studies, and merely wish your sons to study, the result will be that they will do likewise when they grow up. They will neglect the Torah themselves and desire that their sons do the studying."

S. S. K., v, 46.

4. The Drunkards: Father and Son

Rabbi Zeev Zitomirer, the "Or ha-Meir," once saw through a window a man and his son, both drunk, reeling into the gutter.

"I envy that father," said the Rabbi to his son, Israel Dov. "That man has succeeded in his ambition to have a son like himself. But I do not yet know whether you will be like me. See to it that the drunkard does not have better success with his son that I with you."

Beth Phineas, pp. 18-19.

5. Originality

After Rabbi Noah's succession as Rabbi at Lekhivitz, some Hasidim inquired of him: "Why do you not conduct yourself like your father, the late Rabbi?"

"I do conduct myself like him," retorted Rabbi Noah. "He did not imitate anybody, and I likewise do not imitate anybody."

O. Y., p. 46.

6. A Man and His Children

Rabbi Solomon Karliner said: "God treats a man in the same way that the man treats his children. Do not neglect your children, and God will not neglect you."

D. Z., p. 33.

7. A Good Man's Desires

Said the Mezeritzer: "When a child desires something from his father, the latter rejoices if he is able to grant his son's wish. Likewise, when a good man desires something, God takes pleasure in granting it."

Butz. D., p. 233.

8. Noah's Sons

Said the "Yud": "We find that a father strives to help his son to become a learned and pious Jew. When the son grows up, he endeavors to make his own son become a good Jew. But when will the time ever come when the father himself shall strive to be a good Jew, instead of leaving this task to his son? We read: 'These are the sons [1] of Noah: Noah was a just, wholehearted man.' (Genesis 6:9.) Noah himself was what he wished his sons to be."

Nif. Yeh., p. 65.

[1] Or "generations, genealogy."

51. FELLOW-FEELING IN THE RABBI

1. The Record of Sorrows

The Rimanover Rabbi said: "Every Jew who narrates to me his sorrows leaves a mark upon my heart. When I arise to recite the Amidah, I open my heart to God, and I pray that He may read every sorrow recorded upon it."

T. M., p. 31.

2. The Other's Tribulations

A poor man came to the Berditschever and petitioned him to offer prayers for his deliverance from poverty. The Rabbi asked that the man remind him of his request the next day.

"But, Rabbi," protested the suppliant, "today I have a chance for a free trip home."

"What can I do?" replied the Rabbi. "At this moment my heart is full of another man's troubles. When the Lord will aid him, my heart will be free to take up yours. I can assist you only when my heart feels your trouble as much as you yourself."

N. B. L., p. 28.

3. Quicksilver

Said the Riziner: "The true Zaddik should be like quicksilver which instantly records a change of temperature. He must, likewise, instantly recognize the lack of tranquillity and peace of mind among his followers."

N. I., p. 39.

4. The Overflooded Heart

Once when the Hasidim were feasting him from plates of gold, Rabbi Dov Baer, the great Maggid, enlightened them on the hardships of great rule. "Think ye," he said, "it is a comfortable station to be a Zaddik and a leader of the many? Know better, then, that it is a thicket of thorns. For the heart of the true Zaddik is flooded with the life-blood of others, and weighted with the sorrows of the people."

After a little silence, he added with a laugh: "My wish for all evil-doers is that they become Zaddikim and atone by carrying my burden."

Bl., Pr., p. 69.

5. The Heart of Tin

Once the Riziner came to Lemberg for a cure. He visited the Rabbi of the city, Rabbi Jacob Urinstein, and was tendered a great welcome. Rabbi Urinstein expected his famous guest to discuss a profound problem of the Torah, but to his astonishment, the conversation was as follows:

"How are Lemberg roofs covered?" asked the Riziner.

"With tin," answered Rabbi Urinstein.

"Why not with tar paper?" responded the Riziner. Thereupon he bade him adieu and left. Later the Premislaner Rabbi heard of this odd conversation and he explained it as follows: "As the roof protects the building for the comfort of its residents, so should the Rabbi strive for the well-being of the city-dwellers. He should possess a tender and compassionate heart, comparable to the soft tar-paper."

"Why is your heart as hard as tin?" was the Riziner's subtle inquiry to the Lemberg Rabbi.[1]

N. I., p. 23.

[1] See Graetz, v, 614, regarding Rabbi Urinstein. This utterance has a cryptic oracular quality, like many of the Delphic pronouncements, though not open to double meanings.

6. The Musician and the Deaf Man

The Sudilkover Rabbi told the following parable:

"A violinist played melodies for a dance so beautifully that all his hearers began to dance with great ardor. A deaf man who happened to enter the room, could not understand why the people danced with such abandon and enthusiasm. Had he not been deaf, would he not have joined the others?

"Our opponents wonder at the sight of the Hasidim singing and dancing at their assemblies. If they understood our viewpoint, would they not become our comrades?"

Kahana, p. 87.

7. If Nothing Better

The Rimanover asked the Ropshitzer: "Are your lodgings satisfactory?" The latter replied with the expression commonly found in the Talmudical commentaries: "It is possible to agree with this (explanation), if nothing better is in view."

Ohel N., p. 114.

52. FLATTERY

1. A Universal Necessity

Said the Ropshitzer: "I was once loath to accept a Rabbinical post, inasmuch as I believed I would be compelled to resort to flattery. I despise flattery. Then I observed that every one must practice flattery, whether he be tailor, shoemaker, or storekeeper. Hence, I said to myself: 'Since flattery is an unavoidable and universal necessity, I may as well be a Rabbi.'"

M. D., p. 109.

2. Flattery for Peace

Said the Bershider: "My Master, the Koretzer, taught me that flattery is permissible in order to promote peace, but only in the case of a man of the highest character."

M. P., p. 44.

3. The Bratzlaver on "Flattery"

"1. Flattery oftentimes leads to vulgarity and to fear.
"2. Flattery causes heartache.
"3. He who is dependent upon others speedily falls into flattery.
"4. The flatterer is despised by every one.
"5. He who hates flattery will receive salvation."

Sef. Ham., p. 68.

4. Love Reproof; Hate Flattery

The Bershider used to object to the fact that the Cantor waited for him to finish the Amidah before repeating it aloud. He would say: "It wounds me for you to do this." The Koretzer's son, Jacob Simon, expostulated with him: "But if he should not wait for you, you would miss the 'Kedushah.'"

The Bershider answered: "I beg of you, O revered father, to leave me in peace. Force me not to change my conduct." He often quoted the words: "Love him who reproves thee, and dislike him who honors thee." [1] He also quoted from Rabbi Feibish Zbirizer: "Many persons believe they have attained perfection when they are able to cherish the same feelings when praised or abused. This is not so. Thy must actually love abuse and hate praise."

M. P., p. 43.

[1] Derekh Eretz Zuta, chapter 9.

53. FOOLS AND FOOLISHNESS

1. The Idiot's Shoes

The Punideler saw in the vestry of the synagogue a poor idiot who went about bare-footed. He brought him shoes, but the pathetic fellow could make no use of them. When asked where he had placed the shoes, the idiot replied that he had hidden them, since he did not know how to put them on his feet.

The Rabbi, thereafter, made it a habit to put on the shoes for him every morning, and to take them off in the evening.

M. D., p. 297.

2. Solomon's Wisdom

The Berditschever said: "There is a saying to the effect that King Solomon was wiser than any one, even than an idiot. This may be explained as follows: 'Every idiot sincerely believes he is wiser than everybody else, and it is almost impossible to convince him of his fallacy. Solomon, however, was so wise, he could persuade even the idiot to acknowledge himself a fool.'"

S. S. K., iv, 136.

3. The Foolish in Paradise

The Lubliner said: "I dislike the foolish intensely. Were I to see a man of folly in Paradise, enjoying himself thoroughly, I would say to him: 'A man of folly remains a man of folly, and I do not envy your rich share of enjoyments in Paradise.'"[1]

E. O., p. 96.

[1] See Elmer Rice's "The Adding Machine"; Mr. Zero in the Elysian Fields, and in the Last Act; see also "The Paradise of the Unlearned," 1:17.

4. A Man's Garments

Said the Koretzer: "It is possible to recognize an insane man by observing whether his clothes fit him as if they truly belonged to him. The normal man's garments accommodate themselves to the normal movements of his muscles and limbs."

Nof. Tz., p. 11.

5. Good Sense

An author showed his work, "Good Grace," to Rabbi Gershon of Shkliv, and asked his opinion. "It is a good book," replied the Rabbi, "but it has one defect; namely, it lacks the 'sense' mentioned in Proverbs 3:4: 'So shalt thou find grace and good sense.'"[1]

L. H. F., p. 54.

[1] The word "Sekhel" is literally "sense."

6. Fool and Sinner

Said the "Yud": "The Talmud teaches that no man sins until a spirit of folly enters into him.[1] Hence, he in whom folly persistently dwells may be considered a constant sinner."

[1] Sotah 3.

Tif. Yeh., p. 45.

54. FORGETFULNESS

1. Forgetfulness and Repentance

The Lizensker Rabbi was asked by a student how to prevent forgetfulness. "Repent," replied the Rabbi. "The Talmud tells us that repentance reaches to the Throne of Glory,[1] and we say in the New Year's prayer: 'There is no forgetfulness before Thy Throne of Glory.' "[2]

On another occasion, a Hasid complained to the Gerer Rabbi that he forgot what he learned.

"Do you forget to place the spoon with food into your mouth?" asked the Rabbi.

"No, because I cannot live without food," was the reply.

"Neither can you live without learning," retorted the Rabbi. "Remember this and you will not forget."

O. S., p. 9.

[1] Yoma, 86.
[2] Singer, p. 249.

2. A Cure for Forgetfulness

A Hasid complained to Rabbi Israel Isaac of Alexander that he was afflicted with forgetfulness. The Rabbi replied: "We say in the Sh'ma: 'That ye go not about after your own heart and your own eyes, after which ye use to go stray; that ye may remember' (Numbers 15:39). Obey this injunction and you will remember."

M. H. H., p. 4.

3. The Bratzlaver on "Forgetfulness"

"1. He who shames his fellow-man becomes forgetful.

"2. Worries, hardships, sadness and falsehoods cause forgetfulness.

"3. Humility brings a good memory in its train."

Sef. Ham., p. 66.

55. FORGIVENESS

1. The Path to Forgiveness

Rabbi Nahum of Tzernobil had an opponent who habitually insulted him. The man began to suffer business losses, and hence resolved to appease the Rabbi. When he petitioned the latter to forgive him, the Rabbi replied: "I forgive you in the same spirit as you ask me."

The man's losses continued, however, and the Hasidim besought the Rabbi to have compassion and forgive the transgressor wholeheartedly. The Rabbi acceded to their request, but the man lost the remainder of his property and became a pauper. The Hasidim asked the Rabbi why his forgiveness tended to punish the man even more heavily. He replied:

"Moses was the meekest of men. When his sister insulted him, he bore no malice and promptly forgave her. But God punished her the harder for her offense.[1] It is so with me; the more thorough my forgiveness, the more severe was the Lord's punishment, since the man did not regret his offense with his whole heart."

The Hasidim, thereupon, gathered a purse for the pauper, and, his offense having been atoned by his misfortunes, he henceforth prospered and adhered to righteousness.

Beth Nahum, pp. 46-8.

[1] Numbers 12:9.

2. Overlooking the Offense

The Kotzker said: "We read in Numbers 23:21: 'He hath not beheld any wrong in Jacob, nor hath He seen perverseness in Israel: [when] the Lord his God is with him, and the glory of the King dwelleth in him.' This means that the Lord overlooks offenses only if the sinner feels himself near to Him."

S. S. K., i, 74.

3. Too Many Errors

Rabbi Bunam sought to cause a sinner to improve his ways. He invited him to a game of chess and, while playing, the Rabbi made an obviously false move. The man was about to take advantage of the error, but the Rabbi asked him to excuse the mistake. Soon the Rabbi made another wrong move. This time his opponent refused to overlook it. The Rabbi turned to him and said:

"You refuse to condone two false moves in a game of chess, yet you expect the Lord to pardon you regardless of the number of your own transgressions."

The sinner was stricken with remorse and promised to mend his conduct.

S. S. K., v, 58.

4. Forgiveness from Our Fellow-Man

The Amshinover Rabbi said: "To sin against a fellow-man is worse than to sin against the Creator. The man you harmed may have gone to an unknown place, and you may lose the opportunity to beg his forgiveness. The Lord, however, is everywhere and you can always find Him when you seek Him."

S. S. K., iv, 119.

5. God Will Punish

Said the Koretzer: "When a man injures or abuses you, it does not lie within your rights to revenge yourself. It is as if a man stood in the presence of a King, and another smote him on the cheek. The only course open to him is to keep silent. The King witnessed the blow, and, if he believes the man deserved it at the hands of his neighbor, the injured person cannot go counter to the King's wish. If the King, however, believes the blow was undeserved, the King will surely punish the offender. In the same way, remember that you are always in the presence of the King of Kings. He will inflict punishment upon your adversary if you are undeservedly abused by him."

Nof. Tz., p. 56.

6. Forgiveness Through Kindness

A Hasid of the Medzibozer Rabbi who knew his Rabbi's opposition to the Hasidic system of the Ladier, dared insult his Master's opponent. The Medzibozer rebuked him severely and commanded him to petition the Ladier for pardon. The Hasid, alarmed at his Rabbi's displeasure, traveled speedily to the Ladier and besought his forgiveness; he voiced his readiness to chastise his body if the Rabbi ordered him to do so.

"Not by chastisement will you win my forgiveness, but by a deed of kindness," said the Ladier.

Shortly afterwards the Hasid's only daughter, a young bride, became dangerously ill. He regarded this affliction as a punishment and was desperate of heart. His Rabbi could give him no help, and, in a mood of utmost grief, he walked to his home. On the way he heard a little child crying bitterly. He stepped into the house, and found a poor woman about to give birth to a child, with no one but a weeping two-year-old baby at hand. He summoned a neighbor, gave her the baby and ran for a midwife. Not until the child was born did he leave the house. When he returned, he learned that his beloved daughter had improved greatly.

He was forgiven.

Beo. H., pp. 59-62.

56. FORTITUDE (IN TRIBULATION)

1. "I Know No Sorrow"

Rabbi Schmelke and his brother once petitioned their teacher, the Maggid of Mezeritz, to explain to them the words of the Mishnah: "A man must bless God for the evil in the same way that he blesses Him for the good which befalls." [1]

[1] Berakhoth 54.

The Maggid replied: "Go to the House of Study, and you will find there a man smoking. He is Rabbi Sussya, and he will explain this to you."

When Rabbi Schmelke and his brother placed their question to Rabbi Sussya, he laughed and said: "I am surprised that the Rabbi sent you to me. You must go elsewhere, and make your inquiry from one who has suffered tribulations in his lifetime. As for me, I have never experienced anything but good all my days."

But Rabbi Schmelke and his brother knew full well that from his earliest hour to the present, he had endured the most grievous sorrows. Thereupon they understood the meaning of the words of the Mishnah, and the reason their Rabbi had sent them to Rabbi Sussya.

M. D., p. 216.

2. Courage and Melancholy

The Gerer Rabbi said: "We are taught in Pirkei Avoth[1] that impudence is evil and shamefacedness is good. We should bear in mind, however, that seeming impudence may in reality be courage, and that seeming shamefacedness may in truth be melancholy. The distinction is so delicate that oftentimes great men have failed to appreciate it."

S. S. K., ii, 51.

[1] 5:23; Singer, p. 203.

3. The Bratzlaver on "Patience"

"1. A man should believe that everything which happens to him during his lifetime is decreed by God for his benefit in the World of Eternity.

"2. Bitter medicines heal not only a man's body but also a man's soul. Oftentimes, however, a physician seeking to heal the sick body is compelled to abandon all hope, and to confess that no medicines will avail. This does not apply to the healing of the soul. God never sends more pain or tribulation to a man than he is able to bear. If he bears his trials with patience, his soul will be cured, whatever the offenses which may have stricken it with maladies.

"3. Be not discouraged by any tribulations which may assail you. The recognition that they are for the good of your soul will aid you to endure them.

"4. If a man harms you, be patient with him. Endeavor to believe that he may not have intended to injure you. Through patience you may gain his love and also attain peace.

"5. God inflicts pain upon us to remind us to improve our conduct and to cleanse our soul of any impurities of sin.

"6. Remember that man is born unto affliction (Job 5:7). Every man on earth must encounter tribulations and pain. If he takes refuge from them in the Lord, he will be comforted.

"7. Man is born, not to enjoy the world and its pleasures, but to

labor for his Eternal Life. Tribulation is one of the tools intended
for this purpose."

L. E. H., pp. 72-3.

4. *"This Also Is For Good"*

Said Rabbi Joshua Belzer: "When a tribulation overtakes you,
know that God wishes to place you to the test that He may learn
how you will accept it. If you receive the blow with fortitude and
repeat the words of Nahum Ish-Gamzu: 'This also is for my good,'[1]
your distress will vanish. There will be no need to try you further,
and you will then perceive that the misfortune was truly for your
good."

P. v. K., p. 38a.

[1] Taanith, 21.

5. *Dissolving Bitterness*

Said the "Yud": "The Talmud teaches us that if we swallow the
bitter herbs at the Seder meal instead of chewing them, we have not
fulfilled our obligation.[1] I interpret this to mean: 'If we have not
dissolved the sense of bitterness within us by virtue of faith and
fortitude, we have not done our duty as Jews.' "

Tif. Yeh., p. 46.

[1] Pesachim, 115.

6. *Concentrated Anxiety*

Rabbi Leib Dimimles of Lantzut was a wealthy merchant, and
very learned in the Torah. It happened that he lost his money and
was reduced to poverty. Rabbi Leib paid no heed to this calamity
and continued his studies. His wife inquired: "How is it possible
for you not to show the least anxiety?" The Rabbi answered:
"The Lord gave me a brain which thinks rapidly. The worrying
which another would do in a year, I have done in a moment."

P. v. K., p. 29b.

7. *Affliction and Forgiveness*

The Apter narrated the following tale: "A confirmed sinner died,
and his soul came before the Heavenly Tribunal. When the Satan
brought forth the list of his transgressions and asked for conviction,
the sinner argued that his many sufferings on earth should entitle
him to a suspended sentence.

"The Satan made this rejoinder: 'Has this man ever been
prompted to accept his tribulations with calmness, assuming that he
merits them because of his sins? Since he has never cherished this
thought, his excuse is inacceptable.'

"The sinner was sentenced to Purgatory."

P. v. K., p. 37a.

57. FREE-WILL

1. *God Requires Man's Help*

The Kobriner Rabbi interpreted the words of the Psalmist (118: 25) thus: "I beseech you (saith the Lord) help Me (O man) by your repentance, so that I may be able to grant your plea: 'We beseech Thee, O Lord, make us now to prosper.'"

O. Y., p. 107.

2. *Man's Free Choice*

The Apter commented on the verse (Psalm 119:35): "Make me to tread in the path of Thy commandments; for therein do I delight."

"The Lord gives to man free-will to choose his way of conduct; but when He sees that a man has chosen wisely, God assists him to continue in the right paths. The Psalmist implores: 'Since I find delight in Thy commandments, I petition Thee to guide me that I may steadily walk in the path of righteousness.'"

E. O., p. 121.

3. *Choosing the Good*

The Besht and a disciple were walking along a road. The disciple became thirsty, but there was no water available for miles about; he complained of his intense thirst to the Besht. The latter replied: "Do you believe that in the very moment when God thought of creating the world, He foresaw your predicament and provided for it?"

"Yes," replied the disciple.

Thereupon a man appeared, bearing a pail of water, and gave the sufferer a drink from it. The Besht asked the man how he came to be in such an out-of-the-way spot, carrying water from a long distance. The man answered: "My master suddenly fainted not far from here, and I was compelled to bring water from a spring several miles distant."

"You see that your belief is justified," commented the Besht to his disciple. "Before the earth was created, God foreordained every happening. There are no coincidences in the universe. Everything depends upon man's choice of the good, and upon his use of the intelligence and spirit wherewith he was endowed."

O. Y., p. 101.

4. *Freedom and Redemption*

Said the Apter: "We now have the best opportunity to achieve redemption. Until the present time a Jew did not have complete freedom of action, inasmuch as formerly the leaders of the Jewish community had authority to punish transgressors against Jewish customs and communal regulations. Now, however, any one may commit any offense against Judaism with impunity. Hence, he who chooses not to sin through self-control and reverence for his faith is worthier in the eyes of God than the law-abiding Jew of former generations."

M. Hat., p. 78.

5. Economy of Miracles

Said the Medzibozer: "The Lord is sparing of miracles, in order to give wider opportunity to man's exercise of his free-will. Were miracles common, man's fear of God's power would remove his free-will to choose for himself between evil and good."

Butz. D., p. 21.

6. God's Help

Said the Bershider: "If a man sins and is contrite, the Lord will aid him to full repentance. It is well to remember this axiom: 'Man has only the power of free choice; everything else is in God's hands.' Therefore, if a man chooses to repent, God will perform all else required for the accomplishment of his choice. But even the free-will of a man needs the help of God to maintain it intact, lest it lapse into weakness."

M. P., p. 39.

7. Circumstances and Free-Will

Rabbi Samuel Kariver said: "Cherish no hate for thy brother who offends, because you have not offended like him. If your fellow-man possessed your nature, he might not have sinned. If you possessed his nature, you might have offended as he has done. A man's transgressions depend not entirely upon his free-choice, but oftentimes upon many other circumstances."

D. Z., p. 20.

8. "Because Thou Art Come"

The Lizensker was discussing the verse (Ruth 2:12): "May the Lord recompense thy work, and may thy reward be complete from the Lord, the God of Israel, under whose wings thou art come to seek shelter." He drew attention to the comment of the Midrash: "Said Rabbi Hassa: 'because thou art come.'" [1] This comment, he said, requires an explanation. "The reward of the Zaddikim," he said, "is received by them only for their commencement in the service of the Lord. When they have attained an understanding of the Lord, it is natural that they should continue to serve Him. This is the purpose of Rabbi Hassa's teaching. Ruth deserved her reward from God, 'because she came'—because she made the initial commencement."

E. Tz., p. 35.

[1] Ruth Rabba, chapter 5. The reading in the Midrash is, however, faulty. See the commentary "Assifath Maamarim."

9. The People's Free-Will

The Medzibozer commented upon the verse: "And the Lord said unto Moses: 'Write this for a memorial in the book, and rehearse it in the ears of Joshua: for I will utterly blot out the remembrance of Amalek from under heaven' " (Exodus 17:14). He said: "The Lord informed Moses of the future fate of Amalek, and of His decree to blot out in a day to come all remembrance of that nation. This occurred when Haman, the Amalekite, was slain. Yet it was not the Lord's will to mention expressly the time of his extinction, since Mordecai and the Jews would have had no occasion to implore the Lord to save them, and to repent with sincerity. Therefore, it is merely hinted in the written Torah and it is whispered in the ears of Joshua. Were people to know the future, there would be no free-will in their service of the Lord."

Butz. D., p. 6.

58. FRIENDS AND FRIENDSHIP

1. *A True Comrade*

Rabbi Bunam advised every man to endeavor to gain a true comrade to whom he can unfold his heart and disclose even his transgressions. Judah acquired as a friend, Hirah, the Adullamite, and was not ashamed to send a kid at his hand to Tamar in order to redeem his pledge from her.[1]

[1] See Genesis 38:1 and 38:20.

O. Y., p. 197.

2. *The Stork*

The Gerer Rabbi discovered that a custom had developed among his Hasidim to give a helping hand only to one of their associates, but not to an outsider. In his discourse the next Sabbath morning, the Rabbi remarked on this and said:

"Among the detestable birds forbidden as food is included the stork (Lev. 11:9). Its Hebrew name is 'Hasidah,' so-called, according to the Talmud,[1] because of its habit of bringing food to the nests of its friends. But if the bird is a 'Hasidah' and helpful, why is it nevertheless, deemed detestable? The answer is: 'because it feeds its friends only, and no outsiders.' "

[1] Hullin 63.

O. I. H., p. 98.

3. *The Loyal Friend*

The Kossover Rabbi promised to visit the Lubliner on the High Holydays but was prevented from doing so. He sent his son, Hayyim, to present his excuses. The Lubliner remarked: "Had your father considered me his true friend, he would have felt no need to excuse himself."

R. T., ii, 111.

4. *In an Emergency*

When the Ropshitzer came for the first time to the Rimanover, his Master, he found a great crowd in the vestibule. In order to steady himself in the jostling throng, he leaned on a Hasid by the name of Simon. Later his friends reproved him for being so familiar with a Hasid whose reputation was not of the best. The Ropshitzer replied: "We find in the Talmud the expression: 'Rabbi Simeon is deserving to lean on in an emergency.'" [1]

Ohel N., p. 114.

[1] Berakhoth 9a.

5. The Two Strangers

The Medzibozer commented on the verse: "I am a sojourner in the earth; hide not Thy commandments from me" (Psalms 119:19). He said: "A traveler came to a town where everyone was a stranger to him and he had no one with whom to converse. Later another stranger arrived, and both became friends, impelled by their mutual loneliness. They agreed to have no secrets from each other henceforth. The Psalmist says: 'I am a stranger in the earth of evildoers, and Thou, O Lord, art likewise unwelcomed. Let us become friends, and have no secrets from each other.'"

Butz. D., p. 9.

6. Meekness in Friendship

The Besht commented on the verse: "As in the water face answereth to face, so the heart of man to man" (Proverbs 27:19). He said: "When a man stands upright near the water, his shadow is reflected in enlarged form. But when he bends down his reflection is smaller in size. In like manner, when one man looks upon another with pride, the other is also prompted to a feeling of proud aloofness. When, however, a man is meek in his relationship with another man, the latter likewise feels friendship and good-will towards him."

M. R. T., ii, 103.

7. Friendship and the Evil Impulse

Said Rabbi Schmelke: "We read in the Talmud: 'He who is greater than his comrade has a greater evil impulse than his' (Sukkah 52). I paraphrase it: 'Who is great? He who cleaves to his comrades. Whose evil impulse is great? The man who abides by himself.'"

This was repeated by the Ropshitzer when the Lubliner asked him whether the Zaddik has a greater evil impulse than a common man.[1]

Ohel N., p. 43.

[1] The lesson appears to be as follows: if the Zaddik holds himself aloof, his evil impulse is greater. If he is democratic, his impulse is not greater than that of the common man.

59. GAMES

1. Every Move

Rabbi Bunam said: "We should learn to be careful of every move we make in life, just as the chess player takes great precaution before he makes a move. Before a decision is made, we should think in advance whether we will have cause to regret it."

S. S. K., v, 58.

2. Lessons from Checkers

The Tzupenester Rabbi found his Hasidim playing checkers. He said:

"You may learn much wisdom from the rules of this game. You surrender one in order to capture two. You may not make two moves at one time. You must move up, but not down. When you reach the top, you may move as you like."

N. I., p. 69.

3. The Advocate of Gamblers

Rabbi Wolf of Zbaraz was told that some Jews in his hometown spent the entire night at the gaming-table. He said: "Perhaps it is their intention to accustom themselves to the habit of remaining awake all night. After they acquire this habit, they may learn to devote the night to holy study and divine service."

S. H. H., Chapter 4.

60. GOD'S COOPERATION

1. Aiding Good Deeds

The Mezeritzer Maggid commented on the verse: "Behold a people that riseth up as a lioness, and as a lion doth he lift himself up" (Numbers 23:24).

He said: "A people that riseth up with the vigor and zeal of a lioness to perform good deeds, shall surely be aided by the Lord to become as strong and as valiant as a lion, whose strength exceeds that of a lioness, in accomplishing his task."

E. O., p. 31.

2. A Fair Exchange

Said the Berditschever: "We read (Isaiah 40:31): 'They that wait upon the Lord shall exchange strength.' This means that those who seek the Lord give their strength unto Him, and receive in return from Him new strength to serve Him further."

E. O., p. 59.

3. Delivering Our Enemies

Said the Sassover: "We read (Deut. 21 : 10) : 'When thou goest forth to battle against thine enemies, and the Lord thy God delivereth them into thy hands.' We may understand this verse to teach us that when we go forth to battle against our evil impulses, the Lord will deliver them into our hands. The Lord assists in such a battle."

M. Hat., p. 61.

4. Unaided By God

To a man who spoke continually of the cleverness of his business plans and projects, the Kotzker Rabbi said: "Let me explain to you the verse (Ecclesiastes 9: 11) : 'neither yet bread (is given) to the wise.' The Lord says to those who consider themselves to be wise and clever: 'If you are so astute, go and seek your bread of your own accord, and do not look for aid from Me.' "

S. S. K., i, 26.

5. Petitioning for God's Aid

Rabbi Lippe of Lvov asked the Premislaner to aid him in his efforts to persuade the market-women to close their stands early on Friday afternoons in preparation for the Sabbath.

The Premislaner said: "When you endeavor to accomplish a good deed, you ought to offer the following prayer: 'My Lord, I am seeking to do Thy will, and I petition for Thy aid towards success in my endeavors, in order that Thy glory may be increased.' You will then gain the coöperation of God Himself, and you will need no human help. Bear in mind that if you call upon mortal men to assist you, they will undoubtedly commence arguments, and you will soon be engulfed in quarrels. The result will be that obstinacy will defeat your objective, and matters will be worse than before."

O. H., p. 36.

6. The Wishes of God

Said the Koretzer: "I was told of a country where the Jews found it difficult to learn Torah and to pray. I remarked: 'Surely they must study and pray falsely and in a manner unacceptable to the Lord; for, were it desirable in the eyes of God, nothing could have stood in their way. No one is able to overrule the wishes of God."

M. P., p. 14.

7. The Lord's Coöperation

A Hasid came to Rabbi Israel Isaac of Alexander and said to him: "I wish to engage in a trial with the Lord. According to the Sages,[1] God is a partner in my son, and, since He is possessed of great riches, it is proper that He send me the money necessary for the wedding of my son."

[1] Kiddushin, 30; Niddah, 31.

The Rabbi replied: "When a rich man enters into a partnership with the poor man, the former says: 'I will enlist my money in this enterprise, and you your work.' Go out among the richer Jews, and the Lord will induce them to aid you."

M. H. H., p. 4.

8. Over-ruling the Lord

Said the Lizensker: "We read in the hymn chanted in the Sephardic ritual: 'The grace and the triumph to the Immortal One.' This means: it is a grace to God that His Zaddikim overrule Him." [1]

E. Tz., p. 33.

[1] Compare the Talmudical expression: "My sons have triumphed over me." Pesachim, 119; Baba Metziah, 59.

9. Inclining His Ear

The Koretzer commented on the verse: "I love that the Lord should hear my voice and my supplications. Because He hath inclined His ear unto me" (Psalm 116:1). He said: "I love to have the Lord hear me, not because I wish Him to grant me my desires, nor because I expect to receive from Him any benefits, but because He, the Great and Mighty God, has deigned to incline His ear unto me, the lowly supplicant."

Nof. Tz., p. 53.

61. FEAR AND LOVE OF GOD

1. An Idolater

Said the Gerer Rabbi: "If a man has fear of anything except the Creator, he is in some degree an idolater. For to fear is to offer worship to the thing feared; and this form of worship may be offered only to the Lord."

S. S. K., i, 75.

2. Fear Is a Sin

Rabbi Schmelke said: "The Psalmist (90:11) declares: 'And Thy wrath according to the (lack of) fear that is due unto Thee.' This teaches us all that all fear is due unto God exclusively. To fear anything else is to withhold from the Lord that which is due unto Him and thereby to arouse His wrath."

S. ha-Tov, p. 34.

3. Repentance from Fear or Love

Commenting on (Hosea 14:2): "Return, O Israel, to the Lord," Rabbi Schmelke remarked: "Whenever the word 'to' is used, there is always a question whether it is exclusive or inclusive. Here it is both. Repentance from fear reaches to the Lord, but excludes the presence of God, since there is no fear in Him. But repentance from love reaches the Lord Himself since there is love in Him as well."

S. ha-Tov, p. 37.

4. Fear of Man

The Lekhivitzer read the verse (Genesis 32:8): "Then Jacob was greatly afraid and was distressed." Commenting on these words, the Rabbi said: "Jacob was greatly afraid of Esau, and when he realized that this was fear of a man in place of fear of God alone, he was distressed at his shortcoming."

O. Y., p. 14.

5. Fear That Is Pure

Rabbi Henoch Alexanderer explained the verse (Psalm 19:10): "The fear of the Lord is pure, enduring forever," as follows: "If the fear of the Lord is pure, then it will endure."

The Kotzker Rabbi added: "If the fear of the Lord endureth, then we know it is pure."

S. S. K., iii, 26.

6. Change of Heart

The Slonimer used Psalm 114 as a text, and he said: "We read that 'the sea saw it, and fled.' Why? Because of 'the presence of the Lord Who caused the earth to tremble.' We also read that 'the mountains skipped like rams.' Why? Because of 'the presence of the God Who redeemed Jacob.' One verse teaches fear of the Lord; the other love of the Lord. When one person possesses both qualities in combination, then his heart of rock 'is changed into a pool of water; his heart of flint into a fountain of waters.'"

O. Y., p. 184.

7. The Mishnah's First Word

Rabbi Sussya came to Rabbi Schmelke and asked him to teach him the Mishnah. Rabbi Schmelke began: "Mei-eimothai korin eth Sh'ma," and translated: "From what time do we read the Sh'ma?"

Rabbi Sussya stopped him and said: "Rabbi, perhaps it may also mean: 'from fear of the Lord do we read the Sh'ma!'"

Rabbi Schmelke was surprised and exclaimed: "Rabbi Sussya, you are wise enough to do your own studying!" [1]

S. ha-Tov, p. 70.

[1] Both meanings are correct in the Hebrew.

8. Not Figures of Speech

Rabbi Zalman Ladier declared: "Before I was at Mezeritz I had a faith that filled me constantly with love and fear of God. At Mezeritz I advanced to the stage where my whole conscious existence was but love and fear. When I first heard the Maggid say: 'The divine attributes of grace, that is our love of God; the divine attributes of power, that is our fear of God,' I imagined that it was a figure of speech; but later I saw it was a literal fact. God's grace is God's love; God's power is fear of God."

9. Who Is the Real Zaddik?

The Kozmirer Rabbi once overheard several Zaddikim discussing the question: who is the real Zaddik worthy of adherence?

He called them over and said to them: "In the 'Ethics of the Fathers' (4:15)[1] we read: 'Let your fear of your Rabbi be as the fear of the Lord.' This means: let your fear of the Rabbi be according to *his* fear of the Lord. Thus any Hasid may know his true Rabbi. The one of whom you are greatly in fear is the one who is greatly in fear of the Lord."

[1] Singer, p. 197.

Ha-Beer, vii, part i, p. 46.

10. Hasid and Mithnaged

The Kotzker said: "The Hasid has fear of the Lord, and the Mithnaged has fear of the 'Shulchan Arukh.' "[1]

[1] Rabbinical Legal Code.

S. S. K., v, 44.

11. Secret Piety

Rabbi Bunam explained the prayer: "At all times a man should have the fear of Heaven in secret," in this manner: "To the world you should appear as an ordinary man, and be secret in your piety."[1]

S. S. K., i, 11.

[1] Singer, p. 7. "L'olam" means "at all times" or "to the world."

12. Mine and Thine

The Alexanderer Rabbi said: "We read in the 'Pirkei Avoth' (5:13)[1] 'He who says: "mine is thine and thine is mine" is a vulgar man.' We are taught by our Rabbis that everything is in the hands of Heaven except the fear of Heaven.[2] Hence if one says: 'for my fear of Heaven I depend upon Thee, O Lord, to grant it to me, whereas for my worldly gains, I can depend upon my own diligence and ability,' he is an ignorant man. It is the very opposite which is true."

S. S. K., i, 24

[1] Singer, p. 201.   [2] Berakhoth, 33.

13. A Plenitude

A Hasid implored the Kotzker Rabbi to pray that he might be in easier circumstances.

The Rabbi replied: "If you are a Hasid and have the fear of Heaven in your heart, you have plenty."

S. S. K., i, 70.

14. Too Wise for Piety

Rabbi Phineas of Koretz was accustomed to say: "I am constantly in fear lest I become too wise to remain pious."

Dubnow, H. of H., p. 105.

15. The Fly and the Penny

The Gerer Rabbi said: "Many of us possess less fear of a transgression than of a fly. When a fly alights upon us, we take the trouble to brush it away. Likewise, many of us possess less willingness to perform a commandment than to obtain a small coin. If we see a small coin on the ground, we take the trouble to bend over and pick it up."

S. S. K., v, 15.

16. Public and Secret Love

Said the Besht: "Our love of God should be like the love between brother and sister, or between a mother and her child, rather than like the love between man and wife or between lovers. The first may show their love both in private and in public; whereas the latter do so in private only. We should not imitate those who say that our love of God should be demonstrated only in the synagogue or at home, but should not be shown on the street or in public places. In the Song of Songs (8:1), the author conveys the above lesson to us in the words: 'O that thou wert as my brother, or as he that sucked the breasts of my mother! When I should find thee without, I would kiss thee; yea, and none would despise me.' "

M. R. T., ii, 7.

17. Stimulating Our Love for God

Said the Besht: "When you fall in love with an earthly pleasure, consider that the power of love was vouchsafed unto you for the purpose of loving God, not for unworthy things. Then you will find it easy to serve God with the love awakened in your heart. We read (Song of Songs 7:7): 'How fair and how pleasant thou art, O love, for delights!' Without the feeling of love, stimulated by pleasures, it is difficult to feel true love of God."

M. R. T., p. 8, part ii.

18. A. The Bratzlaver on "Fear and Service"

"1. When fear overcomes you, subdue it by drawing over yourself the fear of God.

2. Through fear of God a man is able to pray fervently and to perform all commandments in gladness.

3. Love of God should accompany the fear of God, but the attainment of fear of Him comes first.

4. If you are your own judge and regret your misdeeds, you will not be judged in Heaven.

5. When you are judged in Heaven, the slightest thing may cause you grief and pain. You cannot predict what form or through what intermediary your chastisement will come.

6. Chastisements come to you in order to awaken in you the fear of the Lord. Therefore the voluntary drawing over yourself of the fear of the Lord will save you from grief.

7. The chief point of fear is to feel ashamed of sin.

8. Through fear one may steadily increase in holiness every hour and every day. This is called long life.

9. Perfect fear is a combination of: first, fear of God; second, fear of a man's teacher in holy matters; third, fear of parents.

10. The chief difficulty a man encounters is at the beginning of a new mode of conduct. He must therefore commence with enthusiasm and zeal in attaining a better way to serve the Lord. If he attains every day a higher position, he must commence each day with fervor in order to safeguard the point he has reached. Hence a fresh start must be made each day, based upon the achievements which have gone before.

11. The higher soul of man is thus newly created and matured daily through fear and love of God.

12. The man who cares not to reach his ultimate goal, wastes his days.

13. An important rule in the true service of the Lord, as well as the maintenance of confidence in His Providence, is to think only of to-day, nay, of the immediate hour. Service of the Lord in its perfect form appears to be a heavy burden, but a man will be able to endure it if he bears in mind that it is only for the immediate day he must make the uphill struggle.

14. A man must not delay his start in the right direction until the next day. Do not say: 'To-morrow I will commence to serve the Lord properly; to-morrow I will begin to worship from the heart with all my strength.' A man has only the day and hour in which he stands, and the morrow is a different world into which he enters. We read this in the Psalms (95:7): 'To-day, if ye would but hearken to His voice.'

15. Charity broadens the portal to holiness; therefore a man should give charity before commencing his Service to the Lord or performing a commandment. It eases his path to perform charity in holiness.

16. Through charity a man is granted reverence for the Lord; through reverence a man is granted mercy, and he can labor in the service of God without the hindrance of anxiety for his livelihood.

17. The Lord enjoys the praise and sanctification ascending to Him from men more than the adoration he receives from Angels.

18. He who preaches the fear of Heaven must possess it in his own person; otherwise his words are futile and of no effect.

19. Merely to pass time in this world has no value. Only the goodness acquired during our earthly sojourn becomes an eternal value in the World-to-Come.

20. Even labor for the acquisition of eternal values to benefit him in the World-to-Come is not perfect service by a man. Only labor for the sole purpose of understanding God and becoming more intimate with Him can avail.

21. Since man may or may not serve the Lord in every circumstance and in everything he does, it follows that his free-will is unlimited.

22. The world and all its contents was created to give free play to man's free will."

L. E. H., pp. 44-48.

18. B. The Bratzlaver on "The God-Fearing Man"

"1. He who does not consider himself wise, is able to attain the fear of Heaven.

"2. He who talks little will attain the fear of Heaven.

"3. The words of him will be heeded who has the Fear of Heaven.

"4. Shamefacedness causes fear of sin.

"5. The man by whom the people bless is a God-fearing man.

"6. A God-fearing man is able to subdue arrogant hearts; he draws to himself the Shekinah, and has the spirit of submission within him.

"7. A God-fearing man attains truthfulness and peace.

"8. A God-fearing man need not fear in troubled times.

"9. Pride precludes the fear of God.

"10. A man's yearning to perform a Mitzwah demonstrates that he possesses the fear of God.

"11. Not the people as a whole, but only individuals among them, can become faithless to God."

Sef. Ham., pp. 73-5.

19. Infinite Fear and Love

The Medzibozer said: "Since man is infinite, all commandments relating to humanity are specifically described. But the fear and love of God are bound by no rules since God Himself is limitless."

Butz. D., p. 9.

20. Words Inducing Reverence

The Medzibozer commented on the verse: "The Psalmist says: 'Confirm Thy word unto Thy servant, which pertaineth unto the fear of Thee' (Psalm 119:38)." He interpreted the Psalmist to mean: "Give unto me words whereby I may be induced towards reverence for Thee."

Butz. D., p. 13.

21. Fear As An Offering

The Medzibozer commented on the verse: "Who would not fear Thee, O King of the Nations?" (Jer. 10:7). He said: "Why does not the Prophet ask: 'Who would not love Thee?' The answer is that love cometh from the Lord, and it is natural for us to love God when He loves us. But fear appertains to us, and we should voice it as an offering to Him."

Butz. D., p. 23.

22. The Purpose of Blessings

The Medzibozer commented on the verse: "Behold, surely thus shall the man be blessed that feareth the Lord" (Psalm 128:4). He said: "Since every one who feareth the Lord is happy (Psalm 128:1), then thus shall a man be blessed, namely, that he may be a God-fearing man."

Butz. D., p. 23.

23. Outer and Inner Fear

Said the Besht: "There are two kinds of fear of the Lord: outer and inner. The outer is fear of punishment, and serves to induce a man to repent. The penitent may then gain the inner fear: the fear of displeasing his beloved Father in Heaven, and he will then have no further need of the outer fear."

K. S. T., p. 13a.

24. Why Fear Is Enjoined

A thinker asked the Besht: "Why are we enjoined to fear the King of Kings, when it is known that we stand in fear of a mortal king without any command?"

The Master replied: "The fear we have of a mortal king is but an outer fear: a fear of lacking or losing a material thing. After the loss has occurred, we are no longer in fear of him. Such a fear is common to men and beasts.

"We, however, are enjoined to have an inner fear of the Lord: a fear of lacking proper attachment to God. Such a fear is terminated only by our death. A man without inner fear is spiritually dead."

K. S. T., p. 13b.

25. The Acceptance of Hardships

Said Rabbi Yerachmiel: "A merchant is willing to undergo the hardships of travel in order to gain a livelihood. In the same way, we should be prepared to accept the hardships of this world with complete indifference, in order to gain the fear of Heaven."

Tif. B., p. 8.

26. It Also Is Work

Said the Porissover Rabbi: "We read: 'All study of the Torah without work must in the end be futile and become the cause of sin' (Ethics 2:2).[1] Does, then, the Tanna mean that a man must be a tailor or a shoemaker in order to learn Torah? No. What the Tanna calls 'work' is the work of the 'fear of Heaven.' "

V. S., p. 18.

[1] Singer, p. 187.

27. The Fear of Sin

Said the Koretzer: "The true fear of God is through fear of sin, but not through fear of punishment. As it is written: And they said unto Moses: 'Speak thou with us, and we will hear; but let not God speak with us, lest we die' (Exodus 20:18, 19). And Moses said unto the people: 'Fear not, for God is come to prove you, and that his fear may be before you, that ye sin not.' Moses said: 'Fear not Him because ye are afraid of dying. Let His fear be before you so that ye may be afraid to sin.' "

R. T., ii, 43.

28. False Is Grace

Rabbi Bunam visited Germany, and observed the conduct of the Jews there. Turning to a companion, he said: "It is concerning this land that Solomon said: 'Grace is deceitful and beauty is in vain; but a woman who feareth the Lord, she shall be praised' (Prov. 31:30). I paraphrase it, thus: 'In a land where deceit is considered as graceful, and vanity as beauty, a woman who feareth the Lord, she should be praised.' "

S. I., p. 60.

29. Prosperity and Adversity

Said Rabbi Bunam: "In prosperity and adversity forget not God. We read: 'And the Lord was with Joseph, and he was a prosperous man; and he was in the house of his master, the Egyptian (Gen. 39:2).' Whether prosperous or an Egyptian slave, Joseph was with God."

S. I., p. 74.

30. The Mezeritzer on "Fear and Love"

"1. Fear without love is worthless. He who fears God because the Lord can do him hurt, is as one who fears a wild beast. His impulse is to place a great distance between himself and the object of his fears. But he who fears God because of His majesty loves Him, because in His greatness the Lord descends to take care of him. Such a man feels near to God.

"2. He who loves God but has no proper sense of reverence for Him is likely to forget himself and become careless in the performance of God's commandments.

"3. The Biblical expression: 'The Lord God' stands for Love and Fear, Mercy and Justice.[1]

"4. Love is the right hand; fear the left hand. The right hand draws one near; the left hand restrains him who approaches too closely.[2]

"5. Even the thief has both fear and love: the love of money and the fear of starvation."

T. M. M., p. 203.

[1] Midrash Bereshith Rabba, 33:4.
[2] Sanhedrim 107; Sotah, 47.

31. The Kossover's Oath

The Kossover used to say: "Let us swear that with our whole heart, our whole soul and our entire fortune we shall express the Lord's Kingdom and Unity." [1]

E. Tz., p. 64.

[1] Namely, read the Sh'ma. The Rabbi implies that the second half of the verse (Deut. 6:5) applies not only to the love of God, but also to the preceding verse. For the term "fortune," see Berakhoth, 54.

32. The Unseeing Eye

Said the Kossover: "The custom of closing the eyes when reading the first verse of the Sh'ma indicates that we are prepared to surrender our life for the sake of God. The unseeing eye is likened in the Talmud [1] to the eye of him who has died."

E. Tz., p. 65.

[1] Nedarim 64.

33. Love for Israel

A Rabbi asked the Stretiner to give him a charm whereby he might attain the fear of Heaven. The Stretiner replied: "I can only give you a charm to attain to the love of the Lord." The other said: "But love of God is even more difficult to attain than fear of the Lord."

"Not at all," replied the Stretiner. "Love Israel truly, and you will easily attain the love of God."

E. Tz., p. 138.

34. The Royal Minions

Said the Mezeritzer: "A royal guardsman may be attired in armor, with a sword at his side. He may seem to inspire fear, yet it would be foolish for a man to fear him since he has no power of his own to inflict harm. A pleasant-faced royal messenger may summon a man to the palace. He may speak courteously and graciously, yet it would be equally as foolish to feel pleased at this messenger's demeanor as to fear the guardsman. The messenger can do no favors on his own initiative. Let the man go to the king, and he will know whether he should be afraid or feel pleased. In the same fashion, it is foolish for us to fear or be pleased at anything. God, the Master of all, is the one to whom we ought to look in the mood of fear or pleasure."

T. M. M., pp. 237-8.

35. The Attribute of Fear

The Koretzer commented upon the verse: "And now, Israel, what doth the Lord thy God require [1] of thee, but to fear the Lord thy God" (Deut. 10:12) . . . "and to walk after Him" (Deut. 13:5). "Concerning the latter verse, the Talmud says: 'How may one walk after God? By imitation of His ways. He is merciful; be thou merciful, etc.' [2] But fear is not God's way, since there is no fear in Him. Therefore, the Lord requests Israel: Although fear is not My way, nevertheless endow Me with this trait as well."

Nof. Tz., p. 26.

[1] Or "request."
[2] Sotah 14a.

62. HELP FROM GOD

1. A Dead World

Said Rabbi Bunam: "When I look upon the world, it often seems to me as if the universe were dead, and I had been left, the only living man. From whom, then, can I ask help, outside of God?"

S. I., p. 17.

2. Imitation of God

A poor man came to Rabbi Nahum of Tzernobil and complained that he lacked the money to give a dowry to his marriageable daughter. The Rabbi gave him all the money he had in his house. Later several Hasidim saw the man walk into a tavern and proceed to drink away the Rabbi's donation. They became incensed at his duplicity, and took away the portion of the Rabbi's gift which remained. When they returned it to Rabbi Nahum, the latter exclaimed: "Give him back the money immediately. Every man should imitate God of Whom it is said: 'He doeth good to the wicked as well as to the good,' [1] and you wish to deprive me of the privilege and opportunity of imitating Him now."

F. R. H.-M., p. 37.

[1] New Year Hymn "And all believe."

3. Grace and Honor

A man came to the Trisker Maggid and said to him that his neighbor had found grace in the eyes of a wealthy magnate, and that as a consequence, he had gained a fine livelihood. He asked the Maggid what he should do in order to find favor likewise with the rich landlord. The Rabbi replied: "In Psalms (84:12) we read: 'The Lord giveth grace and glory.' The question arises: 'Doth not the Lord grant everything? Why does the Psalmist specify grace and honor?' The explanation is that in almost all other matters, God sends a blessing if a man labors for them. But grace and honor He vouchsafes without man laboring in their behalf. Hence, my counsel to you," continued the Maggid to the petitioner, "is that you do nothing to gain the landlord's favor. May God Himself grant you grace, as it is said in the conclusion of the verse: 'No good thing will He withhold from them that walk uprightly.'"

B. P., p. 52.

4. A Free Spirit

The Amshinover interpreted (Genesis 21:20) thus: "And God was with the lad, and he grew; and he dwelt in the wilderness, and became an archer." He said: "The lad was successful, and took pride in his achievements; hence he refused to bend to authority and became a free spirit."

O. I., p. 6.

5. The Bratzlaver on "Help from God"

"1. God's help is extended to the man of charity.

"2. A man who gives charity will not need help from others.

"3. Trust and truth will teach you that your help comes from God and not from men.

"4. Meekness, prayer with joy and the dissemination of God's word among the people will bring to you the help of God."

Sef. Ham., pp. 72-3.

6. The Gate of the Lord

Said Rabbi Bunam: "Always implore God to aid you to attain goodness, and He will surely come to your assistance. The Psalmist tells us that if we cry: 'Open to me the gates of righteousness; I will enter into them; I will give thanks unto the Lord,' we shall surely receive a reply: 'This is the gate of the Lord; the righteous may enter into it.'"[1]

¹ Psalm 118:19-20.

S. I., pp. 73-4.

7. How God Helps

Said the Sassover: "While God is able to aid men by extraordinary measures, he first seeks to employ usual means. If, however, our trouble is of an unusual nature, He will respond to our prayer and aid us in an extraordinary way."

E. Tz., p. 58.

8. Wise Persistence

The Tzanzer said to a supplicant: "It is true that if I persist in my desire to obtain the fulfillment in Heaven of my request, I am able to prevail. But I must use wisdom in my persistence."

E. Tz., p. 120.

9. The Aid of God

Said the Stretiner: "We are able to perform the commandments of God only because God enables us by His help to do so. We find these words in the Song of Songs: 'I am (laboring) for my beloved (when) my beloved (aids) me.'" [1]

[1] 2:16.

E. Tz., p. 139.

10. Far and Near

The Medzibozer commented on the verse: "Unto Thee, O Lord, did I call, and unto the Lord I made supplication" (Psalm 30:9). He said: "When I am near to Thee, I need only to call to Thee to be answered. But when I am far from Thee, I must make supplication in order to receive an answer."

Butz. D., p. 14.

11. Not One Only

The Medzibozer commented on the passage in the Haggadah of Passover: "For not one only hath risen up against us, to annihilate us." He said: "What has always saved us when our enemies wished to annihilate us, is that the One Only hath not risen up against us. Had He been against us, we would have been lost."

Butz. D., p. 24-5.

63. GOD'S OMNIPRESENCE

1. In All We Do

The Kobriner paraphrased the verse (Psalms 145:17) as follows: "A Zaddik is one in all whose ways God is found, and a Hasid is one in all whose works the Lord is present." [1]

O. Y., p. 110.

[1] The verse reads: "The Lord is righteous in all His ways, and gracious in all His works." "Zaddik" and "Hasid" are in the Hebrew.

2. Escaping from God

Said the Belzer: "We read that after Korah was swallowed up: 'All Israel that were round about them fled at the cry of them' (Numbers 16:34). This means that they fled to offer their cry before the Lord to save them from being swallowed up also. But it cannot imply that they fled to safety since they must have understood that it is impossible to escape from the Lord."

D. S., p. 83.

3. God in Everything

Said the Belzer: "We read in Isaiah 64:3: 'Neither hath the eye seen a God beside Thee, who worketh for him that waiteth for Him.' This may be interpreted thus: 'God will aid those who wait for Him, to see nought but God in everything that exists in the world.' "

D. S., p. 99.

4. Always Before Us

The Oheler Rabbi said: "In the 'Prepared Table' (Shulchan Arukh), the author, Rabbi Joseph Caro, begins with the words: 'Be strong as a lion to arise for the service of the Lord.' [1] His co-author, Rabbi Moses Isserles begins his 'Table Cloth' (Mappah) with the words: 'Say to yourself: "I shall set the Lord always before me." [2] Now as a rule, the 'Table Cloth' comments upon and completes the 'Prepared Table.' This is the case in this instance also. Rabbi Isserles enjoins us that when we believe the Lord is always before us, we thereby gain strength to arise as a lion."

O. Y., p. 39.

[1] Ethics 5:23; Singer, p. 203.
[2] Proverbs 3:6.

5. A Dwelling for God

The Kotzker Rabbi said: "The verse (Exodus 15:2): 'He is my God, and I will declare His perfection' may be explained thus: 'This is my God, and I shall make a dwelling for Him within me.' "

S. S. K., p. 24.

[1] The Hebrew is: "Zeh Eli we-Anveihu." "Anveihu" is derived from "Noveh" which means either "perfection" or a "dwelling."

6. The Place of God's Glory

The Koznitzer Maggid said: "We read in the Kedushah: 'His glory fills the universe; His ministering angels ask one another: "Where is the place of His glory?" ' [1] (Singer, p. 160.)

"This query requires an explanation. The following parable furnishes it: 'A king traveled into another kingdom and was highly gratified by the acclaim of the populace, though he was always indifferent to the cheers of his own people. He was moved by the fact that a strange populace applauded him, though they owed him no allegiance.'

"Likewise the Angels question one another: 'Is there, nevertheless, any place where glory is not due the Lord? There our own praise would be more welcome.' Receiving no affirmative reply, they praise Him where praise is due Him."

E. O., p. 82.

[1] The Hasidic Prayerbook has the additional words: "to revere Him."

7. Sparks of Divinity Everywhere

"As the atmosphere encircles the earth, so does God comprehend the world, and there is no space where His Majesty is not. As it is said, in Midrash: 'Why did God reveal Himself to Moses in a bush of thorns? In order to make manifest that there is no place where His radiance is not; it may even be found in a thicket of thorns.' [1]

"It is written in Pesikta: [2] We read in Judges that the Children of Joseph went to Beth-El and the Lord was with them (i, 22). Aye, with them, though they carried there Michah's [3] idols. Whatever comes to pass in this world, be it motion, word or thought, is closely bound up with God. To place life in us, there are sparks of divinity everywhere. Hence it is written in the Zohar: 'Nought drops into a void, neither words nor voice of Man; but all have their fountain-head and destiny.'"

Bl., Pr., pp. 21-2.

[1] Shemoth Rabba, 2:9.
[2] Rashi to Judges 1:22; no source stated.
[3] See Judges 17:5; Michah was of the tribe of Joseph.

8. All Nature Exists in God

The Kobriner turned to his Hasidim and said: "Do you know where God is?" He took a piece of bread, showed it to them all, and continued: "God is in this piece of bread. Without the Lord's manifestation of His power in all nature, this piece of bread would have no existence." [1]

O. Y., p. 87.

[1] Contrast this story with the Catholic concept of the Mass.

9. Identical with God

Said the Koretzer: "It is possible for everyone to know who serves the Lord truly and who is thoroughly evil. This knowledge is attained through God, Who includes everyone in himself. The world is identical with God."

Nof. Tz., pp. 12-13.

10. The Title of King

Said the Koretzer: "We call God the Lord, giving to Him a minor title of nobility. This is not due to the fact that God's majesty is limited, but because our world is insignificant. It is like a King whose title is of minor worth because the country over which he reigns is small in size."

Nof. Tz., p. 22.

11. God, Prayer, Torah, and Israel

Said the Koretzer: "God and Prayer are One. God and Torah are one. God, Israel and Torah are one."

Nof. Tz., p. 27.

12. Before and After

A Hasid asked the Ropshitzer to explain the verse: "Before Me there was no god formed, and after Me there will be none." [1] "How

[1] Isaiah 43:10.

can we understand a time before or after God, when He is above time?"

The Rabbi replied: "The words 'before Me' do not mean: 'earlier' but 'in My presence.' Hence the verse should read: 'In My presence no god was formed,' and by this token the words 'after Me' have no significance in terms of time."

E. Tz., p. 90.

13. The Conception of God

Said the Medzibozer: "God is called the God of Gods,[1] in order to demonstrate to us that He is God beyond any conception of Him we may have. In other words, He is higher than any conception of Him of which humanity is capable."

Butz. D., p. 28.

[1] Deut. 10:17.

14. Distinct from God

Said the Bratzlaver: "Others gain authority over you if you possess a will distinct from God's will."

K. L. M., p. 5.

15. The Unknown God

An innkeeper for whose sons Rabbi Nathan Khelmer had served as teacher, became exceedingly poor at the same time that the Rabbi gained great renown. He went to Khelm and observed that the Rabbi seemed to have forgotten him. He begged permission to make a statement, and when this was granted, he said: "We constantly implore God to aid us for the sake of Abraham, Isaac, and Jacob. Once the Angels inquired: 'Wherein is the importance of the Patriarchs? What have they added to the glory of God?' In the meantime the hymn containing the Neilah prayer was heard: 'The Patriarch Abraham made Thee known when Thou wert unknown in the world.' This was a direct reply to the Angels. In the same fashion the Rabbi does not recognize me, since I taught him nothing and added nothing to his renown. But I helped to make the Rabbi known when he was still unknown to fame.' The Rabbi recollected the innkeeper at these words, and gathered a sum of money to establish him again in business."

Hitz. Z., pp. 31-4.

16. God and the Shekinah

Said the Mezeritzer:

"1. Since nothing can exist without God, it follows that God is present in every tribulation. From the midst of your tribulations call upon Him.

"2. God is in every movement, whether towards good or evil.

"3. Only in tangible things can you see or hear God.

"4. When your child leaves you, his picture is always in your mind. Likewise, we are in God's mind constantly.

"5. The Creator and the objects of His creation are a Unity inseparable. Without the power of the Creator, the created would become naught.

"6. Since no space is vacant of the Lord, no movement in the universe can occur that is not ascribable to God.

"7. There is no past nor future with God, since time is movement, and is, therefore, inseparable from God.

"8. The Shekinah is always present within us, and is shown to us whenever God wills it.

"9. Whatever you do, do it in order to please the Shekinah, the spirit dwelling within you.

"10. The Shekinah longs for good deeds, even as a parent yearns to hear the wisdom of his child."

T. M. M., pp. 9-17.

64. THE PROVIDENCE OF GOD

1. Leaning on God

Commenting on the Talmudic phrase: "We have no one to lean on except on our Father in Heaven," [1] the Gerer Rabbi said: "He who knows this does not lack for anything."

S. S. K., i, 86.

[1] Sotah, 49.

2. Bread from Heaven

Said the Kobriner: "The words (Exodus 16:4): 'Behold I will cause bread to rain from heaven for you' mean: 'I will pour down upon you the knowledge that bread, or livelihood, comes to us from Heaven.'"

O. Y., p. 74.

3. Blessing Our Handiwork

Said the Kobriner: "We read (Deut. 15:10): 'Because that for this thing the Lord thy God will bless thee in all thy work, and in all that thou puttest thy hand unto.' If we do not forget God's presence among us when we perform our labors; if we use our hands to acquire what we need, and at the same time leave place within our thoughts for the remembrance of God, then will He, for all this, surely bless our handiwork."

O. Y., p. 88.

4. God's Seekers Are Contented

Said the Kobriner: "The Psalmist teaches us (34:11): 'They that seek the Lord want not any good thing,' because they believe that whatever they possess, is sufficient good to meet their needs."

O. Y., p. 100.

5. "By His Word"

A man who had business worries came to the Kobriner. The Rabbi was at the breakfast table, and he pronounced the blessing: "Everything came to be by God's word." [1]

"This answers your complaints," said the Rabbi.

[1] Singer, p. 290.

O. Y., p. 54.

6. Penniless or Sleepless

Rabbi Mordecai Lekhivitzer used to say: "If a single coin is left over in my house at bedtime, I cannot fall asleep. But if totally penniless, I sleep soundly, knowing that when the moment comes to awaken, I must immediately look to the Lord for aid."

O. Y., p. 4.

7. Trust in the Lord

The Lekhivitzer related the following story: "A man once heard a sermon to the effect that Providence allots to each one his livelihood and does not permit him to be cheated of it. It was the man's custom to arise before daylight on market days, to walk out of the village in order to meet the farmers bringing in their produce, and to drive bargains with them before they reached the market-place. He would, thereupon, resell the produce at higher prices and thus gain his livelihood. Other middlemen did the same, and each strove to buy the entire produce of the farmers at the best prices.

"After hearing the preacher's discourse the middleman resolved to act upon the counsel to have trust in the Lord. He determined henceforth, to await the arrival of the farmers in the town. When market-day came, his wife roused him as usual before sunrise, but he refused to arise, asserting that the farmers would find it necessary to visit his house in order to sell their produce.

" 'I am convinced,' he said, 'that I cannot be deprived of my profit.'

"In a few hours, he was awakened again by loud knocks on his window-shutters, and by repeated cries: 'Where is Herschke? We wish to deal with Herschke, as usual!'

"Here is an example," said the Lekhivitizer, "of the reward meted out to a person of simple heart, with true confidence in the Lord."

O. Y., p. 43.

8. The Horse's Shadow

A storekeeper complained to the Premislaner that another man had opened a store near him and was taking away his livelihood. The Rabbi answered:

"Did you ever notice that when a horse is led to a pool of water to drink, he stamps with his hoof in the water?"

"Yes," said the man.

"The reason is as follows," continued the Rabbi. "When the horse bends down his head to drink, he sees his shadow. He imagines that another horse is also drinking, and fearing there will not be sufficient water for him, he attempts to chase away the other horse. In reality, he is afraid of his shadow, and there is plenty of water for many horses. You, likewise, are afraid of an imaginary foe. God's abundance flows like a river. No one can touch the other's livelihood, since Providence grants sustenance to everyone according to His will."

S. M., p. 38.

9. The Pair of Gloves

Rabbi Sabbatai, the father of the Koznitzer Maggid, was a bookbinder. It was his custom to leave off work on Fridays at ten o'clock in the morning and go to the synagogue to recite the "Song of Songs" and to study the Zohar. When he became old, he could do little work and lived in great poverty.

It happened once that he lacked even a penny for the preparation of the Sabbath, but he resolved to accept no charity and to fast, if need be, on the Sabbath. He persuaded his wife to accept nothing from her neighbors. When he returned home, however, in the evening, he found the room lighted, and the table laid with courses of fish and meat. He asked his wife why she had failed to keep her solemn pledge. She denied she had broken her word, and told him that as soon as he had left, the following had occurred:

Having nothing else to do, she began to rummage in the cabinet-drawers, and discovered there a pair of long-lost gloves, with silver buttons. She sold these, and with the money, provided for the Sabbath meals. Rabbi Sabbatai was overjoyed that he had been able to dispense with charity. He placed his arm about his wife, and together they danced in their happiness. When the Besht heard of this, he blessed the aged pair, and said that a son would be granted them in their old age. It happened as he predicted, and the son became the illustrious Koznitzer Maggid.

N. H. K., p. 25.

10. "Sussya is Hungry"

In his old age, it was Rabbi Sussya's custom, after the Morning Services, to say: "O Lord of the Universe, Sussya is hungry; let nourishment be granted him." This was a signal for his servant to bring him his food. He resented, however, that the Rabbi did not order him in plain words to place the meal before him. Once, therefore, he determined to see what would transpire if he did not bring in the food until expressly instructed to do so.

In the morning on his return from the synagogue, the Rabbi encountered a merchant from another town who did not recognize him. The sidewalk was narrow, and the Rabbi, being poorly dressed, was mistaken by the merchant for a beggar. The Rabbi was engrossed in his own thoughts, and not noticing the merchant, did not make way for him. This incensed the latter, and in a rage, he pushed the Rabbi into the gutter. When he arrived at the inn, he narrated the occurrence, and described the poor man. The innkeeper told him the identity of the supposed beggar. In great distress, the merchant promptly took cake and wine to the Rabbi's home, just as he was speaking his customary words: "O Lord of the Universe, Sussya is hungry." The Rabbi readily forgave the merchant, and the servant was deeply impressed by the timely intervention.

T. H. A., p. 45.
Bl., Pr., pp. 90-1.

11. The Source of Livelihood

Said the Kotzker: "It often happens that a wealthy good man loses his fortune. Perhaps we may explain this occurrence as follows: the Lord wishes to tempt the man to discover whether he believed his riches had come from successful business enterprises or through the aid of the Lord who is the Cause of Causes. If a man is wise, he will understand that it is within the power of God to provide him with a livelihood in one fashion, just as he had done in another, previous to the loss of his wealth."

S. S. K., i, 74.

12. The Uses of Life

A Hasid once asked the Berditschever Rabbi to explain why the Lord did not provide him once a year with sufficient funds for his annual needs, and thus free his mind for spiritual activities.

The Rabbi replied: "We cannot comprehend God's reasons. Perhaps he desires to see what use you will make of the life He has granted you, while you are burdened with the task of carving out a living."

S. S. K., ii, 88.

13. The Rabbi's Wife

The Hakham Zevi was a Rabbi in a German town in the early stages of his career. A manuscript was brought to him for his approval, in accordance with the custom of securing the consent of several Rabbis before the publication of a new book. The Hakham found that the author was an adherent of the Pseudo-Messiah, Sabbatai Zevi, and in his wrath, he hurled the manuscript into a burning oven. This being a felony in the region, the Rabbi was forced to flee with his family to a town in Poland. He had in his possession a number of gold pieces, but since his family was large, it was necessary to spend a gold coin daily.

When only one remained, his wife became discouraged, and loudly bewailed their lot, bemoaning what the future might hold. The Rabbi said to her: "If you have so little confidence in the Lord, I must secure a separation from you. You have not sufficient fortitude to be a Rabbi's wife."

A few hours later, a committee from Amsterdam visited him, urging him to become the Rabbi of their community. The Hakham speedily repented of his hasty decision, and obtained an annulment of it from many Rabbis.

S. S. K., ii, 123.

14. Thanks in Advance

Said the Medzibozer: "We say in the Sabbath Evening Home Prayer: 'I thank Thee for all the favors which Thou didst to us, and for all that Thou shalt do to us.' Why do we not wait until the favors come before we thank Thee? It is because we may not be in the proper mood to thank Thee as we ought when Thy favors are made known; hence we thank Thee in advance while we are in a mood of holiness."

Butz. D., p. 26.

15. God's Abundance

Said the Besht: "God's abundance fills the world at all times, since there is no time above us; and it always seeks a channel through which it may descend unto men. If our words of prayer or learning are concentrated upon God, they unite with His abundance and form the channel through which it descends upon the world."

K. S. T., p. 15b.

16. The Pains of the Shekinah

Said Rabbi Mendel Vitebsker: "Those who fear the Lord cannot lack for anything, for everything in nature has been made for the benefit of man. Since God is omnipresent in nature, the Shekinah has donned innumerable garments in order to provide for the God-fearing man. The properties of things, the instincts of living beings, the aptitude and talents of thinking men—all these are the manifestations of the Shekinah, which endowed them for the good man's benefit. Thus it was that Ben Zoma said when he saw a multitude from the Temple Hill: 'Blessed be He who created all of these to serve me.' [1] God strives by these means to influence a man to use his opportunities to do good. More than this, the Shekinah lowers itself, and makes itself manifest in penalties and punishments, intended to subdue man's heart through fear, and prompt him to perform God's will. Hence when a man is in want, he may know that his imperfections have caused the Shekinah to lessen its power of providence by donning a garment whereby its abundance becomes limited. It behooves him therefore to offer up a prayer that the Shekinah may be relieved of its pain; not, however, that he may be rescued from want. For his lack is evidence that he cleaves inadequately to the Lord."

Tif. Yeh., pp. 26-7.

[1] Berakhoth, 58.

17. Why Doubt Me?

The Premislaner commented upon the verse: "I will tell of the decree: the Lord said unto me: 'Thou art My son; this day have I begotten thee. Ask of Me, and I will give' (Psalm 2:7)." He said: "The man who suffers poverty complains of the harsh decree against him. The Lord answers: 'Thou art My son.' Does the loyal son doubt his father's ability to support him? 'Have I this day begotten thee?' Who supported thee until now? 'Ask of Me, and I will give.' Hence, why dost thou complain? Why doubt Me?"

E. A., p. 50.

65. SERVICE TO GOD

1. The Vessel

Said the Apter: "A man should not choose the form in which he wishes to perform the service of the Lord, but he should perform it in any manner the opportunity affords. He should be like a vessel into which anything may be poured—wine, milk, or water."

M. Hat., p. 80.

2. Food and Wine of the Spirit

Said the Koznitzer Maggid: "We read (Numbers 15:21): 'Of the first of your dough,' namely, of the first of your years, 'ye shall give unto the Lord.' Do not wait until you are old to serve the Lord, but devote yourself to Him in your early manhood as well."

The Kobriner added: "The Talmud declares that until the age of forty, we find more satisfaction in food; after forty, in drink.[1] Should evil thoughts allure you to devote your younger years to physical enjoyments, be reminded that service to the Lord is like unto food, and food is best when fresh. Should you be allured in your later years to relax from labors in the service of God, be reminded that service to the Lord is like unto wine, and wine is best when it is old."[2]

O. Y., p. 192.

[1] Sabbath, 152.

[2] In Proverbs 9:5 we find the words of Wisdom: "Come eat of my bread and drink of the wine which I have mingled." See Ecclesiastes 12:12: "Remember then thy Creator in the days of thy youth."

3. Reverence for God

The Gerer Rabbi interpreted Psalm 147:10 and 11: "The Lord does not desire to be served by the animal strength in a man, nor by the bodily might within him. He does not wish a man ever to exert himself or to serve Him with the limbs. He does take pleasure in those who revere Him and who hope for his kindness."

S. S. K., ii, 44.

¹ The translation is: "He taketh no pleasure in the legs of a man;. The Lord taketh pleasure in them that fear Him, in those that wait for his mercy."

4. Learning from the Thief

Rabbi Bunam said: "We may learn three things from a thief: First, he is not lazy to be active in his work in the middle of the night. Second, if he does not succeed on his first attempt, he repeats the endeavour several times until he has accomplished his goal. Third, he does not despise any article.

"The man who wishes to serve the Lord aright should utilize the same methods." ¹

S. S. K., iii, 5.

¹ See section on "Thief," for other stories.

5. Learn Service from Everything

Said the Kobriner: "The wise man learns how to serve the Lord from every phrase he hears, from every event he observes, and from every experience he shares. We read in Ecclesiastes 12: 13: '(From) everything that is heard (learn how to) fear God.' " ¹

O. Y., p. 91.

¹ The translation of the verse in the J. T. is: "The end of the matter, all having been heard: fear God, and keep His commandments: for this is the whole man."

6. The Nightingale

A man once came to the Lekhivitzer and complained that he was aware of the imperfections of his service to the Lord, and that he was dejected of mood. His only consolation lay, he said, in his knowledge that others were inferior even to himself.

The Rabbi retorted: "How can you gain any consolation from believing that others are worse than you? How do you know they are inferior? Let me narrate to you a parable from which you can honestly derive comfort:

" 'A king had an orchestra which regaled him with music whenever he pleased. He also possessed a nightingale which sang at intervals. The king found himself rejoicing more in the natural untutored melodies of the little bird than the studied harmonies of his orchestra.'

"The King of Kings has hosts of angels who sing before him in perfect harmony, yet He prefers to hear the imperfect and oftentimes, discordant praise of us mortals. As long as we offer our service to the best of our ability, we need never feel disheartened at our inadequacies."

O. Y., p. 40.

7. The Staff of Misfortunes

Said the Radomsker: "We read (Song of Songs, 1:4): 'O draw me; we will run after Thee.' A shepherd employs two methods to draw his sheep to him. He either whistles and they come, or he drives them with his staff, and they move forward. In the first instance, they follow him; in the second, he follows them. We petition that the Lord should draw us nigh unto Him by His voice, and we promise to follow after Him. But we do not desire that He should drive us to godliness with the staff of misfortunes."

O. S., p. 30.

8. Attachment to God

Said the Besht: "Some seek God as if He were far removed from us, and surrounded by many walls. They say (Song of Songs 3:1) 'I sought Him, but I found Him not.' Had they been wise, however, they would have known that 'no space is free of Him.' They can find Him in everything and everywhere, and they should understand that 'one who attaches himself to any part of God is as if he were attached to the All in All.'"

M. G. I., p. 12.

9. Day and Night

The Radviller Rabbi commented on the phrase (Psalm 74:16): "Thine is the day; Thine also is the night." "If our service is for the sake of God only," said the Rabbi, "it is like the shining day. But if we serve God for the expected reward, and also for His sake, then this service is dim, like the night."

E. O., p. 65.

10. Servant and Master

Said the Gerer Rabbi: "We call our prayers 'Services' to demonstrate that we are servants of the Lord. The servant owns no property except what he receives from his master; he has no anxiety concerning the future, since he relies upon maintenance by his master in return for his work. In our own relations with the Creator, we should feel like the servant towards his master, without pride in our possessions, and without anxiety if we lack them."

S. S. K., iii, 43.

11. A Greeting

Every morning after Services the Sassover would call at the home of every widow in town and wish her a good morning.

M. Hat., p. 51.

12. Everything Can Be Service

Rabbi Baruch of Medziboz once expounded the verse: "If a man has two wives, one beloved and one hated" (Deut. 21:15). He said: "Not two wives, but two services are under contemplation.

The one beloved, is doctrine and prayer; the other, hated, is subservience to corporeal needs. But this too, is Law and Service of the Creator. Even toil for the sake of earning money may be part of divine service, but if it be done in avarice, it is like the worship of the golden calf, and the breaking of the Tables of the Law." Of the Neschizer Rabbi it was said, that instruction and prayer, eating, drinking and sleeping were all parts to him of the study of divinity. Part of the Infinite is hidden in all of Man's faculties and actions, in speech and sight and hearing, in walking, standing still and lying down. It is on this account that it is written in the Sh'ma (Deut. 6:7): "Thou shalt speak thereof when thou sittest in thy house; when thou walkest by the way; when thou liest down, and when thou risest up." Rabbi Jacob Joseph of Pulnoe taught: "A man should have converse not only with books, but also with men, providing that he always have the fear of God before his eyes."

Bl., Gem., p. 64.

13. The Impulse of the Heart

Rabbi Ber of Radishitz asked the Lubliner to teach him the best way of serving the Lord. The Lubliner replied: "The best way is the one to which your heart is drawn. Labor in it with your whole strength."

D. Z., p. 41.

14. For Your Own Benefit

A youth came to the Lekhivitzer and asked to be taught how to serve the Lord. The Rabbi replied: "The Lord does not need your service. Do we not say in the Neilah Amidah: 'And if man be righteous, what can he give Thee?' (Singer, p. 267). What you may properly ask me is to instruct you how to serve yourself. You, not the Lord, will receive benefit from your Mitzwoth and your Torah."

O. Y., p. 9.

15. Thanks to God

When a Hasid complained of his small attainments in the service of the Lord, the Radishitzer would say to him: "Offer thanks to God for what you have attained. Others have accomplished less."

D. A., p. 19.

16. In Every Circumstance

Said the Porissover: "It is not permissible to excuse your failure to serve the Lord by calling attention to your tribulations and your poverty. Bear in mind that David wrote the finest Psalms while he was in the direst straits."

He also said: "Do you wish to attain a higher degree in the service of the Lord? Do all you possibly can with your present powers, and I assure you that you will then attain more."

D. Z., p. 19.

17. By His Own Abilities

Said the Besht: "No two persons have the same abilities. Each man should work in the service of God according to his own talents. If one man tries to imitate another, he merely loses his opportunity to do good through his own merit, and he cannot accomplish anything by imitation of the other's service."

K. S. T., p. 2b.

18. Service Without Pride

Said the Besht: "When a man serves God constantly he has no leisure for pride or other disagreeable traits. He feels that he does not belong in this world. Neither the respect or disrespect of men concern him. He is then able to perform any good deed without feeling pride in doing it."

K. S. T., p. 15a.

19. Everything is Equal

Said the Besht: "In the verse: 'I have set the Lord always before me' (Psalm 16:8), the word 'shivithi' may also mean: 'I equalized.' Everything becomes of equal worth to me because I serve the Lord constantly. I care not if I am praised or blamed; whether I eat dry bread or goodly viands. I serve equally in every circumstance and every place; when I am alone, or when I talk to people; when I am at home or on the highway. I believe that God's care is never absent from me. He sends people to talk to me since He wishes me to serve Him through my speech with them. He leads me away from my home because I am wanted for His service elsewhere. Not I, but He, my God, knows what is for my good, and what is not."

K. S. T., p. 16b.

20. The Will to Serve

Said the "Yud": "Possession of the will to serve God is very rare. Even a Zaddik merely possesses the will to have the will to serve God."

Nif. Yeh., p. 40.

21. Service Without Regulations

Said the "Yud": "All regulations concerning the service of the Lord which a person may impose upon himself are not binding, including this regulation as well. Many may serve God in an irregular way, yet it is true service nevertheless."

Nif. Yeh., p. 42.

22. Profane Phrases of Holiness

Said the Riziner: "Abraham wished to enable men to devote a portion of the day to the Lord, and he, therefore, instituted the Morning Service. The Satan conspired against this, and succeeded in capturing it by filling it with distracting thoughts. Isaac said: 'I will institute a brief service, through which men may perhaps be able to pray with the proper concentration.' This proved of no avail. Jacob then said: 'I will proclaim a voluntary evening service; perhaps the Satan will not trouble to introduce alien thoughts into an optional service, since a man may choose not to read it.' But this, too, proved unsuccessful. The 'Ari' said: 'I will institute the practice of silent meditation'; but this too, proved unsuccessful. Hence the Besht said: 'Let the good man who cannot pray properly recite aloud profane phrases or tales, and endow them with a holy meaning.' This proved a successful remedy against the machinations of the Satan." [1]

Tif. Z., pp. 19-21.

[1] See Berakhoth 26 on the institution of Services by Abraham, Isaac and Jacob, and folio 27 on the optional aspect of the Evening Service.

23. *The Mezeritzer on "Service and Worship"*

"1. Service from the heart is a source of great joy to the Lord.

"2. He who gives pleasure to God, receives godliness in reward.

"3. The object of man's creation is that he should lead back all virtues to their source; namely, he should return them to nothingness, even as they were in their origin; this can be done through Torah, worship, and good deeds. Thus can he attach them to God.

"4. We find that our limbs obey our mind. We are as limbs of the Most High and it should be natural for us to obey the Supreme Mind. But our body is so engrossed in materialism that it knows not there is a Supreme Mind. No man should allow his mind to degenerate in order to please the body.

"5. In order to offer proper prayer we must feel ourselves encompassed by the light of the spirit.

"6. Through prayer our thoughts may ascend higher and higher to the very seat of holiness.

"7. In our prayers we must become so absorbed that we see and hear nothing, even as we oftentimes become completely absorbed in something which interests us deeply."

T. M. M., pp. 143-159.

66. GOODNESS, MEN OF

1. *Exceptions Prove the Rule*

"Why does the Bible relate the wrong-doings of good men?" the Besht was asked. "Would it not encourage righteousness to teach that good men are invariably good?"

The Besht answered: "If the Bible failed to indicate the few sins of its heroes, we might doubt their goodness. Let me explain this by the following fable:

'A lion taught his cubs that they need fear no living creature, since they were the strongest on earth. One day the cubs went for a walk and came upon a ruin. They entered and saw on the wall of the deserted castle a picture of Samson breaking in twain a lion cub.[1] In fright they ran to their father, crying out: 'We have seen a creature stronger than ourselves and we are in fear of him.' The old lion questioned them, and on learning what they had seen in the ruin, he said: 'This picture ought assure you that the race of lions is the strongest of creatures, for when once a stronger creature appears, it is pictured as a miracle. Exceptions prove the rule.'"

K. S. T., p. 34b.

[1] Judges 14:5, 6.

2. The "Ehrlicher Yud"

The Belzer said to his wife that an "ehrlicher Yud," a truly pious Jew, a Jew par excellence, was dead. "Who is it?" inquired his wife.

"The Rabbi of Dinov," answered the Belzer.

"Was he then, only an 'ehrlicher Yud,' and not a famous Rebbe?" was his wife's question.

"There are many Rebbes," replied the Belzer, "but few truly pious Jews."

P. v. K., p. 26b.

3. The Nation's Memory

Said the Medzibozer: "The expression: 'Aaron shall be gathered unto his people'[1] means that the nation which produced Aaron will keep sacred the memory of his righteousness and holiness, and will seek to imitate his noble qualities."

Butz. D., p. 29.

[1] Numbers 20:24.

4. God's Image

Said the Koretzer: "The explanation of the verse: 'Let me see thy countenance; let me hear thy voice' (Song of Songs 2:14) is as follows: 'The Lord declares to the good man: 'Let me be seen through thy countenance, for God's image is in the countenance of the good man. Let Me be heard through thy voice, for he who hears the words of good men is moved to improve himself.'"

Nof. Tz., p. 59.

5. In Many Generations

Said the Lizensker: "It is written (Gen. 6:9): 'These are the descendants of Noah; Noah was in his generations a man righteous and perfect.'

"The fact that Noah thought himself to be righteous and perfect made of him a good man of lower degree; he had descended.

"The man who labors in quest of the Lord never stands still: he either increases the purity of his service or he decreases it.

"Every such change marks a different 'generation' in his life. It

is in this way that a good man lives in many generations, as we
read in the case of Noah: 'in his generations.' "

Noam E., p. 6.

6. Rebirth

Said the Berditschever: "We read (Gen. 6:9): 'These are the
generations of Noah: Noah was in his generations a man righteous
and perfect (whole-hearted).' We learn from this verse that the
good man's generations are his good acts, the means by which he
is continually reborn as a better and better man.

"Only this kind of man can be truly called 'born,' as he seeks to
be born again and again in an ever-higher degree. We may thus
explain the words of Rava in Makkoth 17b: 'When birth is given, it
should be given to one like Rabbi Simeon ben Yochai; else there
should be no begetting.' Only an illustrious person like Rabbi Simeon
is properly called 'born.' "

E. O., p. 53.

67. HANUKAH

1. Hanukah and Purim

The Gerer Rabbi explained why a special feast is ordained for
Purim, but not for Hanukah. On Purim we celebrate the annulment
of the royal edict to destroy the body; therefore we partake of an
enjoyable meal in order to give pleasure to the body.

On Hanukah we were rescued from a decree which would have
destroyed our soul. Therefore we chant the Hallel [1] and gratify
our soul.

S. S. K., ii, 46.

[1] Singer, pp. 219-224.

2. The Value of Martyrdom

The Gerer Rabbi gave another reason for the feast on Purim.
"Had the Jews been slain by Haman, their death would have served
no holy purpose; hence we may celebrate Purim with a tasty repast.
On the other hand, had the Jews been killed by Antiochus because
of their fealty to the Torah, they would have sanctified the Holy
Name. Hence there is no occasion to rejoice unduly that we were
not given the opportunity to die gloriously for the sake of the Lord."

S. S. K., ii, 46.

3. Hanukah Candles

The Sachatzover Rabbi was asked: "Why does the Shulchan
Arukh insist that one must buy Hanukah candles even if he is destitute and must beg for the money, whereas other duties are not obliga-
tory on the part of one who lacks the means for them?"

The Rabbi replied: "We find in the Talmud the rule, that if a
person contemplates performing a precept, but is unavoidably pre-

vented from fulfilling his intention, the Creator allocates to him the credit as if he had actually done the deed.[1] Hanukah candles, however, must be lighted, it is commanded, in order to give public testimony to the miracles associated with the Festival. Inasmuch as mere intention to perform the duty will not give public evidence, therefore this precept cannot be assumed to be fulfilled, except through its actual performance."

S. S. K., iii, 28.

[1] Berakhoth, 6.

4. An Important Holiday

Said the Koretzer: "Hanukah is an important holiday. It is the only period of celebration during the last week of any month."

Nof. Tz., p. 14.

5. The Divine Light

Said the Koretzer: "For thirty-six hours, Adam enjoyed the Divine Light that was created on the first day and was superseded later by the sunlight; then It was hidden. On Hanukah this Divine Light inspired the victory of the ancient Hasidim, and for this reason thirty-six lights are kindled during Hanukah as a memorial of the thirty-six hours that the First Man enjoyed It. Since then this Divine Light has inspired the creation of the thirty-six Tractates of the Talmud. The Messiah will redeem us by this Divine Light."

Nof. Tz., p. 18.

68. HAPPINESS

1. Ten Rules on Happiness By the Slonimer Rabbi

"1. Happy is he who studies the Torah and gives satisfaction to his Creator, according to his ability.

"2. Happy is he who constantly searches his actions and regrets every unworthy act.

"3. Happy is he who recognizes the aid His master gives him continuously.

"4. Happy is he who reminds himself at all times to fear the Lord and His retribution.

"5. Happy is he who devotes his life to study.

"6. Happy is he who sanctifies the name of the Lord by his acts and who takes care to avoid the opposite.

"7. Happy is he who increases continuously his devotion in the service of the Lord.

"8. Happy is he who withstands temptations.

"9. Happy is he who serves His God with his whole heart, and who does not consider this out of the ordinary.

"10. Happy is he who ends his days in repentance and holy service, and who dies with a clear conscience."

O. Y., p. 202.

69. HASID AND ZADDIK

1. Hasid and Zaddik
(From Bloch, *Priester der Liebe*, p. 37 ff.)

"The two types of Hasidism trace their origin both to Holy Writ and the Talmud. The Scriptures place the Hasid upon a higher pedestal than the Zaddik, who is regarded (Ezekiel 3:20) as a lapse into a lower sphere. Not before the advent of Hasidism did the Zaddik reach his full significance as the Super-man, and Just man made perfect, the highest within creation. The Hasid, in the goodness of his heart, waived his charter of privilege to be altogether subject to the Zaddik. A few lines taken from the Bible and the Talmud will give their proper lineaments to both the Hasid and the Zaddik.

"God, in Holy Writ, appears as a Hasid: 'I am a Hasid, said the Lord, and will not be angry forever' (Jeremiah 3:12). A Hasidic trait is stressed here: the readiness of the Hasid to be pacified. God is also called a Zaddik: 'A Zaddik and a righteous one is He' (Deut. 32:4). Again in Psalms (145:17): 'A Zaddik is God in all His ways and a Hasid in all His deeds.' Concerning this the Talmud observes: 'He is a Zaddik first and then becomes a Hasid' (Rosh ha-Shanah, 17b). Rashi comments: 'He is at first a Zaddik, in an impartial administration of justice. But when He turns from the Law to perform acts of mercy, he becomes a Hasid.'

"Hasid and Zaddik in one person was King David. (II Samuel 23:3) 'A Zaddik ruleth over man, he ruleth in the fear of God.' And Psalms (86:3): 'Guard Thou my soul, for I am a Hasid.'

"As the first of the Hasidim appears Adam (Erubin 18b), but as the first of the Zaddikim, Noah, of whom Holy Writ gives this account: 'He was a Zaddik entire in his generation, and he walked with God' (Gen. 6:9).

"There are many sayings in the Talmud, characterizing the qualities of Hasid and Zaddik. 'A Hasid is he who says: what is mine is thine, and what is thine is also thine; one slow to anger and quick to be assuaged; who doeth charity and wishes others to do likewise" (Pirkei Avoth, 5:13-16; Singer, pp. 201-2).

"King David made manifest before the Lord: 'Lord of the Universe, am I not a Hasid? Other Kings, both of the East and the West, sleep three hours into the new-born day, but I arise at midnight to praise Thee' (Berakhoth 4a). 'The Hasidim of former generations spent an hour first in turning their hearts to God, before raising their voices in prayer' (*Ibid.*, 30b). 'The Hasidim of the Gentiles also have a share in the World-to-Come' (Tosefta Sanhedrin, Section 13; Maimonides, Mishneh Torah, Section Melakhim, p. 11).

"But even the Hasid, the most praiseworthy among men, is not altogether free of evil inclinations. 'Even the greatest of Hasidim is not free of the taint of sin' (Midrash Rabbah, Wayyikra, Section 14). And 'Even the chief of the Hasidim must not be made guardian over his own kinsfolk' (Talmud Yerushalmi, Kethubhoth, i, 8).

"Of the Zaddik, it is said in the Talmud Babli: 'Before the child leaves the mother's womb, it is placed under oath to become a Zaddik, and not one of the wicked. But if a man be called by another person, a Zaddik, let him esteem himself as one of the wicked' (Niddah, 30b)."

2. Confusion in Numbers

Said the Rimanover: "When one hundred Hasidim come to me, even though half are sent by the Satan, I am able to drive out the evil in them. But may the Lord protect me from the confusion caused by a greater number of visitors."

Em. L., p. 44.

3. How to Attract Adherents

Said the Riziner to the Ropshitzer: "Do you know that flies are drawn to fire?"

"Yes," retorted the Ropshitzer. "And cream draws flies also."

Ohel N., p. 108.

4. True Hasidism

The Riziner asked the Rimanover: "Have you Hasidim?"

"Yes, thanks be to God," answered the latter.

"And wherein does their Hasidism lie?"

"In the deep study of Halakhah and the Tossafoth," said the Rimanover.

"Then in truth, they are genuine Hasidim," commented the Riziner.

Em. L., p. 44.

5. Praise of the Zaddik

The Gerer wrote in a letter to his sons and sons-in-law, while in Harbashov on the way to Brody: "To our sorrow we are surrounded by fools whose entire Hasidism consists in praising their Zaddik to the heavens, and everything else is subordinate to this. May the Lord implant within our heart a true seed of service to Him, and may He remove the unworthy soil which surrounds the kernel of truth and makes it hardly distinguishable. It is our duty to study constantly, and to possess ourselves of the will to perform God's commands as enjoined in His Torah. Everything other than this is vanity and without value."

R. T., ii, 58.

6. Interceding for the Hasidim

The Rozdoler dreamed that his father-in-law, the Ziditzover, appeared to him. He asked the Ziditzover: "Have you been admitted as yet into the right place in Paradise?"

The Ziditzover answered: "No, I am still in the vestibule of Paradise in order that I may intercede for my loyal Hasidim."

The Rozdoler awoke and·said to himself: "I shall do my best to perfect my Hasidim, lest any imperfect Hasidim shame me by keeping me in the vestibule of Paradise. My Hasidim shall have no need of intercession."

P. v. K., p. 43b.

7. Nature and Art

Rabbi Uri Strelisker was asked: "Why is it that the Zaddikim formerly were contented with small donations whereas the present-day Zaddikim ask for large donations?"

"Because a natural rose is cheaper than an artificial one," was Rabbi Uri's reply.

F. U. A. O., ii, 39.

8. Higher Than Charity

A non-Hasid asked the Kozmirer Rabbi: "Would it not be a more virtuous act to distribute for charity the money which your Hasidim spend on communal meals and on wine?"

The Kozmirer replied: "We find that during each period of seven years, we were enjoined to set aside a second tithe for our own enjoyment in Jerusalem, on the first, the second, the fourth and fifth years; whereas it was required to give the tithe for the poor only on the third and sixth years.[1] Hence it may be deduced that enjoyment in an atmosphere of holiness precedes charity and is of double importance."

D. Z., p. 56.

[1] Rosh Ha-Shanah, 12b.

9. The Discipline of Hasiduth

The Mithnaged, Rabbi Zalman Pozner, said to the Vorker Rabbi: "The Talmud enumerates the many degrees of scholarship through which a man must advance before he attains the degree of Hasiduth. Yet your people call themselves Hasidim as soon as they visit a Rebbe." [1]

The Vorker replied: "When a man loves Zion, he calls himself a Palestinian even though he has not yet settled in Palestine as he desires."

When the Kotzker heard this, he remarked: "I do not agree with the Vorker Rabbi. A man should not style himself a Hasid unless he is truly one. It is correct that a few chosen persons may attain the degree of Hasiduth without undergoing the preliminary steps. But when a multitude claim to do so, their pretensions are false, and it becomes imperative to return to the established manner of attaining by discipline and study the state of Hasiduth."

Tif. Yeh., p. 39.

[1] Abodah Zarah, 20.

10. The Farmer's Criticism

A Rav asked the Kozmirer Rabbi why when non-Hasidic Rabbis gather, they are friendly towards each other, whereas when Hasidic Rabbis come together, they usually part in enmity.

The Kozmirer answered with a parable: "A famous artist painted a remarkable landscape of a field with reapers working in it. All who saw it at an exhibition admired it greatly; only a farmer shook his head in disapproval. The artist, who stood nearby, inquired what mistake the farmer found in the picture. The farmer replied: 'Reapers must bend down to do their work, but in your picture they are standing upright.'

" 'Your criticism is correct,' said the artist. 'But had I painted the reapers bending down, their faces would be indistinct.'

"In the same fashion," continued the Kozmirer, "if the Hasidic leaders were constantly in agreement, their teachings would be unclear, and they would tread out no new paths in the service of God. Every leader would believe his road to be the best, else he would not have chosen it. But the variety of opinions gives to the Hasidim an opportunity to choose between them."

Sh. Z., p. 43.

11. In His Father's Footsteps

The Viceroy of Austrian Poland demanded that the Hasidim defend themselves in his presence against the accusation that they were impractical dreamers and mystics who misled the youth. The Ropshitzer determined to send his son, the Linsker, to the Rav of Lemberg where the Viceroy resided, in order to request that the Lemberger's son accompany him to the hearing before the viceroy. The Lemberger acceded to the request on the understanding that the Linsker conceal the fact that he was a Hasidic Rabbi.

When they came before the Viceroy, the Linsker found favor in his eyes by virtue of his wisdom, cultivated speech and admirable manners. The official asked the Linsker whether he was a Hasid, and received an affirmative response. On their return to the house of the Rav, the latter's son reported that the Linsker had made a highly favorable impression, and although he confessed to being a Hasid, this had not injured his cause.

The Lemberger Rav asked the Linsker: "Why did you not keep your pledge not to admit you are a Hasid? You took a grave risk that the Viceroy might reject your testimony on the ground that you were an interested party."

The Linsker replied: "Quite the reverse, Rabbi. Had I denied being a Hasid, the Viceroy would have said to us: 'Since you are not Hasidim, how do you know with such certainty that the accusations against them are unfounded?' But when he knew me to be a Hasid, and yet a man of culture and sense, he was compelled to listen to me. As to the understanding, had I refused to agree to it, you would not have permitted your son to accompany me."

The Lemberger Rav smiled and said: "Not for naught does the world say that the Ropshitzer is a man of wisdom, and that his son is not much different."

P. v. K., p. 32b.

70. THE HEAVENLY TRIBUNAL

1. Speaking the Truth

Rabbi Elimelech Lizensker once said: "I am sure of my share in the World-to-Come. When I stand to plead before the bar of the Heavenly Tribunal, I will be asked: [1] 'Did you learn, as in duty bound?' To this I will make answer: 'No.' Again, I will be asked: 'Did you pray, as in duty bound?' Again my answer will be: 'No.' The third question will be: 'Did you do good, as in duty bound?' And for the third time, I will answer: 'No.' Then judgment will be awarded in my favor, for I will have spoken the truth."

N. E., p. 40.

[1] Sabbath, 31a.

2. The Sinner's One Mitzwah

The Belzer recounted the following story:

"There was once a very wicked Jew who disregarded every law and commandment. He clung, however, to a single Mitzwah: he never ate a meal without washing his hands before.[1] He was once on a journey and became ravenously hungry. He looked about for water, but could find none. Then he recollected a spring in the neighborhood, but remembered that a band of outlaws were concealed in a cave nearby. Nevertheless he resolved not to break his life-long custom, come what may, and he turned aside to the spring. After the ablution, the brigands captured and promptly slew him. His soul came before the Heavenly Tribunal, and without any deliberation, decision was rendered that he should be sent to Paradise.

"May this be a lesson to you," continued the Belzer. "A single Mitzwah, even one unmentioned in the Torah, if adhered to, verily at the cost of one's life, is sufficient to atone for numberless transgressions."

D. S., p. 24.

[1] Hullin, 106: see Mark 7:5 (N. T.) for objection to this regulation.

3. The Rich Thief

Two merchants were on a journey. In the middle of the night, one stole the other's purse. Both chanced to be in Berditschev and visited the Rabbi. The loser complained of his loss and related the circumstances. The Rabbi detected the thief, and exclaimed: "Woe is me! What can the Archangel Michael say?"

He then called the thief aside and said to him: "Did you understand me? Michael is the Counsel for the Defense in Heaven. When a poor man steals, he is able to argue in his behalf, but when a rich man steals, what can he say?"

Kahana, p. 254.

4. Full of Mitzwoth

Rabbi Abraham of Slonim commented on the phrase (Psalm 51:5): "And my sin is ever before me." "Only those good deeds or sins performed with thorough-going intention ascend to the Heavenly Tribunal to be recorded. Those done half-heartedly remain here below. Good people perform their beneficent deeds whole-heartedly, and their occasional misdeeds unintentionally; hence their good deeds ascend on high, and their transgressions remain ever before them.

"On the other hand, the wicked perform their occasional good deeds without the proper enthusiasm, and their wicked deeds with zest. Hence their good works remain below and their transgressions ascend on high. The Talmud (Hagigah 27a) implies this in the words: 'The transgressors of Israel are full of Mitzwoth, as the pomegranate is full of seeds.' They are full of Mitzwoth because, having been performed without the proper spirit, they do not ascend on high, but remain continually with them on the earth below." [1]

O. Y., p. 182.

[1] Also Berakhoth 57; Sanhedrin 37. The simple meaning, however, contains the universalist statement: "The fires of Gehenna shall not affect even the transgressors of Israel for they too are full of Mitzwoth, as the pomegranate is full of seeds."

5. Heavenly Juries

Said the Premislaner: "There are three juries in Heaven. The unlearned man, unacquainted with the teachings of the Zaddikim, is brought before a jury consisting of Angels. Angels have no conception of a mortal man's temptations, and they decide according to the strict letter of the divine law.

"One who is learned in the Talmud and early Rabbinical works is brought before a jury consisting of the souls of Talmudists and illustrious Rabbis, since through study of their teachings, the soul to be judged has a relationship to them. These souls, however, departed from the world so long ago, that they retain only a dim remembrance of worldly desires. Their verdict, therefore, is also harsh, though milder than the judgment of the jury of Angels.

"One who has oftentimes visited the Zaddikim and listened to their teachings, is brought before a jury consisting of the souls of Zaddikim who have died recently, because the soul newly-arrived has been close to them. These souls of the Zaddikim still remember all the snares of the world and its passions. They therefore bring in a mild and compassionate verdict, taking into consideration all the circumstances."

B. Z., p. 32.

6. Only Devotion Counts

Said the Mikolayever: "An old man and a youth died on the same day. When the Heavenly Tribunal inspected their deeds, it was announced that the old man had two years to his credit, and the young man eighteen years. It was explained that only those years which are devoted to the Lord are accounted of merit in Heaven."

E. A., p. 58.

7. All the Day

The Medzibozer commented on the verse: "My tears have been my food day and night, while they say unto me all the day: 'Where is thy God?'" (Psalms 42:4). "How can you enjoy your food and your pleasures when you remember that in the After-Life you will be asked: 'Where was thy God all the day?' Then you will recall that you remembered God only at the time of prayer and did not hold Him in mind all the day."

Butz. D., p. 18.

8. The Weighted Scales

Said Rabbi Elimelech of Lizensk: "People come to me with various plaints: one wishes a livelihood, another a cure. Why do they come to me? What do they wish of me?

"It must be that it is known to all that I am a great sinner, and that, by my transgressions, I have weighted down the scales of the universe towards chastisement.[1] Hence they come to me, exclaiming: 'Give us back the life, the children, the food, of which thou hast robbed us.'"

E. Tz., p. 30.

[1] Kiddushin, 40.

9. The Redeeming Mud

The Riziner sojourned at the home of a certain wealthy man on one of his visits to a neighboring village. The wealthy man complained that the multitudes who came to see the Rabbi brought mud on their feet and soiled his home.

The Rabbi thereupon related to the magnate the following tale: "Once a poor villager came to the town to earn money for the Passover. After nightfall on his return to the village, laden with purchases, his horse and wagon fell into a pit made swampy by the spring rains. A rich man, passing by, heard his cries, and helped his own driver extricate the villager. He roped the latter's wagon to his carriage, and accompanied the poor man to his hut. On beholding the abject poverty in which the villager and family lived, the magnate gave him several hundred thalers.

"When the wealthy man died and was brought before the Heavenly Tribunal, it seemed as if his demerits because of certain business dealings would result in his sentence to Purgatory. Suddenly an Angel of Mercy appeared, and asked that the Heavenly Scales be used to determine whether the worth of his good deeds outweighed his sins. When consent was given, the Angel placed on the Scale of Good Deeds, the poor villager and his family whom the rich man had saved from misery. But this did not suffice. The horse and the wagon were added, but they did not aid. Then the Angel placed on the Scale the mud and mire out of which the rich man had helped rescue the villager, and lo, the Scale of Good Deeds dipped with its weight, and the magnate was saved from Purgatory."

The host understood the Riziner's hint, and complained no more of the mud on the shoes of his visitors.

S. Hay., pp. 36-7.

71. HOLINESS

1. The Life of Holiness Creates Holiness

The Mezeritzer explained that the saying in the "Ethics of the Fathers" (2:1) (1): "Know what is above you," means: "Know that everything above is due to you. It is your life of holiness that creates holiness in Heaven."

Dubnow, H. of H., p. 90.

¹ Singer, p. 187.

2. Rays of the Spirit

Said the Sudilkover: "Every human action sends a ray of the spirit into the realm of divinity like a stream of running water. When the channel is clean, the water running through it is pure. Likewise, if a man's action is worthy, its spiritual influence makes for holiness. Let us beware lest we send up rays of impurity."

Kahana, p. 311.

3. Souls in Holiness

Said the Radomsker: "We read (Exodus 1:6-7): 'And Joseph died, and all his brethren and all that generation. And the children of Israel were fruitful and increased abundantly.' A soul, usually, does not wish to descend to earth in a body, inasmuch as it may easily become corrupted and lose its purity. But when the souls observed an entire generation of souls ascend to Heaven after departing their bodies in increased purity and holiness, a multitude of them petitioned the Lord for permission to enter bodies and gain the opportunity to become holier."

O. S., p. 31.

4. Be Ready

Rabbi Schmelke of Nikolsburg said: "We read: 'Speak unto all the congregation of the children of Israel, and say unto them: Ye shall be holy, for I, the Lord your God, am holy' (Lev. 19:2). I shall give to the word: 'Kadosh' its other meaning: 'to be ready,' and will explain the verse thus: 'Ye shall make yourself ready to

receive My Laws (enumerated further in the Section), for I, the
Lord your God, am ready to give them to you.'"

S. ha-Tov., p. 18.

5. Awakening Holiness

Said the Apter: "Holiness has the effect of awakening holiness.
It cultivates the better nature of those who observe it. We learn that
when the artists who wrought the holy objects for the Tabernacle
reported a surplus of materials, Moses did not ordain that no more
materials should be brought, but that no more work should be done.[1]
This was because the people, aroused to a sense of holiness and dedication, could not be restrained from bringing gifts as long as a holy
work was being performed."

M. Hat., p. 71.

[1] Exodus 36: 4-6.

6. The Farmer's Egg

Said the Besht: "A farmer held an egg in his hand, and mused:
'I shall place this egg under a hen; I shall raise up the chick and
it shall hatch other chicks; I will sell them, and purchase a cow
and . . .' While planning thus, he squeezed the egg and it broke
in his fingers.

"In the same fashion some people are satisfied with the sum of
holiness and knowledge they have attained, and think constantly that
they are superior to others. But they do not perceive that by doing
this, they lose even the little they have attained."

K. S. T., p. 35b.

7. Going Back

The "Yud" declared that if a man does not feel that he has advanced in holiness during the day, it is certain that he has fallen
back. He was better the day before. A man always moves; he
never stands still. If he does not advance, he retrogrades.

Nif. Yeh., p. 66.

8. The Rarity of Holiness

Said the Koretzer: "The learned are fewer in number than the
ignorant; still fewer are the righteous; fewest are those who can
truly pray. Holiness does not care to leave its heavenly abode for
this mundane world, and only a few ardent supplicants can induce it
to descend."

Nof. Tz., p. 3.

9. Our Final Aim

Said Rabbi Bunam: "Two merchants go to the Leipzig Fair.
One goes by a direct route, another by an indirect, but both reach
the same destination. Likewise, the aim of service to God is to attain
holiness, and to arrive at the point where we make God's will our
own. Hence, as long as we reach this point, it makes no difference
how long we have served the Lord. One may die young or in the

prime of life and become just as holy as one who has died in old age. We are taught by the Talmud: 'It is the same whether one does much or little, so long as he has aimed to do God's will.' " [1]

S. I., p. 92.

[1] Berakhoth, 5; Shebuoth, 15.

10. *Exit and Entrance*

Said Rabbi Bunam: "The Talmud teaches us to walk into the synagogue the width of two entrances in order that we may pray; not to stand near the door.[1] This means that we should first open our heart in order that the spirit of worldliness may make its exit; then we must open our heart again to give entrance to the spirit of holiness. After this, we may pray properly."

S. I., p. 80.

[1] Berakhoth, 8.

11. *The Deeper We Fall*

The Stretiner was discussing the worth of repentance. He said: "The Kabbalah teaches us allegorically that there are fifty regions of holiness above and fifty regions of impurity below. When a wicked man has descended to a low region in the section of impurity and there repents sincerely, he is lifted up to the region bearing the same number in the section of holiness. The deeper he has fallen, the higher he ascends through repentance, as we say in the New Year Hymn: 'Our return from afar causes us to ascend His Holy Mountain.' "

E. Tz., p. 139.

72. HOLINESS, SPARKS OF

1. *The Diamond*

The Riziner explained thus the verse (Exodus 10:23): "But all the children of Israel had light in their dwellings." "Each one of us possesses a Holy Spark, but not every one exhibits it to the best advantage. It is like the diamond which cannot cast its luster if buried in the earth. But when disclosed in its appropriate setting, there is light, as from a diamond, in each one of us."

E. O., p. 137.

2. *Sparks of Holiness*

The Mezeritzer explained that the Zaddik acts as the seed of the world. The seed when planted draws its sustenance from the soil and brings forth fruit. Likewise the Zaddik draws forth the holy sparks from every soul and brings them on high as an offering to the Creator.[1]

Dubnow, p. 91.

[1] See "Sayings of the Baal-Shem-Tov," collected by Martin Buber, translated from the German by Clifton P. Fadiman, *Menorah Journal*, xvii, p. 56 ff.

3. The Self-Limitation of God

Said the Mezeritzer: "Were it not for God's self-limitation, creation would not have been possible, and His Divinity would be unknown. It is like a father who places limitations upon his intelligence and descends to the understanding of his small child, when through his love, he wishes to speak with him. In this fashion God limited Himself in order that He might be known in His love for His creatures.

2. There are sparks of holiness in everything, and it is they which constitute the spiritual life.

3. The holy sparks yearn to cleave unto man's intellect.

4. It is the duty of man to restore the holy sparks to their Source. By this act a man may enter the palace of the Source of Sources.

5. A man's conscience troubles him only when he commits a serious offense. This shows that the holy spark is most powerful in the greatest sinner, and compels him to repent speedily with complete sincerity."

T. M. M., pp. 35-42.

4. Nature and Its Sparks

Said the Medzibozer: "The Lord placed sparks of holiness within everything in nature, whether composed of organic or inorganic matter. It is His will that man bring forth these holy sparks by his holy deeds and elevate them to their Source.

"It is for this reason that man may eat the flesh of living beings as well as the food of growing plants. By reciting grace over them, he raises them upwards.

"But how can holy sparks be brought forth from bitter and inedible matter in nature? This is done by their use as medicine for the sick. If the ill man is worthy, he accomplishes this purpose, and is cured of his ailment."

Butz. D., p. 22.

5. The Torah's Clues

Said the Besht: "A king dropped a gem out of his ring, and gave his favorite son a clue as to its whereabouts. Thus he might show his diligence and sagacity in pleasing his father. Likewise, God has dropped sparks of holiness upon the world. Through His Torah He gives Israel clues regarding the places they have fallen on earth, so that Israel may return them to Him."

K. S. T., p. 14b.

6. The Altar In Our Heart

Said the Besht: "The Torah commands us: 'Fire shall be kept burning upon the altar continually; it shall not go out' (Levit. 6:6).

Our heart is the altar. In every occupation let a spark of the holy fire remain within you, so that you may fan it into a flame."

K. S. T., p. 16a.

7. Why Was He Marooned?

The Koretzer had ten "Batlanim" (idlers, subsidized for study) in his synagogue, to each of whom he gave a ruble a week for the sustenance of their families. A certain Rabbi Jacob distributed the money. Once he discovered that he had been given only nine rubles, and when he sought an explanation from the Koretzer, the latter declined to give the reason. Rabbi Jacob distributed the nine thalers, but had nothing left for his own family. Stricken by melancholy thoughts not only on behalf of his household, but also lest the Koretzer had found him wanting, Rabbi Jacob saw before him a flour-merchant. The merchant said: "I hear that you are in dire distress; take some sacks of flour, and sell them in the market." Jacob sold them to good advantage, and soon opened a food and fruit store where he prospered.

The local Count wished to purchase oranges for a celebration inasmuch as they were a rarity in this region of the Ukraine. The Count's servant bought them from Jacob who had just received a shipment from Palestine. The Count was delighted and visited the store in person. Observing the admirably displayed goods, he said to its owner: "Leave your store in the care of your family, and I will make you attendant-in-chief of all my estates."

Jacob's diligence and integrity continued to please the Count, and he said to him: "I have no children, and I wish a monument of life-size to be placed at my tomb. I need large-size pearls for the eyes. These can be purchased only in India; go there for me, and buy them." Jacob asked for three days to consider, and went to the Koretzer for counsel. He left several hundred thalers for the Rabbi, but the latter refused to see him, and he was forced to go on his journey without his Master's advice.

Since only silver bars were acceptable money in India, Jacob arranged that they be shipped in large cases. The Count's servants loaded these on the ship at Odessa and returned home. The captain of the vessel plotted to steal Jacob's baggage, which he surmised was valuable. When the ship stopped for water at an island, he invited the passengers to go ashore, and return at three whistles. Jacob, however, was told to return at six whistles. In this way, the captain left without him. In great peril, he was forced to keep himself alive by eating wild fruits and berries. Eventually he was taken off by a passing ship.

When he returned penniless to Koretz he learned that the Count had died, and that a fire had destroyed all his possessions. Jacob went directly to the Koretzer, and received a hearty welcome. The Rabbi said: "There were sparks of holiness on the island which it was necessary for a good Jew to restore to their source. Regret not the opportunity granted you, for you served the Lord well. Here are your last donations to me; marry off your daughter, and come back to me as my chief 'Batlan.' " [1]

Tif. Z., pp. 51-3.

[1] This tale illustrates the type of story with which the Hasidim of all classes regaled themselves. They combine adventure, fantasy, moral preachment, and other elements popular with the people.

73. HOLY MEDITATION IN SOLITUDE

1. Sayings of the Bratzlaver

"1. Every man should devote much time to meditation between his Creator and himself. He should judge himself and determine whether his actions are correct, and whether they are appropriate before the Lord Who has granted him life, and Who is gracious to him every moment. If he finds that he has acted properly, he should fear no one—no officials, no robbers, no beasts—and nothing in the universe except the Lord. When he learns this, he will have attained, first: perfection in the study of the Torah and in meekness; and second, perfect worship wherein all material considerations are forgotten; worship which asks for no personal benefits, and which prompts one to forget his very existence.

2. He who meditates in solitude before God receives divine inspiration.

3. He who is pure of heart will find new thoughts and new phrases every time he meditates in solitude.

4. A man's longing and intense desire to cast away any evil within himself and to attain goodness recreates his soul in pure goodness. It should be expressed in words in order to give it actual and true expression.

5. Meditation before God brings forth the holy spark that is found in every Jew; it lights up his heart, and thereby deprives him of all desire for evil.

6. The chief object of meditation is truthful confession of a man's every act, and the cultivation of a sense of contrition for his sins.

7. Meditation and prayer before God is particularly efficacious in grassy fields and amid the trees, since a man's soul is thereby strengthened, as if every blade of grass and every plant united with him in prayer.

8. In meditation a man may discuss his tribulations with God; he may excuse himself for his misdeeds and implore the Lord to grant him his desire to approach nearer to God. A man's offenses separate him from his Maker.

9. It is impossible to be a good Jew without devoting each day a portion of the time to commune with the Lord in solitude, and to have a conversation from the heart with Him.

10. Even though a man may feel he cannot concentrate adequately upon the theme of his meditation, he should nevertheless continue to express his thoughts in words. Words are like water which falls continually upon a rock until it breaks it through. In similar fashion they will break through a man's flinty heart.

11. A man should say every day in his meditation: 'I shall commence today to cleave unto Thee, O Lord.' No man can remain in the same position without change, and hence in the achievement of goodness we must frequently alter our place. Whether he falls back or moves forward, he will at least have commenced afresh.

12. In true meditation a man cries to the Lord like a child to his father who is about to take his departure. There is no sadness in this weeping—only longing and yearning."

L. E. H., pp. 29-32.

74. THE HOLYDAYS

1. The Knot

Said the Alexanderer Rabbi: "The Psalmist in 118:27 orders us: 'Bind the feast with cords.' [1] The meaning of this phrase is as follows: Unless the tailor knots the thread, his labor is in vain. Likewise unless we strive to secure in our minds the lessons learned during the holydays, the Rabbi's work is for naught."

S. S. K., i, 103.

[1] The phrase is translated also: "Order the festival procession with boughs."

2. The Second Day

The Libavitzer Rabbi said: "On the first day of the Festival, God invites us to observe a day of rejoicing; on the second day, we invite the Lord to rejoice with us. The first day God commanded us to observe; the second day we instituted ourselves."

S. S. K., v, 70.

3. The Reconciliation

The Koznitzer Maggid told the "Yud" that he felt a greater sense of holiness on the second day of a "Yom Tov" than on the first day, and asked him to explain the reason.

The "Yud" replied: "When a bride has displeased her bridegroom she seeks reconciliation with him by proving that she desires his companionship intensely, and is loath for him to leave her presence. Consequently the bridegroom's love is strengthened.

"Exile is a symbol of God's wrath against Israel. Hence when the Jews in Exile devote an extra day to God and keep it holy, they effect a reconciliation between the 'Bride of Israel' and the 'Holy Bridegroom,' thereby gaining a stronger manifestation of God's love for Israel."

N. H. K., p. 10.

4. The Second Instruction

Said the Koznitzer Maggid: "A festival is called 'a holy convocation' [1] or 'a calling for holiness.' In Palestine the holiness is brought down in one day; in Exile, two days are required. It is as a child who does not understand his teacher's instruction the first time, and needs to be taught again."

[1] Singer, p. 228.

Tif. Yeh., p. 10.

5. Adapting our Services

Said the Medzibozer: "During the Holydays of Tishri we serve the Lord with our entire body. On Rosh Ha-Shanah our Service is with our brain, since memorial is within the mind; on Yom Kippur, with our heart, since fasting weakens the heart most; on Sukkoth with our hands, since we hold the Lulav; on the Rejoicing of the Law with our feet, since it is customary then to dance and march."

Butz. D., p. 24.

75. HONORS, DISLIKE OF

1. Twice-Told Honors

When Rabbi Schmelke came to Nikolsburg to assume his duties as Rabbi, he locked himself in a room and began to pace back and forth. One of the welcoming party overheard him repeating again and again the many forms of greeting he anticipated. When the welcome was concluded, the man confessed that he had overheard Rabbi Schmelke, and inquired if the Rabbi would explain his odd action.

Rabbi Schmelke said: "I dislike intensely honors which tend to self-pride; therefore I rehearsed to myself all the words of welcome. No one appreciates self-praise, and after becoming accustomed to these words of acclaim by frequent repetition, I no longer felt pride in hearing these very phrases uttered by the committee of welcome.

"It is in this fashion that I understand the saying in the 'Ethics of the Fathers': [1] 'May the honor of another be as dear to you as your own honor.' Just as one does not care for the honor he pays to himself, so he should not care for the honor which another pays to him."

[1] 2:15; Singer, p. 189

S. ha-Tov, p. 69.

2. Distasteful Honors

When Rabbi Phineas Hurwitz came to Frankfurt a/M., to take up the post of Rabbi, he received an overpowering welcome. Thousands of people surrounded his carriage. A friend asked how he felt in this hour of triumph. The Rabbi replied: "I imagined that I was a corpse, being borne to the cemetery in the company of multitudes attending the funeral."

S. ha-Tov, p. 86.

3. In the Same Profession

Rabbi Aaron Leib Premislaner went to pay a visit to Rabbi Mendel Rimanover. This became known and some Hasidim went out on the highway to meet him. When he noticed them from afar on his high seat, he speedily changed his clothes with the driver, in order to avoid the undesired honor. His noble mien, however, betrayed him to Rabbi Naftali Ropshitzer, one of the welcoming party. Therefore, while the others shook hands with the supposed Rabbi, he gave greeting to the real Rabbi, and said laughingly: "A thief cannot deceive another one in the same profession."

O. H., p. 13.

4. "Where is this Rabbi?"

The Warden of a Rabbi persuaded him to travel to a certain town where his name was famous, in order to gather donations for his causes. It was necessary to arrange this in secret, inasmuch as the Rabbi would otherwise have refused. When the Rabbi's carriage was a short distance from the city, the Warden halted it on the pretext of making repairs, and sent the driver ahead to announce the coming of the Rabbi.

The townspeople in great throngs hurried out to welcome the Rabbi. Seeing the oncoming multitude, the Rabbi asked the reason. The Warden answered: "They have come out to welcome the Rabbi."

The Rabbi sprang out of his carriage, and hurrying to meet the crowds, shouted:

"Let me join you in the good deed of paying honor to a learned man. Where is this Rabbi?" [1]

[1] Compare 34:3; see Judah Steinberg, in his *Sichoth Hasidim*, pp. 3-5.

5. The Bratzlaver on "Honors"

A.

"1. A man should diminish honors to himself, and strive to increase the honor of the Lord.

2. Do not pursue honors; rather flee from them. Then God will approve your honors, and people will not investigate or question whether you deserve your honors.

3. Through a recognition that your honors are as nothing compared to the glory of the Lord, you will attain understanding of the profundity of the Torah.

4. Through bringing nearer to God those who are far from Him, you will increase the glory of God.

5. You will attain honors by honoring those who fear God.

6. Accept no position of honor unless your faith is perfect. If you are superstitious, you have an imperfect faith in God.

7. The Lord permits no durable leadership to those who accept a position of honor on the plea of reforming the community. The reformer's true desire is rather to attain the honor.

8. Leadership cannot be lasting without respect for wise men.

9. Be careful to give due honor to the sons of the lower classes who engage in the study of the Torah. Your honoring of them will serve to encourage them and bring forth their best abilities.

10. There are so-called leaders versed only in superficialities and outward values. They cannot lead even themselves, and yet their evil impulse prompts them to lead others. They are not so much to be blamed as those who vote for them and support them. These adherents will be called upon eventually to give an accounting for their action.

11. The unworthy leader causes disrespect for Jewish decisions and promotes Jewish migration to new settlements. This is like unto the exile from Palestine, since every place that has been a Jewish settlement for a long time has become in a sense a 'Land of Israel.'

12. The worthy leader causes non-Jews to respect Jewish decisions, and achieves additional holiness for his place of residence.

13. Honor is felt by the soul; therefore place it to holy use, and your soul will increase in holiness.

14. When leadership comes to a worthy man, he is certain to be faced with opposition at the commencement of his term of service.

15. Through charity one may preserve the holiness of honors.

16. One who is well-known is compelled to bear the tribulations of many.

17. When leaders become self-satisfied, the Lord Himself inaugurates opposition to them.

18. One who desires honors is unwise, since honors are nets stretched out to ensnare the soul of men.

19. One who stresses his dignity is far from wisdom.

20. The earnest leader rises to the highest honors.

21. Leadership interferes with inspiration.

22. Holy leadership depends upon mercy. The leader must know, however, whom and how to pity. Murderers, thieves and the thoroughly wicked deserve no compassion. The chief point of compassion is to influence every one to lead a blameless life, and to guide him in it.

23. A careless leader is responsible for many crimes.

24. Envy of another's greatness and honors may lead to the loss of faith in God.

25. Proper reflection will show that honors and leadership bring more heartaches and contempt than pleasures even in this world. They are likely oftentimes to degrade the soul."

L. E. H., pp. 49-51.

B.

"1. He who creates an enlargement of God's glory receives honors.

2. Meekness brings honors.

3. The honors given to the Torah protect the donor from enemies.

4. The despised man is the one who loves falsehoods.

5. The persecuted win honors.

6. Persons who honor each other are worthy of respect."

Sef. Ham., pp. 75-77.

6. Looking Backwards

A man complained to Rabbi Bunam: "The Talmud [1] tells us that when a man runs away from honors, honors run after him. Now I have run away from honors, but honors do not pursue me."

"The reason," explained the Rabbi, "is that you keep on looking backwards."

S. I., p. 57.

[1] Erubin, 13a; Tanchuma, See Wayyikra.

7. Pride in Honors

Said the Koretzer: "If a man honors you, he considers himself less important than you at the moment, and he thereby becomes a better man than you. The more he honors you, the more he actually grows at your expense. How then can you feel pride at being showered with honors?"

Nof. Tz., p. 3.

8. The Unselfish Man

Said the Koretzer: "Fame is constantly seeking a man with whom she can abide, but she avoids a man full of pride and selfishness. Upon the latter she cannot descend, inasmuch as she cannot tolerate a competitor. She seeks rather the man who is unselfish and modest, for there she can rule supreme."

M. P., p. 11.

9. Wait Not for Insistence

Said the Rimanover: "If thou art a person of importance and people invite thee to enter or leave first, and thou art aware this will be insisted on, accept the honor at once without declining it. Do not permit thy thoughts to wander high and low on paths of pride and the desire for honor. Accept the proferred honor immediately and let not thy mind dwell upon it."

Em. L., p. 47.

10. Pursued by Honors

Rabbi Nehemiah, son of the "Yud" said: "I heard from the Riziner an explanation of the statement in the Talmud that when one runs away from fame, honors pursue him (Erubin 13a). It would

seem more just that God should fulfil the desire of them that fear
him (Psalm 145:10), and not cause undesired honors to pursue the
God-fearing man. The Riziner explained that if a man still needs
to run away from honors, he is clearly fearful that honors will make
him arrogant and haughty, and he is therefore not truly a God-fearing man. Honors pursue him for the discipline of his character, so
that no amount of honors can weaken his humility. Then he will
no longer need to flee from them."

Tif. B., p. 8.

11. Increasing and Decreasing Honors

Said the Savraner Rabbi, commenting upon the statement: "He
who enters a city should pray twice: once when he enters and once
when he leaves" (Berakhoth 54): "When it becomes known that a
famous Rabbi is about to visit a city, a small delegation is despatched
to welcome him while he is yet far from his destination. A larger
committee awaits him nearer the city, and a multitude honors him at
the city gate. When he departs the reverse occurs. A crowd bids
him farewell at the city gate; a smaller group accompanies him a few
miles, and a still smaller company remains with him for a distance.
"The Talmud teaches us that the Rabbi should pray for ability to
accept with humility both the ever-increasing honors accorded him
at his arrival and the ever-decreasing honors tendered him at his
departure."

E. A., p. 32.

76. HOSPITALITY

1. Assurance to the Guest

A famous Rabbi chanced to pass through Voydislav where Rabbi
Bunam's father dwelt. Being told of the boy, Bunam's, excellence in
studies, he stopped in to visit him, and asked him to say something
new on the proper conduct of life. The young Bunam replied:
"When a guest comes, the host should show him his bed chamber,
before inviting him to the meal, so that he may enjoy his food without anxiety regarding a place to rest his head."

S. S. K., i, 6.

2. Accepting Hospitality from Sinners

The Apter Rabbi was scheduled once to sojourn in a town for a
few days. The town possessed two men of wealth, and both volun-
teered to welcome the Rabbi. One was known to be very pious, but
he demanded excessive respect and homage, being a haughty and
self-willed man. The other magnate was less pious, and there were
grave suspicions regarding his moral conduct. He was, however,
unselfish, pleasant of manner, and modest.
The Rabbi heard of these two men, and elected to go to the

sinner's home. He explained his choice thus: "We read in the Talmud that the Lord remarks concerning the proud man: 'I and he cannot abide together in the world.'[1] If the Lord is out of place in the home of the haughty, neither can I remain with him. The other may be a great sinner, but we read (Leviticus 16: 16) : 'God[2] abideth among them in the midst of their uncleanness.' If it is agreeable to the Lord to abide amid uncleanness, it surely must be permissible for me."

E. O., p. 118.
(Bl., Gem., p. 225.)

[1] Sotah, 5a.   [2] Yoma, 56b.

3. Service Without Payment

The Berditschever insisted upon serving his guests himself. He would bring them food and prepare their beds for them. When asked why he did not leave these duties to his servant, he responded:

"Hospitality is an excellent deed when performed without payment. The servant would do it for pay, and the intrinsic kindness of the good deed would be lost."

N. B. L., p. 14.

4. The Open Door

The Gerer discussed Genesis 18: 1: "And the Lord appeared unto him, and he, Abraham, was sitting at the open door of his tent." He said: "Abraham kept an open door as a standing invitation to all to enter that they might learn the true and pure conception of the Creator. They might also learn the pathway of rectitude, free from envy, pride and haughtiness, that leads to the perfection of the spirit."

S. S. K., iii, 45.

5. Why He Hid Himself

The Ropshitzer came to a wealthy Jew, known to be a miser, for a donation to a worthy cause. The miser, hearing the coach halt near his home, concealed himself. The Rabbi observed him stealing out to the barn and instructed his Warden to summon him. When the owner appeared, he was deeply ashamed of himself, and gave a good-sized donation. The Ropshitzer remarked:

"The Talmud says that welcoming guests is a greater deed than welcoming the Shekinah.[1] You have, therefore, acted quite properly. When the Lord appeared for the first time to Moses, the Prophet hid his face only.[2] When we appeared, however, you concealed your entire body beneath the hay in the barn."

O. N., p. 58.

[1] Sabbath, 127.   [2] Exodus 3: 6.

6. A Craving for Praise

There was once a hospitable man who, however, was accustomed to say: "Tell me, honored guest, am I not hospitable?" The Besht sent to him his disciple, Zeev Kitzes. When the host made the usual inquiry, Rabbi Zeev replied: "We shall see."

The host fell asleep, and Rabbi Zeev pressed his finger against the sleeper's forehead. The host then dreamed that a high governmental official visited him, and after drinking his wine, fell dead. He ran away and became a water-carrier. While carrying the heavy pails, he stumbled and broke his leg. The imagined pain caused the man to awaken. He related the dream to Rabbi Zeev, who informed him that he, the host, had been privileged to behold his fate if he continued to feed the Satan by his craving for praise regarding his hospitality. The host promised to discontinue this unpleasant habit.

M. H. H., p. 44.

7. The Limits of Hospitality

The Przevorsker Rabbi was accustomed to give his guests two glasses of wine with meals. When wine became more expensive he gave only one glass to each guest. He then dreamed that Elijah rebuked him for this. He retorted: "But this act is only a straw in the Mitzwah of hospitality." "Yes," replied Elijah, "but nevertheless it causes a flaw in the good deed."

A similar story is told of Rabbi Leib Dimimles of Lantzut. His house was open to guests and they were free to eat and drink their fill. Once he discovered a guest lying drunk in the gutter, and he gave orders to furnish him no more wine. From this time onward, his success began to lessen. When he complained to his brother-in-law, the Lubliner, the latter said: "God blessed you when your hospitality was without limits. Now that you have placed boundaries on it, even in the case of one person, your efforts meet with less success. Go, then, and ask for the man's pardon, and treat him as before."

D. E. M. R., p. 14.

8. Eating One's Fill

Said the Medzibozer in comment on the verse: "The righteous eateth to the satisfying of his desire; but the belly of the wicked shall want" (Proverbs 13:25): "What virtue is there in eating one's fill? The meaning is this: 'When a guest arrives at the Zaddik's home, the latter invites him to eat. Even though he himself may have eaten, he partakes of food in order that his guest may do so also. But when a guest comes to the home of a wicked person, even though the host may also be hungry, he suffers pangs of hunger rather than invite his guest to eat with him.'"

Butz. D., p. 8.

9. Hospitality and the Shekinah

Referring to the Talmudical saying that hospitality is greater than welcoming the Shekinah,[1] a Rabbi said: "Were this not so, a man could refuse hospitality on the pretext that the wayfarers may speak

[1] Sabbath, 127.

slander of some persons, thereby causing the departure of the She-kinah. Or, in the event a man's wife is opposed to the extra trouble of caring for passers-by, the husband could excuse himself for his failure not to welcome strangers in his home, inasmuch as the Divine Presence cannot abide where man and wife quarrel.[2] But since hospitality is greater, a man should practice it, even though his guests may be guilty of tale-bearing, and even if his wife may quarrel with him for his generosity."

P. v. K., p. 31a.

[2] Kiddushin 30, in a different version.

77. HOST AND HONORS FOR GUEST

1. A Friendly Visit

The Amshinover was asked: "According to the Talmud [1] the three angels who came to visit Abraham [2] after his circumcision each had a mission, one to save Lot, one to foretell the birth of Isaac, and one to heal Abraham. But since the Lord appeared to Abraham at the same time, why did not the Lord Himself heal him?"

The Rabbi responded with a parable: "A king had great affection and respect for his Premier. Instead of summoning him always to the royal palace for consultations, he often paid the Premier the honor of calling on him at home. Later he began to show him even greater honor: he visited him as a guest without discussing affairs of state.

"In the same fashion, God wished to show Abraham the greatest honor. Therefore He visited him in his sickness as a friend, not on a 'professional visit.' Hence the duty to heal Abraham was assigned to an angel."

Ohel Isaac, p. 6.

[1] Baba Metzia, 86b.
[2] Genesis 18:2.

2. Unwelcome Honors

The Gerer Rabbi was present at a function in the home of a wealthy Hasid. The host wished to bestow a certain honor on his distinguished guest, but the Rabbi declined it.

The host remarked: "But Rabbi, the Talmud [1] teaches that it is good manners for the guest not to contradict his host."

The Rabbi replied: "But the Talmud adds the words: 'except when he tells you to leave.' We are also taught [2] that jealousy, desire and honor compel a man to 'leave the world.' Thus when the host seeks to force honors upon his guest, the latter is entitled to decline them."

S. S. K., ii, 59.

[1] Pesachim, 86.
[2] Ethics of the Fathers 4:28; Singer, p. 198.

3. *"For Himself in the World to Come"*

The Neshchizer Rabbi related the following: "Late at night a man came to the home of Rabbi Liber of Berditschev and asked for lodging. Rabbi Liber extended to him a gracious welcome and began to arrange a bed for the guest. The man asked him: 'Why do you trouble yourself to arrange my bed?' "

Rabbi Liber replied: "It is not for your sake, but for my own that I am doing this."

D. E. M. R., p. 37.

4. *Hospitality for Money*

The Vorker admired the courtesy with which an innkeeper treated his paying guests and praised him. "But he does it for money," he was told. "Surely," was his answer. "He takes money in order that he may be able to continue his admirable conduct; but the warmth of his welcome and the loving care he gives are evidence that he has love in his heart for his guests."

D. Z., p. 55.

78. HUMILITY

1. *The Injunction to be Humble*

"To walk in true humility is the first duty of every Hasid. It is said in Avoth 5:22: 'A good eye, an humble mind and a lowly spirit are the tokens of the disciples of our father, Abraham.' [1] Rabbi Joshua ben Levi [2] set humility above all else, as the surest means of guarding against the evil tongue. The Law abideth only with the meek. [3] 'Be not, like the ceiling, out of reach, but like the threshold that is trodden upon by everyone without stirring.' [4] If offended, seek not satisfaction, but bear with offense in silent humility. [5] Our Ancients said: 'If all the world proclaims you a Zaddik, think of yourself as one of the wicked.' [6] For what says the Zohar: 'Whoever thinks of himself as of small account in this world, will be one of the great in the world to come.' Rabbi Elimelech of Lizensk said: 'The top of the ladder leading to perfection is humility. He who has it, has everything else.'

"Rabbi Aaron of Starasola was once asked: how can man attain humility? Said he: 'By fulfilment of the commandments,' and added a parable.

" 'A tree rich in fruits is dragged to earth by its fruits, and its branches hang downward. But a branch that is barren and withered, stands upright without bending.'

[1] Singer, p. 203.
[2] Avodah Zarah, 20.
[3] Taanith, 7.
[4] Aboth D'Rabbi Nathan, 26:6.
[5] Derekh Eretz Zuta, 2.
[6] Niddah, 30.

"'Humility,' said the Besht, 'leadeth forth to love of Man and love of God, for the truly humble in heart does not feel it a hardship to love one of the wicked, unthinking: for all his wickedness, he is better than I am.'

"It is told of Rabbi Meier of Premislan that a Hasid once came to him, boasting in his pride of being on the way to the Holy Land. The Rabbi chided him, saying: 'What, impudent of face, wilt thou take precedence of the Messiah?' And thus he plucked the root of haughtiness out of his heart."

Bl., Pr., pp. 32-3.

2. Worthy To Obey

"Shall men, then, always walk in meekness? Not so, say the Zaddikim. There are moments when haughtiness becomes a duty. When the Evil Inclination approaches, whispering in the ear: 'You are unworthy to fulfill the Law,' say: 'I am worthy.'"

Bl., Gem., p. 84.

3. True and False Humility

The Belzer said: "There is a true and a false humility. The falsely humble believes himself and all others to be unworthy. He is worse than the one who believes himself and all others to be worthy. The truly humble man is he who feels sure that he is unworthy, but that every one else is worthier than himself."

D. S., p. 50.

4. The Humility of Saul

Said the Gerer Rabbi: "Every virtue is subject to the Lord's command. King Saul hid himself among the vessels from a sense of humility,[1] but the Lord had already commanded him to rule over Israel. Hence his humbleness was out of place, and for this reason his reign was unsuccessful."

S. S. K., i, 76.

[1] I Kings 10:22.

5. Dignity and Humility

The Kotzker Rabbi explained: "There are times when the leader must display dignity in order that the rank and file of the people may have the proper respect for him. This seeming pride, however, must be like an outer garment, and not for a moment must it subdue the humility of his inmost heart. We learn this from the verse (Psalm 93:1): 'The Lord reigneth; He is clothed in dignity.'[1] From this we learn that pride has its place only on the outside, never within."

S. S. K., iv, 21.

[1] "Geuth" means "Majesty, Dignity."

6. God's Nearness to the Lowly

The Strelisker Rabbi said: "We read in Psalm (139:8): 'If I ascend up into heaven, Thou art there; if I make my bed in the netherworld, behold, Thou art there.' [1] We may explain this verse as follows: 'If I possess inner pride and believe myself to be high in virtue and godliness, then this signifies seeing the Lord from a distance. But when I am low in my own esteem and feel myself to be undeserving, then I behold Him near.' "

O. Y., p. 19.

[1] "Hinekha" means "Thou art near; Thou art there."

7. The Meek Zaddikim

The Kobriner explained the verse (Psalm 149:4): "For the Lord taketh pleasure (in aiding) His people; He adorneth the meek with salvation." "Though all salvation is from the Lord," said the Rabbi, "yet it is His wish to manifest it through the Zaddikim, who are meek in spirit, in order to adorn them with the respect of ordinary members of the people."

O. Y., p. 110.

8. Housing the Torah With Humility

The Gerer Rabbi discoursed on the large form of the letter "Beth" which begins the Torah, and he said: " 'Beth' means a house, and the unusual form of the 'Beth' is to teach us to house the Torah within us with proper humility. One who feels proud of his learning is transgressing the commandment: 'Thou shalt not bring an abomination into thy house' " (Deut. 7:26).

S. S. K., iii, 37.

9. More Particular than God?

The Sassover once gave his last coin to a man of evil reputation. His students reproached him for it. Whereupon he replied: "Shall I be more particular than God, who gave the coin to me?"

Reflex, May, 1929, p. 67.

10. In Humble Company

Rabbi Manele was heard to say during the Sabbath morning prayer: "Through the mouth of the upright Thou shalt be praised" [1] —"Manele is not among them." "And by the words of the righteous Thou shalt be blessed"; "Manele is not of them."

"And by the tongue of the pious Thou shalt be extolled"; "Manele is not there."

"And in the midst of the holy ones, Thou shalt be hallowed"; "Manele is not of these."

"And in the assemblies of the tens of thousands of Thy people, the House of Israel, Thy name shall be glorified with song, O our King, in every generation." "One of these is Manele."

The Kobriner added: "Only a holy man like Manele could include himself among the people of God, but we are even too un-

[1] Singer, p. 63.

worthy for this. We must continue the prayer to find our place. 'For such is the duty of all created beings before Thee to thank Thee, etc.' It is among them that we belong, since we are created beings, and therefore, it is also our duty to thank and praise the Lord."

O. Y., p. 129.

11. The Good-For-Nothing

Rabbi Elimelech was accustomed to sit under the trees in the woods and allow his body to be bitten by ants. His body became so wan and bloodless that it no longer attracted the ants, and they let him be. "Melech, Melech, you good-for-nothing," he said, "even the ants no longer care for you."

Bl., Pr., p. 99.

12. Without Protest

Once Rabbi Zalman of Ladi, the "Rav," visited a Rabbi who belonged to the Mithnagedim. The Rabbi related to him that he had placed under the chair on which he sat the volume "Noam Elimelech," written by Rabbi Elimelech.

"What sort of a man is he?" asked the Mithnaged.

"He is the following sort of a man: even if you would place him under the chair on which you were sitting," said the "Rav," "he would be silent, and speak no word in protest."

M. D., p. 46.

13. Treading the Earth Underfoot

Rabbi Sussya, of Anipol, once turned earthward and said: "Earth, earth, thou art of better make than I, and yet I am treading thee underfoot. But softly, yet a while, and I will lie below thee, thy humble servant."

D. E. M. R., p. 20.

14. Accepting Reproof

Said the Koretzer: "He who accepts reproof is greater than the one who reproves him. The latter may do so because he imagines himself better than ordinary persons, and is thereby guilty of pride.

"The former, however, by his acceptance, demonstrates a spirit of humility, and the Lord loves the companionship of the meek."

E. O., p. 41.

15. "Be Very Humble"

Rabbi Nahum Tzernobiler visited a town to deliver a discourse. He looked about the synagogue and waited. Soon a young man, learned, rich and immensely proud of his accomplishments as a singer, entered the synagogue. Immediately the Rabbi began to recite the phrase in the Mishnah [1]: "Rabbi Levitas said: 'Be very, very humble.'" Rabbi Nahum repeated these words again and again to the great astonishment of those present. Finally the proud young

[1] Ethics of the Fathers, 4:4; Singer, p. 195.

man walked over to the preacher and begged for instruction in the conquest of his pride. He used to say that henceforth the Rabbi's reproof sounded unceasingly in his ears.

Beth Phineas, pp. 41-2.

16. Prayer With Humility

The Riziner used as a text (Exodus 20:23): "Neither shalt thou go up by steps unto Mine altar, that thy nakedness be not uncovered thereon." "The House of Prayer," said the Rabbi, "represents the altar. The chief requisite when bringing an offering upon the altar or when praying, is to be contrite of heart, in a humble mood, and full of regret at one's shortcomings. We are forbidden to go up to pray in a frivolous mood, lest our evil thoughts confuse our words of supplication. There is a hint of this in the little letter 'Aleph' in the word 'Way-yikra,'[1] 'and He called to Moses,' because Moses possessed humility."

N. I., p. 56.

[1] Lev. 1:1.

17. The Song of the Lowly

On a Sabbath the Kobriner was chanting the Hymn of Glory.[1] When he came to the verse: "My praise, may it be a crown unto Thy head; and my prayer, may it be set before Thee as holy incense," the Rabbi exclaimed: "O Lord, how utterly undeserving am I, and how without merit my prayer, that they should be a crown unto Thee!"

Then he heard the congregation chant the next verse: "May the song of the lowly be as precious in Thine eyes as the song sung at Thine offerings."

"Yes," the Rabbi continued, "no matter how lowly we are, we implore that our singing may be precious in the eyes of the Lord."

O. Y., p. 131.

[1] Singer, pp. 78-80.

18. The Hour Strikes

A man came to the Lekhivitzer and besought him to teach him humility. At the very moment he was speaking, the clock struck the hour.

The Rabbi commented: "From the sound of the clock, striking the hour, we can receive ample instruction regarding the submission of the heart. Each one of us should ask himself: 'Another hour of my life has departed; have I accomplished any improvement of my soul within it?'"

O. Y., p. 40.

19. Truth, Humility and Love

Rabbi Raphael Bershider used to say: "I learned from my Master that if I will walk with Truth, my soul will instruct me, and I shall need no other teacher."

He also said: "He who wishes truly to live should also wish to be more insignificant than anyone else."

The Bershider heard his wife scolding her maid. He rebuked her, saying: "You have no right to give pain to a Jewess. A child of Israel is very, very precious."

M. P., p. 42.

20. The Lowliness of the Bershider

The Bershider refused to accept any dictate involving dignity if it ran counter to his sense of lowliness. He dressed with exceeding plainness; he stood in the synagogue behind the door; he would be pleased if he made a mistake in his prayers on behalf of the congregation, since this demeaned his dignity. He never summoned anyone to his home, but walked instead to those whom he wished to see. He bought vegetables himself in the market-place, and smiled at those who thought it undignified.

M. P., p. 43.

21. Envying the Water-Carrier

In Rabbi Raphael Bershider's house, Herschel, the Water-Carrier, would often come with fresh water for the Rabbi. The latter once remarked to his wife: "I tremble before the worthiness of Herschel. When he enters with his pails, he feels as the very dust of the earth. When will I be able to attain such lowliness of spirit?"

M. P., p. 42.

22. The Deserving Rebbe

A young Rabbi came to visit the Alexanderer Rabbi. The latter expressed surprise and said: "Were I in your place I would not have used valuable time to visit an insignificant Rabbi like myself."

The visitor answered: "Whom else shall Hasidim recognize as their Rebbe, if not one who holds himself to be undeserving to be one?"

T. T., p. 22.

23. The Philosopher's Counsel

Said the Besht: "A king was told that a man of humility is endowed with long life. He attired himself in old garments, took up his residence in a small hut, and forbade anyone to show reverence before him. But when he honestly examined himself, the King found himself to be prouder of his seeming humility than ever before. A philosopher thereupon remarked to him: 'Dress like a king; live like a king; allow the people to show due respect to you; but be humble in your inmost heart.'"

K. S. T., p. 13b.

24. The Divine Light

The Besht commented upon Daniel 2:22: "He knoweth what is in the darkness, and the light dwelleth with Him." He said: "He who knows himself to be insignificant, even among the uncultured and the ignorant, who live in darkness, shall have the Divine Light dwell within him."

K. S. T., p. 12b.

25. *Intentional Humility*

Said the Kotzker: "All Mitzwoth should be performed with the proper intention. There is one exception—humility."

F. U. A. O., ii, 24.

26. *The Gaon*

Rabbi Solomon of Warsaw sent a letter to a man of wealth in Kutna and addressed him as "Gaon," etc. The man was greatly surprised, and when he was in Warsaw, he visited the Rabbi to inquire the reason for this salutation. The Rabbi opened the drawer of his desk, drew forth a letter, and said: "You can see yourself that I only addressed you as people address me."

D. Z., p. 52.

27. *The Lowly and the Torah*

Said Rabbi Israel Isaac of Alexander: "We read at the conclusion of the Amidah (Singer, p. 54): 'Let my soul be unto all as the dust. Open my heart to Thy Torah.' This teaches us that the lowly alone can truly understand the Torah."

M. H. H., p. 10.

28. *Measure for Measure*

Said Rabbi Hayyim Haikel Amdurer: "We read: 'How shall Jacob stand, for he is small?' (Amos 7:2). This teaches us the following lesson: 'If Jacob possesses the knowledge that he is small, and if he subdues any sense of self-importance, he will stand. For the Lord will repay him in the same measure, and making Himself small, He will provide for him as for a son. But if Jacob holds his head high and forgets meekness, Providence, too, will hold back his abundance on High.' "

M. S. Hag., chapter 5.

29. *The Earth Teaches Us*

Rabbi Uri Strelisker said: "We are taught by our Sages (Ethics of the Fathers 2:2) that the study of the Torah is good with the way of the earth.[1] We find that for all our necessities we must thank the earth. Without the earth we have neither food nor clothing. Yet we tread upon her, dig her, spit upon her, and the earth accepts every abuse without complaint. The student of the Torah should adopt these ways of the earth. No matter how greatly his opinion is sought and esteemed, he should consider himself lowly, and should bear demeanment from anyone without complaint or anger."

E. T., p. 83.

[1] "Derekh Eretz" means "The Way of the World," "Customs," "Good Manners." Singer, p. 187.

30. *The Lord's Lowly*

Said Rabbi Bunam: "Only the lowly are able to comprehend the highness of the Lord. We read (Psalms 138:6) 'The Lord is high, and the lowly see it.'"

S. I., p. 65.

31. *Selfishness or Meekness*

Said Rabbi Bunam: "The haughty and the arrogant fill their mind with selfishness, leaving no room for holiness. The lowly and the meek, however, have adequate room for holiness, and should strive to fill their mind with it. Of what use, otherwise, is their weakness?"

S. I., p. 92.

32. *Demonstrating Goodness*

Said the Berditschever: "In the Machzor we read: 'When there is no demonstrator of goodness.' This means: 'When one thinks of himself as naught, this becomes a demonstration of his goodness.'"

O. E., p. 124.

79. HYPOCRISY AND HYPOCRITES

1. *The Soft-Spoken Enemy*

The Kobriner commented upon Psalm 10:10: "He croucheth, he boweth down, and the helpless fall into his mighty claws." In explanation he told the following fable:

"An old mouse sent out her son to search for food, but warned him to be careful of the enemy. The young mouse met a rooster and hastened back to his mother in great terror. He described the enemy as a haughty being with an upstanding red comb. 'He is no enemy of ours,' said the old mouse, and sent her son out again.

"This time he met a turkey, and was still more frightened. 'O mother,' he said, panting. 'I saw a great puffed-up being with a deadly look, ready to kill.'

"'Neither is he our enemy,' replied the mother. 'Our enemy keeps his head down like an exceedingly humble person; he is smooth and soft-spoken, friendly in appearance and acting as if he were a very kind creature. If you meet him, beware!'"[1]

O. Y., p. 79.

[1] See the story, "He Will Be a Man," 137:4.

2. *Admitting Hypocrites With Reason*

It is told that the Satan came to Rabbi Elimelech in a dream and said to him: "Do you believe you can wrest the rulership of this world from me by making many Hasidim? Behold, I make many more, and some of them are in your own fellowship."

Rabbi Elimelech, armed with a stout club, went to the House of

Study, to eject Satan's emissaries with force and arms. But when he crossed the threshold, he was afraid of falling into error by singling out the followers of the Evil One. He left all the disciples in peace, thinking it better to admit many hypocrites than to eject a single one of the righteous."

B., p. 446t.

3. The Good in a Hypocrite

Said Rabbi Eleazar of Koznitz: "No Jew is evil, not even the hypocrite. Do we not see that the outward semblance of a good Jew is pleasant in his own eyes?"

V. S., p. 41.

4. Unworthy Imitation

Said the Besht: " 'Whosoever shall make like unto that incense to smell thereof,' namely, one who imitates the true Hasidim in order that he may be known as a man of piety, 'he shall be cut off from his people' " (Exodus 30:38).

K. S. T., p. 13b.

80. IDOLS

1. Using Our Lips Improperly

The Makarover Rabbi said: "We read (Psalm 115:4-5): 'Their idols [1] are silver and gold, the work of men's hands. They have mouths,[2] but they speak not.' I will use the other meaning in Hebrew of the first word, and will interpret the verse thus: Their anxieties and sadness come from their quest of silver and gold. Why? Because they believe their wealth comes solely through the work of men's hands. They forget the Providence of God. The only use they make of their mouth is on behalf of their own needs; they take no opportunity to speak words of the Torah and of worship. Therefore God will withhold from them His blessing."

Mif. H., p. 56.

[1] The word: "Atzabehem" means "Their idols" or "Their sadness."
[2] Literally: "mouths for them"; namely, for themselves.

2. The Mitzwoth As Idols

Said the Kotzker: "The prohibition against the making of idols [1] includes within itself the prohibition against making idols out of the Mitzwoth. We should never imagine that the chief purpose of a Mitzwah is its outward form, and that its inward meaning should be subordinated. The very opposite is the position we should take."

F. U. A. O., ii, 82.

[1] Exodus 20:4.

3. Offering Fat and Blood

Said Rabbi Bunam: "We are taught by our Sages [1] that he who fasts for the sake of God is like unto one who offers to God his fat

[1] Berakhoth, 17.

and blood. It follows, therefore, that if a man abstains from food because of anger, or through a desire to be known as one who fasts much, he is thereby offering his fat and blood to a strange god."

S. I., p. 55.

81. INTEGRITY AND HONESTY

1. Dissatisfaction

The Lizensker said: "When a person becomes dissatisfied with his business or profession, it is a sure sign that he is not conducting it honestly."

N. E., p. 37.

2. Light From Decay

The Lizensker said: "Not every idea that attracts you is worthy of acceptance. Not all that glitters is gold. Remember, also, that rotted wood gives out a glow in the dark. Do not in your ignorance mistake a corrupt idea for one of worth."

M. R. T., p. 20.

3. A.B.C.D.

Two men came to the Premislaner Rabbi to ask his advice as to whether they should form a partnership. The Rabbi said to them: "Have you already drawn up a partnership contract?"

"No," was the reply.

"Then," said the Rabbi, "I shall draw it for you."

The Rabbi took a sheet of paper, and wrote down: "A.B.C.D."

When he was asked to explain it, he said:

"A—stands for Agreement.
B—stands for Blessing.
C—stands for Calumniation.
D—stands for Disaster.

"That is to say, if the partners will agree among themselves and will be honest, they will have a blessing. But should they calumniate each other, accuse each other of dishonesty and carelessness, there will be disaster." [1]

S. M., p. 35.

[1] In Hebrew the words are: Emunah; Berakhah; Geneivah; Daluth. The translation of the words is freely made.

4. Without Credentials

The Berditschever once came to a village. A Jewish butcher asked him:

"Are you a Shochet? I need one and cannot wait for the regular man."

The Rabbi answered in the affirmative. The butcher promised him additional payment for quick work. The Rabbi said:

"I will do so on condition that you loan to me twenty thalers, which I promise to return soon."

"No," said the butcher; "I cannot loan money to a man I do not know."

"You have convicted yourself as a careless Jew by the words of your own mouth," said the Rabbi. "You refuse to trust me with a sum of money, yet you are willing to trust my assertion that I am a Shochet, without asking for credentials. You might have invited an unscrupulous man to serve, who would have caused you to eat improperly slaughtered meat."

The butcher acknowledged his error, and promised to be more careful in the future.

N. B. L., p. 16.

5. The Proper Answer

The Dzikover Rabbi stopped a Jew, who was not a Hasid, and asked him what he would do if he should find a purse of money.

"I would return it to the owner, of course," was the reply.

"You have too prompt an answer," retorted the Rabbi. "I am not sure that you are sincere"

He asked another non-Hasid, who said: "I would certainly keep it, if I could do so."

"You are a wicked person; you are too ready to give up the privilege of performing a Mitzwah, even for an imaginary gain," said the Rabbi.

A Hasid of the unlearned class was next asked. "Oh, Rabbi," he exclaimed. "It would be a great temptation. I should implore the Lord to grant me strength to withstand it, and to be able to perform the Mitzwah of returning that which had been lost."

"Your answer is proper and correct," said the Rabbi. "And it is fit for a Hasid to give. Our opponents blame us for accepting unlearned persons as Hasidim. But this demonstrates the influence of Hasidic instruction, even among the unlearned."

K. E., pp. 13-14.

6. Protecting the Weak

The Sadigurer Rabbi rebuked a wholesale merchant for being too harsh in his dealing with the retailers. The merchant remarked: "Rabbi, why do you live in a city and interfere with the merchants? Why do you not live in a village, and commune in solitude with God as the Besht did?"

The Rabbi retorted: "In the time of the Besht, the robbers lived in the forests, and hence the Zaddik lived there in order by his prayers to protect the passers-by. Today, however, the robbers live in the city, and the Zaddik is compelled to live there as well, in order to protect, if he can, the weak."

F. R. H.-E., pp. 112-3.

7. A Troubled Conscience

The Magelnitzer walked to and fro one morning in his room and could not concentrate upon his prayers. Finally he summoned his servant and said: "Israel, two weeks ago we passed a dairy in our carriage, and one wheel suddenly cracked. Do you remember borrowing the dairy-owner's extra wheel, and, if so, have you returned it?"

"We have not returned it," replied the servant.

"Then do so without further delay," ordered the Rabbi.

As soon as the servant left in the carriage, the Rabbi found himself able to pray with concentration. When the servant returned, he reported that a wheel of the dairyman's team had just cracked, and if the extra wheel had not been returned to him, he would have been unable to bring the milk into town, at great loss to his trade and great discomfort to his customers.

Hith. Z., p. 69.

8. The Purse

Said the Koretzer: "If a man finds a purse with money near his doorstep, he may not argue: 'I would accomplish but a single Mitzwah by tracing the owner and returning this purse to him. On the other hand, I could perform many Mitzwoth if I should devote this money to several good causes.' Nay, the finder may not even carry the purse into his own home; he must forthwith deliver it to the proper authorities."

Nof. Tz., p. 16.

9. Aid From Heaven

A man complained to the Porissover that he was overwhelmed with debts. The Rabbi said: "From every dollar profit you make, set aside a portion towards the payment of your debts. When it is noted in Heaven that you wish to pay off your debts, you will receive Heaven's aid in doing so."

D. Z., p. 37.

10. Debts Before Donations

A man who had failed in business came before the Gastininer Rabbi, and laid on the table his "Qittel" or written request, with a donation. The Rabbi refused it, saying: "We read: 'When Israel has paid up his debts, he offered willingly.' " [1]

F. U. A. O., i, 181.

[1] Judges 5:2. The Jewish Translation has: "When men let grow their hair in Israel, when the people offer themselves willingly." The Rabbi in this tale uses the verb: "Bifroa," in its Talmudical meaning of "paying up."

82. INTERMARRIAGE

1. "A Mitzwah Draws a Mitzwah"

The Apter Rabbi related the following tale:
"Once a Jew came to a village to purchase grain. The Countess who owned the town was a widow. Meeting the Jew, who was of handsome countenance and form, she fell deeply in love with him. She persuaded him to divorce his wife, become a Christian and marry her. The Jew succumbed to the temptation, and his Christian wife gave him the title of Count.

"A few years later when the nobility were assembled in the capital to sit in the Seym (The Polish Senate) one nobleman declared that a Christian girl had disappeared in his town, and he accused the Jews of having killed her for ritual purposes. Other noblemen added similar tales and affirmed that Christian blood was in constant demand at the ceremonies of Jews. The King became enraged and issued an edict that all the Jews be banished from Poland. According to the Polish Constitution, every edict had to be signed by all members of the Seym in addition to the King. If there was one dissenter, the edict was nullified.

"The former Jew, one of the members of the Seym, placed his veto on the decree, stating that the 'Blood Accusation' was entirely without foundation in fact, notwithstanding the manifold repetitions of the accusation throughout the centuries, and despite the fact that alleged victims had been canonized by the Popes. The edict was destroyed, and the King vigorously reprimanded the nobleman who had brought the accusation.

"Since one precept when performed draws another in its train,[1] it transpired that the 'Jewish' Count repented of his life as a Christian. He consulted a Rabbi, escaped to Amsterdam, and commenced to lead the Jewish life anew. Soon after this event the Countess died; the penitent remarried his Jewish wife, and henceforth lived as a pious and loyal Jew."

P. I., pp. 7-11.

[1] Singer, p. 195, states the principle: one precept draws another. *Ethics of the Fathers,* 4:2; Singer, p. 195.

83. ISRAEL, BRIDE OF GOD

1. The Bride of Noble Birth

The Berditschever argued before the Lord as follows: "When two persons marry, one of noble but poor family, the other provides the sustenance for their livelihood. Thou, O Lord, hast taken unto Thee as a bride, Israel, descendant of noble patriarchs. It behooves Thee to provide Israel with unfailing nurture."

E. Z., p. 12.

2. *Show Us Again Thy Love*

A woman complained to the Koznitzer Maggid that her husband had ceased to love her. "When he married me," she cried, "he loved me dearly. Now his affection has turned away from me."

The Maggid lifted up his hands and exclaimed: "I have the same complaint against Thee, O Lord. When Thou didst choose Israel to be Thy bride at Sinai, Thou didst truly love her. Now it seems as if Thine affection has departed from her. Be not unto us as this woman's spouse unto her, but show us again Thy love and redeem us."

E. O., p. 80.

3. *The Ring of Betrothal*

Said the Koznitzer Maggid: "A young man presented to his promised bride a jeweled ring of betrothal. She exclaimed: 'You are leaving me, my beloved, to visit your native city; perchance you may forget me and marry another.'

"Her betrothed replied: 'As long as you wear my ring, which is priceless, I shall not lose remembrance of you or leave you. I have given you this ring as a pledge of surety.'

"In the same way, Israel says: 'My Lord hath forgotten me' (Isaiah 49:14).

"And God answers: 'As long as you keep My Torah and its commandments, I shall not abandon you. The Torah is your pledge of surety.' "[1]

E. O., p. 82.

[1] The Talmud remarks that the Torah and the literature of Israel are the love letters of God, which Israel peruses in Exile. See my poem in *"Joyful Jeremiads,"* p. 93.

4. *Undesirable Guests*

Said the Sudilkover: "When guests are invited to a wedding, the purpose is to gladden the heart of the bride and the groom. But there are always present guests who care only for their own pleasures, and who give no heed to the young couple.

"Likewise, the purpose of our life in this world is to strive for the union of God and Israel, His Bride, through the performance of good deeds and acts of holiness. But some of us are neglectful of this obligation, and concern ourselves only with our own enjoyments."

S. ha-Has., p. 312.

5. *The Rabbi's Plaint*

After his beloved wife's demise, the Belzer Rabbi was heard to express the following plaint: "Thou knowest, O Lord, that there is nothing in my power I would not have done, to bring my wife back to life, if it were possible. Yet Thou, the All-Powerful, doth not restore Thy spouse Israel, though Thou art able to do so."

He later added: "The Lord answered me, saying: 'Were Israel

as loyal to Me as your wife was to you, I would long ago have redeemed her.' "

D. S., p. 34.

6. The "Best Man"

The "Yud" explained the phrase in the Zohar: "Aaron was the 'best man' of the Bride, and Moses of the Bridegroom" as follows: "Aaron was seeking to praise Israel's virtues before the Lord, and Moses sought to glorify the Lord before Israel."

Tif. Yeh., p. 20.

7. The Stolen Ring

The following tale is attributed to the Besht: A merchant praised his wife for her loyalty to him. A listener boasted that he would be able to persuade any woman to give him her husband's most precious gift. The merchant retorted that if he could obtain form the wife his wedding ring, his boast could he believed. The man, unable to secure the ring, persuaded the wife's maid to steal it. When the boaster showed it to the husband, the latter began to avoid his wife, took her with him on a journey and abandoned her on the way. The wife suffered many tribulations but at last succeeded in reaching her home once more. It was then proved that the maid had stolen the ring and had given it away.

The Archangel Michael, said the Besht, Israel's patron, praised Israel for her loyalty to God. The Satan thereupon declared that he could secure from Israel the holiness entrusted to her. Through sin and strife, he was successful in snatching it away. Then Michael abandoned Israel after leading her into Exile. But the time will come when it will be proved that Israel did not voluntarily surrender the holiness of her trust, and then she will regain the favor of her patron Angel.

M. R. T., ii, 55.

8. The Return of Holiness

Said the Magelnitzer: "We read: 'When Pharaoh shall speak unto you, saying: "Show a wonder for you," then thou shalt say unto Aaron: "Take thy rod and cast it down before Pharaoh, that it become a serpent" ' (Exodus 7:9). We know from the Midrash [1] that the Children of Israel were idol worshipers in Egypt. When Moses stated that Israel must leave Egypt in order to serve the God of their fathers, Pharaoh exclaimed: 'But Israel worshiped our gods; why then should they be chosen by your God to worship Him? If there is a greater God than ours, why should He chose an enslaved people?'

"And Moses said: 'Look at these holy markings on Aaron's rod. Behold, in your country it is turned into an unclean serpent. This could not happen in Midian where the rod was in my possession many years. It is the same with Israel: they are a holy people, but

[1] Shemoth Rabba 21:7.

residence in unholy Egypt transformed them into idolaters. As soon as they depart, their holiness will be made clear.'"

S. Hay., p. 64.

84. THE JEWISH LIFE

1. Live Like a Good Jew

A man expressed the wish in the presence of the Belzer Rabbi to die like a good Jew. The Rabbi commented: "Such a wish is wrong. It is like the wish of Balaam: 'May my soul die the death of the righteous!' [1] Desire rather that you may live like a good Jew, and it will follow as a consequence that you will die like a good Jew." [2]

D. S., p. 179.

[1] Numbers 23:10.

[2] Compare Spinoza's remark: "A free man thinks of nothing less than of death; and his wisdom is a meditation not on death but on life." (*Ethics,* iv, 67.)

2. A "Jew" Enters

Said the Kobriner: "If I knew that when my soul arrives in Heaven, it will be announced that a 'Jew' has been brought in, I would be contented." [1]

O. Y., p. 164.

[1] See 22:3. Aphorism 3.

3. A Better World

"In the first place God created Heaven and Earth" [1] were the words the Gerer Rabbi used in a paraphrase of the first sentence of Genesis. He explained: "The Midrash [2] comments on this verse to the effect that Israel is called first in the Bible, and the expression 'First' instead of 'Beginning' is used to teach that the Creation came to be for the sake of Israel. Each one of us, therefore, should bear steadily in mind that everything was created for his sake; and that it is his duty to neglect no act which he ought perform as a member of the people of Israel. Thereby he will make the world a better place in which to live."

S. S. K., iii, 38.

[1] Genesis 1:1. [2] Bereshith Rabba 1:6.

4. The Second Donation

A poor man came to Rabbi Bunam to beg for a donation. The Rabbi presented him with a few coins, for which the beggar thanked him heartily. As he turned to leave, the Rabbi called him back and again offered him money. The beggar was astonished and ventured to ask the Rabbi for his reason.

"The first donation," replied the Rabbi, "was because, possessing a Jewish heart, I took pity upon you. The second one was because I am commanded by the Lord to aid the indigent."

S. S. K., ii, 84.

5. The Inner Jew

The "Yud" and the Lelever Rabbi came to a wealthy man for a donation. The man, observing the "Yud's" robust frame, said: "I will give you nothing; you should go to work."

After they had departed, the man was told the name of his visitor. He ran after the two Rabbis and with profuse apology, gave them a large gift.

The "Yud" replied: "You have not offended me, since you did not know that I was a leader known among the people. But you did know that I was a 'Yud,' and the common Jew within me, cannot forgive you, since you are not asking forgiveness from him. Show me by your future conduct that you venerate the everyday Jew, and you will gain my pardon."

The Kotzker, in telling this story, asked that it be borne in mind that there are two Jews in every Jew: the workaday Jew and the higher inner Jew. This is alluded to in Genesis 1:27: 'And created man in his image, in the image of God.' Two images, or forms, are mentioned.

Kotzker Maasioth, p. 12.

6. Transactions Between Jews

The Magelnitzer Rabbi was asked to explain the contradiction contained in two passages of the Talmud. One states that Jews should make their living one from the other;[1] the second states that Jews should not need one the other.[2] The Rabbi replied: "The expression 'one from the other' means that both benefit by the transaction and therefore it is desirable. This also includes the case when the donor to charity feels the profit to his soul gained by his gift.

"But the expression 'one the other' means that only the receiver feels benefited, and this is undesirable."

S. S. K., ii, 80.

[1] Berakhoth, 3.   [2] Yoma, 53.

7. At Home Everywhere

When Rabbi Henoch Alexanderer settled in Alexander, a Hasid inquired if he felt at home in the town. The Rabbi replied: "There is a tale that some passengers on a vessel wished to make a purchase at a foreign port. They asked a Jewish fellow-passenger to do this for them. 'But the place is strange to me,' protested the Jew. 'Nay,' answered the non-Jewish travelers. 'A Jew is at home everywhere. Is it not true that his God accompanies and guides him?'

"It is thus with me. In any place where I may commune with God, I am at home."

T. T., p. 22.

8. Reckoning with the Nations

Said the Sudilkover: "We read: 'He shall not be reckoned among the nations' (Numbers 23:9). I paraphrase the verse thus: 'He shall not reckon with the nations.' The secret of Israel's survival among the nations lies in the fact that he has gone his own way and has lived his own life, regardless of what other nations might think and say of him, in scorn or praise."

F. U. A. O., ii, 51.

85. JOY

1. Joy And Tribulation

The Alexanderer Rabbi said: "We read in Isaiah 55:12: 'For ye shall go out with joy.' This means: 'If we are habitually joyful, we shall be released from every tribulation.' " [1]

S. S. K., i, 99.

[1] Or: "Ye shall go out from every tribulation through joy."

2. Service With Gladness

The Alexanderer Rabbi said: "Do you wish to know how important it is to be full of joy at all times? Moses enumerates a long series of curses (in Deuteronomy 28), and then remarks (verse 47): 'because thou didst not serve the Lord thy God with joyfulness, and with gladness of heart.' "

S. S. K., i, 104.

3. Of Rejoicing

The "Seer" of Lublin said of "Ari" (Rabbi Isaac Luria), that he had two chief merits: that he made plain and translucent the mysteries of the Zohar, and that he placed rejoicing foremost in the service of God, whereby he acquired sufficient merit to be deemed worthy of a sight of Elijah.

Said the Riziner: "I envy the Germans [1] of Czernowitz, because their cheery temper makes them enjoy this world, and marks them for a share in the World-to-Come."

Bl., Gem., p. 68.

[1] Hasidim styled Jews in modern attire: "Germans."

4. Rejoicing at a Single Coin

Said the Riziner: "We read (Psalm 106:44): 'Nevertheless He looked upon their distress, when He heard their cry (of gladness).' [1] This may be explained as follows: it is often easy to recognize a

[1] "Rinatham" means "their cry, their song." Heine has remarked that tears and laughter are very close in the Jew.

person's distress by the measure of his gladness. If a person rejoices because he has earned a single coin, we may discern thereby how poor he is. If he is joyful because his punishment has been suspended, we may know thereby how greatly he feared imprisonment."

E. O., p. 133.

5. Causes for Joy

Rabbi Menachem Mendel, the Vitebsker, said:

"1. Rejoice that you have an opportunity to sing unto God.

"2. Rejoice that you are a Jew.

"3. Rejoice that you are able to pray, to study and to perform God's will.

"4. Before the endlessness of God the highest saint and the lowliest commoner are equal.

"5. Be contented with your achievements in affairs of the spirit, as well as with your worldly status.

"6. Do not doubt yourself, but enjoy the Light of God."

M. R. T., p. 49.

6. The Cheerful Sinner

In Lublin there lived a great sinner. Whenever he conceived a desire to converse with the Rabbi, the latter received him and talked with him as with a confidential friend. Many of the Seer's students were angered at this, and one of them said to another:

"How does it happen that the Rabbi, who can read the heart of any man the moment he first sees him, and can trace the genealogy of a soul upon the forehead, does not see that this man is a sinner? And if he sees this, how can he associate and converse with him as he does?"

Finally the two students plucked up courage to go to the Rabbi and ask him. He answered: "I know these facts as well as you do; but you will recall how I love cheerful, happy men and dislike gloomy and despondent men. This man is a great sinner. Other men repent their sins after they have committed them, and are remorseful for a brief time, then return to their folly. This man, however, knows no remorse and no care, but dwells within his happiness as in a tower. And the charm of his happiness wins my heart."

Reflex, May, 1929, p. 66.

7. The Besht on "Joy"

Said the Besht:

"No child can be born except through pleasure and joy. By the same token, if one wishes his prayers to bear fruit, he must offer them with pleasure and joy."

K. S. T., p. 3a.

"The chief value of a Mitzwah is its performance with pleasure. But continuous pleasure loses its relish, and therefore it is natural for a man to descend at times in his service to the Lord. But when he ascends again to his former place, he experiences new pleasure therein."

K. S. T., p. 9b.

"Weeping is evil indeed, for man should serve God with joy. But if one weeps from joy, tears are commendable."

M. R. T., ii, 35.

8. The Gates of Tears

Said the "Yud": "The Talmud [1] tells us that all the Heavenly Gates are closed except the Gates of Tears. Why this exception? Because tears are a sign of grief, and grief cannot open gates that are closed. The other portals, however, can be open wide by joyous prayers."

Tif. Yeh., p. 35.

[1] Berakhoth, 32.

9. The Joyful Are Immune

Said the "Yud": "We read: 'And it grieved Him at His heart. And the Lord said ; "I will blot out man"'" (Gen. 6:6). In the era before the Flood, men knew not grief and sadness; hence no penalties could be meted out to them, since retribution cannot affect those who are joyous. Therefore the Lord caused each man to feel grief in his heart, and then He was able to blot out humanity."

Tif. Yeh., p. 35.

10. Joy and Sin

Said the Koretzer: "Joy achieves the forgiveness of sins, since it comes from a higher world, the world of Divine Light. And we know that to forgive is divine."

M. P., 38.

11. The Approachable King

Said the Mezeritzer: "When a King is at a celebration he is approachable to many people who otherwise would be denied admittance to the palace. Likewise when we serve God with joy, He is more approachable."

T. M. M., p. 237.

12. The Broken Heart

Said Rabbi Bunam: "We read: 'Who healeth the broken in heart' (Psalm 147:3). The question may be asked: 'Since to have a broken heart is oftentimes desirable in a man, why heal it?' The answer is: it is healed through removing the sadness it contains, since a man should be both broken of heart and joyful to serve the Lord aright."

S. I., p. 87.

13. The Bratzlaver on "Joy"

"1. Joy is attained through Torah and Worship.
"2. Joy is a vessel to draw fresh understanding.

"3. He who judges himself attains joy.

"4. Even repentence should be attained through joy. We should rejoice so much in God that it will arouse in us regret for having offended Him.

"5. Through zealous labor on the performance of a holy deed, we can acquire joy.

"6. God dislikes melancholy and depressed spirits.

"7. Joy is a cure for illnesses caused by melancholy.

"8. It is the duty of the joyful person to endeavor to bring to those in sadness and melancholy a portion of his mood."

L. E. H., pp. 94-6.

"1. Joy opens up the heart.

"2. Joy strengthens our power of thought.

"3. Charity from the heart brings joy.

"4. When does the wicked begin to smile? When he conceives a new plan of wickedness.

"5. Sincerity of the heart brings joy."

Sef. Ham., pp. 149-150.

86. JUSTICE AND CLEMENCY

1. The Sheep's Offense

When Rabbi Bunam was a young man, a friend borrowed a few dollars from the chest established for the repairing of damaged synagogue books in order to donate a gift to a poor man who was collecting funds for the marriage dowries of dowerless brides. This became known and the trustees summoned the borrower to a hearing. The defendant asked Rabbi Bunam to serve as his counsel.

Rabbi Bunam narrated the following well-known fable: "There was once an epidemic among the animals of the forest. The lion, the tiger, the wolf and the fox held a consultation, and the fox affirmed his belief that the epidemic was due to a great sin committed by some resident of the forest. He advised that all the animals assemble and confess their transgressions. The beasts of prey first confessed, and their excuses were accepted. Finally a sheep timidly approached and confessed that she had eaten a little hay from her owner's mattress.

" 'Aha,' roared the lion, 'you are the great sinner. You have abused your master's confidence.' And the sheep was condemned to death."

Rabbi Bunam then turned to the judges, and said: "You, Reb Leo, have been guilty of this and this; and you, Reb Bear, have done so and so; you, Reb Wolf, have acted wrongly in this and this instance. Yet you dare sit in judgment against a kind-hearted man because he has borrowed money for a highly worthy cause."

Everyone present felt ashamed and left without pronouncing judgment against the defendant.

N. R. B., ii, pp. 18-30.

2. God's Love of Righteousness

Rabbi Elimelech of Lizensk comments thus on the verse (Psalm 11:7): "For the Lord is righteous, He loveth righteousness; the upright shall behold his face:" "Usually a man does not care for the qualities which he himself possesses, but the Lord, though Himself righteous, loves righteousness. The last word is in the plural.[1] It denotes different types of righteousness. One man's righteousness is perfect; another's is less perfect, yet the Lord loves every kind. The perfect kind is like the heavens, the imperfect like the earth; yet it was God's will to create both. Yea, even if it is so imperfect that it resembles the unformed earth that was void, it is still beloved on High in the expectation of the improvement to follow."

Noam E., p. 4.

[1] Zedakoth, not Zedakah.

3. Justice For the Orphan

"The wife of Rabbi Wolf of Zbaraz accused her maidservant of having stolen a costly vessel. The girl denied the deed. The woman, being wroth, prepared herself to go out and appeal to the rabbinical court. Rabbi Wolf, seeing her preparations, put on his Sabbath garment also. His wife said that it was not fitting for him to go, too, and that she knew well enough how to bear herself in the court's presence.

" 'Truly,' replied the Zaddik, 'you do. But the poor orphan, your maid, as whose counsel I am going, does not. And who but I will see that justice is done her?' "

T. H., p. 321.
"Cities and Men,"
Ludwig Lewisohn,
p. 205.

4. Restoring the Soul

A widow who had lost her case in the Rimanover Rabbinical Court came weeping to Rabbi Hirsch Rimanover, and complained bitterly against the judgment. Nothing the Rabbi could say availed to console her. The Rabbi thereupon went to the Court and asked the Dayyanim to review the widow's case, saying there must have been an error. The Dayyanim retried the case, and discovered in truth that an error had been made. The widow went on her way rejoicing.

The new Dayyan inquired from the Rabbi how he had discovered the error, and expected in reply a lengthy dissertation on the Code. The Rabbi, however, answered in these words: "We read in the Psalms (19:8): 'The law of the Lord is perfect, restoring the soul.'[1] I understand from this verse that a proper decision, based

[1] The verb in the verse quoted also means "refreshes," when used together with the word "soul." Leeser's Bible has it "quietens," which is more accurate in this instance. Dayyan means a judge.

on God's Law, is refreshing to the soul, and even acceptable to the loser. But this woman was unable to cease lamenting over your decision; hence I knew your judgment had been incorrect."

F. R. H.-E., pp. 114-5.

5. Hearing Both Sides

An intimate of the Zbarazer asked him to rebuke his partner. The Rabbi replied: "All Jews are my intimate friends. I can no more rebuke your partner, who is not my Hasid, because of the presentation you have made concerning the facts in the argument, than I could rebuke you if he presented his arguments against you. Both sides must be heard."

S. H. H., chapter 4.

6. Justifiable Methods

Said Rabbi Bunam: "The verse: 'Justice, justice shalt thou pursue' (Deut. 16:20) teaches us that we may use only justifiable methods even in the pursuit of justice."

F. U. A. O., ii, 107.

7. God's Consideration

Said Rabbi Bunam: "When a judge sentences a man to death, he does not take into consideration the pain he thereby gives to the offender's relatives. God, however, considers all the kinsmen and close friends when He is about to punish the transgressor. We learn this from the verse: 'The ordinances of the Lord are true; they are righteous altogether' (Psalm 19:10)."

S. I., p. 71.

8. The Scale of Merit

Said the Besht: "From the commandment to love thy fellow-man as thyself,[1] we learn the Talmudical commandment to judge thy fellow-man on the scale of merit.[2] Since thou always findest excuses for thy own misdeeds, make excuses also for thy fellow-man."

D. E. M. R., p. 59.

[1] Lev. 19:18. [2] Ethics 1:6; Singer, p. 185.

9. God's Deeds

The Strelisker explained thus the three lines in the Rosh ha-Shanah hymn: "His secret is uprightness; His advice is faith; His deeds are truth": "Because the uprightness and justice of God are oftentimes hidden from us, it is His advice that we have faith that His deeds are always truth."

E. Z., p. 82.

10. Direct and Reflected Rays

Said the Koretzer: "The actions of men send forth either direct or reflected rays. The first are mercy, the second justice. He who lends money sends forth the positive rays; he who repays a loan, merely reflected rays. A father in his mercies towards his son sends forth direct rays; the son who aids his father, merely reflected rays. It is for this reason that the proverb states: 'One father can support ten sons, but ten sons cannot support one father.' The reflected rays are many times weaker than the direct rays, even as justice is many times weaker than mercy."

Nof. Tz., p. 200.

11. Authority to Save

Many persons complained to the Sassover concerning a certain Shochet's conduct, and asked for his dismissal. One man, however, declared that the Shochet was without fault and was merely the victim of jealousies. The Rabbi decided to retain the Shochet, and when the others complained at his taking the word of one person against many, the Rabbi replied: "God Himself commanded Abraham to sacrifice Isaac, yet he listened to an angel and saved Isaac's life. Why? Because to harm a man, a command from a high tribunal is required, but to save a man, only a word from the lowest authority is needed."

E. Tz., p. 61.

12. Difficult and Clear Cases

It was the custom in Poland for Rabbis of small towns to act as judges only in cases not involving more than four hundred zloties. Cases involving larger amounts were to be sent to the District Rabbi.

Rabbi Hayyim Schoenberg, the Rabbi of Stzutzin, broke away from this tradition and decided a case involving eight hundred zloties. The District Rabbi summoned Rabbi Hayyim to Tiktin to explain his conduct.

Rabbi Hayyim replied: "I consider the rule to be false. We read that Jethro counseled Moses and said: 'Every great matter, they shall bring unto thee, but every small matter they shall judge themselves' (Exodus 18: 22). Moses, however, did not follow this regulation. Moses appointed the rules, and according to his instructions (verse 26), 'the hard cases they brought unto Moses, but every small matter they judged themselves.' You, Tiktiner Rav, wish to enforce Jethro's rule, that every matter involving great amounts should be sent to you without reference to the difficulty of the case or its clearness.

"I, however, believe in the rule of Moses, that the amount involved does not matter; only the degree of difficulty in the case or its clearness. Only difficult cases should be sent to the higher court, even if they involve but a single zlota. Clear cases, however, may be left to the lower court even if they involve thousands." [1]

F. U. A. O., i, 160-1.

[1] Compare the Talmudical rule: "The case of a penny is the same as the case of a 'maneh' (a thousand)." Sanhedrin, 8.

13. The Bratzlaver on "Justice and Mercy"

"1. A true decision stands even against the will of the disputants.

"2. Good Dayyanim (Judges) cause the Torah to be beloved.

"3. Four things bring down clemency from the Heavenly Tribunal: charity, prayer, a change of conduct, and a change of reputation.

"4. He who shows the way to God will be acquitted in the Heavenly Tribunal.

"5. Knowledge draws God's mercies.

"6. If any one assails Israelites in your hearing, you must defend them.

"7. Stubborn refusal to repent causes incurable diseases.

"8. Melancholy awakens justice, but shamefacedness suspends it."

Sef. Ham., pp. 47-54.

87. KIND DEEDS

1. Hidden Kindness

Rabbi Hirsch Ziditzover narrated the following story: "Once when I was a Disciple of the Sassover Rabbi, I wished to see the Rabbi's midnight service for the 'Exile of the Shekinah.' I concealed myself in his home, and at midnight, I saw the Rabbi arise from his bed, dress in peasant garments, take some logs of wood and an axe, and walk out of the house. I followed him in silence, and saw him step into a hut where a woman had given birth to a child a few days before. Her husband was not in the town, and no one had come to kindle a fire for her in the cold night. The Sassover said to her in Polish: 'Buy my wood very cheap; you may pay me later.' The woman replied: 'I have no strength to chop it and to light the fire.'

" 'I have an axe and will do it for you,' was the reply.

"While chopping the wood, the Rabbi recited: 'Tikkun Leah,' the first part of the service; and while making the fire, he said the 'Tikkun Rachel,' the balance of it. Then he returned to his home, changed his garments, and commenced his studies." [1]

T. Z. H., p. 39.

[1] Doubtless this is the basis of the famous story in Peretz: *Yiddish Tales.*

2. The Apple-Vendor

One day the Tzanzer passed through the market-place and noticed a weeping woman seated before a fruit-stand. In reply to his questioning the woman told the Rabbi that no purchasers came to buy her apples, and that she faced ruin. The kind-hearted, lame old Zaddik took her place and loudly called out: "Buy fine apples, a dozen for a gulden." The news that the Holy Man was selling fruit soon spread and the wealthiest residents came to buy, deeming it an honor to make a purchase at the hands of the world-famed Gaon and Zaddik. The stock of apples was quickly converted into a pile of guldens, to the delight of the poor widow.

Bl., Gem., p. 333.

3. The Three-Legged Stool

In the record of the town of Rybatits, where the Dinover served as Rav in his youth, he inscribed this comment: "We say in the Amidah: 'the God of Abraham, the God of Isaac, and the God of Jacob.' But the benediction in the Amidah ends with the words: 'Shield of Abraham.' (Singer, p. 44.)

"Abraham was known for deeds of kindness. Isaac was known for service to the Lord, as we read: 'And Isaac went out to meditate in the field at the eventide' (Gen. 24:63). Jacob was known for his love of the study of the Torah, as it is written: 'And Jacob was a quiet man, dwelling in the tents (of the Torah)' (Gen. 25:27). We find, thus, that the Three Patriarchs engaged in kind deeds, service and Torah, the three essentials for the stability of the world (Avoth 1:2).

"In our days we behold very few who are able to study properly day and night. Still fewer are those able to serve God fittingly. All we can ask, even now, is that we perform deeds of kindness to our fellow-men.

"But, it may be asked, can kindness alone suffice to stabilize the world? 'Can a three-legged stool stand upon one leg when the other two are broken?'[1] The answer is in the affirmative. Though all three props are needed, the prop of good deeds is strong enough to keep the stool upright. This thought is suggested by the fact that the Rabbis who tell us that the world rests upon three things, have concluded the first benediction in the Amidah with the words: 'Shield of Abraham.' Interest in the performance of good deeds, a quality which marked Abraham, is a shield and a support to us even when other qualities in our own nature may be weak."

[1] Berakhoth, 32.

E. Tz., p. 117.

88. KOL NIDREI

1. The Lullaby

The Sassover Rabbi was late for the Kol Nidrei Service one Yom Kippur Eve. A group of the congregation went in search of him. Nearby they heard his voice singing a lullaby. It was the home of a widow, and when they entered, they found him lulling a little child to sleep. The Rabbi explained that the mother had left the infant to attend the synagogue. It had awakened and cried as the Rabbi passed by. He had sought to still its cries.

E. Tz., p. 49.

2. A Sober People

On Yom Kippur Eve, the Berditschever would say: "O Lord of the Universe! Hadst Thou enjoined others than Jews to eat and drink to-day, they would surely have over-eaten and become drunk, thereby failing to attend divine worship in the evening. But thy people Israel are sober of mien and body, and all are standing before Thee bare-footed. Hast Thou any other people like Israel?"

Kahana, p. 259.

3. "I Forgive As You Ask"

The Koznitzer Maggid was very frail, but despite his weakness, he insisted upon reading himself the entire order of prayer on Kol Nidrei. Before the words: "And the Lord said: 'I forgive as you ask,'" the Maggid offered the following plea: "O Lord, Thou art aware how weak I am, yet I am standing before Thee to petition for Israel with all my strength. Wouldest Thou not do so little as to say: 'I forgive as you ask?'"

E. O., p. 81.

4. Melody and Repentance

Rabbi Bunam said: "The world of melody is near to the world of repentance. We find that sinners frequently repent on hearing the melody of Kol Nidrei."

S. S. K., iv, 39.

5. The Repentant Renegade

The Kotzker Rabbi told the following story: "An old man who had long before become an apostate was riding on the highway one stormy night. It chanced to be the Eve of Yom Kippur. The rain poured down in torrents, and the old man went under his wagon for protection. To while away the time, he began to sing, and among the songs, he chanted the melody of the Kol Nidrei. Suddenly he recalled that it was Kol Nidrei night. An intense yearning overtook him to be once more with his former brethren. He left the horse and wagon and ran in the downpour towards the nearest town. About midnight he reached the synagogue, pushed open the door, and saw that the synagogue was empty. He realized it was too late for the Services, and in grief, he fell to the floor. There he died soon after of a broken heart."

"Thus, we see," continued the Kotzker, "that as long as there is a spark of life in a Jew, we must not despair of his soul, no matter how low he may have sunk."

Kotzker Maasioth, p. 64.

6. A Song from Sin

On the Eve of Atonement Day, Rabbi Sussya once heard the Cantor's chant, "And It Is Forgiven," sung in such a wondrously sweet voice, that he called out to the Ancient of Days in his glad exultation: "Lord of the World, if Israel had not sinned, would such a song ascend to Thee from below?"

O. E., p. 134.
(B., p. 438m.)

7. The Alphabet

An ignorant villager, having heard it is a good religious deed to eat and drink on the day before Yom Kippur, drank himself into a stupor. He awoke late at night, too late for Kol Nidrei Services. Not knowing the prayers by heart, he devised a plan. He repeated the letters of the alphabet over and over, beseeching the Almighty to arrange them into the appropriate words of the prayers. The following day he attended the Kotzker synagogue. After Neilah [1] the Rabbi summoned him to inquire the cause of his absence at Kol Nidrei. The villager confessed his transgression and asked whether his manner of reciting the prayers could be pardoned. The Rabbi responded: "Your prayer was more acceptable than mine because you uttered it with the entire devotion of your heart."

K. M., p. 70.

[1] Closing Service on Yom Kippur.

8. The Tearful Child

Before Kol Nidrei, the daughter of Rabbi Israel Jacob of Kremenitz awaited her father's blessing, holding in her arms her three-year-old child. The pious woman wept copiously, as is the custom on Yom Kippur Eve, and the child, at the sight of her mother's tears, also began to weep. The Rabbi came over and said to his grandchild: "Why do you weep?" The little girl answered: "I hear my mother weeping, and so I also cry."

The Rabbi entered the synagogue, kissed the curtain before the Ark, and, turning to the congregation, exclaimed: "My little granddaughter wept when she beheld her mother's tears. We are the children of God. Why do we not hear God moaning: 'Woe is Me; My children are driven forth from their home, scattered among strangers, and My House is razed to the ground.' [1] Why are we so hard of heart that we do not weep at the voice of God's lamentations?"

The entire congregation began to shed tears and to bewail the Exile of the Shekinah and of Israel.

Joseph Margoshes, in J. M. J., Dec. 6, 1932.

[1] Berakhoth, 3.

89. LAUGHTER AND GAYETY

1. Gayety and Sadness

Rabbi Bunam said: "The Lord's kindness is attracted to gayety. A gay person is usually blessed with plenty, even though he may be impious. A sad person is usually in want, even though he may be God-fearing."

S. S. K., iv, 114.

2. Smiling at Distress

The Lubliner Rabbi commented on Psalm 106:44: "Nevertheless He looked upon their distress, when He Heard their cry." [1] He said: "The Lord becomes attentive to the man who sings in the midst of his troubles and accepts them good-naturedly and with laughter."

S. S. K., ii, 114.

[1] "Song." "Rinatham" means "Their Cry, Their Song."

3. Laughing Through Tears

Said the Lubliner: "The true Hasid must be like a child who can laugh while weeping. Weeping by itself brings despair, while laughter by itself makes one forgetful of the reverence due the Lord."

N. H. L., p. 25.

4. Poverty and Joy

Said the Kobriner: "If a poor man realized the great good he acquires from his poverty, he would dance with joy."

O. Y., p. 58; see 127:1.

5. Joy and Salvation

Rabbi Bunam saw a Jew in danger of drowning while swimming in the sea near Danzig. He noted that the man was about to abandon the struggle to save himself, and he shouted to him: "Give my greetings to the Leviathan." Unwittingly the drowning man smiled at this levity. Thereby he regained his presence of mind, and was able to hold himself afloat until friends rescued him. Relating this experience, Rabbi Bunam remarked: "We may learn from this that prayer with a joyful heart and a cheerful countenance attains to the Lord, but prayer with outcries and lamentations may be wasted."

O. Y., p. 16.

6. Vanished Joys

Said the Belzer: "When the Temple of God was still standing, pious Jews used to assemble in Jerusalem on Holydays, to eat together the 'second tithe' and the 'peace offerings.' [1] They were filled with happiness in each other's society. Now, however, religious folk have no such enjoyment in their meetings, inasmuch as their tribulations are many, and their joys are few.

"It is only the impious who gain true enjoyment in their gatherings. They assemble for pleasure and extravagance, and find therein hearty satisfactions, whereas the pious, who band together on behalf of worthy causes, find abundant objectors and opponents whose Satanic work oftentimes overcomes their best intentions."

D. S., p. 100.

[1] Singer, p. 13.

90. LEADERSHIP

1. *Turning the Wheels*

Said Rabbi Schmelke: "We read (Numbers 27:18): 'And the Lord said unto Moses: Take thee Joshua, the son of Nun, a man in whom is a spirit.' The nature of the spirit is thus explained by Ezekiel (1:20): 'Whithersoever the spirit was to go, as the spirit was to go thither, so they went; and the wheels were lifted up beside them; for the spirit of the living creature (Hayyoth) was in the wheels.'

"The 'Hayyoth' are the leaders, possessed of spiritual enlightenment and inspiration; the Wheels are the ordinary folk who are influenced by the leaders. Only those are true leaders who possess the skill and power to turn the wheels."

S. ha-Tov, p. 22.

2. *Jethro's Counsel*

The Amshinover commented on Exodus 18:19: "Now hearken unto my voice, I will give thee counsel, and God will be with thee."

"Jethro desired that Moses should have assistants in judging the people. He appreciated, however, that if Moses had inquired of the Lord whether he should appoint aides, the Lord would not give his assent, inasmuch as this would seem derogatory to the ability of Moses to care for the people himself. Jethro therefore counseled Moses to appoint aides on his own initiative. Since he did this of his own volition, God would not oppose it."

Ohel Isaac, pp. 11-12.

3. *The Wise Rabbi*

When the Lizensker Rabbi died, some of his closest adherents left Lizensk in order to seek out a new teacher. They came to Rabbi Hirsch of Ziditzov who invited them to remain as students of his method of serving the Lord. They declined and traveled next to Premislan. The Premislaner also invited them to become his Hasidim, and sought earnestly but vainly to win their allegiance.

Their third visit was in Ropshitz. There they met with a lukewarm reception. Not a word of invitation to remain was uttered by the Rabbi. The Hasidim were considerably piqued, and remained over the Sabbath. The Ropshitzer's ways proved of great attraction, and the visitors became his Hasidim.

Shivchei Naftali, p. 21.

4. *The Minor Zaddikim*

Said the Tzartkover Rabbi: "My father, the Riziner, used to say that because people disbelieved in the greatness of holy men in the time of the Besht, it was decreed that they should be forced to believe in unworthy Rabbis. A parable gives the explanation.

"A man owned an expensive watch which suddenly ceased to keep time. Since it was impossible for him to take the watch to a jeweler for repairs, he began, after a few days, to shake the works from time to time to prevent corrosion.

"Like this man, we give our adherence to a minor Zaddik until we discover a major Zaddik. We must not become unaccustomed to reverence for the Zaddik."

E. O., p. 149.

5. *Next Year Either!*

When the elder Lekhivitzer Rabbi died, his son Noah expected to be called as Rabbi in his father's place. His father's Disciples, however, were undecided as to their choice. In the meantime, the Ladmirer Rabbi aspired to become the Rabbi of Lekhivitz and invited himself to Rabbi Noah's home for the Sabbath. Rabbi Noah strove mightily to please the Hasidim and related many novel items on subjects of the Torah. At the final meal, he recounted the following story:

"A villager was accustomed to go out in the wheatfield to discover if the wheat had reached its height. He and his wife would place themselves at opposite ends of the field, and endeavor to catch sight of each other. If they were unable to do so, they knew that the wheat had reached a satisfactory height. When they returned to their home, the husband would say to his wife: 'Have you seen me?' And the wife was accustomed to answer: 'No, and I pray that I may not see you next year either.'

"The Ladmirer Rabbi took the hint, realized that he was regarded as an interloper, and was not seen in Lekhivitz again."

O. Y., p. 44.

6. *"Fear No Man"*

When the Hamburger Rabbi died and a successor was to be chosen, the leaders of the community met to discuss the matter. The most prominent of them advised the election of the greatest Rabbi to be found, even if it should take a long time before he was available. The others, however, declared that none of the best-known Rabbis would be likely to give up their present positions, and voted in favor of the Rabbi of a nearby small town. In order to pacify the opponents, they compromised by electing him for three years only.

Soon after the Rabbi who was chosen took up his duties, a merchant from out-of-town had occasion to deposit his money with a prominent community leader. When he asked for the return of his money, the leader denied receiving it. The merchant went to the Rabbi with his complaint, and the Rabbi sent a summons to the leader. The latter refused to accept it and threw the process-server out of his house. The Rabbi promptly made out another summons in which he threatened to publish the fact that the magnate had denied the authority of the Rabbinical Court, and therefore should be excluded from the Jewish community.

The leader came to the Rav and said: "Since I see that you fear no man,[1] however prominent, I am convinced that you are worthy to be our Rabbi for your lifetime." Thereupon he placed his signature on the letter of invitation to the Rabbi, and not only returned the money to the merchant, but also paid him for his vexation. He admitted that he had purposely withheld the deposit in order to determine whether the Rabbi would give him special consideration because of his prominence.

S. H., p. 34.

[1] Deut. 1:17. There are humorous variations of this story.

7. The Rocking Boat

A Disciple gave this account of the Great Maggid: "When we journeyed to him, most of our desires were stilled upon entering town. Whoever had a particularly keen desire was soothed upon entering the Maggid's house. But if there was one among us whose soul was still rocking like a boat, when he beheld the Maggid's face, he came to rest."

J. T., Dec. 19, '30, p. 4.

8. The Shepherd

Rabbi Bunam was asked regarding the successorship of the "Yud" as Rabbi of Parsischka. In reply, he narrated this tale: "A shepherd who greatly loved his flock took the sheep to a green meadow near a sparkling spring. He feared that a wolf might come out of the wood and snatch away a sheep. Therefore he resolved to keep a most watchful eye. But after nightfall he lay down by the spring, and fell asleep. Before daylight he suddenly awakened and rushed over to the flock to count the sheep. None was missing, and the thankful shepherd fell down on his knees and cried out: 'Dear God, how can I repay Thee for this? Entrust unto me your sheep and I will guard them as the apple of my eye!' Such a leader," said Rabbi Bunam, "would be a worthy Rabbi for you."

The Disciples recalled the clemency and wisdom of Rabbi Bunam, and thereupon they chose him for their Rabbi.

N. R. B., p. 35 (B., pp. 530-1).

9. Serving or Ruling

Said the Amshinover: "We read in the 'Ethics of the Fathers' (1:10):[1] 'Love service and dislike rule.' When a man enters a society of inferiors, he may choose between serving or ruling it. He is advised to choose the former."

O. I., p. 3.

[1] Singer, p. 185.

10. The Moth-Eaten Fur Hat

Rabbi Bunam was asked by the Lubliner for a remedy to stop the hair from falling out of his fur hat.[1] Rabbi Bunam answered: "If all the moth-eaten hair is combed away, the remainder will not fall out. Otherwise the good hair will also fall prey to the moths."

"Let this be a lesson to you, Bunam," exclaimed the Lubliner, "when you become a leader in Israel."

R. T., ii, 111.

[1] A fur hat (Streimel) is worn by Hasidic Rabbis even now.

11. Leaders and Their Generations

A Hasid asked Rabbi Bunam: "There is a Talmudical allegory that God showed to Adam each generation and its leaders.[1] Why did He first show the generation and then the leaders?"

Rabbi Bunam replied: "Had God shown him the leaders first, Adam would have exclaimed: 'Should such a man as Bunam be a leader?' But when Adam saw the generation first, he said: 'In such a generation Bunam is worthy to be a leader.'"

S. I., p. 61.

[1] Sanhedrin, 38.

12. Seeking the Wicked

Rabbi Bunam commented on the verse: "I have seen the wicked in great power, and spreading himself like a leafy tree in its native soil. But one passed by, and, lo, he was not; yea, I sought him, but he could not be found."[1] He said: "We ought understand why the Psalmist sought out the wicked. This will become clear if we apply the verse to our own times. He who in days gone by was considered wicked would now be regarded as a man of goodness. Hence we seek out such a sinner in the past to make him our leader. But now we cannot find a man of even these qualities, and we are compelled to accept as leaders men of qualities still less commendable."

S. I., p. 65.

[1] Psalm 37: 35-6.

13. The Duty of Leaders

The author of "Tefillah le-Moshe" says: "If God has granted you the privilege of being a leader in Israel, do not rebuke your people with an angry heart, but with a soft tongue. For Israel is a holy congregation, blessed of the Lord. Let every man be important in your eyes, and not inconsequential. For you cannot know who is worthy and who unworthy. Man often looks upon a fellow-man as despicable and worthless, but God looks into the very heart."

D. E. M. R., pp. 9-10.

14. The Bratzlaver on "Leadership"

A.

"In every person who comes to the leader, there is some quality of good will which the leader can bring out and fortify, thereby refreshing his soul. The stronger the good will a man possesses, the more he gains from listening to his leader. The first sign of this gain is his ability to show greater love towards his fellow-men."

K. L. M., p. 18.

B.

"1. A leader who commences a good deed but does not complete it loses his place at the head of his people.

"2. When God wishes to punish Israel, He sends them unworthy leaders.

"3. The word of the lowly, wise and popular man is heeded.

"4. When God wishes to honor a good leader and to bring him fame, he causes quarrels among the wicked.

"5. When a man is able to receive abuse smilingly he is worthy to become a leader.

"6. He who cannot accept reproof cannot become a great man.

"7. He who defends Israel attains greatness.

"8. Good sense and calm trust in troubled times proclaim the truly great man.

"9. He who hates dishonesty becomes great.

"10. He who serves the Lord sincerely and sensibly will become great.

"11. The building of a house in Palestine brings leadership.

"12. He whom God has lifted up to become a leader should receive your homage."

Sef. Ham., pp. 60-1.

15. Worthiness to Lead

When in his sixtieth year after the death of the Kotzker, the Gerer accepted election as leader of the Kotzker Hasidim, the Rabbi said: "I should ask myself: 'Why have I deserved to become the leader of thousands of good people?' I know that I am not more learned or more pious than others. The only reason why I accept the appointment is because so many good men and true have proclaimed me to be their leader. We find that a cattle-breeder in Palestine during the days when the Temple stood was enjoined by our Torah [1] to drive his newborn cattle or sheep into an enclosure in single file. When they went to the enclosure, they were all of the same station, but when over the tenth one the owner pronounced the words: 'consecrated unto the Lord,' it was set aside for holier purposes. In the same fashion when the Jews pronounce a man to be holier than his fellows, he becomes in truth a consecrated person."

M. E. H., ii, 29-30.

[1] Lev. 27: 32 and Berakhoth, 58b.

16. *New Paths for the People*

Said the Bratzlaver: "A king had two sons, one wiser than the other. He appointed the less intelligent son to be his treasurer, but the wiser he gave no official appointment, except to be seated at the side of his father. When a nobleman inquired the reason, the king replied: 'Merely to distribute monies already available requires no special wisdom; even a simpleton can do this. But my wise son is seated with me, and plans new avenues for procuring wealth for my treasury. Keen intelligence is required for this task.' In the same way, merely to follow routine does not require a great Zaddik, but to discover new paths for the people to approach God, a wise leader is needed."

D. D., p. 179.

91. LOVE

1. *Without a Reason*

Said the Belzer: "When the Lord wishes to preserve Israel from a calamity, the advocates of Heavenly Justice endeavor to dissuade Him, citing the evil deeds of Israel. But the Lord replies: 'Israel observes many of My commandments without knowing the reason for them. Therefore it is fit that I should save them without a reason for doing so.'"

D. S., p. 103.

2. *An Eternal Love*

The Magelnitzer Rabbi heard that the Vorker Rabbi often visited the Kotzker Rabbi. The Magelnitzer who was known to hold a poor opinion of the Kotzker, asked the Vorker: "What reason have you for liking the Kotzker?"

"I love him without a reason," replied the Vorker, "and, as you know, such a love lasts forever." [1]

S. S. K., iv, 86.

[1] See the "Ethics of the Fathers" 5:19; Singer, p. 202: "Whenever love depends upon some material cause, with the passing away of that cause, the love too passes away; but if it be not dependent upon such a cause, it will not pass away forever. Which love was that which depended upon a material cause? Such was the love of Amnon and Tamar. And that which depended upon no such cause? Such was the love of David and Jonathan."

3. *Beyond Human Strength*

Rabbi Mendel of Rimanov once inquired of his teacher, Rabbi Schmelke of Nikolsburg: "Is it not beyond human strength to love the wicked?"

He explained: "One must love their souls."

Another Zaddik once cried from the depth of his heart: "Would I could love the best of men as tenderly as God loves the worst." [1]

Bl., Pr., p. 84.

[1] Compare 94:1.

4. Love Them First

Said the Bershider: "Do you desire that people love you? Love them first."

M. P., p. 45.

5. Love the Wicked

Said the Bershider: "Love the man of wickedness. Why? Because he will then love you, and love will unite his soul and yours. As a consequence, inasmuch as you hate wickedness, you will transfer your hate to him, thereby causing him to repent and turn from evil to good."

M. P., p. 51.

6. Love Is the Chief Thing

The Besht was asked: "What is the chief point in service to the Lord, if it be true, as you teach, that fasting and self-chastisement are sinful?"

The Besht answered: "The main thing is to encompass oneself in the love of God, the love of Israel, and the love of the Torah. A man may attain this if he secures enough nourishment to preserve his health, and if he makes use of his strength to battle against evil inclinations."

Butz. D., p. 22-3.

7. The Bratzlaver on "Love"

1. "When there is no love among men, there is slander, mockery and false accusations.

2. "Terror and ruin come through hate.

3. "Everyone loves the man who prays for Israel with his whole heart.

4. "Repentance enables a man to love God.

5. "The man whom you strengthen in his service to God will love you. The way to strengthen him is to love him.

6. "If you beware of petty quarrels and unfounded dislikes, even influential persons will be willing to entrust you with the problems of arbitration.

7. "He who does not swear falsely will not transgress the prohibition against revenge.

8. "God is present whenever a treaty of peace is signed.

9. "When the sages of a generation meet in amity at frequent intervals, their unanimous decisions will endure, for God Himself becomes their Chief Justice."

Sef. Ham., pp. 17-18.[1]

[1] The work *Sefer ha-Middoth* is based upon the Bible and the Talmud. A commentary which accompanies the text designates the source of the aphorisms. Oftentimes, however, the source is merely suggested.

92. LOVING OUR NEIGHBORS

1. The More Deserving

Said the Belzer: "Only the man of humility who believes that the other person is more deserving than he, can truly fulfill the commandment: 'Thou shalt love thy neighbor as thyself' (Lev. 19:18). The man of humility will feel unable to disregard his comrade's request when he is in a position to grant it." [1]

D. S., p. 82.

[1] The Rabbi finds a suggestion of this idea in the fact that the next letters in the Hebrew Alphabet following רֵעֲךָ are שָׁפָל.

2. What Brings Our Comrade Pain

Rabbi Moshe Leib of Sassov declared to his Disciples: "I learned how we must truly love our neighbor from a conversation between two villagers which I overheard.

"The first said: 'Tell me, friend Ivan, do you love me?'

"The second: 'I love you deeply.'

"The first: 'Do you know, my friend, what gives me pain?'

"The second: 'How can I, pray, know what gives you pain?'

"The first: 'If you do not know what gives me pain, how can you say that you truly love me?'

"Understand, then, my sons," continued the Sassover; "to love, truly to love, means to know what brings pain to your comrade."

E. Tz., p. 52; Bl., Gem., p. 178.

3. Thine Own Hand

Rabbi Schmelke of Nikolsburg said: "It may sometimes happen that thine own hand inadvertently strike thee. Wouldst thou take a stick and chastise thy hand for its heedlessness, and thus add to thy pain? It is the same when thy neighbor, whose soul is one with thine, because of insufficient understanding, does thee harm: shouldst thou retaliate, it would be thou who wouldst suffer."

Spiegel, p. 120.

4. Rejoicing With Our Brother

Said the Radviller Rabbi: "The commandment to love our fellow-men as ourselves [1] does not necessarily imply that if one buys himself a garment he must buy one also for another person. Most of us cannot afford to do so, and the Torah does not contain a command that only the wealthy are able to observe. What we are capable of doing, rich and poor alike, is to participate in a fellow-man's joys or griefs. If we hear that another man is prospering, we must rejoice as if we ourselves had greatly benefited. If another man is in distress, we must come to his aid, just as if we were ourselves in trouble, and were praying that he aid us. 'Jerusalem was destroyed because of hatreds without cause,' [2] instead of love; men were apparently happy at the misfortunes of their companions. We are all children of God, and He sorrows at the pain each one of us suffers."

E. O., p. 66.

[1] Lev. 19:18.　[2] Yoma, 9.

5. *The Head and the Limbs*

The "Yud" was asked: "How does the commandment: 'Love thy neighbor as thyself' [1] harmonize with the command to love one's Rabbi more than any other man?" [2]

The "Yud" replied: "The verse teaches us to love our fellowmen in the same degree as we love ourselves. But as a man loves his head more than his other limbs, so he may love his Rabbi more than any other man."

N. H., p. 40.

[1] Lev. 19:18.　[2] Pesachim 22 compares the Rabbi to God with respect to our fear and love of him.

6. *The Evil-Doing Neighbor*

A student asked Rabbi Schmelke: "We are bidden to love our neighbors as ourselves. How can I do this when my neighbor does me ill?"

The Rabbi answered: "Thou must understand the command aright: love thy neighbor, as something that thou art thyself; for all sons are one. Each is a spark from the original soul, and that original soul is in all of you, as the soul is in all the limbs of thy body.

"It may sometimes happen that thy hand slips and strikes thee. Wouldst thou then take a rod and beat thy hand because of its blunder, and thus add to thy pain? So it is if thy neighbor, whose soul is part of thy soul, does thee ill in his blindness. If thou dost retaliate upon him, thou merely injurest thyself." [1]

The scholar asked him again: "But if I see a man who does ill to God, how can I love him?"

"Dost thou not know," said the Rabbi, "that the world-soul issues from God, and that every human soul is a part of God? And wouldst thou not pity it, didst thou see one of the holy sparks from that soul caught fast and likely to be extinguished?"

Reflex, May, 1929, p. 65.
Spiegel, p. 147. v.s.
Spiegel, p. 120.

[1] See 92:3.

7. *What We Dislike in Others*

Rabbi Schmelke interpreted the famous saying of Hillel (Sabbath 31a): "What is hateful to thee do not cause to be done to thy neighbor." He paraphrased it saying: "What is hateful to thee in thy neighbor, do not do thyself."

S. ha-Tov, p. 154.

8. In Mortal Danger

Rabbi Aaron, the son of Rabbi Hayyim of Tzanz, journeyed once to Gorletz on a bitterly cold day, wrapped in a bearskin. One of his fellow-travelers had no overcoat, and suffered dreadfully from the cold. He fell sick unto death. When Rabbi Hayyim heard of this, he reproached his son severely. "Why did you not give him your bearskin?" he asked.

Rabbi Aaron answered: "Father, I had only one skin."

"You should nevertheless have given it to him," continued Rabbi Hayyim.

Rabbi Solomon of Radomsk heard the colloquy and said: "Then you would rather your son imperil his own life, though it is written: 'Everyone is his own neighbor.' " [1]

"That is doubtless true," said Rabbi Hayyim, "but know, Radomsker Rabbi, that when it is a question of a man's life or death, we need not proceed according to what is written."

Bl., Pr., p. 228.

[1] Sanhedrin, 9; also Baba Metzia, 62; "Self-preservation is the first rule."

9. Prayers for Others

The Berditschever was asked why he lived in such straitened circumstances, whereas other Rabbis, not so well-known, lived in affluence. The Rabbi replied as follows:

"The Talmud [1] teaches that when we pray for something on behalf of our neighbors, and we ourselves are in need of the very thing we seek in our prayer, we are answered first. Now my adherents wish me to pray for them, so that the Creator may aid them to subdue evil desires and selfishness, and at no time do they crave riches and pleasure. Hence I am granted their wishes in my own person. But the Disciples of other Rabbis implore wealth and worldly delights, with the consequence that the Rabbis obtain the objects they ask for their followers." [2]

Joseph Margoshes, Jewish Morning Journal, Sept. 4, 1931.

[1] Baba Kamma, 92.

[2] Isaac Ber Levinsohn paraphrases the Talmudical quotation, thus: "The Zaddik who prays on behalf of another receives the benefit first, inasmuch as he receives his payment in advance."

10. Why Mortals Precede

A Hasid asked a Zaddik: "Why is it customary to say: 'Le-Hayyim,' 'For Life,' before reciting the benediction over a drink of wine? Is it not disrespectful to bless mortals before blessing the Immortal One?"

The Zaddik opened the Prayer Book [1] and showed the Hasid the passage wherein we are enjoined to accept the Mitzwah of loving our

[1] See *Siddur Derekh ha-Hayyim*, p. 104.

neighbors before accepting the Mitzwah of loving God. The reason doubtless is that mortals need our love and sympathy more than God.

D. Z., p. 36.

11. Loving All Others

Rabbi David of Lelov said: "I am not worthy as yet to be called a Zaddik since I still feel more love for my own children than for other people."

On the same subject, the Gastininer Rabbi said: "The Kotzker Rabbi, my revered teacher, labored to instill in me a love of mankind in such perfection that I might be able to love my enemy as much as my dearest friend."

D. E. M. R., p. 13.

12. For the Love of His Soul

Said the Lentzner Rabbi: "Thou shalt love thy neighbor's soul as thine own. Thou repentest of thy sins for the love of thy soul. Labor, then, with thy neighbor that he may also repent of his sins for the love of his soul."

E. A., p. 29.

13. The Lord Is Thy Shade

The Besht commented upon the verse: "The Lord is thy shade" (Psalm 121:5). He said: "As thou conductest thyself towards others, so doth the Lord conduct Himself towards thee. If thou art kind and merciful, the Lord will be kind and merciful towards thee."

M. R. T., ii, 102.

14. Broadening the Heart

Said the "Yud": "Accustom thyself to good-heartedness by degrees. At first refuse not a request for a pinch of tobacco, for the light of a match, or for other small gifts. Little kindnesses like these will broaden thy heart so that thou wilt thus habituate thyself to helping thy fellow-man in many ways."

Nif. Yeh., p. 58.

15. God in the Compact

Said Rabbi Israel Isaac of Alexander: "The verse reads: 'Thou shalt love thy neighbor as thyself; I am the Lord.' This indicates that the Lord says: 'Love thy neighbor as thyself and include Me also in the compact of love.'"

M. H. H., p. 7.

16. Loving the Wicked

Rabbi Benjamin Halevy and Rabbi Raphael Bershider engaged in a disputation. The latter declared that one must love even the wicked, and the former argued that it is incumbent to pray for their downfall. When Rabbi Benjamin departed from the synagogue, he said to a friend: "Rabbi Raphael, to be sure, was right, and it is truly a praiseworthy attribute to love all Israel. Before the multitude, however, it is desirable to preach that evil-doers will receive their punishment speedily. Moreover it is a trait which few persons possess. My Master (the Koretzer) told me that Raphael has the unique quality of loving even coarse doers of evil." He further declared: "When Raphael comes to me, I surrender to him my desk and my table, yet I know I have not done my full duty to him."

M. P., pp. 41-2.

93. LOYALTY

1. The Wiles of Satan

Said the Pulnoer: "A king wished to test the loyalty of his subjects. He ordered one of his servants to head an apparently rebellious army, and to invite other towns to join the revolt. The ostensible rebel succeeded in winning several cities to his side. When he arrived near a certain town, many of its citizens were prepared to enter his ranks. But a man of wisdom in the town, who had given the matter much thought, said: 'Is it not strange that the king permits this revolt, and dispatches no army to end it? Perhaps it is a trap against us.' He visited the 'rebel' general, and persuaded him to depart.

"The apparent insurrectionist," said the Pulnoer, "is the Satan, who seeks by wiles to entrap us. Words of wisdom and persuasion can head him off."

Kahana, p. 134.

2. The Loyal Kossak

The Kozmirer with his following of Hasidim once turned out of doors on a bitter cold evening to bless the New Moon. At the wall, he met a Kossak, standing guard as motionless as a statue.

"How now, Master Sentinel," exclaimed the Rabbi. "What if you freeze to death, standing in this bitter frost without stirring hand or foot?"

The Kossak replied: "If I die, another will come and stand guard in my stead."

The Rabbi turned to his Hasidim in exhortation: "Look what is done for a master as frail as you or I. Will you do as much for the All-Powerful as this Kossak for one of his liegemen?"

Bl., Gem., p. 76 (F).

3. Not Blood, but Service Warms

The Kobriner Rabbi said: "A general who had been an officer for over fifty years once met the King. The monarch greeted him with a friendly smile, and said: 'Are you in good health, General? Does your blood still warm you?'

"The old general replied: 'No, your Majesty, my blood does not warm me, but service does.'

"Comment is superfluous," said the Kobriner.

O. Y., p. 40.

4. Serving the Rebbe

Rabbi Hirsch of Rimanov was left an orphan in his early boyhood. Once he saw the Rebbe Menachem Mendel Rimanover at the synagogue and was so impressed by his holiness that he resolved to devote himself to his service. He visited the Rebbe's house and persuaded the servants to allow him to chop wood for the Rebbe's oven; later he was permitted to sweep the floors; but his chief ambition was to make up the Rebbe's bed. This, however, he was not allowed to do, as the servants feared the Rabbi's displeasure. One day, however, the Rebbe's personal servant was called away, and he ventured to entrust the lad with the care of his master's room.

Hirsch took great pains in smoothing the Rebbe's bed with care, and when the Rebbe retired to rest, he noted the difference. The next morning he made inquiries, and, being informed of young Hirsch's devotion, enlisted him as his closest attendant. Hirsch soon became indispensable, and his Master grew so attached to him that in his will he designated Hirsch to be his successor as Rebbe, though he had learned sons and many famous disciples.

T. M., p. 32.

5. The Zaddik's Reward

The Lizensker spoke on the text (Exodus 21:33): "And if a man shall open a pit, or if a man shall dig a pit and not cover it; and an ox or an ass fall therein, the owner of the pit shall make it good; he shall give money unto the owner of them.'

"If the Zaddik makes an opening in the heart of his followers or if he strives to dig an opening among the hard-hearted, and continues his efforts lest they grow harsh again, thereby overthrowing the spirit of worldliness, then the Lord who has endowed the Zaddik with the power to influence human hearts, shall grant him his reward.

"He shall repay him by vouchsafing unto him the longing to increase his loyal devotion to the Lord." [1]

Noam E., p. 20.

[1] The Hebrew words: "Kheseph" means both "money" and "longing."

6. Loyalty to One Occupation

A man who was a Shochet and also a Cantor asked Rabbi Bunam's advice as to whether he should become a Sopher (a writer of scrolls).

The Rabbi replied: "The Satan found it difficult to tempt each person individually; therefore he devised a plan to mislead the Shochet and the Cantor and the Sopher in each community. They became unfaithful in their labors, thereby causing the plain people to stumble in the way. Later, however, he improved his plan of action: he induced a single man to become both a Shochet and a Cantor. Thus he was freed from the annoyance of being compelled to tempt two persons. At present, I perceive the Satan proceeds another step forward in his strategy: he persuades one man to unite all three positions in himself. Were you loyal to your communal work, you would have all you can possibly do to accomplish one function in the proper fashion."

S. S. K., v, 53.

7. Serving Other Gods

The Besht commented on the verse: "And ye turn aside and serve other gods" (Deut. 11:16). He said: "The moment ye turn aside from God, ye serve other gods. For all your living forces are from God, and if ye use these forces for purposes not desirable in the eyes of God, it means that ye wish to please other gods."

M. R. T., ii, 72.

8. The Steadfastness of Israel

The Ropshitzer gave another meaning to the Hebrew words in Lamentations (1:3): "All her pursuers have overtaken her in the narrow passes." He said: "All persecutors of Israel have appreciated him when he was in dire straits. When they behold that notwithstanding all persecutions, Israel holds fast unto the Lord, then they understand his merit."

E. Tz., p. 97.

94. LOYALTY TO ISRAEL

1. God's Love for Israel

The Karliner said: "May I be able to love a good Jew as much as God loves a wicked one."[1]

M. D., p. 217.

[1] Compare 91:3.

2. Loving Our Fellow-Jews

The Besht was seated with his disciples, listening to their half-hearted praise of Israel.

"You are like a step-mother who praises her step-son, not because of affection for him, but in order to please her husband," said the Besht. "Israel is a holy and good nation, a people versed in the Torah, a gracious and upright people."

He continued in this strain until the Hasidim were thoroughly instructed in true love for their fellow-Jews.

M. R. T., p. 45.

3. Speak No Evil of Jerusalem

Said the Staliner Rabbi: "When a Jew speaks or thinks evil of his fellow-Jews, he shall be expelled from the Heavenly Abode, even as one who speaks evil of the king's sons is driven from the royal palace. He who loves a person, loves also his children. Likewise, one who loves God, also loves Israel, His son."

O. Y., p. 213.

4. Loyalty Unto Death

The Kobriner related the following tale: "When Napoleon's army invaded Russia, a Saxon officer was captured by the Russians. The Russian commander lacked the facilities to house an officer, and therefore gave the latter a choice between surrendering his commission and death. The officer exclaimed: 'I will never disgrace my king by a promise not to serve him,' and he was executed.

"Let this be a lesson to the Jew," added the Rabbi. "Let him never become an apostate, or transgress the major commands of God, even if death be his portion."

O. Y., p. 109.

5. God's Tephillin

Said Rabbi Schmelke: "An allegory of the Talmud says that God wears phylacteries on his forehead and on his hand, whereon are written the words: 'Who is like unto Thy people, Israel, one nation?' Israel being the only nation on earth which observes God's commandments in the Torah. But when an Israelite sins, the Lord exclaims: 'I am ashamed of my forehead; I am ashamed of my forearm,' as the writing thereon does not conform with strict truth." [1]

S. ha-Tov, p. 41.

[1] Sanhedrin 46a, where, however, another meaning is given to the verb.

6. God's Tephillin Are Fallen

The Berditschever, breaking off his prayer, turned to God, saying: "Lord of the World, Thou art bound to forgive Israel its sins. If Thou wilt do so, it is well. If not, I will inform all the world that Thou art walking about in Tephillin that are unlawful and of no effect. For what said David, Thine anointed one? 'Who is like Thy people Israel, a people set apart on earth?' [1] But if Thou wilt not forgive the sins of Israel, their privilege is of no avail, the word carried in Thy Tephillin untrue, and the Tephillin unlawful."

Another time he exhorted the Divinity as follows: "Lord of the Universe, the people of Israel are the Tephillin of Thy head. When a Jew drops his Tephillin, he lifts them up with loving care, cleanses them of every stain, and then, with a kiss, makes amends for their abasement. Lord of the World, Thy Tephillin are fallen to the ground!"

N. B. L., p. 25; see also B., p. 455.

[1] II Samuel 7:23.

7. Speak No Evil of a Jew

Said the Apter: "It is a grave sin to speak evil, even of the most wicked Jew. Such malignment brings grief to the Shekinah."

M. Hat., p. 72.

8. The Long Arm

Said the Kozmirer: "When all Jews cherish love for each other, they become together as one giant man and their arms together become one long arm. Then in truth it is possible for this mighty arm to reach into Heaven itself and bring down to earth all gracious things."

V. S., p. 45.

9. The Influence of Esau

The Magelnitzer Rabbi said: "When Jacob was about to meet Esau he experienced greater fear of the Lord, but was distressed that it should come through the influence of Esau (Gen. 32:8). Many times we, the descendants of Jacob, begin to reverence God and attach ourselves closely to the people of Israel when our adversaries, the descendants of Esau, threaten us. But, like Jacob, we should feel distressed that this return to Israel should have been caused by the influence of Esau's offspring, our foes."

S. Hay., p. 62.

10. The Preventive

A man of wealth lost his fortune and was unable to provide for the marriage of his daughters. He complained to the Lubliner who counseled him to go forth to ask for donation. The man said: "But, Rabbi, I shall become a hater of Jews. Every time one gives me nothing or less than I think he should, I will hold hate in my heart for him."

"Here is a preventive," said the Lubliner. "Believe that the Lord has decreed how much you are to receive from each person, and you will bear no ill will towards any one."

M. H. H., p. 19.

11. True Proof

Said the "Yud": "The true proof regarding our advancement in service to the Lord lies in our own knowledge as to whether we have advanced in our love for Israel."

Tif. Yeh, p. 40.

12. The Itinerant Preacher

The Berditschever heard an itinerant preacher accusing Jews of violating Jewish laws. He lifted up his eyes and exclaimed: "Lord of the Universe: this Maggid is compelled to make bitter complaints against Thy children because he needs the few coins that are usually given to a wandering preacher. Give him, O Lord, his few coins in another way, and save him from the necessity of speaking evil of Israel."

F. U. A. O., i, 258.

13. Balaam and the Prophets

Said the Pulnoer: "Balaam showered praises upon Israel while the Prophets rained reproofs upon them. Who was the better friend? The ultimate intention of each gives the answer. Balaam intended to persuade the Israelites that they had already attained perfection and need not improve themselves. Had they accepted his counsel, they would have deteriorated and become like other nations.

"The Prophets, however, intended to spur Israel into attaining a state of higher purity and goodness. They, therefore, rebuked them even for minor sins, and did not hesitate to exaggerate their shortcomings."

F. U. A. O., ii, 53.

95. MAN

1. False Commentaries

Said Rabbi Bunam: "It was my intention to write a treatise under the title: 'Man.' It was to require merely a quarter of a page, and the whole meaning of the term 'man' was to be included therein. But after consideration, I changed my decision, lest my treatise might lead to false commentaries."

S. I., p. 29.

2. The Power of Man

Said the Koretzer: "Man contains within himself all the worlds that exist; he is, therefore, able to have contact with them all. Man possesses within himself all good and all evil traits, but they are in an unborn state; it is within his power to give them birth. If he is angelic in character, he will transform evil traits into good. If he is demonic, he will transform good traits into evil. It is the study of the Torah and the performance of Mitzwoth that aid us to become as holy as angels."

M. P., p. 38.

3. A Small World

Rabbi Noah Lekhivitzer said: "Man is often called 'a small world.' This title is to be explained as follows: If a man is small in his own eyes, he is indeed a 'world.' But if a man is 'a world' in his own eyes, then is he indeed small."

Z. Z., p. 13.

4. Man's Creation

Said the Koretzer: "Man was created last for the following reason: if he is deserving, he shall find all nature at his service; if he is undeserving, he shall find all nature arrayed against him."

Nof. Tz., p. 52.

5. Will He Choose Good?

The author of "Keli Yakar" explains why after the creation of man, there are not written the words: "And God saw that it was good" (Gen. 1:25) as in the case of the cattle. All other creatures received their final nature at the time of creation. But man was endowed with the faculty of free-will or self-improvement. Hence it was impossible to declare concerning him that he was good at the time of his creation. It was fitting to discover first what he would make of himself.[1]

F. U. A. O., i, 9.

[1] See Material on Free-Will, 57.

6. A Single Mitzwah

Said the Koretzer: "A man may often live out the entire span of his life for the purpose of performing a single Mitzwah or gaining a single chosen end."

M. P., p. 13.

7. Feet, Hands, and Mind

Said the Koretzer: "Humanity may be likened to the form of a man. Israel is the head, since his importance lies in the achievements of his mind. Other nations are the hands, since they are valuable for their manual works. Animals are the feet, since their worth derives from their feet.

"A man's life may also be compared to the form of a man. In his youth his strength is in his feet; in middle age, in his hands; in old age, in his head."

M. P., p. 9.

96. MARRIAGE

1. The World Is Like a Wedding Hall

The word of the Sages: "This world is like a Wedding" (Erubin, 54a) Rabbi Jacob Joseph of Pulnoe explained as follows:

"Just as it is the goal of the wedding to unite the bridegroom with his spouse, so it is the duty of man to unite himself in this world with Godhead."

Bl., Gem., p. 163.

2. No One Can Be Happy All the Time

Commenting upon the Talmudical saying: "This world is like a wedding hall,"[1] the Alexanderer Rabbi said: A villager came to an inn in Warsaw. In the evening he heard the music and tumult of a wedding coming from the next house. The same occurrence was repeated for several evenings. The villager asked the inn-keeper:

[1] Erubin, 54a.

"How is it possible that a single householder should have so many weddings?"

The innkeeper replied: "It is a wedding hall; to-day one person holds a wedding there; to-morrow another."

"This is symbolic of the way of the world," commented the Rabbi. "There are always those who enjoy themselves. But some days it is one person, and on other days, it is another. No one is happy all the time."

S. S. K., i, 107.

3. The Coachman's Charity

The Lubliner told the following story: "A coachman heard music coming from a house, but suddenly it was succeeded by sounds of a quarrel. He went into the house to investigate, and discovered that the wedding of a poor couple had been interrupted when it was learned that the Tallith [1] promised by the bride to the bridegroom had not been furnished. The coachman promptly gave all his money towards the purchase of a Tallith, and the ceremony continued with music and jubilation.

"This was the highest form of charity," commented the Rabbi. "It affected the welfare and entire future of two children of Israel."

N. H. L., p. 14.

[1] Prayer Shawl.

4. Adding Beauty to Mitzwoth

Rabbi Isaiah Kalman Halberstadt said: "We read in the Talmud (Taanith 30b): Said Rabban Simeon ben Gamaliel: 'There were no holidays in Israel like Yom Kippur and the Fifteenth Day of Ab.' On the latter day (Midsummer Day) the maidens were privileged to ask the young men in marriage. They would arrange an open-air dance in the vineyards; all were dressed in pure white garments, and when the youths would approach, the maidens would divide into three groups. The handsome girls would say: 'Observe our beauty for it is fitting that a wife should be of comely appearance.' Those of noble family would say: 'Observe our high-born lineage for this forebodes good children.' Those of unprepossessing countenance would say: 'Take unto yourselves wives for the sake of obeying the will of God, and adorn us with gold.'

"The phrases of the handsome maidens and the last words spoken by the unhandsome may seem to be frivolous. But they will not appear thus on closer scrutiny and explanation.

"When a man wishes to donate a Scroll of the Torah, he usually desires to do so in a generous fashion. He may either spend additional money to obtain excellent parchment and fine script. This may be accounted 'beauty of the body.'

"Or he may seek for a scroll written by a man of rare piety and holiness. This may be accounted as 'beauty of lineage,' since the value of the Scroll lies in its distinguished associations.

"Or he may strive to obtain a beautiful coverlet, or a fine pair of holders, or decorative adornments for the Scroll. This may be accounted as 'beauty of the exterior.' In each instance the man endeavours to perform the Mitzwah in a beautiful manner.

"So it is with the maidens. The first group says: 'When you seek to perform the Mitzwah of taking a wife to yourself in a fitting manner, consider beauty of the body.'

"The second group says: 'Consider the beauty of noble descent.'

"The third group says: 'We have neither beauty of body or noble descent. But if you wish to marry solely for the sake of the Mitzwah and not for ulterior motives, then demonstrate this by marrying us. As for the beauty you may wish to add to the Mitzwah, it will be sufficient to adorn us in costly garments and jewels."

Tif. Haz., pp. 66-67.

5. The 15th of Ab and Yom Kippur

Said the "Yud": "The reason that the Talmud (Taanith 30b) compares the 15th day of Ab to Yom Kippur is as follows: the 15th day of Ab commemorates the permission of marriage between the various tribes of Israel,[1] and the sins of the young people are forgiven on a wedding day, as on Yom Kippur."

Nif. Yeh., p. 67.

[1] Numbers 36:8 prohibits it.

6. The Careless Prayer

When the "Yud's" first wife died, he waited two years, and then married her younger sister. He grieved greatly, however, over the loss of his first wife. Once he said: "The death of my first wife may be due to her own mother. My mother-in-law professed to be so pleased with me that she prayed within her heart: 'O Lord, send my younger daughter a husband like unto the husband of my older daughter.' Her prayer was heard, and since there seemed to be no other man who would have satisfied her as much as I, her older daughter was compelled to die, thereby giving place as my wife to her younger sister."

Tif. Yeh., p. 6.

96. A. BRIDES, BRIDEGROOMS AND DOWRIES

1. The Family Stem

A man came to the Gerer Rabbi asking his advice whether he should permit the marriage of his son to a maiden whose uncle had become an apostate. The Rabbi replied: "You may safely accept the maiden as your daughter-in-law. So long as the family stem is sound, one need not mind about the branch."

S. S. K., p. 78.

2. Nuts Without Cultivation

The Gerer Rabbi said: "The custom in many congregations of showering the bridegroom with nuts when he goes up to read the Torah on the Sabbath preceding his wedding, is founded on the following principle: the Talmud teaches that one who assumes the yoke of learning Torah is freed from the yoke of profane labors.[1] Thus, the bridegroom is reminded that should he decide to occupy himself solely with study, his livelihood will come to him as free from labor as nuts that grow without cultivation."

S. S. K., i, 83.

[1] Ethics of the Fathers, 3:6; Singer, p. 191

3. Welcoming the Bride

The Alexanderer Rabbi was once reading the Talmudical enumeration of acts of kindness,[1] among which are to be found the following three: visiting the sick, welcoming the bride, attending the funeral. He was asked: "Why does the Talmud interpose welcoming the bride between the sick and the dead?"

The Rabbi replied: "The Talmud seeks to teach us that when we visit a sick person dear to us, we should give charity towards the wedding expenses of a poor bride. By virtue of this good deed, the Lord will preserve us from the necessity of attending the funeral of the friend who is ill."

S. S. K., i, 101.

[1] Based on Sabbath 127, with additions in the Morning Prayers; Singer, p. 5.

4. Dowries for the Poor

Rabbi Baruch of Gorletz, a son of the Tzanzer Rabbi, came to his father, asking aid for the dowry of his daughter. The Tzanzer replied that he lacked the money. A few days later Rabbi Baruch learned that some wealthy Hasidim had rewarded his father with large sums of money for his excellent words of counsel. He again visited his father and besought his monetary aid. The Rabbi said: "I have already distributed the money among the poor for dowries."

"But, father, why am I worse than a stranger?" asked the son.

"You are my son," responded Rabbi Hayyim, "and can easily secure assistance from my Hasidim if you will appeal to them. But these poor folk have no well-known father."

N. Haz., p. 37.

5. The Rabbi's Daughter

The Tzanzer had everything in readiness for his daughter's wedding, when a widow entered, lamenting that her daughter was about to marry, but that she lacked the wedding gown. The Rabbi promptly gave to her everything he had prepared for his daughter. The girl complained but her father comforted her saying: "Do not concern yourself about what you bring your bridegroom. You will be acceptable to him because you are my daughter."

M. D., p. 282.

6. Sharing His Fame

The Kotzker Rabbi told his brother-in-law, the Gerer Rabbi, that he had misgivings regarding the validity of his marriage. His wife, he believed, undoubtedly had consented to marry him because she thought him to be a Rabbi, whereas in his inmost heart, he knew that he was not great enough to be a Rabbi.

The Gerer replied: "My sister did not care whether you are worthy to be a Rabbi or not. She merely desired to share your fame as an illustrious Rabbi, and the populace will always speak of you as the 'Kotzker Rabbi.' "

S. S. K., p. 77.

7. The Wise Choice

Rabbi Isaac of Hamburg desired that his daughter should marry the son of Rabbi Isaac of Linsk, and promised a dowry of six hundred gold eagles. When the prospective bridegroom's parents perceived that the maiden was unprepossessing of looks, they wished to abandon the entire matter. Rabbi Isaac of Hamburg persuaded them to discuss it with their son. The youth had been impressed by the girl's nobility of character, and insisted that he take her to wife. It had been previously agreed that Rabbi Isaac of Hamburg should transmit the promised dowry before the betrothal. The bride's father, however, did not adhere to this condition. Again the Rabbi of Linsk wished to abandon the matter, but once more his son insisted that the betrothal should take place. Immediately afterwards, Rabbi Isaac drew the dowry from his purse.

"If the money was in your possession," inquired Rabbi Isaac of Linsk, "why did you vex me with vain worry?"

Rabbi Isaac of Hamburg replied: "The Talmud teaches that when a man takes a wife for the beauty of her countenance or for her wealth, their children will lack good character.[1] I noted that your son did not wish to marry my daughter for her looks. Now I see also that he does not desire her for her money either. There is every hope, therefore, that they will have admirable children." [2]

O. N., p. 46.

[1] Kiddushin, 70; Sanhedrin, 107.
[2] The Ropshitzer was the son of this couple.

8. A Pearl or a Pea

A friend of the Oheler Rabbi proposed that the latter give his daughter in marriage to the author of "Aryeh d'bei Illaah." The author agreed to become the Oheler's son-in-law, but he stipulated that a settlement be made, so that he might continue his studies in peace of mind, the income from the settlement to be sufficient for his livelihood. The wife of the Oheler opposed the settlement of so large a sum upon a "Batlan." [1] Her husband answered: "A peasant was digging in his field, and discovered a jar containing what he believed to be peas. He tried to cook them but they remained hard. Thereupon he went to a neighbor, and received in exchange peas that were edible. The neighbor had recognized the supposed 'peas' for what they were, namely, precious pearls. He moved away from the vicinity, and realized a great fortune from their sale.

"I, too," said the Oheler Rabbi, "have found a pearl for my daughter. Shall I exchange it for merely an edible pea?"

P. v. K., pp. 15b-16a.

[1] Subsidized scholar; an unworldly person.

9. The Tzanzer's Payment

A dangerously ill man sought the blessing of the Tzanzer, and soon after regained his health. He desired to reward the Rabbi with a gift of 300 thalers, but the Tzanzer declined it.

A few years later, a poor man lamented to the Tzanzer that his daughter remained unmarried because he could not present her with a suitable dowry. The Rabbi gave the father a letter to the magnate who had been restored to health on receiving his blessing. The man could not at first understand why the Tzanzer requested a gift of 300 thalers, but his wife reminded him of the Rabbi's kindness, and said: "It behooves you to give the money as the Rabbi enjoins. He is only asking what is rightly due him."

E. Tz., p. 128.

10. Both Said the Same

Once the Ropshitzer endeavored to link in marriage the families of two noted Zaddikim. The father of the prospective groom said: "I demand that the father of the girl give the young couple twice the dowry I present, inasmuch as my son is a great scholar." The father of the prospective bride likewise demanded twice the dowry on the ground that his family was of higher pedigree. The Ropshitzer remarked to each father separately: "You are quite right; the other one says exactly the same thing."

Eventually the two fathers came together, and after many misunderstandings, they reached an agreement. When the Ropshitzer appeared, they demanded an explanation. He replied: "I merely spoke the truth to you, namely, that each of you said exactly the same thing. I knew that when you would meet, you would not demand double payment from each other, for only a thief is required by law to pay double" (Exodus 22:3).

Ohel N., pp. 126-7.

96. B. WORTHY WIVES

1. The Berditschever's Wife

It was said that the Berditschever's wife excelled even the Rabbi himself in holiness. Once she was overheard saying: "O Lord, may I be worthy that my Levi Isaac may have the same holy thoughts when he says grace over the bread that I have when I form the loaves."

Kahana, p. 252.

2. A Loyal Wife

The wife of one of the Berditschever's enemies met him one day on the street and poured over his head a pail of water. He ran to the synagogue and prayed: "O Lord, do not punish the 'good woman'; she must have done this by the order of her husband, and she is therefore to be commended as an obedient wife."

Kahana, p. 252.

3. Do Not Lose Courage

The Slonimer related the following story:
"A Commander-in-Chief received a message telling him that his main line of defense had been broken by the enemy. He was greatly distressed and his emotions showed plainly on his countenance. His wife heard the nature of the message, and entering her husband's room, she said: 'I too at this very moment have received tidings worse than yours.'

'And what are they?' inquired the Commander with agitation.

'I have read discouragement on your face,' replied the wife. 'Loss of courage is worse than loss of defence.'

By the same token, loss of the will to battle our evil impulses is worse than the offense we commit when we are overpowered by them."

O. Y., p. 109.

4. The Same Dish

In bidding adieu to a group of young men who were his visitors, the Riziner said to them: "Be careful to pray betimes. If you ask why on occasion I am late with my prayers, I will explain it by a parable:

'A certain woman was in the habit of cooking daily the same dish of soup. Once she was late with dinner, and her husband was forced to wait. When he found on the table the same dish, he exclaimed angrily: "I waited with patience because I thought you were preparing a new dish which requires more time. I beg of you, however, not to keep me waiting for the usual dish."'

"We, the Zaddikim, offer prayers with different devotional thoughts daily. It requires time for proper concentration of the mind upon these; hence, we pray late. You, however, have the same inadequate concentration day after day; hence, for such prayers you must not keep the Lord waiting."

When another Rabbi heard of this, he commented: "If the husband truly loves his wife, he readily forgives her tardiness."

The Riziner was told of this comment, and praised the second Rabbi for his defense of ordinary Jews.

N. I., p. 77.

5. Her Wise Choice

When the future wife of the Oheler Rabbi was about to become a bride, her father said to her: "I have had requests for your hand from three young men. One is poor, but a scholar; another rich, but of little scholarly attainment; the third, very wealthy, but unlearned in Hebrew."

The maiden replied: "What matter a man's wealth if he be ignorant, or of limited learning! The third youth may be poor, but he must be truly brilliant, if you, father, praise him!"

She married the Rabbi, Moses Teitelbaum, who became worldrenowned as the Oheler.

P. v. K., p. 9b.

6. A Fresh Share

The father-in-law of the Rimanover wished him to become a merchant instead of a "Batlan," and demanded that he abandon his life of study and piety. The Rimanover refused, and since his wife agreed with his decision, her father drove them both from their home. For three days the Rimanover ate no food. Finally his wife asked the baker for a loaf of bread, and the baker replied: "You are already in great debt to me. I shall cancel the amount if you will give me your share in the World-to-Come."

The woman agreed, and when she brought the food to her husband, she began to weep. The Rimanover learned the cause of her tears, and said: "By rescuing me from starvation, you have earned for yourself a fresh share in the World-to-Come."

Em. L., p. 26.

96. C. UNWORTHY WIVES

1. The Excessively Good

Once the Kobriner narrated the following story: "On his deathbed a father warned his son to beware of the excessively good.

"The son married a beautiful girl. Once he invited her to go walking with him, but she declined, saying she did not wish to have men admire her. 'She is too modest,' thought the husband.

"He announced that he was taking a journey, but returned unexpectedly to discover that his wife had been unfaithful to him with an officer. The latter threatened to kill the unfortunate husband, who left the house, and wandered through the streets all night. In the meantime the king's jewels were discovered to have been stolen, and the wanderer was arrested by the police on suspicion of being the thief.

"He could not say where the jewels were hidden, and was therefore condemned to death. On the way to execution, he overheard a bystander remark to his guard not to tread upon some worms on the ground. He felt sure this over-kind person was a villain, and accused him to the guard of having stolen the royal jewels. This flash of intuition proved correct, and the gems were found on his premises. The judge asked the man how he had singled out the true thief. The man related the story of his father's warning, and, pouring out his heart, told also the story of his wife's infidelity. The disloyal wife and her lover were arrested for their threats, and the husband was restored to his property."

O. Y., p. 80.

2. Two Counsels

A man on his way home from a long journey stopped over to visit the Berditschever. He was impressed by the Rabbi's piety and benevolence, and presented him with a goodly donation. The Rabbi said: "I will repay you by giving you two bits of counsel. The first is: when in doubt, turn to the right; the second is: when you see a young woman married to an old man, look for murder."

The man took his departure in his carriage, and soon came to a junction in the roads. He saw a group of the gendarmerie standing in hesitation, and was informed that they were searching for a thief who had stolen a large sum of money. The traveler advised them to take the road on the right, and followed them also. The thief and his booty were soon discovered, and a substantial reward was presented to the traveler for his counsel.

He continued on his way, and at nightfall halted at an inn. The old landlord wished to give him lodging, but the young wife informed her husband that no rooms were available. The traveler could find no other accommodations, and since it was raining heavily, he lay down beneath the eaves of the inn. About midnight he was awakened by the noise of a wagon. He quietly stole out and saw a man descend from it, knock at the window, and whisper for some time to the young wife of the innkeeper. Scraps of conversation which reached the watcher's ears convinced him that they planned the innkeeper's death. He immediately began to shout "Murder, murder." The culprits escaped in the wagon, and the old innkeeper rewarded his rescuer handsomely. He also sent a gift to the Berditschever who had forseen the consequences of his unwise marriage.

E. O., p. 53.

3. A Wife's Importunities

The "Yud" narrated the following tale: "A Hasid died and was taken before the Heavenly Tribunal. His earthly conduct seemed to have been exemplary and he would have been assigned to Paradise, except for the testimony of an Angel that he had once committed a serious misdeed. The Hasid excused himself on the ground that his wife had compelled him to commit the offense. The Prosecuting Angel laughed aloud at this statement. The Hasid was sentenced to undergo a period of punishment before departing for the Garden of Eden. The Angel, also, was punished for ridiculing the Hasid. He was sentenced to become a mortal man, since the Heavenly Tribunal wished to convince the Angel that sometimes it is well-nigh impossible to withstand the importunities of a wife."

Nif. Yeh., p. 57.

96. D. DIVORCE

1. The Tears

Rabbi Sussya's wife was a quarrelsome woman, and persistently urged him to separate from her.

One night he called to her and said: "Hendel, look here!" He showed her that his pillow was quite damp. Then he said: "Our Sages declared: 'If a man puts away his first wife, the very altar pours forth tears over him.'[1] Do you still wish the letter of divorce?"

From this moment henceforth Rabbi Sussya's wife was quiet, amiable and good.

Bl., Pr., p. 92.

[1] Sanhedrin, 22.

2. Forgiveness and Consolation

After the death of Rabbi Abraham, the Angel, the night following her seven nights of mourning, the widow in her dreams ascended to Heaven. She entered an ample hall, and there she beheld a number of throne-chairs ranged in a semi-circle, and on each throne a man of might. There entered one, like in face and bearing unto the others—her husband, Abraham. He said:

"Know, my companions, that my wife hath this just grievance against me! On earth I lived with her as one apart from her, and for this I stand in need of forgiveness."

"It is yours!" cried the widow, "with all my heart I grant you forgiveness!" And presently she awoke consoled.

Shivchei Besht, p. 44 (B., p. 419).

97. MASTER AND DISCIPLE

1. In Their Hearts

The Kobriner visited the Slonimer Rabbi and asked him: "Have your teachers left any writings as a heritage?"

"Yes," replied the Slonimer.

"Are they printed or are they still in manuscript?" asked the Kobriner.

"Neither," said the Slonimer. "They are inscribed in the hearts of their Disciples."[1]

O. Y., p. I (In introduction).

[1] This is a typical statement and indicates the methods of the Hasidic Rabbis. Just as the New Testatement was written from the heritage received by the Disciples from their Master, so were many of the Hasidic teachings transmitted.

2. *Baring His Heart*

The Rozdoler was asked to tell something regarding his Master, the Strelisker. The Rozdoler bared his heart, and said: "Look into my heart, and you will know what my Master is."

E. Tz., p. 78.

3. *A Burning Coal*

Said the Besht: "The influence of a leader is likened, in the Talmud,[1] to a burning coal. Do not hold yourself aloof from your Master; you will remain cold. Do not approach him too closely; you may be burned. This applies also to your relationship with your friends."

M. R. T., ii, 80.

[1]Ethics 2:15; Singer, p. 189.

4. *Traits in Common*

Said the Besht: "We are told by our Sages[1] to cleave unto the wise. But how can a vulgar man attach himself to one who is wise? By searching out those gracious traits which are common to himself and the Sage. These will furnish both with a point of contact, and a mutual interest in a form of goodness."

M. R. T., ii, 104.

[1] Kethubhoth, 111.

5. *The Man of Purity*

Rabbi Bunam heard the "Yud" oftentimes repeat: "Whosoever attaches himself to a pure man becomes pure."[1] Rabbi Bunam asked: "Where does the justice lie in this? A man who has not labored to purify himself may become as pure as one who has labored diligently to achieve purity?"

The "Yud" answered: "It is often more difficult to remain attached to a man of purity than to purify oneself."

Nif. Yeh., p. 42.

[1] Baba Kamma, 92.

6. *A Reversal of Place*

Rabbi Mordecai Tzernobiler said: "Though the 'Yud' was a disciple of the Lubliner in this world, he is greater in the eyes of posterity than his Master. Oftentimes the positions of Master and Disciple are reversed in Heaven."

Tif. Yeh., p. 13.

7. Holiness Versus Wit

The Ropshitzer voiced a witticism which pleased his Master, the Rimanover, and the latter complimented the Ropshitzer on his wisdom. The Ropshitzer said: "My Master is a man of holiness. How then can he understand a witty saying?"

The Rimanover felt piqued and the Ropshitzer was forced to labor hard to appease him.

Ohel N., p. 29.

8. The Cherished Disciple

Rabbi Benjamin Wolf Halevy narrated the following: "My Master, the Koretzer, said: 'No one can appreciate how deep is the brain of my Disciple, Raphael Bershider.' On another occasion, he said: 'The Besht remarked that God would thank him for giving him such a 'Yossele' (Jacob Joseph Pulnoer); I say that God will thank me for giving Him such a Raphael.' A third time, the Koretzer said: 'I cannot guarantee that anyone I praise will not become spoiled, with the exception of my Raphael.' "

M. P., p. 41.

9. The Disciple's Atonement

When the Besht heard of the holy conduct and the greatness of Rabbi Jacob Joseph, he desired to number him among his society of Hasidim. He invited him to a Sabbath meal, and there related the following tale: "A learned Rabbi in a village was preparing his sermon for the 'Great Sabbath.' [1] After rehearsing it several times he became very thirsty. He walked over to the window and called out to a passing water-carrier. The latter refused to heed his summons, and the Rabbi became indignant. When the water-carrier passed the house again and still refused to give heed, the Rabbi went outside and struck the man on the cheek. The Rabbi greatly regretted this outburst of anger, and it still weighs heavily upon his conscience. If he should come to me, I could indicate to him a path of repentance."

Rabbi Jacob Joseph confessed that he was the Rabbi of the story, and thereupon became the Besht's most enthusiastic adherent.

D. D., pp. 77-8.

[1] Preceding Passover.

98. MELANCHOLY

1. The Sin of the Melancholy

A Hasid bemoaned to the Lubliner that evil lusts plagued him and made him melancholy. The Master said to him: "Above all else, rid yourself of melancholy, for it is more pernicious than sin. When the Evil One rouses men to lust, it is not his aim to make them sin, but to draw them through sin into the pit of melancholy."

E. O., p. 101 (B., p. 481m).

2. Aphorisms on Melancholy and Sadness

Said the Alexanderer:

"1. Sadness is not a sin, but no sin hardens the heart so much as sadness.

"2. A Jew who is not always full of joy because he is a Jew, is ungrateful to the Lord.

"3. One who looks into his inner self whether he is a proper Hasid is guilty of pride. All he needs to know is if he is a proper Jew.

"4. Sadness is the worst quality in a man. It is the attribute of an incurable egotist. He is always thinking: 'Something should rightfully come to me; something is wrongfully lacking to me.' Whether in relation to substance or spirit, it is always 'I.'

"5. There is only a hair's breadth between sadness and bitterness, and bitterness leads to heartbreak.

"6. To the one obsessed by sadness, his very body feels heavy to carry around. He cannot abide himself; he cannot abide the other Jew.

"7. The most delicate dissatisfaction with himself is associated in a man's life with sadness, but the most complete joy is born out of holiness."

S. S. K., i, 115.

3. Signs of Melancholy

Said the Koretzer: "The man of melancholy may be known by these signs:

1. A lack of desire to visit Palestine.

2. A lack of interest in Holy Studies, except for study in order to fulfil the commandment to study Torah.

3. An inability to serve God through everything he hears and knows.

4. An inability to shed tears."

Nof. Tz., p. 12.

4. Repentance and Melancholy

Said the Bershider: "It is not easy to repent of the sin of melancholy. When one begins to repent of it, he falls into deeper melancholy by the knowledge that he has sinned. The sole remedy is to think only of the moment of repentance, and not of the later consequences of his sin."

M. P., p. 50.

5. The Bratzlaver on "Melancholy"

"1. Man's talk often brings him tribulations and sorrows.
"2. Sadness weakens a man.
"3. Melancholy oftentimes presages illness.
"4. God does not abide with the man of sadness.
"5. A man does not attain his hope through sadness.
"6. Sadness leads to heartache.
"7. He who is sad brings upon himself many afflictions.
"8. The study of the Hagadah [1] removes sadness.
"9. Sadness leads to quarrels; joy to peace."

Sef. Ham., pp. 115-117.

[1] The narrative and imaginative lore of the Talmud.

99. MERCY OF GOD

1. Endless Mercies

Said the Psedburzer Rabbi: "If we realize that our very existence is only by reason of God's grace and mercy, we may easily understand that God will grant us other mercies as well. God's power is endless and his mercies are without limit."

O. Y., p. 67.

2. Mercies for the Undeserving

A man came to the Rozdoler with a donation accompanying his written request for the blessing of happiness. The Rozdoler said to him: "You are giving me a donation because you believe that I am a 'Good Jew' (a Rebbe or Zaddik). I know, however, that I am not a Rebbe and do not merit your gift. But one of God's attributes is that he has mercy even on the undeserving. Hence if you give to an undeserving person, God will repay you in the same measure and will aid you even though you may not merit His help. A good deed performed on the earth below brings down from Heaven the Divine mercy." [1]

E. K., p. 63.

[1] The last phrase is an important axiom of the Kabbalah.

3. Making God's Mercies Known

Rabbi Mordecai of Tzernobil commented thus on Psalm 118: 1-4: "In truth God's mercy fills every occurrence of our life. But this is not always apparent to each one of us. The Psalmist says: 'O give thanks unto the Lord, for He is good, for His mercy endureth forever.' But if the mercy is not perceived by all, 'Let Israel so say'; if Israel cannot perceive it, 'Let the House of Aaron say so.' If even they do not observe it, 'Let those that fear the Lord then s; it.' "

Beth Phineas, pp. 38-40.

4. Why We Prosper

Said the Belzer: "We read in Psalm 24:5: 'He shall receive a blessing from the Lord and righteousness [1] from the God of his salvation.' When we succeed in business or study let us remember that our success has come not because of our sagacity or good sense. Furthermore, let us not imagine that we have deserved the blessing because of our goodness. We have received it because God in His mercy has desired to aid us."

D. S., p. 50.

[1] "Zedakah" means also "Charity."

5. The Compassion of God and Man

The Tzartkover Rabbi said: "If a man obtains the compassion of his fellow-men, he also obtains the compassion of God. For the Angels of Mercy argue: 'If a mortal man takes pity on him, surely the All-Compassionate should have mercy upon him.'"

E. O., p. 148.

6. Mercy Through Effort

Said the Koretzer: "When a man is in a state of tribulation, God's mercies emanate from Him, but they remain on high. It requires the effort of repentance, prayer, tears and good deeds to bring them down God's mercy on behalf of the suppliant."

M. P., p. 17.

7. Kindness With Pain

Said the Lentzner: "There are two forms of kindness. A kind man may give money to a person who is sick, and allow him to use his own efforts to improve his circumstances. Not so, however, the kind father and his ill son. The father labors through every means to cure the malady of his son, even though a painful operation may be necessary.

"The Lord is not satisfied merely with forgiving our sins and granting us an opportunity to do better. He wishes to take a hand in our improvement. Therefore He sends us teachers to rebuke and instruct and influence us. If this proves inadequate, He sends down tribulations, even as the mortal father permits his son to suffer pain as a prelude to recovery. Oftentimes, however, we are unable to bear the Lord's punishments, even though we may know they are the height of compassion. We therefore entreat Him to limit His kindness according to our ability to bear it."

R. T., ii. 26.

8. Trust and Fear

Said the Besht: "Trust in God's mercies, and His kindness will encompass you. Fear God's punishments, and His strict judgment will surround you. Wherever your mind abides, you will find yourself cleaving unto it. Serve the Lord in love and in complete trust, and you will receive His mercies."

K. S. T., p. 17a.

9. Boundless Mercies

The Berditschever read in the Machzor the words: "We are full of sins, but Thou art full of mercies." [1] The Rabbi thereupon exclaimed: "O Lord! Consider how insignificant we are and how insignificant are the sins which we are able in our littleness to commit. But Thou art Unlimited and there is no boundary to Thy mercies. How art Thou able to limit them towards us?"

L. I. B., p. 83.

[1] Yom Kippur Prayer.

10. The Conduit

Said the Mezeritzer: "The good man who desires to receive the constant inspiration of God's benevolence must be like a conduit laid from a spring on a hilltop to water a field. In this conduit there must be no blemish of the smallest size. It must be laid straight and it must be carefully linked to the spring."

T. M. M., pp. 248-9.

11. Whoso Is Wise

Said Rabbi Bunam: "The Psalm (107) enumerates various misfortunes which God may send upon man, and concludes with the verse: 'Whoso is wise, let him observe these things, and let him consider the mercies of the Lord.' [1] From this we learn never to lose hope in the midst of misfortune, but to believe that it is truly meant for good. Let us have fortitude and patience to await better days, and we shall perceive that all was a sign of God's mercies."

S. I., p. 72.

[1] Psalm 107:43.

100. THE MESSIAH

A. The Messianic Hope

1. Be Prepared Today for Redemption

A Hasid placed this question before the Berditschever:
"Does not the verse in Malachi 3:23, which states that Elijah will appear before the great day of the Redemption to prepare the hearts of the fathers and their children, contradict the statement in Sanhedrin (98) that the Messiah replied to a query concerning the time of his advent with the verse in Psalm 95:7: 'Today, if you will obey His Voice?'"

The Rabbi replied: "The Messiah could come today without being preceded by Elijah, if we ourselves prepare our hearts without troubling the Prophet to do it for us. Let us make ourselves ready, then, to receive the Messiah any day by obeying the Voice of the Lord." [1]

E. O., p. 60.

[1] Compare Pesachim, 153: "Repent every day," and Browning's poem: "Ben Karshook's Wisdom."

2. *Today as Yesterday*

The Rabbi of Rozniatov, Rabbi Eliezer Lippmann, persistently inquired from Rabbi Mendel of Kossov why the Messiah has not come, and why the Redemption promised by the Prophets and Sages has not been fulfilled.

Rabbi Mendel answered: "It is written: 'Why has the son of Jesse not come, either today or yesterday?' [1] The answer lies in the question itself: 'Why has he not come? Because we are today, just as we were yesterday.' "

E. Tz., p. 65 (Bl., Pr., pp. 177-8).

[1] I Samuel 20:27.

3. *Compelling Messiah to Come*

Before his death, the Apter said: "The Berditschever declared before he passed over into 'his world,' that, when he arrived in Heaven, he would urgently make demands regarding Redemption until the Messiah would be dispatched. When, however, he crossed over into the Heavenly Abode, the Angels were wise enough to place him in a Hall of the highest delights, so that the Berditschever forgot his promise. I, however, faithfully pledge myself, when I attain the Heavenly Heights, that I will not allow myself to be beguiled by pleasures, and will compel the advent of the Messiah."

Bl., Gem., p. 230.

4. *The Bird's Nest* [1]

The Besht narrated this parable: "A migratory bird of rare beauty flew past the royal palace and alighted on the top of a high palm tree. The king yearned to possess this beautiful creature and instructed his courtiers to form a human ladder, one to stand on the shoulders of the other, until the highest could throw a net upon the bird. Though only men of strength were chosen, one weakened, and the entire human structure collapsed to the ground. By virtue of one man's fault, the king's desire could not be fulfilled.

"It is the same with us. The man of holiness depends upon the support of a lesser man, and the latter depends upon men of even lowlier quality in order to attain the summit of holiness and to bring down God's love. But when one person weakens, the whole structure totters and falls, and the Zaddik must begin anew."

M. R. T., p. 42.

[1] This is a famous parable and occurs in many versions. See Marvin Lowenthal, *M.J.*, x, 521.

"And the Temple of the Messiah is called in the Zohar 'the Bird's Nest.'"

Cohen-Buber, pp. 15-16.

5. Redemption Before Atonement?

Said the Riziner: It is told of the Grandfather of Spola, that he once exclaimed: 'Messiah, why tarriest thou? Art thou waiting for repentance and atonement? Verily, I swear the Jews will not make atonement.'

"I will not gainsay the Spoler, O Lord, but this I vow before Thee: let King Messiah come, and we will all make atonement. And for this we have fair warrant: *before* we sinned, four exiles[1] have been decreed against us, in the days of Abraham; it is, therefore, only fair that redemption should be ours before atonement."

On another occasion, the Riziner said:

"It is required of us that we repent and atone before redemption, but we have lost the power, for we are staggering under the burden of our sufferings like drunken men who cannot walk the way. Our Sages have demanded, not in plain words, but by plain implication, redemption before atonement, when they said[2] that crushing poverty makes men avert their faces from a knowledge of the Creator."

Bl., Gem., p. 283.

[1] Bereshith Rabba 54:2: of Egypt, Babylonia, Greece and Rome.
[2] Erubin, 41.

6. Pray for Messiah's Coming

On the Second Day of the New Year, Rabbi Schmelke preached on the text (I Samuel 20:27):

"Wherefore cometh not the son of Jesse to the meal,[1] neither yesterday, nor today?" "Why has not the Messiah, Son of Jesse, come yesterday or today, in former generations and in this generation? Because we petition the Lord merely for bread, for our material well-being. Had we wholeheartedly implored Him to send the Redeemer, and forgotten our individual needs, the Lord would assuredly have sent us the Messiah."

S. ha-Tov, p. 44.

[1] "Lechem" means "meal" or "bread."

7. Within Each Of Us

Said the Stretiner: "Each Jew has within himself an element of the Messiah which he is required to purify and mature. Messiah will come when Israel has brought him to the perfection of growth and purity within themselves."

E. Tz., p. 138.

8. Let Messiah Come!

Before Kol Nidrei, the Oheler stood before the Ark and said: "Lord of the Universe! Thou art well aware of my unworthiness, but Thou also knowest that I do not speak falsehood and that now, before the advent of Yom Kippur, I wish to relate to Thee my true thoughts. Had I known that the Messiah would not come in my own days, long ago I would have surrendered my soul to Thee. All that has held me to life is my expectation that the Messiah would speedily come. Let Messiah come now, not for our sake, but for Thy sake, so that Thy name may be glorified. I am prepared to die at once, if it has been decreed that I am unworthy to behold his coming, and if my living delays for even a moment the Redemption."

P. v. K., p. 11a.

9. The Bitter Exile

Rabbi Meir Apter and the Ropshitzer were at a wedding-feast. Said the Apter, holding forth a bottle of brandy: "When Messiah comes, we will go out to him with strong drink, and we shall show him the manner by which we awakened our religious emotions in the bitter Exile."

The Ropshitzer replied: "Nay, my dear friend. We will go out to him together, and show him the kind of religious leaders Israel possessed as guides in the bitter Exile."

Ohel N., p. 131.

10. The Harp and the Discourse

Rabbi Yekuthiel Teitelbaum narrated the following: "The Rimanover Rabbi assured his Disciples before his death that he would refuse to enter Paradise unless the Messiah would come. When he died, King David was ordered to play upon his harp, and the sweetness of the melody caused the Rimanover to forget his promise.

"When my grandfather, the Oheler, died, he said before his departure: 'David's harp shall not prevail over me.' On arrival, he was asked to deliver a discourse and was informed that the Messiah would come as soon as he had finished it. But since above us there is both unlimited time and unlimited wisdom, the discourse still continues, and the preacher believes that he has just begun."

P. v. K., p. 16b.

11. Elijah Will Explain

Commenting on the Talmudical passage (Erubin 43) that Elijah will not come on the Eve of the Sabbath or of the Holydays, the Belzer said:

"I anticipate his coming every day, even on the Eve of the Sabbath. As for the statement of the Talmud, it must be explained by Elijah when he comes. Do we not have many other statements in the Talmud awaiting his explanation?"

P. v. K., p. 35b.

12. Redemption of Prayers

A Zaddik once inquired of the Prophet Elijah why the Messiah fails to make an appearance and to redeem the people of Israel from its servitude in exile. He made answer: "Let the Israelites cease from praying without making sense of their supplications, and the Messiah will forthwith appear. Behold, the letters and words of holy prayer are held in captivity by heedless worshippers; let the Jews redeem them first and their own redemption will follow." [1]

[1] See "Unity in Prayer"; 187:9.

Cf. B., p. 649 ff.

B. False Messiahs

1. Akiba and Bar Kochba

An unbeliever asserted to the Rabbi of Berditschev that the great masters of old were steeped in error. For instance, Rabbi Akiba believed that Bar Kochba was the Messiah, and enrolled under his banner.

Thereupon the Berditschever narrated this parable: "Once upon a time the only son of an Emperor fell ill. One physician advised that a piece of linen be smeared with a burning salve and wrapped around the bare body of the patient. Another physician, however, discouraged this, because the boy was too weak to endure the pain the salve would cause. Thereupon a third physician recommended a sleeping-draught; but a fourth physician feared this might endanger the heart of the patient. Upon this, a fifth physician advised that the sleeping-draught be given by teaspoonfuls to the patient, as often as he awakened and felt the burning of the salve. And this was done.

"Thus, when God saw that the soul of Israel was sick unto death, he wrapped it in the biting linen of poverty and misery, but laid upon it the sleep of forgetfulness, in order that it might endure the pain. However, lest the spirit expire utterly, he awakens it from hour to hour with a false hope of a Messiah, and again puts it to sleep until the night shall have passed and the true Messiah shall appear. For such reasons the eyes of the wise are sometimes blinded." [1]

[1] "Rabbinic Wisdom," from Martin Buber; in *The Reflex*, May, 1929, p. 65. In N. B. L., p. 22, we find the same story, and the lesson drawn from it is as follows: "The Jewish nation—God's first-born—became dangerously ill with immorality and wickedness. The Prophets and the later Sages were unable to achieve any improvement, with the result that God prescribed Exile to purge us of our spiritual maladies. In order, however, that we, in our weakened state, may be able to bear it, He has permitted false Messiahs to mislead even the noblest Jews in order to sweeten the Exile by a hope of Redemption."

2. Sabbatai Zevi's Downfall

Of Sabbatai Zevi, the false Messiah and Pseudo-Redeemer of Smyrna, the Besht said:

"Many have trodden the same steep path [1] and have attained the fortunate goal. He, too, had a holy spark in his being; he fell, however, into the net of Samael, the false deceiver, who thrust him into the rôle of a Redeemer. This overtook him only because of his arrogance."

[1] In the study of the Kabbalah.

Bl., Pr., p. 68.

C. The Messiah's Character

1. The Loyal Wife

Rabbi Mordecai Lekhivitzer divorced his wife. His enemies who had vainly hunted for excuses to defame him, believed that the woman would not hesitate to inform them of any of her former husband's misdeeds.

Her reply, however, greatly surprised them. "I have nothing to declare regarding him," she said, "except to say that if he is not great enough to be the Messiah, no one in this generation is."

O. Y., p. 4.

2. The Holiness of the Berditschever

Rabbi Moshe of Zlotzov visited Rabbi Baruch of Medziboz. At the meal he noticed a Hasid imitating the bowings and movements of the Berditschever Rabbi at prayer. Instead of rebuking him, Rabbi Baruch laughed uproariously. Rabbi Moshe reproved him for ridiculing so holy a man.

Rabbi Baruch replied: "I well know his great holiness, but it is for this very reason that I am ridiculing him. The Satan frequently argues: 'What need is there of a Messiah and a Beth ha-Mikdash,[1] when the divine services of the Berditschever fully equal the divine services of the High Priest at the Holy Temple.'

"Therefore I ridicule his services to counteract the Satan's argument."

[1] Holy Temple.

Kahana, p. 248.

3. Hasid or Mithnaged?

Said the Kotzker: "I believe the Messiah will come as a 'Mithnaged.' If he came as a Hasid, the Mithnagedim would not be likely to accept him, whereas the Hasidim would quickly recognize him as Messiah, even though he came as a Mithnaged, and would gladly accept him."

Kotzker Maasioth, p. 33.

4. The True Zaddik

The "Yud" said: "When Messiah will come, all the Zaddikim and their Hasidim will go forth to meet him. Some of them will be received cordially; others will be turned aside. The Hasidim of the unwelcomed Zaddikim will cry out: 'Our intentions were good; we believed our Rebbe to be a true Zaddik. Why do you repel us?' Messiah will answer: 'A Hasid should daily implore the Lord to send him knowledge concerning the true Zaddik to guide his soul. Had you been sincere, and prayed in this mood, the Lord would have aided you to find the true guide.' "

Tif. Yeh., p. 12.

5. The Omnipresent Messiah

Said Rabbi Moses Sopher: "In every generation there lives a man great enough to be the Messiah. This man knows not his own greatness; but should he be summoned, he will be endowed with the Messianic spirit whereby he will be able to select worthy aides. If the generation is unworthy, the man dies, and another man arises great enough to be the Messiah."

P. v. K., p. 11b.

6. Keep His Commandments

The "Yud" commented on the verse: "The end of the matter, all having been heard: fear God and keep His commandments: for this is the whole man" (Ecclesiastes 12: 13). He said: "At the end of time (in the Messianic period) all that will be heard is this: fear God and keep His commandments."

Nif. Yeh., p. 38.

7. The Difference

The Lubliner was asked concerning the Talmudical saying of Samuel (Sabbath 63a) that the difference between the present and the Messianic times is only in the freeing of Israel from the domination of non-Jews: "The Tossafoth comment: 'The word "only" in Samuel's statement cannot be taken literally, since in Messianic times Jerusalem and the Temple will be rebuilt; hence there is more difference than in freedom from the domination of non-Jews.' In other passages, however, the Tossafoth write that 'only' must be taken literally. Why is this?"

The Rabbi answered: " 'Only' is to be taken literally in this passage as in others. It should, however, be understood thus: 'the difference in what Jews have now, and what they will not have under the Messiah is only in foreign domination. This we have now and will not have in the Messianic age. Yet the difference between what we have not now, but will have in the Messianic era is very great indeed." [1]

Hith. Z., pp. 22-23.

[1] The statement of Samuel is often quoted, and it is therefore important to note this Hasidic interpretation.

D. *Messianic Tribulations*

1. *Signs and Portents*

Rabbi Bunam said: "Before the Messiah will come, there will be Rabbis without Torah, Hasidim without Hasidism, rich men without riches, summers without heat, winters without cold, and grainstalks without grain."

S. S. K., i, p. 129.

2. *The World's Redemption*

The Rozdoler paraphrased the verse in Proverbs 31:30 thus: "When Falsity will be accepted as Grace, when Vanity will be looked upon as Beauty, and when the woman who fears the Lord shall be ridiculed, then will the Redeemer be compelled to rescue the world from utter corruption, and to uplift it, since it can fall no lower." [1]

O. Y., p. 19.

[1] The verse is: "Grace is deceitful and beauty is vain; but a woman that feareth the Lord, she shall be praised." In Hebrew "Tishalal" means "she shall be praised, or ridiculed."

3. *Prosperity and Poverty*

The Besht explained the adversities which, according to the Talmud,[1] will befall us before the advent of the Messiah as follows:

"Before the coming of the Messiah, there will be a period of great prosperity and Jews will become wealthy. They will grow accustomed to extravagant living and forget all their habits of frugality. Later, a terrible depression will arise, and the means of livelihood will be scarce. Poverty will descend upon those who no longer know how to live sparingly. These will be the Messianic tribulations."

O. Y., p. 19.

[1] Sanhedrin, 97.

4. *The Goal of Prayers*

Said Rabbi Schmelke: "When one prays to God for his personal wants, the Satan interposes by displaying the petitioner's iniquities, and the prayer may not be heard. But when one prays for the redemption of the Shekinah from exile, his prayer ascends higher than the Satan's domain, and he may then also pray for his own needs, since the Satan is not present to accuse him.

"It is thus that we can interpret Psalm 102:12: a prayer was offered at first for the 'afflicted one,' namely the Messiah, who is described as the 'afflicted one who rides on an ass';[1] this prayer is offered because he delays his advent, and a 'complaint was poured

[1] Zechariah 9:9.

out' because God is in exile. After these words, the Psalmist adds:
'O Lord, hear my prayer' for my own needs.' "

S. ha-Tov, p. 34.

5. *Evil Portents*

It is related of the Riziner by Rabbi Herzl of Luck:

"Once I remained with the Riziner over the Sabbath and he sat
at the meal with ten Hasidim, which was not his wont. He made
lament of a near day, when the common run of people will prosper
in body and soul, but the just and the elect will suffer and be in
such straits for their daily bread, that they will scarcely have
strength to recite a Psalm."

"Said the Riziner: 'Why do I tell you this? So that you may
be prepared and that you may not lapse into doubt, for it must be
so.' "

Bl., Gem., p. 286.

6. *Working for the Messiah*

Rabbi Bunam once said to the Gerer Rabbi, then his Disciple:
"I am convinced I can petition the Lord so earnestly for the advent
of the Messiah that He would grant my request. Nevertheless I picture to myself the order of the Messiah's advent in this way: He
will notify all the Zaddikim to assemble at the home of the oldest
Zaddik, the Apter Rabbi. All the Zaddikim will sit at the table,
with the Messiah at its head and the Apter at his right hand. The
Apter will surely ask the Messiah whose prayer was responsible for
his coming. The Messiah will answer: 'It was the prayer of Bunam
Parsischer who is seated at the end of the table.' This will greatly
vex the Apter Zaddik. Hence I do not work for the coming of the
Messiah."

M. E. H., i, 36.

7. *The Messiah as a Hasid?*

The Gerer Rabbi visited the Riziner and other Zaddikim. When
he returned, he paid a visit to his Rebbe, the Kotzker. When the
latter inquired regarding his long journey, the Gerer informed him
that every Zaddik seemed to be hotly opposed both to the Kotzker
Hasidim in their territories and to their Master.

"So?" exclaimed the Kotzker. "And what will they say if the
Messiah proves to be a Kotzker Hasid?"

M. E. H., i, 106.

101. THE MIND AND THOUGHTS OF MAN

1. *"The Holy of Holies"*

"In every action," said the Berditschever, "a man must regard
his body as the Holy of Holies, a part of the supreme power on

earth which is part of the manifestation of the Deity. If he does, he will ward off the Evil Impulse. The brain of man is like unto the Ark and the Two Tables of the Covenant. It is the noblest part of man. Whosoever thinks unholy thoughts is placing an idol in the Holy of Holies. Whenever a man lifts his hands to do a deed, let him consider his hands the messengers of God."

Bl., Gem., p. 64.
N. B. L., p. 35.

2. The Holy Dwelling

Said the Riziner: "The Psalmist laments (78:60): 'And He forsook the Tabernacle of Shiloh, the tent which He had made to dwell within [1] men.' When the Lord gave Israel the Law, He intended to live in the hearts of men; He did not desire a dwelling erected for Him. But when Israel sinned He ordered a Holy place to be built to house His holiness. Ezekiel indicates this when he says (43:10): 'Thou, Son of Man, show the house to the house of Israel, that they may be ashamed of their iniquities.' They should feel shame because their sins had made necessary the building of a Holy House."

E. O., p. 136.

[1] J. T. has "among."

3. The Mind's Divinity

The Berditschever Rabbi interpreted thus the verse (Exodus 34:6): "And the Lord passed by before him, and proclaimed: The Lord, the Lord": "When the thought of the Lord passes through the mind of the good man, it becomes divine, and Divinity exclaims: 'O Thou that art divine.' "

E. O., p. 60.

4. God's Thoughts and Man's

The Riziner interpreted Isaiah 55:8: "For My thoughts are not your thoughts, neither are your ways My ways, saith the Lord." His paraphrase was: "For are there not My thoughts to give you what is in your thoughts? Why, then, are not your ways, as My ways?"

E. O., p. 135.

5. A Stable

A Hasid told Rabbi Bunam that he had become an expressman. The Rabbi remarked: "Your head will now be occupied with the horse; hence it appears you have made of your mind a stable."

S. S. K., v, 48.

6. On the Way to Karlin

A Hasid was on his way to visit the Karliner Rabbi. A Rav met him, and said: "Cannot you find a Rabbi nearer than Karlin?"

"No, I cannot," answered the Hasid. "I read the thoughts of all the Rabbis, and I find them to be spurious."

"If you read thoughts," said the Rav, "then tell me what I am thinking now."

"You are thinking of God," answered the Hasid.

"No, your guess is incorrect; I am not thinking of God."

"There you have it," remarked the Hasid. "You yourself have stated the reason why I must go to Karlin."

O. I. H., pp. 47-8.

7. Disciplining Our Thoughts

Rabbi Elimelech commented on Genesis 18: 12-15, and said: "We may understand the laughter of Sarah as a sign of joy rather than of unbelief. The verse will then have the following meaning: Sarah rejoices to hear the angel's prophecy that after she had waxed old, her youth would be renewed. At this moment, however, an impious thought crossed her mind: 'But my lord is so old.' She immediately dispelled this unworthy thought, however, inasmuch as it implied disbelief in the power of God. She believed she had not sinned because she had regretted her thought without delay. And she said: 'I did not deride,' since she knew she had feared the improper thought and did not retain it. But God explained to her that it had been derision on her part.

"The truly good person must discipline himself so that he will be unable to think impure and unworthy thoughts."

Noam E., p. 14.

8. Concentrate the Mind

Said the Besht: "It is desirable that a man should frequently interrupt his occupation for a moment, whatever it may be, and concentrate his mind upon the fear of the Lord. This should be practiced even if one is engaged in a sacred occupation."

K. S. T., p. 12b.

9. The Solid Foundation

Said the Besht: "Mind is the foundation of man. If the foundation is solid, the building is secure. By the same token, if a man's mind is filled with holy thoughts, his actions will be sound. But if his mind is occupied with selfish thoughts, even his good actions are unsound, being built on a weak foundation."

M. R. T., ii, 50.

10. Sinful Thoughts

Once Rabbi Sussya said to Rabbi Elimelech: "Melech, pray, explain this to me. I read in a Holy Book that all souls were included in the soul of Adam. Why was Adam allowed to sin, placing thereby a blemish on all souls, including your own?"

The Lizensker answered: "Had Adam not sinned, he would have continued to carry in his mind the thought that all his frailties are due to the fact that God, desiring no rival, had refused him permission to eat of the fruit of the Tree of Knowledge. Had he eaten of it, he would have become as powerful as God. And since sinful thoughts are worse than sins,[1] I preferred that Adam actually sin rather than carry in his mind evil thoughts."

F. U. A. O., i, 11.

[1] Yoma 29.

11. *The Bratzlaver on "Understanding"*

A.

"1. When the eye sees it is easy to comprehend.

"2. He who walks in humility has clear thoughts.

"3. Faith and the fear of the Lord lead to understanding.

"4. If we perform no kind deeds, we have no understanding.

"5. If we are deserving we will learn how to find God in all our enjoyments, even in eating.

"6. The greater our good deeds, the greater our understanding."

Sef. Ham., pp. 43-6.

B.

"1. The chief source of understanding lies in the heart.

"2. The chief goal of understanding is to know God in our heart, not in our brain. The heart is conscious of fear and awe, and induces to pure service.

"3. Lack of proper understanding is the cause of all tribulations; perfection of knowledge will banish them.

"4. The happiness awaited after the Resurrection will exist because 'understanding will fill the earth.' All men will know God, and will thereby be included in His Unity and Immortality. He who knows God is included within God. Therefore beware lest you employ your mind and your heart for unholy thoughts. Holy thoughts lead to an understanding of God.

"5. Enthusiasm within the heart is born out of the movements in the nerve centres of the brain. The more we exercise our brain with thoughts of Torah and divine service, the more enthusiastic does our heart become in its desire to serve the Lord.

"6. The holy enthusiasm of a man's heart balances its unholy enthusiasm for unworthy passions, and purifies it.

"7. Perfection of understanding is possible only to the man who keeps his five senses holy. Holy inspiration and enlargement of the mind's powers may be attained thereby.

"8. Universal mind surrounds us, but cannot be grasped by mortal man. Mortal mind cannot solve all problems of the universe, since it lacks omniscience.

"9. Were we in possession of the Universal Mind we would know beforehand everything that is to be; then there would be no free will. In the Millenium there will be no free will since human beings will become immortal like the angels, and like them, will possess the mind of the universe.

"10. The essence of a man is his mind and understanding. Hence where his thoughts are, he is. Let him but think holy thoughts, and he will be in a holy place.

"11. Anger and cruelty testify to a defect in a man's knowledge. With increased understanding come calmness, peace, kindness and contentment.

"12. The essence of joy awaited at the Redemption and in the Future Life is the attainment of holiness and the knowledge of God. The better the man, the more he will attain. The people of Israel will be granted more than the nations.

"13. He who thinks holy thoughts in the Torah and in divine service is rewarded by the ability to understand more and more. This means that a man gives entrance in his own mind to that part of the Universal Mind which immediately surrounds him, and this may continue even unto his death. He absorbs more of the Universal Mind and is able to attain a higher degree in the World-to-Come, whereas another person must be satisfied with less of it. Such understanding warms his soul, as garments warm the body.

"14. A kind deed brings the blessing of understanding from the Lord. But since our understanding is limited we must add faith to it. Enthusiastic and joyful performance of a Mitzwah brings the attainment of spiritual light, which is divine inspiration.

"15. A man must strive to subdue his bodily desires wherein he resembles the beasts, and endeavor rather to improve his mind.

"16. A man must make use of his mind's powers and bring hidden faculties into play by study in affairs of the spirit. His understanding of metaphysics remains with his soul after the physical life is over. This holy understanding constitutes life after death, or the immortality of the soul.

"17. No one is entitled to excuse his lack of service to the Lord by affirming that he is engaged in business and must associate with vulgar folk. God is everywhere. He is among the most common of men; he is to be found in the lowliest occupation. Delve deeper and you will find a way to serve God in everything and in every work and place.

"18. By the same token, no matter how low you may have fallen in your own esteem, bear in mind that if you delve deeply into yourself, you will discover holiness there. A holy spark resides there which through repentance you may fan into a consuming flame which will burn away the dross of unholiness and unworthiness.

"19. Without God's presence, no existence is possible. Whether it be organic or inorganic matter, it has existence only because of the divinity within it.

"20. He who conquers his evil impulses is like unto an angel. He can behold divinity in all things. He receives a taste of the Light of Love which resides in understanding. This Light is above time and is without limits.

"21. Join your heart in alliance with your understanding. If your heart is submissive to your understanding, your knowledge that the Divine Presence is within everything at all times, will aid you to subdue all your unworthy impulses and the undesirable traits of your heart.

"22. The mind is the soul: if we improve our mind through holy studies, we improve our soul. Other studies are of no value to the soul. Repentance means the expulsion of all thoughts which are outside the domain of holiness.

"23. Holy studies continually renovate the mind and the soul.

"24. He whose brain nerves grow weary of metaphysical thoughts may rest them either through sleep, through the study of the Torah in its simple meaning, or through occupation with mundane problems. Faith in God, honesty, dependability and trust must, however, pervade his every action.

"25. Passion and desire surround understanding as the shell, the kernel; break through the shell and thereby attain understanding.

"26. Unholy thoughts are the foundation on which the Satan builds.

"27. In metaphysical research, a man must combine understanding with faith. In repose from this labor, faith must be the master.

"28. The Lord by his decrees gives to a man the suggestion that he approach more closely. Look into everything that transpires in your life, and heed the suggestions contained therein.

"29. Be careful that your performance of good deeds at all times equals your knowledge; otherwise your heart will be unable to keep your understanding holy, and it may turn into the sinful channels of doubt and unfaith.

"30. Knowledge may become firm through three things: through instruction; through practice; through the beauty of form it assumes.

"31. He who possesses firm knowledge can aid those of weaker understanding and become their leader.

"32. A man without understanding is a mere brute. Give consideration to this thought and you will return unto the Lord.

"33. In the spirit of joy a man may direct his brain to holy thoughts. In the spirit of sadness, the brain is in exile, and refuses to obey a man's commands.

"34. The man of great understanding knows full well that time has no significance for the values that are real. Equip yourself with whatever you can that you may bear it into the World-to-Come.

"35. He who demonstrates his understanding has given true proof of himself."

L. E. H., pp. 21-7.

12. Minds Great and Small

A man told the Strelisker that he knew the entire Zohar by heart. Rabbi Uri replied: "I am unable to retain within my mind so great a number of ideas, since a single idea often engrosses my mind for a thousand days."

The Koznitzer Maggid said: "The difference between a great mind and a small mind is this: a great mind is able to cling to one idea for a long time, and to perfect it; whereas within a small mind ideas chase each other about like strokes of lightning."

D. D., p. 252.

13. The Research of Reason

Rabbi Bunam was an advocate of sober thought and of profundity in the learning of the Torah. He was also opposed to the teaching of Kabbalah to the rank and file. Once he remarked: "The Kabbalists discover innumerable secret meanings and suggestions in the letters of the Torah. But the Talmud permits the recital of the Sh'ma in any language.[1] Where can they look for meanings and suggestions in other languages? In addition to the Torah it is necessary to teach morality and the research of reason."

D. D., p. 276.

[1] Berakhoth 13a.

102. MIRACLES

1. Deviations from Nature's Laws

Rabbi Bunam said: "The Lord created nature and inspired the Torah. We find that there are deviations from the strict laws of the Torah. Thus the Sabbath may be desecrated to save human life. Likewise, there exist some deviations from the laws of nature. When the Lord pleases to perform them, miracles sometimes occur which seem to contradict natural laws."

S. S. K., ii, 83.

2. The Miracle Worker

A Hasid told the Kotzker Rabbi about another Rabbi who was credited by rumor with the power to work miracles.

"I would like to know," said the Kotzker, "if he is able to perform the miracle of making one real Hasid."

S. S. K., ii, 29.

3. Without an Intermediary

The Hasidim of the Koznitzer Maggid informed him that an elderly woman had borne a son, though she had not gone to a Rebbe for a blessing.

"Well, what of it?" commented the Maggid, "the Lord is sometimes desirous of demonstrating that He can accomplish a miracle, the same as a Rebbe."

O. I. H., p. 134.

4. A Man of Wonders

The Lentzner Rabbi declared that the Sassover Rabbi was a man of wonders: he was broken of heart and whole of heart at one and the same time.

E. Tz., p. 45.

5. Before He Was Born

A Hasid visited the Premislaner. The Rabbi inquired the name of his Rebbe, and he replied that he was accustomed to visit the Dzikover regularly. The Premislaner exclaimed: "Your Rebbe, Eliezer, is a great Zaddik. He precedes me in Heaven."

The Hasid repeated this to the Dzikover, and the Rabbi's sons importuned their father to tell him whether the Premislaner was right in his statement.

"It may have once been true," responded the Dzikover.

"When?" asked his sons.

"Before I was born," was the reply.

Ohel N., p. 32.

6. The Lord Dislikes Miracles

Said the Vorker: "It is said (Gen. 26:12): 'And Isaac sowed in that land, and found in the same year a hundredfold; and the Lord blessed him.' This means: The Lord thanked Isaac for tilling and sowing his land, and thus enabling Him to provide for Isaac in a natural manner. For had Isaac not worked his field, the Lord would have been impelled to provide for him in a supernatural manner."

R. T., ii, 117.

7. A Miracle Explained

Rabbi Meir Nathan, son of the Tzanzer, told his father-in-law, Rabbi Eliezer Dzikover, that last Shevuoth, he had heard his father, the Tzanzer, declare that the Ropshitzer sat at his table. When the Tzanzer came to visit the Dzikover, the latter asked: "Pray, explain to me how it was possible for my late father to be present at your table, seeing that he has been dead many years?"

The Tzanzer replied: "My meaning was metaphorical, to be sure. I conducted the meal according to the custom of your revered father, the Ropshitzer." [1]

Ohel N., p. 32.

[1] The more learned Hasidic Rabbis cared little for miracles, and explained the true facts when among their own group. They permitted, however, the circulation of tales of wonder-working among the common people in the belief that thereby they might become attached to an ethical life.

8. A Genuine Miracle

The Lizensker commented on the expression: "Show a miracle for yourselves" (Ex. 7:9). He said: "When a magician performs his acts on the stage, they are magical in the eyes of the audience. The magician himself, however, knows them to be merely tricks. But when the man of God is commanded to perform a miracle, he himself is greatly astonished at the wonder. The Lord intended to say: 'Pharaoh will invite you to demonstrate a miracle that will be a marvel even in your own eyes, unlike the magical tricks of his court magicians.'"

E. Tz., p. 35.

9. *The Greatest Miracle*

Rabbi Solomon of Karlin said: "The greatest of all miracles is to bring into the heart of a Jew the holy influence whereby he may be enabled to pray properly unto his Creator."

D. D., p. 170.

10. *"The Lord is God"*

Rabbi Baruch of Medziboz was informed of the many miracles accredited to the Lizensker. He said: "How utterly useless they are! When Elijah performed miracles, we are told that the people exclaimed: 'The Lord is God.' [1] But nowadays the people grow enthusiastic over the reputed miracle-worker, and forget entirely to say: 'The Lord is God.'"

[1] I Kings 18:39.

D. D., p. 174.

11. *Fools and Miracles*

Rabbi Hirsch Leib Aliker said: "We find in the Talmud the saying: 'Since the day of the destruction of the Holy Temple, prophecy has been taken away from the Prophets and given over to fools' (Baba Bathra, 12b). How is this to be explained? In this way: 'Since the destruction of the Temple, it is known to every sensible person that Prophecy is no longer manifested; it is only the foolish among the Hasidim who expect their Zaddikim to prophecy and foretell the future.'"

D. D., p. 176.

12. *An Incentive to Superstition*

In the presence of the Riziner, Hasidim once related the many miracles which the Zaddikim were reported to be performing. The Riziner said: "The more miracles are attributed to the Zaddikim, the more the ground is prepared for deception by clairvoyants, fortune-tellers and charlatan doctors. A Zaddik should merely offer prayer to the Lord, and if he is a true Zaddik, his prayer will be heard."

D. D., p. 308.

13. *Better Without Miracles*

The Gerer said to his closest Hasidim: "It were evil indeed were we in our time in such a position that we required miracles to be shown us."

M. E. H., ii, 62.

14. The Zaddik's Will and God's

A Hasid heard much regarding the renown of Rabbi Israel Meir ha-Cohen, the "Hafetz Hayyim," as a great Zaddik.

He chanced to meet a resident of Radin, where the "Hafetz Hayyim" resided, and inquired: "Does your Zaddik perform miracles?"

The Radiner Jew answered the Hasid: "You deem it a miracle when God does the will of your Zaddik; we, however, deem it a miracle if it can be truthfully asserted that our Zaddik does God's will."

J. M. J., Oct. 2, 1933.

103. MITZWOTH

1. Celebrating a Mitzwah

Rabbi Mordecai Tzernobiler said: "The banquet which we Jews give to celebrate a Mitzwah is more worthy than the Mitzwah itself. A parable illustrates this:

" 'The Satan brought many serious accusations against the Jews, and their defender, the Archangel Michael, knew of no arguments in their behalf. After a while he bethought himself and said: "The few Mitzwoth which Jews perform, offset their many transgressions. When a Jew performs a circumcision, he gives a banquet, because he is overjoyed at having done a Mitzwah. Have you ever seen a Jew, however, celebrating when he transgresses? This demonstrates that he feels no joy in his offense, and only succumbs because of weakness. In the Mitzwah he feels intense happiness." This defense before the Heavenly Tribunal proved successful.'

"Hence you see," continued the Tzernobiler, "how important is the celebration of a Mitzwah!"

A. H., p. 17.

2. The Fur-coat

A Rabbi related the following tale: A man died and was brought before the Heavenly Court. His sins and good deeds were placed on the scales, and the sins far outweighed the good deeds. Suddenly a fur-coat was piled on the scale containing the good deeds, and this side becoming heavier, the man was sent to Paradise. He said to the Angel who escorted him: "But I cannot understand why the fur-coat was brought in." The Angel replied: "One cold wintry night you traveled on a sled and a poor man asked for a ride. You took him in, and noticing his thin clothes, you placed your fur-coat on him to give him warmth. This act of kindness more than offset your transgressions."

T. H., pp. 20-21.

3. The Value of a Mitzwah

The Besht explained (Psalm 62:13): "And unto Thee, O Lord, belongeth mercy; for Thou renderest unto every man according to his work." "We see frequently a Jew hurrying to the synagogue on a week-day, but stopping to purchase an article which he happens to see for sale at a cheap price. He can only hope to gain a half thaler by the transaction, and the delay may cause him to miss the 'Borekhu' response or the 'Kedushah.' Yet if one should wish to purchase from this very Jew the Mitzwah of saying: 'Borekhu' or the 'Kedushah,' offering a hundred thalers, he would refuse to sell it. The Lord in His kindness recompenses every man according to the value which a man places upon a Mitzwah after he has performed it, not according to its worth to him before it is performed."

M. R. T., p. 70.

4. The Reward for a Mitzwah

The Dinover Rabbi related the following story: A Jewish girl ran away from home with a non-Jewish general. Later he left her. Then she married a miller and had a son by him. Many years passed; her husband died, and her son succeeded his father as the miller. Two Jewish merchants were caught in a snowstorm near the mill, and took refuge at the miller's home. This was on a Friday afternoon. They sent the miller to bring them food. A little before sunset, an old woman entered and kindled the Sabbath lights. This astonished the Jewish merchants, and they inquired how she came to be there. Thereupon she related the story of her life, and added that throughout all the years, she had never forgotten to kindle the Sabbath lights in tribute to her Jewish birth. The sad memories of the past proved too grievous for her; her heart broke, and she died within a few hours. When the miller returned, the merchants told him that his mother had been born a Jewess and expressed the desire to be buried as one. The miller agreed, and the body was taken to the nearest Jewish cemetery.

"I was told of the circumstances," said the Dinover Rabbi, "and I ordered that Kaddish be said for her soul, since she had never failed to keep at least the one Mitzwah of kindling the Sabbath lights."

L. S., pp. 15-18.

5. The Helping Hand

It was the custom of Rabbi Meyer Hurwitz, grandfather of Rabbi Schmelke, to perform an act of mercy before he ate his meal. One day no opportunity came to him and he refused to break his fast. Toward night he heard a wagon halt at his door. He went outside and saw that the wagon was loaded with excellent lumber. The driver informed him that, owing to a misadventure, he had come late to town, and seeing a lighted house, had stopped to offer the tenant his lumber at an unusually low price. The Rabbi awakened a carpenter, and loaned him the money to avail himself of the bargain. Then, he ate his meal.

S. ha-Tov, p. 111.

6. Minor and Major Good Deeds

Said the Radviller: "We read in the 'Ethics of the Fathers': 'Run to do even a slight precept.'[1] What is meant by a slight precept? I believe it may be explained by the saying in the Talmud (Kiddushin 39b): 'One who sits and does not transgress is rewarded as if he observed a commandment.' This is, therefore, a minor good deed, and we are told to be as careful to abstain from doing evil as to exercise care in performing good."

E. O., p. 66.

[1] Ethics 4:2; Singer, p. 195.

7. Intention and Action

The Lizensker Rabbi used the text (Gen. 22:7): "Behold (here is) the fire and the wood, but where is the lamb for a burnt-offering?" He said: "An explanation is due to the question: 'Why did Abraham carry wood and fire for a distance of three days' travel, and why did he chop the wood before leaving home, when a log is easier to carry on the shoulder?' To understand this, we must first comprehend that the Lord appreciates most in a man his zeal in performing a commandment, and his readiness to do it with his whole heart and soul. Therefore should a man's heart yearn to do a good deed, but he fails to perform it because circumstances prevent, the Lord accepts his fervent desire as equal to actual success in performing it. It is, however, almost impossible for a man, as a rule, to concentrate his entire being on the performance of a Mitzwah, and the enthusiasm with which he commences, soon wanes. Hence the actual performance of a Mitzwah is necessary to the mind as a stimulus to the effort at pleasing God.

"Isaac saw that his father, fearing lest his ardor to perform God's command would cool, and eager to obey while his mind was full of determination, cleft the wood and prepared the fire at once. Hence he thought that the intention to sacrifice his son was sufficient to fulfil the Lord's injunction, and that a lamb could be substituted. And Abraham answered: 'You may be correct regarding my intention in the matter. I fully intended to sacrifice you and also acted upon my resolve, by cleaving the wood and preparing the fire. I hoped that the combination of intention and partial fulfilment might be sufficient to please the Lord. But you also were included in the command, since I was not ordered to bind you and sacrifice you against your will. Hence it is necessary that you actually perform your share by going up to the altar, and making yourself ready for the sacrifice. Then if it be God's will, He will provide the lamb.'"

Noam E., p. 15.

8. The Difference

Said the Kotzker: "The difference between my Disciples and others is this: Other Hasidim do Mitzwoth in the open and transgressions in secret. Mine transgress in the open and do Mitzwoth in secret."

M. D., p. 254.

9. Generous With a Mitzwah

Rabbi Israel Salanter [1] saw a servant maid carrying upon her shoulder two pails of water. When dinner was ready, he washed his hands sparingly. He was asked why he did not use more water, and he replied: "One must not be generous with a Mitzwah upon another person's shoulders."

S. Rosenfeld, in "The Day," June 25, '32.

[1] Rabbi Israel Salanter, may be called a "Near-Hasid." Another of his utterances was: "Honors and trustfulness are akin. For myself I avoid honors and am filled with trust in God. As for others, however, I give them due honor, and must aid them to provide for the morrow."

10. The Acceptable Mitzwah

Said Rabbi Yerachmiel: "A Mitzwah is acceptable only if it is performed for the sake of pleasing the Lord, but not for the sake of a reward. Nevertheless, we should do our utmost to perform every Mitzwah within our power, even if we feel ourselves unable to be rid of the expectation of rewards. For among a multitude of Mitzwoth there may perchance be a few acceptable ones.

"It is the reverse with transgressions and evil traits of character. Anger, for example, is an evil trait, comparable to idolatry. But when one hears blasphemy he may show his anger, provided it is made known for the sake of honor to the Lord, and for no other reason. Nevertheless, if a man is not quite certain, or if he feels unable to distinguish another reason for anger from his desire to defend the Lord's honor, he must not indulge in anger.

"In short, when in doubt regarding the purity of your motive, act affirmatively in the case of a Mitzwah, and negatively in the case of an offense."

Tif. B., pp. 3-4.

11. Avoid Pettiness

Said the Bershider: "Many a time my Master, the Koretzer, counseled me to bear in mind the words in the Besht's Testament: 'Do not indulge overmuch in pettiness while performing thy religious duties.' He added: 'This rule sustained me in my youth.'"

M. P., p. 41.

12. A True Reward

Said the Bratzlaver: "Rejoice so much in a Mitzwah that you will desire no other reward than the opportunity to perform another Mitzwah."

K. L. M., p. 6.

13. The Perfect Mitzwah

Said the Koretzer: "A perfect Mitzwah should be performed in three ways: in action, in talk, and in thought. The Mitzwah of kindling the candles on the Sabbath is performed in action by the women; in talk by the recital of the Mishnah on kindling the Sabbath lights; [1] and in thought by the concentration of our mind upon longing for the restoration of the Menorah in the Holy Temple."

Nof. Tz., p. 33.

[1] Sabbath, chapter 2.

14. The Divinity of Every Mitzwah

Said the Medzibozer: "We learn from the verse: 'Behold, I set before you this day a blessing and a curse: the blessing, if ye shall hearken unto the commandments of the Lord your God' (Deut. 11:26), that we will receive the blessing if we look for the indwelling presence of God in every commandment; if we will understand the divinity of every Mitzwah."

Butz. D., p. 21.

15. Unhurried Obedience

Said Rabbi Bunam: "We should not go about in haste to do a Mitzwah, but we should first consider and observe the proper way and the proper spirit for its performance, as we are taught: 'And it shall be righteousness unto us, if we observe to do all this commandment before the Lord our God, as He hath commanded us' (Deut. 6:25). Through deliberation we can properly perform the Mitzwah as God hath commanded us."

S. I., p. 67.

16. The Supreme Sacrifice

The "Yud" said: "A man should choose two Mitzwoth that he may perform them with his whole heart and soul, and even be ready to die for them."

The Magelnitzer added: "Choose one Mitzwah for which you are ready to die, namely the Mitzwah which you are in the act of performing."

Nif. Yeh., p. 41.

17. The Sculpture

Said the "Yud": "A Mitzwah or a prayer may be performed in a spirit of great-heartedness or of pettiness. It may be asked: wherein lies the difference, as long as it is performed? The difference may be discerned from the following illustrations: a sculpture may be done in clay and the same figure poured out in gold. Does not the statue of gold captivate your appreciation more than the same figure in cold clay?"

Tif. Yeh., p. 11.

18. The Three Sages

The Kotzker narrated the following excerpts from the Midrash:

"A fine ornament was hung upon a very high tree and no one could climb up to bring it down. A wise man ordered that one ladder should be tied to another ladder until it was possible to reach the top. It was then easy to reach up and take hold of the ornament (Wayyikra Rabba, 19:2).

"Some healing mineral waters were flowing in a deep ravine, and none could draw them up. A wise man ordered that one rope be tied to another rope to which a vessel was attached, and the waters with healing properties were drawn up (Bereshith Rabba, 93:3).

"A nobleman called for workmen to fill with wine barrels that had holes. The workmen grumbled and wished to know the reason for such a command. A wise man said to them: 'As long as you are compensated, of what concern to you is the nobleman's reason?'" (Wayyikra Rabba, 19:2).

The Kotzker explained this Midrash as follows:

"The first sage reasoned that the ornament had been placed on the tree by human hands, and therefore other men might follow the same procedure and bring it down. This applies to moral laws which were observed by people even before the Torah was given.

"The second sage went further. He reasoned that since we understand the worth of healing waters, we should make an endeavor to draw them forth, even though no one has done so before. This applies to the laws of the Torah the reason for which we understand.

"The third sage was willing to obey even when the reason for certain laws was not understood by him. This applies to laws of the Torah which seem to have no reason. The third sage was the wisest."

F. U. A. O., ii, 165-6.

104. MODESTY

1. The Punishment of Fame

When the Great Maggid perceived that he had become a man of wide renown he inquired of God: "What sin have I committed to incur the punishment of widespread fame?"

J. T., (B-F), Dec. 19, '30, p. 4.

2. Favorable Testimony

Rabbi Mendel Vitebsker received a call to become a Maggid in Minsk. The letter styled him a pure, holy, saintly man, and it bore upwards of a hundred signatures.

"Would that I were able to take this document with me after my death and present it to the Heavenly Court!" said the Rabbi. "I can hardly conceive that a hundred men should testify that I am holy and pure."

M. D., p. 243.

3. Learning from Another

A Hasid asked the Gerer Rabbi why he still visits the Kotzker Rabbi though he himself is more renowned. The Rabbi replied: "As long as a man finds that there is someone from whom he can learn, he should not teach others."

S. S. K., ii, 28.

4. Teaching Modesty

Rabbi Nahum Zeev proudly announced to the Kotzker Rabbi that he had been elected Rabbi of Biala. The Kotzker began to shout at him: "You have become a Rabbi? How dare you accept such a position? Are you fit for it? By whose influence? By whose intervention?"

The Bialer Rabbi left the room dazed, and took his Rabbi's disapproval deeply to heart. In a few moments, however, the Kotzker's Warden called him back to the Rabbi's presence, and his Master met him with hearty congratulations on his election.

S. S. K., v, 62.

5. Deference Towards a Greater

When Rabbi Isaac was Rav of Brody there lived in the city a learned man named Joshua. The scholar heard that the Rav had accepted a call to become Rabbi at Hamburg, and petitioned him for a recommendation concerning a book he had written on rabbinical law. When Rabbi Isaac on the journey perused the manuscript, he recognized it at once as a work of brilliancy and scholarship. As soon as he arrived at Hamburg, he informed the community leaders that he had just discovered a man greater than himself, and advised them to elect him instead. The leaders did not accept this recommendation, but Rabbi Joshua was appointed Dayyan of Rabbi Isaac's Court.

S. N., pp. 24-5.

6. The Leader's Meditation

The Kaminker said: "We read in the Song of Songs (1:6): 'They made me keeper of the vineyards, but mine own vineyard have I not kept.' The leader complains that multitudes come to him for guidance, though he still needs guidance for his own conduct of life. He then muses: 'Because I have not yet perfected my own ways, I must suffer the punishment of guiding others. It is painful, also, that I must lead others to perfection while I must constantly endeavor to perfect myself. Every day, therefore, I must set aside many hours for self-improvement.' "[1]

B. P., pp. 33-4.

[1] Cf. Rabbi Azrael's words in the "Dybbuk."

7. *Without Special Worth*

Said the Lubliner: "The reason a Zaddik may accept money when asked to pray for someone is as follows:

"When the Zaddik offers a prayer on behalf of another person, it may be asked in Heaven: 'By what right may one person pray for his comrade, and thereby give the impression that his prayer is more acceptable?' And when the Zaddik is rewarded for offering the prayer, he may reply: 'I offer this prayer for my fellow-man because he has engaged me to do so, not because my prayer is worthier.' This is suggested by the verse (Psalm 72:15): 'He will give them of the gold of Sheba, that they may pray for him continually.'"

N. H. L., p. 24.

8. *Modest Piety*

The Kozmirer Rabbi visited Rabbi Akiba Eger of Posen. The latter asked him to define a Hasid. The Kozmirer replied:

"A Hasid is one of whose Hasiduth or piety, only he and his Creator know."

S. S. K., v, 117.

9. *Considering Himself the Half*

The Lubliner Rabbi said:

"A true Hasid is very rare. Two Hasidim are not likely to be found in one place. One Hasid in a place is not sufficient. Every place should have a Hasid and a half of a Hasid, and each one should consider himself as the half, and the other as the whole."

S. S. K., v, 14.

10. *The Bold and the Shy*

The Medzibozer Rabbi quoted the "Ethics of the Fathers" (5:23) (Singer, p. 203): "The bold-faced are for Gehinnom (Purgatory), the shame-faced for the Garden of Eden" (Paradise). He explained it as follows: "We see oftentimes that one is impudent and bold-faced when he is about to commit a transgression, which leads him to Gehinnom. But one who is about to perform a good deed which leads him to the Garden of Eden, is quite shy and shame-faced about it. The reverse would be more natural."

O. Y., p. 135.

11. *The Gates of Righteousness*

The Medzibozer commented upon the verse: "Open to me the gates of righteousness; I will enter into them; I will give thanks unto the Lord" (Psalm 118:19). He said: "When the Zaddik declares: 'I have not yet entered into the domicile of righteousness; open the gates unto me,' he receives the response: 'Thy knowledge that thou hast not yet begun to perform good deeds—this will open the gates of the Lord.'"

Butz. D., p. 7.

12. *From One Another*

A Hasid who was an intimate of the Alexanderer, asked him why he did not admit the Hasidim who came to him until many hours had elapsed. The Rabbi replied: "As long as they wait in the vestibule they talk among themselves on Hasiduth, and they learn from one another. But what can they learn from me?"

T. T., p. 23.

105. MONEY AND SUSTENANCE

1. *Sayings of the Bratzlaver on "Money and Sustenance"*

A.

"1. Poverty comes to a man through unworthy talk and through pride. Charity corrects these influences and brings riches.

"2. A man will obtain sustenance through fervent worship.

"3. Charity cools the heat of desire for riches.

"4. He who is constantly engrossed in money-getting, and allows himself no rest or respite for worthier activities, involves himself in the curse of the words: 'In the sweat of thy face shalt thou eat bread' (Gen. 3 : 19).

"5. Desire for money is like the worship of idols.

"6. A man should believe that God does not require him to concentrate his entire mind on earning a livelihood. A little effort on the part of the man who has faith that all sustenance is from God, suffices for him to attain his necessities.

"7. Desire for money degrades a man from his true ethical plane.

"8. True faith is demonstrated by a man's readiness to spend money on the performance of a good deed.

"9. Those sunk in desire for money are always in debt. They either borrow to make more money and carry the load of debt, or they fall into obligations to this desire for money. Oftentimes we perceive men of wealth toiling arduously and assuming risks in order to acquire more money, as if they were compelled to pay off a debt. This debt they owe to their desire, and since a man has not yet died who was half-satisfied with his possessions, they are always in debt to their own desire. These slaves to gold suffer irritation, bitterness, sadness and anxieties because of their desire. The more gold they own, the more anxiety they feel. Their money consumes the days of their life.

"10. The money of the rich who do not give sufficient charity is like the sport of madmen. The money plays with them as with children, and then slays them in This-World and the After-World.

"11. He who dislikes superfluous money attains wisdom, intelligent understanding, and inspiration.

"12. He who is honest in his business dealings is like one who brings incense unto the Lord.

"13. The desire for good eating leads to poverty, contempt and shame.

"14. Wealth comes through truth.

"15. Those who are dissatisfied though they possess every necessity, are those concerning whom it is written (Proverbs 13:25): 'But the belly of the wicked shall want.'

"16. The desire for gold diminishes understanding, life, longevity and the call of conscience.

"17. The melancholy which the desire for money brings in its train, makes the limbs heavy and weakens the pulse. The weaker the pulse, the heavier the limbs; the heavier the limbs, the weaker the pulse. This continues until it causes death.

"18. He who covets is guilty of robbery in thought.

"19. He whose livelihood is straitened should contribute to charity. This good deed will act like a medicine.

"20. Only the man of folly marries for money. He will pay for his sin by suffering through his wife and children.

"21. Desire for money brings enmity.

"22. The lowly and the meek cannot be curtailed in their livelihood by anyone.

"23. He who deals honestly, keeps the commandment: 'Thou shalt love thy neighbor as thyself' (Lev. 19:18).

"24. He who does not keep the law in his thoughts during his business transactions will be forced to go to law.

"25. Desire for money corrupts the mind.

"26. He who employs others should enforce a reasonable authority, and he will find it easier to provide them with a livelihood.

"27. This-World is merely a passage-way to the Eternal World. He who possesses and he who lacks money pass through it just the same. Profits are mere imagination.

"28. The man and his money cannot both be in the same person. Either he loses his money and remains a man, or he loses his dignity as a man, and the money is left.

"29. The will to attain immortality is precious in the eyes of the Lord. In your passage through life, take hold of an added prayer, a good deed or a page of the Torah, so that your journey will be of benefit to you."

L. E. H., pp. 52-57.

B.

"1. He who is accustomed to mock others will possess no wealth.

"2. Wealth will not remain with him who has no pity on others.

"3. Poverty is worse than fifty plagues.

"4. The nations have power over Israel because they study the Bible.

"5. Wine brings poverty.

"6. The man who possesses knowledge will prosper.

"7. He who breaks the fence of the Sages will become poor.

"8. He who controls his desire to eat will receive a fine home.

"9. To gain a livelihood is as difficult as dividing the Red Sea; it is more difficult than the Redemption, and twice as difficult as giving birth.

"10. He who is appointed a leader oftentimes becomes wealthy.

"11. Do not be anxious lest your competitors remove from you your livelihood. Against their will, people will seek you out in your place and call upon you, for your livelihood has been allotted to you.

"12. For four things do householders lose their property: because they rob the wages of their hirelings; because they delay their wages; because they transfer their own obligations to the shoulders of others; and because of haughtiness.

"13. A change of name and residence oftentimes aids in securing a livelihood.

"14. Through faith a man's livelihood will be increased.

"15. When prosperity arrives, weakness is decreased.

"16. Drought comes, when people promise to give to charity and give not.

"17. Uncleanliness in the home leads to poverty.

"18. Honoring the Torah and the Sabbath brings wealth in its train.

"19. To gain success, enter into partnership with a man of success.

"20. He who dislikes money will live long.

"21. He who seeks treasures, hastens the day of his death.

"22. Constant joy brings success.

"23. Poverty saves from Purgatory.

"24. When your livelihood is endangered, try to give to charity.

"25. He who engages in building, becomes poor.

"26. Modesty brings riches.

"27. A man's livelihood is decreased if he judges not his fellow-man in the scale of merit.

"28. He who dislikes money receives inspiration from Heaven.

"29. Dishonesty leads to poverty.

"30. He who deliberates not on his actions is embroiled in debt.

"31. He who removes another's livelihood is as if he had slain him.

"32. Atheism leads to poverty.

"33. Melancholy decreases sustenance.

"34. Overmuch sleep leads to poverty.

"35. Honor your wife and you will become wealthy.

"36. He who has no livelihood should study the Torah, and then pray for sustenance. His prayer will be heard on High.

"37. He who engages in unfair competition is wicked.

"38. For all things, including wit, wisdom, wealth and children, a man must strive according to nature, and pray that God may send him prosperity.

"39. He to whom another's possessions are as dear as his own, can pray with concentration of heart.

"40. A man's wealth will remain with him if he gives generously to Palestine." [1]

Sef. Ham., pp. 95-101.

[1] Many of these sayings are derived from the Talmud.

2. An Informal Prayer

Said the Mikolayever: "In many prayer books, two informal prayers are inserted in the middle of the benediction in the Amidah, beginning with the words: 'Hear Our Voice' (Singer, p. 49). One pleads for forgiveness, and the other for sustenance. But why was not the plea for forgiveness inserted in the benediction for forgiveness? Doubtless this may be explained as follows: we see that the impious are oftentimes more wealthy than the pious; hence we petition: O Lord, we too have sinned; hence we also are entitled to wealth."

_E. A., p. 69._

106. MONEY AND ITS USE

1. The Use of Money

The Premislaner said: "It is true that a Jew oftentimes offers most earnestly those prayers which plead for a livelihood and for money. But to what use does he place the money? He keeps God's commandments therewith; he donates it to charities; he engages a teacher to instruct his children in the Torah; he spends it on meals appropriate to the Sabbath; he contributes it to the support of students of the Talmud. Is it improper, then, for him to pray for money?"

_M. D., p. 222._

2. The Favors of the Satan

The Rimanover Rabbi dreamed that he ascended to Heaven and heard an angel pleading with the Lord to grant Israel wealth, saying: "Behold how pious they are in poverty; vouchsafe unto them riches, and they will be many times as pious."

The Rabbi inquired the name of the angel. The reply was: "He is called the Satan."

The Rabbi then exclaimed: "Leave us in poverty, O Lord. Safeguard us from the favors of the Satan."

_O. I. H., p. 186._

3. With Silver and Gold

Said the Gerer Rabbi: "We read in Psalm 105:37: 'And He brought them forth with silver and gold; and there was none that stumbled among His tribes.' The Psalmist wishes to tell us that the money did not spoil them."

_S. S. K., ii, 60._

4. *Treasure At Home*

A man asked the Kotzker's advice regarding the wisdom of moving from his native town in order to improve his circumstances. The Rabbi told the following story:

"A certain Jew of Cracow dreamed several times that there was a treasure near a mill awaiting his arrival to dig it up. He left his house early in the morning, and dug carefully, but did not find the money. The miller asked the reason for digging near his mill, and when the explanation had been given, he exclaimed: 'Why, I dreamed that there is a treasure in the courtyard of a certain man in Cracow,' and he named the digger himself. The man promptly returned to his home, and uncovered the treasure in his own yard.

"You see now," added the Rabbi. "Sometimes a man can find a treasure in his own home." [1]

Kotzker Maasioth, p. 105.

[1] Compare the motif of Maeterlinck's "The Bluebird."

5. *The Maggid and the Miser*

The Khelmer Maggid observed among his congregation, in the front row, a wealthy beardless man, who was known to be a miser. Looking hard at this person, he narrated the following parable:

"I dreamed that I was walking on the street, and an ox met me. He greeted me in a friendly manner. 'What friend of mine are you?' I asked. 'I give you of my flesh,' replied the ox.

"Next a cow greeted me. 'I give you of my milk,' she said.

"Next a he-goat greeted me, and said: 'Both of us wear long beards.'

"A swine came next to greet me. I cried at her: 'Keep away, thou swine; I do not eat thy meat; I do not drink thy milk, and thou hast no beard; what then hast thou to do with me?'"

The miser left his seat and walked out.

O. I. H., p. 188.

6. *The Power of Money*

The Zlotzover Maggid remained a few weeks in Brody. It was observed that he walked to and fro in the synagogue, carrying his Tallith, and that he waited until every one else had completed Services before he began to pray himself. This odd conduct piqued the curiosity of the synagogue's frequenters, and they induced a rich and learned member to ask the Maggid for an explanation.

The Maggid said: "Are you the most learned man in the city that you were selected to question me?"

"No," replied the member. "I was chosen as the richest man in the congregation. The poorer members did not dare to approach you."

"It seems, then," said the Maggid, "it is money that questions me. I do not care to answer the queries placed to me by money."

The Apter Rabbi explained that Rabbi Michael of Zlotzov prayed so late in order to include all half-hearted prayers together with his own, and thereby to make them all acceptable on High.

Yeshuath Israel, pp. 14-15.

7. A Disbursing Agent

A wealthy man visited the Kossover. The Rabbi questioned him regarding a poor teacher, one of his adherents, but the rich man affirmed that he knew him not. The Rabbi reproved the magnate, saying: "God, by vouchsafing riches to you, has appointed you as His disbursing agent to aid the poor. Yet you aid not even your fellow-Hasid."

E. Tz., p. 61.

8. Jacob and Esau

The Ropshitzer discussed Jacob's purchase of Esau's birthright. He explained that this world is the birthright of Esau and the World-to-Come, the birthright of Jacob. But Jacob found that in order to attain the World-to-Come, he must labor in this world in the service of the Lord. Inasmuch, however, as he entirely lacked the wealth of this world, he would not be able to serve the Lord. Therefore he asked Esau to sell him some of his birthright in this world.

E. Tz., p. 99.

9. Avoid Wastefulness

Said the Izbitzer: "We learn that most of the holy furnishings of the Tabernacle were of gold, but when it was ordered that the trumpets be made, Moses was told (Numb. 10:2): 'Make thee two trumpets of silver.' The reason is that the trumpets were also used in war: 'When ye go to war in your land against the adversary that oppresseth you, then ye shall sound an alarm with the trumpets' (Numb. 10:9). This teaches us not to waste our subsistence in the event of tribulation, but to deliberate how we can best meet it, according to the circumstances which confront us."

Nif. Haz., p. 32.

107. MORAL INSTRUCTION

1. Lighting the Candles

When Rabbi Schmelke and Rabbi Phineas came to the Mezeritzer Maggid, they were already great students of the Torah, but they gave little attention to the study of ethics. The Mezeritzer convinced them of the importance of devoting adequate time to these studies as well. After they had left him, the Maggid turned to his Disciples, and said:

"I found a house full of candles that were unlit. I have kindled them, and the house is filled with light."

M. R. T., p. 10.

2. The Bratzlaver on "Moral Influence"

"1. Every man should frequently converse with his friend on the subject of the fear of the Lord. Each man possesses good points which the other lacks. Through such conversation both receive the benefit of the other's judgments. Oftentimes this influence may be transmitted in ordinary conversation.

"2. Our understanding becomes as perfect as it is possible for mortals to attain, if we seek to bring others near unto God.

"3. Almost everyone possesses the influence to draw others to the fear of the Lord. Some may be able to affect only their near ones; others may have power over multitudes. He who does not utilize his influence towards faith and morality is punished for the misdeeds which his influence might have prevented.

"4. Through written words we can influence those of whom we have never heard.

"5. He who seeks to influence others should frequently judge himself.

"6. He who influences others for good erects a Holy Temple unto the Lord, and builds an altar whereon is offered unto God the goodness which has been awakened.

"7. In admonition let no anger escape your heart.

"8. Those whom we influence for good become our spiritual children.

"9. There are persons so wicked that to befriend them is dangerous to your own spiritual peace. Pray to God to keep them far from you.

"10. Even though your fellow-men may not heed your admonition, you will have benefited yourself. By admonishing others your own higher impulses are awakened more than by the effort at self-admonition.

"11. When we wish to influence another person, we ought to begin by commending his good traits, and help him find excuses for his misdeeds. In this fashion we may hope to succeed in improving him.

"12. We ought to have the greatest compassion upon him who has a burden of transgressions to bear. If we help him to rid himself of it, he becomes our disciple in holiness. We will then be destined to arrive in the After-World with a precious gift for the Lord."

L. E. H., pp. 114-6.

3. The Broom

The Besht was accustomed to send forth his Disciples to endeavor to improve people. Once his Disciple, Rabbi Mendel of Bar, returned to Medziboz from a journey. The Besht said to him:

"A broom sweeps the courtyard clean, but it becomes soiled itself. Go now and cleanse yourself of any offenses in which you may be guilty."

M. R. T., p. 70.

4. Three Kinds of Jew

The Radomsker Rabbi visited a spa in Austria on the Sabbath when the Sedrah "Kedoshim" was read in the synagogue. He was asked to deliver a brief discourse. Noticing in the congregation a goodly number of irreligious Jews, he said: "We read today the portion in Leviticus, chapter nineteen. The second verse commands us to be holy, and ends with the words: 'I am the Lord your God.' The third verse commands us to reverence our parents and to observe the Sabbath; 'I am the Lord your God.' The fourth verse commands us not to turn unto idols, and also concludes with the words: 'I am the Lord your God.' Why does this repetition occur?

"It may be explained thus: God speaks to three kinds of Jews: the saints, the persons of average character, and the irreligious. To the first group He says: 'Lead a saintly life; do more than you are required; I am your God, the Master of Holiness.'

"To the second group, He says: 'Keep My commandments; I am your God Who commands you to do so.'

"To the third group, He says: 'Even though you refuse to keep the entire Torah, at least do not become apostates. I am your God, and if you do not wish to obey Me, at least do not turn to strange Gods.'"

O. S., p. 32.

5. Seize the Opportunity

Said Rabbi Bunam: "If by chance an opportunity comes to you to better yourself, do not hesitate to seize hold of it. It is so decreed in Heaven. Cling to it until another opportunity comes to you."

S. I., p. 37.

6. The Need for Company

A Rabbi was asked: "Why is it that the pious man seems less eager to persuade others to become religious than the impious man to gain companions in wickedness?"

He replied: "The man of piety walks in light and is not afraid to walk alone, whereas the man of impiety walks in darkness and is anxious for company."

L. H. F., p. 38.

7. The Seed Will Bloom

Said the Bershider: "Despair not if you preach and behold no result. Be assured that the seed you have planted will blossom in some listener's heart."

M. P., p. 47.

8. A Mature Jew

Said the Bershider: "I asked my Master, the Koretzer, how to strengthen my faith and trust in God in times when it seems that God has hidden his countenance and left me in want.

"He replied: 'Only the young require such advice. A mature Jew has had sufficient experience to trust in God's constant watchfulness over him.'

"On another occasion I told him of the pride in my heart when people show me respect. He answered: 'Indulge not yourself in minor, but rather in major thoughts, and your pride of heart for minor reasons will disappear.' "

M. P., p. 41.

9. Time to Clarify

A young Hasid was ready to return to his home after a visit to the Dinover. He began to meditate: "With what am I going home?"

The Rabbi read his thoughts and said: "Young man, it is at home that you will become aware of your gain."

E. Tz., p. 108.

10. No Exchange

A Hasid said to the Riziner: "The Hasidim who visit Rabbi N. have both worlds, whereas your Hasidim have neither."

"How is this?" asked the Riziner.

"He lives near his Hasidim, and they therefore visit him in comfort. They find few visitors there, and hence the Rebbe can instruct them with thoroughness in proper service to the Lord. But this is not the case with you," explained the Hasid.

"Know then," retorted the Riziner, "that you should not exchange my Purgatory for that Rebbe's Paradise." [1]

D. Z., p. 45.

[1] The Riziner's few words were worth more than the other Rebbe's long tirades.

11. Freedom for Moral Instruction

Said the Porissover: "Let us be thankful that the Rabbis of old have already clarified and explained the Halakhah. This leaves us the opportunity in our days to occupy our minds with the principles of Ethics according to the teachings of the Besht."

D. Z., p. 32.

12. A Letter of Instruction and Reproof

The following letter was sent to an unknown Hasid by Rabbi Eleazar at the command of the Lizensker, his father:

"My father was greatly distressed on reading your epistle to see that among the Hasidim there are to be found such foolish and unwise persons. We note that you do not visit the Zaddikim in order to observe their holy conduct, their constant repentance over each step, look or word for which they are responsible, lest these be not wholly for the sake of the Lord. You do not observe their lack of concern whether a good deed or a blessing is better or preferable above others, as the Talmud teaches: 'We must not declare this saying or instruction is admirable and another inferior.' [1] Nor do you

[1] Erubin 64.

see that they seek solely to serve God with their every act, movement and word, as it is written: 'Know Him in all thy ways.' [2]

"What you observe, however, is not their mode of service, but the manner in which they move about, dress, eat, and so forth. You think that he who imitates the Zaddik in these outward actions is a proper Hasid. If you were not known to us as an earnest man who seeks the way to God, we would not have answered you with a single word. Hence my father said: 'He who inquires whether to chant these or other hymns, whether to recite the Song of Songs at this or that time, and the like, is still ignorant and foolish.' And he commanded me to write you several regulations concerning your conduct in order that you may know how to serve the Lord aright.

"Learn Talmud and the Code 'Orach Hayyim,' and pray that you may understand it correctly.

"Arise before daylight and commune with thy God in solitude, weeping over the pain of the Shekinah. Confess your sins with a broken heart. Tear your heart into twelve pieces by considering how much anguish your sins have brought to the Shekinah, and how you have lengthened its Exile.

"Devote, also, an hour during the day for communion with God in solitude. You will soon be able to perceive before your eyes your sins, great as mountains, which you have overlooked. Repeat this many times, and you will receive Heaven's mercy.

"Pray to the Lord that He may lead you on the pathway of truth, that you may no longer waste your days in unworthiness.

"Guard your soul against flattery, falsehoods, mockery, the evil tongue, jealousy, hate, rivalry, arrogance, anger, and frivolity with women. Remember constantly the day of your demise.

"After you have come to believe that your soul has been purified of its contamination by sins, and that your thoughts no longer turn to worthless and impure desires, you may study some of the Kabbalistic works of the Ari. But be not impatient, for the study of the Kabbalah is a veritable poison for impure persons. Learn steadily the Haggadah of our Sages, for it achieves purification of the soul.

"If you persist in this, you will be vouchsafed the ability to chant praises to the Lord aright.

"Know that if a man serves the Lord with every form of service, but nevertheless retains a vestige of pride therein, he is an abomination to the Lord.

"If your heart becomes pure, the Shekinah itself will sing within you.

"As for the proper conduct of a man, I am able to write you only a brief suggestion. Each virtue, quality and trait has an unlimited number of branches.

"A very important rule is to guard yourself against drinking intoxicating liquors. The Talmud teaches: 'Avoid intoxication and you will avoid sin.' [3]

[2] Proverbs 3:6.   [3] Berakhoth 29.

"Another important rule is to avoid evil thoughts, sadness in any form, and hatred of any person except the thoroughly wicked.

"Love other persons as much as you love your own kinsmen and children. Aid them with your person, your wealth and your endeavors.

"If you hear your praises sung, feel truly downcast of heart. Think in truth whether others would have praised you, were every act, intention and motive of yours known to them as it is known to the Most High.

"If you hear yourself abused, feel truly glad of heart. God has been merciful to you and has sent you some one to reprove you for your ugly deeds.

"Believe that every other person is superior to you. Let it seem to you that your every movement is being constantly observed and that you are ashamed to do anything you will not wish to become known. Remember that God sees your every movement and knows your every thought.

"Beware of uttering a single word before your prayers, as your mind must be wholly engrossed in contemplation of God to Whom you are about to offer prayer.

"Show not an angry mood to your household or to any person. If you feel anger, believe it to have come because of your sins.

"Pray to the Lord that you may not be summoned by death without true repentance. Pray also that all Israel may become sincere penitents.

"Be careful lest you utter God's name in vain. Take care not to think of Holy subjects of the Torah in an unclean place. Engage in no talk in the synagogue; do not speak even words of admonition as they will lead you to unseemly words as well.

"At all times abstain from unnecessary talk. Think always of your lowliness and of God's grandeur.

"May the Lord, Blessed be He, guard us in His mercy and kindness from folly and unworthiness. May we deserve to serve the Lord in truth, awe and love, without any evil inclinations, and without any hindrances, until the coming of the Redeemer, speedily in our days."

Signed by Eleazar ben Elimelech.
E. Tz., pp. 36-38.

108. MUSIC AND MUSICIANS

1. Harmony in the Community

Said the Lekhivitzer: "We read (II Kings 3:15): 'And it came to pass when the minstrel played, that the hand of the Lord came upon him.' The musician, the leader of the orchestra of community affairs, should be as unselfish and unprejudiced as music—as the melody which is pleasing to all. Then will the Lord's inspiration come to him to assist his efforts and to achieve every desirable and harmonious end."

O. Y., p. 15.

2. Variations or Monotone?

The Bialechziger Rabbi said: "Some persons wonder at the various methods of the Hasidic Rabbis in serving the Lord. But the explanation is simple. It is the musical variations which make for melody, not the monotone."

S. S. K., iv, 123.

3. Imperfect Instruments

A Rabbi asked the Lubliner: "Why do you stop to take snuff in the midst of prayers, when interruptions are forbidden?"

The Rabbi replied with the following story: "A king heard a street singer playing his violin and singing. He found it to his liking, and invited the troubador to sing at his court. In the middle of a song, however, a violin string would frequently break, and the king was forced to wait until it was replaced. Finally a courtier asked the violinist why he did not have the entire instrument restrung in order to avoid interruptions.

"'I will tell you,' replied the street singer. 'The king has many musicians with perfect instruments, and could order anyone of them to entertain him. Yet he seems to prefer my playing. Hence it appears as if he were willing to hear me play my imperfect violin.' Likewise the Lord has many hosts of singing angels, yet when He orders us mortals to pray unto Him, it is clear He is willing to endure our frailties."

N. H. L., p. 30.

4. Melodies from Shepherds

The Kalever Rabbi learned from the Mezeritzer Maggid a melody for the hymn in the Haggadah "The Mighty in His Kingdom," and was greatly pleased with it. The Maggid said he had learned it from a shepherd. From then on, the Kalever made it a habit to walk in pastures to listen to the melodies sung by the Shepherds. His melody for the Psalm (137:1): "By the Waters of Babylon" was heard by him on the lips of a shepherd, and is now well known. He used to say: "Many a melody once chanted by the Levites in the Holy Temple is now in Exile among the unlearned common people."

E. Tz., p. 72.

5. The Singing Brigands

Rabbi Meir Margulis visited the Besht with his young son, Saul. The father went to transact some business in the suburbs and left his son with the Besht for a few days. The Besht took the boy Saul with him on a brief journey. Passing an inn, they heard the sound of beautiful singing. They entered and saw a group of peasant lads entertaining a large audience with their songs. The boy Saul was asked to sing, and his sweet voice charmed the listeners. The lads were introduced and shook hands in token of friendship.

In later years Saul became a merchant, and passing through a forest, was set upon by brigands and robbed of his valuables. Suddenly he recognized among the brigands the lads who had pledged him their friendship at the inn. He called them by name and reminded them of the occurrence. They invited him to sing again, and, in token of their enjoyment, they returned to him the goods they had seized.

Nif. Yeh., p. 84.

6. Song Without Words

The Ladier noticed an old man among his listeners who obviously did not comprehend the meaning of his discourse. He summoned him to his side and said: "I perceive that my sermon is unclear to you. Listen to this melody, and it will teach you how to cleave unto the Lord." The Ladier began to sing a song without words. It was a song of Torah, of trust in God, of longing for the Lord, and of love for Him.

"I understand now what you wish to teach," exclaimed the old man. "I feel an intense longing to be united with the Lord."

The Rebbe's melody became part of his every discourse henceforth, though it had no words.

Beo. H., pp. 47-50.

109. THE NINTH OF AB

1. The Truthful Transgressor

The Berditschever on the Ninth of Ab encountered a Jew who was eating in public. He stopped him and said: "You must have forgotten that to-day is the Ninth of Ab."

"No, I have not forgotten," was the reply.

"Then perhaps you are unable to fast because you are unwell?" continued the Rabbi.

"Oh, no," answered the man.

The Rabbi lifted his eyes skyward and exclaimed: "O Lord, behold how Israelites love the truth. Even while transgressing, a Jew declines to speak a falsehood."

Kahana, p. 264.

2. Hope for Jerusalem

The Alexanderer Rabbi was present at a banquet in celebration of the completion of a Talmudical treatise, held during the mournful period before the Ninth of Ab. He spoke as follows:

"It has been customary to set aside this period for sad contemplation regarding the destruction of the Temple. We Hasidim, however, do not hesitate to hold banquets during these days. We say: there was a Temple in days gone by; there will be a Temple in days to come. Let me narrate to you a parable in this connection:

" 'King Solomon, according to a Talmudic tale,[1] lost his throne to Ashmedai, the King of the Demons. He was compelled to escape from Jerusalem and to wander about among the villages. He chanced to come to a wealthy farmer who believed his statement to the effect that he was the King. The farmer gave a banquet in his honor, but bewailed his mournful lot so dolefully that Solomon was unable to partake of the viands set before him.

" 'On leaving the rich man's house, Solomon encountered a poor peasant, and related his misfortunes. The peasant comforted him, and persuaded him not to lose hope of restoration to the throne. "Thou hast been king, and thou shalt be king," said the peasant with confidence. Solomon's heart rejoiced once more, and he ate with zest the frugal meal served him by the peasant. He found more to his taste the dry bread of the peasant than the luxurious viands of the wealthy farmer.'

"In the same fashion we Hasidim do not feel we please the King of Kings by overabundant sadness and gloom during these nine days. The Lord was King in Zion, and He will again be King in Zion."

S. S. K., i, 105.

[1] Gittin 68.

3. God's Secret Tears

Rabbi Bunam narrated this parable: "A king beheld the evil conduct of his only son, and he concealed his most precious valuables in an inner chamber of the palace. He thought to himself: 'When my son improves his ways, I will reveal the treasure to him.' Later the palace was consumed by fire, and nothing was saved. Everyone bewailed the heavy loss, but the king lamented most in secret. He alone knew of the magnitude of the loss.

"Likewise when the Holy Temple was destroyed, everyone wept at the loss of outward possessions, but God lamented most in secret. He alone knew of the precious spiritual treasures which He had hidden there, as it is said: 'My soul shall weep in secret for your pride' (Jer. 13:17)."

S. I., p. 87.

4. Mourning with Joy

The Ropshitzer used to say during the three weeks before the 9th of Ab: "It is not fitting that we should deplore the loss of the Holy Temple with our entire heart, for the Lord, who endowed this edifice with holiness, is with us in Exile. We should mingle mourning with joy because our Lord is present among us."

Ohel N., p. 114.

5. A Day for Peace-Making

The Bershider narrated this experience: He came once to a town on the 9th of Ab. The townspeople informed him of a bitter quarrel between two factions, and asked him to act as peacemaker. "We suppose, however," they said, "that you will not care to consider this matter on the 9th of Ab."

"Quite the contrary," replied the Rabbi. "The destruction of the Temple was caused by unfounded hatred, according to the Talmud.[1] What can be more appropriate than to abolish unfounded hatred on this day?"

[1] Yoma 9.

M. P., p. 44.

110. NOBLE BIRTH

1. Three Pre-requisites

The Kotzker Rabbi said: "There are three things desirable for success: the first: to be well-born; the second: to be a good worker; the third: to have the aid of Heaven."

S. S. K., ii, 23.

2. The Palace Murals

The Riziner told the following tale:

"A king built a palace and summoned four artists to paint murals on the walls. Three artists painted murals, but the fourth painted his wall with such a beautiful coloring substance that all the murals were reflected in it as in the clearest mirror. The king admired most the fourth wall."

"Noble birth," continued the Riziner, "may be admired only when it reflects by its own worth the fame of a man's forebears."

N. I., p. 80.

3. Overstepping Our Sires

A Rabbi visited Rabbi Shalom of Belz. During the course of the conversation the Belzer Rabbi mentioned that his forebears had been distinguished men and belonged to a famous family. The visiting Rabbi, who was of humble descent, expressed surprise that his pious host should express pride in his family, where the true "good Jew" knows only humility.

The Belzer Rabbi made the following reply: "You are quite mistaken in attributing to me pride for speaking of my high descent. It is really the contrary. We are taught by our Sages that a man should say to himself: 'When will my deeds equal those of my sires?'[1] It follows, then, that one, whose parents are famous, always feels humble, believing that he has not yet reached the height of his parents' fame. On the other hand, one with humble parents, as soon as he became favorably known, would feel proud of being a self-made man who had overstepped his father."

S. S. K., iv, 17.

[1] Midrash Tanna d'bei Eliyahu.

4. The More Renowned Family

The Ropshitzer related his genealogy to his Hasidim and declared: "I doubt if there is a family more renowned than mine."

A Hasid, however, retorted: "Rabbi, I come from a nobler family than even yours!"

The Rabbi invited him to describe his family.

"Let me explain, Rabbi," declared the Hasid. "Of my entire family, I am the only one who dons the phylacteries and washes his hands before meals."

The Rabbi laughingly admitted the superiority of the Hasid's family connections, and respected him for his wit.

O. N., p. 60.

5. Brandy That Is Bitter

The Ropshitzer remarked to a Zaddik: "You, who are of lowly descent, are better off than I, who am of noble lineage. When you have performed your Services in a holy fashion, you can enjoy a little brandy afterwards, and think to yourself that you are superior to your forebears. Not so with me. After I complete my Services and partake of a little brandy, the taste is bitter within me, inasmuch as I think to myself: 'Is this simple Service all that I can offer to God? Have not my Sires far outshone me?' Hence you see that noble birth does not aid in the performance of Services to the Lord, but merely helps to embitter the brandy after prayers." [1]

E. Tz., p. 90.

[1] A similar story is told by the Belzer; 110:3.

6. Independent of Each Other

Said the Premislaner: "Concerning the verse (Exodus 6:3): 'And I appeared unto Abraham, unto Isaac and unto Jacob,' Rashi comments: 'And I appeared unto the Patriarchs.' It may be asked: What did Rashi intend to explain by this comment? The answer is: It is customary for one whose father was a man of holiness, to be lax in his efforts to improve his own service to the Lord, inasmuch as he depends upon the greatness of his father. This is all the more true when his grandfather was also a saintly man. He contents himself with being the son and grandson of illustrious personages. This was not the case with Isaac and Jacob. They labored hard at self-improvement, and paid no heed to their parents' fame. They desired to be great Patriarchs in their own right. This is the meaning of Rashi: they were all Patriarchs, and no one of them received his fame by reason of his parents."

H. G., p. 7.

7. Three Noble Families

The Besht declared that three families in Israel gave more noble sons to the Holy Rabbinate than any other: the family, Margulis, the family, Shapiro, and the family, Hurwitz. He, therefore, respected most his disciples, Meir Margulis, Rabbi of Lemberg and Chief Rabbi of Ukraine; Phineas Shapiro, the famous Koretzer Zaddik

and thinker; and Zevi Hirsch Halevy Hurwitz, the Rabbi of Tzartkov, father of Rabbi Schmelke and Rabbi Phineas.

Nif. Yeh., p. 88.

8. The Parents' Struggles

Said the Zablitover: "The sons of famous men are usually unsuccessful, because they believe they may begin where their fathers
left off, and they do not care to undergo their parents' struggles."

E. A., p. 62.

111. NON-JEWS AND JEWS

1. The Poverty of Israel

Said the Lubliner: "The Talmud tells us that 'poverty becomes
Israel like a red ribbon becomes a white horse.'[1] When the horse
is for sale, the owner decorates him to please the eye of the pur-
chaser. Likewise when Jews look poor, it pleases the non-Jews, and
they do not do us harm because of envy."

[1] Hagigah 9.

N. H. L., p. 36.

2. Help from Naught

Said the Gerer Rabbi: "During many periods of Israel's history,
they turned for help in their need to other nations, or to those in
authority. This rarely brought satisfactory results. Only when
Israel comprehended that 'from naught shall come my help,' namely,
that there is no man or people in whom they can place their trust,
did it come to pass that they declared in song: 'My help is from the
Lord' (Psalm 121:2)."

S. S. K., ii, 41.

3. Jewish Inns

The Rimanover Rabbi greatly opposed the residence of Jews in
the villages since their children were forced to associate with non-
Jews and grew up in ignorance of Judaism. He induced many of
his Hasidim to leave the villages and move into the town. Those
who did not follow his injunction he threatened with excommunication. They related their troubles to the Ropshitzer, explaining
they could not throw away their opportunity for a livelihood for
themselves and their families.

The Ropshitzer hired a sled and journeyed to the Rimanover.
The snow was deep and the cold severe. When he arrived at the
Rimanover's home, he found the Rabbi absent. He removed his
garments and laid himself in the Rabbi's bed. When the Rimanover
prepared to retire, he found the Ropshitzer occupying his bed. He
tried to awaken him, but the Ropshitzer merely groaned and refused
to move.

"What ails you, Ropshitzer Rabbi?" asked the Rimanover.

"I am frozen with cold despite my warm fur coat," replied the

Ropshitzer. "Before you compelled the Jewish innkeepers to move to the town, a Jewish traveler could find a place to halt his journey and warm himself. Now I can find no Jewish inns near Rimanov. I can provide for myself since I own warm clothes, but I shudder to contemplate the plight of the less warmly-dressed travelers."

The Rimanover saw the point, and promised to recall his threat of excommunication.

O. N., p. 64.

4. The Lord Will Provide

The Ladier Rabbi in his youth was on a journey one wintry morning and his feet became frostbitten. The driver brought him to an inn, where the aged innkeeper rubbed his feet with snow and brought warmth to them again. The future Rabbi questioned his benefactor, who seemed to be a pious Jew, about his affairs. The innkeeper related that for fifty years he had been an innkeeper in the village, where he was the only Jew.

"How often do you attend public worship?" asked the Ladier.

The innkeeper replied that every year at Rosh ha-Shanah and Yom Kippur he attended the synagogue at the nearest town.

The Rabbi sought to persuade him to move to the town in his old age, where he would be able to attend Services daily, and listen to the preaching.

"But how will I earn a living there?" asked the old man.

"How many Jewish families live in the town?" inquired the Rabbi.

"About a hundred," was the reply.

"Do you not believe," asked the Rabbi, "that the Lord who provides for a hundred families, is able to provide a livelihood for one more?"

The old man immediately assembled his belongings, and journeyed to the city.

S. ha-Has., p. 204.

5. Who Is Superior?

Rabbi Aaron Livanier related the following experience of his early manhood: "In my student days I attended the Talmudical Academy at Prague. Once a wealthy man visited the Academy and requested the dean to recommend him a studious, clever youth as a son-in-law. I was selected and soon after married the rich man's daughter. My father-in-law promised to support me in great comfort on condition that I continue my rabbinical studies.

"But the luxurious living made me indolent and I began to neglect my books. In reply to my father-in-law's reproofs, I said: 'No matter how little I study, I know more than any other person in the town.'

"An itinerant Rabbi who sojourned for a time at my father-in-law's home was urged to discuss the matter with me. The Rabbi remarked to me: 'It is true that in this town you are the most learned person. But suppose I should counsel your father-in-law to send you back to the Academy, would you not feel shame at your backwardness in comparison with the progress of your fellow-students?"

"These words convinced me of my error, and I speedily mended my ways. I then understood the verse: 'Be holy, for I the Lord am Holy.' [1] I used to wonder how man's holiness can be compared to God's. The Rabbi's words clarified my doubt.

"A Jew who is careless in his duties as a Jew believes that, no matter how neglectful he may be, he is still superior to the non-Jew. This may perhaps be true in this world. But when his soul comes before his God after death, how will he feel in the holy realm above—the Academy on High—when he observes the superiority of his friends?"

O. Y., p. 81.

[1] Lev. 17:2.

6. Extra Covering

Said the Koretzer: "In the synagogue the Jews make use of an extra covering, the Tallith (Prayer-Shawl), so that they may the more separate the nakedness of the body from the spiritual. Non-Jews, however, remove their coats and their hats. They do not realize that the body and the soul are distinct from each other."

Nof. Tz., p. 11.

7. Gifts for Justice

The Duke of Mannheim complained to a Rabbi that the Jews made gifts to the judges. The Rabbi replied: "When your judges have before them a Jew and a non-Jew, they are inclined to decide in favor of the non-Jew, but the gifts induce them to mete out justice."

L. H. F., p. 42.

8. The Town's Owner

The Polish nobleman, Radziwill, who owned the little town of Nishwiz, chanced to be out of funds while in Warsaw. He entered a Jewish banking house and asked for a loan. The clerk refused on the plea of not knowing him. The nobleman asked: "Did you ever hear of a town named Nishwiz?"

"Yes," answered the clerk.

"Do you know to whom it belongs?"

"Surely I do. To the Rebbe of Lekhivitz," said the clerk.

The nobleman left in disgust.

L. H. F., p. 122.

9. The Unwelcome Jew

The author of "Homer Ledrush" writes: "We read in Genesis (26:16): 'And Abimelech said unto Isaac: Go from us; for thou art much mightier than we.' Isaac did not open a shop, so that the Gentile shopkeepers might have the excuse of complaining against his rivalry. He did not open a tavern in the village so that there might be complaint that he demoralized the peasants. He did not establish a bank so that there might be talk of usury. All Isaac did in Gerar was to engage in agriculture. Yet it did not prevent the natives from protesting against his sojourn in their midst, and the men of authority said to him: 'Go from us; for thou art much mightier than we.' "

F. U. A. O., i, 60.

10. Who Will Be Punished?

The Gerer overheard several zealous Hasidim condemning the untraditional ways of the Jews of Germany, saying that they should be banished from the face of the earth. The Rabbi summoned one to his side and said: "Yossel, when you visit Prussia on your next trip, I could give you a Kabbalistic phrase with power to turn into dust all the impious ones of Prussia. I hesitate to do this, however, since you will have no one with whom to trade."

"But, Rabbi," said Yossel. "I will trade with the Gentiles."

"Aha!" exclaimed the Rabbi. "You wish Jews to die that you may turn to non-Jews! I do not wish it so."

M. E. H., ii, 53.

11. The Garments of Esau

Several university students, unmistakably Jews, passed the Belzer Rabbi on the thoroughfare. The Rabbi sighed and said: "I am not opposed to non-Jewish education. Even our father Jacob adopted Esau's garments in order to obtain a blessing. I sigh, however, because, unlike our father Jacob, they do not return to the culture of Israel after they have received the blessing of secular learning. For the most part, they decline to remove the garments of Esau."

D. D., pp. 311-12.

12. When Enemies Rule

The Riziner once prophesied that the time would come when every country would be ruled by the enemies of Israel who would force us to return to the Holy Land. "It will be a disgrace," he added, "if, after so long an Exile, we return for this reason. Be this as it may, however, honors will attend us in Zion, if for once we can escape from our adversaries."

D. D., p. 310.

112. OBEDIENCE

1. For the Sake of Certainty

Rabbi Hayyim Tzernovitzer, the author of "Siddurah shel Shabbath," narrates the following parable: "A king wished to visit an outlying town and wrote its officials to prepare for him and his retinue. The inhabitants spoke a dialect unlike the cultured speech of the capital city, and did not comprehend clearly the royal instructions. A discussion ensued among the leaders, and many explanations were offered.

"A sage advised them to follow all the explanations of the message, and they did so. When the king saw the abundance prepared in his honor, he inquired the reason. The reply pleased him greatly. In the same way, if we do not understand a commandment clearly, we should obey it according to all the explanations."

M. R. T., pp. 13-14.

2. Obeying the Record

A Rabbi who accepted a call to become the Rabbi of Metz asked that the Community Record (the Pinkhas) be brought to him. When this was done, he proceeded to write therein the Ten Commandments.

The leaders were astounded, and asked the Rabbi to explain his action. He replied: "My experience in the Rabbinate has shown me that the words written in the Community Record are more readily obeyed than those written in the Torah."

F. U. A. O., i, 167.

3. The Worm

Said the Ropshitzer in his first sermon: "I am a worm, not a man, as the Psalmist [1] states. But you Hasidim are afraid of worms. I shall, therefore, expect from you fitting obedience." [2]

E. Tz., p. 93.

[1] Psalm 22:7.

[2] Hasidim are scrupulously careful to cleanse vegetables, fruits and even water from worms, however tiny, in conformance with the law forbidding the swallowing of creeping creatures (Lev. 11:43).

113. OCCUPATIONS

1. Loving God's Ways

The Besht narrated the following parable: "A son came to his aged father and asked his counsel regarding the occupation in which he should engage. The father replied: 'Seek a different occupation from mine. I labor hard at it and earn a mere pittance.'

"The son's friend marveled at this, inasmuch as his own father had earnestly advised him to follow the paternal vocation in order to learn a comfortable livelihood. The son replied: 'My father apparently dislikes his work, while yours has affection for it.' God says regarding Abraham (Gen. 18:19): 'For I have known him, to the end that he may command his children and his household after him, that they may keep the way of the Lord, to do righteousness and justice.' Abraham loved God's ways and asked his children to walk in the same path."

M. R. T., p. 6, part ii.

114. OFFERINGS AND SACRIFICES

1. Offering His Spirit

Said the Amshinover: "We read (Exodus 25:2-3): 'Of every man whose heart maketh him willing, ye shall take My offering. And this is the offering which ye shall take of them: gold and silver and brass.' If you observe a man," explained the Rabbi, "who is earnest in his piety and worships Me from his heart, bring him as an offering unto Me, and make it possible for him to continue in this way. And the way to bring him as an offering to Me is by removing from him the desire for gold, silver and brass. Give him a position of security, display to him due regard, and he will be content to devote his life unto God."

O. I., p. 9.

2. Neither Leaven nor Honey

The Kotzker Rabbi commented on the verse (Leviticus 2:11): "No meal-offering, which ye shall bring unto the Lord, shall be made with leaven; for ye shall make no leaven, nor any honey, smoke as an offering made by fire unto the Lord."

He said: "In your devotion unto the Lord be neither tasteless like leaven, or too sweet-mannered like honey."

S. S. K., ii, 23.

3. Over-abundant Offerings

Said the Gerer Rabbi: "We read (Exodus 36:6-7): 'And they caused it to be proclaimed throughout the camp, saying: Let neither man nor woman make any more work for the offering of the sanctuary. So the people were restrained from bringing. For the stuff they had was sufficient for all the work to make it, and too much.'

"Two things need explaining here," said the Gerer. "First: why proclaim against bringing more work; it would be useful later. Second: why does it say: 'sufficient' and then 'too much.' It may be explained in this fashion: Every man and woman in Israel was eager that his or her contribution be employed in furnishing the Holy Tabernacle. Moses regretted to disappoint any one by returning a gift or having it left over for later use. There were already more gifts than sufficient, and the workmen were hard pressed to plan the use of everything offered. Hence Moses was most eager to halt the flow of donations."

S. S. K., ii, 40.

4. "Behind" and "Thicket"

Said the Sassover: "Abraham was not commanded to offer up a ram instead of his son, Isaac. But he was a Prophet and he foresaw that his children would worship a calf, and he offered up a ram as an atonement for them in advance. A suggestion is given in the words (Gen. 22:13): 'And behold, behind him a ram caught in the thicket.' The Hebrew word for 'thicket' is composed of the letters: 'Samekh,' 'Beth' and 'Kaph'; and the letters following each of these, respectively, in the alphabet are 'Ayin,' 'Gimel' and 'Lamed,' composing the Hebrew word for 'calf.' "

M. Hat., p. 60.

[1] Seeking such hints took the place of chess problems among the Hasidim. In עגל and סבך, "Ayin" follows "Samekh"; "Gimel" follows "Beth," and "Lamed" follows "Kaph."

5. A Substitute

Said the Dinover: "We read (Leviticus 1:2): 'When any man of you bringeth an offering unto the Lord, ye shall bring your offering of the cattle.' The words: 'of you' seem superfluous, but the meaning is this: the reason for an offering is that God in His mercy permits us to offer an animal as a substitute for our own life, of which we have deprived ourselves by sinning against God. But the sinner must thoroughly repent of his sin before the offering. Hence the verse may be understood thus: If a man offers himself wholeheartedly as an offering unto the Lord, then he may bring 'of the cattle' as a substitute."

H. G., p. 9.

6. A Rescue from Punishment

Rabbi Baruch of Medziboz was seated at his meal, when a man entered. The Rabbi ordered him ejected and began to abuse him. His friend, Rabbi Abraham Dov of Chmelnik, said: "And what have you to say of the statement in the 'Ethics of the Fathers' (3:15) (Singer, p. 193): 'He who puts his fellow-man to shame in public has no share in the World-to-Come?' "

Rabbi Baruch answered: "That man had committed a serious offense, and I have ordered him ejected and have abused him in order to save him from God's punishment. To rescue a Jewish soul I gladly surrendered my own share in the Future World."

Butz. D., p. 32.

7. Learning the Law of the Offering

Said the Koretzer: "It is written (Lev. 7:37): 'This is the law of the burnt-offering, of the meal-offering, and of the sin-offering, and so forth . . .' Repentance while the Temple stood was accompanied by an offering. Nowadays, however, it should be accompanied by the learning of the Law regarding the offering which in the times of the Temple it would have been a man's obligation to bring." [1]

Nof. Tz., p. 26.

[1] Based on Menachoth 110a.

115. OSTENTATION AND LUXURY

1. The Playing Card

The Alexanderer Rabbi said: "An overdressed man, who tries to imitate blindly his betters is like the poorly drawn imitation of a man on a playing card."

S. S. K., iii, 81.

2. The Three Funds

The Riziner lived in great luxury. A Rabbi inquired the reason, and the Riziner explained as follows:

"I have three kinds of funds: one is from the real Hasidim, and this goes for my necessities. One is from the householders of middling piety; this I give away to the needy. The third is from habitual sinners; and this goes for luxuries. Is it my fault that the third fund is the largest?" [1]

O. I. H., pp. 63-4.

[1] It is said that the real reason was the same which prompted the command to the High Priest to wear gold-embroidered vestments, and the Tabernacle to have gold appointments, namely to gain the deference of the people.

3. The Pearl in the Ash-heap

Ere leaving for the land of Israel, Rabbi Menachem Mendel Vitebsker called upon the great disciple of the Besht, Rabbi Jacob Joseph of Pulnoe. He came to the tavern in a carriage drawn by three horses, which scandalized the Hasidim not a little, for their teacher had taught them to live austerely. The guest gave further offense, going from the inn to the Zaddik's house without a fur hat or girdle, a long-stemmed pipe in his mouth. They all knew Rabbi Joseph for a short-tempered man, and fully expected him to forbid his house to the free-mannered guest.

But the old man received him at the threshold right lovingly, and remained with him for hours in earnest discourse. The Disciples asked him the next day: "Who is this man, making bold to enter your house without a fur hat or girdle, with a pipe in his mouth, and silver buckles on his shoes?"

Said the Zaddik: "A certain king going to war placed his treasures behind locks and bars. But his choicest pearl he hid in an ash-heap where no one was likely to search for it. Rabbi Mendel hides his great humility in the ash-heap of worldly vanity, where the powers of evil cannot meddle." [1]

N. I., p. 72. See Fuchs, J. T., Dec. 19, '30, p. 5.

[1] Hasidic Rabbis wear a fur hat and gird their loose garments.

4. The Zaddik's Opulent Living

The Riziner gave another explanation for living like a prince in a richly-appointed home. He explained his manner of life by declaring that when a Zaddik lives in poverty, he has only limited ideas of people's needs, and prays for mere sustenance. When, however, he enjoys riches, he feels bold enough to pray that his adherents also may have a life of comfort." [1]

N. I., p. 45.

[1] See "The Meal of Stones," 177 : 1.

5. The Maggid's "Worldliness"

After grave deliberation, Rabbi Schmelke and Rabbi Phineas resolved to remain in Mezeritz. But the longer they tarried, the less they found the conduct of the Maggid to their liking. They noted with disfavor, that he kept court like a potentate, and busied himself overmuch with the concerns of his house and landed estate. Before morning prayer, belatedly said, he looked after his horses and cows, assigned tasks to his servants, and saw to it that they greased the wheels of his carts. In other matters, also, his ways appeared strange, for he held converse in the streets with people of little worth and even with some of evil repute. This gave offense to the Rabbis, and they made ready to leave, until Rabbi Sussya, by expounding a passage in the "Ethics of the Fathers" [1] prevailed upon them to remain with the Maggid.

"Our fathers," remarked Sussya, "have said: 'The froward to Gehinnom; the shamefaced to the Garden of Eden.' [2] How is this to be understood? Is it not as follows: The bold, the froward, is he whom men call the Zaddik; his sanctity emboldens him to descend hellward to carry aloft that which is low; he is not afraid of wickedness on the streets and at county fairs. But the shamefaced who fears infection must continually keep on a level with Paradise; he must always pray and study and shun contact with those whom the Zaddik lifts from the mire."

Bl., Gem., p. 120.

[1] 5 : 23 ; Singer, p. 203.
[2] See 104 : 10.

6. Inner Worth

Rabbi Bunam in his early manhood was a timber merchant, and as such, wore business clothes of German style. He chanced to be in Lemberg on business at the same time that the Sudilkover Rabbi, the grandson of the Besht, was there. Hearing of this, he longed to partake of the Sabbath meal at the Rabbi's table. He heard of the Sudilkover's presence, however, too late to change into Hasidic garments, and was, therefore, not permitted to take a seat in front. The Rabbi, passing by, recognized his noble character, and invited him to sit at the head of the table, next to himself. He said:

"We find (Gen. 25:25) that when Esau was born 'they called his name Esau.' Rashi explains that everybody who saw him called him thus. 'Calling' means 'drawing to oneself, becoming attracted to one.' Esau, who stands for falsehood, for evil conduct, for unethical living, attracted people.[1] Many came to name him. But Jacob, who stands for truth, self-restraint, and purity of life did not attract the by-standers. His naming was left to the one person who understood his worth, and who was drawn to truth and morality."

He then turned to Rabbi Bunam and said: "Have no ill feeling for those who refused you a fitting place. One among many is attracted to the true worth of a person, regardless of his appearance."

S. I., p. 26.

[1] In verse 25, concerning Esau, the plural is used; 'they called him'; in verse 26, about Jacob, the singular is used in the Hebrew, literally 'he called him.' "

7. Garments and Their Meaning

Said the Bratzlaver: "Soiled clothing is an indication of the wearer's character. Ostentatious garments mark their wearer as an adherent of the Satan. His clothes are more important to him than his God."

L. E. H., pp. 7-10.

8. Lead Not to Envy

Said the "Yud": "Display neither your material nor your spiritual wealth, lest those who lack it be led by you into envy and covetousness."

Nif. Yeh., p. 42.

9. Broadening the Understanding

A Hasid asked the Zlotzover Maggid why he lived in great luxury. The Maggid replied: "We are told in the Talmud (Berakhoth, 57) that a fine dwelling, fine clothes and a beautiful wife broaden a man's understanding, and I need all the understanding I can acquire to serve my Master fitly."

D. D., p. 85.

10. When Understanding Is Absent

A Hasid complained to the Riziner that he lacked fine garments, a fine dwelling, and a beautiful wife, the three things which serve to broaden understanding according to the Talmud (Berakhoth, 57).

"But these things only serve to broaden a man's understanding, not to create it in him," replied the Riziner. "Therefore of what use will they be to you?"

D. D., p. 309.

11. In His Element

Rabbi Nahum Tzernobiler noticed that his stepson, Rabbi Shalom Shakhna Prohobister, the son of the "Angel," enjoyed fine clothes and residence in a finely furnished home. He appreciated that Rabbi Shalom believed himself an aristocrat and a Prince of the Captivity. Nevertheless he warned him against his mode of living as contrary to Hasidic conventions. Rabbi Shalom replied: "A hen sat on goose eggs, and the chicks believed themselves young hens. Once when they chanced to wander to a pool, the goslings entered it immediately. The hen shouted a warning, but the young geese exclaimed: 'We are in our element.' I, too, am in my element in a fine home and fine garments."

D. D., p. 303.

116. PALESTINE

1. Land of Abraham

The Kozmirer Rabbi said: "The Lord gave Canaan to Abraham on the condition that his heirs should follow in his footsteps. When Ishmael did not adhere fully to his father's teaching, Isaac received the inheritance. When Esau did not comply with the true tradition, Israel was given the heritage. When Israel became habitually delinquent, his heirloom reverted to Esau [the names given to Rome and Christendom in Hebrew literature]. When Esau's followers degenerated, they were compelled to surrender Canaan to Ishmael [the Moslems]. At the present the process is reversing itself: the land was lost by Ishmael to Edom [Esau] and will shortly be given up by Edom to its rightful owner—Israel."

S. S. K., v, 15.

2. The Return

Rabbi Bunam explained the verse (Psalm 37:34): "He will exalt thee to inherit the land." He said: "The Lord tells us that He will raise the people of Israel to a high place of fame among the nations before they will be fit to inherit the Holy Land. Let us, therefore, become great enough to arouse the admiration of the peoples, and we shall be ready to return to our Land."

S. S. K., ii, 18.

3. Like Abraham

Said the Riziner: "The purpose of Rabbi Mendel Vitebsker's journey to Palestine was the same as the purpose of Abraham, namely, to tread out the way for Israel."

O. Y., p. 54.

4. Palestinian Fruit

The Kobriner visited his teacher, the Lekhivitzer, on the day of the New Moon of Elul. The Lekhivitzer handed him a piece of fruit from Palestine, and said to him, paraphrasing Judges 6:14: "Go thee with this symbol of the rejuvenation of the Land of Israel, and with the strength derived from it, labor for the salvation of Israel." [1]

O. Y., p. 164.

[1] The verse reads: "Go in this thy might and save Israel."

5. The Dignity of Palestine

A discussion was once held at the home of the Mezeritzer regarding the inability of the Besht to visit Palestine. The Maggid said:

"I interpret it in this fashion: some souls need Palestine for their greatness; but others must stay in Exile in order to develop their souls to a high degree of excellence."

At a later time a Rebbe was asked by a Hasid if he should settle in Palestine. The Rabbi advised him against it, saying:

"Since the greatness of Palestine was weakened, it requires a holy person like Rabbi Mendel Vitebsker to revive it. Others are likely to lower the dignity of Palestine by improper living."

M. R. T., p. 71.

6. The Irreligious and Palestine

The Berditschever learned of certain irreligious Jews who had become interested in the restoration of Palestine to Israel. He narrated the following parable:

"A certain wealthy man sought a bridegroom for his daughter. A friend said to him: 'If you follow my advice, marry your daughter to a poor youth who will appreciate the rich dowry you give and who will hold your daughter dear. A rich youth would care little for the dowry and might abuse your daughter. The father followed his friend's counsel and married his daughter to a poor youth. Soon after the daughter complained to her father that her husband did not show her sufficient respect. The father compelled his son-in-law to take his departure, but was later persuaded to receive him back. A second time the daughter complained and the son-in-law was commanded to leave. Later the son-in-law came to demand the money he had received as his dowry. His father-in-law replied: 'I gave you the fortune in order that you might be able to keep my daughter in comfort. But if you do not appreciate my daughter, the fortune does not belong to you.'"

The Berditschever explained the parable as follows: "The Lord desired to give his daughter, the Torah, to a nation that would respect her. Moses said: 'I counsel you to give her to a poor landless nation which will show her due appreciation. Other nations have sufficient land, and the small strip of territory, Palestine, which you will give them as a dowry, will not interest them.' God acted upon the advice of Moses. When Israel showed disrespect for the Torah, He exiled them again and again. Now some Jews have appeared to demand Palestine without the Torah. And the Father in Heaven answers: 'I gave Palestine to you to enable you to respect and prize the Torah. But if you do not care for the Torah, you have no claim to Palestine.'"

N. B. L., p. 23.

7. *The Bratzlaver on "Palestine"*

A.

"1. Prayers are more acceptable when offered in Palestine.
2. All holiness comes by way of Palestine. Only there is it possible to mount the ladder of holiness higher and higher.
3. Through the merit of studying Torah a man attains the opportunity to visit Palestine.
4. No one can go to Palestine except through sufferings. They chiefly arise through the discouragement of unfavorable tidings regarding the Land. The study of the Torah, however, completely removes all obstacles.
5. He who conquers all hindrances and remains in Palestine is a true hero.
6. Those who donate to Palestine are embraced in its very atmosphere.
7. By earnest prayer one gains the ability to go to Palestine.
8. It is in Palestine that we will see the downfall of the wicked.
9. In Palestine the good shall see befall the wicked what the wicked desire should befall the good.
10. One who goes to Palestine to attain holiness will achieve his aspiration, but one who goes there for other ends can gain no benefit.
11. The holiness of Palestine aids in the attainment of faith and patience; it strengthens a resolution to be done with anger, melancholy and heaviness of heart.
12. A man should pray that he may always yearn for Palestine so that he may thereby merit the attainment of his desire to go there.
13. In Palestine one can convince himself that God provides for every one.
14. Palestine is the nerve center of Israel. Each one has a share in it as long as he honors the Lord. If he desecrates God's name he loses his association with Palestine, and becomes a source of quarrels.
15. The brain-nerves of Palestine work for calmness and peace. Through gifts to Palestine these qualities are absorbed by brain-nerves elsewhere. But when the donors are careless of the honor of God, and permit blemishes to appear, they taint the brain-nerves of Palestine and cause quarrels there also. This is the cause of the present-day controversies in Palestine and in Exile."

L. E. H., pp. 9-11.

B.

"1. The settlement of Palestine best demonstrates God's loving care of the world.
2. The desire to go to Palestine draws affluence in its train.
3. He who gives sustenance to the multitude, draws blessings from Zion to other countries."

Sef. Ham., p. 25.

8. Outside of Palestine

Said the "Yud": "Rabbi David of Lelov said: Outside of Palestine a man may attain success, but not blessing, for 'the Lord bless thee from Zion.'[1] Success means mundane prosperity, and blessing, prosperity from on High. Rabbi Moses of Lelov added: He who surrounds himself with holiness may obtain a blessing even outside of Palestine, since holiness sanctifies the very ground beneath his feet, making it as if it were Palestine itself."

Nif. Yeh., p. 41.

[1] Psalm 134:3.

9. Land and People

Said Rabbi Bunam: "It is written (Nehemiah 9:8): 'And madest a covenant with him to give the land of the Canaanite . . . even to give it unto his seed.' The phrase: 'to give' is repeated, for it means that God vouchsafed a gift to Palestine by giving it a holy people to dwell in it."

R. T., p. 116.

10. Building Jerusalem

Said the Ropshitzer: "By our service to God we build Jerusalem daily. One of us adds a row, another only a brick. When Jerusalem is completed, the Redemption will come."

Ohel N., p. 60.

11. Admitting the Blessing

Rabbi Abraham David Butzatzer said: "Since the Holy Land was granted to Israel, every Israelite by virtue of his share in it may demolish the boundaries of any land where he resides and give entrance into it for the blessings from Zion."

D. Z., p. 4.

12. From Holy to Profane

A Palestinian merchant brought to the Medzibozer a few bottles of wine made from the grapes grown in a Jewish vineyard in Palestine. The Medzibozer said to his son: "What shall we drink when we have finished these few bottles?"

"The wine we ordinarily drink," answered his son.

"Then remove the gift from our table," commanded the Medzibozer. "After drinking holy wine, it would be profane to return to ordinary wine."

E. Tz., p. 129.

13. Holy and Unholy

Said the Savraner: "He who serves the Lord earnestly and thoroughly despises worldly affairs should go to the Holy Land if he is able. The holiness there will enable him to attain a higher position of holiness.

"But he who is as yet unseparated from worldliness and has not fastened his entire mind upon service to the Lord, will do better to

remain outside of Palestine. God has permitted the unholy forces
to be equal with the holy forces. Hence in the Holy Land where
holiness is more powerful, the Evil Impulse is also stronger and
harder to resist."

E. A., p. 33.

14. The Good Aspects

Said the Koretzer: "We read that Moses prayed: 'Let me go
over, I pray Thee, and see the good land' (Deut. 3:25). Moses
meant by these words: I shall not imitate the Spies who saw the
unpleasant aspects of Palestine; nay, I wish to see the good aspects
of the land."

F. U. A. O., ii, 81.

15. Hasidim on Palestine

The Great Maggid said: "Zion is absolute in the world; it is the
life of all countries; therefore all countries have a part in Palestine."

Rabbi Israel Polizker said: "At last the day has come for which
we have waited with such impatience; how happy we are here in our
wonderful land, in this country which is the Holy of Holies."

Said a Zaddik: "Once the land was exalted, and it exalted the
man who came there. Now it has sunk low, and man must exalt it
again; this can be achieved only by an exalted person, after the
pattern of Rabbi Menachem Mendel."

Once when Rabbi Menachem sojourned in Palestine, a foolish
fellow, unnoticed, climbed the Mount of Olives, and blew a blast on
a Shofar. Among the terror-stricken populace, the word spread like
wildfire that it was the trumpet-blast announcing the Redemption.
When the report came to the ears of Rabbi Menachem, he opened
the window, looked out upon the world, and said: "I see no renewal
there." (B., p. 423.)

Rabbi Menachem was accustomed to say: "It is true that the air
of the Land of Israel makes one wise.[1] As long as I lived outside
its boundaries, my whole being yearned for the power to recite a
prayer once in the right fashion. Since, however, I am in the Land
of Israel, my sole wish is that I may once say 'Amen' in the way it
should be uttered before the Creator." [2]

Rabbi Menachem also remarked: "I have attained to this wisdom
in the land of Israel: if I see a bundle of straw lying in the street,
the fact that it lies according to its length and not its breadth, is to
me a sign of the Divine Presence." (B., p. 423.)

Rabbi Schneur Zalman of Ladi said: "The love for Zion must be
as a fire burning in the heart of the Jew. He who wishes to be a
true Jew must go to Palestine; and if there be obstacles in the way,
he must overcome them all and go there." [3]

It is told that the Sheptev Rabbi came to visit his friend, Rabbi

[1] Baba Bathra 158.
[2] B., p. 423. Compare a similar statement by Rabbi Menachem Mendel of
Premislan, in A. Z. Rabinowitz, *Toledoth ha-Yehudim be-Eretz Yisrael,* p. 124.
[3] Rabinowitz, *op. cit.,* p. 126.

Wolf Zbaraz in Tiberias. On entering the courtyard he noticed that the Rabbi's wife was washing linens. The visitor expressed his sorrow that so distinguished a lady must wash clothes. "Rabbi," exclaimed the woman. "These linens are not mine; I am washing them for others, and I am being paid for the task. But I feel no regret. No sacrifice is too great for the privilege of living in Eretz Yisrael." [4]

The Bratzlaver said: "While I am breathing and alive, I must go to Palestine. The absolute spirit and wisdom are found only in Palestine. There a man can attain to his highest estate, to be like Him, Praised be His Name." "All that has been before me was as the life within the fruit before it is ripe." "The only place for me is Palestine." "The chief of everything is Palestine." When his Disciples asked if he was thinking of a spiritual Palestine, he answered: "No, I mean the real Palestine, with its houses and its streets, as we see it with the human eye." "The life I possess is due only to my having been in Palestine." [5]

[4] Rabinowitz, p. 126
[5] Horodetzky, pp. 85-7; Buber, Cohen, Levin, pp. 184-5.

16. The Unorthodox and Palestine's Rebuilding

The Bendiner Rabbi wrote: "I fail to understand those orthodox Jews who preach against Zionism because its leaders are not from the camp of the ultra-orthodox, and who believe it to be an act of impiety to associate with them. I ask: if the love of the Holy Land and the good deed, namely giving a dependable livelihood to many Jews, may be invalidated because of the partnership of less religious Jews, why should not the opposition to Zionism likewise be invalidated, inasmuch as Reformers and assimilationists are partners and co-workers in agreement with you. Hatred of Zion and abandonment of poor Jews—both impious matters—become virtues even when those who run away from Judaism share in them. On the other hand, love of Zion and helpfulness to the poor—both pious matters—become defects, because the less religious are aiding those who declare: 'We wish to be Jews.'" [1]

The Zakrotziner Rabbi wrote: "Many ultra-orthodox parents are so bitter in their hostility to Zionism that they force their sons, who are Zionists, to overthrow paternal authority, and thereby to lose the paternal guidance so essential to them. Yet we read in the Torah (Gen. 18:19) that God loved Abraham because he taught his son to walk in the ways of the Lord. Do these anti-Zionists who dispense with the love of God realize what they are doing?" [2]

Rabbi Mordecai Ashkenazi said: "We find that Ezra did not discriminate against any Jew who wished to join him in migrating to Eretz Yisrael. Only afterwards did he preach against the sinners." [3] "We find in the Talmud that a Tanna advised Herod to expiate his

[1] Mordecai Ashkenazi, Geulath ha-Aretz, Warsaw, 1904, p. 5.
[2] Ashkenazi, p. 15.
[3] Ibid., Book i, p. 7.

crime of murdering learned Rabbis by restoring the Temple.[4] Why, then, should modern orthodox Jews refuse to permit sinners to atone by restoring the Holy Land?" [5]

[4] Baba Bathra 4a.
[5] Ibid., p. 9.

17. The Task of Restoration

The Shepser Rabbi wrote: "It is the duty of every Jew either to migrate to Eretz Yisrael, or to help support the colonists. The Holiness of the Land is broadened as the number af Jews increases. In the Talmud (Kethubhoth 75), we are taught that one who demonstrates his yearning for Eretz Yisrael by aiding its Jews contributes to the broadening of its holiness, just as if he himself went to reside there. We are also taught that the Lord says: 'I shall not enter the upper Jerusalem—of the truly pious—until they shall come to the lower Jerusalem [1]—they, meaning the common people who are enjoined to perform daily labor.' " [2]

When the Kalisher Rabbi, Hayyim Eleazar Waks, arrived in Jerusalem, he preached to the Jews residing there, urging them to engage in agriculture rather than to rely upon the dole (Halukah). They answered that the uncertain benefits from tillage of the fields did not appeal to them; they preferred the steady dole. The Rabbi thereupon inquired: "And what will you do, if for some unexpected reason, the dole is not forthcoming?"

"Oh, we do not concern ourselves about the morrow," was their reply.

"Then," exclaimed the Rabbi, "you are like the wicked person who says: 'What care I for the morrow or the World-to-Come; I shall live only for to-day.' " [3]

Rabbi Mordecai Ashkenazi declares that the Talmud teaches in at least two passages [4] that there is no more genuine sign that Redemption is near than the sight of groves in Eretz Yisrael, loaded with fruit; as it is said (Ezekiel 36:8): "But ye, O mountains of Israel, ye shall shoot forth your branches, and yield your fruit to My people, Israel; for they are at hand to come." [5]

18. No Permanent Home

Rabbi Eliakim Getzel, the son of Rabbi Jacob Joseph of Ostroah (Yibi) lived in a small room for which he paid hire. The townspeople of Ostroah wished to build a home for him, but he refused, saying: "I do not wish to possess a permanent home outside of the Land of Israel."

D. D., p. 195.

[1] Taanith 5.
[2] Ashkenazi, p. 4.
[3] Ibid., p. 26.
[4] Sanhedrin 98; Kethubhoth 112b by implication.
[5] Ibid, Book i, p. 2. For a comment on the Berditschever's attitude towards the rebuilding of Palestine and the place of the Torah, see 116:6. For further material regarding the Hasidim and Palestine, see article by Louis I. Newman in the Avukah Annual, 1932, pp. 316-326.

117. PARENTS AND CHILDREN

1. The Ship of Life

The Radomsker told the following parable: "A passenger on a ship impatiently awaited the day when it would reach port. When the ship was nearing the harbor, a storm drove it back to sea, much to the chagrin of the traveler.[1]

"Likewise a man is afflicted with anxiety for his sons and daughters until he succeeds in rearing them to maturity. Then he hopes to be freed from worry regarding their lot. But his oldest son comes with his troubles, seeking paternal counsel and the father's retirement is delayed. The daughter also comes with her problems, and once more his hope of a quiet life is postponed.

"Few of us are ever entirely freed from worry and the necessity of continuous labor in this world."

O. S., p. 47.

[1] See the Talmudic parable, quoted in Hertz, *A Book of Jewish Thoughts,* p. 310, wherein the simile of a ship is used.

2. The Three Partners

Commenting on Leviticus 19:3: "Ye shall fear, every man, his mother and his father; I am the Lord your God," Rabbi Schmelke said: "The Talmud teaches that there are three partners in a man, God, his father and his mother.[1] And the Lord tells us: 'You could truly attain holiness if my share in you predominated, for I am Holy.' But it is essential that you retain also the share you have inherited from your father and your mother. Refuse, however, to succumb to bodily desires, but maintain an equilibrium between matter and spirit."

S. ha-Tov, p. 18.

[1] Kiddushin, 30.

3. Obeying His Mother

A disciple of the "Yud" perceived that his Rabbi had become engrossed in a problem of interpretation of the Torah. The youth knew from experience that such concentration was of long duration, and he returned home for his meal. When he had finished, his mother asked him to perform an errand for her, but the boy refused to stop on the plea of not caring to miss the Rabbi's lesson.

When he had departed, however, the boy bethought himself: "Is not the object of learning the performance of good deeds? Obedience to my mother is more important than haste for my lesson."

He returned and performed the errand for his mother. Then he hurried to his Rabbi. When the latter saw him, he exclaimed: "You must have done a good deed, for the moment you entered, a complicated matter became clear to me."

N. H., p. 45.

4. *Even in Old Shoes*

A bride gave a dance in Tzanz. The Rabbi's daughter asked him for money with which to purchase new shoes, but the Rabbi refused to give it. He noticed, however, that her companion, a daughter of a Hebrew teacher, wore old shoes, and he asked her: "Are you invited to the dance?" "Yes, Rabbi," she answered.

"Here, then, take this money and buy yourself stylish shoes," and the Rabbi urged her to accept his gift.

One of those present inquired from the Rabbi why he treated a stranger better than his own daughter. He answered:

"I know that my daughter's friend comes from excellent parents, yet should she wear old shoes to the dance, she will be scorned. But my daughter will be treated with deference even in old shoes."

M. D., p. 283.

5. *Ungrateful Children*

A rich fur merchant married his son and daughter into wealthy families, and rejoiced in his successful life. But the wheel of fortune turned; his wife died, and his business collapsed. Neither his son nor his daughter wished to give him assistance. He complained of this to the Riziner Rabbi, who enjoined his Hasidim by letter to aid him. With the money thus assembled, the father reëstablished himself in business and prospered. Soon after he married a widow and lived in great happiness.

Hearing of his prosperity both the son and daughter began to urge him to live with them and to give their stepmother a divorce. On the way to the Leipziger Fair, he stopped over to visit the Riziner and told him of his children's importunities. The Rabbi said: "On your way back, stop again here, and I will advise you what to do."

When he returned the Rabbi said: "Write a letter to your wife; another to your son; and a third to your daughter. Each letter should read as follows: 'A great misfortune has befallen me. My fur became moth-eaten and worthless. I sold some of my clothes in order to enable me to leave Leipzig, and I had just enough money to reach the home of the Riziner Rabbi. I beg of you to send me sufficient money for my fare home.' Then," continued the Rabbi, "show me the answers you receive."

The merchant followed the Riziner's advice. Both the son and daughter gave excuses for failing to forward him any money and advised him to remain with the Rabbi. His wife, however, sent him sufficient money, and comforted him with her promise to work faithfully with him to earn a livelihood anew. When he returned home, only his wife welcomed him. Then he told her that he was richer than ever, and willed to her his entire property. When his children protested, he showed them the three replies to his letters, and ordered them out of his home.

M. G., pp. 7-9.

6. *Never Go Back*

It is told of Rabbi Zalman of Ladi that immediately after his marriage he received free board from his parents-in-law, according to custom. But his solitary meditations and strange ecstatic prayers were an offense to them, and they declared him to be a fool, his great learning notwithstanding. They urged their daughter to demand a divorce from him, but in vain. Therefore they made his life miserable, stinting his maintenance. They refused him candles, and he was forced to study by moonlight. In winter nights they let him freeze. And so they kept on tormenting him until he reached his twentieth year. Then he took to the road and journeyed to the great Maggid of Mezeritz.

When, in later years, Rabbi Zalman's fame began to spread, his mother-in-law repented of her ill-usage, and she begged him, with tears in her eyes, to return to her home, and to abide there. She promised, with many protestations, that she would serve him hand and foot there, and be hospitable to his Hasidim. Rabbi Zalman would not consent, and when she did not cease her entreaties, he said:

"Look you, who can be better off than the child in the mother's womb? It careth not for food or drink and knows the whole Torah. But when the babe is born, an angel touches its lips, and it forgets its learning. Yet no one, if such a thing could be, would return to the mother's womb. Why not? Because babes, once born, soon outgrow the measure of their erstwhile habitation." [1]

[1] "From a Hasidic Treasure Trove," *Jewish Tribune*, Dec. 19, '30; "Der Grosse Maggid," by Martin Buber, translated by James Fuchs.

7. *The Premier's Demotion*

The Kotzker read from the Dubner Maggid's book the following story:

"A courtier, the nephew of the Premier, was guilty of misbehavior on several occasions. The Premier interceded for him with the king and won the royal forgiveness. Once, however, the courtier's misconduct was so heinous that his uncle was ashamed to approach his master on behalf of the culprit. He loved his nephew, nevertheless, and desiring to save him, he went to the king and said: 'The offender's reason for misbehaving was his belief that I would intercede for him. The best remedy, therefore, would be for you to demote me. The knowledge that I shall no longer be able to secure his immunity from punishment will cure him of his evil behavior.' Moses interceded many times for Israel, but when they worshiped the Golden Calf, he begged the Lord: 'Blot me out, I pray Thee.'" [1]

S. S. K., ii, 27.

[1] Ex. 32: 32.

118. THE PASSOVER

1. Reasons for Its Names

Rabbi Zevi Meir of Radomsk said: "The Lord calls the Spring Festival: 'The Feast of the Unleavened Bread,' but we usually call it 'The Feast of Passover.' The reason is as follows: We read (Deut. 26:17): 'Thou hast acknowledged the Lord this day to be thy God, and the Lord hath acknowledged thee this day to be His own treasure.' Hence the Lord names it 'The Feast of the Unleavened Bread' to commemorate our promptness in obeying his command to leave the Land of Egypt, without even storing up food. And we name it 'The Feast of Passover' to remind us that God passed over our houses, when he smote the Egyptian first-born (Exodus 12:27)."

O. S., p. 10 in Introduction.

2. Time for Redemption

Rabbi Bunam commented upon Exodus 6:6: "I am the Lord, and I will bring you out from under the burdens of the Egyptians."

"A burden," he said, "is usually carried with ease after one has become accustomed to it. When the Lord observed that the Israelites were growing accustomed to their tasks and labored at them without complaint, then He deemed it high time they were liberated."

S. S. K., iii, 130.

3. The Miracle of the Exodus

Thus taught Rabbi Elimelech of Lizensk: "At the pronouncement of laws, Holy Scripture always makes mention of the Exodus out of Egypt, and never of the Creation of the World. How is this? Was not the Creation out of a void a greater miracle than the Exodus? Understand, then, that the Creation, properly speaking, was not a miracle. All nature is in God, and subject to Him, and whatever sprang into being at His behest, did so in a natural way. But the Exodus was a wonder, for to deal with the Egyptians according to their merits, God had to divest Himself, for the time being, of His Goodness, and let evil prevail."

Bl., Pr., p. 23.

4. Miracles Beyond Imitation

Said the Belzer Rabbi: "We find that Pharaoh's magicians were able to perform by their secret arts the miracles of turning water into blood and of bringing up frogs. The other miracles they were unable to duplicate. The question arises: Why did the Lord cause Moses to perform miracles that could be duplicated by magic? Could He not have enjoined that all the ten plagues be beyond imitation?

"The answer is as follows: the Lord knew that in later times unbelievers might arise and say: 'The Egyptian soothsayers were possessed of little sagacity, and hence Moses was able to deceive them. We, however, would not have been victims of his chicanery.' Then we believers might retort: 'If you are wiser than the Egyptian sages, accomplish at least as much as they. Turn water into blood and bring up frogs. If you cannot do this, you must admit their superiority, and at the same time recognize that they acknowledged the divine power resident in the acts of Moses.' "

D. S., p. 78.

5. Dividing the Waters

The Gerer Rabbi said: "We find that the division of the waters of the Red Sea accomplished the beneficent result of instilling into the Israelites the virtues of the fear of the Lord and of true belief in Him. As it is said: 'And the people feared the Lord, and they believed in the Lord' (Exodus 14:31). By means of these virtues, they were able to overcome seemingly insurmountable obstacles. It were well for us to bear this lesson constantly in mind, namely that nothing can withstand the union of genuine fear of the Lord, and sincere belief in Him."

S. S. K., iii, 66.

6. The Body Overpowers the Soul

Said Rabbi Schmelke: "We read in the 'Song of Songs' (1:9): 'I have compared thee, O my love, to a steed in Pharaoh's chariots.' The Talmud[1] explains that when the chariots of the Egyptians entered the Red Sea, the force of the current became so powerful that the horses were pulled along by the chariots. Likewise, the soul within us has its own life, and the body can be compared to inert matter. Yet we permit our bodies to draw our souls into the torrent of pleasures, even as the living horses were dragged along by the chariots."

S. ha-Tov, p. 7.

[1] Mekhilta to Exodus 14:25.

7. Angelic Music

Said Rabbi Schmelke: "We read in the Talmud[1] that when the Egyptians were drowning in the Red Sea, the Angels wished to sing for joy, but the Lord silenced them, saying: 'The works of my hands are perishing. How can you wish to sing?' This may signify that the Angels desired to sing so loudly that the souls of the Egyptians would take their departure through the sweetness of their celestial melodies. And the Lord said: 'They have caused my children to perish; should they not perish of themselves, rather than die from your singing?' "[2]

S. ha-Tov, p. 7.

[1] Megillah 10.
[2] This is a variation of the Talmudic story, which I have placed in verse: *Joyful Jeremiads*, p. 69.

8. *Higher Than Justice*

Said the Gerer Rabbi: "We read in Exodus 19:4: 'Ye have seen what I did unto the Egyptians, and how I bore you on eagles' wings.' Rashi remarks: 'The eagle carries his offspring above his wings, as if to say: "If an arrow be shot in my direction, let it enter into me, and not into my son." ' This, however, does not explain the use of the simile or the connection between an eagle and the Lord. It may be explained thus: The Attribute of Justice, the Midrashic allegory [1] runs, complained to the Heavenly Tribunal that the Sons of Israel did not merit deliverance at the expense of the Egyptians, both being as yet pagans.

"The Lord responded: 'I have lifted Israel above the wings of strict justice. If you question my act, direct your arrows at Me, not at my son.' "

S. S. K., ii, 38.

[1] Shemoth Rabba 21:7.

9. *Manna Still Comes Down*

Rabbi Bunam said: "Manna still comes down daily in quantities sufficient for the minimum needs of each person. In the desert it came to a person without toil; to-day, however, it is distributed to each one of us through our physical or mental labor."

S. S. K., ii, 83.

10. *"The Hametz" of Idolatry*

Said the Koretzer: "Why does Scripture say (II Kings 23:22) that no Passover has ever been performed as in the days of King Josiah? Because Josiah first burned all the altars and the pagan temples. In other words, he cleaned out the 'Hametz' [1] properly."

Nof. Tz., p. 23.

[1] Leavened bread; metaphor for evil.

119. PASSOVER INCIDENTS

1. *Charity Without Ostentation*

The Berditschever learned that a poor Jew who earned a few cents daily by digging clay and carrying it by horse and wagon to builders, had lost his horse, and was compelled to transport the clay in a box upon his shoulders. The claydigger refused to accept charity though his earnings became insufficient for even dry bread. The Rabbi bethought himself how to give him aid before Passover so that he might not lack the holiday necessaries. Finally he conceived a plan. He disguised himself as a peasant, placed on his shoulders a bundle of fagots, dropped it in the poor man's hovel, and then ran quickly away. The poor man hastened to recall his benefactor, but without avail. When he returned to his home, he placed the wood in a corner, and as he did so, noticed a cloth hidden in it. When he untied the knotted cloth, he discovered it contained a sizable amount of money. The claydigger went to the Rabbi and asked his counsel. The Rabbi enjoined him to have no hesitancy in using the money since it must have been sent by the Lord in reward for his trust and faith. The man bought a kiln, began to bake bricks for houses, and henceforth greatly prospered.[1]

N. K. L., p. 25 (M 12).

[1] See Peretz' story "If Not Higher" and v. s.

2. A Prayer from the Haggadah

The Radomsker was visited by a Hasid, who complained that he had suffered heavy losses in his business, and was unable to meet his debts. Moreover, he could not secure any more goods on credit. The Rabbi replied: "In a case of this kind, I will pray to the Lord on your behalf, in the words of the Haggadah of Passover, as I paraphrase them: 'To the one who has no one from whom to borrow, do Thou, O Lord, open up a credit account.' A few days later, the merchant received a favorable business opportunity, and henceforth he prospered.[1]

K. E., pp. 47-8.

[1] In the Haggadah the verse reads: "But for him who knows not what to ask, thou shalt open up." "Ask" and "borrow" is the same word in Hebrew.

3. Smuggling Hametz

Before Passover, the Berditschever summoned together the merchants and asked them whether much smuggling was being practiced. They replied that there was considerable. The Rabbi then exclaimed: "O Lord, behold what a good nation is Israel. The king has many officers, and they cannot halt smuggling. Thou hast none, and yet Thou wouldst find no Hametz smuggled into any Jewish home on Passover."

O. I. H., p. 37.

4. Partnership with a Horse

Rabbi Meir Margulis walked along a muddy street on the Eve of Passover towards the river, carrying a large pitcher. The Maggid, Rabbi Jacob Joseph of Ostroah, was likewise on his way towards the river, but he rode in a wagon. He noticed Rabbi Meir and exclaimed: "Why do you walk in the mire, O Chief Rabbi?"

The latter replied: "The Mitzwah of drawing water for the baking of the Matzoth for Seder comes only once a year. I do not care to share it with a horse."

The Maggid descended from his wagon, and walked beside the Rabbi to the river.

Nif. Yeh., p. 89.

120. PEACE

1. *Peace and Truth*

Rabbi Bunam related the following tale from the Midrash:[1] "When the Lord planned to create man, Truth objected because man is deceitful, and Peace objected because man is quarrelsome. The Lord, thereupon, ordered Truth to depart.

"The question arises: 'why was Peace allowed to remain?' The answer is that after Truth has departed and Falsehood has taken its place, there is automatically Peace, inasmuch as false foes hide their true sentiments and give the appearance of friendship for each other."

S. S. K., ii, 86.

[1] Bereshith Rabba 8:5.

2. *Peacemaking*

Said the Pulnoer: "We are taught[1] it is a great 'Mitzwah' to achieve peace between two men who quarrel. I will tell of an even greater 'Mitzwah,' namely to make peace between your body and your spirit, so that materialism does not conquer the spirit."

Kahana, p. 126.

[1] Peah, 1; Mishnah, 1.

3. *The Value of Coöperation*

Said the Karliner: "The entire progress of mankind depends upon loyal coöperation. If quarrels are absent from a company of men, no evil can overtake them."

D. E. M. R., p. 14.

4. *The Full Truth*

A Hasid asked the Bershider: "You teach that a man should always tell the truth. How can one do this if he wishes to make peace?"

The Rabbi replied: "To make peace, I demand the full truth, and with the full truth, I make peace."

M. P., p. 49.

5. *The Bratzlaver on "Peace"*

"1. The Sabbath candles increase peace.

2. The pursuance of peace brings honors in this world, and a goodly share in the next.

3. That which is done for the sake of peace is immune from the prohibition to avoid untruth. (Yebamoth 65.)

4. When people are forced to give to charity, it increases peace in the community.

5. The pursuance of peace leads to trustfulness.

6. Peace comes through truth.

7. The building of Jerusalem depends upon peace.
8. Peace brings good tidings.
9. When reproof is heeded, there is peace.
10. Through education peace is increased.
11. Prayers are not heard where there is no peace.
12. Peace is a sign of the good life.
13. The pursuance of peace saves from death and exile.
14. Blessings come through peace.
15. Where there is peace there is no terror.
16. Even the wicked who live in peace enjoy prosperity.
17. Peace is a sign of prosperity."

Sef. Ham., pp. 152-3.

121. PENALTIES AND PUNISHMENTS

1. *The King's Treasure*

Three officials were assigned to guard the king's treasures. They proved to be corrupt, and, dividing the valuables, ran away. One thought better of it, and returned of his own accord. The second was persuaded by a friend to return. The third witnessed the execution of an embezzler and returned out of fear. The first was restored to the king's confidence; the second received a less responsible post, the third was appointed executioner of the embezzlers.

"There are three kinds of people in this world who act like these three officials with respect to the fulfillment of God's injunctions," explained the Pulnoer.

Kahana, p. 89.

2. *Rigor Versus Kindness*

Rabbi Nachman Horodenker said: "There are two ways of curing offenders. Some claim a cure by inflicting privations, but these usually result in the transgressor becoming embittered against society, and cruel henceforth. Others effect a cure through persuasions which oftentimes transform the sinner into a man of kindness and helpfulness."

Dubnow, H. of H., p. 103.

3. *Punishment to Fit the Crime*

Said the Belzer: "The Lord fits the punishment to the crime. Korach opened his mouth to utter rebellion and dissension; therefore 'the earth opened her mouth and swallowed him' (Num. 16: 32)."

D. S., p. 83.

4. *Only in Ourselves*

In the town of Bausk an epidemic occurred. Some Jews wished to organize a committee to investigate whose grave sins had brought so great a calamity upon the city.

The Rabbi, however, dissented. He said: "It is true that penalty implies sins, but we must not search for the sins in others. We must seek them only in ourselves."

F. U. A. O., ii, 126.

5. The Long Piyyutim

The Ropshitzer was told that one of his Hasidim ate Matzah that had been dipped in soup on Passover. He ordered a Holiday Prayer Book to be brought to him, and laughingly said: "If you eat like a Mithnaged, then say the long Piyyutim [1] that the Mithnagedim say." [2]

Ohel N., p. 123.

[1] Liturgical Poems, chiefly from Medieval Jewish Literature.

[2] The Hasidim object to dipped Matzah on Passover, inasmuch as a tiny piece may remain raw, and therefore be liable to leaven if moistened.

6. In Genuine Need

The Ropshitzer needed money for his son's marriage, and asked the residents of Ropshitz to aid him. The leader of the community asked the Rabbi why in this instance he wished the residents of Ropshitz to assist him, whereas on other occasions he was accustomed to visit his rich Disciples in other towns, and to receive their abundant donations. The Rabbi replied: "On other occasions, I did not need the money badly; hence the people gave me freely. But this time I am in genuine need, and I fear that I shall receive only a little from free-will offerings.

"I explain thus the Mishnah (Peah 1): 'He who needs no charity and asks for it, will in the end be compelled to ask people for charity.' What punishment is there in this statement for a man who is accustomed to live on charity? The answer is: 'One who does not need aid and asks for it, receives alms in abundance. And his punishment in the end will be that when he really requires aid, he will encounter only refusals.'"

P. v. K., p. 42b.

7. The Merchants' Atonement

A clerk in the employ of two wealthy merchants accumulated his modest savings and purchased a small house. His employers wished to purchase this house in order to demolish it and add the grounds to their garden. The employee declined to sell it, however, and was dismissed. He opened a small shop with the remainder of his savings, but was unsuccessful and lost everything. He petitioned his erstwhile employers to reinstate him, and they did so on condition that he sell them his home for a third of its value. The clerk succeeded in inserting within the bill of sale a hint that it was not a voluntary sale on his part. Deprived of his home and compelled to work at a smaller salary, the clerk fell sick and died before the new owners took over his house.

The clerk's heirs did not believe he had sold his home voluntarily for a third of its value, and they brought a complaint before Rabbi Michael, the Zlotzover Maggid. The merchants brought with them the bill of sale. On examining it, the Maggid noticed the clerk's hint, and rendered a decision that the heirs should repay the purchase money and retain the house. This angered the merchants greatly, and they resolved on revenge.

They informed the Duke of the country that the reason for his failure to obtain satisfactory rents for his inns or a better price for his lumber and produce was due to the Maggid's prohibition of competition among the Jews, on the ground that it was a severe sin to take away another's livelihood by outbidding him. The Duke took counsel with other noblemen, and it was decided within a short time to punish the Maggid.

Suddenly the Duke's daughter was stricken with paralysis, and no physician was able to aid her. The Duke bethought himself of his designs against the Holy Man. He sought him out and begged him to pray for his daughter's recovery. The Maggid's prayer proved successful, and the Duke solemnly promised never to injure a Jew or to demand exorbitant rents. The two informers were ostracised and compelled to move away. They lost their wealth and soon wandered from town to town, begging food. When they came to the Lizensker Rabbi, he persuaded them to confess their sin in public. Having atoned for it, they were given shelter for the rest of their days in the Rabbi's house.

Hith. Z., pp. 41-5.

122. PERFECTION

1. *Attaining Perfection*

Said the Lizensker: "We read (Gen. 6:10): 'And Noah begat three sons: Shem, Ham and Japheth.' We may give to this verse an allegorical interpretation: Noah means the pleasing one, hence the good man; he begat three sons: three degrees of perfection. Shem is 'the name': the first degree is to sanctify the Holy Name within ourself through repentance of those sins which make a flaw in our holiness.

"Ham means 'warmth': the second step is to be warm in our worship by battling against the return of our former faults.

"Japheth means 'beautifying' or 'perfecting'; this is the third step: to offer to the Lord perfect devotion, a devotion that burns within us.

"We can find this allegory also in the designation of the Angels in Ezekiel, chapter one. The lowest degree is the Ophanim, the Wheels. One whose devotion is through fear of God's punishment cannot be sure of himself. Like a wheel he may roll down, and succumb to temptation.

"Those who are devoted because they begin to love God are like the Hayyoth, moving back and forth (verse 14) but not up and down. They are sometimes nearer, sometimes further away from perfection. But the highest degree is the position of the Seraphim, who constantly flame with devotion. The pure love of God within them cannot be extinguished."

Noam E., p. 6.

2. Only God Is Perfect

Said the Lizensker: "Only God is perfect. Man's actions must be basically defective in part. If one believes his good deed or holy study to be thoroughly pure and perfect, this is a sure sign that they are thoroughly bad."

O. E., p. 130.

3. Wicked for a Moment

Said the Koretzer: "He needs no penance who acts upon the Talmudical axiom: 'I would rather be called a fool all my days than be wicked for a moment before my Maker.' " [1]

Nof. Tz., p. 28.

[1] Mishnah, Edioth, v, 6.

123. PHILOSOPHY AND PHILOSOPHERS

1. The "Guide to the Perplexed"

The Sassover observed his Disciple, the "Yud," reading Maimonides' "Guide to the Perplexed." He said to him:

"My advice is that you read it in the same order the author had in mind when he wrote it. Maimonides was convinced of his conclusions and questioned the axioms in order to clarify them. But one who reads the questions first may be led to doubt the validity of Jewish doctrines, if only for the length of time it requires to reach the answers."

M. Hat., pp. 59-60.

2. Aristotle and Ezekiel

The Riziner said: "Maimonides holds in great admiration both the Prophet Ezekiel and the Philosopher, Aristotle. The difference between the two can be explained by a parable:

" 'Two men were invited to make their obeisance before the king. The wiser went straight to the royal throne room. The less sagacious halted to marvel at the splendors of the royal palace, and forgot his obligation to the king.' [1]

"Maimonides believes that Aristotle was better acquainted with less essential matters, but Ezekiel stood higher in his knowledge of holy things. We must, therefore, not be surprised when we perceive that at times Maimonides allows himself to praise the Philosopher more than the Prophet."

E. O., p. 129.

[1] For the use of a similar parable with reference to "Seeking Communion with God," see 157:8.

3. Spinoza and the Animals

Once it was told to Rabbi Pinchas of Koretz that there had lived a sage by the name of Spinoza who asserted in his works that man has the same nature as animals, and that he stands in no way higher than them.

The Rabbi laughed and said: "One should ask this free-thinker whether the animals can also bring forth from their midst a Spinoza."

Bl., Gem., p. 151.

124. PHILOSOPHY AND SCIENCE

1. Sayings of the Bratzlaver on "Philosophy and Science"

"1. The chief goal of human understanding should be to comprehend the nature of Divinity.

2. General philosophy suggests understanding that has fallen to a lower plane.

3. The Science of Divine Knowledge is the only true science.

4. The more one acquires the secular sciences, the less room there is in his brain for holy studies.

5. Into the brain cells utilized by the secular sciences gather and unite all passions and evil traits.

6. Since understanding is the soul, he who devotes his understanding solely to holy subjects sanctifies his soul.

7. Philosophy may become dangerous when the development of the mind it encourages is not accompanied by a similar degree of self-improvement through the medium of good practice.

8. He whose understanding is greater than his practice of good deeds lapses into grave sins and unbelief.

9. Man should not neglect the intelligence which God has granted him, but he should utilize it to the utmost. Nevertheless there is a limit which the human mind may not transgress without danger to a man's sanity and his faith in God.

10. It is because of God's ineffable greatness that we are unable to comprehend many truths which seem self-contradictory and unjust. The reasons prompting God are inexplicable.[1]

L. E. H., pp. 41-3.

[1] For the benefit of those readers who may wish to compare these aphorisms with the original, the following remarks must be made: (1) Only those thoughts with special merit for a modern reader have been utilized. (2) The constant repetitions of the same idea have been omitted. (3) Kabbalistic references have been ignored. (4) References to sexual offenses, to the Evil Eye, to the Powers of the Satan and his hosts of unholy beings, and similar themes have been omitted. (5) The constant emphasis upon the influence of the Zaddik and his powers of mediation has been minimized and utilized very sparingly. (6) While ideas intertwine, some have been dropped for the sake of clarity. (7) Entire subjects have been left out of the quotations from the Bratzlaver, for the reasons stated, but a large part of the meritorious material has been presented. This applies to the various items quoted in this work from the Bratzlaver.

2. Decay and Rebirth

Said the Koretzer: "When seed is sown, it must decay and its elements decompose until it becomes naught to the eye, before the power of rebirth hidden within it begins to function. At the very moment of complete decomposition, this power comes into immediate action. It demonstrates the formula of the Kabbalah: 'putting off form and putting on form,' teaching that everything in both the material and spiritual worlds is constantly changing form.

"This is the meaning of the allegory that the Messiah was born on the day when the Holy Temple was destroyed.[1] Since the holiness which had existed had fallen into naught, the hidden holiness immediately began to sprout forth. To symbolize this idea, we sit on the ground on the 9th Day of Ab to demonstrate how we have fallen to earth. Then we go to the cemetery where our forefathers lie buried underground. After showing symbolically that we have sunk to the utmost depths, we await the emergence of the force which revives and redeems."

Nof. Tz., p. 14.

[1] Ekhah Rabba 1: 57 (to Lam. 1: 16).

125. PHYSICIANS

1. A Permanent Cure

A Hasid once discussed with the Tzupenester the fact that one who is ignorant is usually more humble than one who is learned. In reply the Rabbi narrated this parable:

"A man was afflicted with a distressing abscess. He went to a physician who gave him a salve which healed the sore. A year later it reappeared and another physician prescribed a stronger salve which likewise did not effect a permanent cure. The sufferer went to a great specialist who gave him an internal medicine. This caused the growth of the sore, and the patient complained to the specialist. The latter assured him that as soon as the diseased matter would come out of his system, he would be able to cure him permanently.

"In the same fashion, the ignorant man may think he is cured of the sin of pride, but numerous experiences prove this to be false. Whereas the learned may be guilty of pride at first, he acquires true and abiding humility when he delves deeper into his studies."

N. I., p. 71.

2. The Generous Physician

Said the Alexanderer Rabbi: "We find in the Midrash the expression that courtesy preceded the Torah.[1] We should love the Lord not because we were so commanded in the Torah, but as a matter of courtesy and appreciation. If a physician not only cured

[1] Wayyikra Rabba 9: 3.

a poor patient, but also donated to him a sum of money, would not the sick man feel everlasting love for the generous friend? The Lord gives us life, and the means of maintaining it, and our love for Him need not be dictated by the Law alone."

S. S. K., i, 25.

3. The Cheap Physician Is Valueless

A Mithnaged came to Rabbi Bunam with a complaint that he attracted young men as students and thereby led them away from their study of the Torah. "People say," remarked the complainant, "that you teach ethical precepts, but they can learn these from ethical writings with less waste of time."

The Rabbi related the following story:

"When I was an apothecary, I was acquainted with two physicians at the hospital. Both settled in the same city, and though their knowledge was equal, their characters were different. One cared little for money, accepted any fee tendered, and earnestly desired to cure the sick. The other demanded his fee beforehand, refused to repeat any instructions, and seemed to care more for the money he received than for his patients. Yet I heard that the first physician became unpopular and was rarely summoned; the second, however, was in constant demand and hence difficult to secure.

"I inquired the reason for such odd behavior on the part of the townsfolk, and received the following explanation: the first physician, being cheap, was often called for slight indispositions; when he gave a prescription, it was not used inasmuch as the patient did not care to spend money for medicine. The result was that the patient became steadily worse, and the physician was summoned again. The latter did not imagine that his prescription had not been followed, but gave the patient another medicine, which caused his death.

"The other physician's prescriptions were invariably filled, and his patients were cured."

"When a man is spiritually sick and seeks to find a remedy in well-known ethical writings, he has no patience to follow the instructions they contain. He delays from day to day, and before he realizes the seriousness of his moral defects, his soul is lost.

"But when such a man comes to me and finds it difficult to approach me because of the many demands upon my attention, he is willing to follow my practical counsel, which I vary according to his particular need and ability. Before he knows it, he is cured of his malady."

N. R. B., p. 38. (B., pp. 531-2).

4. The Kindly Soldier

The Gastininer Rabbi recounted the following episode: "A poor mother fell asleep at the cradle of her sick baby. Suddenly she opened her eyes and beheld a soldier standing near the cradle and giving medicine to the ill child. The mother screamed in her fright and the soldier hurriedly departed. The distracted woman ran to the Rabbi with her story and he sent for the soldier and questioned him. The soldier described how he had become a doctor. 'I was walking one day,' he said, 'with my non-Jewish comrades on a road. The soldiers forgot I was a Jew, and when they met a Jew on the highway they robbed him and hanged him to prevent his complaining to the authorities. I lagged behind and when the robbers had left, I cut down the Jew and gave him my own money. This delayed me, and I was missed at the roll-call. My comrades were dispatched after me, and fearing their revenge, I fled and came to this town. I had learned a little medicine in the army, and therefore, I engaged secretly in healing the sick hoping, thereby, to gain forgiveness for my sin in associating with bandits.'

"So you see," continued the Gastininer, "a holy man may be concealed even beneath the uniform of a man whose trade is war."

S. S. K., ii, 77.

5. The Surgeon and the Rabbi

Said the "Yud": "In the same way that a surgeon may shed a man's blood in order to heal his body, a leader may shame a sinner even in public in order to cure his soul. And just as the surgeon may not operate when he knows it will not avail the sick patient, the leader may not shame a sinner when he knows that his rebuke will accomplish no good."

Tif. Yeh., p. 45.

126. PIETY, PUBLIC AND SECRET

1. Special Piety and Servants

The Ropshitzer once walked abroad late at night and passed a watchman. He asked the watchman his employer's name. The watchman gave it, and then, to the Rabbi's astonishment, asked him the same question.

The Rabbi bade him come to his house the next morning, and forthwith engaged him as his servant. The Ropshitzer appreciated that such a "golem" [1] would be unable to understand anything before his eyes, and that it would be unnecessary to seek concealment when he performed any acts of special piety.

S. N., p. 37.

[1] "Golem" means a "dull clod."

2. True Piety

A young Hasid complained to the Kotzker Rabbi that many Hasidim speak of him with contempt as a "pietist."

The Rabbi responded: "The reason they feel contempt for one who openly exhibits his piety is that the pious man usually changes the proper places of important and unimportant things in religious conduct."

S. S. K., i, 75.

3. The Deceiving Cloak

The Tzupenester Rabbi was informed that a certain man was renowned for his piety. He remarked: "Piety that is renowned is a cloak, the cloth of which is pride; it is lined with anger, and sewn with the threads of melancholy."

N. I., p. 70.

4. Who Is More Pious?

Said the Riziner: "One Jew may be praised that he does not attend to his business on the Sabbath; another Jew may be blamed because he talks during the Services on a week-day. Who is the more pious? Who is the better Jew?"

M. D., p. 225.

5. The Bridge of Life

When asked how to be truly pious, the Riziner answered with this parable:

"Two rebels were condemned to death, but their sentence was commuted to the following: they were to cross the river by a rope stretched from one bank to the other. The first crossed in safety. When the second was about to follow, he shouted to the first: 'Can you give me any counsel so that I may not fall from the rope and drown?'

" 'The only advice I can offer you,' the first shouted to the second, 'is that when I felt my body was about to incline too much in one direction, I strove to lean over to the other.'

"Likewise," commented the Riziner, "when we incline too much towards a fault, we must bend towards the opposite extreme." [1]

N. I., p. 27.

[1] This is taught by Maimonides. For the figure of the crossing of a river on a rope, see "The Tenuous Cord of Life"; 172:4.

6. Piety on a Journey

The Karliner used to say: "He who is a complete Jew at home is only half a Jew on a journey. He who is half a Jew at home is only a quarter Jew on a journey."

The Alexanderer added: "When a man is on a journey, he conducts himself according to a Shulchan Arukh different from the code he follows at home. The Talmud [1] says: 'And it came to pass when the Ark went forth' [2] is a separate book.' "

D. Z., p. 59.

[1] Sabbath 116.
[2] Numbers 10:35.

7. Silence and Secrecy

Said the Bershider: "Two things I learned from my Master during my last visit to him: 'The less one talks, the nearer he is to holiness'; and 'Only that good deed is valuable of which no one knows.'"

M. P., p. 49.

8. Outside and Inside

Rabbi Judah Zevi of Stretin remarked: "One should keep his special piety hidden; otherwise he is guilty of pride. The word: אֲנִי 'I' which denotes the proud and haughty person, and אַיִן 'naught' which denotes the meek and humble one, have the same letters. But in the first word, the 'Yud' [1] is on the outside, while in the second word, it is inside."

E. Tz., p. 141.

[1] "Jew" or the letter "Yud."

9. Hidden Holiness

After the death of the Koznitzer Maggid, his Disciples hesitated to accept for their leader, Rabbi Moses, his eldest son, inasmuch as they have never perceived anything extraordinary in his conduct and character. He was considered a man of mediocre scholarship, and was known as the "Psalm Chanter," the impression being that he understood nothing higher. Nevertheless they resolved to send three scholars to test him. When they entered his presence, Rabbi Moses recited the verse (Psalm 138:6): 'For though the Lord be high, yet regardeth He the lowly, and the haughty He knoweth from afar.' The delegation then understood that the Rabbi in his meekness had concealed his learning and his holiness during his father's lifetime. They recommended him as a worthy successor."

S. Hay., p. 56.

10. Why He Boasted

The Ropshitzer took the utmost care to conceal his great piety. Once when he recited the Midnight Services, lying with outstretched hands and feet on the ground and crying bitterly over the Exile of the Shekinah, a householder unexpectedly entered. The Rabbi turned to him and said: "If the townsfolk but knew the greatness of their Rabbi, they would respect him all the more."

The man then related that the Rabbi was a vain boaster, just as the Rabbi intended.

E. Tz., p. 88.

127. POVERTY

1. The Poor Man's Wisdom

Rabbi Bunam commented on the verse in Ecclesiastes (9:16): "The poor man's wisdom is despised." He said: "It is the poor man's wisdom that he should have no feeling of false pride, and be willing to do any honest work to earn a livelihood."

S. S. K., i, 11.

2. Cause to Sing

Rabbi Mordecai of Lekhivitz was exceedingly poor in his early manhood. His wife and children oftentimes went hungry. A relative found the Rabbi in the synagogue singing hymns.

"Your wife and children weep," he said, "and you sing."

"Well may they weep," replied the Rabbi, "since they depend upon a mortal man. I however, depend upon the All-Powerful, and I have cause to sing."

M. D., p. 238.

3. The Wrong Emphasis

A man came to the Pulnoer Rabbi, complaining about his poverty. "It is true, however," added the complainant, "that my evil deeds are responsible for my lack of money, as the Tanna says in the Talmud." [1]

"You may be correct," replied the Rabbi. "But you have not quoted the Tanna correctly. He emphasized in his complaint 'the evil deeds' but you have placed the emphasis upon 'the lack of money.' "

[1] Kiddushin 82.

Kahana, p. 110.

4. Not Riches, but Fervor

Rabbi Mendel of Kossov was once a guest at the home of his brother-in-law, and noticed that all the people who came to the latter were poor. He inquired from Rabbi Uri: "Brother-in-law, why are your adherents not blessed with riches?"

Rabbi Uri responded: "They lack the desire for riches."

When the two Zaddikim sat together at meal-time, Rabbi Uri turned to a Hasid and said to him: "Ezekiel,[1] now that I am seated with my brother-in-law, you have a suitable opportunity to express your heart's wishes; I assure you that every one of them will be fulfilled."

The Hasid replied with fervor: "I beg the Rabbi to make it possible for me to utter the prayer: 'Praised art Thou who spoke and the world appeared' [2] with the same devotion as yourself."

[1] Probably the Kozmirer Rabbi.
[2] Singer, p. 16.

E. Tz., p. 79; Bl., Gem., pp. 245-6.

5. The Shoe-Button

Among the adherents of Rabbi Uri was a Hasid by the name of Wolfsche of Lemberg. He was the only one who was well-to-do. Once the Rabbi said to him: "Wolfsche, you would please me better if you were poor."

The Hasid was terrified and cried, trembling: "Rabbi, leave me in peace. If I would lose a single button of my shoe, I would no longer know how or what to pray."

E. Tz., p. 80; Bl., Gem., pp. 246-7.

6. Disdain for Wealth

Once the wife of Rabbi Uri said to him: "Your adherents waste your time for you while their families famish at home. Why do you not seek to improve their resources, so that they may have no difficulties in making both ends meet, and can serve God with a joyful spirit?"

Rabbi Uri replied: "My followers do not yearn for earthly goods; I will demonstrate this to you tomorrow."

The next day at the morning prayer, when he came to the passage: "Riches and honor are from Thee," [1] he spread out the folds of his robe (Chalat), stepped up to each Hasid and said: "Whosoever wishes money, let him place his hand into the fold, and he will have it."

But not a single one of the Hasidim stirred from his place.

E. Tz., p. 79; Bl., Gem., p. 246.

[1] I Chronicles 29:12.

7. Why the Pious are Poor

The Besht was asked why the pious are poorer than the impious. In reply he narrated the following parable:

"A king desired to please his loyal courtiers and announced that to each would be granted his particular wish. Some asked for honors; others asked for wealth. But one of them said: 'My wish is to speak to the king three times a day.' "

"We the pious prefer communion with the Lord thrice daily above all honors and riches, and God grants unto us our wish."

M. G. I., p. 12.

8. The Foundation

A Rabbi was asked why the true Zaddik is always so poor. "Because," replied the Rabbi, "he is the foundation of the world,[1] and the foundation is built in the ground."

O. I. H., p. 166.

[1] Proverbs 10:25.

9. A Morsel of Bread

Rabbi Nahum Tzernobiler's Hasidim could no longer endure the sight of the abject poverty in which their Rabbi lived, and they begged permission to build him a decently-furnished home. He refused their request on the plea that he wished to remain a Hasid. They asked him to explain, and received the following reply: "The Talmud [1] says: 'One who desires to be a Hasid should perform the

[1] Baba Kamma 30.

commandments of the 'Ethics of the Fathers.' In this work we are taught (6:4) : 'This is the way that is becoming for the study of the Torah: a morsel of bread, water by measure, sleep on the ground.' " [2]

[2] Singer, p. 206.

F. R. H.-M., pp. 39-40.

10. The Children of Our Home

Rabbi Nahum Tzernobiler's wife came to him weeping and complained that there was not a piece of bread in the house. She said: "You promise to others wealth and possessions, and your blessings are fulfilled. But your wife and children alone must remain in want."

He sighed from the depths of his heart. Then he bethought himself and said: "It is written: 'And the poor shall be—the children of your home' " (Ethics of the Fathers, 1:5; Singer, p. 185).

His wife left the Rabbi's little room, comforted.

Bl., Pr., p. 80.

11. See No Excuses

Said Rabbi Schmelke: "Look not for offenses in the poor man who asks thy aid, as an excuse for not helping him. For then will the Lord surely look for offenses in Thee, and He is certain to find them in abundance. Remember that thy suppliant's sins have been erased by his poverty, whereas thine still remain with thee."

F. U. A. O., ii, 99.

12. Joy in Poverty

Said the Porissover: "If a man is poor and meek, it is easy for him to be joyful, inasmuch as he has nothing to guard against losing."

D. Z., p. 18.

13. The Choice of Poverty

Said Rabbi Nahum Tzernobiler: "Between poverty and wealth I always choose poverty. It is the best shield against egotism and against every evil of the spirit. It is the least costly, the most easily attainable; it need not struggle against jealousy and competition; it need answer no questions or suspicions; it is understood without comments and without explanations. I beg of you, my good friends, not to deprive me of this great treasure."

D. D., p. 96.

14. God's Will and Man's

The Gerer Rabbi in his younger days was extremely poor, his father-in-law having been unsuccessful in business. His wife complained and entreated him to pray to the Lord for money. The Rabbi refused, saying: "It is my desire to do the will of God, but not that God should do my will."

M. E. H., i, 33.

128. PRAISE OF GOD

1. Adon Olam

The Kotzker Rabbi was asked: "Why do we begin Services with 'Adon Olam' and finish them with 'Adon Olam'?"

He answered: "We do so in order to demonstrate that the conclusion of the Services does not imply we have praised the Lord sufficiently. Nay, it is fitting that we should repeat the Services again and again. There is no limit to the praise we ought render the Creator."

S. S. K., iii, 26.

2. Praise and Thanksgiving

The Mezeritzer Maggid said: "We read in the Sabbath prayers: 'Though our mouths were filled with song as the sea . . . yet would we be unable to thank Thee. . . . Therefore the limbs which Thou hast planted in us. . . . Lo, they shall thank Thee' (Singer, pp. 125-6).

"There seems to be a contradiction in these two statements. But it may be made clear by the following parable: A king informed one of his generals that he wished to lunch at the latter's home. The general showed the confusion he felt, inasmuch as he did not know the proper dishes for the royal food. The king noted this and added: 'My cooks will prepare the food, in order to save you the trouble.'

"Likewise the Lord desires our praise, and we tremble at the thought that our mouths are ignorant of the proper words, and that we lack the proper spirit. But then we remind ourselves that our limbs have been formed by the Lord, and we feel that He will accept our words through His vessels."

E. O., p. 30.

3. At All Times

The Radziminer Rabbi said: "One who crosses the ocean and is rescued from a shipwreck gives thanks unto the Lord. But why should we not thank God if we cross without a mishap? One who is cured of a dangerous illness, blesses the Lord. Why should we not bless Him, when He grants us health and preserves us from illness."

M. N., p. 10.

4. "Greet My Father"

The Lizensker met a group of Jews, who were traveling to Warsaw. "Greet [1] my Father, please," requested the Rabbi.

"Who is he?" the Rabbi was asked.

"He is mine and yours—our Father in Heaven," said the Lizensker.

M. D., p. 217.

[1] "Forget not."

5. The King's Son and the King's Courtiers

Said the Besht: "The courtiers of a king are accustomed to converse with their royal master only seldom, and then with a few brief phrases. If they observe that the king is angry, they do not approach him. The prince, however, does not hesitate to speak with his father even when the King is in anger, and he holds lengthy converse with him.

"The angels are the courtiers of God, and their singing unto Him is limited. Israel, however, is His son, and he is permitted to praise Him as often as he desires."

K. S. T., p. 18a.

6. The Ever-Broadening Spring

Said the Lizensker: "To relate the goodness of God and His wonders draws forth ever greater goodness and wonders. It is like a spring that gushes forth water increasingly and grows wider and wider, the more frequently its water is drawn. We read: 'The fame of Thy great goodness they shall pour forth' (Psalm 145:7)." [1]

O. E., p. 53.

[1] The translation of this verse is according to Singer, p. 29. "J. T.," uses the word "utter" instead of "pour forth."

7. Thanksgiving for Our God

Said Rabbi Baruch of Medziboz: "We read in the Grace After Meals: [1] 'We thank thee, O Lord our God, because Thou didst give . . . the Land, Redemption from Egypt, the Covenant, the Law, Thy Statutes, Life, Grace and Lovingkindness, food . . .'; then we continue: 'For all this, O Lord our God, we thank Thee.'

"This last passage may be translated thus: 'And above all, for being the Lord our God, we thank Thee; for our not having erred as other peoples have done.'"

Mif. H., p. 38.

[1] Singer, p. 280.

129. THE ECSTASY OF PRAYER

1. Fiery Words

The Lubliner asked the "Yud": "Why do you pray so fast?"

The "Yud" replied: "I love the words of the prayers; hence I swallow them quickly."

"But," retorted the Lubliner. "I too enjoy the prayers, and yet I enunciate the words slowly."

"Your words," exclaimed the "Yud," "are like flaming fire, hence you must allow them to cool."

N. H., p. 44.

2. *A Lesson from Dancers*

A village innkeeper complained to the Kobriner that he lacked a private room for praying, far enough from the noise made by the patrons of his inn. The Kobriner told him in reply this experience: "Once I chanced to visit an inn, and the time for the afternoon prayers arrived. It was a Catholic holiday, and the inn was filled with noisy merrymakers and dancing couples. Still I prayed there with complete devotion, thinking to myself: 'If so much enthusiasm is given to physical enjoyments, why cannot I be even more enthusiastic in activities of the spirit?' "

O. Y., p. 155.

3. *"Father, O Father"*

A Hasid was praying with great enthusiasm, and frequently interjected the exclamation: "Father, O Father!" A second Hasid argued: "We know from the Talmud [1] that when we obey God, He is called our Father; otherwise He is our Master. How is this Hasid so certain that he is worthy enough to call upon the Lord as his Father, not his Master?"

The Kotzker Rabbi who overheard this remark, said: "If one cries out: 'Father, O Father' many times, at last God becomes in truth his Father!"

S. S. K., iv, 29.

[1] Kiddushin 36.

4. *A Single Amen*

Said the Kobriner: "If I knew that I have answered a single 'Amen' as it ought be said, I would be contented."

O. Y., p. 164.

5. *Noiseless Prayer*

A Hasid asked Rabbi Pinchas of Koretz why he prayed without motions of the body, and without a single sound, whereas other Zaddikim oftentimes prayed with many gestures of enthusiasm and in a loud tone of voice.

The Koretzer answered: "When a Zaddik prays, he cleaves in truth to God, and loses all sense of corporeality, as if his very soul had departed from his body. The Talmud [1] tells us that in some people the soul leaves the body only after great agonies and convulsions, whereas in others it departs as quietly as one draws a hair out of milk or offers a kiss." [2]

M. H. T., p. 3.

[1] Berakhoth 8.
[2] Compare: Last Paragraph, 133:13.

6. *The Unheeded Knife*

Said the "Yud": "Do you wish to know what is proper prayer? When you are so engrossed that you do not feel a knife thrust into your body, then you are offering prayer aright."

Tif. Yeh., p. 45.

7. A Consuming Flame

Rabbi Feibush Hobnover was possessed of a burning desire to serve the Lord. Once he slept in the Ropshitzer's House of Study. The Ropshitzer told his other Disciples: "Watch and you will see him awake at the dot of midnight to perform the 'Midnight Service.'" At the stroke of twelve, Rabbi Feibush awoke, tore at his collar, and began to shout: "O Mother, I am burning."

Later the Hobnover became a Disciple of the Apter. The Ropshitzer regretted this, and said to his intimates: "Feibush is a consuming flame; I strove to cool him a little; but the Apter himself is fiery, and will increase the conflagration." Shortly after, the Hobnover fell dead while praying. His heart could not endure his burning ecstasy.

Ohel N., pp. 107-8.

8. The Lame Foot

The Tzanzer was a Disciple of the Ropshitzer in his youth. Once he was praying with enthusiasm and was stamping on the floor. The Ropshitzer's wife said to her husband: "Why do you not counsel the youth to stamp only with his healthy and not with his lame foot?"

The Ropshitzer replied: "If I had known that he was aware with what foot he was stamping, I would have told him."

Ohel N., p. 110.

9. The Linen and the Cotton Wick

Said the Medzibozer to his grandson, Israel, who was accustomed to gesticulate in his prayers:

"A wick of linen burns quietly and gives a better light than a cotton wick which burns noisily. Believe me when I say that a sincere movement of your smallest toe is sufficient to show your enthusiasm."

Butz. D., p. 32.

10. Speedy Prayer

Said the Besht: "A man sometimes becomes drunk with the ecstasy of rejoicing over the Torah. He sometimes feels his love for God burn within him. The words of prayer come pouring out of his mouth, and he must pray quickly to keep pace with them."

K. S. T., p. 16b.

11. The Dry Logs and the Wet

Said the Besht: "We read in the Talmud that Fastday Services in which men of impiety take no part are not genuine Services.[1] How is this to be explained?

"A wet log placed in a stove will not burn, but if placed between ten dry logs, it will also burn if the kindling is adequately

[1] Kerithoth 6.

done. Likewise the worship of pious men who cannot kindle by its ardor a similar fervor among men of impiety is not genuine worship."

K. S. T., p. 30a.

130. PRAYER: ITS HOURS

1. Tardy Prayers

The Riziner was once asked why so many Zaddikim are heedless of the hours of prayer fixed by tradition. He answered with a parable: "The king has appointed an hour for all who come upon their own business, and after this hour, they are barred from his presence. But those who come, not upon their own private affairs, but on matters of the common welfare, require no special hours; they are welcome at any time." [1]

[1] See 130:3.

Bl., Gem., p. 277.

2. The Proof of a Deed

The Gerer Rabbi was asked why the Hasidim are wont to hold their prayers at an hour later than that established by the Shulchan Arukh. He replied: "There is a proof of everything, even of our actions. In Pirkei Avoth,[1] Ben Azzai teaches us that one good deed leads to another, and a transgression draws a transgression in its train. This, then, is the proof of whether or not a deed is good or evil. Since we engage in acts of piety after divine worship, it follows that there is no sin in our deviation from the Code."

[1] 4:2; Singer, p. 195.

S. S. K., p. 74.

3. The Public Welfare

The Riziner explained why the Zaddikim are tardy with their morning prayers, offering the following parable:

"A judge, who was also mayor of his city, issued an order that all cases would be heard by him in the forenoon only, so that he might devote the afternoon to public affairs. A citizen of public spirit, however, came to the court just a few moments late and asked to be heard. The judge replied that he could not change the rule. The citizen then said: 'Your rule was made for the purpose of leaving you time for public affairs. My case is of public concern, and I bid you therefore to hear me.'"

"A rule was established," continued the Riziner, "stating the proper hours for prayer, so that a person should not delay it and perhaps forget about it. But this is only applicable to those who have private business during the day—other than serving the Lord. The Zaddikim, however, have no other business but service to the Lord and service to Israel; hence, they may be heard even after the established hours."

N. I., p. 8.

4. The Time for Prayers

A man who was not a Hasid desired to witness for himself the behaviour of the Apter Rabbi. He visited the Apter synagogue, and found the Rabbi buried in thoughts and smoking his pipe. He dared not interrupt the Rabbi, but recited the morning prayers to himself, and then took the *Hok le-Yisrael,*[1] studying in it for some time the portion of the day. When noon came and the Rabbi made no movement to begin his Morning Prayers, the visitor whispered to him:

"Rabbi, the time for the Morning Prayers is past."

The Apter replied: "A man like you is satisfied to enter the synagogue and to commence his worship immediately. As for myself, it is different. I began the order of prayers earlier than you with the words: 'I give thanks before Thee'[2] and commenced to think: 'Who am I to give thanks before the Lord?' I am still thinking of the same matter."

M. D., p. 211.

[1] A collection of extracts from the Bible and Talmud.
[2] These words begin the Morning Prayers in the Orthodox Prayer Book, but Singer does not include them. The sentence in full is: "I give thanks before Thee, King, living and ever-existent, that Thou has restored in me my soul with pity. Great is Thy faithfulness."

5. "All Prayer"

Rabbi Bunam narrated this parable: "A man of handsome raiment came into an institution to ask for charity, and was compelled to make considerable explanation as to the reason for his need. Another man, poorly attired, entered, and he was given aid at once. In the same way, a self-satisfied man who asks God for help needs to do much entreating. But he who is broken of heart and meek is answered at once. We read: 'But I am all prayer' (Psalm 109:4). 'My broken heart is in itself a prayer, and I hardly am required to entreat Thee.'"

S. T., p. 80.

6. The Tardy Soldier

The Sidlovtzer Rabbi was opposed to those Hasidim who declared that they required a long time to prepare themselves for prayer. He said: "A soldier received an order to arise daily at sunrise and to stand guard before the royal palace. He arrived at his post late, and pleaded that he needed to brush his clothes and make himself ready before appearing at the palace. He was, nevertheless, punished for disobedience. We, too, are commanded to commence the day with prayers, and a plea that we require preparation, will not avail us if we delay our worship beyond the appointed hours."

Tif. B., p. 14.

7. The Best He Can

Said the Ropshitzer: "A man should not declare: 'I cannot pray at this moment because my thoughts are astray; I shall wait until I can pray with the proper concentration.' He should pray at the appointed time to the best of his ability. It is written: 'But from thence ye will seek the Lord thy God' (Deut. 4:29). This means: at any place, at any hour where thou art."

Ohel N., p. 60.

8. Shall Prayer Be Punctual Or Tardy?

Rabbi Eliezer of Tarnigrad narrated the following parable: "A prince chanced to sojourn overnight in a village. He commanded his servant to procure for him palatable food for breakfast from the nearest city. When the prince awoke, he waited for the meal, but it did not arrive. He then ordered a peasant woman to bring him simple food.

"In the same fashion, the soul of a Hasid would rejoice to offer worship of the highest degree of holiness; but if it cannot attain this, it prays in a simple manner. Therefore why wait with prayer until it is too late?"

Rabbi Leib, the Zaklikover, told this parable: "A man had two sons. To the elder he gave a coin and commanded him to make a purchase; the boy did so and returned immediately. The next time the father gave a coin to his younger son for a purchase. The boy was alert, and observed that the object his father desired could be secured in better quality for more money. He, therefore, performed errands for a neighbor, and with the additional amount, purchased the superior article. The father had grown impatient, but when he saw the purchase his son had made, he was filled with affection and admiration for him.

"In the same way, the man who requires more time to prepare himself for worship is more beloved by God even if his worship be offered late."

Tif. Yeh., pp. 37-9.

131. PRAYER: ITS LENGTH

1. A Long Prayer

The Strelisker stopped over in a town and visited the synagogue. There he prayed at great length, and the congregation was forced to wait for him before proceeding further. The Rav of the town said: "We read in the Talmud [1] that Rabbi Akiba when praying with the congregation was accustomed to pray quickly, but when praying alone, he prayed slowly. Why do you compel the congregation to wait?"

[1] Berakhoth 31.

The Strelisker replied: "The Talmud means the following: When Rabbi Akiba felt that the members of the congregation prayed with him, namely, with his own intensity and fervor, then he prayed rapidly. But when he prayed alone, namely, when he sensed that the congregants did not offer their prayers wholeheartedly, he was forced to pray at length, so that their prayers might also prove acceptable."

O. O., pp. 30-31.

2. Worship At Length

The Nadvorner Rabbi was accustomed to worship nearly the entire day. His Morning Services lasted until nightfall. Once he visited Rabbi Moses Teitelbaum at Ohel. The Oheler said to him: "I am also a Jew, and yet my praying does not consume more than an hour. Why does yours require the whole day?"

The Nadvorner replied: "Both rich and poor alike use bread. The rich man eats a small slice since he has other food. The poor man eats three slices, since bread constitutes his entire meal. Likewise you spend your time in study; hence worship does not occupy so important a place in your day's activities. As for me, I have no other occupation but worship. I am not acquainted with the learning of the Torah, and therefore I must devote the whole day to worship."

M. D., pp. 212-3.

132. PROPER PRAYER

1. Praying to Pray

The Tzanzer was asked by a Hasid: "What does the Rabbi do before praying?"

"I pray," was the reply, "that I may be able to pray properly."

M. D., p. 212.

2. Service From the Heart

A Hasid complained to Rabbi Bunam that he oftentimes is afflicted with severe headaches after praying.

"What has worship to do with the head?" exclaimed the Rabbi. "Worship is service from the heart, not a labor of the head."

M. D., p. 212.

3. Refreshing Worship

The "Yud" declared: "When one feels fatigued after prayer, it is a sign that his devotion has been inadequate. We read in Isaiah (40:31): 'they that wait for the Lord shall renew their strength.'"

N. H., p. 49.

4. The Power of Prayer

A Hasid once complained to the Kotzker Rabbi that he found it exceedingly hard to earn a living. The Rabbi counseled him to pray to the Lord to have mercy upon him. The Hasid thereupon declared he did not believe his own prayer would avail with the Creator.

"If this be your sentiment," answered the Rabbi, "you are the victim of an affliction greater than the problem of a livelihood. You should feel distraught that you do not know how to give utterance to true prayer."

S. S. K., i, 68.

5. "And With All Your Soul"

Rabbi Hirsch of Rimanov suffered the heavy tribulation of losing his children in their youth. The last one, a daughter, died in childbirth. His son-in-law, her husband, said to the Rabbi: "You offer prayers for others that their offspring may be blessed with long life, and the Lord grants your petitions. Why do you not pray for yourself?"

"I shall explain this to you," replied the Rabbi. "We read that Abraham prayed that the people of Sodom be preserved from destruction. But we do not find that he prayed that the Lord save his son Isaac from being offered as a sacrifice. The reason is that the true Zaddik serves the Lord in every way pleasing unto the Lord, even at the cost of his own life and of those most precious to him."

M. T., p. 21.

6. Sensible Prayer

The Medzibozer Rabbi said: "We are taught by our Rabbis that 'the gates of tears are not closed'; [1] namely, that tearful pleas to God for mercy are accepted by Him. It may be asked, since they are not closed, of what use are gates? The answer is: If one begs tearfully but without intelligence, the gates are then closed."

M. G., ii, 32.

[1] Berakhoth 32.

7. Oiling the Wheels With Prayer

The Berditschever saw a teamster dressed in Tallith and Tephillin, lubricating the wheels of his wagon. The Rabbi exclaimed: "O Lord, what a holy people is Thine! Even when they oil the wheels of their wagons they pray unto Thee in Tallith and Tephillin!" [1]

E. Z., p. 12.

[1] A frequently quoted story; attributed also to the Sassover.

8. Chatter or Prayer?

Whenever a certain Rabbi perceived anything evil, he always spoke charitably to God in favor of the wrongdoer. Once some people in his vicinity interrupted him with shallow chatter while he was praying. Thereupon he added to his prayer the words: "Lord, they call unto Thee even in the midst of their eager conversation."

Reflex, May, 1929, p. 67.

9. The Prayer of the Perfect

"Great is the prayer of the Perfect, for it turns brutishness into compassion" (Moed Katan, f. 16a). As has been told by our Fathers: "When the winter-rains in the Holy Land were delayed, Honi Hamagel stepped into a foss of his own digging and spoke: 'Lord of the Universe, Thy children have appointed me spokesman to pray for rain, and I will not budge from here, until my prayer is heard.' A downpour came, and Rabbi Simeon ben Shetach threatened the overbold man with excommunication, but thought better of it, saying: 'If, in your quality of spoilt child, you have privileges on High, I will allow them here below.'"[1]

[1] Taanith 19 and 23.   *Bl., Gem., p. 70.*

10. The Bridge to God

In the Talmud, Rosh ha-Shanah 17b, we are taught: "God wrapped Himself into a prayer-shawl and taught to Moses the order of supplication, together with this revelation: 'Whenever Israel sinneth, let them pray to Me according to rule, and their sins will be forgiven.'" And the Talmud Yerushalmi exhorteth in Berakhoth (9:1): "When ill befalls a man, let him not turn to Michael or Gabriel, but invoke the Lord Himself." Our forefathers, Abraham, Isaac and Jacob have instituted prayer and it has come to us as a tradition.

"Prayer is the bridge that carrieth Man to God, but he must not, while praying, think of a guerdon in the world to come. Quoth the Zohar: 'He who loves the King, does not do him homage for a fee.' The fate of the Jewish nation, and with it, the fate of all the world, depends upon prayer. . . . It is written in the Torah: 'And the people saw and moved about.'[1] Wherefore it was taught by a Zaddik: "If you see one praying, standing upright without emotion, know that he does not pray with thoughts inviolate and with a whole heart, his mind is not with God."[2]

[1] Exodus 20:18.   *Bl., Pr., p. 27.*
[2] See 187:9.

11. The Sh'ma: Its Words and Its Time

Said the Ropshitzer: "Some Mithnagedim are careful not to pass over the time of reciting the Sh'ma, but they are prone to pass over the Sh'ma itself, without giving their hearts to its words. The Hasidim are likely to pass over the time of the Sh'ma, but they are careful not to pass over the words of the Sh'ma itself with inattention."

Ohel N., p. 100.

12. The Power of the Sh'ma

The Koretzer told the Bershider that his grandfather would visit the impious and say to them: "I care not what deed of impiety you do; but perform for me one request: say the Sh'ma daily. It is such a little request." Many did so and became men of faith. It is a comforting lesson to those sinners who recite the Sh'ma that through its power they may escape perdition.

M. P., p. 41.

13. The Privilege of Prayer

Said Rabbi Abraham Moses, the son of Rabbi Bunam: "One Talmudical passage praises him who puts his mind into his prayer;[1] but another passage states that he who is thoughtful in his prayer causes his deeds to be meditated on in Heaven.[2] The explanation is: he is praiseworthy who prays earnestly because God has commanded us to call upon Him in tribulation; but he does not expect God to fulfil his pleas of necessity, in the same way that he does not anticipate immediate compensation for any other commandment he has performed. But he who believes God ought grant his petition because of his fervent prayer, is judged in Heaven, whether or not by his other acts he deserves to have his petition granted. A man's right to the petition of prayer is a privilege, not something that is due him without merit. A man cannot dictate to the Lord unless he has earned the right."

[1] Sabbath 127.
[2] Berakhoth 55.

S. I., p. 36.

14. The Thirst of Plants and Trees

The Ziditzover told the following story: "Rabbi Joseph Caro was accustomed to express a holy intention in words before doing anything. Once he arose in the night for a drink of water, but he could remember no words of holiness to utter. Finally he said: 'As I am about to quench my thirst with this water, may it please the Lord to still the thirst of plants and trees.' This prayer was accepted and rain which was sorely needed, came down in abundance."

P. v. K., p. 44a.

15. Pray Without Reasons

Said Rabbi Jacob Zevi Porissover: "Had Moses simply prayed for Israel without giving a reason why God should save them from annihilation, the Israelites who went forth from Egypt would have entered Palestine. Moses, however, gave as a reason the injury that might be done to God's reputation as a God of Power. To refute this, it sufficed that the young generations that followed should conquer Palestine."[1]

[1] See Numbers 14: 16, 29, 31.

D. Z., p. 51.

16. The Shekinah and the Shofar

Said the Koretzer: "It is written: 'Lift up thy voice as a Shofar' (Isaiah 58: 1). As the Shofar cannot emit any sound except when blown by man, no man can raise his voice in prayer except when the Shekinah prays through it."

Nof. Tz., p. 54.

17. The Emissary of the Shekinah

Said the Besht: "The true worshipper is he who discovers the Shekinah in all his supplications. He acts as the emissary of the Shekinah to bring thoughts into words."

K. S. T., p. 21b.

18. Out of the Depths

Said Rabbi Yerachmiel, the son of the "Yud": "We read: 'Out of the depths have I called Thee, O Lord' (Psalm 130: 1).

"A traveler lost his way in a wilderness and his provisions gave out. After a few days of hunger he found traces of a rider who had just passed. His misery reached the depths when he noticed containers of food which, however, were empty.

"He encountered another traveler and with his last strength ran up to him and begged for food. The other misunderstood his actions and thought him a robber. As he whipped up his horse, the wanderer fainted. This second depth of misery was too much for him; there was no one else to whom he could appeal. The rider noticed his plight, revived and fed him.

"When we call upon the Lord, we should do so from the abyss of two depths: from the depths of contrition for our transgressions; and from the depths of our knowledge that God is the only Source of succor."

Tif. Yeh., p. 60.

19. Our Head Erect

Said the Medzibozer: "We need not bow down before the Lord with our body. Let us bow with our heart and keep our head erect."

Butz. D., p. 13.

20. An Acceptable Time

Said the Medzibozer: "We read: 'And as for me, may [1] my prayer unto Thee, O Lord, be in an acceptable time' (Singer, p. 175). And as for me, who am I? And as for my prayer, what significance is there in it before Thee, O Lord? But may it be in an acceptable time, when even an insignificant prayer by an unworthy person like myself is accepted."

Butz. D., p. 32.

[1] The word "may" is transposed in the interpretation.

21. A Fresh Miracle

Said the Besht: "The first time a thing occurs in nature, it is called a miracle; later it becomes natural, and no attention is paid to it. Let your worship and your service be a fresh miracle every day to you. Only such worship, performed from the heart, with enthusiasm, is acceptable."

K. S. T., p. 9b.

22. The Shekinah Enters

Said the Besht: "When a man begins the Amidah and says the opening verse: 'O Lord, open Thou my lips!' [1] the Shekinah immediately enters within his voice, and speaks with his voice. Remember this, and you will have no fear."

K. S. T., p. 15a.

[1] Singer, p. 44.

23. The Bratzlaver on "Prayer"

A.

"1. When you cannot pray with proper concentration, try your utmost to speak the words in a spirit of belief in their truth."

K. L. M., p. 12.

"2. Let your heart hear what your mouth speaks if you wish to offer proper prayer."

K. L. M., p. 6.

B.

"1. The prayer of the flatterer is not heard.

2. The student of the Torah in poverty will have his prayer heard.

3. The prayer of the lowly in mind is heard.

4. Pray that no tribulation befall you before it comes.

5. The prayer of another for your sake aids you more than your own prayer.

6. The prayer of an individual is not heard unless he concentrates upon it, but the prayer of the many is heard, even if not all of them are whole-hearted.

7. In your prayers ask not for more than one thing at a time.

8. Do not ask that God change the laws of nature for you.

9. He who forgives will find his prayer heard

10. Limit your requests for your material needs, but ask all you wish in Torah and piety.

11. It is a good deed to be properly attired at the time of praying.

12. A man should pray that he be not afflicted with poverty.

13. Praying in a loud tone of voice brings feeling into all of your limbs.

14. The prayer of the trustful person is heard.

15. Before prayer, give to charity.

16. A man receives divine powers according to the place in which he prays.

17. Visit the synagogue early and late, and long life will be granted you.

18. He who deprives another of his belongings or he who shames another, will find his prayers unheard.

19. A prayer offered in tears will be accepted.

20. If you are not at peace with the world, your prayer will not be heard.

21. Pray for the welfare of the city in which you live.

22. He who prays not concerning the tribulations of Israel is a wicked person.

23. Be not ungrateful either to a Jew or a non-Jew.

24. The sick man who prays for himself will be heard.

25. Through joy will your prayer enter the Palace of God.

26. He who prays with all his strength will be heard.

27. He who has not paid his vow will find his prayer unheard.

28. The prayer of him who has no faith will not be heard.

29. Before prayer let your soul cleave to your Maker.

30. If you remain silent when you hear abuse of yourself, God will answer your prayer.

31. A joyful prayer has a sweet fragrance to God.

32. The prayer of the meek, even if not uttered in words, will be heard.

33. A man can offer more adequate prayer if his eyes are turned Heavenward.

34. By hymns and praises, the Shekinah is drawn down unto us.

35. He who is distressed by the tribulations of Israel and offers prayers to dispel them is permitted to complain against God.

36. Often a prayer is not heard until many people recite it together."

Sef. Ham., pp. 162-7.

C.

"1. Clothe the words of your prayers in grace; namely, pronounce them carefully and with sincerity. Would you mumble your words and ignore their meanings when addressing a superior? Take no advantage of the good nature of God if you wish Him to accept your worship.

2. The main weapons of a Jew are his prayers. All his battles against evil impulses and against obstacles he wins through prayers. The holiness of Israel comes through prayers.

3. God listens to every word of prayer. No word goes to waste, and the effect of prayer accumulates until God's mercies are brought down.

4. Since all good deeds are performed with God's aid, no reward should be expected as if it had been earned. Any salvation comes solely through God's mercies and through no merit of our own.

5. The heart should hear what a man prays, and should respond with joy at its ability to hear.

6. Fear other than fear of the Lord prevents the joy of proper prayer. Strive to overcome this fear through faith.

7. Impure worship lengthens our Exile.

8. Pure worship depends upon pure faith.

9. Words of prayer spoken with fervor will open for themselves a door through the foreign thoughts which encompass you.

10. A man should pray with such devotion that his heart is as if it were poured out like water before the Lord.

11. Our every act, even that of worship, should be intended for the benefit of our soul. Since the soul cannot abide in this world outside a body, the profits of our soul will automatically bring profit to our body. Body without soul is as mere clay.

12. When we lack means, children or health, the proper remedy is to pray to God, and not to rely overmuch on other remedies. God is ever-near, and ever-present, whereas other remedies may not be attained except by chance.

13. Through self-judgment and through nullifying our self-importance, we can attain spiritual light.

14. Pray not for your own profit but in order to bring pleasure to the Lord by your worship.

15. It is God's mercy that we may call Him by attributes suitable to a human being. Pronounce, therefore, these attributes with devotion and thanks.

16. A man should pray warmly before commencing discussion of the Torah in order that God may place in his words the warmth of sincerity.

17. A man should not stubbornly demand that God grant his prayer, and should not feel disappointment if it is unanswered.

18. A man should pray fervently that God may constantly increase his understanding of holy subjects. His soul will thus increase in holiness.

19. A man's mundane thoughts of the day crowd into his mind when he offers prayer. It requires strength of character to avoid them. Be strong and valiant in this task.

20. Since your donation to Palestine embraces you within the clear and holy air of Palestine, you will be thereby able to pray without the disturbance of foreign thoughts.

21. Bind your thoughts to the words of your prayers, and you will gain God's abundance.

22. The good man should intend to achieve through his prayers three things: first, to bring back doubters to the true faith; second, to assist the philosophers to maintain the true faith; third, to transform those who abuse him into those who honor him.

23. A man should know that during his prayers he stands in the King's Palace and sees only the King. He will then forget his own existence.

24. Pray in words, not in thoughts. God's Providence and His abundance descend through the medium of words.

25. By defending sinners, a man may properly pray that his own sins be overlooked.

26. Know that God stands above you, and listens to every word of your prayers. Worship with your whole heart, as is fitting.

27. Every word of your prayer is like a rose which you pick from its bush. You continue until you have formed a bouquet, a complete blessing. From them you form new bouquets of blessings, until you have pleated a wreath of glory unto the Lord.

28. Every word is reluctant to leave your soul. For example, the word 'Blessed' talks to you; implores you to consider the meaning of 'Blessed'; to remember whom you bless and why, and it begs you not to forget it even when you recite the other words. If you heed it, your prayers become a unity of holiness.

29. Forget everybody and everything during your worship. Forget yourself and your needs. Forget the people of whom you have need. Then in truth you may worship the Lord.

30. Feel your words in all your bones, your limbs, and your nerves. The Psalmist exclaims: "All my bones shall say: 'Lord, who is like unto Thee?'" (Psalm 35:10).

31. When you offer prayer, imagine yourself as one who is newly-born; without achievements of which to be proud; without high family descent to make you arrogant. Forget all dignity and self-esteem. Remember only your Maker.

32. When you chant the great Psalm (148) in your prayers, pray with intense devotion and with glowing heart. In it you command the angels and all nature to praise the Lord (Singer, p. 32).

33. Just as your fervor arouses a similar fervor in your fellow-worshiper, so it arouses fervor in yourself again and again.

34. In thy greatest trouble, strengthen thyself to call upon thy God; then it is that thy prayer is most acceptable.

35. Before thy prayers, remember any good qualities thou hast, or any good deeds which thou hast performed. This will put life into thee and enable thee to pray from the heart.

36. If a man endeavors to complete his prayers with utmost speed, he exiles his prayers from his presence.

37. Three things destroy worship: First, contempt for any man; second, deficiency in faith; and third, an unclean life.

38. True devotion will heal a malady in its inception and as yet unrecognized by any physician.

39. The presence of many worshipers heightens devotion.

40. Devotion is the gate to the dwelling of the Lord.

41. Everything may be attained through devotional prayers.

42. Make every effort to pray from the heart. Even if you do not succeed, the effort is precious in the eyes of the Lord.

43. If you feel no joy when you are beginning your prayers, compel yourself to be joyful, and real joy will follow. A joyful melody is of genuine aid.

44. If you are unable to pray in the proper spirit, say the words slowly, and explain them to yourself, even as a child reads them in school. Eventually the spirit of true devotion will come.

45. Feel the tribulations of the individual and of the multitude, and implore God to ease their burden."

L. E. H., pp. 104-114.

24. The Lizensker's Prayer

The Lizensker offered the following prayer:
"O Lord! Guard us from selfish motives and from pride when we do Thy will. Guard us from anger and chagrin, from sadness and from talebearing and from other evil traits. May no jealousy of our comrades enter our heart, and may no jealousy of us enter the heart of our fellow-men. Grant us the ability within our own heart to behold no defects but only virtues within our comrades."

D. D., p. 127.

25. Prayer After Discussion

The Tzanzer visited the Dzikover one afternoon, and was engaged by the Dzikover's brilliant sons in a Talmudic discussion. At its conclusion, the Tzanzer began to offer the Afternoon Services with the greatest enthusiasm. The Dzikover inquired: "Did not your mind still retain during your prayer a recollection of the discussion?"

"In no wise," replied the Tzanzer. "When I pray I forget there is Torah in the world, and when I study, I forget that there is anything else in the world."

Once the Tzanzer was sitting in judgment of an important civil suit with two other Rabbis. The disputants had chosen to accept a decision according to the Jewish law. One of the Rabbis suddenly exclaimed aloud: "Master of the Universe, One and Unified!"

The Tzanzer displayed his displeasure and said: "When you are engaged in deciding a case according to law, leave the Master of the Universe alone, and give attention to the authorities!"

D. D., p. 332.

133. PRAYER IN TRIBULATION.

1. The Heavy Heart

Rabbi Bunam used to say: "When a man's heart is heavy and full of anxiety, he may lighten it through ardent prayer and a belief in God's mercies."

M. N., p. 37.

2. Intercessions and Evil Decrees

When Emperor Joseph of Austria decreed against the Hasidim, Rabbi Elimelech wrestled so powerfully with Heaven, that a murmur like thunder growling afar went through all the upper worlds. His teacher, the Maggid of Mezeritz, appeared to him in a dream, saying:

"Dost thou recall how I entreated you and the others of my retinue to pray for my life, that I might avert, while yet alive, the evil decree, hanging over you, by prayer?"

"But look you, Master," argued Elimelech, "our Sages have taught the contrary doctrine: that Zaddikim are more powerful after death than during their lifetime." [1]

"True," said the Maggid, "but once dead and raised on High, they are not always inclined to make intercession as you wish. As long as I walked on earth, I saw nought in an evil decree, save a misfortune to be turned. In the upper worlds I know better. Why should I pray to shield you from blessings in disguise?"

Bl., Gem., p. 71 ff.

[1] Hullin 7.

3. Crying to the Lord for Rescue

A Hasid said to the Besht: "The Psalmist (145:19) says: 'He will fulfil the desire of them that fear Him; He also will hear their cry, and will save them.' But after He fulfils their desire, what need is there for their cry?"

The Besht replied: "Frequently a thief calls upon the Lord to help him, and the Lord permits him to accomplish his nefarious deed, in the same way that He hears those who are law-abiding.[1] The difference lies in this: when the thief is caught and again calls upon the Lord, He refuses to aid him. But if a good person asks to be permitted to do that which is evil for him, and the Lord grants him consent, then, when he discovers that he has walked into a veritable hornet's nest and cries unto the Lord to save him, the Lord aids him out of his tribulations."

M. G., I, p. 12 13.

[1] Doctrine of Free-will.

4. The Teaching of Phineas

Said the Radomsker: "We read (Psalm 106:30-1): 'Then Phineas stood up and prayed [1] and the plague was stayed. And that was accounted unto him for righteousness unto all generations for evermore.' The question arises: Aaron also stayed the plague,[2] yet we find no such recompense for him as for Phineas. The explanation is: Aaron used incense, and that was available only in the days of the Temple. But Phineas used prayer which may be utilized even today, even for the halting of an epidemic. Hence the great reward meted out to Phineas."

O. S., p. 32.

[1] The phrase is "And Phineas wrought judgment"; but the Targum has "And Phineas prayed."
[2] Numbers 17:12.

5. Nearest to God

After the Rimanover was disclosed as a Holy Rabbi, a Polish noblewoman came to him and entreated him to pray for the life of

her son who was dangerously ill. The Rabbi said: "Do you come
to me as a worker of miracles?"

"Nay," replied the mother, "I come to you as to a man who is
nearer to God than any other living person."

The Rabbi prayed for three hours and sweat covered his entire
body. At noon he said to the noblewoman: "I hope that my prayer
has been heard. Return home."

When she arrived at her home, she was told that the child had
opened its eyes and had asked for a drink. In 1883 when the boy
had become a man of eighty years, he came to Rimanov accompanied
by his own son, the Cardinal of Lemberg, to visit the grave of his
early benefactor.

Em. L., p. 30.

6. Rescue First and Prayer Later

A woman came to the Belzer Rabbi entreating him to pray for
her. The Rabbi said: "But have you sufficient belief in the efficacy
of my prayer?"

The woman answered: "We find that Israel at the Red Sea was
first saved [1] and then believed." [2]

The Rabbi smiled and offered prayer on her behalf.

P. v. K., p. 31b.

[1] Exodus 14:30: "Thus the Lord saved Israel."
[2] Exodus 14:31: "And they believed in the Lord."

134. PRAYER WITHOUT CONCENTRATION

1. Hunger Amid Prayers

The Medzibozer Rabbi said: "If one feels hunger while he is
praying, it is a certain sign that he has not prayed properly. The true
supplicant cannot feel any material needs when he communes with his
Creator."

M. R. T., p. 77.

2. Business and Prayers

Rabbi Nachman Kossover taught that we should always have
the Lord in our thoughts. He was asked: "Can we think of the
Lord when we are engaged in buying and selling?"

"Surely we can," answered the Rabbi. "If we are able to think
of business when we are praying, we should be able to think of
praying when we are doing business."

Dubnow, H. of H., p. 102.

3. Greetings to the Returned

The Berditschever walked over to a group of his Hasidim in the
congregation when they had finished the Amidah, and shook hands
with them, greeting them with the words: "Shalom Aleikhem." They

were greatly surprised at such an unexpected salute, inasmuch as they had not left the city, and were not guests, who usually are thus accosted.

The Rabbi noted their surprise and explained himself as follows: "The reason for this salutation is that I could read in your faces while you were reciting the Amidah, that you did not have in mind the meaning of the words of the prayers, but were thinking of the grain market in Odessa or the woolen market in Lodz. Now that you have returned from so long a voyage, it is appropriate for me to extend to you a welcome home."

Margoshes, J., J. M. J., Sept. 4, 1931. B., p. 456b.

4. Bounds to Good Counsel

The Disciples of the Besht were told of a certain man who was known as truly wise. There were several of the Disciples who were prompted to call upon this man in the town of his residence and to profit by his doctrine. The Master gave them leave, but they inquired: "How shall we know him for a true Zaddik?"

"Ask him to counsel you," said the Besht, "how to keep your thoughts from going astray when praying or learning. If he offers counsel, you will know that his wisdom is nought; for it is part of man's bondage, until the hour of his death, to wrestle with alien thoughts, time and again, and to subdue them in any ascent of the soul."

J. T., Dec. 19, '30; B-F.

5. The Insulted Guest

Said the Tarnigrader Rabbi: "He who worships and allows his thoughts to stray from God is like him who prepares a banquet for the king and then leaves his home."

D. E. M. R., p. 25.

6. Lip Worship

The Strelisker commented on the Sephardic version of the Amidah, reading: "For Thou hearest the prayer of every mouth." He said: "We praise the Lord for hearing our prayers, even if they come only from the mouth, and not from the heart."

E. Tz., p. 82.

7. Attention in Meditation

The Besht was asked: "If a man prays without concentration upon the meaning of the words because of foreign thoughts, should he say the prayer over?" The Besht replied: "Since even foreign thoughts contain a spark of God's Holiness, it is not fitting that a worshipper should audibly repeat his prayer. This would be a slight on the holiness of his first prayer. Let him add in meditation the attention lacking in his words, and thereby complete the holiness of the prayer."

Tif. Yeh., p. 31.

135. PREACHING

Simple Preaching and Its Uses

1. Telling Tales

The Riziner Rabbi said: "There are two ways to influence men for good. One is by sermons of a serious and profound character—when the hearers are of high intelligence. The other is by sermons of a light nature, interpolated with tales and parables—when the listeners are ordinary men and women of little learning.

"We may thus understand the verse (Song of Songs 8:8) : 'We have a little sister'; namely, an audience of but little education. 'And she has as yet no breasts'; namely, is undeveloped and immature as yet. 'What shall we do for our sister?' How shall we influence such a gathering? 'In the day': on the Sabbath or Holyday, 'she shall be spoken to'; namely, told tales." [1]

O. Y., p. 42.

[1] The Riziner makes use here of a decided paraphrase: "We have a little sister," is the Biblical verse, "and she hath no breasts; what shall we do for our sister, in the day when she shall be spoken for?"

2. Folk-Stories For the People

The Besht was narrating folk-stories to his Disciples. Noting their surprise he told them the following parable:

"A king sent his son to take charge of a fortress situated near the frontier. He informed him that the enemy was planning an attack in the near future, and instructed him to store within the fortress all food procurable. If he could not secure food of superior quality, he was to fill every storehouse with food of poor grade. Though the king's counsel did not seem necessary to him, the prince obeyed. The siege of the fort continued a long time, and the coarse food in the end proved the safeguard against surrender.

"Likewise, my friends, store in your memory those common tales I narrate to you, as well as the teachings which seem to you profound. In your work among the people everything will prove useful." [1]

M. G. I., p. 11.

[1] For comment on this item see Introductory Essay. Another version of this story is: "A king noticed that his sons cared little for the viands set before them. He ordered the left-over bread and cake to be stored in sacks. Later the enemy besieged the city, and in the ensuing scarcity of food, the left-over food was consumed with gratitude. Likewise store in your mind," said the Besht, "the popular tales and sayings which you hear from me. The time will come when you will appreciate them." M. R. T., p. 70.

3. The Popular Sermon

Said the Riziner: "Various methods were utilized by the Sages in order to prompt the people to devote earnestly a part of their time to religious thoughts. At first sacrifices were ordered to be brought before the Lord. It proved evident, however, that the pure sentiment of faith was absent, and hence prayers were substituted. These also failed oftentimes to hold the full of attention of the worshipers. It became necessary, therefore, to add sermons by the Rabbi. And it becomes the duty of the preacher to expound his message in easily understood terms, interpolated with parables and stories, clever expressions, epigrams, aphorisms, and even secular matters. Every listener seems to possess an antagonistic spirit which bids him turn away his thoughts from interest in faith and worship. But the same spirit of mischief is apparently beguiled by an effective discourse, and it fails to command loss of interest by the listener until it is too late: the religious teaching has already penetrated his mind and is retained by his memory."

N. I., p. 15.

4. The Horse Doctor

Rabbi Elimelech of Lizensk once came to the city of Nikolsburg where Rabbi Schmelke was officiating. On being asked to deliver a sermon, he said to the congregation: "Your Rabbi's method is to cure your spirit by means of delicate medicines, like the good physician. I am but a horse doctor, and I cannot do otherwise than treat you with plain and homely medicines. I must adjure you to beware of breaking the Ten Commandments: not to steal, not to bear false witness, not to covet, and the like."

S. S. K., v, 52.

5. Miracles or Sermons

The Gerer Rabbi heard that another Rabbi specialized in performing miracles. He said:

"Nowadays our people cannot be brought near to God through the working of miracles, but through appropriate sermons and ethical teachings."

S. S. K., v, 63.

6. Cutting the Earth In Vain

Said the Riziner: "We read in Psalm 141:6: 'And they shall hear my words, that they are sweet, as when one cleaveth and breaketh up the earth.' This means that when a preacher expects his listeners merely to enjoy his clever phrases, caring naught whether his words bear fruit, it is like cleaving the earth—a useless and vain process."

N. I., p. 38.

7. Parables for the Soul-Sick

Said the Pulnoer: "A man in good health when he is thirsty drinks pure water. One whose constitution is weak requires milk or wine. In the same fashion a healthy-minded man thirstily absorbs words of exhortation and reproof in a sermon, welcoming their explicit and frank message. But he whose soul is sick finds direct reproof too bitter and too personal. It is necessary for the preacher to clothe his admonition to the soul-sick in a garment of parables or tales. At the same time it is necessary to guard against the danger that those who hear, absorb merely the outer meaning and miss the inner message."

Kahana, p. 137.

8. Exhortation and Reproof

Said the Pulnoer: "It is the Rabbi's duty to exhort and reprove his congregation. If a direct reproof is displeasing to most of his congregants, he should not resort to it against their wish, and acquire thereby their enmity. In such a case, he should use words of admonition and warning found in the Torah, without adding words of his own. If his congregants then become angry, their displeasure is against the Lord Who has inspired the Torah." [1]

Kahana, p. 137.

[1] See "The Advocate"; 154 : 1.

9. Speech at a Banquet

Said the Pulnoer: "It is proper for a Rabbi or a sage to say a few words at the commencement of a banquet in order to overcome the usual tendency towards gossip, and to give a praiseworthy tone to the conversation. But some Rabbis, unfortunately, endeavour to display their erudition and enter into a learned disquisition. This method is entirely wrong. The Rabbi's purpose should be to subdue the self-satisfaction and complacency encouraged by a rich meal. But if he is himself guilty of these faults through his vanity, how can he subdue similar inclinations in others? Moreover, only a few understand his erudite references. On the other hand, if he speaks a few words of ethical and spiritual content, indirectly reproving undesirable qualities, he will doubtless meet with success."

Kahana, p. 137.

10. Secular Studies

When Rabbi Schmelke became Rabbi of Nikolsburg he preached on his first seven Sabbaths concerning seven different sciences. On the eighth Sabbath he preached on a theme related to the Torah. He explained his selection of topics as follows:

"We read in Ecclesiastes (7:5): 'It is better to hear the wise admonition from a man who understands the song of the unlearned.' [1] If I should counsel you to study the Torah rather than secular learning, you might retort that had I known the niceties of secular knowledge, I would not have offered such advice. Now, however, that you have heard I am acquainted with the sciences, and

[1] The verse reads: "It is better to hear the rebuke of the wise than for a man to hear the song of fools." Rabbi Schmelke has indulged in a paraphrase.

prefer the Torah nevertheless, you will appreciate that my counsel comes from experience."

S. ha-Tov, p. 72.

11. *Ingathering the Multitude*

A famous Rav asked the Lubliner: "Why do so many thousands come to you and not to me? I have learned more Talmud than you, and I can discourse on the Halakhah more profoundly."

The Lubliner replied: "I am likewise surprised at the multitudes who come. Who am I that thousands should seek to learn godliness from me? But perhaps they come to me because I know how little is my worth, and they do not come to you because you are surprised at their failure to come."

Niflaoth ha-Choze Lubliner, p. 23.

12. *The Lover of Money*

A Maggid addressed the congregation at Premislan and was heartily congratulated by his hearers. But after the discourse, when the Warden passed among the congregation in order to gather a sum of money for the preacher, only a small amount was donated. Before his departure from the town, the preacher went to Rabbi Meier to bid him farewell. While sitting in the Rabbi's room he observed with intense envy the piles of money given to the Rabbi by his visitors. The Rabbi noticed this and said to him:

"Every man is able to transfer some of his personality into the minds of his hearers. As for myself, I have no use for money and I receive it only to distribute it among the indigent. Therefore some of my disdain for gold is transferred to my visitors and they become generous. As for yourself, however, it appears that you love money for your personal use, and when your characteristic is transferred to your listeners, they feel the desire to retain their money for themselves, and hence they do not care to part with it." [1]

O. H., p. 21.

[1] Buber, p. 499, tells this story of the Lubliner and a wandering Maggid. The Lubliner's retort is: "Belike we both awaken in the hearts of men what we carry in our own; I, hatred of money; you, love of money."

13. *The Tailor and the Garment*

Said the Mikolayever: "In the same way that a tailor sketches the design and cuts away the extraneous material before making up a garment, so the preacher must first outline his subject of discussion, and with questions eliminate the non-essentials before he brings his analysis to a point."

E. A., p. 57.

14. The Rooster and the Goose

A preacher decided to settle in a small town. When he met the Rav of the community, he explained his purpose. The Rav was surprised and protested: "But the community pays its Rav an exceedingly small amount; how will you make a living here as well?" The Maggid narrated the following parable by way of answer: "A goose belonging to a thoughtless owner often suffered from hunger because her master forgot to feed her. One day the man bought a rooster and placed him in the same coop with the goose. The goose was greatly concerned. 'Now I shall surely starve. There are two of us to eat from my small portion.'

" 'Do not worry,' retorted the rooster, 'I can crow when I feel hungry, and this will be a reminder to our owner. Then we shall both be fed.' "

L. H. F., p. 103.

15. Short and True

The Ropshitzer was a scholar of great learning and would sometimes study a single verse for weeks. This caused him considerable difficulty when he began to preach. He commenced one of his first sermons as follows:

"It is fitting that a Rabbi always preach the truth; that he speak briefly, and that his theme be taken from the 'Sedrah.' I wish to say that I do not know what 'Sedrah' is to be read on this Sabbath. This is true; it is brief, and has the 'Sedrah' for its theme. Amen."

Ohel N., p. 29.

16. Inspired Preaching

Rabbi Joshua Belzer invited a visiting Rabbi to say a few words. The Rabbi replied: "To speak words of Torah one must receive inspiration. Moses said: 'This is the word that the Lord commanded to say.' [1] If the Lord commands one to say a word, he should speak it; otherwise he should keep silent."

P. v. K., p. 39a.

[1] Leviticus 17:2.

17. Hovering Interpretations

The Medzibozer was asked: "Why does the Zaddik in his interpretation of Biblical verses paraphrase them so decisively that he almost deprives them of their plain meaning?" The Medzibozer answered: "It is written (Gen. 1:2): 'And the spirit of God hovered over the face of the waters.' Likewise those receiving an inspiration from God, hover over the Torah, which is likened to water, coming near, but not touching it."

Butz. D., p. 28.

18. The Preacher's Reward

Said Rabbi Bunam: "We understand from the Midrash [1] that Rabbi Abuha was discouraged with his work of admonishing the people, since he found that he accomplished but little. Then he dreamed he went up to Paradise and was shown his great reward. He then applied to himself the verse (Isaiah 49:4): 'But I said: I have laboured in vain; I have spent my strength for naught and vanity; yet surely my right is with the Lord, and my recompense with my God.' It is like the counsellor or the physician who receive payment, even if they are unsuccessful, inasmuch as they have done all within their power."

S. I., pp. 71-2.

[1] Bereshith Rabba, chapter 62.

19. Belated Influence

A rich merchant came for a Sabbath to Rimanov. On Sunday the Rimanover's wife asked the Rabbi for some money, but he replied: "Wait until this wealthy merchant has taken his farewell. He will surely leave me a sizable donation." Several hours passed and the merchant failed to come. The Rabbi sent for him, and on his arrival, the merchant declared: "Rabbi, your sermon influenced me so much, I have resolved to abandon business and remain a student at the Beth ha-Midrash."

"Nay," replied the Rabbi. "This will not do. Yesterday we were in an elevated world of the spirit, and nothing mundane was required. To-day, however, we are in the world of reality, and we are in need of many things. Return, therefore, to your business, and study at your leisure."

The merchant left his donation, received the Rabbi's blessing, and took his departure.

D. D., p. 219.

20. Curses and Blessings

An itinerant preacher came to Ostroah and delivered a sermon where he showered blessings upon the inhabitants. He anticipated a goodly reward, but received only modest gifts. Incensed at this disappointment, the Maggid commenced to pour forth curses. Rabbi Eliakim Getzel halted him, and said: "How much worse than Balaam you are! Balaam sold his curses dearly but gave his blessings free. You, however, wish to be paid highly for your blessings, whereas your curses you give without payment."

D. D., p. 195.

136. PRIDE

1. Dying of Pride

A Rabbi was told that a certain man had died of hunger. "No, he died of pride," replied the Rabbi.

S. S. K., iv, 121.

2. False Pride

A young man complained to the Kobriner that he could not rid himself of pride.

"Are you very rich?" asked the Rabbi.

"No," was the answer.

"Are you a great scholar?"

"No," replied the youth.

"Do you know many foreign languages?"

"No," was the answer.

"Then," concluded the Rabbi. "What reason have to you to be proud?"

O. Y., p. 159.

3. The Conceited Student

The Gerer Rabbi said: "When a man learns the Torah, prays much and begins to think: 'I am perfect; I am truly pious; I am a Hasid; I overlook nothing in the performance of my religious duties,' he then transgresses the words (Numbers 15: 39): 'that ye go not about after your own heart, and your own eyes, after which ye are used to go astray.'"

S. S. K., ii, 51.

4. The Ball

Ere the great Maggid began to teach the two brothers, Schmelke and Pinchas, he told them how to order themselves all day long, from rising to falling asleep, and by command and prohibition made manifest his miraculous knowledge of their ways, as if they had been known to him long before. In the end he said: "Before retiring to rest at night, the Disciples of the Wise are accustomed to cast accounts of their doings during the day. And if a Disciple's heart swells within him at the thought of having made excellent use of the day, the Angels in Heaven knead all his good works into a ball, and hurl it into the abyss."

B., p. 412b.

5. Pride Within Meekness

A merchant who was a Hasid of the Riziner was proud of his apparent meekness. He began to suffer great reverses and complained to the Riziner. The Rabbi warned him to abandon his weakness of giving ostentatious display of his humility. But the merchant soon forgot this warning, and in his pride refused to ask his friends for temporary loans to bide him over the crisis. This necessitated the liquidation of his business. Still the merchant failed to alter his character, and soon after his home was burned to the ground. Instead of appealing to his friends, he left the town, and wandered from place to place. He was arrested on suspicion as a vagrant and jailed. Buried deep in his melancholy thoughts, the destitute prisoner allowed the cigarette he was smoking to fall upon his cloak and he was severely burned. In the hospital a relative visited him, and for the first time, the former merchant broke through his pride, and weeping, described his miserable state. The relative promised him assistance, and little by little the unfortunate man was able to overcome his difficulties. In the end he prospered greatly. When he next visited the Riziner, the Rabbi said: "Be sure that you maintain the mood of sincere meekness, and your success will endure."

M. G., iii, 15-16.

6. The Bratzlaver on "Pride and Humility"

A.

"1. The humble man understands that everything that happens to him happens for good.

2. The humble man is able to rid himself of materialism.

3. Pride leads to poverty.

4. Only the humble man is able truly to repent.

5. One who must fast and scourge his body is not yet a Zaddik, since he has not yet rid himself of bodily desires.

6. To overcome pride one must cleave to the Zaddikim.

7. By overcoming pride, one receives faith, joy and understanding. This also contributes to length of life.

8. The Torah itself becomes coarse in the mouth of the man of pride.

9. Because of pride were we exiled; because of pride and the quest for glory, we are still in Exile.

10. One who appears to be humble in order to win praise, is guilty of the highest degree of pride.

11. One cannot be a genuine student unless he is meek; since a student must abase himself before his teachers and his companions; at times even before his inferiors.

12. The man of meekness must beware of pride in his strength, in his riches and in his learning.

13. Meekness leads to peacefulness.

14. Pride leads to a man's fall.

15. Meekness attracts a man's fellow-man to worthy causes.

16. The man of meekness should regard himself as even more lowly than he thinks himself to be.

17. No one envies the meek or plans to injure them.

18. The leader of democratic qualities strengthens his power.

19. Pride dies with the man. Meekness survives him and will accompany him at the Heavenly Tribunal.

20. Meekness is born within every man; by drawing near to the Zaddik, it is revealed in him.

21. Severe study is required to recognize true meekness. The ne'er-do-well's humility is undesirable. Pray to the Lord to teach you how to be meek.

22. If your affairs are not well with you, meekness will restore them to strength."

L. E. H., pp. 19-21.

B.

"1. Through faith and truth a man attains humility.

2. Humility brings greatness and long life.

3. Humility removes the fear of enemies, quarrels and pains.

4. Everyone is at peace and friendly with the humble.

5. The humble has no fear of losing his leadership.

6. The soft-hearted is able to attain humility.

7. God remembers and fulfills the desire of the humble.

8. By his voice a man can be recognized as haughty or meek.

9. Messiah will come when pride will end.

10. Pride leads to drunkenness and to terror.

11. To break thy pride partake in the tribulations of Israel.

12. Pride leads to a lapse from faith.

13. Pride closes the heart and the eye from seeing God's wonders; thus it leads away from reverence for Him.

14. Good food and much drink bring pride in their train.

15. The wisdom and the inspiration of the haughty man are doomed to disappear.

16. Pride is a blemish.

17. Through faith a man can subdue pride.

18. The proud man's plans are unsuccessful.

19. A poor and lowly man who gives nothing to charity is preferable to a rich haughty man who gives to charity."

Sef. Ham., pp. 40-1; 113-115.

7. Without Foundation

Said the Bershider: "One must beware of pride, since pride needs no foundation on which to build. A man may be lying on his bed; his house may be cold; he may be covered with a torn blanket, and yet he may think in his heart: 'I am great! I am great!'"

M. P., p. 54.

8. A Play on Words

Said the Bershider: "A book on the 'Transmigration of Souls' declares that the proud man after death will become a bee. The reason a bee was chosen appears to me to be the following: an arrogant man is wont to say: 'I am a writer; I am a scholar; I am a sinner.' 'I am' in the Yiddish is 'Ich bin,' and a bee in Yiddish is a 'bin.'"

M. P., p. 54.

9. Pride and Anger

Said the Bershider: "Anger, like pride, is the chief weapon of Satan. It brings impurity to the soul and leaves not a pure thread in it. As to pride, it is the garment of the Lord.[1] He who possesses pride makes a flaw in the Lord's garments."

M. P., p. 48.

[1] Psalm 93:1.

10. God's Garment

Said the Stretiner: "The Lord clothes Himself with the pride which good people cast off" (Psalm 93:1).

E. Tz., p. 138.

11. A Greater Offense

Said the Koretzer: "A wise man was asked by his Disciples for instruction how to avoid sin. He replied: 'Were you able to avoid offenses, I fear you would fall into a still greater sin—that of pride.'"

Nof. Tz., p. 50.

12. "Yud" or "Waw"

Rabbi Bunam said: "A 'Yud' that is too big (too proud) is no longer a 'Yud.'"[1]

F. U. A. O., ii, 25.

[1] A play upon words: "Yud" or "Y" (the letter), and "Yud," Jew.

13. The Worst Pride

Rabbi Mendel Libavitzer was accustomed to say: "The worst pride is pride of piety."

F. U. A. O., ii, 91.

14. Revaluing Ourselves

Said the Zablitover Rabbi: "When you are unknown to fame, think of yourself as a mediocre person; but when you are called a Zaddik, think of yourself as wicked. You will thereby keep yourself from falling into pride."

E. A., p. 62.

15. The Extreme Point

The Savraner said: "In all traits of character it is best to walk in a middle path. The exception is in the case of pride. We should go to the extreme point, farthest from pride."

Butz. D., p. 23.

16. Pride Is Falsehood

Said the Lubliner: "The prohibition against falsehoods includes within itself an admonition against pride, since haughtiness is false.

He who is truthful in his heart and knows his own shortcomings must of necessity be humble."

Em. K., p. 58.

17. Lowering the Proud

Said the Kotzker: "The Lord brings the proud low, but the man of pride remains haughty even in his lower state; once more the Lord lowers him, and this continues until he is humbled to the very earth. On the other hand, the Lord lifts up the lowly, and he remains lowly of spirit even in his higher estate. Again he is lifted up until he attains the highest station. For this reason we say in the Hasidic Prayer Book: 'Who bringeth low to the ground the haughty, and raiseth up to the peak the lowly.'"

R. T., ii, 40.

18. The Traveler

Said the Besht: "It is so natural for a gifted man to attain pride that he scarcely is aware of it. It is only when he strives to humble himself in his intercourse with people that he realizes how full of pride he has been. It is like a man who travels in a stagecoach and falls asleep. The driver has to ascend a hill; after he reaches the summit, there is a long stretch of smooth road. When the man awakes and is told he is now on a hill, he can hardly believe it. Only when the descent is made, does he realize how high he had been."

K. S. T., p. 17a.

19. A "Perfect Character"

Said the Besht: "False humility can be illustrated by this story: 'A man was learned, gifted and charitable, but he was afflicted with the blemish of pride. He was told that if he learned humility he would become a perfect man. He acted upon this counsel, and studied humility until apparently he had learned it by heart. One day a man failed to show him deference. The man of supposed humility turned to him and said: 'You fool! Do you not know that since I have learned humility, I am a man of perfect character?'"

K. S. T., p. 23a.

20. Pride As a Hindrance

A tailor was summoned to the Count's court to measure him for a suit of clothes. The Count remarked: "I have purchased expensive cloth abroad for this suit; be careful with it." The tailor replied: "Am I not known as the best tailor in the province?"

When he returned with the suit, the Count refused to accept it, declaring it a poor fit. The tailor was perplexed and sought out Rabbi Yerachmiel for counsel. The Rabbi advised him to take the suit apart and carefully to make it again.

When the remade garment was brought to the Count, he was delighted with it and paid the tailor handsomely. On his next visit to the Rabbi, the latter explained the reason for the Count's change of opinion: "When you made up the suit first, you did so in a spirit of pride, and became careless of the details, which serve to give the master's touch to any article. The second time in a contrite mood you took especial care and therefore achieved worthy workmanship. Over-confidence and pride tend to make the best workman unsympathetic and slovenly in his labor."

Tif. B., p. 11.

137. PRODIGIES

1. Discerning a Prodigy

Rabbi Meier of Apt once saw among his visitors a youth from Vlostzov. He called his companions aside and bade them never to bring the young man again. The next time the company from Vlostzov were ready to leave for the Rabbi's home, the youth wished to join them, but they forbade. Finally they consented to permit him to travel with them as far as a village near Apt. They continued on their way and soon arrived at the home of Rabbi Meier. The latter inquired whether the youth was in their midst; the visitors explained the reason for his absence.

"Do you know why I opposed his coming to me as a Hasid?" said the Rabbi. "It is because he is a greater Zaddik than myself. When you can boast of such a youth in your native city, it is absurd for you to come to me."

The youth was compelled to become a Rebbe, and won fame as the Radomsker Rabbi.

Beth Shelomo, pp. 3-11.

2. The Slap on the Cheek

In his younger days, the Gerer studied under the Koznitzer Maggid. It happened once that the Maggid propounded before his Hasidim a certain passage in a Talmudical commentary which lacked clearness. The elderly Hasidim were unable to explain the troublesome portion. Thereupon, the young student arose and expounded correctly the knotty problem. Instead of praise, however, he received from his Master a sound slap on his cheek, and was told that even if his elders did not know a subject, it was improper for a youngster to "show off."

S. S. K., 78.

3. The Cap Aslant

In his boyhood Rabbi Mendel of Vitebsk was a student of Rabbi Dov Baer's following in Mezeritz, and was much in favor with the Master because of his great diligence in learning. Scholarship and the Master's favor went a little to his head, and his teacher noted it. One Sabbath after dinner, young Mendel paced the room with a cocky strut, his cap aslant on his head, which is against the Hasidic rule of humility. The Maggid, who was standing at the door, said: "Mendel, how many folios of the Talmud did you learn to-day?" The student said: "Six." The Maggid, with a shrewd glance at him, said: "If six folios suffice to set a cap aslant, how many will make it fall off the head altogether?"

The lad perceived that his pride had drawn reproof; he wept and vowed amendment. Rabbi Mendel used to tell this story of his early years himself, adding how the Master bade him be of good comfort, and how the remembrance of his youthful error served him through life, as a pillar of fire lighting his path.

Bl., Gem., p. 157.

4. *"He Will Be a Man"*

A youthful prodigy visited the Koznitzer Maggid and began to exhibit before the Disciples his profundity of learning. The middle-aged adherents of the Maggid jokingly belittled his talents. When the youth returned home, he complained to his father-in-law. The latter, who took immense pride in his son-in-law, laid the affair before the Maggid, saying that "those who do not reach to his knees" in learning dared ridicule the remarkable youth.

The Maggid replied: "Let me relate to you this fable. A lioness instructed her cub, saying to him: 'You need fear no living being except the man.' The young lion saw an old man, bent with age, and inquired from the mother: 'Is he dangerous?'

" 'No,' retorted the mother. 'He *was* a man.'

"The cub soon after saw a child and placed the same query.

" 'No,' answered the mother-lion. 'He *will be* a man.'

"Then a hunter, tall and powerful, appeared.

" 'This is the dangerous being,' exclaimed the lioness, and ran with her cub to their den.

"In the same fashion, your son-in-law is yet to be a man, while the Disciples are men now. It was unseemly for a youth to show off before his elders as if he were superior. Modesty becomes the young."

E. O., p. 82.

5. *"What Does the Lord Say?"*

A young scholar who was proud of his knowledge, visited the Lizensker. The Rabbi observed his conduct and wished to cure him of his arrogance. He called him over and remarked: "Young man, what does the Lord say?"

The scholar became confused by the question, and knew not what message the Rabbi wished to convey to him. The Lizensker repeated the question several times, but did not elucidate it.

When the young man came to bid the Rabbi farewell, the latter said to him: "We read (Jeremiah 23:24): 'Can any hide himself in secret places, that I shall not see him? saith the Lord.' I interpret this phrase thus: Though one hides his piety in secret, but thinks 'that I' am a scholar, a good Jew, 'I shall not look at him,' saith the Lord." [1]

Mif. H., pp. 54-55.

[1] The pronoun "I" is repeated in the Hebrew sentence. Literally it is: "I, I shall not see him."

138. PROSELYTES TO JUDAISM

1. *The Prince Who Became a Jew*

"A woman who had long yearned in vain for motherhood at last gave birth to a son; but after two years of happiness she lost the child. Thereupon the Baal-Shem told the weeping mother the story of a childless king in a distant land who had vainly consulted all his magicians on how he might secure an heir to his throne. Finally one of them advised him to forbid the Jews of his realm to exercise their faith; for only the prayers born of their despair would be able to move God to give him a son. The king issued the prohibition. The pious community was shaken with grief and terror—the dreadful cries of the Jews rose to heaven. Then one of the transfigured souls in Paradise was seized with compassion and came before God, offering to return to the nether spheres as the son of the king.

"The prince was born; but because his soul was supernal, he stood so high above all men that his father could find no teachers who would be able to do him justice,—until a stranger instructed him in the Jewish faith and he, burning with holy fervor, abandoned the palace and became a Jew.

"When, after the prince's death, the soul whose compassion had moved it to sacrifice itself for Israel stood before the divine tribunal, only a trifling charge was brought against it: that it had spent the first years of its life on earth amid the pomp and worldly vanity of the royal court. In order to atone it would have to descend to earth once more, to be nursed for two years by a pious Jewess.

"The story closes with the Baal-Shem's words to the sorrowing mother: 'Dost thou, pious woman, regret having nourished a sainted soul for two years?'"

Spiegel, pp. 157-8.

2. *The Proselyte's Persistence*

Said the Gerer Rabbi: "The Torah forbids the admission of an Ammonite or a Moabite to the congregation of Israel.[1] When Ruth came to Judea, this prohibition was told her, but she persisted in becoming a proselyte, even if the Hebrew community would not recognize the legality of her affiliation. This attitude compelled the Israelitish leaders of the time to promulgate a new interpretation of

[1] Deut. 23:4.

the Biblical law, namely that only males are excluded, but not females.

"In the future also, in Messianic times, those proselytes will not be admitted [2] who obviously seek entrance only when Israel is prosperous. But those who persist in becoming Jews, though unwelcomed by the community of Israel, will eventually force the adoption of a more liberal policy, and will later gain acceptance as Jews."

S. S. K., ii, 43.

[2] Yebamoth 24.

3. The Half-Hearted Proselyte

A Hasid came to the Tzechinover Rabbi to ask his blessing that he might draw the winning number in a lottery. The Rabbi refused and chided him for possessing an illegal lottery ticket.

The Hasid exclaimed: "But Rabbi, I have already bought it. If I win, I promise never to buy another."

The Rabbi replied: "You are like the would-be proselyte, who had already undergone circumcision and was lacking only in immersion. As he is about to enter the ritual bath, the proselyte says: 'I have a store of excellent pork left over; wait until I eat it; then I will immerse and never eat any more henceforth.'"

S. S. K., ii, 72.

4. Refusing Aid to the Traveler

Said a Rabbi: "The Torah forbids the admission into the congregation of Israel to the Ammonites and Moabites,[1] even after conversion, because they did not set bread and water before Israel when they passed through their land. The question arises: 'Perhaps they lacked sufficient resources to offer sustenance to an entire nation.' The answer is: 'Yet they employed Balaam for a large sum to curse Israel. Since they could afford to set aside a fortune in gold for Balaam, they could not give the excuse of poverty as a reason for refusing Israel bread.'"

O. I. H., p. 187.

[1] Deut. 23 : 4.

139. PROSPERITY AND SUCCESS

1. The Lord Guards Us

The Tzechiver Rabbi commented on the verse in Numbers 6:24: "The Lord shall prosper thee and guard thee." "Oftentimes," he said, "prosperity brings evil results in its train, and therefore the priests bless us, to the end that we may enjoy prosperity and avoid its resultant evils through the Lord's guardianship over us."

H. Fridling, ha-Beer, vii, part i, p. 44.

2. The Bratzlaver on "Prosperity and Success"

"1. Success comes only by the aid of Heaven.
2. Study of the Torah brings success.
3. He who divorces his wife will have no success.
4. He who speaks no vain words will succeed.
5. He who speaks the truth will find success.
6. Confession brings success."

Sef. Ham., pp. 62-3.

140. PUBLICANS AND SINNERS

1. The Future Rabbi in Taverns

When the Sassover Rabbi was a young man, he made it his custom to visit the taverns every evening, and to participate in the enjoyments of his fellow-youth. When they proposed, however, to commit a serious offense, he would dissuade them.

After he became a Rebbe, one of his former companions visited him, and perceiving the honor and reverence showered upon his former friend, he wondered greatly at the transformation of a former habitué of the public house into a man of holiness.

He pondered the matter a moment, and then walked over to the Rabbi and said to him:

"A thousand thanks unto you, Holy Rebbe, for saving me from many grievous iniquities which would have stained my soul except for you."

II. II., pp. 21-22.

141. PURIM

1. The Sanctity of Purim

Rabbi Samuel Abba of Slovita said: "There is a saying that when other memorable days are no longer observed, Purim will still be commemorated.[1] This means that all our festivals are demonstrations of God's miracles, but Purim is in commemoration of a natural event. Though we may not merit it that God deliver us in a miraculous manner, nevertheless we may still hope for aid in a natural way."

Beth Phineas, pp. 14-15.

[1] Piyyut to Sabbath Zakhor. (Special Prayers on the Sabbath Preceding Purim.)

2. The Upright Sheaf

The Gerer Rabbi said: "The twelve months are the same in number as the sons of Jacob; each month is a symbol of one of the tribes. The month of Adar represents Joseph, and inasmuch as two tribes are descended from him, we have two months of Adar in leap years. Haman held the same high position as Joseph, but when he wished to annihilate the Jews in the month of Joseph, the latter's dream was fulfilled: 'my sheaf arose and also remained standing upright' (Gen. 37:7)."

S. S. K., iii, 67.

3. Overcoming Israel's Enemies

The Kobriner was accustomed to command his Hasidim to give Purim gifts to each other, and to pay for the messengers by a special donation to the poor of Palestine.

"This is the best way to strike at Haman," said the Rabbi.

O. Y., p. 134.

4. The Common Soldier

Once on Purim the Kobriner in his youth visited the home of the Lekhivitzer Rabbi. The latter said to him: "The Talmud teaches us that to-day any one who stretches forth his hand for something, must have his request granted.[1] What shall I give to you?"

The Kobriner replied: "I wish nothing whatsoever as a gift. I desire merely to be like the common soldier who elevates himself from the ranks by virtue of his loyal service, and not through undeserved influence, exerted by others in his behalf."

O. Y., p. 55.

[1] Yerushalmi, Megillah, i, 4.

5. Drinking for a Month

The Sachatzover Rabbi was accustomed to relate this story on Purim: "In Cracow there lived a drunkard who was in the habit of drinking more than usual, a fortnight before and a fortnight after Purim. He gave the following reason: Haman was no fool. He understood that it was not possible to find all the Jews in a single day for slaughter. It would require at least a month to ferret them out of their hiding places. Hence his original plan was to devote the entire four weeks of Adar for this purpose. Later it occurred to him that if his plan miscarried, and the Jews would have occasion to celebrate their deliverance, they would enjoy a month's festivity. This Haman could not countenance, and he therefore issued an order for a single day's execution. For this reason, I deem it proper to defeat Haman's evil plan to limit our enjoyment, and I celebrate the whole month."

S. S. K., ii, 81.

6. The Lowest in Rank

Said the Belzer: "We read in the Book of Esther: 'And those next to him were Carshena, Shethar, Admatha, Tarshish, Meres, Marsena, and Memucan' (Esther 1:14). We read further (1:16): 'Then said Mumchen.' Why is his name spelled differently in these two verses?[1]

[1] In the Hebrew.

"The explanation is that though he was the last of the seven nobles, he was the first to offer his opinion, ahead of the six nobles of higher rank. And the author of the book gives us a hint as to the explanation by spelling the name: 'Mum chen,' 'a fault is this.' "

D. S., p. 106.

7. *Sir Moses Montefiore and the Gerer Rabbi*

Sir Moses Montefiore visited the Gerer Rabbi in Warsaw and discussed with him various subjects. Sir Moses complained that the Polish Jews did not learn the language of their native country. If Mordecai had been averse to the learning of languages, he declared, he would have been unable to frustrate the plot of the King's servants against their master.[1]

The Rabbi replied: "The story of Mordecai clearly indicates that the knowledge of languages was rare among Jews. Had it been known that Jews were adepts in languages, the plotters would not have spoken in Mordecai's presence. It is, therefore, preferable that only a distinguished Jew like yourself should be a linguist, and be able to place it to use for the benefit of the people."

S. S. K., i, 95.

[1] Esther 2: 21-22, as explained by Rashi.

8. *Afflicting the Mind and the Body*

Said Rabbi Bunam: "Purim is greater than Yom Kippur. On Yom Kippur we are ordered to starve our bodies, but on Purim, the Talmud [1] enjoins us to imbibe more than usual, thereby starving our minds. The affliction of the mind is greater than the affliction of the body."

S. S. K., ii, 17.

[1] Megillah 7.

9. *Purim and Yom Kippur*

One Purim many Hasidim assembled at Medziboz in order to celebrate the joyful day in company with their Rabbi. Rabbi Baruch, however, was depressed of mood and spoke no word. The Hasidim were greatly dismayed: they had hoped to see their Master in good spirits at least on this day, so that out of this joy a stream of happiness and heavenly grace might pour forth over the world.

Yet the spirit of sadness had overwhelmed him and he sighed deeply. His heart was troubled, and therefore the waggish Hirsch Ostropoler had to be called to the holy chamber.

"Rabbi," he said, "tell me, I beg of you, how does it chance that the sacred Day of Atonement on which the Jew must castigate his body, is called 'Yom K'Purim,' a 'Day like Purim'? Has our holy Torah no nobler designation to give to this honorable and serious day, than to compare it with the unrestrained and cheery Purim day when every Jew may be drunk?"

The Rabbi looked at him and said in a low tone of voice: "I do not know; tell me!"

"It is all very simple," answered the rogue. "It is because on both of these days the Jews change places: on Purim Jews conduct themselves as Gentiles; on the Day of Atonement, however, Gentiles conduct themselves as Jews, since they visit the synagogue and act with piety."

The Rabbi raised his eyes and gazed at Hirsch for a moment; then a gentle smile came over his countenance.

Then for the first time the Hasidim sang the Purim melody: "The Lily of Jacob Rejoiced." [1]

[1] Singer, p. 277.

Bl., Br., pp. 111-12 (F).

10. The Day After Purim

On the day following Purim, the Porissover would call the poor to his home early in the morning and distribute money to them. He gave as his reason the following: "Because it is a special Mitzwah to make gifts to the poor on Purim, every one neglects this Mitzwah on the next day; and I deem it an excellent deed to perform a neglected Mitzwah."

D. Z., p. 32.

11. The Scroll of Esther

The sons of the Belzer were away from home on Purim. One of them, Rabbi Eleazar, remarked: "How I miss the reading of the Megillath Esther by our father!"

The other, Rabbi Joshua, said: "To-day we have performed the Mitzwah in perfection. While at home, we hear the Megillah not only because it is a Mitzwah, but also because we take pleasure in our father's reading of it. Mitzwoth and pleasure may not be combined if the true spirit of performing a Mitzwah is to be maintained."

P. v. K., p. 41a.

12. Preparation for Holy Days

Rabbi Eleazer, the son of the Lizensker, commented on the Talmudical statement that Haman informed Ahasuerus that the Jews neglected their duties to the King because they professed to be occupied throughout the entire year with their religious duties. When asked to do their share of work for the King, they offered the excuse: "To-day is the Sabbath"; "To-day is Passover." [1]

"But how do the Sabbath and Passover constitute the entire year? The answer is that during all the days of the week they busy themselves with preparations for the Sabbath and the Festivals."

E. Tz., p. 33.

[1] Megillah 13. The Talmud has the words in initials: "Sahay Pehay"; and Rashi gives them in full: "Sabbath hayom, Pesach hayom."

142. QUARRELS AND CONTROVERSIES

1. Angels and Mortals

The Gerer Rabbi recounted the allegory in the Talmud [1]: "When the Creator desired to create man, He asked the advice of the Angels. Some favored, others opposed the plan. [2] Then, added the Rabbi, the Lord exclaimed: 'Since even Angels have differences, why not create man?'"

S. S. K., i, 131.

[1] Sanhedrin 38.
[2] On the plea that men would engage in strife.

2. Opposition to the Great

The Mezeritzer said: "Let no one be discouraged by violent opposition. Brigands attack the one who carries jewels on his person, not the one who drives a wagon-load of fertilizer. Like the carrier of gems, we must be prepared to repel our assailants."

M. R. T., p. 34.

3. Only Experts Decide

Rabbi Nachman Kossover was once an adversary of the Besht. One day he overheard several commoners talking against the Besht, and he related to them the following story:

"Two jewelers of renown were working on a royal crown. A dispute arose between them regarding the proper place for a certain gem. A passer-by ventured to express his concurrence with the opinion of one of the artists. Both rebuked him, saying: 'If we have an argument, it is because we have trained ourselves to be experts in the art of fashioning crowns. But how is it that you, who apparently know nothing of this art, venture to express an opinion?'"

Kahana, p. 54.

4. The Lion's Trap

When the Tzanzer and the Sadigurer Rabbis indulged in a long-standing quarrel, many of the Dzikover Hasidim began to take sides. Their Rabbi, Rabbi Meier, read to them the following fable from the "Yalkut":

"A lion was compelled to forego food so long that the breath of his mouth was no longer sweet. He met an ass, and said to him: 'Place your head near my mouth and tell me if my breath is sweet.' The ass did so and reported unfavorably.

"'How dare you insult me?' exclaimed the King of Beasts, and promptly slew and ate him.

"A few days later he encountered a wolf, and put the same question to him. The wolf replied favorably. 'How dare you lie to me?' roared the lion, and devoured him also.

"Later he questioned a fox, but the shrewd animal was not to be caught in the trap. 'I am sorry,' said the fox to the lion. 'I have a catarrh, and I cannot smell.'

"Acquire for yourself," said Rabbi Meier to the Hasidim, "a convenient catarrh and you will be saved from the lion."

O. N., p. 49.

5. Leaders in Confusion

Rabbi Bunam was the favorite disciple of the "Yud" and was privileged to sleep in the Master's anteroom. One night he heard the Master sighing and sobbing at short intervals until the hour of dawn, when he made inquiry regarding his distress. The "Yud" answered: "I am sore aggrieved at the thought of those who are the leaders of Israel in our own days. After Moses came the Judges; after the Judges the Prophets; after the Prophets the Men of the Great Synagogue; then the Tannaim and the Amoraim, and after them the Zaddikim. To all of these who have gone before us, the people look for guidance. But to whom are they to look for guidance now, when the Zaddikim have lost the way, and all is in confusion?"

Nif. Yeh., p. 46 (Bl., Gem., p. 266).

6. The Satan in the Quarrels

Rabbi Bunam explained the origin of the controversies between the adherents of the numerous Hasidic groups, by means of the following allegory:

"The Baal Shem left a tradition that with him began the tenth and last form of leadership in Israel prior to the Advent of the Redeemer. They were: 1. Prophets. 2. Judges and Elders. 3. Kings. 4. Priests. 5. Patriarchs.[1] 6. Tannaim. 7. Amoraim. 8. Gaonim. 9. Rabbis. 10. Zaddikim.

"The Satan asked in Heaven for an explanation of the leadership of the Zaddikim, inasmuch as every Jew should be a Zaddik. It was explained to him that there are many Hasidic groups, and that each group has a teacher in Godliness, whom they name the Zaddik. The Satan was vastly distressed, and feared that his plans and projects would utterly collapse. But his fertile mind quickly came to the rescue. He instigated jealousies among the various groups. Now the Hasidim in our group malign and deride the leaders of other groups, and they believe it to be a worthy act."

S. S. K., iv, 39.

[1] The Patriarchs are supposed to be the Chief Justices of the Sanhedrin.

7. The Jealous Adversary

Rabbi Moses Teitelbaum, the Oheler, had been in his youth a wrathful enemy of Hasidic doctrine, which, according to his opinion, was the worst of heresies. One day he stopped at the house of his friend, Rabbi Joseph Asher, who was, like himself, an adversary of the Hasidic innovations. In those days the Prayerbook, according to the Sage, Rabbi Isaac Luria, whose word had been a precursor and foreheralding of the Hasidic doctrine, had appeared in print. When the book was handed to the two teachers, Rabbi Moses tore the bulky volume out of the messenger's hands, and hurled it upon the floor. But Rabbi Asher lifted it up, saying: "After all, it is a Prayerbook, and should not be handled disdainfully."

When word of this was brought to the Lubliner, he prophesied: "Rabbi Moses will turn Hasid, but Rabbi Asher never. For he who burns this day with enmity, will burn to-morrow with love of God, but the road is closed to him whose hatred is cold."

And it came to pass in truth as the Lubliner had foretold.

B., p. 476 m.
Reflex, May, 1929, p. 67.

8. Insincere Peace

Said the Lubliner: "Better is an insincere peace than a sincere quarrel."

F. U. A. O., i, 229.

9. Unworthy to Interfere

Two men quarreled on the thoroughfare and one struck the other. The Zbarazer was importuned to stop the quarrel. He replied: "I am unworthy to interfere in a quarrel between men who may be greater Zaddikim than I am."

S. H. H., chap. 4.

10. Quarrels and Insults

Whenever the Bershider heard of a domestic quarrel, he would repair to the home and make peace between husband and wife.

Once a man read to him from a Hebrew book that we should love non-Jews since God had created them. This pleased him immensely.

A man insulted the Rabbi. The latter extended him his hand and thanked him for the opportunity to practice his preachment, namely, to receive abuse with undisturbed mien.

M. P., p. 44.

11. Every War a Holy War?

The author of "Kol Omer Kera" said: "We read in a Midrash that Cain and Abel quarreled for the reason that each wished to establish the Holy Temple on his land. This excuse ever since has been brought forward for every shedding of blood and for every war. It is always maintained that the fight is on behalf of a holy purpose."

F. U. A. O., i, 16.

12. Prepared for More

The Vorker and a friend were traveling on a stage coach during their younger days. His friend complained that the driver hurried and insulted them when they wished to pray earnestly. "How can you bear this so calmly?" asked the Vorker's friend. "The reason is that I was prepared for even more insolence and abuse than we are receiving."

D. Z., p. 50.

13. Words of Kindness

The "Yud's" wife was high-tempered and often quarreled with him. The "Yud" would never answer back with a single word. Once, however, when his wife harassed him more than ever, he replied with a few words. Rabbi Bunam asked him: "Why have you departed from your custom of not answering?"

"Because I perceived that my wife's greatest vexation lay in the fact that I did not concern myself with her nagging," replied the "Yud." "The few words which I addressed to her were truly a kind deed."

D. Z., p. 52.

14. Accusations to Fit the Person

Rabbi Bunam learned that he had been accused of a misdeed. He turned to his Hasidim and said: "Usually accusations fit the persons accused. A person of low estate is accused of a low crime; a distinguished man of a higher offense. When Joseph's brothers were accused of stealing the goblet, Judah exclaimed: 'A person like me you accuse of stealing?' I may say the same: of all possible accusations, they accuse me of a crime entirely unsuited to my character!" [1]

S. I., p. 61.

[1] Genesis 44:18 begins Judah's speech in Hebrew with the words "Bi," "Me."

15. Self-Satisfaction and the Law

The Alexanderer Rabbi suffered much from a certain opponent. The Hasidim advised him to proclaim an edict of excommunication against his adversary, and assured him that if he should be fined by a non-Jewish court for this act, they would pay the fine. The Rabbi replied: "It is true that according to Jewish law my opponent deserves excommunication; but it should be pronounced only on condition it is for the Lord's sake, inasmuch as He desires that an example should be made of those who abuse a scholar. How can I be sure, however, that my motive will be as pure as the law requires? Perhaps some satisfaction for my own sake will be mingled therewith?"

Sh. Z., p. 40.

16. Unreasoning Hostility

The Ropshitzer said: "Moses led the life of a hermit and established his tent outside the camp. As a consequence his critics condemned him for exclusiveness and aloofness. Aaron, on the other hand, took pains to pacify all who quarreled and went freely among the people. He was, in his turn, condemned for being too democratic and unmindful of his high position. The opponents of a good man will blame him, no matter what his behavior." [1]

E. Tz., p. 97.

[1] See Fleg, *Life of Moses*, p. 131.

17. The Tribulations of the Ladier

As Told by a Ladier Hasid

A. *The First Battle*

"When Samael [1] learned that the Ladier had achieved great success in disseminating Hasidism in Lithuania and White Russia, he resolved to combat him by arousing quarrels. He induced some Hasidim to become over-enthusiastic, to shout their prayers, insult students, dance on the street and roll on the ground. This aroused the anger of the Gaon.[2] The Samael further induced false informers to declare that the Hasidim turned the 9th of Ab into a day of rejoicing, in imitation of the adherents of the Sabbatai Zevi.

Forgetting that the 9th of Ab chanced to fall on a Sabbath that year, when no mourning is permissible, the Gaon excommunicated the Hasidim without listening to their defense. For this, the Gaon was summoned to the Heavenly Tribunal to give an account of his action. Samael had lost the first battle."

Beoh. H., pp. 22-5.

[1] The name given to the Satan in mystical literature.
[2] Elijah Wilna Gaon, the great Rabbinic opponent of Hasidism.

B. *The Second Battle*

"Twenty-five years after the death of the Gaon, the Samael renewed the battle by inducing Rabbi Avigdor of Pinsk to become an informer to the Czar—an unheard-of thing. The Ladier was accused of disloyalty and imprisoned in a Petersburg fortress.

"It was decided in Heaven that only the Czar himself was great enough to release the holy prisoner. The Governor of the fort went into the Rabbi's cell and beheld a sight which stunned him. When he had recovered, he reported to the Czar Paul that a divine light had illumined the cell, and that divine voices had chanted in it. The Czar likewise visited the Ladier's cell and also beheld a vision which left him powerless to move. It was like unto the rays of divinity which Moses received from the Most High. The Czar found his voice at last and asked the Holy Man if God speaks to mortals to-day as of yore. 'Surely,' replied the Rabbi. 'Daily His Voice asks: 'What, O man, hast thou accomplished this day? Hast thou done thy daily task whereby thou art entitled to live?' The Czar freed the Ladier, and the Samael thus lost the second battle."

Beoh. H., pp. 25-32.

C. *The Third Battle*

"The Ladier was freed on the 19th day of Kislev, 1799, just as he was chanting the verse: 'He delivereth my soul in peace from the battle against me' (Psalm 55:19). Once more, however, the Samael commenced his nefarious work. He induced a Jew, a fanatical opponent, to invite the Ladier to his home for a glass of tea, and to threaten his death unless he swore to abandon Hasidism and its teaching. A passing Hasid heard the Rabbi's groan, broke open the door, and was about to stab the fanatic. The Rabbi prevented this, and wishing to show his pardon, asked for the glass of tea, even before the fanatic repented. This was a wrong step, and the Samael won a minor skirmish.

"As an atonement, it was decreed in Heaven that the Ladier should be imprisoned a second time. The Czar ordered that he be brought in chains. The Ladier said: 'Since the Emperor knows my innocence and treats me like a criminal, death will overtake him shortly.' The Crown Prince Alexander also visited the Holy Man, and he, too, beheld a vision. As soon as he became Czar, he freed the Rabbi."

Beoh. H., pp. 33-46.

18. *The Bratzlaver on "Quarrels and Discords"*

A.

"1. A man should also seek the good in another and judge every man in the scale of merit; this applies even to those who abuse and quarrel with him. Thus he will never be embroiled in quarrels, and will thereby fashion a crown for the Lord containing many priceless jewels.

2. He who heeds not insults, abuse, or strife against himself, performs the true act of repentance and self-correction. He is truly wise and attains honors from the Lord.

3. He who is as yet unclean and has not purified himself of inclination towards evil, must not interfere with the wicked or enter into quarrel with them.

4. The greater a man's understanding, the further does he remove himself from quarrels.

5. Sometimes a man pays no attention to his opponent in order to vex him the more by his silence. There is no holiness in this behavior. If you understand that a soft answer will calm your foe, do not withhold it from him.

6. When a man quarrels with you, do not imitate him, for then your opponent will discover that he spoke the truth concerning you. Revenge yourself through kind deeds towards him, and it will be proved that he lied.

7. Poverty and illness follow in the train of discord.

8. Bear in mind that life is short, and that with every passing

day, you are nearer to the end of your life. Hence how can you waste your time on petty quarrels and family discords? Restrain your anger; hold your temper in check, and enjoy peace with every one."

L. E. H., pp. 59-62.

B

"1. The side which breaks a truce in a war is destined to lose.

2. When a man pursues another to injure him, God directs tribulations against the pursuer.

3. When you remember the poor, victory will be yours.

4. The man who stubbornly rejects proof that he is wrong, is forgotten by God.

5. The stubborn man becomes forgetful.

6. If a man does not accept the opportunity to perform a Mitzwah, he will find a quarrel on his hands.

7. He who has enemies should submit, and God will save him.

8. When a man seeks to the utmost for ways to love his enemies, their enmity disappears.

9. When a man does not think of his enemies, but cleaves to the Lord in joy, they will be rendered harmless.

10. Incurable diseases come to the stubborn.

11. He who honors the aged will be saved from controversies.

12. Quarrels bring poverty.

13. He who quarrels with his neighbors will become an object of derision in their eyes.

14. He who keeps silence in the face of abuse is a true Hasid.

15. He who has led a good life will find many allies in a controversy.

16. If you confess your errors, you will banish enmity.

17. If you have trust, it will be impossible for your enemies to injure you.

18. Submission will frequently cause your enemies to fall into the trap which they have laid for you.

19. If you have trust, your enemies will not rejoice over your tribulations.

20. He who shames not his fellow-man will not be put to shame by his enemies.

21. He who has faith fears not his enemies.

22. Even thy friends will quarrel with thee if thou fallest into sadness.

23. Even though a quarrelsome man be learned, show him no honors.

24. Where there is quarreling, there the Satan is to be found.

25. Through prayer, Torah and kind deeds, a man will see the downfall of his enemies.

26. Always give succor to the persecuted.

27. The world stands firm because of the man who closes his lips during a quarrel.

28. He who suffers hurt in silence will see God espouse his cause.
29. He who is able to halt wickedness and fails to do so, is considered as if he performed the evil himself.
30. Unfounded hate multiplies quarrels.
31. There are many famous men whose fame has come to them through controversies."

Sef. Ham., pp. 87-95.

19. Black and White Roosters

In the revolutionary years of 1848 and 1849, the Hasidim were the objects of heavy persecutions on the part of the populace. They assembled in the Riziner's home. Rabbi Hayyim Kossover exclaimed: "We must defend ourselves; we cannot act like roosters."

The Riziner replied: "White roosters, according to the tale, once met to discover a way to abolish the custom of choosing their fellows for the meal after Yom Kippur.[1] An old rooster remarked: 'Let us fly to the roof through the chimney, and our feathers will become black. Thus we shall be saved.' As for ourselves, let us take off our white silk garments and intermingle with the public. Then we will not be singled out as targets for their persecution."

D. D., p. 309.

[1] White, according to Isaiah 1, is the symbol for sinlessness and forgiveness.

20. The Silk Belt

Rabbi Bunam's teaching of rationalism and learning prompted many of his adherents to ridicule the opposite qualities among adherents of other Zaddikim. A Hasid of the Apter Zaddik received from him a snow white silk belt as a charm against recurring misfortunes. His neighbor, a Disciple of Rabbi Bunam, in ridicule of the charm, once dyed it black by stealth, thereby destroying its virtue, according to the believers.

M. E. H., i, 42.

21. The Sabbath-Breaking Cow

Rabbi Bunam's new system greatly vexed the Apter, and the latter remarked to a Hasid of his opponent, that a leader is responsible for the conduct of his adherents. Therefore Rabbi Bunam should be condemned for the unseemly acts of his Disciples. "We find in the Talmud," [1] he added, "that a Tanna was blamed for a cow of his neighbor which carried a load on the Sabbath, contrary to the Fourth Commandment, inasmuch as the Tanna had authority over his neighbor."

Rabbi Bunam's Hasid answered: "In Apt, your Hasidim dared to insult my Rebbe, Rabbi Bunam. Is it permissible to insult a scholar?"

[1] Sabbath 54.

"But I knew it not," retorted the Apter.

Quick as a flash, the Hasid exclaimed: "But, Rabbi, the cow!"

M. E. H., i, 42.

22. Leaves of the Trees

Rabbi Simon Deutsch was a conservative Hasid and greatly opposed any new system. He was responsible for the disagreement between the "Seer" and the "Yud" and later sought to break the friendship of the Apter and Rabbi Bunam. The Apter refused to listen to him, and said: "I believe that if you were alone in a forest with no man to engage in quarrel, you would enter into an argument with the leaves on the trees."

M. E. H., i, 42.

23. The Defamation of Enemies

The Kotzker's last twenty years were passed in solitude. Very rarely did he venture forth from his home, and it was only on exceptional occasions that he saw his Hasidim and spoke a few words. The enemies of the Kotzker disseminated false rumors regarding him, and cast doubt upon his sanity. The Gerer Rabbi comforted the distracted Disciples of the Kotzker, and said: "From the defamations by our enemies we may truly learn our Rebbe's greatness and influence. Were his system commonplace, it would not provoke such fervent opposition. Let us adhere loyally to his teachings."

M. E. H., i, 69.

143. THE RABBI (CALL TO BE)

1. Unsolicited Offers

The Radishitzer Rabbi told the following tale: "A friend of mine came to me for counsel whether he should accept a certain call to be Rabbi. I asked him: 'Have you solicited this call?' His reply was in the negative. 'Then,' said I, 'accept it, but always act in accordance with your conscience, and Heaven will guard you. Let me narrate to you my own experiences. On my way home from visiting my Rabbi, a rich Hasid proposed that I become tutor to his children. 'This suggestion is from Heaven,' said I to myself, and accepted the offer. I made no request for payment, leaving it to the will of Heaven, and the Hasid sent sufficient money to my family. After two years, my services were no longer needed, and I settled in Radishitz. I studied constantly in the synagogue and became known as a 'Batlan.'

"Once a neighbor's child became grievously ill. The mother gave me some money to pray for her son's recovery. The boy regained his health, and other persons came to me with their tribulations. In this way I became a Rebbe. If it had not been the will of the Lord that you should become a Rabbi, the call would not have been extended to you."

L. S., pp. 21-26.

2. Prevailing Against God's Will

When a vacancy occurred in the position of Rabbi at Pressburg, a call was extended to Rabbi Isaac Harif of Sambor. The letter was received by the community secretary, who gave it to the President of the community. The two resolved not to show the offer to their Rabbi, so that he should not leave Sambor for the much larger city. Receiving no reply, the Pressburg community sent their offer to Rabbi Meshullam Igro of Tismenitz. Hearing that the Samborer Rav had been the first choice, Rabbi Igro went to Sambor to investigate the reason for his failure to accept the call. Rabbi Harif denied ever receiving the communication. The President was compelled to admit his offense. Rabbi Igro proposed to yield to Rabbi Harif since the latter had not declined the position, but Rabbi Harif refused the proffer, declaring that if it had been God's will for him to become Rabbi at Pressburg, no human intervention would have availed to prevent it.

H. H., pp. 3-10.

3. Impatient to Lead

The Ropshitzer heard that Rabbi Zevi Elimelech of Dinov had become a Rebbe. In great displeasure the Rabbi remarked that the Dinover had acted foolishly. When pressed for an explanation, the Ropshitzer said: "Every leader is allotted by Heaven a term of service lasting for a certain number of years. Had the Dinover waited to commence his term at a more mature age, he would have enjoyed a longer life.'"

It happened exactly as the Rabbi had surmised: the Dinover was summoned by death while still young.

E. Tz., p. 89.

4. Moses in the Spirit

Said the Koretzer in comment on the verse: "And Moses spoke in the ears of all the assembly of Israel the words of this song until they were finished" (Deut. 31:30): "And Moses speaks the words of his Torah to all Israel until the end of all generations. Every teacher in Israel is Moses in the spirit."

Nof. Tz., p. 53.

5. Love Work, Not Lordship

Said the author of "Lev ha-Ivri": "We read in the 'Ethics of the Fathers' (1:10; Singer, p. 185): 'Love work and hate lordship.' This means that if a man accepts a call to a rabbinical post, he must consider as the reason for his acceptance his love of endeavor on behalf of the community's spiritual betterment, not his love for lordship and authority."

D. E. M. R., p. 90.

144. RABBI, COUNSEL BY THE

1. The Rabbi's Good Sense

About a hundred years ago there was a Polish rebellion against Russia. Some of the rebels came to a rich Hasid near Radomsk and demanded that he buy for them hay and food. The Hasid refused to do so, and the rebel leaders condemned him to death. The Radomsker Rabbi was notified and he sent a messenger to the leader, asking permission for the Hasid to ransom his life by giving the rebels all his money. The leader agreed.

When the Hasid came to the Rabbi he told him that by chance he had had a large sum of gold in the house and the rebels had seized the entire amount. The Radomsker pondered for a moment and said:

"Since the sum is so large, a record of it will be kept in the treasury office of the rebels. Hence you may hope to receive it back."

This shrewd surmise proved correct. When the Russians captured the treasury of the rebels they found the money intact with the entry that the Hasid had been fined this sum for refusing to aid them. The Czar was informed of the incident, and he returned the entire sum to his loyal subject.

H. H., pp. 27-31.

2. The Cripple on the Lonely Road

A merchant came to the Apter Rabbi and asked his blessing for his trip to a foreign city. The Rabbi said: "Follow this counsel: if a healthy pedestrian should stop your coach and ask you for a ride, you may give it to him; but if a lame one should do so, do not halt, but drive on as quickly as possible."

The merchant did not understand the reason for this bizarre advice, but resolved to obey it, because of his thorough confidence in his Rabbi's wisdom. When he was on a lonely road, a lame man limped towards him and shouted a request to be given a ride. The merchant instructed the driver to hasten the gait of the horses. Then he looked back and saw the supposed cripple drop his crutches and point a musket at him. Fortunately the carriage was too far ahead already, and the bullet failed of aim. On his return home, the Rabbi explained to him the reason for his counsel: a healthy man may be expected to be a poor but honest wanderer, whereas a lame man has no business to walk out of a town, relying upon rides he may solicit. In all probability, he may be a disguised brigand, as the merchant's experience had proved.

N. Haz., pp. 24-25.

145. "REBBE," RABBI AND "RAV"

1. The Word "Rabbi"

In the Hasidic book: *Sifthei Zaddikim* the word "Rabbi" is interpreted through its initials. If one who becomes a Rabbi is sincere and dutiful, he is the "*R*evered of the *B*egotten of *I*srael. If he, however, is insincere and neglectful of his duties, then he becomes "*R*epellent (to those) *B*eholden (by) (the) *I*mmortal (One).[1]

S. B., p. 15.

[1] There is here a play upon words:

רבי = ראש בני ישראל

or   רבי = רע בעיני יי

2. The Rebbe and Mortal Desires

The Rozdoler Rabbi was asked: "Wherein does the desire to become a Rabbi differ from other desires?"

He replied: "Before one attains the desire to become a Rebbe, he must break himself of every other desire."

E. K., p. 61.

3. The Rav and the Rebbe

When the Rozdoler was a student of Rabbinical law, he observed a fellow-student endeavoring to imitate the Rebbe in the hope of learning to become one. He took him aside and earnestly counseled him to abandon the effort as futile, and to apply himself to study instead. He argued as follows:

"One who intends to become a Rav may properly announce the fact, and if he is needy, he may request aid. But one who wishes to become a Rebbe must keep his special piety to himself. The student of Jewish law knows when he has matured, but the Rebbe has no curriculum and his work is never finished. The student may be tested to determine whether he is sufficiently learned to be a Rav, but a Rebbe cannot be examined as to his fitness. Only by hearing a divine command may one truly announce himself as a Rebbe. The matured student induces only a single community to select him as its Rav, but the Rebbe must extend his influence over many communities, and his livelihood is a difficult problem. Finally a Rav who feels the urge to teach godliness has the opportunity to commence with his own community. If his work is successful, he becomes renowned, and attracts adherents eager to learn from him. But one who is not a Rav rarely finds listeners to his teachings."

E. K., p. 64.

4. Gaon and Zaddik

The Volozhiner Rav disliked the Hasidim intensely. Once he said: "Our Rav is called 'Gaon'; a Hasidic Rebbe is called 'the Zaddik.' The first is like a headache; the second like a stomach-ache.

When a little boy wishes to play truant from school, and complains of a headache, his mother feels his forehead, and if it is not hot, she sends him to school. But when he complains of a stomach-ache she has no choice but to believe him.

"Likewise, when a man claims to be a Gaon, we can examine him, and determine whether he is a great scholar in rabbinical learning. But when a man claims to be a Zaddik, there is no way to prove it; it is only a matter of belief."

M. D., p. 48.

5. Is a Rebbe a Gaon?

Rabbi Enzel of Stry observed a fellow-Rabbi writing a letter to the Strelisker Rebbe with the address: "To the Gaon of Strelisk, my Teacher." "Why do you address the Rebbe as Gaon?" he asked. "Only those proficient in Rabbinical law merit this title. The Hasidic Rabbis, as a rule, are proficient only in ethical instruction."

Rabbi Ziskind, the writer, replied: "The title 'Gaon' implies a thorough knowledge of the Torah. A young pupil understands merely the superficial meaning of a commandment of the Torah, whereas the Gaon knows its deeper significance and its application in practice. Though you may be properly styled a Gaon for your thorough knowledge of the Halakhah, the practical law, you are still on the level of the young pupil in your understanding of the Spiritual Law. My teacher, the Strelisker, is a Gaon in the Spiritual Law. If you wish evidence of this, it can be secured if you will discuss with him such commandments of the Torah as: 'to love God; to fear God, and to cleave to God.' [1] His explanations and his teachings will amaze you."

O. O., pp. 32-33.

[1] Deut. 30 : 20, paraphrased.

6. Rebbe and Hasidim

Rabbi Israel Salanter said: "Both the Hasidim and their opponents are in error: the opponents for thinking that they do not need a Rebbe, and the Hasidim for believing that they have a Rebbe."

J. M. J., "Series of Great Jews," by Masliansky.

7. Deserving the Title

When the Kotzker heard that the Radomsker had become a Rebbe, he said: "Rabbi Shelomo is surely deserving of the title: 'Rebbe.' There is a saying: 'Words which emerge from the heart of one man enter into the heart of others.' My explanation is: Before one may reprove a fellow-man, he must first be certain that the misdeed which he corrects in others cannot find a place in his own heart. This is the case with the Radomsker."

Niflaoth Tifereth Shelomo, p. 32.

8. Knowing the Rabbi's Ways

The Berditschever Rabbi and his disciple, Rabbi Aaron Zitomirer, once visited Rabbi Elimelech of Lizensk. The Lizensker said: "Why do you draw away my disciples? Many have left me to go to your city."

"But Rabbi," exclaimed the Berditschever, "am I not myself your disciple? And are not, then, my disciples the disciples of your disciple?"

This reply appeased the Lizensker.

After the Berditschever had departed, his companion Rabbi Aaron remained in Lizensk. Rabbi Elimelech inquired why he did not accompany his Rabbi.

"Oh, I know my Rabbi's ways already," was the reply. "Now I wish to learn your methods."

"What!" exclaimed the Lizensker. "You know your Rabbi? Why, you do not even know correctly his outer-jacket!"

Kahana, p. 247.

9. The Rabbi's Fee

A woman came to the Ropshitzer, laid a sum of money on the table as her "Pidyon," and talked without interruption for an hour. When she had finally left, the Rabbi's brother, Rabbi Yokele, remarked: "How can you listen to so long a tirade in patience?"

The Ropshitzer smiled, and said: "That is how I earn my own 'pidyon.'" [1]

O. N., p. 58.

[1] "Pidyon" means "Fee" or "Redemption Money."

10. The Pseudo-Rabbi

Rabbi Bunam asked his Disciples the following question: "The Talmud teaches us that one who simulates blindness in order to obtain additional charity really becomes blind.[1] Hence it seems logical to assume that one who simulates the state of being a Rebbe should really become a Rebbe. Wherein, therefore, does the punishment lie in his case for counterfeiting a Rebbe?"

No one of the Disciples could give a reply.

Rabbi Bunam thereupon related this parable: "A rich Protestant desired to make fun of the ignorance of the Catholic priests at the time of Luther. Seeing a drunken peasant on the ground, he ordered his servants to carry the sot into his home. He then purchased priestly vestments and laid them out in the bedroom where the drunkard was carried. He also instructed his servants to address the peasant as 'Father.' When the peasant awoke, he rubbed his eyes in amazement at the furnishings of the home in which he found himself. He believed he was dreaming, but inasmuch as the servants addressed him as a priest, and clothed him in priestly garments, he

[1] Mishnah Peah, chap. 8, last paragraph.

began to think that his recollection of having been a peasant was a dream. He bethought himself of another proof, and ordered that the Vulgate be brought him. He discovered he could not read it, and again began to doubt himself. But he soon reminded himself that he had heard many priests were illiterate. This convinced him and henceforth he paraded as a priest, to the vast merriment of the Protestants.

"It is the same with the false Rebbe. He cannot read the Holy Books and he thinks that others are as ignorant as he is himself. This leads him to neglect opportunities to learn from others who have knowledge, and to seek the advice of true Rabbis. Hence he dies unrepentant, and is subject to severe punishments."

N. R. B., ii, 31-35.

11. The Four Heads

When the Lizensker died, his Disciples desired to accept Rabbi Sussya as their Master. Rabbi Sussya, however, refused and said: "We read: 'And a river went out of Eden to water the garden, and from thence it was parted, and became four heads' (Gen. 2:10). The Besht is the Eden; the Great Maggid is the river that went out to water the garden, namely, my brother Elimelech; and there it was parted and became four heads, namely, the Lubliner, the Rimanover, the Koznitzer, and the Apter. They no longer need a Master."

Ohel N., p. 132.

12. Judgment Regarding Greatness

Rabbi Zevi Margulis, son of Rabbi Joseph, succeeded his father as Rabbi of Yazlivitz at the age of sixteen, and was Rabbi in the same town for eighty-four years. He lived to the age of one hundred years (1637-1737). His son, Rabbi Meir, became a disciple of the Besht, before the latter won renown.

When his father asked him what he saw in the Besht, he replied: "He is wiser and more pious than any one in the whole world."

Nif. Yeh., p. 91.

13. Attracting Real Scholars

The Lubliner Rav was a vigorous opponent of the Lubliner Rebbe because he did not devote sufficient time to the study of the Torah. When the great Talmudical scholar, the Oheler, visited the Lubliner Rebbe, he was invited by the Rav to speak in his synagogue. After the discourse, the Rav accosted the Oheler, and said: "How can you, a real scholar, find anything of real merit in the Hasidim and their Rebbe?"

The Oheler answered: "Think of it from the other angle, my dear Rav! How great the Rebbe must be, that he can attract to himself real scholars!"

P. v. K., p. 10b.

14. The Rav's Rejoinder

Rabbi Ezekiel Landau of Prague, according to the tale, once sojourned in the same town where the Besht chanced to be. They both met in the synagogue. A chicken was brought in to the Praguer Rabbi for his judgment as to its "kashruth." The Rav examined it and pronounced it "kasher." The Besht agreed with this opinion. Rabbi Ezekiel was surprised and said: "But you have not examined it!" The Besht answered: "I can see a spiritual vision of holiness on this bird. Were it 'terephah,' a vision of uncleanliness would hover over it."

Rabbi Ezekiel, a great opponent of mysticism, then laughingly remarked: "I understand now the meaning of the Talmudical passage [1] which tells that in times to come, a woman will bring a loaf of holy bread to the synagogue to inquire whether it is ritually clean after falling into a profane vessel. I used to question: 'What reason can the woman have for bringing the loaf to the synagogue? Cannot any one look up the case in the code?' Now, however, the reason has been made clear to me by your words: she will bring the loaf so that it may be decided whether a spirit of cleanliness or uncleanliness hovers over it. For, as the Talmud continues in the passage, they shall be unable to decide for lack of sufficient knowledge of the Torah."

[1] Sabbath 138.

P. v. K., p. 16a.

15. The New Leader

An old Kotzker Hasid came to the Gerer after his Rebbe's death and complained that he could not appreciate the mild ways of the Gerer, so different from the uncompromising, awe-inspiring ways of the Kotzker. The Gerer answered: "When a leader dies, his ways are no longer in force. Pack them up well, and you will soon learn to appreciate the new leader."

M. E. H., ii, 30-31.

16. Bending Hearts Towards Heaven

The Gerer once made this declaration on Passover: "I am not a professional Rebbe. I need neither more money or more fame than I now possess. All I wish is to bend the hearts of Jews towards Heaven, that truth may enter in. I wish it to be known that I care not to be visited by those who come to me for health, wealth or offspring; in these matters, there are others to visit. But if a man feels that he is unable to serve the Lord properly because he lacks health, wealth or offspring, he may come to me. I shall strive to aid him in his effort to remove the hindrance."

M. E. H., ii, 34.

146. REPENTANCE

A. *Contrition*

1. *Two Forms of Repentance*

Said Rabbi Schmelke: "He who regrets his transgressions may do so for two reasons: one, that he stands in fear of punishment; the other, that he is contrite for having displeased his beloved Father in Heaven. In the first instance, the sin becomes suspended, but a record of it remains. In the second, it is thoroughly erased, and no trace remains, as if no sin had ever been committed."

S. ha-Tov, p. 36.

2. *The Unworried Mind*

Said the Kobriner: "In Psalm 90: 3, we read: 'Thou turnest man to dejection and sayest: 'Repent, ye children of men.' But I say: 'O Lord, if Thou turnest man to dejection, how can you expect him to repent? Grant him his necessities, and his heart will be free to turn to Thee.'" [1]

O. Y., p. 105.

[1] The Kobriner makes use of a paraphrase here, translating the Hebrew: Dakha to read "dejection" rather than "contrition."

3. *Genuine Repentance*

Rabbi Bunam was asked: "How can a man know if his repentance is genuine?"

"If he loses the desire to commit these very offenses again," answered the Rabbi.

S. I., p. 55.

4. *The Impulse of Self-Judgment*

Rabbi Bunam narrated the following parable: "A father loaned his son a thousand thalers to establish him in business. When the time for repayment came, he perceived that his son had used the money wisely and successfully, and he therefore made him a gift of the money loaned. On another occasion he lent the same amount to a second son. When the time for repayment had arrived, he found that the youth had used the investment unwisely; in order to prevent further losses he withdrew his money and the son was compelled to abandon the business.

"It is the same with us. God loans us the impulse to judge ourselves and to repent of our unworthy deeds. If we use this impulse wisely and increase it through sincere study, pure worship and admirable conduct, God leaves this impulse with us. But if we do nothing and make no use of this impulse ourselves, He takes it back, and we remain unrepentant and sinful."

S. I., pp. 59-60.

5. Three Major Crimes

Said the Sassover: "We read: 'Thou turnest man to contrition' (Psalm 90:3) (עַד דַכָּא). This may be interpreted: Thou causest man to repent of his sins and acceptest his repentance, unless he commits the heinous crimes of shedding blood (דָם); denial of God (כְּפִרָה); or adultery with a married woman (אֵשֶׁת אִישׁ). To atone for these crimes, repentance is not so easy, since a Jew must suffer martyrdom rather than commit them." [1]

E. Tz., p. 54.

[1] The Hebrew words: "Tashuv ad Dakha" may also mean: "Causest us to repent up to 'Dakha'." This last word contains the initial letters of the Hebrew words which mean "blood, atheism, and wife of a man."

6. The Throne of Glory

Said the Koretzer: "The Talmud teaches us that 'Great is repentance, for it reaches the Throne of the Glory of God.' [1] It means: it unites with the Throne of Glory and becomes itself a part of the Throne of Glory."

Nof. Tz., p. 52.

[1] Yoma 86.

7. The Opinion of God

Said the Mikolaycver: "We read: 'At the mouth of two witnesses or three witnesses, shall he that is to die be put to death; at the mouth of one witness he shall not be put to death' (Deut. 17:6). We also read in the Talmud: [1] 'Wisdom was asked: 'What shall become of a sinner?' She answered: 'May evil pursue the sinner.' [2] Prophecy was asked the same question and she replied: 'The sinner shall die.' [3] The Torah was asked and retorted: 'Let him bring a sin offering and he shall be forgiven.' Then God was asked, and he said: 'Repentance will be his salvation.'

"Thus the verse may mean allegorically that according to two or even three opinions (since we have no offerings now), the sinner will be put to death. But according to the one opinion of God, he shall be saved through contrition."

E. A., p. 59.

[1] Yerushalmi, Makkoth 2:6.
[2] Proverbs 13:21.
[3] Ezekiel 18:20.

8. The Two Horses

Said the Mezeritzer: "One man was influenced by the call of conscience to repent. Another went to a tavern to drown his conscience in strong drink. The first is like a horse which, guided by the reins, turns into the right road; the second is like a horse, which, feeling the pull of the rein, steps from the road into a ditch."

M. R. T., ii, 46.

9. Turn About

Rabbi Nathan David Sidlovtzer, son of Rabbi Yerachmiel, said: "We read: 'As far as the East is from the West, so far hath He removed our transgressions from us' (Psalm 103 : 12). When a man stands facing the east, he needs but a turning about to face west. Likewise a sinner needs but a slight mental turning-about to be far removed from his transgressions."

Tif. B., p. 9.

10. The Bratzlaver on Repentance

A.

"1. The chief point of repentance is to bear with patience abuse and public ridicule. By it a man may slay the evil nature within him and attain holy honors.

2. Previous to repentance a man has no real existence, and it were better for him not to have been born; it is repentance which gives him existence. By repentance he declares: 'I am ready to exist as a man of worth.'

3. He who begins to repent is admonished by Heaven not to do so hastily, inasmuch as God desires to cleanse him who wishes to cleanse himself. It is like a mother who counsels her child not to wash himself too rapidly so that he may become truly clean. Hence the penitent discovers more and more offenses in himself; and if he is sincere he tells himself: 'You are not yet thoroughly purified' until his improvement is thorough.

4. Genuine repentance is performed through fear and love of God, not because a man wishes to become virtuous. Hence a man must be contrite even if he repents for his own sake.

5. After repentance a man understands God better, and he knows that his repentance was performed in the light of his lack of understanding; hence he must repent again in the light of his greater understanding. Again he attains higher understanding, which leads him to repent once more. Hence there is no limit to penitence. For this reason we pray day after day three times: 'Bring us back in perfect repentance unto Thy presence. Blessed art Thou, O Lord, who delightest in repentance' (Singer, p. 46).

6. There are three requisites for repentance: seeing eyes, hearing ears, and an understanding heart, ready to return and be healed (A paraphrase of Isaiah 6 : 10). Let your eyes see your conduct; your ears hear words of admonition by our Holy Rabbis; and let your heart understand its eternal purpose. Then you will attain perfect penitence.

7. Repent even when you have ascended to a high state of holiness. Repent even when you have descended to a low state of uncleanness, as we are told: 'If I ascend up into Heaven, Thou art there; if I make my bed in the netherworld, behold, Thou art there' (Psalm 139 : 8). Whatever your state, you must return unto the Lord.

8. There are many scholars who not only fail to repent but who even quarrel with men of justice. It is because their learning has been gained for the ends of pride, false honors, and the authority and ability to provoke and sneer at others. Their learning sharpens their wit, and they use it for unworthy purposes. We read: 'For the ways of the Lord are right, and the just do walk in them, but transgressors do stumble therein' (Hosea 14:10). Hence though learning is good, it may be employed for self-destruction.

9. Converts and penitents who enter the dwelling of holiness bring glory to God.

10. The evil spirits, created by your offenses, hinder you when you wish to liberate yourself from them. Be strong to overcome all obstacles.

11. Repent also of offenses which you have committed unintentionally, for they also make you impure.

12. All sins come because we do not guard our thoughts well lest they depart from the bounds of holiness.

13. The resolution to think aright is repentance.

14. The penitent must labor harder in the service of the Lord, in order to compensate for the time he did not serve Him.

15. True repentance is shown to a man when he is once more in the same position and circumstances as in his first submission to temptation, and when he can triumph and remain virtuous (Yoma 86).

16. True repentance is attained through the sense of shame and heartache over our sins.

17. The chanting of Psalms with attention aids us to feel the urge for repentance. For this reason it is the universal custom among Jews to recite Psalms during the months of Elul and Tishri.

18. There is no sin that will not be forgiven by sincere repentance. Every saying to the contrary in the Talmud and the Zohar is not to be understood literally."

L. E. H., pp. 118-121.

B.

"1. He who resides in Palestine is sinless.

2. The penance of sinners should be made easy.

3. Sin weakens man's power of resistance.

4. When two Mitzwoth come before you, perform the one that requires more control of your impulses.

5. He who aids men to repent will sit in God's Academy.

6. Contrition for sins is a greater penance than fasting.

7. He who deals honestly has his sins forgiven.

8. A sigh over our transgressions transforms us into newly-born creatures.

9. He who aids the fatherless breaks down the strength of the wicked and prompts them to repent.

10. He who causes people to improve is honored by God and renowned among the nations.

11. Untruth strengthens the hands of the wicked.

12. He who repents with his whole heart gains an understanding heart wherewith to know God.

13. A penitent should owe no debts.

14. Many of the non-Jewish nations are near to repentance.

15. The study of the Torah aids in the forgiveness of sins.

16. Enemies, sickness and wealth are obstacles in the path of perfection.

17. There is no comparison between even a great Mitzwah performed by an individual for his own good, and a small Mitzwah, the performance of which brings benefit for the many.

18. The lazy man thinks that the path to repentance is hidden from him.

19. He who is ashamed of his sins draws God's charity upon him.

20. Kindness and truth cause sin to be forgiven.

21. Ask God's love and He will overlook your sins.

22. A man should reprove himself every morning.

23. A year's service of God in youth is worth more than many years in old age.

24. A man should begin his service of God by doing all the Mitzwoth through love of God without knowing the reason for them. When goodness becomes habitual, God will disclose to him the secret reasons.

25. If you are sincere in your wish to serve the Lord, you will not wish your service to be known.

26. Lies prevent self-improvement.

27. God prefers the Mitzwoth from which your fellow-men derive a benefit to those which are only between your Maker and yourself.

28. Strengthen your body before you strengthen your soul.

29. Purgatory is not seen by these persons: the poor; the sufferers from sickness; those who are heavily in debt; and those whom the government afflicts unjustly.

30. Repentance is a cure for the ills of humanity.

31. Repentance brings Redemption near and lengthens life.

32. He who forgives is forgiven.

33. It is easier to turn young people to good than the aged."

Sef. Ham., pp. 155-161.

B. Sincerity of Repentance

1. Repent All Your Life

Said the Belzer: "We are commanded [1] to bring daily two offerings, one in the morning, and one in the evening. A sacrifice unto the Lord is a symbol of repentance, and we may learn from

[1] Numbers 28:4.

this commandment, that we should repent of our transgressions both in the morning of our life as well as in its evening." [2]

D. S., p. 85.

[2] Cf. Browning's poem "Ben Karshook's Wisdom," as well as the Talmudic story.

2. Holy Sparks Within Sin

Said Rabbi Dov Baer of Mezeritz: "Sparks of divine splendor dwell even in sin, else it would be unable to subsist or to move even the smallest member.

"And what are the sparks that dwell in sin? Repentance. At the hour of thy repentance and of thy turning away from sin, the sparks that were in it are raised to the upper regions."

Spiegel, p. 146.
S. S. K., iii, 146.

3. Oil Within the Olive

Rabbi Dov Baer of Mezeritz said: "Sin contains repentance as the olive contains the oil. At the hour of thy repentance and of thy turning away from sin, the sparks of divine splendor that were in it are raised to the heavenly regions."

S. S. K., iii, 146.

4. The Gate of His Enemies

The Gerer Rabbi commenting on Genesis 22:17: "And thy seed shall possess the gate of his enemies," said: "We find in the Talmud [1] that a sinner who becomes a sincere penitent receives credit for his transgressions, as if they had been transformed into virtues by repentance. Hence it follows that the penitent of the seed of Abraham actually inherits spiritual riches from his worst enemies, his iniquities."

S. S. K., iii, 43.

[1] Yoma 86.

5. Admitting Our Prayers

Rabbi Schmelke commented on the phrase (Song of Songs 2:9): "He looketh in through the windows."

"A poorly dressed man wished to present a petition to the governor, but the doorkeeper refused to admit him. The petitioner then walked to a window of the room where the governor sat, and loudly begged for admittance.

"Likewise our uncleanness prevents our petitions from being heard by the Lord; but if we open our heart before offering our prayers, the Lord will vouchsafe them entrance."

S. ha-Tov, p. 26.

6. Receiving Credit

The Gerer Rabbi said: "The righteous man loves to perform every good deed within the range of his ability. There is, however, one good deed he should not desire to accomplish, namely, repentance, inasmuch as it requires sin to precede it. Nevertheless a way may be found for earning the credit of repentance without its prior delinquency. The Talmud [1] teaches that he who studies the laws on offerings, receives the same reward as one who actually brings the offering. Hence one who studies the methods of repentance receives the same credit as the penitent."

S. S. K., iii, 63.

[1] Menachoth 110.

7. Joyful Repentance

Said the Lekhivitzer: "True repentance brings joy. If repentance is genuine, the person is joyful though contrite and humble. If it is insincere, the penitent is melancholy and irritable. He will repulse in anger as an intruder anyone who comes to speak with him. Sadness is more deserving of rebuke than serious transgression, since one forgets to regret it."

O. Y., p. 10.

8. The Free-Will of the People

Said the Belzer: "We find in the Talmud [1] the expression: 'The Holy One, Blessed be He, prays: "May it come to pass that My compassion overcome my anger, so that I may redeem My people."' The Lord prays: 'May it come to pass that Israel make use of his free-will to return unto Me. Thereby he will cause My attribute of compassion to triumph over My attribute of impartial justice, and allow Me to redeem Him.'"

D. S., p. 100.

[1] Berakhoth 7.

9. Sweetening the Torah

The Gerer explained the prayer: "And sweeten, O Lord, the words of Thy Torah in our mouth." [1] His comment was: "The same viand which is sweet to the taste of a person in good health is bitter to the sick. Likewise the healthy mind appreciates the Torah which the morbid mind disdains. We, therefore, petition the Lord to aid us in ridding ourselves of all sin through repentance. Then will God's word be sweet to our mind, cleansed and purified and made healthy."

ha-Beer, vii, part i, p. 45.

[1] Singer, p. 4.

10. The Lying Sinner

Said Rabbi Bunam: "I believe I have the power to transform any sinner into a penitent, provided he is not a liar."

S. I., p. 45.

11. Moments Without Number

Said Rabbi Bunam: "Failure to repent is much worse than sin. A man may have sinned for but a moment, but he may fail to repent of it moments without number."

S. I., p. 47.

12. Wise Utterances

Said the Koretzer: "When I desire to admonish a person, I recite to him words of wisdom and thereby strengthen his soul with encouragement to repent sincerely."

M. P., p. 19.

13. Intentional Sin

Said the Besht: "If a man sins unknowingly, his sincere repentance and the declaration of his offenses in his confession wipe away his transgressions. For the regret accompanied by a full intention never to repeat the sin can overcome offenses performed without intention. But if a man sins purposely, how can he know whether his intentional repentance can overcome his intentional sin? The remedy lies in maintaining his mood of repentance for a long time until he is confident his sins have been forgiven."

K. S. T., p. 9b.

14. God's Way

Said Rabbi Bunam: "We read: 'Then will I teach transgressors Thy ways; and sinners shall return unto Thee' (Psalm 51:15). This means: I will teach transgressors God's ways. He appeals to sinners to repent, and I shall cause transgressors who have accepted God's ways in other respects to accept His way in this also: namely, to appeal to other sinners to follow their example, and like them to return unto the Lord."

S. I., p. 75.

15. The Prodigal's Return

Said the Mezeritzer: "A king had two sons. One was contented to be constantly in attendance on his father; the other preferred to enjoy himself away from home. There evil companions led him astray. The king was prompted to send his officers to fetch him for chastisement, but out of paternal love, refrained from doing so. Later the prodigal regretted the anguish his conduct had caused his father, and of his own free will, returned with a plea for pardon. The king was overjoyed and showed him more love and favor than to the other son who had never absented himself. Likewise, when a grievous sinner returns unto the Lord, He receives greater joy and favor than those who have never sinned."

T. M. M., pp. 244-5.

16. The Straight and the Crooked Road

Said the Mezeritzer: "He who always walks on the straight path of righteousness feels no special pleasure in it. He does not know there is a crooked path. But he who has at first walked on the crooked path and later finds the direct path rejoices greatly in his discovery. In the same fashion, the penitent appreciates righteousness more than the saint who has never transgressed."

T. M. M., pp. 229-31.

17. The Soul's Impulse

Said the Koretzer: "Since all souls are part of the One All-Embracing Soul, and since whatever is in the whole is in every part of it, it follows that if one soul resolves to repent, its resolution resides also in every other soul. The leader obtains command of the soul of him who appeals to him, and is able to strengthen its resolution until it is put into effect. But were there no impulse towards penitence within the soul, all the efforts of the Zaddik would be fruitless."

Nof. Tz., p. 11.

18. A Pretense

A confirmed sinner visited the Ropshitzer, saying he had been sent by an erring friend who was too shy to come himself. His friend had committed certain offenses, and he desired to learn the appropriate means of repentance. The Rabbi at once divined that the visitor was himself the sinner, and he said:

"What a foolish person is your friend! Could he not have come himself to me, and pretended that the sinner is a friend?"

O. N., p. 51.

19. Spiting God

A man came to the Ropshitzer and said: "I am a great sinner. I have offended this person and that, and I beseech the Rabbi to teach me how to repent."

The Rabbi replied: "Tell me, my man, what harm has God done to you, that you have done so much to spite Him?"

M. D., p. 250.

20. The Ropshitzer's Skill

A great sinner came to the Ropshitzer. He complained that though he wished to repent, the course in self-denials assigned him by the Rabbi of Kalev was too severe for him. The Ropshitzer replied: "I am confident the Kalever underestimated the gravity of your sins and gave you too easy a course in the ways of repentance."

The Rabbi, thereupon, began to weep copiously at the seriousness of the visitor's transgressions. Seeing this, the sinner himself burst into lamentations, and fainted several times from emotion. The Ropshitzer turned to him, and said: "Since you have shown wholehearted contrition for your sins, God has forgiven you."

Several Hasidim from Hungary were present at this scene, and they said to the Ropshitzer: "Since you are able to draw forth a man's very soul, and restore it again to its place, we acknowledge you to be our Rabbi."

S. N., pp. 21-22.

C. Reformation of Sinners

1. Envying an Opportunity

The Berditschever once met on the street a certain high official, whose evil deeds were as notorious as his great power. Tugging him by the sleeve, he said: "I envy your Excellency very much. For if you repent and return to God, out of every one of your blemishes will go forth a ray of light, and you will be luminous altogether. You are destined to be a shining light, and for this I envy you." [1]

E. O., p. 53 (B., p. 458b).

[1] This story is continued by humorists thus: The sinner replied: "Wait another year and you will envy me more."

2. The Fast Horse and the Slow

The Besht asked a man: "Why is a fast horse worth ten times as much as a slow one?"

"Because he runs ten times as fast," was the reply.

"Yes, but if he loses his way, he loses it ten times as fast."

"Yes?" queried the man, not knowing what the Besht would say next.

"Well, but do not forget that when he finds the right road, he makes up for lost time ten times as quickly."

"When a sagacious man repents, he attains his former state of righteousness much faster than the dull man."

Kahana, p. 51.

3. A Fresh Start

The Kobriner commented on the verse (Song of Songs, 2:8): "Hark! my beloved! Behold, he cometh, leaping upon the mountains, skipping upon the hills." "The Midrash [1] tells us that when Moses announced the Redemption to Israel, they said: 'How may we be redeemed when on every mountain and on every hill stand our altars to the false gods?' And Moses replied: 'When God calls you, He does not look upon your idolatrous temples. His eyes leap over the mountains, and skip over the hills.'

"Nowadays when a Jew is influenced by the sermon of the preacher, and earnestly desires to improve his ways, the evil thought within him declares: 'How can you become a good Jew when you have neglected God's commandments and precepts for so long a time?'

"Then the spiritual leader tells him: 'God desires only your repentance. He will overlook and forget what has transpired, if only you resolve sincerely to embark anew upon the road to godliness.'"

O. Y., p. 89.

[1] Shir ha-Shirim Rabba 2:19.

4. The "Lord of Repentance"

The Levite [1] once met in Warsaw a notorious vagabond named Benisch, a man of many evil deeds. He turned to him and spoke: "Brother and man of highest destiny, follow me and take root in the world of love and fear, for beyond it there is no life." A miracle happened. The heart of the evil-doer melted and he became a Lord of Repentance. He of whom this tale runneth became famous afterwards as Rabbi Benisch, disciple of the Berditschever." [1]

Bl., Gem., p. 84.

[1] This story has a strong New Testament flavor, but was in no wise influenced by it. The Berditschever is sometimes called "The Levite."

5. Repentance Hints

Rabbi Sussya of Anipol said: "There are five verses in the Bible which constitute the essence of Judaism. These verses begin in Hebrew with one of these letters: 'Tav, Shin, Vav, Beth, Heh,' which comprise the Hebrew word for Repentance: 'Teshuvah' (תְּשׁוּבָה).

1. Thou shalt be whole-hearted with the Lord, thy God (Deut. 18:13).
2. I have set the Lord always before me (Psalm 16:8).
3. But thou shalt love thy neighbor as thyself (Lev. 19:18).
4. In all thy ways acknowledge Him (Prov. 3:6).
5. To walk humbly with thy God (Micah 6:8). [1]

"Therefore," said Rabbi Sussya, "resolve to act accordingly, so that your repentance may be sincere."

Mif. H., p. 49.

[1] The "Vav" in Micah 6:8 is omitted.

6. The Heart of Repentance

Said the Bratzlaver: "Contrition at our offenses is the heart of repentance."

L. E. H., pp. 17-19.

147. REPROOF

1. Loving Rebuke

Said the Besht: "One who sees faults in another and dislikes him for them is surely possessed of some of these very faults in his own person. The pure and good man can see only the goodness in others. We read (Leviticus 19:17): 'Thou shalt not hate thy brother in thy heart; thou shalt surely rebuke thy neighbor, and not bear sin because of him.' This teaches us: Rebuke thyself first for seeing faults, and thus being to a degree impure; then thou wilt not hate thy brother, but feel love towards him. If thou rebukest him, it will be in the spirit of love. He will become attached to thee, joining the goodness within him to thine own goodness, and all his faults will disappear. If he should refuse to listen to thee and to admit his fault and abuse thee, he shall lose thereby his goodness to thee and remain wholly evil.

"Thus through a loving rebuke, either of these two courses is open: both of ye shall join in love, and both of ye shall attain improvement. Or if there is hatred left, it shall be in his heart."

M. R. T., ii, 9.

2. Twice as Long a Time

Rabbi Yerachmiel said: "There is a proverb in the Talmud: 'Words are worth a Selah; silence is worth two.'[1] Selah means a shekel, or a rock. If one must reprove a man whose heart is hard as a rock, he should first think over in silence how to influence him for twice as long a time."

V. S., p. 44.

[1] Megillah 18.

3. Reasons for Misconduct

Said the Besht: "A prince was banished from his father's realm. Two servants were assigned to him, and were commissioned to report on his conduct. One servant made a dry report of facts unfavorable to the prince. The other made the same report, but added that the youth's misconduct was the result of his exile and his sense of disgrace and melancholy. The father took compassion on his son, restored him to the palace, and rewarded the loyal servant.

"In the same fashion, when a sage or a preacher reproves Israel, let him always employ the method of the second servant. It is in this way that he will surely please the Father in Heaven."

K. S. T., p. 10a.

4. A Good Example

Rabbi Mendel Vorker said: "It must not be thought that Joseph maligned his brethren.[1] He merely behaved better than his brothers, and it was inevitable that thereby Jacob was prompted to notice their inferior conduct, and reprove them."

D. Z., p. 50.

[1] Genesis 37:2.

5. The Bratzlaver on "Reproof"

"1. Reprove not the apostate, for it will not avail.

2. Be wise in your reproof, lest you do more harm than good.

3. Include yourself in any reproof.

4. He who accepts not admonition, will surely die before his time.

5. Reproof that is heeded draws in its train clemency and kindness.

6. Reproof brings down contentment and blessing."

Sef. Ham., pp. 161-2.

148. RESPECT FOR FATHERS

1. *Retirement Rather Than Contradiction.*

The Gerer Rabbi gave an involved decision on a Rabbinical rule, and asked the persons present whether they understood him. All replied in the negative. He then addressed his son, Abraham Mordecai: "And you, too, did not understand me?"

His son remained silent, and the Rabbi left for his room. From there he heard his son explaining the decision. He returned to the Study Room and demanded of his son an explanation. "Why did you not gladden my heart before, when I made inquiry of you?"

Abraham Mordecai responded: "Had you asked whether I did understand, I should have replied in the affirmative. But since you asked whether I did not understand, I did not presume to contradict my father."

S. S. K., v, 35.

2. *Aaron and David*

The Radomsker said that David was greater than Aaron. When Aaron's sons died, he kept silent. But when David was in trouble, he sang Psalms.

S. S. K., ii, 92.

3. *Reciting Kaddish*

Rabbi Israel Salanter was supposed to recite the Kaddish in memory of his father. Another Jew, who did not know this, asked permission to recite the prayer, and was chagrined to learn that he must yield to the Rabbi. Rabbi Israel, however, granted to the other man the privilege, saying: "I know I will have pleased my father by performing a kind deed by means of his Kaddish." [1]

[1] This is the story of a "Near-Hasid." S. Rosenfeld in "The Day," June 25, 1932.

149. RESPECT FOR PERSONS

In Extending Hospitality

1. *Barring the Shekinah*

Rabbi Aaron of Karlin one terrible winter-night, entered a village which had only one Jew residing among the peasants. When he asked for shelter at the home of the Jew, he was not recognized as the Karliner. Admission was delayed, and words were bandied between the Rabbi's servants and the domestics of the villager. When finally Rabbi Aaron proved his identity, he was admitted, half-frozen, and was well-entertained. Said the Karliner:

"It is plain to me now, why our Sages [1] attribute more merit to hospitable demeanor to man than to God. When the Shekinah finds

[1] Sabbath 127.

the door barred, it returns to Heaven and no harm is done, save only to the unwilling host. With man it is different; if denied access, he may perish." [2]

Bl., Gem., p. 167.

[2] See the Amshinover on "Forgiveness," 55:4.

2. Man and His Equipage

When the two brothers, Rabbi Elimelech and Rabbi Sussya, were yet wandering about from place to place, poorly dressed and still unknown to fame, they halted at nightfall in Lodmir. The only one who gave them any attention was a poor Hasid, Rabbi Aaron, who welcomed them in his home. A few years later when they had become famous, they arrived in Lodmir with a fine equipage. The richest man in town invited them to sojourn in his home, but they went instead to the house of Rabbi Aaron. When the wealthy man protested, they replied:

"We are the same persons to whom you paid no attention when we stopped here a few years ago. Hence it appears that it is not so much we who are welcome, as our coach and horses. We are entirely willing to accept your hospitality for the horses."

N. E. L., p. 38.

3. Lot's Hospitality

Once the Berditschever on his journeyings came to Lemberg. He called upon a man of wealth and influence, asking for a night's lodging. The magnate, not knowing the stranger for a man of great renown, denied his entreaty, saying there were inns aplenty in Lemberg. The Rabbi said: "I have no money to go to an inn." The rich man thereupon sent him to a poor teacher of children who had an excellent reputation for hospitality to indigent travelers. There the Rabbi was received with great kindness and made welcome, though he did not make known his name and position until the following day.

Soon thereafter the word spread throughout the town and there was great rejoicing: "Behold the holy Rabbi dwells among us!" Large throngs called at the teacher's house to see the holy man face to face and to receive his blessing. Among the visitors was also the man of wealth who had denied the Rabbi shelter the night before. He did not recognize his petitioner standing before him now in his customary Rabbinic attire, and said with a reverential bow: "Let your Worship come to my house; I have comfortable lodgings and all men of fame and substance, on coming to Lemberg, sojourn with me. Surely it would be unbefitting if your Worship were to tarry longer under the roof of a poor teacher, as if the men of means in the community had denied him entertainment."

The Rabbi answered: "Your hospitable entreaty is like that of Lot, and this poor teacher's like Abraham's. What is the difference between Abraham and Lot? It is reported of both that they entertained the angels of the Lord. But of Abraham, Holy Scripture says: 'When he raised his eyes, he saw three *men* standing before him.' [1]   He did not know they were angels, but entertained them through a sense of duty to his fellow-men. Of Lot, Scripture says: 'The two angels came to Sodom.' [2] Lot, unlike Abraham, was well aware of the heavenly character of his visitors. When I came to you as a commoner, you bade me depart, first to an inn, and then to this poor teacher. Now, however, that you know me as the Rabbi of Berditschev, you invite me to partake of your hospitality. Yours is Lot's, not Abraham's way, for Abraham, our Patriarch, was no respecter of persons."

Bl., Gem., p. 201.

[1] Gen. 18:2.
[2] Gen. 19:1.

4. Respect for an Opponent

The Radviller had an argument with his friend, the Kossover. Neither was willing to retire from his position. Later the Radviller chanced to be invited to the home of a rich Hasid. There the host introduced to him his four sons-in-law, all great in learning and piety, and all adherents of the Kossover. The Radviller then exclaimed: "One must have respect indeed, for a Rebbe who has such Disciples."

E. Tz., p. 53.

5. Generosity Versus Respect

The Lubliner Rabbi presented the "Yud" with a shirt of silk. A poor man came to the "Yud" and complained that his only shirt was falling into rags. Without hesitation the "Yud" handed to him the shirt of silk. This was told to the Lubliner who made inquiry regarding the episode. The "Yud" replied to him: "When a poor man asks me for a garment, I would not hesitate to give him even a priestly habiliment."

"You may be generous with your own possessions," retorted the Lubliner. "But should not my gift have been held dear by you?"

Tif. Yeh., p. 52.

6. Who Is a Sage?

Said the Ropshitzer: "Who is a sage? 'One who knows his place,' [1] say our Sages. I shall paraphrase it: 'Who is a sage? One who makes his place known.' A town becomes known throughout the entire world by the presence within it of an illustrious sage."

Ohel N., p. 28.

[1] Ethics 6:6; Singer, p. 206.

7. As a Slave Before a Master

The Bershider would say: "When a man dies he shall be asked: [1] 'Have you studied Torah? Have you done kind deeds? Have you acknowledged twice daily the Kingdom of God? Have you ac-

[1] Based on Sabbath 31.

cepted your fellow-man as your king in a meek manner?' " He would add: "We should especially note the final phrase: 'In a meek manner.' Accept not your fellow-man as your superior because it is a duty, but because you feel that he is in truth your superior, and that you are verily as the dust of the earth." His son spoke to him once, and his father was standing before his own son as a slave before a master.

M. P., p. 43.

150. REWARDS

1. Double Reward

Said Rabbi Schmelke: "The Lord hath pleasure in rewarding the godly man, and it is a good deed to give pleasure unto the Lord. Therefore he who performs a good deed is doubly rewarded: once for the good deed, and secondly, for affording the Lord the pleasure of rewarding him for it. The same applies to the transgressor, since the Lord does not desire to punish."

S. ha-Tov, p. 20.

2. Temporal Discomforts and Heavenly Reward

The Besht once journeyed to Turkey and on his travels sojourned in a small town. A Jewish merchant invited him to his home, and showered hospitality upon him, though he was unaware of his guest's identity. Before his departure, the Besht inquired what blessing his host desired. The merchant answered: "May I have a goodly share of the blessings of the World-to-Come."

The Besht made himself known and promised to give the merchant the desired blessing if he would visit his home in Medziboz. The merchant embarked on the journey. He took along wine and other products of Turkey, stopping on the way to Medziboz to engage in trade. One day he halted at a little inn in a lonely spot, where the drivers of his wagons were compelled to sleep in a nearby barn. In the morning when he sought the barn, the merchant could not find his way in the morning fog, and was soon completely lost. He saw no human being for miles, and knew not which way to turn. He lay down in the grass and fell asleep from exhaustion. When he awoke his rich garments had disappeared and he was clothed in ragged clothes. Finding a piece of bread in a pocket, he breakfasted upon it. A few moments later a troupe of wandering beggars passed by; he joined them and soon forgot about his own personality and problems. After wandering about for several weeks, the troupe arrived in Medziboz.

The Besht summoned his former host into his presence, and reminded the erstwhile merchant of his promise to bless him. Soon after the blessing had been pronounced, the merchant's wagons arrived safely, and he made highly profitable trades. The Besht assured him that his tribulations had served as an atonement for his sins, and had earned for him a much larger share in the "World-to-Come."

Beth Shelomo, pp. 11-23.

3. The Heritage

Concerning the text (Genesis 15:5, 6) Rabbi Elimelech of Lizensk said: "Abraham heard the Lord say to him: 'Thy reward shall be exceedingly great.' He understood it in the sense of material rewards, and he pleaded for a son to inherit them. And the Lord explained to him: 'It is not material wealth which you should desire as an inheritance for your seed. Look up towards Heaven, and think of celestial riches. Such should be the heirloom you transmit to your son.' 'And Abraham believed,' namely, he became convinced."

Noam E., p. 12.

4. For the Sake of the Lord

The Tzernobiler Rabbi on one of his periodic journeys on behalf of the dissemination of Hasidism, was compelled to pass through a Lithuanian town, a stronghold of its opponents. He wished to avoid angry discussion, and commanded his driver to whip up the horses of the carriage. A passer-by, however, recognized in him a proponent of Hasidism and picked up a stone to hurl it at the Rabbi. The Tzernobiler ordered the driver to drive still faster, and the missile missed its mark. The driver commenced to curse the stone-thrower; the Rabbi, however, halted him. "But he wished to kill you," grumbled the driver.

"Surely it was his intention, and had you not driven away rapidly he might have accomplished this wish. Now were it God's will for me to die, I should not have run away from it. The reason I did flee was that I did not wish this non-Hasid to kill me as an enemy of Judaism. He would, by this act, have gained a share in the World-to-Come instead of punishment, for he was thoroughly convinced his deed was for the sake of the Lord."

F. R. H.-M., i, 44-46.

5. The Joy of Being Alive

Said the Koretzer: "We read: 'What profit hath man of all his labour wherein he laboreth under the sun?' (Ecclesiastes 1:3). What reward is due man for all his labors in God's service in addition to the recompense of being alive, and of beholding the sun shine upon him, to bring him the joy of life and light?"

Nof. Tz., p. 53.

6. The Seer

Rabbi Meir Margulis in his younger years was Rabbi of the town of Yazlivitz. The owner of the town, Prince Poniatovsky, and his son Stanislav August visited the town one day, and his tenants went forth to welcome him. When Rabbi Meir and his son Saul approached the nobleman, the youth, Saul, exclaimed: "Your Highness! Your son, I am confident, will be elected King of Poland; his countenance is truly that of a noble ruler." The prince and his son were delighted, and took account of this "prophecy."

When, later, Poniatovsky was chosen king, he was called upon to ratify the petition of the Jewish communal leaders of Ukraine on behalf of their choice of Rabbi Meir as Chief Rabbi. He commanded that the confirmation be written in golden ink, and presented to the Rabbi. When the King was informed that Saul, then Rabbi of Lublin, was in Warsaw for his health, he commanded his own physicians to attend him.

Nif. Yeh., p. 89.

7. Expect No Rewards

Said the Bratzlaver: "It is improper for you to expect rewards for your piety, since all your good deeds and all your prayers come from the Lord."

K. L. M., p. 5.

8. True Claims and Spurious

The Riziner related the following story: "A man determined to devote his son to God as if he were a son of the Lord himself. When the lad grew to maturity, full of learning and holy deeds, his father wished to gain for him as wife the daughter of the holiest man of the generation. He went into the fields, and fervently implored the Lord to send him wealth, so that the holy man might be willing to become his son's father-in-law. With this wealth he would be enabled to gain renown as a philanthropist. The Lord hearkened to his prayer and sent him exceptional blessings in all his works.

"A neighbor marveled at the man's sudden rise to wealth and succeeded in ascertaining the reason. He, too, entreated the Lord for bountiful gifts, claiming also learning and holy deeds for his son. But the Heavenly Tribunal soon discovered the falsity of his pretensions, and no riches or honors were meted out to him.

"On the Day of Judgment," continued the Riziner, "the nations will observe the rich rewards granted to Israel and will also claim them for themselves. But the Tribunal will speedily disregard their pretensions as spurious."

Tif. Z., pp. 17-9.

9. His Unaided Efforts

The Besht commented on the words: "Also unto Thee, O Lord, belongeth mercy; for Thou renderest to every man according to his work."[1] He said: "The question arises: where is His mercy, if He

[1] Psalm 62:13.

pays according to man's work? The answer is that it is God who makes it possible for man to perform good deeds. Man's work is of slight merit, yet He rewards man as if he achieved it by his own unaided efforts."

K. S. T., p. 14b.

10. Aiding Man in Goodness

The Medzibozer commented on the words: "Abounding in loving-kindness and truth" (Singer, p. 144). He said: "Loving-kindness denotes undeserved giving. How can this be reconciled with truth, which implies truly deserved rewards? The explanation lies in the following: it is the Lord's loving-kindness to reward man according to his true deserts. In order to do so, He aids each man in his efforts to do good, and causes opportunities to come to him to achieve it."

Butz. D., p. 26.

151. ROSH HA-SHANAH

1. A Colloquy With the Lord

The Berditschever would hold the following conversation with the Lord on the Eve of Rosh Ha-Shanah:

"Tell me, O Lord, what hast Thou against Israel? Thou hast written in Thy Torah: 'Speak.' Unto whom? Unto Israel. Thou hast written: 'Say.' Unto whom? Unto Israel. 'Command.' Whom? Israel. Hast thou no other nation to instruct in Thy laws? Hence it must follow that Thou lovest Israel. Have mercy upon him, and fulfill his great needs!"

Kahana, p. 258.

2. God's Verdict Is True

The Vorker Rabbi explained the words in the Rosh ha-Shanah Hymn: "His counsel is belief; His verdict is truth." The Lord desires to acquit every Jew on the Day of Judgment, and He counsels us to believe in the doctrines of faith, namely that there is reward and punishment, and that sincere repentance is acceptable to the Lord. If we believe and act upon our faith, we shall receive a favorable verdict; we will know, also, that God's decree is truly merited by us. We will also understand that since His verdict is always true, any misfortune which may assail us is according to our deserts."

Sifthei Kodesh, p. 58.

3. The Divine Nature

Commenting on the words in the Rosh ha-Shanah Hymn: "His garment is charity; His mantle is wrath; He is girded with vengeance; His hidden character is compassion," the Rozdoler Rabbi said:

"The author explains in these words the Divine Nature. Only outwardly is our Lord clothed with wrath and girded with vengeance; but hidden within, He wears the garment of charity and compassion."

E. K., p. 67.

4. Wicked and Good

Rabbi Bunam explained the verse in the New Year's Hymn: "And All Believe," reading: "He is good and He is kind to the wicked and the good." He said: "This means: 'God is kind to those who are sometimes wicked and sometimes good.'"

S. S. K., iv, 43.

5. A King Without a People

The Amshinover spoke on Rosh ha-Shanah thus: "All of us are filled with sins. Should strict justice prevail in the Heavenly Tribunal, all of Israel would merit doom. We find, however, that the Lord rejoices in the sincere praises offered him by Israel, and that He calls Himself our King even in our wickedness. We read: 'If Thou, O Lord, shouldest mark iniquities, who could stand?' (Psalm 130:3). If Thou shouldest refuse us forgiveness, who will be left over to stand up to praise Thee? We also read: 'They stand this day according to Thine ordinances, for all are Thy servants' (Psalm 119:91). All Israel stands in prayer before Thee on this Day of Judgment and hopes for Thy pardon. For shouldest Thou convict those who are Thy subjects, Thou wouldst become a King without a People." [1]

O. I., p. 4.

[1] In the Hebrew "ordinances" and "judgments" are both the same word; so are "subjects" and "servants." Therefore the interpretation of the verse by the Rabbi is simple. This remark applies to many other such interpretations.

6. "Inscribe Us For Life"

When Rosh ha-Shanah occurred on a Sabbath, the Berditschever exclaimed:

"O Lord, Thou forbiddest us to write on the Sabbath except in order to save life. Write us down, then, for life, as otherwise even Thou mayest not write on the Sabbath."

O. I. H., p. 17.

7. "Remember Us For Life"

Said the Belzer: "It is customary in synagogues on Rosh ha-Shanah and Yom Kippur for the congregation to respond, when the Reader repeats the Amidah, only at the special prayer: 'Inscribe us for a good life.' [1] The congregation does not respond when the Reader says in the earlier portion: 'Remember us for life.' [2] The reason is that one first requests a lesser favor, and later asks for a

[1] Singer, p. 52.
[2] Singer, p. 44.

greater. Thus, when we have already said in the silent Amidah: 'Inscribe us for a good life,' it would be unseemly for us to respond later: 'Remember us for life,' wherein we petition for any sort of life, even for that which may not be good."

D. S., p. 105.

8. Forgetting and Repenting

Said the Riziner: "We read in the New Year Prayer:[1] 'For Thou rememberest all forgotten things, and there is no forgetfulness before Thy Holy Throne.' This means that when a person performs a good deed, but forgets it and demands no reward, then the Lord remembers it; but if the man keeps it in his memory and expects a reward for it, the Lord forgets it. Also, when a man transgresses and remembers it, and repents of it, then the Lord forgets about it; but if the man pays no heed and forgets his sin, the Lord remembers it."

N. I., p. 62.

[1] Singer, p. 249.

9. Too Much Merriment

A Hasid complained to the Koretzer Rabbi that he was destitute and unable to purchase food. The Rabbi asked him: "What is your occupation?"

"A merry-maker at festivities," was the reply.

"Abandon this occupation," said the Rabbi, "and your circumstances will improve. On New Year's Day, the measure of merriment for the coming year is allotted to each person.[1] Since you waste so much of it at your trade in a few evenings, the balance, divided among the days when you have no festivities in which to participate, is too small for your necessities."

E. O., p. 40.

[1] Based on Baba Bathra 10.

10. The Shofar Blower

The Berditschever Rabbi was seeking a Shofar-Blower. Many applied for the post, and he asked each one his mystic thoughts[1] during the Shofar-blowing. No one's answer pleased him. Finally one man said:

"Rabbi, I am unlearned, and I know no mystic thoughts, but I have four daughters to marry, and I have no money for their dowries. Therefore when I blow the Shofar, I think: 'O Lord of the Universe; I have done my duty in obeying Thy command; do Thou also Thy duty and send me worthy mates for my daughters.'"

The Berditschever appointed him to blow the Shofar.

O. I. H., p. 15.

[1] "Kavvanah" in this story means "Kabbalistic thought."

11. How the Lord "Bought" The Berditschever

A Rabbi narrated this tale at a Rosh ha-Shanah meal:
"I dreamed once that I was attending the Heavenly Court, and saw the Satan bringing up bundle after bundle of Jewish sins. The Counsel for the Defense was the Soul of the Berditschever, since only a Soul like his can defend Israel. The Soul was standing near the door leading to the burning cauldron of Gehenna, and when the Satan turned his head, the Soul snatched away all his papers and hurled them into the cauldron.

"The Satan finally caught the Soul doing this, and he demanded that it be brought to trial. It was convicted and sentenced to be sold into servitude, according to the law of the Torah: 'If the thief cannot make restitution, he shall be sold as a servant to work out the value of his theft.' [1]   An auction sale was announced. Many were the Zaddikim who wished to redeem the Soul of the Berditschever, but the Satan outbid them all. Finally the Lord Himself 'bought' the Soul as His own servant. This is what is meant by the author of the Piyyut: 'To the One who buys His servant at the Judgment Place.' "

Kahana, p. 250.

[1] Exodus 22:2.

12. A Mitzwah Before Death

It was told to Rabbi Bunam that a famous Rabbi had been on board a ship on Rosh ha-Shanah. The ship sprang a leak and the water poured in. The Rabbi took up a Shofar and blew a blast; at once the hole was located and the ship repaired. Rabbi Bunam commented: "The Rabbi's intention was to perform another Mitzwah before he died. Hence the Mitzwah saved him from death. But had his intention been to blow the Shofar to rescue himself, it would not have availed, since then it would have been no Mitzwah."

S. I., p. 46.

13. As Helpless Children

Said the Koretzer: "It is proper to weep on the High Holydays in order to show that despite all our seeming wisdom and learning, we are as helpless as children who weep for what they desire."

Nof. Tz., p. 19.

14. The Meaning of "Le-Rosh"

The Dzikover Rabbi explained the phrase recited at the Rosh ha-Shanah table: "May it be the will of God that we become the head, not the tail." He read the word: "Le Rosh" (the head) as the initials of four words: "La-asoth Ratzon Ovinu She-Ba-shammayim," namely, "To do the will of our Father in Heaven."

E. Tz., p. 99.

15. Hiding From Supplicants

Said the Koretzer: "It is the royal etiquette that if guilty persons succeed in seeing the King, he pardons them. To prevent wholesale pardons, the King hides himself from the supplicants. It is thus with the King of Kings: He conceals Himself on the Judgment Day, and we seek for the key which will open the door to the place of His hiding. We try our customary prayers, our hymns and special prayers, the blowing of the Shofar, and the varied intonations for the reading of the Torah. And when the traditional keys have all been used, one of them will surely open the hiding place of the Lord."

Nof. Tz., p. 19.

16. The Foolish Soldier

Rabbi Joshua Dzikover narrated the following story: "During the Crimean War the Czar Nicholas stood on a bastion to watch the progress of the battle of Sebastopol. A common soldier noticed a flying shell and bent over the Czar's body. The shell almost grazed the Czar's head. In gratitude for his rescue, the Czar asked the soldier: 'What reward can I give you for your deed?'

"'I beg of you, Little Father, order me placed under another Corporal, since my present superior treats me badly.'

"'What a foolish fellow you are!' exclaimed the Czar. 'Become a Corporal yourself!'

"In the same fashion," continued the Dzikover, "we are granted at the High Holydays an opportunity to ask favors from God, our King. Instead of beseeching Him to send us the Redeemer, we ask instead for minor favors. Are we not as foolish as the soldier?"

Ohel N., pp. 52-3.

17. The Scales

Said the Koretzer: "The Zodiac sign for the month of Tishri is the Scales or Balances. The first of Tishri, Rosh ha-Shanah, is the exact middle of the Biblical year. If a man's conduct during the preceding six months has been average, the scale keeps its balance level."

Nof. Tz., p. 28.

18. The Boy's Response

Rabbi Sussya left the synagogue one Rosh ha-Shanah before the blowing of the Shofar, and meeting a little Jewish boy, barefooted and dressed in a ragged jacket, said to him: "Look, my lad, at the non-Jewish boy over yonder. See how well-dressed and well-nourished he is. Have you no envy of him in your heart?"

"Surely not," answered the boy. "I am much better off, for I am a Jew."

Rabbi Sussya returned to the synagogue, and relating the boy's response, he added: "This reply opened every gate of Mercy to all Israel."

M. H. H., p. 67.

19. The Dilapidated Bundle

The Oheler dreamed on Rosh ha-Shanah Eve that he was gazing through his window at the crowd hurrying to the synagogue. He said to himself: "I have no need for haste, thank Heaven, for I have studied the Torah the entire year and have prayed well. I have nothing to fear on Judgment Day."

Immediately there appeared before his eyes a torn, dilapidated and soiled bundle, and a voice cried out: "These are your good deeds for the past year." He rose quickly, and ran to the synagogue in great terror.

P. v. K., p. 12b.

20. Men and Cattle

The first Mishnah of the Tractate "Rosh ha-Shanah" enumerates various New Year days. One paragraph reads: "On the New Moon of Elul is the New Year day for the tithe of cattle, but Rabbi Eliezer and Rabbi Simeon say that it is on the New Moon of Tishri." The Lizensker discussed this text, and said: "Those who are distant from God the entire year but on the first day of Elul commence to devote a portion of their time to God are verily as the cattle; they have no sense to remember God until the Day of Judgment approaches. Rabbi Simeon and Rabbi Eliezer say that even those who arouse themselves a month before Rosh ha-Shanah are still men; those who wait until the very Judgment Day are as cattle."

O. E., p. 139.

21. The Royal Messenger

One New Year Day before the blowing of the Shofar, Rabbi Joshua of Belz asked a Hasid to repeat what he had heard from Rabbi Solomon Kluger of Brody. The Disciple complied, and said: "The Broder Maggid, illustrating the desirability of expressing in a few words one's readiness to perform a Mitzwah for the sake of pleasing the Lord,[1] narrated the following parable:

" 'A royal messenger carried a valuable gift to the King. Wherever the opportunity presented itself, he announced himself as the King's messenger. This served to protect him from malefactors who might otherwise have robbed him. In the same fashion, let us solemnly proclaim that we are about to bring a valuable gift to the King of Kings, and the Evil Impulse will fear to molest us.'

"The Maggid learned this also from the verse: 'My heart overfloweth with a goodly matter; I say: "My work is concerning a king": my tongue then is as the pen of a ready and facile writer' " (Psalm 45:2).

Joseph Margoshes in J. M. J., Dec. 9, 1932.

[1] See for such preambles especially the Passover Haggadah.

22. *Blasts on the Shofar*

The Gerer once dreamed that he was in Kotzk on the day of the New Year. When it came time to blow the Shofar, the Kotzker began to blow it; the tones were perfect in quality, but he was unable to finish. Then the Gerer blew blasts on the Shofar, of inferior quality and smaller in volume. But he was able to complete the entire Order of the Shofar ritual. When the Rebbe related this dream, a Hasid intrepreted it as follows: "The Kotzker's call for repentance and purity of heart was of a quality higher than the Gerer's. But it was the latter who succeeded in influencing for good all of the Kotzker's adherents, thus completing his work."

M. E. H., ii, 55.

152. THE SABBATH

1. *The Chief Purpose*

The Gerer Rabbi said: "The Talmud [1] enumerates thirty-nine different kinds of work necessary for the construction of the Tabernacle. All these forms of labor had one supreme object—the Tabernacle.

"In our various activities during the week-days, we should likewise emphasize the one chief purpose—namely, the duty to honor the Sabbath. Then our every action will become sacred."

S. S. K., iii, 52.

[1] Sabbath 73.

2. *Appreciating the Sabbath*

Said the Gerer Rabbi: "We say in the Sabbath morning prayer: 'May Moses rejoice in the gift of his lot.' [1] When the giver of a gift sees that the recipient appreciates it by caring for it earnestly, he rejoices. Likewise, when Moses discovers that Israel appreciates the Sabbath and the Holydays, which he presented to us, he is pleased."

S. S. K., ii, 44.

[1] Singer, p. 138.

3. *The Ministering Angels*

The Lemberger Rav, Rabbi Hayyim Rappaport, stopped over for the Sabbath with his brother-in-law, Rabbi Hirsch of Tzartkov, the father of Rabbi Schmelke and Rabbi Phineas of Frankfort a/M. His sister prepared the evening meal for him, and invited him to partake of it without waiting for the return of her husband who was accustomed to remain late in the synagogue. Rabbi Hayyim chose to await his host, and read in a holy book to pass the time. About midnight the host arrived, dressed in white silk garments, wearing white shoes, and with his Tallith about his shoulders. Rabbi Hayyim said to his sister: "Never before have I appreciated the innovations which the Hasidim have introduced; instead I have condemned their leaders for altering traditional customs. But I shall do so no longer. When your husband entered, I could almost feel the presence of the two ministering angels, who, according to the Talmudic allegory,[1] accompany every good Jew from the synagogue to his home on the Sabbath."

[1] Sabbath 119.

S. ha-Tov, p. 107.

4. Not the Ninth of Ab

A Hasid was seated near the door of the Gerer synagogue on a Sabbath, and seemed inclined to melancholy. The Rabbi went over to him and said:

"The Sabbath is known to offer hospitality to guests. If the New Moon occurs on the Sabbath, she offers to it portions of the prayers; to the Intermediate Festival she yields the Musaph; to the Festivals and to Yom Kippur she yields the entire service. There is one guest, however, to which the Sabbath will not grant admittance, namely the Fast of the Ninth of Ab. The Sabbath is eager for joy, but she has no place for sadness."

S. S. K., iii, 113.

5. Our Super-Soul

The Besht said: "The Hasidic custom of eating the third Sabbath meal in company with comrades rather than in the midst of one's own family, is founded upon the following reason: among good Jews, it is eminently desirable that a man offer up his soul in the presence of ten Jews. At the conclusion of the last Sabbath meal, we offer up our super-soul, received by us on the Sabbath. We desire to do this in congenial company."

S. S. K., iii, 55.

6. The Sabbath Meal

The Pulnoer Rabbi said: "The young son of a lord, while at school, received a splendid gift, which he had long desired, from his father. He would have danced for joy, except that he feared the comments of his school-comrades. Therefore he invited them to a festivity, and they all danced joyfully together.

"The soul of the Jew receives from his Father a priceless gift— the spirit of the Sabbath. It desires to express its delight, but is ashamed to do so unless its mate, the body, also enjoys itself. Therefore we are enjoined to give joy to the body on the Sabbath by partaking of the Sabbath meal."

Kahana, p. 88.

7. The Master's Household

When an old woman, who had served in her youth in the household of Rabbi Elimelech, was importuned for stories about the Master and his ways, she said:

"Nought has remained with me in my remembrance, save only this. During the week, there were often quarrels in the kitchen, and upbraidings between the maidenfolk, as in other households. But in this we differed from others: on the eve of each Sabbath, we fell around each other's neck, and we begged forgiveness for any harsh words spoken during the week."

E. Tz., p. 22 (B., p. 443).

8. Without the Sabbath Spirit

The Sassover Rabbi narrated the following parable: "A man invited an important personage for a Sabbath meal, and prepared a sumptuous meal for him. Later, however, he changed his mind, and did not call for his guest.

"In similar fashion, many persons make elaborate preparations to welcome the Sabbath, but the atmosphere at their table is the same as on a week-day, and no Sabbath hymns are chanted."

O. Y., p. 194.

9. Sabbath Solitude

"Rabbi Bunam was wont to say: 'When on the Sabbath day my room is full of people, I find it hard to interpret the Law. For each man needs his own law, and needs to be perfected therein; and what I interpret for all, I withdraw from each.'"[1]

[1] Quoted by Ludwig Lewisohn, *Cities and Men*, pp. 205-6.

10. The Sabbath Candlesticks

The Medzibozer Rabbi was journeying over his customary route to gather money from his Hasidim. For the Sabbath he sojourned at the home of his brother, the Sudilkover. Noticing the humble candlesticks on his brother's Sabbath table, he remarked: "Is it not time you secured silver candlesticks for yourself?"

The Sudilkover replied: "I prefer to remain at home, and the candlesticks elsewhere, than to have the candlesticks in my home, while I absent myself."

S. ha-Has., p. 309.

11. A Sabbath Hymn

Rabbi Orele Vitebsker was accustomed to sing on the Sabbath this song:

> "Sollen Sie froehlich sein,
> Nicht mit Gold und Silber,
> Nicht mit Schaff und Rinder,
> Nicht mit Weib und Kinder,
> Nur mit dein Koenigreich allein."

This is a comment on the first few words of the prayer: "Let them rejoice with Thy kingdom." [1]

O. Y., p. 130.

[1] Singer, p. 163. The translation, freely done, is:
"Let us rejoice, not in gold and silver,
Not in sheep and cattle,
Not in wife and children,
But in Thy Kingdom alone."

12. *The Unhappy Sabbath*

The Besht and three of his Disciples came to an inn in answer to an anonymous summons. It was on a Friday afternoon, and they hoped to spend the Sabbath there. In the meantime they sought also to discover who had called them. The innkeeper at first refused them permission to remain, but finally agreed on the stipulation that they would not annoy him with Hasidic ceremonies. As if in spite, the innkeeper did everything possible to thwart their efforts to observe the Sabbath according to their customs, and subjected them to one indignity after another.

On the morrow as they were about to leave without having learned the identity of the person who had summoned them, they were addressed by a woman.

"Do you recognize me?" she asked the Besht.

"No," was his reply.

"I am Ohre, the orphan girl whom you once employed as a maid in your home," said the woman. "It was I who summoned you here. Once your wife became angry at me and slapped my face in your presence, yet you remained silent. I mentioned this to my husband, who is a Zaddik in secret, and it was he who planned to make you suffer an unhappy Sabbath as punishment for condoning the ill-treatment of an orphan. Since the Sabbath is a miniature of the 'World-to-Come,' your suffering yesterday will save you unhappiness in the After-Life."

P. I., pp. 4-7.

13. *Darkness and Light*

Said the Sassover: "Sabbath should be the 'Delight of Our Hearts.' If, however, it has become a Sad Day, it is surely because of our uncleanness on the days of the week. It is like a man who comes out of a dark place and cannot endure the light."

E. Tz., p. 55.

14. *"My Crown"*

The Razvidover related that in his youth he visited the Tzanzer on a Sabbath. The Rabbi took the cup of wine in his hand, and began to sing in an agreeable tone the words: "O Creator, Thou Art My Crown." For three hours his singing continued until the candles were nearly burned down.

E. Tz., p. 123.

15. A Partial Cure

Said the Koretzer: "The Talmud [1] teaches us that with the advent of the Sabbath we feel like shouting forth: 'Woe unto us; our soul is lost.' This may be explained as follows: when we are thoroughly sick, we feel no pain, since there is no healthy limb to feel it. But when we are only partially afflicted, the healthy part feels the ache. It is thus with us: on week-days our spirit is entirely sick. The Sabbath cures us partially, and hence we feel the loss of our soul."

E. Tz., p. 8.

[1] Taanith 27.

16. Feeding the Birds

Said the Premislaner: "It is customary to throw food to the birds on the Sabbath when the story of the Manna is read in the synagogue. The reason is as follows: Dathan and Abiram wished to prove false the assertion of Moses that no Manna would be found on the Sabbath. Hence they spread out on the ground some of the Manna they had gathered on Friday. The wild birds came and ate it, and the malicious purpose of Dathan and Abiram was frustrated. As a reward, Moses instituted the custom to feed the birds annually on the Sabbath when the Sedrah of the Manna is read."

E. A., p. 51.

17. A Branch of the Sabbath

Said the Medzibozer: "The Sabbath is greater than the World-to-Come, since the future world takes its source from the Sabbath, and is thus merely a branch of it."

Butz. D., p. 21.

18. The Conclusion of the Sabbath

Said the "Yud": "A king informed some of his vassals that he wished to pay them a visit. The wiser henchmen abandoned their private pleasures and worked vigorously to prepare a suitable reception for the royal guest. The foolish, however, made only scant preparations. The King reproved the latter, and they begged his forgiveness, promising to show him more respect henceforth.

"In the same fashion, the Lord advises us that He will visit us on the Sabbath. Some of us prepare the entire week for the reception of the Holiness of the Sabbath. Others, however, are unprepared to receive its Holiness properly, since their hearts are steeped in mundane affairs. It is fitting that at the conclusion of the Sabbath, they repent and resolve to improve themselves. This is the reason why we then chant many hymns and eat a 'Farewell to the Queen' meal."

Nif. Yeh., p. 44.

19. The Sabbath Rest

Rabbi Meier Shalom of Porissov said: "If we avoid thought of money on the Sabbath, we shall not lack it on week days." He also said: "Sabbath is a day of rest. Abstain from hard work on it, even in the service of the Lord."

D. Z., p. 15.

20. The Cripple and the Porter

Said Rabbi Sholem: "A famous musician once came to a town and posted announcements for a concert. All the well-to-do folk hurried to buy their seats. In the town there lived a man who was a great lover of music, but both his legs were crippled and he was so poor that he had not the price of a seat. He had just about enough for standing room which was of no use to him. However, he could not bear to miss this event, and for a few groschen, he induced a poor porter to carry him, perched on his back, to the concert hall. And thus seated on the porter's shoulders he listened with unbounded delight; but now and then he was so carried away by the player's genius and the beauty of the music that he forgot where he was sitting; he danced about, clapping his hands, until the porter began to complain: 'You are breaking my neck; stop kicking my sides; don't press so on my shoulders!' But the cripple forgot these complaints in the intervals of playing until finally the porter said: 'I cannot bear you any longer; I am going to set you down.' The cripple implored his indulgence and in the next intermission asked the porter to carry him to a nearby wine-shop. There he ordered a large brandy for the porter and they returned to the concert hall. Now the porter, cheered and enlivened by the drink, was himself so touched by the music that he swayed and capered to its rhythms, no longer mindful of the antics of his burden. And thus a blissful peace was established between them, and both enjoyed the concert to its end."

"Thus it is clear," continued the Rabbi, "that the important thing on the Sabbath is indeed to praise God with a pure soul; but the soul is unfortunately crippled without the body; lacking the body it can neither praise nor thank God. Now, should the body be impatient, dissatisfied, the soul will not achieve its Sabbath delight. Hence we are taught to satisfy the body, to cheer it with wine and good food, so that it too may be free to join the spirit in praise of the Almighty, to sustain the soul in joyful contemplation. Then only will the Sabbath be perfect." [1]

[1] This story is told by Mendel, one of the characters in *Hear, Ye Sons*, a novel by Irving Fineman, published by Longmans, Green and Company, 1933, pp. 238-9 (New York). It illustrates the type of story current among the folk-masses even today, and is in direct line of descent from other Hasidic tales. Perhaps it may be called "Jewish" rather than "Hasidic," inasmuch as homiletical illustrations of this kind abound in Jewish literature throughout the ages.

153. SABBATH DESECRATION

1. The Spirit of Hospitality

Rabbi Eliezer, father of the Besht, was a village innkeeper, renowned for his hospitality. A poor Jew came to him on the Sabbath, a staff in hand, and his belongings in a bundle slung over his shoulder. Rabbi Eliezer spoke no word of reproach for his guest's desecration of the Sabbath, but invited him to the Sabbath meal, and on the morrow gave him a donation.

This act of hospitality and forbearance was pleasing in the eyes of the Lord, and He granted to Rabbi Eliezer a holy son.

M. R. T., p. 45.

2. Sitting in Judgment

A man without foreknowledge or guilty intent, had desecrated the Sabbath, inasmuch as his cart had broken down on the road, and he did not (though running afoot and out of breath) reach the town ahead of the "Coming of the Bride." The youthful Rabbi Michael—he who afterwards became known to fame as the Zlotzover—punished him with hard and long-continued severities. Under these inflictions the sinner, after a while, began to suffer in health. When report of the visit of the Besht to the neighboring countryside reached his ears, he took courage, narrated his sin to the Master, and asked him to impose a fine. This the Besht did, bidding him give a pound of candles to the House of Prayer. At this light penalty, the offender wondered not a little, fearful of Rabbi Michael's disapproval. But the Master said: "Do my bidding and tell Rabbi Michael to come to me at Chvostov where I will tarry over the next Sabbath."

A wheel of Rabbi Michael's cart broke on the road to Chvostov and he had to do his errand afoot. He sought hard to make good speed, but hasten as he might, he did not reach his goal before sundown. As he reached the threshold of the Master, behold, there stood the Master, with cup lifted on high to make *Kiddush*. The Besht turned to the visitor, standing on the threshold in consternation, and said: "Good Sabbath sinner, your hand, before you sinned, was heavy upon other sinners, but henceforth it will be light, for you have tasted of their inward pain and outward shame. Therefore, good Sabbath to you, and a hearty welcome!"

B., p. 326-7 (F).

3. The Rabbi Who Forgot the Day of Sabbath

The Yanover Rabbi was invited to the wedding of a relative in a distant city. While the stagecoach was passing through a forest, the Rabbi requested the driver to halt, so that he might recite the afternoon prayer. He looked about for a stream of water at which to wash his hands, and in doing so, lost his way. The stagecoach driver endeavored without success to find him. The Rabbi walked on and on for days, eating berries and nuts for nourishment. He became so confused of mind that he lost count of the days, and kept Friday as the Sabbath. Finally he came to a settlement, and thence returned to Yanov. He refused, however, to believe that his count of the days was incorrect, and insisted upon observing Friday as the Sabbath. This greatly embarrassed his friends and the townspeople, and they sought the advice of Rabbi Schmelke of Nikolsburg, a former school-friend of their Rabbi. Rabbi Schmelke arrived in Yanov, and, after investigating, advised the people to humor their Rabbi.

On Thursday evening, Rabbi Schmelke sat down to the ostensible Sabbath meal with his friend, and unbeknown to him, dropped into the wine a sleeping draught. As soon as he drank of it, the Yanover fell into a profound slumber, and slept throughout the entire Friday. In the evening, the table was laid for the real Sabbath meal. The Yanover Rabbi was carried over to his chair and was awakened. He opened his eyes, excused himself for falling asleep and continued with the meal. When he noted that the townspeople now kept the Sabbath on the same day as himself, it was his impression that they had become convinced his reckoning was the correct one. He was never told of his long slumber.

S. H., p. 38.

4. Souls in Lament

At the time Rabbi Elimelech was living, Rabbi Dov Mordecai occupied the post of Rabbi at Lizensk. Once Rabbi Elimelech said to him: "Rabbi Dov Mordecai, let us go walking a bit," and they went into a forest at the edge of the city. At the end of the forest road, Rabbi Elimelech halted his conversation and recited the afternoon prayer. Rabbi Dov Mordecai suddenly heard a terrible lamentation, coming from many voices. He was terror-stricken, but did not move, in order not to disturb Rabbi Elimelech at his worship.

After a few moments Rabbi Elimelech stepped up to him and inquired: "Did you hear the sound?"

He replied: "I heard a tragic lamentation, but knew not whence it came."

"It was the lamentation," said Rabbi Elimelech, "of Jewish souls, who at some future time will be compelled to profane the Sabbath as soldiers."

Bl., Pr., p. 98.

5. The Baal Shem's Dream

The Sadigurer Hasid, Reb Leibush Istriker, related the following legend, while seated at the communal third meal of the Sabbath:

"When the Besht was still seeking the proper way to serve the Lord, he found that the observance of the Sabbath according to the injunctions of the later Rabbis practically prohibited any movement, and filled a man with anxiety lest he transgress some strict regulation. He believed that this contradicted the command of Isaiah to 'call the Sabbath a delight' (Isaiah 58: 13). He pondered on this for a long time, and in the night he had a dream:

"An Angel took him up to Heaven and showed him two vacant chairs in the highest place in Paradise, brilliantly illumined, as if with vari-colored gems. 'For whom are these intended?' he asked. 'For thee,' was the answer, 'if thou makest use of thy intelligence; and also for a man whose name and residence I am writing down for thee.'

"He was next taken to Gehenna at its deepest spot, and shown two vacant seats, burning with a hellish flame. 'For whom are these intended?' he asked. 'For thee,' was the answer, 'if thou makest no use of thy intelligence; and also for a man whose name and residence I am writing down for thee.'

"In his dream the Besht visited the man who was to be his companion in Paradise. He found him living among non-Jews, ignorant of Judaism, except that on the Sabbath he gave a banquet for his non-Jewish friends, wherein he greatly rejoiced.

"'Why do you hold this banquet?' asked the Besht. 'I know not,' replied the man, 'but I recall that in my youth, my parents prepared admirable meals on Saturday, and sang many songs; hence I do the same.' The Besht wished to instruct him in Judaism, inasmuch as he had been born a Jew. But the power of speech left him for the moment, since he realized that the man's joy in the Sabbath would be marred if he knew all his shortcomings in the performance of religious duties.

"The Besht then departed, in his dream, to the place where his companion in Gehenna dwelt. He found the man to be a strict observer of Judaism, always in anxiety lest his conduct was not correct, and passing the entire Sabbath day as if he were sitting on hot coals. The Besht wished to rebuke him, but once more the power of speech was taken away from him, since he realized that the man would never understand that he was doing wrong.

"Thereupon the Besht meditated on the whole matter, and evolved his new system of observance, whereby God is served in joy which comes from the heart."

F. R. H.-E., p. 91-4.

6. *Tied Hand and Foot*

Said the "Yud": "It is almost impossible not to desecrate the Sabbath in a minor fashion, unless one were tied hand and foot. But this would prevent the 'Delight of the Sabbath.'"

Nif. Yeh., p. 62.

7. *The Angel of Tales*

A certain man in Kolomeya learned that the Besht was in the town for the Sabbath. He told this to his wife at the evening meal for the Sabbath and began to deride the Besht's work. Next morning the Besht halted him, and to his surprise asked: "Is it fitting for a good Jew to deride a fellow-Jew on the holy Sabbath?"

The man retorted: "Do Angels, then, engage in tale-bearing, that they have told you what I said and did in my own home?"

"Verily," answered the Besht, "derision and an evil tongue create an Angel who does not hesitate to tell how and why he was formed."

D. D., p. 31.

154. THE SABBATH OF REPENTANCE

1. The Advocate

A preacher came to Tiktin on the Sabbath of the Penitential Period, the Sabbath of Repentance, occurring in the ten days between Rosh ha-Shanah and Yom Kippur, and reproved the congregants for being great sinners. Rabbi Meyer Hurwitz, Rabbi of the city, said to him: "Why did you not reprove me among ourselves, instead of shaming me in public?"

The preacher replied: "I meant no one in particular. I spoke in general terms."

"Nay," retorted the Rabbi. "All your hearers are good folk. You could have had in mind only my sins."

.   .   .

On the Sabbath of Repentance another year, a preacher gave a discourse in Tiktin and accused his listeners of cheating by the use of false weights and measures. The Rabbi ascended to the pulpit and exclaimed: "All of us here are average folk: neither good nor evil. We are now being judged in the Heavenly Court of Justice, and I declare before the Judge on High, that this preacher's accusation is false."

S. ha-Tov., p. 114.

2. When the Lord Is To Be Found

Said the Belzer in a Yom Kippur sermon: "We read in Isaiah 55:6: 'Seek ye the Lord while He may be found; call ye upon Him while He is near; let the wicked forsake his way, and the man of iniquity his thoughts.' The question arises: why does the Prophet begin in the plural and continue in the singular? Moreover, he begins to address his hearers in the second person, and continues in the third.

"We are told in the Talmud that on Yom Kippur even the Satan can find no fault with Israel,[1] and must admit that their actions on that day are divine in character.

"The Talmud also tells us: 'When is the Lord to be found and when is He near? In the Ten Days of Penitence.'[2]

[1] Yoma 20.
[2] Rosh Ha-Shanah 18.

"Therefore we may interpret the verse as follows: 'Seek ye the Lord with your whole heart. Then even the Satan, the source of wickedness and unrighteousness, will forsake his way and his designs against you, as on Yom Kippur.'"

D. S., p. 105.

3. Take With You Words

In his Yom Kippur sermon, the Belzer said: "When the sinner feels contrition for his offense, the gravity of it is lightened. Yet this is insufficient, for confession by word of mouth is necessary, and we are commanded by the Lord to pronounce in words our admission of guilt.

"We may interpret Hosea 14:2: 'Return, O Israel, unto the Lord thy God' to indicate repentance within our own heart, such repentance being known to the Lord alone.

"The second step follows: 'Take with you words, and return unto the Lord; say unto Him: "Forgive all iniquity and accept that which is good." Accept our repentance graciously when we substitute for sacrifices the sincere words of our lips.'"

D. S., p. 105.

155. THE SATAN

1. The Satan's Hasidim

The Alexanderer Rabbi, observing the unruly conduct of many of his Hasidim, related the following allegory:

"When the Baal Shem Tov originated his Hasidic system, the Satan feared he would be humiliated by reason of the holiness of the new system of faith. He, therefore, induced many of his own adherents to join the few true Hasidim, with the result that the Satan's Hasidim became the ruling majority."

S. S. K., iv, 45.

2. Who Imprisoned The Satan?

The Riziner said: "When I was imprisoned as a political prisoner, I understood why the Midrash describes the Satan, the Evil Impulse, as a fool.[1] Even in prison the Evil Impulse would not leave me for a moment. Is he not, then, a fool? I was compelled to remain in prison, but who compelled the Satan to do so?"

M. D., p. 222.

[1] Commenting on Ecclesiastes 4:13; in Koheleth Rabba 4:15.

3. The Omnipresent Satan

The Berditschever was invited in his youth to read the "Atta Hareitah" prayers on Simchath Torah. He ascended the "Bimah," but stood there silently. Finally he returned to his seat without reciting a word. His father-in-law wished to know the reason for such an action.

The Berditschever explained: "When I was ready to begin my prayers, I suddenly felt that the Evil Impulse, the Satan, wished to recite them with me. Therefore I asked him: 'Who are you to dare recite these important prayers before the whole congregation?'

'And who are you?' was his reply.

'I am a man learned in the Torah,' I answered.

'So am I, and when you studied, I kept you company,' answered the Satan.

'But I am also a Hasid of the Mezeritzer Maggid,' I rejoined.

'So am I; I kept you company then as well,' he said.

'Since this is so,' I replied, 'if you are both a 'Lamdan' and a 'Hasid,' go and say the prayers yourself.'

"And I descended from the Bimah." [1]

Kahana, p. 251; B., p. 452.

[1] "Bimah" is the Pulpit of the Synagogue; or the Reading-Desk. "Lamdan" is the scholarly student. "Atta Hareitah," "Unto thee it was shown" (Deut. 4:35); a collection of verses recited on Simchath Torah, previous to the opening of the Ark. The collection bears the name of the first two words.

4. Each to His Work

The Satan came to the Lizensker with the warning that unless he did not stop persuading people to repent, he would set aside all other labors and use his every power to tempt the Rabbi. The Lizensker replied: "I am sure that you are already doing your utmost to lead me into transgression. I shall leave you to your work, and I shall go on with my own."

E. Tz., p. 29.

5. The Evil Impulse Has No Satan

When Rabbi Eliezer Dzikover was a young boy, he once became unruly. The Ropshitzer, his father, rebuked him. The lad answered: "Father, it is not my fault; the Evil Impulse tempted me, and I succumbed."

"Learn from the Evil Impulse how to do your duty," said the Ropshitzer.

"But, Father," replied the boy, "the Evil Impulse has no Satan to tempt him away from his duty."

Ohel N., p. 36.

6. Satan's Chief Joy

Said the Besht: "The chief joy of the Satan is when he succeeds in persuading a man that an evil deed is a Mitzwah. For when a man is weak and commits an offense, knowing it to be a sin, he is likely to repent of it. But when he believes it to be a good deed, does it stand to reason that he will repent of performing a Mitzwah?"

K. S. T., p. 6a.

156. THE SEDER

1. Burning the Hametz

On the Eve before Passover, the Riziner explained the rules of the search after leavened crumbs in the following manner:

"This evening we make search after Hametz, but we do not burn it before the morrow. The search and the burning are allegories of the things to come. Galuth is the night during which we suffer the Hametz,—the meaner qualities of our people—to remain in the house. But when the morning of our Redemption comes, they are cast into the fire of our return, and altogether consumed. Then the words of Isaiah (25:8) will become truth: 'Death will disappear forever and the tears of man will be wiped away.'"

N. I., p. 58; Bl., Gem., pp. 286-7.

2. Matzah and Bitters

Rabbi Bunam said: "We eat the Seder meal in the following order: the Matzah first and the Bitter Herbs next, though it would seem the reverse order is proper, since we first suffered and later were freed. The reason for this, however, is that as long as there was no prospect of being redeemed, the Israelites did not feel keenly the bitterness of their lot. But as soon as Moses spoke to them of freedom, they awoke to the bitterness of their slavery."

S. S. K., i, 53.

3. Grain That May Become Hametz

Said the Apter Rabbi: "There is a Talmudic rule that one may fulfill his duty to eat Matzah only with grain that may be leavened and become Hametz.[1] We may learn from this fact ethical principles of value. A man can perform his duties of full service to the Lord, only if he serves Him also in his daily works—in his occupation, his eating and drinking, and in the conduct of his possessions. All of these may be performed in a profane manner: a man may cheat, he may eat unlawful food, he may purchase forbidden pleasures. Therefore if he engages in these activities in the spirit of obedience to God's commandments, he has performed a high duty indeed. But one who merely serves the Lord by studying Torah and by prayer has not performed his complete duty—since these cannot be turned to unlawful purposes."

M. G., ii, 31.

[1] Pesachim 35.

4. The Water-Carrier's Seder

A famous Rabbi was known throughout the region for his elaborate Seder ceremony. One day, following Passover, a stranger came to him and said: "There is a certain Isaac ben Jacob whose Seder this year has been even finer than yours." His curiosity piqued, the Rabbi summoned the Isaac ben Jacobs of the community, but each was found to have performed the ceremony in the customary fashion. Finally the Rabbi learned that in the town there was a certain Isaac ben Jacob, a humble water-carrier, addicted to drunkenness. He was called into the Rabbi's presence.

"What kind of a Seder did you have this year?" inquired the Rabbi.

The water-carrier burst into tears. On further questioning, the Rabbi discovered that the water-carrier had received an unusually large number of gifts of Passover wine from his patrons. He imbibed freely of them before the Seder, became intoxicated, fell asleep and did not awaken until the next morning when he saw the townsfolk entering the synagogue. In great distress of spirit and sincerely repentant, the water-carrier placed four cups of wine on the Seder table, and cried out: "O Lord, Thou art the greatest God in the Heavens, and I, I am the greatest drunkard on the earth!"

One moment of genuine contrition, say the Hasidim, is worth the most ostentatious and elaborate ceremonies.[1]

[1] Told to Rabbi Newman by Rabbi I. Tabak, descendant of a famous Hasidic "dynasty." The Yiddish of a similar version, told with variations regarding the Berditschever, is to be found in *Or Zaddikim,* pp. 31-34. See Buber, "Der Seder der Unwissenden," *Buecher,* p. 463.

5. *The Rabbi's Seder*

On the eve of Passover, it transpired that the Premislaner Rabbi gave away all his money to the poor, and his wife had nothing with which to buy meat for the Holyday. She discovered an article of value, pawned it, and with the money bought a small chicken. When Rabbi Meyer came from the synagogue, he informed his wife he had heard of a poor woman who had just given birth to a child, and who had no chicken or soup in her house.

"Give me the chicken and the soup for her," said the Rabbi. "We are able to eat Matzah and potatoes." He carried the food to the woman, and then returned home to conduct the Seder, with contented heart.

O. H., p. 42.

6. *The Gentile's Impatience*

Two neighbors, a Jew and a Gentile, being without employment, resorted to begging from door to door. Close to Passover, the Jew instructed the Gentile, who knew Yiddish, to pretend to be a Jew, and thereby receive an invitation to a Seder. The Jew also instructed his friend to follow the host's example during the ceremony. The Gentile was duly invited to a Seder and on arriving at the house, smelt with delight the appetizing foods. He hoped soon to partake of them, since he was famished. To his disappointment, however, the food was not served. Instead a glass of wine was given him, and it whetted his appetite still more. To his disgust he was given some bitter herbs soaked in salt water, was compelled to dissemble reading the Haggadah, and then received more wine. At last a piece of Matzah was given him, and he anticipated that solid food would soon follow. Instead he was offered some horse-radish and later a horse-radish sandwich.

The hungry man could endure it no longer. He rose angrily from his place, and with imprecations upon his host, hastily left the house, as hungry as when he entered it. A few hours later his companion arrived at their sleeping quarters and with great surprise listened to his disappointing experience.

"You impatient fool," exclaimed the Jew. "Had you waited another moment, what beautiful viands would have been yours. If you pretend to be a Jew, you must learn the first requirement of being a Jew—to be patient and to trust in a better future."

Kotzker Maasioth, p. 108.

7. Loquacity and Silence

Said the Koretzer: "Loquacity is proper at a banquet, and silence at a house of mourning. It is for this reason that we must strive to persuade the 'one who knows not what to ask' [1] to talk also at the celebration of the Seder."

Nof. Tz., p. 24.

[1] In the Passover Haggadah.

8. The Two Seder Meals

Rabbi Samuel Kariver, though very poor, resolved to ask aid from no one, whatever betide. His Master, the Lubliner, became aware of this, and instructed a rich Hasid to buy goods requisite for Passover, and to deliver them to his Disciple, the Kariver. So pleased was Rabbi Samuel that the Lord had permitted him to adhere to his resolution to ask no man's aid, that he recited the Seder Service in high spirits. It seemed to him that he had attained a rare state of holiness.

The second evening, Rabbi Samuel was weary and worn, and lay down for a rest before the Seder. He fell asleep and awoke a few moments before midnight. He wished to partake of the Afikomen [1] before midnight, and therefore was compelled to recite the Seder Service very rapidly. This made him feel low of spirits, and he wondered whether any other Jew had ever been compelled to perform a Seder so hurriedly. When he related the episode to his Master, the Lubliner said: "Your first Seder was of little merit. Your belief that you had flown straight to Heaven was a sign of arrogance. Your second Seder, however, was of higher worth, inasmuch as humility and a knowledge of your frailties accompanied it."

Hith. Z., pp. 66-7.

[1] Afikomen is the last morsel of a Matzah, eaten at the end of the Seder meal in memory of the morsel of the Paschal lamb which was eaten after the meal in the days of the Temple.

9. The Ordinary Matzah

At the Seder meal, the Zbarazer ate only a special Matzah [1] which is baked from special flour on the afternoon of the same day. A Hasid brought with him some ordinary Matzah and began to eat it. The others rebuked him, and the Rabbi said: "Do you believe that the millions of our fellow-Jews who eat plain Matzoth at their Sedarim are not fulfilling their obligation, and that we are exceptionally good?" He took the ordinary Matzah and ate of it, contrary to his life-long habit.

S. H. H., chapter 4.

[1] The Hebrew name for the special Matzah is "Matzah Shemurah."

157. SEEKING COMMUNION WITH THE LORD

1. Where He Is Invited

The Kotzker Rabbi said: "Do you know where the Lord is to be found? He is in the place where He is invited to enter."

S. S. K., i, 71.

2. God Alone Is Desired

While absorbed in his devotions, the Ladier Rabbi was heard to say: "My Lord and God. I do not desire Thy Paradise; I do not desire the bliss of the After-World; I desire only Thee, Thyself."

S. ha-Has., p. 203.

3. The Joy of the Quest

The Apelier Rabbi made the following comment on the verse (I Chronicles 16:10): "Let the heart of them rejoice that seek the Lord": "When one seeks a certain object, he feels no gladness in his heart until his quest is successful. But when one seeks the Lord, the very act of seeking Him rejoices the heart of the seeker."

S. S. K., v, 48.

4. No Strange God

The Kotzker Rabbi paraphrased the verse (Psalm 81:10): "There shall no strange god be in thee," as follows: "God shall not be a stranger in thee."

S. S. K., iii, 77.

5. Opening to the Beloved

The Lekhivitzer Rabbi thus explained the verse (Song of Songs 5:5): "I rose up to open to my beloved": "I am endeavoring to admit the Lord: all my good deeds serve only as an effort to open my companionship to the Most High. 'My hands drop with myrrh'; then I please Him by knowing how little value my actions have. But when I believe that 'I have opened to my beloved indeed,' that by my conduct, I deserve communion with Him, then 'my beloved had turned away and was gone.' "

O. Y., p. 19.

6. The Former Days

Said the Kobriner: "Some people say: 'Nowadays it is difficult to serve the Lord. Formerly there were many good and pious folk whose example could be imitated.'

"This notion is absurd, and I say to them: 'Have you truly endeavored to seek the Lord without avail? Endeavor to seek Him in the manner of those in former days and you too will find Him, even as they did.' We may learn this from the verse (Ecclesiastes 7:10): 'Say not thou: "How was it that the former days were better than these?" for it is not out of wisdom that thou inquirest concerning this.' "

O. Y., p. 91.

7. The Miraculous Palace

The Sudilkover Rabbi narrates this parable (in *Degel Machne Ephraim*) which he heard from his grandfather, the Baal Shem Tov:

"A wise king built a vast palace which he adorned with beautiful trappings. It possessed many rooms, and the door of each was exactly opposite the door of the next room. The King's throne-room was in the farthest room. The nobles were invited to enter the presence of the King. As soon, however, as they entered the gate of the court, they observed that all the palace doors swung closed. They did not know how to enter the King's presence through so many intervening doors. Finally a page came over and said to them: 'All these doors appear only to be locked; in reality, a vigorous push will open them, and you may easily proceed into the presence of the King.'

"We are told that our Lord dwells on high, and that our greed, deceit and sinfulness intervene between us and our Father. This, however, only seems to be true; in reality a genuine and wholehearted effort on our part to break away from our faults, will bring us near to God."

Kahana, p. 86.

8. Treasures That Impede

"There was once a king who built himself a glorious palace. By means of magical illusion it seemed as if the palace were filled with devious corridors and mazes, preventing the approach to the royal presence. But as there was much gold and silver heaped up in the entrance halls, most people were content to go no farther but to take their fill of treasure. The king himself, they did not notice.

"At last the king's intimate had compassion upon them and exclaimed to them: 'All these walls and mazes which you see before you do not in truth exist at all. They are mere illusions. Push forward bravely, and you shall find no obstacles.' "

Schechter, Studies in Judaism, p. 34.

9. The Unlearned Near to God

Rabbi Sussya of Anipol was not learned in the Torah like his brother, the Lizensker, but he became a Hasid earlier. Once the Lizensker asked his brother: "Why do you waste your time with Hasidism? If you have spare time, you should increase your knowledge of the Torah."

Rabbi Sussya replied: "I shall tell you a story. There was once an artisan who saved up a sum of money and decided to move to the royal residence where he could see more often his greatly-beloved master, the King. On his arrival, he induced the Chamberlain to assign him to the task of furnace-man in the palace, so that he might be near the king. He strove to keep the palace at an even temperature and to do everything to make the ruler comfortable. The king became aware of this, and asked to see the furnace attendant. The man told him he had given up his trade to accept a post which would bring him into association with the ruler, and he asked for permission to see the latter whenever he wished. The king replied he could not be disturbed in this way, but he permitted the loyal servant to bore a hole in the ceiling of the throne-room, whence he could behold him. In the meantime, a prince had displeased his royal father and was banished from the palace. The prince wished to catch a glimpse of his royal sire, and therefore accompanied the furnace-man to the garret, whence he could look at the king through the crevice. He could understand, however, what he beheld in the throne room better than the other man.

"We both love our Master, the Lord," continued Rabbi Sussya. "Through following the instructions of Hasidic Rabbis, I, the unlearned, feel myself near to God. How much the more will you, a learned Rav, be able to understand the Lord if you but employ the proper methods."

Rabbi Elimelech, the Lizensker, thereupon joined Rabbi Sussya when he next went to the Maggid of Mezeritz, and he likewise became a famous Rebbe.

N. E., p. 19.

10. The Labyrinth

Rabbi Bunam narrated this parable: "A king who wished to be untroubled by the curiosity of visitors, built a labyrinth about his palace. Once he heard a man who had lost his way, crying for help. He took pity on him and led him out of the maze. Another man numbered the turns with indelible marks, and thereby avoided passing the same turn twice; he advanced easily on his way and soon reached the King. Both came into the royal presence, but the King also made a pathway for others as well.

"In the same fashion, a man may attain holiness through crying aloud unto the Lord after turning backward and forward; he does not know, however, the direct path. The truly wise Zaddik teaches his adherents the proper manner of advancing directly to the goal without the need to retrace steps."

S. I., p. 55.

11. The Thickness of a Needle

Said Rabbi Bunam: "The Midrash teaches that God declares to us: 'Open thy heart unto Me as much as the thickness of a needle, and I will open it for thee as wide as the portal of a vast hall.'[1] I add this thought: 'But God wishes this opening of needle-thickness to be not merely a scratch, but through and through.' "

S. I., p. 56.

[1] Shir ha-Shirim Rabba 5:3.

12. God's Complaint

The Medzibozer's grandson, Yechiel Michel, was playing hide and seek with another child. He hid himself for some time, but his playmate did not look for him. Little Yechiel ran to Rabbi Baruch and said amid tears: "He did not look for me."

The Rabbi said: "This is also God's complaint, that we seek Him not."

Butz. D., p. 32.

13. Thoughts of Home

Said the Mezeritzer: "Two young men left their homes to seek their fortune. After the lapse of considerable time, both began to think of returning. One cherished thoughts of home when he met with failure, reminding himself then of the quiet and pleasant life among his family in contrast to his present tribulations. The other youth thought of home when he prospered: he dwelt upon the pleasure his homecoming would bring to his parents.

"The lesson is clear: some think of God only in times of tribulation; others in prosperity as well."

T. M. M., p. 245.

14. Perfect Concentration

Said the Besht: "When you are laboring on work which brings you either pleasure or wealth, you know you must concentrate upon it all your thoughts. Do likewise when you are laboring on that which will bring you into communion with the Lord and His holiness. If you fail to do so, your work is fruitless."

M. R. T., ii, 58.

15. The Royal Palace

Said the Besht: "A king built himself a palace and surrounded it with guards. Many of the people came to behold the King, but when they saw the guards, they departed. Others gave presents to the guards, and were permitted to enter. But when they saw the ornaments in the great halls, they halted to look at them and forgot their mission to see the King. Still others looked neither at the guards nor the decorations, but walked straight into the presence of the ruler. "Some people," continued the Besht, "who wish to commune with the Lord, retreat at the first hindrance. Others bring the gifts of charity and kind deeds before they commence their prayers, but they become engrossed in a wise comment or fine saying in the Prayer Book. Still others, however, concentrate their mind immediately upon God, and refuse to be diverted by any distraction, however appealing."

M. R. T., ii, 90-1.

16. Food with Struggle

Rabbi Bunam was asked to explain why the serpent which beguiled Adam received the comfortable punishment of finding his food everywhere without labor or struggle, whereas human beings were commanded to eat their bread in the sweat of their brow.[1]

The Rabbi replied: "The sentence upon the serpent was the greatest possible punishment. God said to him 'Dust shalt thou eat, and thou shalt have no further intercourse with Me, since there will always be plentiful food for thee, and thou shalt have no need to turn to Me.' But Adam and Eve were compelled to look to the blessings of God for food, and if they lacked bread, they turned to Him with entreaties. Thus they and their descendants will always be in communion with God."

S. I., p. 60.

[1] Genesis 3:14-19.

17. Indolence and Pleasure

Said Rabbi Bunam: "We can find God and achieve holiness only if we devote our leisure to holy studies and lead an exemplary life; not if we repose indolently in our homes, or waste our time in the pursuit of city enjoyments. We read:[1] 'By night in bed I have sought Him whom my soul loveth; I sought Him but I found Him not. I will rise now, and go about the city, in the streets and in the broad ways; I will seek Him whom my soul loveth; I sought Him but I found Him not. Scarce had I passed from them, when I found Him whom my soul loveth.' As soon as a man puts away indolence in bed and pleasure-seeking in the city, he finds God."

[1] Song of Songs 3:1-4.

S. I., p. 73.

158. SELFISHNESS (EGOTISM)

1. The Hedge

The Zlotzover Maggid commented upon the words (Deut. 5:5): "I stand between God and you." "A person who thinks of his own importance and of his own ego entertains an idea which stands between the Lord and himself. It places a barrier, a hedge between Godhead and him. The word 'I' only God can utter."

O. Y., p. 86; Bl., Pr., p. 76 and 84.

2. The "Zaddik in Furs"

The Kotzker said: "In freezing weather one man keeps warm by donning a fur-coat; the other by heating his house. The first cares merely for himself; the other cares for others as well. The first is the 'Zaddik in furs' of popular report."

S. S. K., iv, 109.

3. The Vanity of Personal Desires

The Bratzlaver said: "The Evil Impulse is like a boy who teases his friends by asking them to guess what is in his closed hand. Each person guesses that the hand conceals whatever is particularly desirable to himself. But when the hand is opened, it is found to contain nothing."

Dubnow, T. H., p. 303.

4. Struggling With Egotism

The Midrash tells us that when God instructed Moses to collect a half-shekel for the ransom of each soul, He showed to Moses a coin of fire, and said to him: "Such a coin they shall give." [1]

The Kotzker offered the following explanation: "Moses could not understand how so small a donation would suffice to ransom a soul. Hence the Lord told them that it would suffice if given with burning enthusiasm."

The Kobriner added: "It suffices because they give it after a struggle with fiery egotism and self-interest."

[1] Tanchumah to Wayyikra.

O. Y., p. 77.

5. The Nature of Selfishness

The Hobnover Rabbi told the following tale: "A beggar woman was accustomed to say to her benefactors: 'Whatever one does, he does for himself.' A wealthy noblewoman who befriended her, became thoroughly incensed at this remark, and resolved to teach her a lesson. She inserted a harmful drug into a freshly-baked cake, which she gave to the beggar woman. The latter set it aside for the Sunday meal.

The following day the noblewoman's son lost his way in the forest while hunting, and staggered, hungry and footsore, into the beggar woman's hut. The woman recognized the youth, and, desiring to be hospitable, gave him the cake which his mother had presented to her. On eating it, the young man became unconscious. The beggar woman in terror ran to the noblewoman and told her of the youth's mishap. After a long illness, he recovered, and his mother ruefully confessed her guilt.

"You were right," she said. "Whatever we do, we do for ourselves."

Geulath ha-Aretz, p. 69.

6. His Private Personality

Said the Gerer Rabbi: "The proud man is of small profit to the community; he is too much occupied with his private personality. We read in Ecclesiastes (9:15): 'Now there was found in it a poor man and wise, and he by his wisdom delivered the city.' It was because he was poor, and thus devoid of pride and egotism, that he was able to deliver the city."

S. S. K., ii, 53.

7. The Incurable Egotist

Said the Alexanderer: "Sadness is the worst quality of a man. It is the attribute of an incurable egotist. He always thinks: 'Something should rightfully come to me; something is wrongfully withheld from me.' Whether in relation to substance or spirit, it is always 'I.'"

S. S. K., i, 115.

8. The Mirror and Its Silver

"One day a Hasid came to the Rabbi; he was rich, but a miser. The Rabbi took him by the hand and led him to the window.

"'Look out there,' he said. And the rich man looked into the street.

"'What do you see?' asked the Rabbi.

"'People,' answers the rich man. Again the Rabbi takes him by the hand, and this time leads him to the mirror.

"'What do you see now?' he says. 'Now I see myself,' answers the rich man.

"Then the Rabbi says: 'Behold—in the window there is glass, and in the mirror there is glass. But the glass of the mirror is covered with a little silver, and no sooner is the silver added than you cease to see others but see only yourself.'" [1]

[1] From S. Ansky's *"The Dybbuk,"* p. 65; see my poem "Add a Little Silver" in *Joyful Jeremiads*, p. 96.

9. The Gilt Foliage

Before Rabbi Eisig succeeded his uncle Hirsch in the wardship of Ziditzov, he used to travel the countryside. He was welcomed everywhere and received gifts in coin and kind, enough to lift him beyond all straits for his sustenance. Once he came to a village where only one Jew lived, and that a poor one. There was a downpour of rain, and Rabbi Eisig was forced to halt and seek shelter. His host gave him supper and prepared a couch for him.

"You have been sighing all this while," said the guest. "Why are you sighing?"

"Because I am too poor to do you proper honor," answered the host.

The Rabbi, much affected, gave him his blessing, calling upon Heaven to endow the poor man with riches in order that he might be able to care for the needy in generous fashion.

The Rabbi's blessing proved effective. The poor villager prospered in his business from day to day; he was fortunate beyond the reach of his boldest expectations in his every venture, and he soon became the wealthiest man within a compass of several miles. But with his wealth grew his avarice, and with his avarice a new haughty bearing toward the poor, whom he disdained now as much as he had regarded them before. In the hardness of his heart he engaged a Warden giving him strict orders to stand at the door and to allow no poor man to go beyond the gate.

In the meantime, Rabbi Eisig had achieved renown as an illustrious Zaddik and as head of a well-known community. When he heard of the villager's change of heart, he journeyed toward his abode. At the gate he was halted by the Warden, shouting: "Forbear; my Master is in private discourse with a noted person."

"Tell him, nevertheless," insisted the Rabbi, "that the man who brought him riches by his blessing is awaiting his welcome at the gate!"

He was admitted, but his reception at the hands of the wealthy host was by no means friendly. Thereupon Rabbi Eisig invited his host to step to the window, bidding him to look out.

"What do you see?" asked the Rabbi.

"I see the people going about their business upon the streets," answered the rich man.

"Now look into the mirror, and tell me what you see," continued the Rabbi.

"Only myself do I see," said the host.

The Rabbi laughed and said: "Both the window and the mirror are squares of glass; yet you see others through the window and only yourself in the mirror. Know ye why? Because the mirror is a square of glass with a gilt foliage behind it. It is time to scratch off the gilt."

And with this the Rabbi turned to the rear side of the mirror. "Stop, I beg of you," cried his host, who understood his meaning. "Leave me my riches, and I will consider the poor from this day forward, as in duty bound."

His change of heart was sincere, and, from having been a miser, he became a veritable father to the widow and the orphan.

Bl., Gem., p. 337 (F).

10. Forgetting Our Existence

Commenting on the "Ethics of the Fathers" (Singer, p. 187): "If I am not for myself, who will be for me? And being for my own self, what am I?" the Besht said: "If at the time of worship, I do not feel any material existence, what foreign thoughts can come to me?

But if I think of my own self at the time, what am I, seeing that I do not serve the Lord even for the duration of my devotion?"

M. R. T., ii, 26.

11. The Wall Between God and Ourselves

Rabbi Michael of Zlotzov expounded the verse:[1] "I stand between God and you." He said: "What stands between you and God like a wall is your Ego. This I, this consciousness of a separate existence, is a wall between you and the Divinity. For the Majesty of God rests only upon him who conceives of himself as a speck in the universe. 'I' is a word that has proper meaning only in the mouth of God."

"Shall man, then, always walk in meekness? Not so, say the Zaddikim. There are moments when haughtiness becomes a duty. When the Evil Inclination approaches, whispering into the ear: 'You are unworthy to fulfill the Law,' say: 'I am worthy.'"

Bl., Pr., p. 84.

[1] Deut. 5:5. See 158:1.

12. Selfish Prayers

Rabbi Michael of Zlotzov lived in great poverty. Once a man asked him: "Since the Lord hearkens to the prayers of the Zaddikim and fulfills their requests, why do you not ask Him for sustenance?"

The Maggid replied: "There was a king who proclaimed a feast during the wedding festivities of his daughter. He decreed that savory food and drink be given every one who called at the court during the stated period. But the princess became dangerously ill, and the king's joy turned into mourning. Several visitors from other cities arrived at the palace at this time. Those of finer nature left at once on hearing the sad tidings and did nothing to disturb the court's grief. But one man, of unsympathetic nature, asked for the promised viands. He received them, but all the courtiers regarded him with contempt.

"Likewise God's Shekinah is grieving at the Exile and the tribulation of God's daughter, the Congregation of Israel. How, then, have I the heart to ask for selfish comforts?"

M. H. H., p. 8.

159. SELF-IMPROVEMENT

1. Do Better

Rabbi Bunam went to the market to purchase grain. The farmer was dissatisfied with the price the Rabbi offered, and said: "Do better." This phrase captivated the Rabbi's imagination, and many times afterwards he persuaded his adherents to repent by repeating the farmer's plea: "Do better!"

S. S. K., i, 33.

2. Making the Earth Into Heaven

Said the Alexanderer Rabbi: "The expression in Psalms (115: 16): 'The Heavens are the Heavens of the Lord; but the earth hath He given to the children of men' means: 'The Heavens are already heavenly, but the earth hath the Lord given unto men that they may make of it the Heavens.' "

S. S. K., i, 99.

3. Inspiration to Improve

Said Rabbi Bunam: "There is a saying:[1] 'If a man remains at home, he will have no occasion for remorse.' This may be understood to mean that when a Hasid leaves home to journey to the Rabbi, he encounters other persons there. By observing the virtues wherein they excel him, he feels remorse at his own shortcomings and attempts to do better. But when the Hasid remains at home, he finds no reason for self-condemnation."

S. S. K., iv, 43.

[1] Popular; non-Talmudical.

4. The Watch

Rabbi Yerachmiel narrated the following story: "When I was a youth, newly married, I lived with my father-in-law, a watchmaker. I desired greatly to visit a famous Rabbi, but had no money for the journey. I said to my father-in-law: 'If you will give me a few dollars, I will repair the little watch with which you have had no patience to bother.' He agreed and I took apart the watch to discover the cause of the difficulty. I soon saw that nothing was lacking, but that a tiny hairspring was twisted. This I soon made straight, placed everything together and the watch began to keep time once more. Does this not teach that a slight twist of the heart oftentimes halts the normal moral feeling? A little adjustment and the heart beats properly again."

S. S. K., ii, 123.

5. The Candle

Rabbi Sussya and Rabbi Elimelech once came to a village inn to spend the night. The innkeeper was repairing Rabbi Sussya's coat by candlelight. "Make haste," called out the innkeeper's wife. "Repair the coat quickly or the candle will soon be consumed."

"How true is this with regard to the betterment of our life," commented the Rabbi. "According to the Bible, 'the spirit of man is the lamp of the Lord, searching all the inward parts' (Proverbs 20:27). When it is consumed, every opportunity for self-improvement is past."

S. S. K., ii, 80.

6. Self-Reliance

When thousands of Disciples came to Gerer on a festival, the Gerer said to them: "Let me be candid with you. You cannot depend upon me as an intermediary between God and ourselves. I can merely attempt to point out to you the right paths in good conduct, leading to Godliness. But you must walk thereon without my aid. Learn to stand on your own feet, and even if your Rebbe is not a great man, you will not fall."

M. E. H., ii, 58-9.

160. SELF-KNOWLEDGE

1. The Lantern on the Highway

A young Rabbi complained to his Master: "During the hours when I am studying, I feel filled with light and life, but as soon as I cease to study, this mood disappears. What ought I do?"

Thereupon the Rabbi replied: "It is like a man who journeys through a forest on a dark night, and part of the way is accompanied by a companion who carries a lantern. At length they come to the point where their paths divide, and they must go on alone. If each carries his own lantern, he need fear no darkness."

Reflex, May, 1929, p. 67.

2. Self-Instruction

A man of piety complained to the Besht, saying: "I have labored hard and long in the service of the Lord, and yet I have received no improvement. I am still an ordinary and ignorant person."

The Besht answered: "You have gained the realization that you are ordinary and ignorant, and this in itself is a worthy accomplishment."

M. R. T., p. 106.

3. A New Order

Rabbi Eleazar commented on the verse (Genesis 12:1): " 'Get thee out of thy country'—do not hesitate to leave thy country because there reside in it famous persons. 'And out of thy birthplace'—out of the place where a spirit of breeding aids in the cultivation of intellectual people. 'And from thy father's house'—from the place where you are respected as a member of a noble family. But go 'unto the land which I will show you'—to found there a center of culture, learning and nobility, by your own labors."

O. Y., p. 82.

4. His Letters

It was the habit of Rabbi David Talner to spend half an hour early each morning reading his mail in his private room. An intimate asked why he did this before prayers the first thing of the day. The Rabbi answered: "I wish to commence the day aright. As you know, the more important a man is, the harder are his struggles against his evil thoughts,[1] since the Satan striveth hardest to tempt

[1] Sukkah 52.

him. Hence when I look over my letters and read in the salutation that I am called a Zaddik, a Leader, a Holy Man, and the like, I pray to the Lord: 'You and I know that I do not merit these titles of honor. But since so many good men believe them in all sincerity, I beseech Thee to aid me to avoid the snares of Satan, so that these men may not feel shame!' "

F. R. H.-M., ii, 123.

5. Self-Dissatisfaction

The Talmudical saying: "As for the disciple of the wise who becomes angry—it is the Torah that enkindles him," [1] was explained by the Ropshitzer, thus: "The Torah shows him that he has not fulfilled his duties, and he becomes angry at himself."

E. Tz., p. 94.

[1] Taanith 4.

6. A Wise King

A Rabbi told the following stories to illustrate the verse that the heart of a ruler is in the hands of the Almighty: [1]

Some priests complained to a king that the synagogue in the community was taller than the church. He replied: "I rule in the length and breadth of the land. In the height, however, there is another Ruler."

The king visited a prison and talked to the prisoners. Each asserted his innocence, except one who confessed to theft. "Throw this scoundrel out," exclaimed the king. "He will corrupt the innocents." [2]

L. H. S., pp. 46 and 51.

[1] Proverbs 21:1.
[2] Proverbs 28:13, vide.

7. The Sensitive and the Coarse

Said the Bershider: "There are two kinds of men. One possesses a character of nobility. He is sensitive to every slight offense, and is pained at every unworthy thought. He discovers within himself much requiring self-criticism.

"Another type of man is coarse of character. He feels only offenses that are serious, after they are pointed out to him. For him a preacher is required to reprove him, since he does not indulge in self-study."

M. P., p. 40.

8. Seeing Our Own Defects

Said the Besht: "It is not good for a man to be alone, for he cannot know his own defects. By observing the acts which he dislikes in a fellowman, he can see his own defects as in a mirror. He would not have been given the opportunity to note his comrade's offense if he had not been unconsciously guilty in some degree of the same offense. Likewise, if a man is disturbed in his study or worship by his neighbor's revelries, it is a sign from Heaven that his interest has been turning in the wrong direction, and he should commence afresh with the proper intention."

K. S. T., p. 21b.

9. The Highest Joy

Said the Besht: "What if thou hast never transgressed, if the source of sin is in thy heart! Thou mayest not have offended because thou wast not tempted by circumstances and opportunities, or because thou wast prevented by shame. Dost thou know that anger is like unto idolatry? That pride is like unto adultery? Dost thou know that evil thoughts are worse than evil acts, for thoughts give life to deeds? Thou art righteous only when thou feelest more joy in cleaving unto the Lord than in any material pleasure."

M. R. T., ii, 59.

161. SELF-MASTERY AND THE EVIL IMPULSE

1. Mastering Evil Desires

A villager lamented to the Kobriner that his evil desires constantly overcame him and caused him to fall into transgression.

"Do you ride a horse?" the Rabbi inquired.

"Yes," answered the villager.

"What do you do if you happen to fall off?"

"I mount again," said the villager.

"Well, imagine the Evil Impulse to be the horse," remarked the Rabbi. "If you fall, mount again. Eventually you will master it." [1]

O. Y., p. 108.

[1] This is an excellent example of the manner in which the Hasidic Rabbis made use of simple, homely folk-material to drive home their ethical lessons.

2. From Furrow to Furrow

Said the Kobriner: "In our struggle against the Evil Impulse we are like men who walk on a field from furrow to furrow. Now they go up, now down. Likewise, there are times when men are on the top of their impulses, and times when they are under them. We must make sure that the struggle ends when we are on top."

O. Y., p. 54.

3. The Battle

The Kobriner once interpreted the verse (Deut. 20:1): " 'When thou goest forth to battle against thine enemies'—against thy evil impulses; 'and thou seest horses and chariots and a people in greater number'; thou feelest the attraction of a multitude of evil desires; 'from thee'; though they came to you, because you permitted them to grow and multiply within you. 'Be not afraid of them; for the Lord thy God is with thee, Who brought thee up out of the land of Egypt'

—out of the land full of impurity and iniquity. Moreover, He will bring you out victorious in your present struggle."

O. Y., p. 88.

4. "Man of War"

Said the Kobriner: "In the Red Sea Hymn (Exodus 15:3) we read: 'The Lord is a Man of War.' This may be interpreted thus: 'The Lord is *with* the man who makes war against his evil desires, and gives him aid to overpower them.'"

O. Y., p. 73.

5. The Evil Impulse

The Lekhivitzer commented on Jeremiah 31:11: "For the Lord hath ransomed Jacob and He redeemeth him from the hand of him that is stronger than he." "This adversary is the Evil Impulse in man. He becomes strong and overpowering when man makes no struggle against him, and allows him to grow within him, though it lies within man's power to weaken him. Despite this, however, the Lord redeems man from him."

O. Y., p. 20.

6. Do Not Investigate

The Kobriner said that the phrase (Numbers 15:39): "'And that ye go not about after your own heart and your own eyes' teaches us this lesson: when an evil thought comes to us, or when we chance to see an unworthy thing, we should not pause to contemplate or investigate it, but we should instantly remove the thought or the sight from our heart and from our eyes."[1]

O. Y., p. 91.

[1] The verb used in Hebrew in the above phrase: "we-lo sa-suru" means to explore, to spy out, to search, etc.

7. Combatting Inner Evil

The Kotzker Rabbi said: "The battle in a man's heart against evil impulses may be likened to warfare. Strategy must be employed in the inner battle exactly as in war. When the general succeeds in entrenching his position against the foe at one place, he does not rest content with this achievement lest the enemy assail him elsewhere. Likewise if a man immunizes himself against a particular fault, he must guard himself against succumbing to another."

S. S. K., iv, 20.

8. Nails in the Wall

The Besht related the following parable: "A man asked permission of a house-owner to dwell in his house. When this was refused he asked permission to hammer a nail into the wall. This request being granted, the man hammered the nail in one place, removed it, declaring the place unsuitable. Then he nailed it into place after place until finally he had spoiled the entire wall. The Evil Desire behaves in a similar fashion. If a man allows it to enter his life in the least objectionable way, it will soon fill him completely with evil."

S. S. K., i, 13.

9. The Lost Men

Rabbi Jonathan of Hamburg recounted the following parable: "A man was lost in the woods. After a long time he espied another man and ran hastily to him for direction. The latter said: 'I am sorry to disappoint you, inasmuch as I am likewise lost. This, however, I can tell you: there is no highway to the north; I have just come from there.' In the same fashion one who is a sinner may properly warn another man against pursuing evil paths. He has had the bitter experience."

S. S. K., ii, 119.

10. Breaking Rocks

A youth asked the Riziner to aid him in breaking off his evil habits so that he might better serve the Lord.

The Riziner replied: "It is much harder to break off one's evil habits than to split rocks. Be earnest in your praying and your study, and the evil will disappear of itself."

N. I., p. 26.

11. Good and Evil

The Gerer Rabbi said: "We are told by the Psalmist first to leave evil and then to do good.[1] I will add that if you find it difficult to follow this advice, you may first do good, and the evil will automatically depart from you."

S. S. K., ii, 93.

[1] Psalm 34:15.

12. The Rescue

The Gerer Rabbi said: "The Zaddik endeavors to the utmost to lift the sinner out of the mire of materialism, but he can accomplish little if the transgressor does not coöperate in the effort at redemption. The drowning man who loses command of himself and hinders the work of rescue, is likely to drag down his savior with him to destruction."

S. S. K., iii, 53.

13. Escape or Capture

Said the Besht: "We find the words: 'Who is mighty? He who subdues his passions' (Ethics 4:1; Singer, p. 195). They may be illustrated as follows: 'A watchman heard a thief seeking to break into a house; he cried out, and the burglar escaped. Another watchman who heard of this, prepared handcuffs. When the thief sought to break in, he captured him and bound him with the chains.

"One good man, when an evil desire overtakes him, drives it away. Another Zaddik subdues the desire unto service of God.

Hence we are taught: 'Who is Mighty? He who forces his passions, his desires and his every quality of character to serve the Lord.' " [1]

K. S. T., p. 12b.

[1] For abbreviated version, see the *J. E.,* ii, 385-6, and *T. M. M.,* p. 203. "The Besht once commented upon asceticism as follows: A thief tried to break into a house, the owner of which, crying out, frightened him away. The same thief soon after broke into the house of a very strong man, who, on seeing him enter, kept quite still. When the thief had come near enough, the man caught him, and placed him in prison, thus depriving him of all opportunity to do further harm."

14. Look Not on Evil

Said the Besht: "The sight of unworthy pleasures leads to remembrance of them. Remembrance leads to covetousness. Covetousness leads to performance. Look not upon evil, and you will not do evil. Despise bodily pleasures and combat your profane desires. You will find joy in the victory."

M. R. T., ii, 61.

15. Sureties for Each Other

Said the Besht: "Our Rabbis say: 'All Israelites are sureties, one for the other.' When an influence for good descends on earth from the Source of Good, every Jew receives a share thereof. The Zaddik then labors his hardest; the man of moderate qualities is awakened from his indifference, and even the wicked feels a twinge of conscience, and is susceptible to repentance. It is the same when an evil influence descends. The wicked succumbs to it without a battle. The Zaddik, also, admits some evil thoughts into his mind. Who, shall we say, is more responsible? We may say that the Zaddik is more to be condemned. Were he strong enough utterly to subdue the evil influence, the wicked would not have sinned. Or, we may say, the wicked man is responsible. Had he combatted and weakened the evil influence, the Zaddik would have been able to deny it admittance to his mind.

"When the Israelites worshiped the Golden Calf, Moses blamed himself for not weakening the influence of the Satan so that the common people would not succumb. And Moses begged the Lord to erase his name from the Torah. But the Lord replied that he was not at fault, since he had not admitted such thoughts into his mind."

M. R. T., ii, 105.

16. Why Abandon the Struggle?

A Hasid succumbed to temptation and committed a grievous offense. He became desperate and no longer cared to continue the struggle against his evil desires.

The Magelnitzer Rabbi summoned him to his private study, and said: "If a ruffian encounters a passer-by and beats him, shall the victim remain to suffer further mistreatment? Does he not use his first opportunity to escape? Why do you abandon the struggle? Why do you not seek to escape further punishments?"

The Hasid resolved to heed the Rabbi's counsel and became a man of uprightness.

V. S., p. 18.

17. Judge and Officer

Said Rabbi Bunam: "We read: 'Judges and officers shalt thou make thee in all thy gates' (Deut. 16:18). Thou man, first judge well how thou shouldst conduct thyself with all thy gates, namely, thy limbs and senses; then make thyself an officer, to enforce thy judgments."

R. T., ii, 116.

18. The Evil Impulse ("Yetzer Ha-Ra")

Said the Mezeritzer:

"1. Understand that your evil impulse hinders you from attaining a high degree of spirituality.

2. The Evil Impulse comes in two ways: like water to cool your desire to perform good deeds; and like fire, to persuade you to transgress prohibitions.

3. Oftentimes the Evil Impulse leads you to believe that you have sinned gravely, though this be untrue. It seeks to encompass you in melancholy and thus hinder your true service to the Lord.

4. The Evil Impulse may not be able to persuade you to learn no Torah, since you do not wish to feel the shame of ignorance. But It may persuade you that you need not learn Ethical Books and the Code, in the belief that learning may be limited to the Talmud.

5. You may attain a compromise between the impulses towards evil and good by the enjoyment of your bodily pleasures and their dedication, at the same time, to the service of God.

6. The words: 'Restore our Judges as at the first' (Singer, p. 48) means this: When Israel received the Law, his Evil Impulse was turned into good. When a man performs a Mitzwah in perfection, even the Satan is compelled to praise him. Therefore we pray that, as in the early period, both our impulses should jointly and in agreement judge us. Both should praise us."

T. M. M., pp. 121-2.

162. SERVICE WITHOUT REWARD

1. With Love and With Pride

Rabbi David Leikes of Bar narrated the following parable:

"A king sent forth several armies against his enemy, one of them under his son's command. The son loved his father deeply, and concerned himself only with pleasing him, rather than with his own glory. Hence the victory of his army gave him little joy unless the other armies were also victorious. The commander of another royal army, however, cared only for his own reputation, and welcomed the tidings that his companion-armies were repulsed, since this heightened his own prestige.

"By the same token, the truly pious man rejoices to hear that another is greater than himself, since he seeks only to please the Lord, and it matters not to him who gives the Lord this satisfaction. But the falsely pious man envies another's fame and seeks to detract from his repute, desiring that only his own goodness shall be praised.

"In the service of the Temple we find [1] that the superior priests cared not whether a holy task fell to their own lot, or to the portion of another priest, provided it was performed properly. But the more ignorant priests sought to thrust others out of their way in their haste to receive the merit of performing sacred duties, even though this ill-mannered behavior sometimes led to serious injury."

O. Y., p. 192.

[1] Yoma, 39.

2. He Heard—He Came

Said the Belzer: "When describing a journey, it is the custom of the Bible to state that the person it mentions 'went' to his place of destination. But in the case of Jethro, nothing is said of his going. The statement is that he heard and he came to Moses.[1] The reason for this is that Jethro made no plans for his journey, but as soon as he heard of the Exodus, he immediately took the road to travel to Moses. Had he paused to deliberate, he might have hesitated to journey through the desert with his daughter and grandsons, and he might not have joined the people of Israel in accepting the Lord's teachings.

"Herein lies a lesson. When we have an opportunity to join a good and holy cause, we should do so without deliberating upon its merits and disadvantages. Otherwise we may never participate in it."

D. S., p. 108.

[1] Exodus 18:1.

3. Without Thought of Reward

The Gerer Rabbi said: "The chief wish of a worthy man should be to receive the ability to serve the Lord without thought of reward. If he prays for this whole-heartedly, he may be assured he will be granted all necessities as well, the lack of which would prevent his service from being pure."

S. S. K., iii, 46.

4. Measure for Measure

A contractor was accustomed to visit Rabbi Sussya of Anipol, and to present him gifts in return for his blessing. Once he did not find the Rabbi at home and learned that the latter had left to visit his Rabbi, the Mezeritzer. The contractor deliberated for a moment, and resolved to discontinue his visits to the disciple, but to go to the Master instead. Henceforth, however, the prosperity which had until now attended him, dwindled away, and he suffered severe losses. Again he visited Rabbi Sussya and asked him:

"Why have I become unsuccessful ever since I began to visit the Mezeritzer whom you yourself acknowledge as your superior?"

Rabbi Sussya answered: "As long as you gave your support to any good man without calculating the degree of his goodness, the Lord likewise granted you a portion out of his abundance without calculating your just deserts. But since you began to look about for a better man to whom you might offer your tithe, the Lord in His turn also looked for a man better than yourself whom He might endow with His riches."

S. Hach., p. 155. (See J. T., Dec. 19, '30, p. 5,
for the translation from Buber, by James Fuchs.)

5. The Thraldom of Reward

When the Great Maggid's wife pressed her starving child to her bosom, the Maggid heaved a rebellious sigh. Forthwith a voice from Heaven thundered into his ear: "Thou hast lost thy share in the World-to-Come."

"It matters not," said the Maggid joyfully. "The thraldom of reward has gone; henceforth I will serve God as a freeman."

J. T., Fuchs, Dec. 19, 1930, p. 4.

6. A Deathbed Utterance

Rabbi Ber Radishitzer was dangerously ill and awaited death. He spoke to his Disciples, saying: "It is usual in these circumstances to make a deathbed confession. But what shall I say? Shall I declare that I have sinned when I know not of any sin; shall I speak falsehood in my condition? Shall I vow to devote more time to the service of God, and to serve Him with more diligence? But I know that I have done all in my power. All I can do now is to vow that if my days are lengthened, I shall strive to improve my service; I shall make it adhere more and more to the pure motive of serving God for His sake only, since the more one does so, the more he perceives room for betterment."

The Rabbi recovered.

Hith. Z., p. 38.

7. With Money, Not With Piety

Rabbi Teitelbaum said: "The true Zaddik does not derive personal gain from his piety. We find in the book 'Hovoth ha-Levavoth' the story of a pious man who entered a shop where he was known, to make a purchase. The storekeeper asked him a ridiculously low price, and the Zaddik remarked: 'I came, my friend, to purchase with money, not with piety.' "

F. U. A. O., i, 49.

8. Sacrifice for God

Said the Kossover: "Inasmuch as proper service of God includes the readiness to die for Him, it follows that service of God for an anticipated reward is not proper service.

"For he who labors for a reward is not willing to die for his master, any more than he would take his own life for money. Thus he who anticipates a reward demonstrates that he is not willing to give his life for the sake of God; whereas he who is ready to die for God, does so for love of Him, not for a reward."

E. Tz., p. 66.

9. The Acrobat's Skill

One day an acrobat came to Krasny and announced that he would cross the river on a rope stretched from bank to bank. Rabbi Hayyim Krasner, a disciple of the Besht, stood by and watched the performance. His friends noticed his deep preoccupation and inquired what element in this sight caused him to be buried in thought. The Rabbi answered:

"I was thinking of the acrobat's readiness to submit his life to danger. You may say that he does so for the money which an admiring crowd will shower upon him. This is not true, for if he thought this, he would surely tumble into the water. His entire thinking must be concentrated upon one idea only, namely, to maintain his balance, to prevent his body from inclining a hair's breadth to one side. His safety depends on his determination to keep upright without thought of reward. In this fashion men should cross over the narrow cord of life." [1]

[1] Compare 172: 4.

Tif. Yeh., p. 9.

10. With the Proper Intention

Said the Besht: "A king announced that every subject of his realm might petition him on his birthday. Men brought their requests for money, position, justice, revenge or honors. One man, however, petitioned for the privilege of free access to the king at all times. The king soon became very intimate with him, and asked his friend what he might confer on him. As a consequence, this man received more benefits than any other petitioner.

"We learn that God said to Solomon that because he asked for wisdom, he would also receive riches and honors (I Kings 3: 11-12).

"When we petition God, let us ask for understanding and firmness to do His will. Then we shall also obtain other favors in a form as unlimited as is God Himself."

"We should be cautious, however, lest we be deceitful in our intention: we must not affirm that we offer prayer and acts of piety for love of God, and not for anticipated rewards, whereas in our heart we remember that we will profit thereby. There is a story to the effect that a poor man asked his rich brother: 'Why are you wealthy, and I am not?' The other answered: 'Because I have no scruples against doing wrong.' The poor brother began to misconduct himself but he remained poor. He complained of this to his elder brother, who answered: 'The reason your transgressions have not made you wealthy is that you did them not from conviction that it matters not whether we do good or evil, but solely because you desired riches.'

"How much more applicable is this to doing good with the proper intention!"

M. R. T., ii, 36-37.

163. NO SHAMING OF SINNERS

1. *Consideration for a Sinner*

A man to whom the Rabbi of Lublin was describing all the secret weaknesses of the soul interrupted him, saying: "Rabbi, thou shamest me."

"If I shame you," said the Rabbi, "if I shame you, I beg your pardon."

Reflex, May, 1929, p. 67. B.

2. *The Eavesdropper*

Rabbi Sussya once came to an inn owned by a noted sinner of many years of evil-doing. The story of his life and his chief offenses was known to him, but he could not call the offender to account in public, inasmuch as putting a man to shame before his neighbors is likened to murder in the Talmud,[1] nor did he care to rebuke him face to face in private. But he knew that his host was an eavesdropper, and this he turned to profitable use.

When he knew the innkeeper was listening at the keyhole, Rabbi Sussya interrupted himself in the midst of psalm-singing, and made a self-accusing outcry: "Sussya, thou servant of evil, where art thou going?" And then he recited the innkeeper's many misdeeds as if they were his very own, weeping and beating his breast in token of contrition. The listener, terrified at seeing his deeds held up before him as if in a mirror, recoiled from the door, and from that day onward mended his life.

[1] Baba Metzia, 58.

Fuchs (B), J. T., Dec. 19, '30, p. 5.

3. *The Hasid's Radishes*

A Hasid entered the synagogue of Rabbi Wolf Zbarazer one Sabbath afternoon, took his seat among the crowd, and began to eat radishes, loudly smacking his lips. Other Hasidim whispered him to stop, inasmuch as the noise might disturb the Rabbi's meditations, but he continued his chewing. Rabbi Wolf heard the whispering and observed that the Hasid grew red of countenance. He spoke aloud: "I feel a craving for radishes. Has anyone radishes?"

Thus the Hasid was enabled to draw to himself the envy rather than the contempt of the Hasidim.

S. H. H., chapter 4.

4. The Rabbi as Partner

A shopkeeper came to Rabbi Isaac of Alexander with a complaint that his business brought him no livelihood. The Rabbi declared: "Take me in as a partner, and you will prosper." When the man agreed, the Rabbi continued: "I am entitled to a part of the profits; will you give me a seventh?" When the man agreed again, the Rabbi said: "Then close your store on the Sabbath as I do not care to draw any share of profits."

When it became known that the Rabbi was a partner in the enterprise, the merchant's shop prospered.

M. H. H., p. 6.

5. The Returned Jewels

Rabbi Yekuthiel Teitelbaum was informed by a Hasid that while his wife was giving birth to a child, he had hired a Jewess for the housework. During this time his wife's jewels and other valuables had disappeared, and though he was not certain, he believed that the hired woman had stolen them. The Rabbi counseled him to keep silent and await developments. He then summoned the woman secretly to his Study, and succeeded in inducing her to return the stolen articles. After a few days, the Rabbi enjoined the Hasid to make another search of his home, and the missing goods were found.

P. v. K., p. 16b.

6. The Bratzlaver on "No Shaming"

"1. He who shames another person becomes foolish and forgetful.

2. Rabbis who pay to secure positions deserve no respect. Their gowns are like the yoke of an ass.

3. It is better not to obey a commandment of the Torah than to shame an Israelite.

4. You are shamed when you have been guilty of rejoicing in a fellow-man's tribulation.

5. Trustfulness will prevent shame.

6. He who robs the poor will be disgraced.

7. God punishes for contempt of lawful authority.

8. When you hear your friend telling an untruth, shame him not. Merely give him a hint.

9. He who feels shame does not sin easily.

10. Shaming another in public is like shedding his blood."

Sef. Ham., pp. 35-6.

164. SHEVUOTH

1. The Third Month

Said the Alexanderer Rabbi: "The fundamentals of Judaism were given to Israel in gradations. In the first month of the Exodus, Israel learned that the Lord is Almighty; in the second month, that the Lord is a Provider;[1] in the third month, they were prepared to learn that the Lord is Just, and they received the Torah."

S. S. K., iv, 58.

[1] The Manna began in the second month.

2. Giving or Receiving

The Kotzker Rabbi gave two reasons for our naming the Feast of Shevuoth "The Time of the Giving of Our Torah," and not "The Time of Our Receiving the Torah."

The first reason is that while the Torah was given us in the time of Moses, we continue to receive the Torah all the time henceforth.

The second reason is that, while the Torah was given to every Jew alike, it was not received by everyone in equal proportion, since the receiving depends upon the power of understanding in each individual.

S. S. K., i, 60.

3. The Gift

The Sadigurer Rabbi explained that the Torah does not name the Feast of Shevuoth "The Feast of the Receiving of the Law" for the reason that it is unmannerly for one who presents a gift to another person to ask him to rejoice over the gift.

E. O., p. 143.

4. On Mount Moriah

A Rav asked the Tzanzer Rabbi why the Holy House of God was built on Mount Moriah rather than on Mount Sinai where the Torah was given. The Rabbi answered: "The place where a man served his God in readiness to die for Him,[1] is dearer to the Lord than even the place where the Torah was received."

E. O., p. 127.

[1] The Sacrifice of Isaac.

5. Following the Zaddik

Many Hasidim who had heard of the piety and holiness of the Radomsker, visited him on the eve of Shevuoth. The Radomsker declined to receive them and departed in order to visit the Kozmirer Rabbi for the Holyday. The latter reproved him for leaving his guests, and asked him to remember the example of Moses, the faithful shepherd of Israel.

"But Rabbi," retorted the Radomsker, "Moses went to Sinai and the Israelites followed him. Why, then, do not my visitors follow me here?"

The Kozmirer appreciated the compliment, and permitted his guest to remain.

B. S., p. 31.

6. Dairy Foods

Said the Koretzer: "We eat dairy food on Shevuoth to welcome the Day of the Giving of the Torah with humility. Dairy food denotes that we consider ourselves like young children who are still too young to eat meat."

Nof. Tz., p. 36.

7. Herbs on the Moor

Rabbi Asher Zevi Ostroher gave the following reason for decorating the synagogue on Shevuoth with green boughs and grass:

"We read in the Talmud (Erubin 22): 'Rav Ada bar Mathnah left home for the Academy.' His wife said: 'How shall I feed the children?' Rav Ada replied: 'Edible herbs can be found on the moor.' Israel likewise inquired of God: 'If we spend all our time studying Thy Torah, how can we feed our children?' And the Lord replied: 'Food can be secured without much labor.' On Shevuoth, therefore, we spread out herbs and grass to remind us that we should devote our life to the Torah, even though we have nothing but edible herbs to keep us alive."

D. D., pp. 189-90.

165. SHEMINI ATZERETH

1. In the Book-Case

The Lubliner declared that on Shemini Atzereth the Ropshitzer held fine processions with the Scrolls of the Torah, inasmuch as his ancestor, the "Shalho" [1] was with him in spirit. When the Ropshitzer visited him later, the Lubliner inquired concerning the former's observance of Shemini Atzereth.

"Oh, we had excellent wine, tasty fish and delicious birds," was the Ropshitzer's reply.

"But was not the 'Shalho' present?" persisted the Lubliner.

"Yes," replied the Ropshitzer, "but he must have been angry with me, for his back was turned and he spoke not."

"How could that be?" inquired the Lubliner.

"Why," said the Ropshitzer, "he was standing in the book-case."

Ohel N., p. 30 (also 36).

[1] "Shalho" contains the initials of the famous book: "Shenei Luchoth ha-Berith" (by Rabbi Isaiah Halevy Hurwitz). The Ropshitzer seemed to care little for mysticism. The "true believers," however, attribute this denial to modesty.

2. The Additional Day

A Rabbi explained: "In the Talmud the Festival of Shevuoth is termed 'Atzereth,' while in the Pentateuch the term is applied to the Eighth Day of Tabernacles. 'Atzereth' means 'Hold Over.' The Lord says to Israel after the week of Tabernacles: 'Abide with Me another day,' even as a father who is visited by his son, begs him to remain another day. Why, however, is the 'Hold Over Day' of Tabernacles celebrated immediately after Sukkoth, and the 'Hold Over Day' of Passover six weeks after Passover?

"The 'Yalkut' explains this by a parable: 'A father was visited by his grown children. Some had a difficult, and others a comfortable journey. Those whose visit was marked by hardships were requested by their father to lengthen their sojourn, but those who had made the journey easily, he merely invited to visit him again soon. Likewise, the celebrants at the Pilgrimage Festivals traveled to Jerusalem afoot during the Temple period. And those who came on Passover could easily come again on foot six weeks later, since the ground was dry, there being no rain in Palestine during the summer.'

"Those, however, who came on Sukkoth would find it difficult to walk a few weeks later in the rainy season. Therefore they were invited to celebrate an additional day immediately."

S. S. K., v, 90.

165a. SIMCHATH TORAH [1]

1. The Omnipresent Satan; 155:3

[1] In Palestine, Shemini Atzereth is called "Simchath Torah." The Hasidim have the "Procession with the Scrolls of the Torah" on both days.

2. The Battle; 31:9

166. SIN AND TRANSGRESSION

1. No One Is Without Sin

Said the Besht: "No true saint would be able to see wickedness in others. The real Zaddik would not know if men and women are guilty of offenses. He could not, therefore, under these circumstances serve as an example to others, and could not teach the people. It is for this reason that there is no man on earth who does not sin. The sin makes the Zaddik humane and enables him to guide others."

M. R. T., p. 68.

2. Public Versus Private Sins

Rabbi Samuel Kaminker said: "We read (Isaiah 1:18): 'Though your sins be as scarlet, they shall be as white as snow; though they be red like crimson, they shall be as wool.' It can be read: 'Though your sins be like scarlet thread, they shall whiten like snow; if they redden like the worm that emits crimson dye, they shall become like wool.'

"There are two kinds of sin: sin in private and sin in public. When one repents of a private sin, his repentance is contagious. But if his sin is known, others will not imitate his repentance on the plea that they have not been guilty of his particular sin.

"And Isaiah says: If your sin be like the dyed thread that does not dye other articles, namely, if the sins are private and hold forth no evil example, then your repentance of them shall whiten, namely, shall purify others as well, even as the snow which cleanseth other things.

"But if your sins be done in public, as the worm issues a dyeing substance which colors other articles, then your repentance will be only as wool, that may itself be white and pure, but which does not cleanse other things.

"This explains why the causative verbs, 'whiten' and 'redden' are used (in the Hebrew) instead of the passive: 'become white' and 'be red.' "

Beth Phineas, pp. 28-33 (above line).

3. Only Half-Guilty

Rabbi Bunam said: "We are commanded by the Lord[1] to give half a shekel as the ransom of our souls. Why only half? Because one-half of the guilt belongs to God Himself for endowing us with the impulse to sin."

F. U. O. A., i, 196.

[1] Exodus, 21:13.

4. Sin Is Implied

The Vorker was listening to the complaints of the Hasidim regarding their meager livelihood. His friend, Rabbi Feivel Gritzer, remarked: "No one complains about his low spiritual estate."

"They need not shame themselves by explicitly admitting their offenses," replied the Vorker. "Does not the Tanna tell us:[1] 'Because my deeds are poor, my livelihood is poor. Hence, when they complain of their livelihood, by implication they confess their sins.' "

D. Z., p. 54.

[1] Kiddushin, 82.

5. The Holiness in Sin

Said the Ropshitzer: "Before the Most High no wickedness may be brought. How, then, does the Satan bring before the Lord the sins of men? The answer is that he brings only the holiness contained in sin, since sin contains the seed of repentance which turns a transgression into a good deed. And the Satan declares: 'This man owes repentance of this kind.' If the man fails to repent, he remains in debt, and cannot come before the Holy One, Blessed be He."

E. Tz., p. 94.

6. God's Worthiest Attributes

Said the Koretzer: "If men did not sin, the Lord would have no occasion to employ His attributes of mercy, compassion, and the like, but only his attributes of justice. Therefore, it follows that even sinners please the Lord: they bring into play His worthiest attributes."

Nof. Tz., p. 17.

7. Intentional and Unintentional Sins

Said the Savraner: "Many persons show more anxiety and regret over their unintentional than over their intentional sins. If they unintentionally desecrate the Sabbath, they are regretful and broken-hearted, but if they intentionally speak untruths, or revile each other, they feel no true regret, but merely mumble the prayers concerning these offenses. The opposite, to be sure, is the proper course."

E. A., p. 35.

8. God in Sin

Said the Besht: "There is a suggestion that God is found in sin, but is not active therein. The letter 'Aleph,' or 'The Source,' is found in the word 'Het,' 'Sin,' but it is not pronounced."

M. R. T., ii, 41.

9. Unable to be Angry

Said the Bershider: "Our Sages declare: 'One who is angry may be sure that his sins are more numerous than his good deeds.'[1] Therefore, how can a man have time to be angry, when it behooves him to be diligent in repentance and add to his good deeds? And just as soon as he thinks of repentance, his good deeds overweigh his sins and he is unable to be angry."

M. P., p. 51.

[1] Nedarim, 22.

10. The Torah and Transgressions

The Radziminer, a Disciple of Rabbi Bunam, once said to his friend, the Gerer: "I cannot understand how the Children of Israel could sin so grievously in the Wilderness after receiving the revelation at Mount Sinai."

"Has it ever occurred to you," answered the Gerer, "that their sins were of a quality superior even to our Mitzwoth? From their sins the Torah was composed. But what, pray, is done with our good deeds? Inasmuch as the Israelites were on a high altitude of the spirit, they oftentimes erred, even as great mentalities frequently err on the rarefied heights of reason. But for us their deeds appear to be ordinary transgressions."

M. E. H., ii, 73.

167. SINCERITY

1. Wisdom and Sincerity

The Lubliner asked the Ropshitzer Rabbi:
"Why does the Torah command us to be sincere [1] with the Lord [2] and does not order us to be wise with Him?"

"Because," replied the Ropshitzer, "it requires wisdom to be sincere with the Lord. Hence wisdom is included under any circumstances."

T. H., p. 321.

[1] Or "whole-hearted."
[2] Deut., 18:13.

2. Overdoing His Chanting

Rabbi Bunam said, when he heard that a certain man chanted daily the entire Book of Psalms: "If after reading half the Book of Psalms, he says (Psalm 78:36): 'Nevertheless they beguiled Him with their mouth, and lied unto Him with their tongue,' how much the more is this true when he says the whole Book of Psalms?"

S. S. K., ii, 13.

3. Sincere Students

The Gerer Rabbi spoke at the dedication of the Gerer Synagogue. He said: "We read [1] that Rabban Gamaliel was deposed from the presidency of the chief academy, and thereupon the number of students greatly increased. During Rabban Gamaliel's tenure, only picked and sincere students were admitted. Seeing so many new students, the former president of the academy became sad at heart for having excluded them hitherto. This requires an explanation. Did he not know before that many students sought admittance? If he believed his regulation correct, why did he now feel sadness? The explanation is that he had convinced himself that the insincere student became sincere under the ministrations of an efficient and inspiring instructor."

S. S. K., i, 131.

[1] Berakhoth, 28.

4. Innocence versus Wiliness

The Ropshitzer said: "Innocence is usually a highly desirable trait, but a little wiliness is also needed. Isaac was earnest and unsophisticated; therefore he became the victim of Esau's wiles, for Esau made it a habit to ask Isaac questions regarding petty rules of conduct, while he was transgressing major ones. Rebecca, however, was born into a wily family, that of Laban, and she soon perceived the hypocrisy of Esau and cherished greater affection for Jacob."

F. U. A. O., i, 59.

5. Returning to Sincerity

Said the Sassover: "We read: 'And Laban departed, and returned to his place. And Jacob went on his way' (Gen. 32:1). As long as Jacob lived with Laban, he was compelled to encounter trickery with trickery. But when Laban departed, Jacob went on his way, namely, the way of integrity and sincerity."

F. U. A. O., i, 75.

168. SLEEP

1. Sleep and Its Purpose

Rabbi Sussya said: "Even sleep has its purpose. The man who wishes to progress in his service always forward, from holiness to holiness, from world to world, must first put aside his life-work in order to receive a new spirit, whereby a new revelation may come upon him. And therein lies the secret of sleep. Yea, even sleep has its service."

Bl., Pr., p. 92.

2. Sleep and Study

The Lekhivitzer commented on Psalm 127:2: "It is vain for you to be early in rising, to be late in sitting up, eating the food of sadness; for so doth He give unto His beloved sleep."

"Many pious folk," remarked the Rabbi, "attempt to serve the Lord by arising before sunrise and remaining up late in order to learn the Torah. They eat the food of the spirit in sadness, and their brain is bemused for lack of sleep. The Psalmist, however, teaches us that this is the wrong way to study. He counsels us to give to the Lord sufficient sleep that we may thereby gain a clear head for sacred studies. Then his sleep is as acceptable to the Lord as his study." [1]

O. Y., p. 18.

[1] The Jewish Translation has: "It is vain for you that ye rise early and sit up late, ye that eat the bread of toil; so He giveth unto His beloved in sleep." "Sadness" is more literal than "toil."

3. Morning Sleep

Said the Koretzer: "Morning sleep is sweet, for the brain is then vacated of thoughts in order to make room for fresh ones."

Nof. Tz., p. 7.

169. SMOKING

1. The Pipe

The Belzer Rabbi gave the following explanation for abandoning the habit of smoking a pipe:

"I was sitting in the Study Room and a companion was busy cleaning his pipe and filling it. In the time it took him to do this, I learned a folio of the Talmud. Hence I said to myself: 'If a pipe requires me to waste so much time, it shall not enter my mouth again.'"

D. S., p. 18.

2. *The Smoke of the Pipe*

The Kobriner found the Riziner sitting in his chamber on a Friday before sunset, and smoking so furiously at his pipe that the room was filled with smoke. The Riziner noticed his friend's displeasure, and narrated to him the following story:

"A man lost his way in a forest and chanced upon the hut of a brigand. Near the door stood a table on which a loaded gun was lying. The man seized the gun and thought to himself: 'If I kill the robber, I save myself; if I miss him, I may be able to escape in the smoke.'

"By the same token, in order to purify my brain for the Sabbath, I think holy thoughts, and smoke my pipe. If my thoughts fail me, the tobacco fumes may at least dull my brain, so that I do not think unholy thoughts." [1]

N. I., p. 26.

[1] See the remark of the Lubliner to the Hasid, when the latter asked him for a remedy against losing his temper. "Smoke a pipe," replied the Rabbi. "Smoking mellows a man." See 3:13.

170. SOLDIERY AND ITS MESSAGE

1. *The Cavalry and the Infantry*

The Sudilkover Rabbi (Son of Adel, daughter of the Besht) relates in his work: *Degel Machne Ephraim*, the following parable:

"The royal army consists of cavalry and infantry. In battle the infantrymen stand in compact ranks, and lacking horses, they bear the brunt of the struggle against the enemy; if need be, they die for their king. In the event of victory, they cannot carry away much plunder on their shoulders. On the other hand, the cavalry men can ride away from superior forces of the enemy; if they are victorious, they can load their horses with great booty. The infantrymen who know they were in the thick of the battle and whose hand-to-hand fighting defeated the foe, hope that the cavalrymen will share the booty with them. What would you think if the horsemen should claim credit for the victory and refuse any share of the plunder to the men on foot?

"By this token, we may say that the Jews who engage in learning the Torah and who are careful to attend services thrice daily are the infantrymen who devote their lives to the honor of God. It is for their sake that the Lord sends prosperity into the world in recognition of their triumphs over everything evil. They have a right to expect that the men of means who ride proudly on their possessions, will contribute a portion of their wealth to students and pious men. What can we think of those rich men, who believe it is their own hand which brought them their wealth, and refuse to aid the pious? They must expect the displeasure of a just King." [1]

Kahana, p. 85.

[1] Cf. story of the wealthy man who prayed on Yom Kippur out of his "division." 198:2.

171. SOLITUDE AND SILENCE

1. The Withered Tree

Once several Hasidim came to the Great Maggid, Dov Baer, and harassed him greatly, each with his own request. Together they consumed the time which ordinarily he spent in learning and praying. Finally he said to them: "David, the King, calls the Zaddik a palm-tree.[1] If you do not allow me time to devote myself to the Torah, then you will have before you not a palm tree, but only a withered trunk."

Henceforth the Hasidim were careful not to disturb the Master during his customary hours of study and meditation.

Bl., Pr., p. 75.

[1] Psalm 92:13.

2. The Cry in Silence

Said the Besht: "We should strive to pray and sing hymns in a low voice, but with all the strength in us. This applies also to learning. Any cry to the Lord from a heart at one with Him should be in silence, as we read: [1] 'Their heart hath cried unto the Lord.' "

K. S. T., p. 12b.

[1] Lamentations, 2:18.

3. Torah Through Silence

The Tzartkover Rabbi failed to preach Torah for a long time. He was asked his reason and replied: "There are seventy ways of reciting Torah. One of them is through silence."

V. S., p. 33.

172. SOUL AND BODY

1. The Kernel and the Husk

When Rabbi Schmelke and his brother, Rabbi Phineas, returned home from the Maggid of Mezeritz, their father said:

"Children, speak truly, what have you learned and received there?"

They answered: "Only one thing. Until now we have mortified our body, for we believed it was the kernel, whereas the soul, on the contrary, was only the husk. In Mezeritz, however, we discovered the opposite: the soul is the kernel; the body, however, is merely its shell."

Bl., Pr., p. 70.

2. A Spotless Garment

The Besht taught that in the lowliest of men there dwells a soul, a sacred mystery, the garment of the Living God. It behooves man to keep this garment spotless in order that he may return it whenever bidden, without blemish. Purity of heart, rectitude of mind and love for all creatures preserve the soul from defilement.

Bl., Pr., p. 25.

3. Keep Thy Soul Diligently

The Kotzker Rabbi explained the verse (Deut. 4:9): "Only take heed to thyself, and keep thy soul diligently." He said: "Give some care to thy body, but guard thy soul with scrupulous attention."

S. S. K., i, 68.

4. The Tenuous Cord of Life

One day there came to Meshibach [1] a troupe of German acrobats who gave their performance in the streets of the town. They stretched a rope across the river and one of them walked along the rope to the opposite bank. From all sides the people came running to behold this ungodly marvel, and in the midst of the crowd of onlookers stood the Holy Baal Shem himself. His Disciples were greatly astonished, and asked him the meaning of his presence there. And the Holy Baal Shem answered them thus: "I went to see how a man might cross the chasm between two heights as this man did. And as I watched him I reflected that if mankind would submit their soul to such discipline as that to which he submitted his body, what deep abysses might they not cross upon the tenuous cord of life!" [2]

[1] "Medziboz" (?).
[2] From S. Ansky's "The Dybbuk," p. 98. See 162:9.

5. Matter and Spirit

The Pulnoer wrote: "The main duty of a man is to transform his impulse towards materialism into a dedication to affairs of the spirit. If he is successful for himself, let him aid others to the same goal. He then becomes a true Zaddik." [1]

Kahana, p. 126.

[1] See "Peacemaking," 120:2.

6. Damage to the Soul

The Koznitzer Maggid visited the Lizensker and on his arrival heard the Rabbi sighing aloud: "I am the worst of men." The Koznitzer exclaimed: "Why do you consider yourself so wicked?" The Lizensker answered: "If a man thrusts a pin through a thick article, it does it little damage, but if he thrusts it into a thin substance, it pierces it through and through. In the same manner, a

minor transgression causes more damage to the soul of a Zaddik than
a major sin to the soul of a commoner."

E. Tz., p. 18.

7. Elevating the Soul

Said Rabbi Schmelke: "We find in the Amidah after the words:
'Thou revivest the dead, Thou art mighty to save,' the phrase: 'He
causeth the wind to blow and the rain to fall' (Singer, p. 44). While
the Talmud gives a reason for placing this phrase in the Blessing for
the Revival of the Dead, another explanation is at hand, by giving
the words their other meaning: 'He causeth the soul to soar upward
by bringing the body low.'

"When materialism is at a low level in a man, his spiritual interest soars to great heights and quickens him." [1]

S. ha-Tov, p. 43.

[1] This is an interesting instance of the manner in which the Hasidim spirit-
ualized the concept of the "Resurrection of the Body." "Geshem," rain, is also
used in medieval Hebrew to denote "Matter" or "Body." "Ruach" means in
Hebrew both "wind" or "spirit."

8. Yourself and Another

Said the Kotzker: "Take care of your own soul and of another
man's body, but not of your own body, and of another man's soul."

F. U. A. O., ii, 82.

9. Refreshment for the Soul

Said the Besht: "Do not consider the time you spend for eating
and sleeping wasted. The soul within you is rested during these
intervals, and is enabled to renew its holy work with fresh enthusiasm."

K. S. T., p. 4a.

10. The Strong Body

Said the Besht: "You may be free from sin, but if your body is
not strong, your soul will be too weak to serve God aright. Maintain your health and preserve your strength."

K. S. T., p. 17a.

11. Half-Heartedness

Said the Mezeritzer: "Half-hearted study and the performance
half-heartedly of Mitzwoth are of no real value to a man's body and
soul. He who is half-hearted is like unto one half-asleep."

M. R. T., ii, 59.

12. One Soul and the All-Soul

The Koretzer was asked: "How can we pray that a man repent,
since we are taught in the Talmud that the fear of Heaven is not
in Heaven's hands." [1] The Rabbi replied: "All souls are included

[1] Berakhoth 33.

in One Soul; hence if a man repents himself, he may give rise to an impulse towards repentance in another soul which he envisages. We know that when one Jew is elevated to a high place, all Jewish souls are elated. It is because one soul is included in the other; because both are parts of the Once Inclusive All-Soul. Hence we pray that the impulse enters within us."

M. P., p. 26.

13. The Ghost, the Spirit and the Soul

Said the Koretzer: "Man is possessed of a ghost, a spirit, and a soul [1] in this order of importance. At the Sabbath Meal, the eating is the ghost; the singing of hymns is the spirit, and the discussion of Torah is the soul.

"Abraham is the ghost of Israel; Moses, his spirit, and the Messiah, his soul.

"Of the Sabbath, the evening is the ghost; the morning, the spirit, and the afternoon, the soul.

"Of Torah, the Bible is the ghost; the Mishnah, the spirit, and the Talmud, the soul.

"Of the student of Torah, the words are the ghost; the proper intention is the spirit, and the holiness of his study is the soul."

Nof. Tz., p. 25.

[1] In the Hebrew "Ruach," "Nefesh," "Neshamah."

14. The Three Caretakers

Said the Besht: "Three noblemen were commanded by the King to care for one of the royal kennels. The wise nobleman understood that if the previous caretaker did not know of a change in masters, he would continue to feed the dogs in his trust; and he therefore spent the money on a new crown for the king. The second man spent some of the money given him for the kennel and with the remainder he purchased a gift for the king. The third nobleman spent all the money on the dogs and overfed them, so that they became unfit for the hunt.

"God commands us to care for our body. The Sages believe that He who has fed our bodies in childhood will continue to do so in manhood; and they therefore spend their time creating a crown for God. Persons of moderate understanding also bring to the Lord gifts of Torah study and the performance of Mitzwoth, though they spend much of their time earning a livelihood. But the unwise use their entire time for bodily pleasures, and become unfit for spiritual activity."

K. S. T., p. 8a.

173. STRENGTHENING OURSELVES

1. *A. The Bratzlaver on "Strengthening Ourselves"*

"1. No matter how low we may have fallen, we can strengthen ourselves and return unto our God.

2. The Lord is greatly pleased by the return of those unto Him who were furthest away. The leader can aid those who are separated from God to cleave again to Him.

3. The disciples of the good leader should advise and encourage each other in true repentance.

4. God finds something of which to be proud in every Jew, however grievous his sins. Resolve, then, to serve Him through utilizing every passion and desire.

5. If we had no impulse and passion to do evil, our service to the Lord would be worthless. The Lord has endowed man with an overwhelming passion which acts as an obstacle against his resolution to come nearer to God. Though this impulse may bring a man to grave offenses, it is worth every sacrifice when a man at times succeeds in bending his passion and desire towards the service of God. This occasional victory is more pleasing to the Lord than a thousand years of service by a passionless man, lacking the impulse towards evil. The Universe was created only for the sake of man's battle against his inborn evil. This struggle is the chief occupation and objective of a man's life.

6. Be strong and stubborn against the persuasion of the Evil Impulse, even though it assails you for a long time. When you finally succeed in overcoming it, it will leave you in peace. This is also true of foreign thoughts during prayer.

7. He who admits he is far from the Lord need not despair. Woe to him who does not know he is far, and who thinks that he is an upright man.

8. In his every state, a man has different impulses and desires. The better a man becomes, the more he is compelled to fight off strong impulses. A man should not imagine he has lost his place because he feels even stronger impulses than heretofore; he should anticipate this because he has reached a higher state of moral character.

9. No two persons can occupy the same position of integrity. Every position is occupied, and therefore if one steps into a certain place, the other occupant ascends to a higher status.

10. The Evil Impulse of the common people is ordinary and vulgar. A man of understanding battles it with ease. The Evil Impulse of superior people is of a higher and higher quality. The Evil Impulse of the Zaddik is veritably a Holy Angel.

11. Overdoing our enthusiasm in service to the Lord is the handiwork of the Satan. Reverence and awe before the Lord disappear.

12. The Satan finds it easier to entrap men and women when they are in tribulation. Be strong and avoid sadness.

13. He who desires to approach nearer to God may discover many obstacles, tribulations and maladies. Let it not appear to him that God sends these obstacles because he does not wish him to come nearer to Him. It is the very opposite. God assists him in his struggle, since the way to approach closely to God is through victory over obstacles. Were it a light matter to do this, it would contain little merit.

14. In intercourse with non-Jews, a Jew must strengthen within himself his sense of the holiness of Judaism; he must pray not to be lured away by that which is not Judaism.

15. Every man should search out his in memory the good deeds he has performed, and forget his transgressions after he has repented of them. This will give him strength, and aid him to serve the Lord with joy.

16. If a man succumbs to temptations, he must not surrender to melancholy, but he should take hold with enthusiasm of that which remains of his former state, and gather himself together anew.

17. Sadness because of our sins leads to despair. It prevents us from striving after self-improvement and for worship from the heart.

18. The duty of the leader is to strengthen those who have fallen, and to teach them that the Lord is near to them. It is also his duty to demonstrate to those who imagine themselves in a high state of goodness that their knowledge of the Lord has not yet begun.

19. The questioning by the fallen: 'Where is the place of God's glory?' serves to elevate them higher and higher. Those who have fallen low may attain a higher position than those who have never succumbed and do not seek God's glory.

20. The slightest movement towards goodness by one steeped in materialism is precious in the sight of the Lord.

21. Song and melody aid a man to conquer melancholy.

22. Man's path through life is over an exceedingly narrow bridge. Be strong and believe that God's mercies fill the universe."

L. E. H., pp. 32-7.

B. *The Bratzlaver on "Hindrances"*

"1. Hindrances are given to man on the path of goodness, in order to increase his desire to achieve the good deed. It is man's nature to desire more that which is hard to attain.

2. There is no hindrance or obstacle that a man may not overcome if he intensely desires to do so.

3. The man of understanding will discover God even in the hindrance to a holy act.

4. The battle against obstacles moulds a man into a vessel ready to receive holiness.

5. Hindrances are merely imaginary obstacles. God sends no hindrances which man cannot overcome.

6. The greatest hindrance arises when our reason and heart do not agree on the worth of the holiness we seek to achieve.

7. When a man's heart is in his service to the Lord, every place in the world is the proper place for it."

L. E. H., pp. 62-4.

2. Before and After

Said the Mikolayever: "Consider yourself worthy before you perform the Mitzwah and unworthy immediately after. Thus you will frustrate Satan's wiles."

E. A., p. 58.

3. Overcoming Obstacles

Said the Dinover: "When men of impiety are being urged to change their ways and become God-fearing, many protest that the place where they reside makes it difficult to perform religious duties. Others declare that their wives are opposed to their pursuance of piety, since it entails additional labor, and stands in the path of many pleasures. Still others affirm that the age in which they live makes it arduous to be loyal servants of the Lord. It is to these three groups that our Sages [1] addressed their teaching: 'How should you return unto God? In your place, with your wife, and in your age.' Every penitent meets with obstacles, hindrances and difficulties. It is the duty of the sincere Jew to overcome them, even as others have succeeded in doing."

E. Tz., p. 116.

[1] Yoma 86.

4. Weakness and Strength

Said the Koretzer: "Oftentimes apparent weakness denotes strength that is to come. At the moment of birth, no living creature is as weak and helpless as man, yet man grows up to be master of all life.

"The horse secures his rest through sleep while standing; the cattle rest while kneeling; only man is so weak that he must lie down with his entire body. This also denotes his superiority, since he rests his mind and nerves in this fashion, and awakens with renewed strength.

"We thus behold that there is frequently weakness before strength. We fast on Yom Kippur and on other days: to create weakness in order to attain the strength which follows it. It is preferable to become weak through fasting than through controversies and illness. But in any case a man's troubles though they weaken him for the moment oftentimes cause him to be stronger, both physically and mentally, than before.

"The man who is popular and influential needs to fast at regular intervals. He cannot remain masterful of spirit for a very long time without weakening it at interludes.

"A man who was constantly cheerful and in happy mood became

very ill. The Rabbi commanded him to fast and he was cured. Thus, fasting became a substitute for sickness by lowering his exorbitant good cheer at times.

"Sometimes a singer cannot reach the higher notes. Another man comes to his aid and sings in a loud tone. This gives to the first man, also, the ability to raise his voice. It is a result of the communion of two spirits, wherein each becomes a partner in the other's strength.

"Sometimes a man does not understand the theme of his study. But when he discusses it with a comrade, it suddenly becomes clear. This results, also, from the cleaving of two souls: it gives birth to new understanding and to new wisdom."

Nof. Tz., pp. 5-7.

174. STUDY, STUDENTS AND TEACHERS

1. Study and Devotion

Thus taught the Besht: "Study for the sake of scholarship is desecration; it is a transgression of the commandment against bowing before alien gods, the idol being mere learning. The study of the Torah is a matter of the heart's devotion."

He was answered in dispute: "Our Sages tell us that the study of the Torah for the sake of worldly advancement is not to be discouraged altogether, inasmuch as he who studies at first to seek his own fortune, will study in the end for love of the Law." [1]

The Besht chided the disputant: "I do not gainsay what our Sages have said, but the application you suggest turns wisdom into folly. In the days of our Sages, a single day's task over the Torah turned a man from his own ends to those of the Law; now, however, a whole life of study will not always suffice."

[1] Pesachim 50.

Bl., Gem., p. 74.

2. Study and Practice

The Kotzker said: "We are told in the Midrash [1] that Korah asked Moses: 'Is a house filled with Scrolls of the Torah free from the obligation to have a Mezuzah nailed to the doorpost?' The answer was in the negative.

"This question may be explained allegorically thus: 'Is a scholar who understands the reasons for the precepts of the Law, free from the obligation actually to perform them?' The answer is that he is not free, but he must observe them in practice."

[1] Tanchumah, Korah.

S. S. K., iii, 15.

3. The Diligent Blacksmith

The "Yud" related the following experience of his youth:

"Near my home was the shop of a blacksmith who was exceedingly diligent, working early and late.

'Should I not give as much time to my study of the Torah,' I told myself, 'as this workman gives to his material labors. If he is so diligent to provide his bodily needs, does it not behoove me to be at least as diligent in order to obtain spiritual treasures?' "

N. H., p. 23.

4. Food and Learning

Once in a year of drought, the price of food had risen high, and there was general suffering. Several Hasidim who visited the Kotzker Rabbi on a Sabbath, wished to receive his farewell blessing and leave for their homes, but the Rabbi refused to permit them to depart. The Rabbi's wife inquired why he held them over at a time when inn prices are prohibitive.

The Rabbi replied: "The reason food is high and learning is cheap is because everyone demands food, but few are anxious to learn. Let people care more for study and less for food, and you will perceive that food will be cheap and learning expensive."

Kotzker Maasioth, p. 103.

5. Study Without Teaching

Rabbi Zevi Ezekiel Michelson explained the passage in "Pirkei Avoth" (1:14; Singer, p. 186) : "If I am not for myself, who will be for me? But if I care only for myself, what am I? And if not now, when?" He said: "If I am not learning for myself only, but teach others as well, then the pupils who profit by my teaching will be a credit to me; but if I study myself without teaching others, what profit is my learning? And though its futility may not be clear while I live, it will be discovered when I die."

S. S. K., iii, 93.

6. Business and Learning

The Gerer Rabbi was asked by a youth if he should devote his entire time to study or learn a business in addition. The Rabbi replied:

"Since Isaac saw that Jacob was a quiet, studious lad, why did he love Esau more? The answer is: Isaac believed that Jacob was simple-hearted by nature, thereby making it easy for him to lead a quiet life; whereas Esau was a hunter, and endeavored nevertheless to please his father by inquiring what he ought do. When, however, Esau complained to Isaac that Jacob had outwitted him twice, Isaac said: 'If this be so, that Jacob is of a practical turn of mind, but leads a quiet life from preference, he may receive my blessing.' "

S. S. K., i, 131.

7. Near the Door

Said the Koretzer: "All the knowledge I have acquired I have studied near the door. Now when I must go to the front to study I know not what is written."

M. P., p. 32.

8. To Learn Versus to Be

Rabbi Samuel Shinaver came to Rabbi Bunam for the first time and introduced himself. Rabbi Bunam said: "If it is thy wish to be a good Jew, thy coming was for naught; but if thou wishest to learn to be a good Jew, it is well that thou hast come to me."

R. T., ii, 113.

9. The Improvement of Conduct

A man complained to the Ropshitzer that he studied hard, but could not understand much of the subject matter. The Ropshitzer replied: "We are commanded to study day and night,[1] but we are not enjoined to become scholars. Isaiah teaches: 'Learn to do well' (1:17). If your conduct is being improved by your study, you need not be disturbed if you cannot understand every intricate detail."

[1] Joshua 1:8.   *Ohel N., p. 39.*

10. The Diamond in the Hay

Said the Kotzker: "The Sages teach us that we should not believe the man who professes to have labored hard in the study of the Torah and found himself unable to comprehend it.[1] How do they come to make this statement? From the statement of the Torah saying that God's words are not in Heaven but are near to man.[2] Hence since every Jew is near to the Torah, it follows that if he makes a sincere effort to understand it, he must attain his wish, else it would be as if it were in Heaven, at least for this man.

"It is like one who has lost a diamond in a stack of hay. He does not abandon his effort to find it, no matter how long it requires, for he is sure the diamond is there. Likewise, the Torah assures you that the Word of God is near to you, and is within your comprehension. Do not leave off your effort, for you will surely discover eventually that you understand it."

[1] Megillah 6.   *R. T., ii, 39-40.*
[2] Deut. 30:12.

11. Teacher or Companion?

The Sidlovtzer Rabbi said: "We read: 'Provide thyself a teacher, and get thee a companion, and judge all men in the scale of merit' (Ethics 1:6; Singer, p. 185). When a Rebbe dies, the learned Hasid often hesitates to accept the newly-elected Rabbi as his teacher. He is told that if he does not care to acknowledge him as his teacher, let him accept him as a companion. Nevertheless the Hasid may hesitate because he thinks: 'I may accept him merely as a companion, but he may think of himself as my teacher, and thus a false situation is created. How shall I seek the companionship of a person who harbors untruthful thoughts?' He is told, therefore, to judge all men in the scale of merit, and to believe that though he calls him 'Rebbe,' he seeks his friendship as a companion."

Tif. B., p. 12.

12. Outward Signs

Said the Zakilkover Rabbi in his work "Likkutei Maharil": "Some persons when visiting a great man, observe closely his outward actions, and believe that these display his greatness. This is false. To know a man's greatness, one must observe the creative powers of his inner spirit. Do we not read: 'And all the people perceived the thunderings, and the lightnings, and the voice of the horn, and the mountain smoking; and when the people saw it, they trembled, and stood afar off. But Moses drew near unto the thick darkness where God was.'[1] The people saw only the outward signs; hence they were far from knowing God. Moses, however, went into the inner region, and there he found God."

D. E. M. R., pp. 24-5.

[1] Exodus 20: 18-21.

13. The Funnel

Said the Mezeritzer: "A teacher must oftentimes imitate the man who pours liquid from bottle to bottle by means of a funnel. In the same way, the teacher must concentrate his wide knowledge into words, chosen for the understanding of his people. But if he is unwilling to narrow his own mind and attempts to convey his own broad comprehension of the subject, his pupils will learn nothing, for his instruction will be beyond their grasp."

T. M. M., p. 246.

14. Students into Scholars

Said Rabbi Meier Shalom of Porissov: "A man may pray to the Lord for aid to become an honest Jew, namely a perfect Jew, but the Lord deigns not to heed him. Why? Because perfect Jews are exceedingly few, and not every person may become one. Can all soldiers become officers? The Midrash says that one out of a thousand students becomes a real scholar.[1] And the others; what of them? They serve to form the thousand from whom the one scholar goes forth. Without them, he would not have the opportunity to emerge." And he added: "Do you know who emerges as the true scholar? Not the one who is expected to emerge, but he whose thoughts were devoted to aid the development in their midst of the great man."

D. Z., pp. 18-19.

[1] Koheleth Rabba, vii, 49.

15. Accepting the Rain

Said the Koretzer: "We read: Moses said: 'My doctrine shall drop as the rain' (Deut. 32:2). We see that rain falls upon many kinds of plants, and each grows according to its own nature. In the same fashion, let instruction be accepted by all persons, and each one will profit according to his inherent ability."

Nof. Tz., p. 28.

16. The Forgetting of Sin

Said the Koretzer: "We read: 'An excellent thing is the study of the Torah combined with some worldly occupation, for the labor demanded by them both makes sin to be forgotten' (Ethics of the Fathers, 2:2).[1] Why is it an excellent thing to make sin to be forgotten, when a sinner who forgets his sin does not repent of it and thereby causes his sin to be remembered in Heaven?

"This is the meaning of the statement: 'In your worldly occupation, do not forget the Torah; let both be as one. For should they be two separate things in your mind, you will forget to repent of your sins.' We read this further on in the text: 'All study of the Torah without work must in the end be futile and become the cause of sin.'"

[1] Singer, p. 187.

Nof. Tz., pp. 44-59.

17. Qualifying for Torah Study

Said the Medzibozer: "We read: 'Qualify thyself for the study of the Torah, since the knowledge of it is not an inheritance of thine' (Ethics 2:17).[1] How does this saying harmonize with the verse: 'My words which I have put in thy mouth shall not depart out of thy mouth, nor out of the mouth of thy seed' (Isaiah 59:21). Does not this verse indicate that the words of God shall be inherited by our offspring? The answer is: 'the desire to learn Torah is often inherited, but it is fitting that each man should not merely repeat what others have said, but that he should originate new thoughts in the Torah. For this task a man must qualify.'"

[1] Singer, p. 189.

Butz. D., p. 18.

18. The Palace Treasures

Said the Besht: "Two persons went into the royal palace to see the king. At the entrance they were informed that the king would not see petitioners on that day. One left immediately, but the other obtained permission to view the beautiful paintings and other valuable objects in the palace.

"In the same fashion, since mortals cannot comprehend God, there are some teachers and philosophers who declare that there is no need to study and to keep the Torah and its commandments: no matter, they affirm, how much a man may study, he cannot know God. This is wrong. Even if we do not behold the King face to face, we may view His treasures in His palace, and enjoy them through observing the prescribed regulations. That is to say, we may study God's world, God's Torah, God's creatures, and thereby at least be near to His Presence."

K. S. T., p. 2b.

19. For the Sake of Love

Said the Besht: "A certain prince disliked his studies and all his teachers departed from him. The tutor who remained at his side observed that the prince had fallen in love with a beautiful maiden. When he informed the king, the monarch said: 'Since he has developed an affection, it may be possible to turn it into the channel of learning. He commanded the girl to refuse the attentions of the prince until he had promised her to devote himself to diligent study. She continued to decline his admiration until he had trained himself thoroughly in the field of learning.

"In the same way, the Lord instils within us a desire for a long life, but He tells us in the 'Sh'ma' that we may not enjoy it until we have learned the Torah."

K. S. T., p. 5b.

20. Littleness and Greatness

Said the Besht: "In every good deed, there is both littleness and greatness. If a man studies with inattention, it is littleness. If he concentrates upon his study, it is greatness."

K. S. T., p. 15a.

21. The Chariot of the Lord

Said the Besht: "If a man fastens his whole attention upon the words of the Torah which he studies, his soul is attached to the life of the Torah's inner light and he becomes a chariot unto the Lord. Rabbi Jochanan ben Zakkai is described [1] as being versed in every phase of learning, including the study of the Chariot. This means: he included all phases of Torah in the Chariot of the Lord."

[1] Sukkah 28.

K. S. T., p. 26a.

22. A Chosen Few

Said the Pulnoer: "We read in the Talmud: Rabbi Simeon ben Yochai said: 'If a man occupies himself with his material labors, when will the Torah be studied? Therefore one should do God's will and his livelihood will come to him through the labor of others.' 'But,' adds the Talmud, 'many have tried it and were unsuccessful.' [1]

"It is because there have been many to try it that they have been without success. Only a limited number of students may be students all their life and be supported by the endowment of others."

M. R. T., ii, 80.

[1] Berakhoth 35.

23. Two Kinds of Students

Said the Bratzlaver: "Some students criticise others through sheer love of derogating their fellows. They seek in the Torah only that which they can utilize in unfair comments. They fail to remember the other and worthier side of the Torah, and that the Shekinah which cleaves to the Torah feels itself in exile as a consequence.

"Other students learn for the sake of acquiring knowledge; they unite their souls with the souls of the Tannaim and Amoraim whose teachings they study. They repent of their misdeeds, and they light up their days of darkness. They see only the beneficent side of the Torah, and the makers of this Torah hearken in Paradise to their voices. The soul of the Tanna dwells in him who learns aright."

K. L. M., pp. 15-6.

24. *The Bratzlaver on "Study of the Torah"*

A.

"1. Through study all prayers are accepted.

2. Study strengthens our good impulses for victory over the evil.

3. Through study we find our way to serve God everywhere.

4. Study cures nervous maladies caused by sins.

5. Torah and worship strengthen and illumine each other.

6. Study draws down God's Providence upon the student.

7. For the sake of study a man may gain the opportunity to go to Palestine.

8. A man should offer fervent prayer before preaching a sermon, to the end that the souls of his listeners may be united to his own.

9. He who discovers new meanings in the Torah should elicit them in public for the profit of his hearers.

10. A man should be both a scholar and a man of piety. He is then like unto an angel. One without the other is worthless.

11. A man should pray to God to send his children an excellent teacher, so that their study may be holy.

12. Through sharpening his wits by the study of the Torah, a man understands better the greatness of God; he feels more shame for his sins, and is able to repent in truth.

13. Inadequate faith oftentimes interrupts study through the necessity of travel or migration.

14. A man should know even in study when he has attained sufficiency. He should not attempt to study too much lest he become confused; he cannot learn all there is to be known.

15. Study brings longevity; it should be expressed in words.

16. The object of study is to learn good conduct, for the use of the student, as well as for the instruction of others.

17. The object of study is to teach true values and sound judgment.

18. Every book on Torah is useful and holy. Some understand better one book; others find different volumes preferable.

19. He who discovers new meanings in the Torah should have confidence that God takes pleasure therein, and should strive to search deeper and deeper, and to publish his findings in a book.

20. He who works untiringly on the study of the Torah until he understands it, heals his soul, and raises it to its Source, thereby increasing God's glory.

21. Even he who does not understand the Torah should read it aloud, inasmuch as this pleases the Lord.

22. Study of the Torah cools off the heat of passions.

23. Simple language easily understood, should be employed in explaining the Torah.

24. A man should apply to himself all the admonitions of the Torah, and thereby demonstrate that his study is for the purpose of obedience to God's will.

25. Some deliver a discourse on the Torah which is elaborated at length on the earth below, but is found to contain very little truth when estimated in Heaven. Others lecture in the opposite way: they are terse below, but great above.

26. No matter how occupied a man may be, he must snatch at least one hour for study daily.

27. A man should learn the law as contained in the code. Through the study of the law a man is enabled to distinguish the good from the evil, and to know the proper conduct of life.

28. Learning the Torah and discovering fresh meanings within it grant pleasures comparable to those we anticipate in the World-to-Come. Through them we can be rescued from all tribulations.

29. An aid to the ability to study with steadfastness is to seek only the virtues in another person, never to speak evil of anyone, and to regard everyone as admirable and noble.

30. Through refusing all honors, a man will recognize sweetness in the Torah. He should direct honors to the Lord.

31. A man must bear in mind that the finest words of the Torah lose their true clear light as soon as they are written down. The writing conceals and disguises their true and full meaning. Hence a man should endeavor to rediscover and reveal the inner meanings.

32. Even the sinner who is sunk in offenses, may elevate himself out of the mire by the study of the Torah.

33. A man should study even though he forgets quickly. He will find many occasions to recall what he has learned."

L. E. H., pp. 97-103.

B.

"1. He who has a liking for study will gladden the heart of his father.

2. Our new interpretations of the Torah gladden the heart of the Lord.

3. Every iota of knowledge of the Torah, whether it concern the laws governing the relationships of man to man, or of man to God, contributes to the success of the spirit.

4. A man will not forget his knowledge if he is not too proud to inquire regarding that which he does not understand, and if he teaches others what he knows.

5. A man who says: "This tradition is good, and this one is not," destroys the wealth of the Torah.

6. Learning Torah is of more importance than building the Temple and honoring parents.

7. Holiness leads to understanding; understanding, to repentance.

8. Learning should precede piety; piety should precede research into the learning.

9. He who learns and does not review his studies, is like one who sows and does not reap.

10. He who learns Torah for its own sake builds a palace unto the Lord.

11. He who prays without concentration also studies without attention.

12. Charity from the heart leads to study from the heart.

13. He who holds falsehood in abomination will have an affection for the study of the Torah.

14. Torah for which a man spends money will be remembered longer by him.

15. He who separates himself from the Torah attaches himself to the Satan.

16. Cleave to the teacher who punishes your negligence, for in the end you will learn much from him.

17. If your will has become obedient to your teacher's will, it is a sign that you have understood him.

18. If you have lost every emotion except the desire for Torah, it is a sign that you have understood.

19. Torah leads to faith. Faith leads to the sanctification of God's name, which may be martyrdom."

Sef. Ham., pp. 79-85.

25. The Missing Page

The Gerer Rabbi once studied Talmud with a Dayyan, Rabbi Aryeh Leib Zinz. The Dayyan was an exceedingly ingenious student. Once while the two were studying, the Gerer noticed that a folio was missing in the volume of Gemarah. Rabbi Zinz, however, failed to observe the omission, and connected the previous page with the following by a clever interpretation. The Gerer was indignant, and refused to study with him any longer.

M. E. H., i, 13.

175. SUKKOTH

1. The Season of Our Joy

The Kotzker Rabbi said that joyfulness is the outcome of holiness. Therefore Sukkoth, coming after Yom Kippur when we become holy and sinless, is called "the season of our joy" (Singer, p. 228).

S. S. K., i, 126.

2. Publicly and in Secret

Said the Slonimer Rabbi: "We read in Micah 6:8: 'And to walk secretly with thy God.'[1] This verse teaches us to observe those commandments which concern only us and our God in secret. It does not signify, however, that we should not attend public worship, or that we should conceal ourselves when we bless the Ethrog or sit in the Sukkah, thereby seeming in the eyes of our fellow-men to be neglectful of the Torah. We must perform these injunctions publicly and hold forth an example to others.

"Only extraordinary piety should be in secret."

O. Y., p. 66.

[1] Usually translated "humbly."

3. Sukkoth and Sabbath

Rabbi Bunam said: "The command to dwell in a Sukkah during the Festival of Tabernacles is highly important, inasmuch as this is the only precept which we fulfil with our whole body. The Lentzner Rabbi commented on this, saying that the Sabbath Day is of greater merit, inasmuch as it surrounds us everywhere; whereas the command of the Sukkah is limited to the indoors, and cannot be fulfilled out-of-doors."

S. S. K., iv, 29.

4. Myrtle and Lulav

Said the Gerer: "Each one of us should know his place. You cannot make a Myrtle into a Lulav. A man, however, can join himself unto one who is known to be of more consequence. He then becomes attached to him, even as the Myrtle is to the Lulav."

S. S. K., ii, 46.

5. The Blessing Over a Horse

Rabbi Mordechai of Neschiz before he attained leadership, was a merchant. Then it was his custom from time to time to set aside a sum, in order to buy a beautiful Ethrog for the Sukkoth Festival. Once during the "Ten Penitential Days," he journeyed to Brody, in order to buy an Ethrog for the festival. There he met a coachman, who stood by the side of his fallen horse, and wept. The Rabbi did not deliberate long. He gave to the man the money which he had set aside for the purchase of the Ethrog, in order that he might buy another horse, and he took his departure in a cheerful mood. When he came home, he was asked regarding the Ethrog.

"The whole world," he said, "may recite the blessing over the Ethrog, but unto me only has the privilege been granted to recite it over a horse."[1]

Bl., Gem., p. 171.

[1] V. s., regarding the Ethrog "Without Anger," 3:2.

6. The Tzanzer's Charity

The Tzanzer said: "I visited many Zaddikim in order to learn wherein each excels. I wished to learn the spirit of perfect charity from Rabbi Hirsch, of Rimanov, but I was unsuccessful. Rabbi Hirsch would be just as joyful when he lacked money for charity as when he possessed it. I, however, feel anguish in my whole body when I have no money for the poor."

On Sukkoth Eve the Tzanzer would borrow great numbers of thalers, and distribute them among the poor. When asked why he insisted upon special charity for Sukkoth, the Rabbi replied: "We are commanded to adorn the Sukkah. And what better ornament can there be than the distribution of charity among those who lack the means wherewith to be glad in the 'season of rejoicing'?"

E. Tz., p. 124.

7. Warmth and Coolness

Said the Tzanzer: "After we are warmed by the glow of our fervent service to the Living God during the High Holydays, we are commanded to find coolness in the Sukkah."

"After our exhausting labors in the service of the Lord during the Fearsome Days, we are commanded to recuperate by a week's rest in our tent-home."

E. Tz., p. 130.

8. The Purpose of the Ethrog

Said the Savraner: "The initials of the words: 'Let not the foot of pride overtake me' (Psalm 36:12) in the Hebrew, spell the word: 'Ethrog.' Herein lies a suggestion that we should not feel pride in the purchase of a fine Ethrog. We should not buy it to demonstrate that we are also included among those who strive to perform the Mitzwoth in perfection, but solely to please the Lord by the faithful observance of His commands."

E. A., p. 34.

9. The Trembling Heavens

The Ropshitzer said: "I am the grandson of Rabbi Isaac Hamburger, and I accomplish naught when I wave the Lulav. But my servant Hirsch, who was once a tailor, and who possesses an inferior Lulav, causes all the heavens to tremble when he waves it." [1]

Ohel N., p. 33.

[1] Rabbi Hirsch, "The Servant" was destined later to succeed the famed Rabbi of Rimanov.

10. Essentials for Sukkoth

A Hasid asked the Dzikover before Sukkoth to grant him a blessing so that he might have an exceptionally fine palm branch, ethrog, myrtle twigs and willows of the brook for the festival. The Rabbi replied: "What you need for Sukkoth is a kind heart, a humble spirit, a truthful mind, and the will to perfect yourself. After you have attained these, it will be time to concern yourself regarding an exceptionally fine set of the symbols for Sukkoth." [1]

D. D., p. 327.

[1] Namely, "First attain 'Arba Middoth,' and then acquire 'Arbaa Minnim.' "

176. SYMBOLS

1. Protector of the Home

The author of "Teshuath Hein," Rabbi Gedaliah of Lintz, writes: "We find inscribed on the outside of the Mezuzah the letters of God's Name: S D I.[1] This word is used because it also has the initials of "Shielder" (Shomer); Doors (Delathoth); Israel (Yisrael). It is ordained that the Mezuzah shall be nailed at every Jewish door, serving as a visible symbol of God's protection over the home. When we enter our home, we are reminded by it to struggle against the impulse towards wrong conduct, and to avoid anger and quarrelsomeness. When we leave our home, we are again reminded by it to curb our egotism in dealing with our fellow-creatures, and in striving to acquire substance. The Tephillin and the Tzitzith are symbols of a similar character."

[1] Pronounced "Shaddai."

O. Y., p. 76.

2. Symbols for the Priest

Said the Apter: "We find in Leviticus (14:4) that the priest was commanded to take for him that is to be cleansed two living clean birds, and cedar-wood, and scarlet, and hyssop. These are symbols, and teach us the following: he who wishes to become pure must raise his impulse towards goodness on high like the cedar tree; he must become lowly like the hyssop. He should, however, balance himself carefully between loftiness of mood and humility, drawing a line between the two (the scarlet line) over which he must not tread."

M. Hat., p. 82.

177. SYMPATHY

1. The Meal of Stones

A rich Hasid came to Rabbi Dov Baer for his blessing.

"What is the conduct of your household, and what table do you set from day to day?" asked the Maggid.

"My household is conducted with great simplicity," said the rich man. "My own meal consists of dry bread with salt."

Full of indignation, the Maggid looked at him, and asked: "Why do you not favor yourself with meat and wine, as becomes a man of wealth?"

For a long time he berated the rich Hasid until the latter finally promised that henceforth he would serve meals of more becoming viands.

When the Hasid had departed, the Hasidim asked the Maggid: "What matters it to you whether he eats bread with salt or meat with wine at his meal?"

The Maggid answered: "It matters a great deal. If he enjoys a good fare and his meal consists of fine viands, then he will understand that the poor man must have at least dry bread with salt. But if, being wealthy, he renounces all enjoyments of life and lives so stingily, he will believe it is sufficient for the poor to eat stones."

Bl., Pr., p. 70.

2. *Sympathy From Experience*

Rabbi Hayyim Auerbach of Luntzitz one winter night heard a knock at his door. He dressed quickly, and then admitted his visitor, a poor shoemaker, who told him that his wife had just given birth to a child. With tears of anxiety, however, he explained that there was no wood with which to heat the room where his wife and the new-born babe lay.

The Rabbi went forth and awakened a wealthy neighbor by knocking on the window of his home. The neighbor invited the Rabbi to enter, but the latter refused. The rich man dressed himself and went out to greet the Rabbi. The cold was bitter, and the magnate was sharply discomforted. Once more he bade the Rabbi enter, but the Rabbi said: "This poor man's wife and new-born child are suffering from the cold. Now that you have felt it yourself, you will appreciate truly the situation in which they are."

Wood and money were promptly supplied to the destitute man, and he returned home rejoicing.

S. ha-Tov, p. 139.

3. *Two Hearts*

The "Yud" told the following story: "A general crept into a city during a rebellion to discover the means of subduing it for its rebellion. He was recognized and fled to the home of a loyal subject of the king. The searchers were unable to find him, and the general escaped in disguise. The loyalist feared to remain in the city and also succeeded in making his departure. He came to the general and was treated as he deserved for his loyalty.

"The man then asked the general: 'How did you feel when the searchers were in my house?'

"The general seemingly resented this inquiry, and gave orders that the man should be executed, despite the latter's piteous pleas for mercy. When the noose had already been placed about his neck, the general released him, and said: 'Now you know how I felt.'

"The only way a sated man may know how the hungry one feels is to be compelled to go without food himself for some time. The

Talmud [1] tells us: 'Before a man eats and drinks, he has two hearts,' that is to say, he feels his own hunger and also another's. After he eats and drinks, he has only one heart—namely, his own, and it is concerned with his own comfort."

N. H., p. 59.

[1] Baba Bathra 12.

4. Face to Face With the Poor

When Rabbi Levi Isaac accepted the call to become Rabbi of Berditschev he stipulated that he be invited to participate only in those meetings when new ordinances were to be decided. Once it was resolved to vote upon a prohibition against house-to-house begging by the poor. It was suggested that a public fund be substituted to aid them. The Rabbi was called, but he protested, saying: "Why do you summon me upon an old matter?"

"But it is new," they said.

"You are mistaken," was his reply. "It is as old as Sodom and Gemorrah, where direct aid to the poor was forbidden. Perhaps they also had a public fund, the object of which was that the wealthy should be freed from the necessity of coming face to face with the poor."

Kahana, p. 253.

5. The Sympathetic Poor

Said Rabbi Schmelke: "We read: 'He hath scattered abroad (or dispersed); he hath given to the poor' (Psalm 112:9). The verse means: the trait of dispersing, of aiding and assisting others, He hath given to the poor."

F. U. A. O., i, 53.

6. The Two Farmers

Said the Besht: "A farmer sowed a large quantity of seed and felt confident that he would reap a great harvest. Instead of caring for his field, however, he wasted his time in the taverns. As a result weeds clogged up the stalks, and the birds ate up the seed.

"Another farmer sowed a smaller quantity, but took constant care of his field. He harvested manifold the grain produced in the other peasant's field.

"One man gives a large sum to charity without inquiring into the merit of the cause or the manner in which the money is administered. As a consequence, little good is achieved. Another gives less in amount, but interests himself in the enterprise of charity, and excellent results ensue.

"One man assembles many Mitzwoth and prayers without proper attention; another performs fewer, but he shows concentration and sincerity. As a consequence more rewards attend him."

M. R. T., ii, 35-6.

7. Joy When Others Sorrow

The Vengrover Rav asked the Vorker: "Why does Rabbi Zayra give as a reason for his long life that 'he never rejoiced at his fellowman's tribulation' (Megillah, 28a)? Are we to understand that the other Sages were guilty of this offense?"

"Nay," answered the Vorker. "What Rabbi Zayra means is that he never found enjoyment at occasions of gladness, such as weddings and the like, when he knew that any fellow-man was then suffering affliction."

The Vengrover Rav exclaimed: "Seventeen times have I completed the Talmud and have never understood this passage. And the Vorker who gives less time to the Talmud, promptly expressed its true meaning."

D. Z., pp. 55-6.

178. THE SYNAGOGUE

1. The Busy Rabbi

Said the Besht: "When the Berditschever was about to be born, the Satan complained that henceforth he would have no work to do, inasmuch as the Berditschever would be able to induce every Jew to become a Zaddik.

"'Do not worry,' replied the Lord. 'He is destined to become a Rabbi, and hence he will be busily occupied with congregational affairs.'"

Kahana, p. 250.

2. Synagogue Attendance

A teamster sought the Berditschever's advice as to whether he should give up his occupation because it interfered with regular attendance at the synagogue.

"Do you carry poor travelers free of charge?" asked the Rabbi.

"Yes," answered the teamster.

"Then you serve the Lord in your occupation just as faithfully as you would be frequenting the synagogue."

N. B. L., p. 32.

3. Story of a Near-Hasid

An epidemic ravaged Kovno, and all the hospitals were filled with patients. Rabbi Israel Salanter went to the synagogues and preached: "It will please God more to turn the synagogues into hospitals than to conduct services in them." [1]

[1] S. Rosenfeld in "The Day," June 25, 1932.

4. The Overfilled Synagogue

The Besht was about to enter a synagogue but he halted at the door and exclaimed: "This place is overfilled with prayers and learning!"

"Why, then, do you hesitate to enter such a holy place?" inquired his disciples.

"Were this a truly sacred place," replied the Besht, "the prayers and learning would have ascended heavenward, and this synagogue would be empty of them. Only the prayer and learning which does not come from the heart can fill an earthly abode."

M. R. T., p. 96.

5. The Belzer Synagogue

The Belzer gave many years of his life to build his synagogue. With his own hands he mixed the mortar and fashioned bricks, and the other workers were Hasidim of long-standing. The synagogue was not completed either by Rabbi Shalom of Belz, or by his son and successor, Rabbi Joshua, or by the latter's successors. Legend declares that it will not be completed until the Messiah will come, and it will then be transported to the Holy Land. Many persons of wealth have offered to give money towards its completion, but the Belzer determined to allow all comers to have a share in it, rather than the few.

A legend declares that the Belzer Count told the Belzer Rabbi that he was a second Haman, and that he would build a church close to the synagogue. A competition began, inasmuch as each wished to build a taller edifice. But misfortunes began to rain upon the Count. His title to the land was lost through the decision of a court of law, and finally he was killed in a duel by the Count of Hobnov.

Another legend declares that Elijah taught the Belzer how to build the synagogue in holiness.

P. v. K., pp. 25a-26a.

179. THE THEATER AND ITS MESSAGE

1. The Play and the Playbill

When Rabbi Bunam was still a timber-merchant, several tradesmen in Danzig asked him: "Why have you wandered so far from your literary studies as to turn to the Zaddikim? How could they tell you what you might not discover just as well from other books?" He gave them an answer, but they did not understand him. In the evening they invited him to accompany them to a play, but he refused. When they returned home, the merchants related to Rabbi Bunam that they had seen much that was quite remarkable.

"These remarkable things I also know," said the Rabbi. "I have read the playbill."

"But you cannot know, Rabbi," they said, "what we have seen with our own eyes, merely by reading the playbill."

Rabbi Bunam replied: "Your comment applies in just the same fashion to the Zaddikim and the books you have mentioned."

S. S. K., i, 48. (B., p. 530.)

2. *Straightening Young Treelets*

Rabbi Bunam said of a certain Zaddik, by name Rabbi Meier of Apt: "He hath been of godly ways and conversation from childhood upward and does not know the snares of sin. How then can he know what ails the men and women reaching out to him for help?"

"But I—I have been in Danzig and have met with the play-actors. I have been made conversant with the bypaths of sin, and hence I know how to straighten young treelets that are bent." [1]

S. S. K., iii, p. 14. (B., p. 400b.)

[1] For another story relating to the understanding of Human Nature, see "The Lost Men," 161:11.

180. THIEVES

1. *Wishing Thieves No Harm*

Rabbi Wolf Zbarazer once saw thieves robbing his home. He remained still and murmured: "I do not wish to cause you to be guilty of a sin, and therefore I make you a gift of everything you take."

In a moment he noticed that they were taking a jar containing medicine. He then approached them and said: "Do not fear to take away whatever you can place in your bag, for I am presenting these things to you as gifts; but, I beg of you, do not consume the contents of the jar you have included. It is medicine and may harm you."

Mif. H., p. 64. (Bl., Pr., p. 161.)

2. *Who Saw Him?*

A Rabbi was traveling in a carriage, when the driver stopped near a field where the hay was piled high. He said to the Rabbi: "Look about, and if any one sees me, shout!"

He then gathered a considerable amount of hay, but, in doing so, he heard the Rabbi shout. He dropped the hay hastily and drove away. After a moment he looked back, but saw no one.

"Why did the Rabbi speak an untruth?" exclaimed the driver.

"It is the truth, my man," answered the Rabbi. "I shouted to you that you were seen, and you were seen, by Him who dwells in the Heavens above."

M. D., p. 240.

3. *"Let Him Keep It"*

Rabbi Nachman Horodenker gave shelter one cold night to a poor traveler. In the morning he noted that the visitor had gone, and with him, the Rabbi's overcoat. When he arrived at the synagogue, a youth exclaimed: "Rabbi, a moment ago I saw a man in your overcoat. I was not sure before, but since you are not wearing it, it must have been stolen from you."

"Did it fit him?" asked the Rabbi.

"Yes," answered the youth. "It was a good fit."

"Then let him keep it," said the Rabbi. "He is a poor man, and the winter is hard."

No search for the thief was made.

M. D., p. 290.

4. Repentance Before Sin

Several peasants had stolen several valuable articles at the Court of the Count, and they concealed them with a certain Jew. The robbery was discovered, and the Jew was in great terror. He hurried to the Baal Shem. He was ashamed to admit the truth and pretended to fear a false accusation.

"Wait," said the Baal Shem, "until I return from the bath."

When he had returned, he took the troubled Jew by the hand and said: "Why do you speak of a false accusation, when the stolen articles are still in your possession?" The Jew confessed and begged for counsel.

The Baal Shem said: "God pardons and helps. But you must promise me never to commit another transgression of this kind in the future." He then counseled him how to make restitution.

After several years the same Jew came to Rabbi Jacob Joseph of Polnoe, and complained of his business difficulties.

Rabbi Jacob raised his eyes and said to the Jew: "Do penance!"

"Alas," cried the man, "would that the Holy Baal Shem were still living!"

"And what would happen then," asked the Rabbi in astonishment.

The man replied: "The Baal Shem knew that I was a receiver of stolen goods, and yet he spoke to me with kindness. You, however, address me angrily and demand penance from me, before I have stolen anything at all."

Bl., Pr., pp. 64-5.

5. Instruction from a Thief

"In seven things take instruction from the thief," said the Great Maggid. "He goes about his business at night-time. If one night will not yield, he puts in another. He and his fellows are at amity with each other. He stakes his life at a trifle. What he takes he sells for scant reward. He is patient of misfortunes, and esteems his handicraft above all others." [1]

J. T., Dec. 19, 1930, p. 5.

[1] See "Learning from a Thief"; 65:4.

6. The Thief's Gratitude

The "Yud" told the following tale: "A thief in his old age was unable to ply his 'trade' and was starving. A wealthy man, hearing of his distress, sent him food. Both the rich man and the thief died on the same day. The trial of the magnate occurred first in the

Heavenly Court; he was found wanting and sentenced to Purgatory. At the entrance, however, an Angel came hurrying to recall him. He was brought back to the Court and learned that his sentence had been reversed. The thief whom he had aided on earth, had stolen the list of his iniquities."

Kotzker Maasioth, p. 57.

7. The Minyan's Experts

A Rabbi ordered his Warden to assemble ten men for a Minyan [1] to chant Psalms for the recovery of a sick man. When they entered, a friend of the Rabbi exclaimed: "I see among them notorious thieves."

"Excellent," retorted the Rabbi. "When all the Heavenly Gates of Mercy are closed, it requires experts to open them."

L. H. F., p. 55.

[1] Quorum for Prayer.

8. The Heavenly Gates

Said the Mezeritzer: "Every Heavenly Gate requires the proper key to open it, namely the proper prayer with sincere intention. This, however, is a slow process. Let us act like the thief who breaks through every door without keys. Let us open all Gates of Heaven by breaking through our hearts of flint."

K. S. T., p. 18a.

9. The Guilty Curser

The Koznitzer Maggid counseled a man from whom a valuable article had been stolen, to inquire regarding his loss from everyone under suspicion. "Those who deny knowledge of the article in a calm spirit are honest," said the Maggid, "but he who begins to abuse and curse is the thief, and his house should be searched. This advice resulted in the discovery of the stolen article."

R. T., p. 247.

10. The Bratzlaver on "Thievery"

"1. He who is ready to steal is prepared to commit every offense.

2. He who is uncharitable will suffer from robbery.

3. He who cares not to prevent waste of another's property is equivalent to a thief.

4. He who accepts a share in stolen goods will be discovered.

5. A city where thieves abound, is sure to possess judges who are bribed and police who are corrupt."

Sef. Ham., p. 42.

181. THOUGHTS

1. Sayings of the Bratzlaver

A.

"1. Unholy thoughts prevent devotion and joy.

2. Subduing unworthy thoughts leads to perfection of the mind.

3. Holy thoughts bring holiness to the soul.

4. Unworthy thoughts corrupt the heart.

5. Holy thoughts are the good influences; unholy thoughts are the evil impulses of the soul, the Satan.

6. Through good thoughts a man is led to perform good deeds; he is able to worship from the heart and to repent.

7. When evil thoughts assail us during our prayers, we should pay them no heed. We should not seek to combat them, since the more we battle them, the more they will afflict us. Your Leader will instruct you how to avoid them.

8. Feel no sadness because of your evil thoughts; it will only serve to strengthen them.

9. There is no room for more than one thought at a time. Think of a subject of Torah or even of a transaction of your business, and the unworthy thoughts will find place in your mind.

10. No one can think while he speaks or chants a melody. Silence and a pure heart are necessary for a pure thought.

11. Charity saves a man from unworthy thoughts.

12. Man is master of his thoughts and may guide them in the right direction.

13. Thinking of God prevents unworthy thoughts.

14. Thought is more precious than all the five senses.

15. A fine thought sometimes enters the mind only to disappear. Strive to bring it back through diligence and courage."

L. E. H., pp. 57-9.

B.

"1. A man obsessed by evil thoughts should always judge his fellow-man in the scale of merit.

2. Prayers from the heart open all doors in Heaven.

3. If you pray solely on behalf of the Shekinah, you will have only worthy thoughts."

Sef. Ham., pp. 55-9.

2. The Mezeritzer on "Thought and Wisdom"

Said the Mezeritzer:

"1. Wisdom is God's garment.

2. Wisdom constantly receives influence from above and gives out spirituality below.

3. 'The Lord by wisdom founded the earth' (Prov. 3: 19). There-

fore if you wish to elevate yourself, you must ascend through wisdom, namely, fear of the Lord.

4. Wisdom is the Effective Power of God. Without it, everything is theory and without existence.

5. If you cleave to wisdom, you cannot cleave to desires.

6. There is no existence in the world that existed not first in thought.

7. Man receives from above the outlines of thought, and gives them out below in detail.

8. To do this, man must concentrate his thought upon certain details. This is oftentimes arduous labor, but success brings joy. This joy is exceedingly great in the world of the spirit.

9. Thought is higher than words; thought rides on words and directs them.

10. Thought is a world of freedom.

11. Oftentimes when you elevate a man's thoughts to God, you may transform them.

12. When God wished to speak through a Prophet, He concentrated Himself in the Prophet's thoughts."

T. M. M., pp. 45-58.

"13. Just as a man cannot look at the sun face to face but is able to utilize its light, in the same fashion he cannot comprehend God, but he is free to utilize His light, namely his own thoughts and spiritual emotions."

T. M. M., p. 249.

3. The Parapet

Said the Savraner: "We read: 'Thou shalt make a parapet for thy roof' (Deut. 22 : 8). Thou shalt not think evil thoughts in thy head, for evil thought is worse than transgression" (Yoma 29).

E. A., p. 29.

4. God's Thoughts and Man's

Said the Medzibozer: "As one thinks of God in his heart, so does God think of him."

Butz. D., p. 27.

He also said: "We read: 'O God, the heathen are come into Thine inheritance; they have defiled Thy holy temple' (Psalm 79 : 1). O Lord, foreign thoughts are come into the brain which I have inherited from Thee; they have made unclean the heart which is Thy holy temple."

Butz. D., p. 17.

5. A Miniature Inspiration

Said the Besht: "When a man's thoughts are concentrated on God, and into the midst of them there enters another thought: verily, this is a miniature inspiration from on high. Act upon it."

K. S. T., p. 15a.

6. Goodness Through Reason

Said the Gerer: "An inclination towards goodness attained through calm reasoning is worth more than an inclination attained through the ecstasy of prayer. The first is rational and lasting; the second contains much untrue imagination, is not enduring, and is prone to lead to pride." [1]

R. T., ii, 58.

[1] This statement, coming from a foremost Hasidic Rabbi, is of distinct importance. He is closer in this opinion to the view of the Mithnagedim than of most Hasidim.

182. TOLERANCE

1. Many Ways to Choose

Rabbi Schmelke thus interpreted the saying in "Pirkei Avoth" (ii; 1): [1] "Rabbi Yehudah ha-Nasi said: 'Which is the right course that a man should choose for himself? That which he feels to be honorable to himself, and which also brings him honor from mankind.'

"Nevertheless, he must not believe that this is the only correct course. He must be prepared to admit that there may be other ways in which other men may take pride and feel to be honorable."

S. ha-Tov, p. 41.

[1] Singer, p. 186.

2. The Other's Arguments

Said the Apter: "We find that when Abraham spoke in defense of Sodom, he enumerated fifty just men, forty-five, and so forth.[1] The Lord could have replied to him at once that Sodom did not contain a single just man, but He wished to teach a lesson, namely, that permission should be granted to one who argues, to bring out all his points. These should be answered one by one, with patience. It is not fitting that a man should give an abrupt answer immediately in order to silence his adversary."

M. R. T., ii, 28.

[1] Gen. 18:24-32.

183. TORAH

1. The Torah Is Spice

Said the Mezeritzer: "The Talmud tells us that the Torah is spice to the Evil Impulse.[1] Like spice, the Torah makes our impulses palatable by forcing the naturally evil urge into the service of the good."

E. O., p. 32.

[1] Kiddushin 30.

2. Learning Torah

A young man was asked by the Gerer Rabbi if he had learned Torah. "Just a little," replied the youth.

"That is all any one ever has learned of the Torah," was the Rabbi's answer.

S. S. K., ii, 29.

3. The Tree of Life

The Gerer Rabbi related this parable of the Midrash:[1] "A man fell from a boat into the sea; the skipper of the vessel threw him a rope and shouted: 'Take hold of this rope, and do not let go; if you do, you will lose your life.'" The Rabbi then remarked: "This parable explains the verse (Proverbs 3:18): 'It[2] is a tree of life to them that lay hold upon her.' If you let go of her, you will lose your life."

S. S. K., iii, 40.

[1] Bemidbar Rabba 17:7.
[2] The Torah.

4. Past and Present

The Gerer Rabbi explained the difference between the Jewish philosophers in the past and in the present. Those of former days believed in the sanctity of the Torah and strove to find in it evidence supporting their investigations. Those of to-day believe in the truth of their investigations, and look to them for support of the truth of the Torah. But when their investigations do not give this support, they are uncertain of the truth of the statements of the Torah."

S. S. K., i, 87.

5. Hovering Over the Torah

Said the Besht: "We read: And the spirit of God hovered over the face of the waters. And God said: 'Let there be light.'[1] If a man's brain, the divine spirit, hovers over the Torah that is likened to waters, then God commands that light come to it."

K. S. T., p. 3a.

[1] Genesis 1:2, 3.

6. Better than Gold and Honey

Said the Besht: "The words of the Torah, we are told by the Psalmist,[1] are more desirable than gold and sweeter than honey. Gold is highly desirable, but it is unsatisfying, as no man is ever contented with the amount of gold he possesses. Honey is exceedingly sweet, but it is unpleasant to the sated man. The Torah, however, is both satisfying and pleasant."

K. S. T., p. 23b.

[1] Psalm 19:11.

7. Work in the Palace

Said the Besht: "A greatly beloved king desired to satisfy the intense wishes of his loyal nobles to serve him with the actual labor of their hands. He, therefore, subdivided all manual services among them. One became Lord of the Garter; another, of the Order of the Bath; the third, of the Seal. The work of kindling the chandeliers was also divided. Some lit the corner lamps; some the center; still others the lamps in the vestibules which threw light into the courtyard and beyond. The king was pleased with the illumination which lighted up every part of his palace, leaving no dark corners.

"The Torah is the palace of the King of Kings, and its sincere students who labor to discover its hidden meanings and secret suggestions, are the kindlers of its lamps. Some of the searchers bring to light suggestions unacceptable to the majority, yet they illumine the Torah as well as those adopted. Without the labor of the first group of seekers, the latter would not be able to discover the true results of their quest. It requires thorough and complete discussion to arrive at the light of a disputable subject.

"We must not say, therefore, that the opinion of the minority is worthless and undeserving of study.

"The letters: M-o-S-he-H (Moshe or Moses) stand for 'Mahalokoth Shammai Hillel,' the controversy between the School of Shammai and the School of Hillel. 'Moses received the law from Sinai'; both sides represent the law as received from Sinai (Ethics 1:1).[1] 'Blessed be He who made choice of them and their Mishnah' (Ethics 6:1)[2]: namely, that chose for his enlighteners all of the Tannaim, with all of their opinions, as stated in the Mishnah, whether adopted as law or not."

K. S. T., pp. 24a-26a.

[1] Singer, p. 184.
[2] Singer, p. 204.

8. The Torah Is Everything

Said the "Yud": "We read in Selichoth: 'And nothing but this Torah was left us.' But since the Torah has been left us, we have everything. For from the Torah we should be able to regain our former state of holiness."

Nif. Yeh., p. 42.

9. Study of the Torah and Fear of God

Said the "Yud" in comment on the verse: "The fear of the Lord is the beginning of wisdom" (Prov. 1:7): "I came to fear the Lord through my study of the Torah; but my friend, Rabbi David of Lelov, came to study the Torah through his fear of God. He is, therefore, greater than I am."

Tif. Yeh., p. 32.

10. Dark Places

Said Rabbi Bunam: "We find in the Talmud[1] the expression that the verse (Lamentations 3:6): 'He hath made me to dwell in dark places' means: 'He gave me the Talmud of Babylonia.' Why should

[1] Sanhedrin 27.

the Talmud call itself a dark place? The answer is that the Talmud means the following: 'In the darkness of exile, He hath refreshed me by means of the Torah which I studied in Babylonia.' " [1]

R. T., p. 152.

[2] The verb in Hebrew "Hoshivani" means "made me to dwell" or "refreshed me."

11. Purpose of the Torah

Said the Lizensker: "In order to accept the sovereignty of the Lord, we must perform all His commandments. We learn this from the words: And God spoke all these words to say: 'I am the Lord, thy God' (Exodus 20:1). The whole Torah was spoken in order to enable us to say that the Lord is our God." [1]

O. E., p. 56.

[1] "To Say" is the literal translation; in the J. T., the word "Saying" is used.

12. Torah and Mitzwah

Said the Mezeritzer:

"1. God concentrated Himself in the Torah.

2. The Torah was given to us in spoken words. Words proceed invariably from thoughts. When we fulfill the words of the Torah we complete the three conditions requisite for a Mitzwah: thought, words and performance.

3. Cleaving unto the Lord is possible only through Torah and Mitzwoth.

4. He who keeps the commandment: 'In all thy ways know God,' observes the countless Mitzwoth.

5. Each Mitzwah is a branch of the Torah.

6. A Mitzwah is the vessel by which holiness is received."

T. M. M., pp. 83-97.

13. Left-Overs

The Dzikover Rabbi commented on the line in Selichoth: [1] "And nothing but this Torah was left us." He said: "I explain it thus: Nothing is accounted to us as left-overs except the Torah. Everything is more important in our eyes than learning Torah."

E. Tz., p. 93.

[1] See note to 199:1.

14. The Patriarchal Standard

Said the Strelisker: "We should so sanctify ourselves that we may attain the standard of the Patriarchs, whose every story became holy Torah."

E. Tz., p. 80.

15. A Different Torah

Said the Koretzer: "I find myself able to recite profound Torah only if the listener is an ignorant man who understands but little of what I say. When, however, a learned person is present, I cannot discuss the same Torah. Why? Because when the Torah comes to

the Zaddik, it is an intimate conversation between them, and this may
not take place in the presence of people who understand."

Nof. Tz., p. 21.

16. Torah and Science

Said the Koretzer: "We learn that the Torah is higher than all
other sciences from the fact that he who is learned in Torah finds it
easy to understand any other science; but he who has learned other
sciences finds it difficult to understand Torah."

Nof. Tz., p. 30.

17. Misdirections

The Besht narrated the following parable: "Several merchants had
lost their way and lay down to rest. A passer-by gave them directions and they journeyed further on the road. But again they lost
their way, and a second man gave them directions. But his instructions were incorrect, and led the travelers into impassable swamp-
lands.

In the same fashion, the words of the Torah may be directed into
beneficent channels of study, or they may be misdirected into the
swampy paths of false interpretations or unworthy purposes."

M. R. T., ii, 15.

18. The False Mother

A man asked a Rabbi: "What need is there of the Haggadah[1] in
the Talmud? Why not cut it out?"

The Rabbi answered: "The woman who consented to have the
baby cut in twain, according to Solomon's judgment, was not the true
mother."

L. H. F., p. 39.

[1] Haggadah is the legendary, narrative, homiletical lore, of the Talmud.

19. According to His Own Ability

Said the Medzibozer: "We read the words: 'In the sight of all
Israel' (Deut. 34:12). The Torah concludes with these words to
indicate that each Israelite may see into the Torah according to his
own ability."

Butz. D., p. 16.

20. The Living Listeners

Said the Medzibozer: "We read: And Moses assembled all the
congregation of the children of Israel, and said unto them: 'These are
the words which the Lord hath commanded' (Exodus 35:1). Moses
told the Israelites: 'These children of Israel are the Torah. Not the
dead written words, but ye, the living listeners to the words, are the
Torah, when 'ye should do them.' "

Butz. D., p. 6.

21. The Cherubim Who Guard

A Rabbi said: "The Cherubim placed on the cover of the Ark, according to the Talmud, had the likeness of a boy and a girl.[1] This teaches us that the proper guardians of the Ark of the Law are our children. They must, however, be placed on the cover of the Ark, namely, they must receive a sound Jewish education."

F. U. A. O., i, 187.

[1] Sukkah 5. The word is given its Aramaic meaning: "Ke-rubim," "like children."

22. A Drop of Ink

Rabbi Mendel Libavitzer was once asked by a Russian Cabinet Minister why there are many exaggerations in the Talmud; for example, the legend of the leaping ashore of a dying whale whereby sixty towns were destroyed.[1] The Rabbi replied: "Recently an order of the Czar banished Jewish residents from towns located on the boundary line, thereby ruining six hundred settlements of Jews. Is it not true that if a writer should now record that a drop of ink drowned six hundred communities, would this not seem an inexplicable exaggeration centuries later?"

F. U. A. O., ii, 77-8.

[1] Baba Bathra 73.

183. REVELATION

1. Revelations of Elijah

The Gerer Rabbi, a Disciple of the rationalistic Rabbi Bunam, cared little for mysticism and the so-called "practical Kabbalah." He once said to a Hasid: "Before I was thirteen years of age, when I was under the influence of the Koznitzer Maggid, I frequently received 'revelations of Elijah.' But when I grew to maturity, I was no longer thus privileged."

On another occasion he said with a smile: "A true 'revelation of Elijah' is rare indeed. Elijah's loyal disciple, Elisha, must also be revealed with him. Moreover, Elisha's disloyal servant, Gehazi, must in truth call upon the person who professes to receive the revelation, and inquire if his Master has been seen. It is Gehazi's punishment always to miss his Master by a moment."[1]

M. E. H., i, 11.

[1] The boastful and mercenary Gehazi doubtless represents in the Gerer's statement, the boastful and mercenary Zaddikim. They always just miss attaining holiness.

2. In Elijah's Spirit

The Rabbi of Kolbiel said: "At the conclusion of the Prophets, the Lord says: 'Behold, I send you Elijah' (Malachi 3:24).[1] Israel

[1] J. T., "I will send," but the Hebrew has the verb in the continuous present tense.

might think in his heart that God had abandoned him since He terminated Prophecy whereby he manifested concern with Israel's affairs. He therefore proclaimed through Malachi: 'Keep the Torah of Moses, and I will not abandon you. From time to time I will send unto you worthy men to whom will be granted the insight of inspiration, symbolized by Elijah. This inspiration has within it a portion of prophecy.' "

Tif. Z., p. 48.

3. A Share of Elijah's Spirit

Rabbi Elimelech Lizensker declared that a pious Hasid had informed him he received "revelations of Elijah." The Rabbi was asked: "We find in the works of Ibn Ezra that he denies such a 'revelation' to be possible; since Ibn Ezra did not see Elijah, how can a man of lesser merit behold him?"

The Lizensker replied: "Because Elijah prompted the Israelites to proclaim the Lordship of God, he is privileged to induce within every Jew a portion of his holiness. The greater and finer the man, the greater portion does he acquire. This Hasid attained a small share of Elijah's spirit, and his good life sufficed to prepare the way for the revelation of it. Ibn Ezra, however, deserved a large share of Elijah's spirit, but since he did not labor adequately to purify his soul, the revelation was withheld from him."

Tif. Z., p. 48.

184. TRIBULATIONS AND SORROWS

1. Poor Merchandise

Said the Lekhivitzer: "Sorrow is a poor piece of merchandise, both in this world and in the After-World." [1]

O. Y., p. 10.

[1] In Yiddish: "More Sechorah is Shlechte Sechorah."

2. The Shekinah's Sorrows

A lumber dealer shipped a load of wood down the river and much of it was lost. He expressed his grief to the Lekhivitzer. The Rabbi rebuked him, and said: "Do you not know that the Shekinah participates in every one's sorrows? Is it then worthy of you to bring sorrow to the Shekinah for the loss of some lumber?"

M. D., p. 251.

3. Not Bad, but Bitter

Said the Kobriner: 'When a man suffers tribulation, he should not say: 'This is evil,' for the Lord sends no evil. He should rather say: 'I am undergoing a bitter experience.' It is like a bitter medicine which a physician prescribes in order to cure the patient."

O. Y., p. 57.

4. Aid in Tribulation

The Kobriner said: "We read (Leviticus 25:49): 'Either his friend [1] or his friend's son may redeeem him, or any that is near to him or his family may redeem him.' If we find ourselves in trouble, we should pray to the Lord, our Friend, to aid us; we may also go for aid to the Rabbi, the son of our Friend; or we may discuss it with a sympathetic comrade, a member of the same society. We may receive benefits from them all."

O. Y., p. 82.

[1] The Hebrew word "Dod" means uncle, friend, or beloved.

5. Holiness and Suffering

Said the Belzer: "The Lord says to us: 'Ye shall be holy.' [1] If we do not choose to be so, He compels us through suffering. Therefore we should endeavor to avoid suffering by honoring our parents, keeping the Sabbath holy, and performing other injunctions mentioned in the chapter."

D. S., p. 82.

[1] Leviticus 19:2.

6. The Measure of Suffering

Boundless was the Apter's love for Israel. Once he broke into great lamentation and wept almost a half day without cease.

On this day Rabbi Sussya of Anipol visited Apt and came directly to Rabbi Abraham Joshua. "What is the cause of your weeping?" he asked the Apter in his compelling fashion. "Has not the Holy Baal Shem commanded us to be always gay and cheerful?"

The Apter cast a mournful glance at his friend and cried: "Sussya, Sussya, what will befall you? Do you not feel the dreadful suffering and the bitter persecutions to which the people of Israel are subjected?"

"I feel them," answered Rabbi Sussya, "but it is written in the Book of Zohar, that God inflicts upon mankind only as much suffering as it can endure."

Bl., Pr., p. 149.

7. The Lost Manuscript

The Basher Rabbi told this story: Rabbi Heshel gave a manuscript he had written to a disciple for publication in Jerusalem. A storm damaged the ship and the passengers were transferred to another vessel. Their possessions, including the precious manuscript, were lost. The Disciple returned to the Rabbi and asked him: "Why does the Talmud teach us that one should bless the Lord for the evil as well as for the good." [1]

"Because the Lord does everything for the good of man," replied Rabbi Heshel. He was thereupon told of the loss of the manuscript, and he promptly fainted away.

[1] Berakhoth 54.

"It may be asked why the Rabbi did not act according to his own statement. The answer is that only such misfortunes are good for a man which do not interfere with his ability to study.[2] The loss of the manuscript, however, was a severe obstacle to the Rabbi's studies; hence he took it deeply to heart."

N. I., p. 73.

[2] Berakhoth 5, paraphrased.

8. The Sorrows of All Living Creatures

On Yom Kippur Eve, the Tzidnover Maggid called in Rabbi Samuel of Kaminka, and showing him his sick grand-daughter, said: "Is not the new dress she wears very beautiful and does it not become her greatly?" Rabbi Samuel also complimented the girl on her new gown, and for a few moments she forgot about her incurable malady. When the girl had left the room, the Tzidnover said:

"I know that we gave her only a few moments of gladness, but even these few are pleasing in the eyes of the Lord, since we have done all we can for her. We are taught in the 'Ethics of the Fathers' (6:4): 'This is the way that is becoming for the study of the Torah: a morsel of bread with salt thou must eat, and water by measure thou must drink; thou must sleep upon the ground, and live a life of trouble the while thou toilest in the Torah.'[1] Hence it is not sufficient for thee to eat nothing but bread, and sleep upon the ground, but in addition thou must also feel the troubles of all living creatures, and thou must seek to minimize them as much as thou art able."

Z. H., pp. 12-15.

[1] Singer, p. 206.

9. The Value of Suffering

It is told of a Zaddik that robbers overtook him on a journey and stripped him of all his possessions. He did not lament his loss, did not repine, but said smiling that the robbers had come into their own. Those of his household protested, but he replied:

"They have taken by force what was theirs by rights as decreed in Heaven. As for my cognizance and right understanding of what has befallen, the Baal Shem has said: 'Suffering makes for proper insight and compassion.'"

Bl., Pr., p. 23.

10. Afflictions From Love

Said the Porissover: "Some Hasidim are so proud of their piety that they cannot believe the Lord sends them hardships in order to awaken in them penitence for their sins. They affirm: I am a perfect Jew, and I will accept these hardships as 'afflictions from love.' But afflictions from love are not sent in vain; they are intended as a means to arouse penitence. When the Riziner was imprisoned, he wept. He was asked: 'Why do you not accept this affliction as intended in love?' He answered: 'When God sends bitterness, we ought to feel it.'"

D. Z., p. 19.

11. Tribulations to Doubters

Said the Besht: "We say in the Rosh Ha-Shanah Hymn: 'Certainty is His name.' It follows, then, that 'doubt' is not from God. Most tribulations come to those who are wavering in their beliefs and in their resolutions, whether they concern matters of substance or spirit."

K. S. T., p. 35b.

12. A True Cure

Said the Besht: "He who suffers tribulations and believes he can dispel them by moving to another place, is like a sick man who imagines his illness will depart if he moves. The truth is that his malady will pursue him to his new place as well. The real cure is obtained by repentance, by prayer from the heart, and by petitions for God's mercies."

K. S. T., p. 8b.

13. Joy and Anxiety

Said the Porissover: "The Talmud declares that the expression 'It was' is a sign of sorrow, and the phrase: 'It shall be' is an omen of joy.[1] Why? Because when we look upon our deeds that 'were,' we are filled with grief at their imperfection. But we hope that our deeds that 'shall be' will be excellent."

A Hasid added: "What should cause us anxiety? The sorrows that have passed over us are no longer felt, and they have done us the incalculable benefit of wiping out our sins. We should, therefore, feel joy in them as well as in the good works we have resolved to perform in the future. Let us leave worry to those who possess great riches."[2]

D. Z., p. 18.

[1] Megillah 10b.
[2] See Buber, pp. 638 ff. "Von Leid und Freude" for other items. See also "Prayer in Tribulation," Rubric 133.

14. Pride and Sorrow

Said the Koretzer: "Sadness and bitterness are the result of pride. The proud man who suffers tribulations cannot understand how a person of his quality merits tribulations. But the humble man accepts whatever betides with calmness and philosophic resignation."

D. D., p. 91.

185. TRUTH AND FALSEHOOD

1. Truth Near to Earth

Commenting upon the phrase: (Psalm 85:12) "Truth springeth out of the earth," the Slonimer said: "Truth is near you on the ground, but you do not wish to bend down to reach for it."

O. Y., p. 183.

2. When Falsehood Is Buried

Commenting on the same verse, the Gerer Rabbi in response to the inquiry: "How can anything sprout forth when nothing is placed within?" made the comment: "When Falsehood is buried, Truth springeth forth."

S. S. K., iv, 102.

3. The Seal

Said Rabbi Bunam: "The Lord selected truth as his seal,[1] because any other virtue may be a clever imitation of the true form, whereas any imitation of the truth is falsehood."

S. S. K., i, 53.

[1] Sabbath 55.

4. "Falsehood Hath No Feet"

The Lubliner commented upon the Talmudical saying that he who endeavors to do good is assisted from Heaven, and he who seeks to do evil is allowed to do so, but receives no aid.[1] He said:

"One who does good is assisted by 'truth,' the patron of good; and truth brings with it enthusiasm. But the evil man is associated with untruth, and there is a folk proverb which says: 'falsehood hath no feet,'[2] that is to say, it lacks enthusiasm and vigor."

N. II. L., p. 31.

[1] Sabbath 104.
[2] Rashi to Proverbs 12:19.

5. Who Is More Lovable?

The Lubliner declared: "I love more the wicked man, who knows that he is wicked, than the righteous man who knows that he is righteous. The first one is truthful, and the Lord loves truth. The second one falsifies, since no human being is exempt from sin; and the Lord hates untruth."

N. H. L., p. 25.

6. True for the Moment

Rabbi Azriel Hurwitz, hearing the Lubliner say that he was not a "Rebbe," asked him:

"If you are not a 'Rebbe,' why do you teach thousands to follow in your footsteps?"

"What can I do?" replied the Lubliner; "they refuse to leave unless I give them instruction."

"Then tell them you are not a 'Rebbe,' and they will leave you," said Rabbi Hurwitz.

The Lubliner promised to do so. Later he met the Rav, and told him that the more he humbled himself, the more his followers clung to him.

"The Hasidim indeed love the humble. Tell them, then, that you are a Zaddik, and they will depart from you."

"But, my dear Rav," replied the Lubliner, "though I am not a 'Rebbe,' neither am I a liar, and I cannot call myself a Zaddik. Should I be called a Zaddik even by a holy man, it may be true for the moment. The next minute, however, I may have an evil thought."

N. H. L., p. 23.

7. The Bratzlaver on "Truth and Falsehood"

A.

The Bratzlaver said:

1. "Faith can be attained only through adherence to truth; he who adheres merely to the power of reason has no faith.
2. "The chief way to discover truth is by cleaving to the Zaddikim and by separation from the impious.
3. "He whose faith is weakened is susceptible to false beliefs. True faith is the seal that guards holiness.
4. "Truth and faith work for cheerfulness and length of life.
5. "Wealth is earned through truth; the falsifier lacks possessions and suffers ignominies.
6. "Falsehood corrupts the blood; truth purifies it.
7. "Falsehood leads to vain regrets, and brings hurtful tears to the eyes.
8. "Falsehood is evil and impure; it removes the Providence of God.
9. "Falsehoods are many, but truth is one. In the unity of truth, there is strength; truth is divine and it will surely triumph.
10. "He who wishes to prevail in a dispute cannot possibly see the truth. He will give no credence to that which he beholds with his own eyes.
11. "A man of truth knows no difference between service of the Lord in public or in private. Such a man is troubled by no doubts.
12. "In time of tribulation falsehood must be guarded against most zealously. Tribulation weakens truth."

L. E. H., pp. 3-7.

B.

"1. He who adds to truth decreases it.
2. The breath of a lie creates the Satan.
3. A lying man of wealth has no one's respect, not even his own.
4. The world would be rescued from all injuries were truth its sovereign.
5. Flattery leads to falsehoods.
6. The liar hates meekness.
7. Often a master is led to lie to cover up his subordinates' misdeeds. More often subordinates are led to transgress through the lies of their chief.
8. Where there is no truth, there is no kindness.
9. Truth redeems from all tribulations.

10. Where there is no truth, there is no peace.

11. He who is far from truth is far from charity.

12. Truth leads to fame.

13. In a family where the parents are untruthful, the children oppose each other.

14. Lies are usually caused by undue fear of men.

15. Through lies God is forgotten.

16. He who possesses no confidence, utters falsehoods, and he who utters falsehoods, possesses no confidence.

17. He who is untruthful regards the man who avoids evil as a fool.

18. He who cleaves to vanity becomes forgetful.

19. He who guards himself against falsehoods usually is victorious over his adversaries.

20. The fear of the Lord brings truthfulness.

21. No slander can touch the man who is known to be truthful.

22. He who is not proud is saved from falsehoods."

Sef. Ham, pp. 13-16.

8. The Power of "Falsehood"

A Hasid was asked by the Kobriner: "Where is your aged father?"

"On the way to Kobrin," replied the Hasid.

"How old is he?" asked the Rabbi.

"Seventy years old," was the response.

"How far is it from your city to Kobrin?" asked the Rabbi.

"Sixty miles," said the Hasid.

The Rabbi turned to his Disciples and said: "Observe how great is the power of falsehood. It attracts a man of seventy years to walk sixty miles to visit me!"

O. I. H., p. 184.

9. Walking with Truth

Rabbi Bunam once explained that humility means that a man should consider himself a nobody. A Hasid remarked: "But, Master, I am truly a nobody; hence what use would it be for me to consider myself a nobody?"

"If this is the case," retorted the Rabbi. "You will walk with truth if you obey me."

S. I., p. 45.

10. The Stamp of Approval

The Lubliner said to Rabbi Bunam: "He who knows his true worth is deserving of every one's approval. When a man imports goods and pays the duty, the goods are stamped: 'Approved.' Likewise God's seal is 'truth,' and the man who knows his true worth bears God's stamp of approval."

S. I., p. 48.

11. Truth in Measure

Said the Kossover: "Pure truthfulness does not exist in this world. One man is far from falsehood, and another man still farther. But no one is altogether truthful."

E. Z., p. 64.

12. The Study of the Truth

The Strelisker was a disciple of the Karliner. After his marriage Rabbi Uri left his wife and went to Karlin. His wife was given shelter by the Strelisker Rav. When Rabbi Uri returned home for Passover, he was invited to the Rav's home for the Seder. The Rav noticed the ecstasy of Rabbi Uri's conduct of the Seder, and he inquired of him: "Since you are so God-fearing, why do you not fulfill your duties to your wife? Does it not say in the Marriage Contract: 'And I solemnly promise to work for thee, to respect thee, to give thee food and other necessities of a woman?'" Rabbi Uri replied: "Read on, Your Worship, and you will find written: 'As the custom of Jewish husbands who support their wives in truth'; hence I went to Karlin to be taught the truth."

E. Tz., p. 80.

13. When Elijah Comes

Said the Medzibozer: "We read: 'Two men have deposited money, one a hundred zuzim, and the other two hundred, and later each claims to have put in two hundred: if there is no proof, the money shall remain unpaid until Elijah comes' (Talmud: Baba Metzia, 34a). What can Elijah do about it? Must there not be two witnesses for legal evidence? The answer is: When Elijah comes, the inhabitants of the world will become truthful, and the man who deposited the lesser amount will testify to the truth."

Butz. D., p. 18.

14. Harmony of Heart and Mouth

Said the Berditschever: "He who has an opportunity to gain a profit by lying, but holds fast to the truth because he remembers the prohibition against falsehood, is rewarded not only for adhering to the prohibition, but also for retaining it in his mind. Thus he who abstains from a sin or performs a good deed receives also the reward for learning the portion of the Torah concerning it.

"He whose mouth and heart are not in perfect harmony cannot expect his prayers to be acceptable on high. The Satan will claim that though he prays with his mouth, he does not believe in the Lord's powers in his heart."

Em. K., p. 56.

15. Admit Your Untruth

Rabbi Mordecai of Tzernobil said: "If you wish to acquire the habit of truthfulness, make it a point when you catch yourself telling

a falsehood, to say unashamedly: 'I have just been guilty of a lie.'
In this manner you will speedily discipline your tongue."

Em. K., p. 56.

16. Acknowledge the Truth

Said Rabbi Bunam: "We read in our Morning Prayers: 'At all
times let a man fear God, in private as well as in public, and
acknowledge the truth.' [1] If a person asks if you have performed a
certain act of piety, let not your modesty prompt you to deny that
you have really done it. Avoid ostentation in your deeds of piety,
but if asked, acknowledge the truth."

Em. K., p. 61.

[1] Singer, p. 7.

17. What Is Truth?

Said the Ladier: "I have labored twenty-one years on truth; seven
years to learn what truth is; seven years, to drive out falsehood; and
seven years to acquire the habit of truthfulness."

Em. K., p. 74.

18. A Daily Prayer

The Koretzer would often remind his sons to offer this prayer
daily: "O Lord, lead me in the path of truth."

M. P., p. 17.

19. The Power of Truth

Said the Trisker Rabbi:
"1. God's seal is truth. If thou utterest a lie, thou art guilty of
forging His seal.
2. Thy words are food to the Shekinah. Nourish her with truth
and with words of holiness.
3. Man is either ruled by truth and peace, or by falsehood and
quarrel. Make thy choice."

Em. K., p. 62.

20. Indispensable Truth

Said the Bershider: "We read 'Acquire truth and do not dispense
with it.' [1] Some virtues may be dispensed with temporarily for the
sake of acquiring others. But if you dispense with truth, how will
you know that you are acquiring a worthy trait of character? Perhaps you are deceiving yourselves."

M. P., p. 39.

[1] Proverbs 23:23.

21. The Friend and the Angel

Said the Bershider: "The Sages teach that the greatest labor of
man should be to avoid self-deceit. But how can a man do so when
he is deceived and believes his action to be right? By obeying the
counsel of his friend, since his friend cannot profit by permitting the
deceit to continue. We are also taught that he who labors for truth,

creates for himself an Angel of Truth who acts as a monitor to warn him of falsehood."

M. P., p. 49.

22. Nothing But the Truth

Said the Koretzer: "Nothing has been so difficult for me to conquer as the habit of telling at times an untruth. Each limb and each bone in my body protested against my resolution to avoid lies. But once for all, I came out victorious: there must be no lies within me, not a single time."

He would tell his new Disciples: "A man who fell into evil traits began with lying and continued with pride. He who wishes to uplift himself should do the reverse: begin with telling the truth, and continue with meekness.

"I could give you further advice in the service of God, but I cannot counsel you until you become masters of your words, and force them to utter solely the truth. How can I know whether your worship and holy studies are of truth and for the sake of serving God, if you have not yet gained the ability to hold unswervingly to truth?"

And he continued: "After you have left untruth behind you, you will find it easy to abandon all other undesirable habits."

To children, the Rabbi would distribute gifts and declare: "Say aloud: 'I must tell no lies.'"

He would also teach: "May my soul leave my body, ere falsehood leaves my mouth."

M. P., pp. 52-3.

23. Unable to Hear Untruth

Two men came with a money dispute to Rabbi Leib Koveler. The Rabbi said to them: "My father, the Rabbi of Neschiz, taught me from my childhood that God is Truth and the Torah is Truth. If a man tells the truth, he is associated with God and His Torah, but if he lies, he has no association either with God or His Torah. This lesson, repeated for many years every day, has worked so deeply upon me, that I am unable even to hear a lie. Now if you will tell me truth, I will hear you; otherwise, your words will fall on deaf ears."

D. Z., p. 43.

24. The Older Generations

A Rabbi made the following comment: "When a Rabbi is asked concerning his father, he praises him as a very learned man. His grandfather in his eyes was even greater. But when a man unlearned in Torah is asked the same question, he replies: 'My father was a superstitious fool, and my grandfather was an idiot. He believed in everything.'

"We may apply to them the Talmudical saying[1] that with the wise, the older, the wiser; but with the unlearned, the older, the more foolish."

L. H. F., p. 39.

[1] Sabbath 152, paraphrased.

25. Higher Than Any Majority

Rabbi Solomon Kluger of Brody read in the Midrash [1] that Kindness favored the creation of man; Truth disapproved; Charity was favorable; but Peace opposed it. God then "threw Truth to earth," and thus there remained a majority in favor of man's creation. The Rabbi remarked: "Since Peace was also in opposition, why was Truth selected to be thrown to earth? The reason is that were Truth left in opposition, a majority against man's creation would not have availed. Truth is higher than any majority against it."

F. U. A. O., i, 9.

[1] Bereshith Rabba, 8:5.

26. False Speech

Said the Sassover: "We read (Exodus 23:7): 'Keep thyself far from false speech.' This may be interpreted thus: 'Your false speech will keep you far from God, for God is truth.'"

Told to Samuel Spitz by the Mirapoler Rebbe, Grandson of the Kaminker.

27. Rather Die Than Lie

This story is told regarding one of the disciples of Rabbi Pinchas of Koretz, Rabbi Raphael of Bershid:

The latter was once invited to the house of a nobleman to tell what he knew of a certain Jew. Through a single false word he could have made the Jew happy for his whole life, but by speaking the truth he would have brought him grave harm. The Rabbi felt he could neither speak the truth under the circumstances nor do a man an injury, and, therefore, with tears, he begged God to take away his life. To this degree did he seek to guard himself from straying off the path of truth.[1]

Bl., Pr., p. 85.

[1] There is another version that two Rabbis were invited; one was willing to utter an untruth in order to save the Jew's family from destitution. But the other hesitated; thereupon the Jew resolved to save the Rabbi from untruthfulness and confessed the crime.

28. Arrogance and Untruth

The wife of Rabbi Pinchas of Koretz once bought a gilded Kiddush-Goblet.[1] On Friday evening, when he saw the goblet, he called to his wife indignantly: "Since when do we have golden utensils in our house?"

His wife sought to justify herself, saying: "See it is not genuine, but only a gilded goblet!"

"Then," said the Rabbi, "you have not only brought arrogance, but also deceit and falsehood into the house," and he refused to use the goblet for the sacred ceremony.

Bl., Pr., p. 85.

[1] Sanctification Cup, used at the Sabbath and Festival Meals.

186. UNBELIEVERS

1. The Value of Atheism

The Sassover taught thus: "There is no quality of mind in men that is altogether without its uses. Even the meanest errors and those most fit to be abhorred have a goal of their own and may lead to God. But how about infidelity? Aye, even infidelity is not altogether barred. For if someone comes to you entreating aid, do not say in refusal: 'Trust in God; He will help,' but act as if there were no God, and none to help but you."

E. Tz., p. 53 (Bl., Gem., p. 189).

2. Denying God

The Kaminker was accustomed to journey to neighboring towns for the purpose of preaching. After his discourse a collection would be made in his behalf. Once after an absence of several weeks he returned home penniless. His wife asked him: "How shall we pay our debts?"

The Rabbi answered: "Had I been willing to deny God, I could have returned with sufficient money."

His wife pressed him for an explanation, and he said: "We find in the Talmud the saying that one who closes his eyes to charity is as one who denies God" (Kethubhoth 68).

Beth Phineas, pp. 34-35.

3. Reward and Punishment

A scholar of distinction came to the Berditschever and explained that he was assailed by doubts, particularly regarding the doctrine of Reward and Punishment after death.

The Rabbi replied: "I cannot, of course, lay before you on this table, Paradise and Purgatory, in order that you may be convinced. But remember that it is quite as logical to believe that the soul is judged before a Heavenly Tribunal, as to prove the opposite. In the event that the first interpretation is correct, where, pray, will you stand?"

The skeptic was moved by this declaration, and departed in peace.

E. O., p. 57.

4. The Worthy Man

Rabbi Bunam said: "The man of learning is frequently a heretic; the good-hearted man is often a lover of the pleasures of the flesh; the pious man is usually an egotist."

"What then constitutes the worthy man?" the Rabbi was asked.

"To be all of these together," was the reply.

S. S. K., i, p. 6.

5. The Prosperity of Unbelievers

A heretic asked the Gerer Rabbi the following question: "In the 'Sh'ma' I read that the religious will prosper and the irreligious will be famished. Now I am an unbeliever and yet I am quite well-to-do, whereas deeply religious people frequently petition me for charity."

The Rabbi replied: "I perceive that once you read the 'Sh'ma' with attention. The reward for this act is more than your present possessions. There is more coming to you yet."

S. S. K., ii, 19.

6. The Royal Revenge

The Pulnoer said: "A man of great intelligence revolted unsuccessfully against his king. Instead of executing him, the king placed him in a high state position, and continued to advance him higher and higher. With every promotion the former rebel felt keener and keener remorse. Therein lay the royal revenge.

"Sometimes one who denies the Lord is vouchsafed an increasingly clearer insight into the glory and power of the Lord, and he becomes unhappy through the very intensity of his remorse."

Kahana, p. 90.

7. The Heretic's Repentance

Said the Lubliner: "The Talmud declares that Rabbi Elisha ben Abuya became an unbeliever. A former disciple sought to persuade him to repent, and Rabbi Elisha answered: 'I heard a Voice from Heaven calling: 'Repent, ye transgressors,—except Elisha.' "[1]

The Lubliner made comment: "If Elisha had been but wise, this was his opportunity to become the greatest of all men. Believing that his repentance was unacceptable, and therefore expecting no reward from it, had he returned to the service of the Lord despite this, his service would have been the most pleasing in the eyes of the Lord, and he would have become the most perfect of mortals."[2]

N. H. L., p. 30.

[1] Haggigah 15, paraphrased.

[2] Bloch, *Priester der Liebe*, p. 68, attributes this story to the Besht. A verse from the *Ethics of the Fathers* speaks of perfect service as a "servant who anticipates no reward." (1:3; Singer, p. 184.)

8. The Penitent Heretic

A heretic said to Rabbi Asher Staliner: "I should like exceedingly to become a penitent and return to Judaism, but I fear the Talmudical statement[1] that a heretic who repents will not live." The Rabbi answered: "To believe in a heretic's sincerity is indeed difficult. Therefore the Talmud states that such a penitent shall not live, that he may have no chance to relapse into apostasy once more. If, however, his repentance is so sincere that he is willing to take a chance of dying rather than to continue his life in error, it may be assumed in

[1] Abodah Zarah 17.

Heaven that he is an exception to the general rule of heretics, and he may be granted the boon of life."

Z. Z., p. 34.

9. Learn from the Scoffers

The Koretzer said: "In our code we read that we should not avoid the proper religious rites because we are ashamed of those who ridicule us. This means that we should not be ashamed to perform any religious rite. How do we know this? We learn it by observing those who scoff at us. If they are bold in their ridicule of those who serve the Lord, how much bolder should we be in serving Him!"

Mif. H., p. 58.

10. Who Is an Unbeliever?

Said Rabbi Bunam: "The greatest scoffer among Jews is not a genuine unbeliever, since he utters a plea unto the God of Israel when he finds himself in tribulation. The true unbeliever was Pharaoh of the Gentiles. God smote him ten times, and still he continued to say: 'Who is God that I should obey Him?' (Exodus 4:2)."

S. I., p. 17.

187. THE UNITY OF ISRAEL

1. The Fusing Flame

The Pulnoer Rabbi said: "Jews are likened in the Torah to sand.[1] Each particle of sand is distinct, and only through fire do they become fused into glass. Likewise the Israelites are usually divided among themselves, and it requires calamities to unite them."[2]

Dubnow, T-Ha-Has., p. 101.

[1] Genesis 32:13; in earlier verses the word "dust" is used.

[2] Another story in which Jews are likened to sand is the following: A Jew came to a Rabbi and said: "I encounter prejudice everywhere and therefore am thinking of becoming baptized. What difference would this make in me, seeing that I will continue to disbelieve in Christianity?" The Rabbi replied: "You know that the Bible likens Jews to sand. As long as sand is dry, it is sand, but the moment water is poured over it, it becomes mud." M. D., p. 84.

2. Unity Through Torah

The Sachatzover Rabbi said: "In our present Exile, as in the Babylonian, the Israelites are scattered among other nations, whereas in Egypt, they dwelt together in Goshen. The reason is that before we received the Torah there was no force sufficiently strong to bind Israelites together as a particular people, and therefore the Creator decreed that they should sojourn in the same territory. To-day, however, our study of the Torah serves to unify us in our dispersion."

S. S. K., iii, 123.

3. The Hasid's Leadership

"It is incumbent upon the true Hasid to lead his people back to unity by making no account of whatever disunites them—the differences between the learned and the vulgar, between rich and poor. For God and Israel are one, and their unison above will be restored by a reunion below. Nothing more precious exists in the sight of God than the Unity of His Chosen People—as it is said in Midrash Tanchuma to Deuteronomy: 'If the nation only lives in unity, God will not punish it, even for worshiping idols.' [1] And at another point, it says: 'Israel will not be redeemed until united.' "

[1] Hosea 4:17.   Bl., Pr., p. 37.

4. The Letters of the Torah

The Berditschever said: "When a Scroll of the Law is sewn together, it becomes holy, and it is forbidden to erase a letter in it. But when it is still in several parts, it is permissible to make an erasure in it. The letters represent the souls of Israel; when united none may be blotted out." [1]

N. B. L., p. 25.

[1] This story is also allocated to the "Maggid," Rabbi Dov-Ber of Mezeritz. See Bloch, Gemeinde, p. 128.

5. The Letter "Yud"

The Sassover said: "Why do we find that in many prayer books the name of God is represented by the union of two letters 'Yud' and 'Yud.' The explanation is to be found in the fact that thereby we have demonstration of this principle: if Jews are united, the Name of God is fashioned, and no erasure can be made in it even if it is written by mistake in a wrong place. It is different, however, if Jews are disunited and each one stands separate and apart. They do not then create the Name of God, and if they do not stand in their right position, it is permissible to erase them." [1]

[1] Compare 34:5.   Bl., Gem., p. 190.

6. Precious Stones

Once the Baal Shem said: "There are precious stones beyond cavil; every one can see the gleam and the lights they shed in their different colors; their genuineness can be recognized at once. These are the Jews who are true Hasidim. There are also false gems: these are the hypocritical pietists. Finally there are stones, 'treasures concealed in the sand,' which cannot at once be identified as precious. These are the Jews who easily surrender to untrammeled desires and passions, and who do not follow the injunctions of the Law. Nevertheless, they, too, carry in their heart the treasure of abiding love for humanity."

He meditated for a moment, and then continued: "But they are all precious gems."

Bl., Pr., pp. 52-3.

7. Why the Israelite Is Called a Jew

Rabbi Meier of Premislan once explained why the Israelite is called "Yud" (a Jew), as follows: "The Hebrew letter 'Yud' (י) is the smallest in the Hebrew alphabet; also, the man, 'Yud' must consider himself among the least significant of mortals on God's earth; he must bear himself with humility towards every one.

"Moreover, the letter 'Yud' has a short 'little foot.' If, however, something is erased from it, there remains only a spot. Likewise, if the Jew turns slightly away from his Judaism, there remains only a spot."

Bl., Gem., p. 312.

8. Communion With Israel

Before prayer Rabbi Michael of Zlotzov was accustomed to say: "I unite myself with all Israel. with those greater and those smaller than myself. With the great ones, that through them my prayer may be raised on high; with the smaller, that through me, their prayer may ascend to the Heavens."

Bl., Pr., p. 77.

9. Unity In Prayer

"If all of Israel, without schisms and dissensions, were to pray only once in whole-hearted devotion, the hour of the Messiah's coming would be nigh. It is Satan, the Evil Inclination, that keeps Israel from uniting in prayer."

Bl., Gem., p. 27.

10. The Branch of the Tree

Said the Kobriner:[1] "An Israelite in his relationship to the synagogue may be likened to a branch growing on a tree. As long as the branch is still attached to the tree, there is hope it may renew its vigor under favorable conditions, no matter how withered it may have become. But once the living branch falls away all hope is lost."[2]

O. Y., p. 96.

[1] The item is also ascribed to the Besht concerning the Frankists.

[2] Dr. Ben Zion Mossinsohn once compared the individual Jew to leaves on a tree. The leaves may drop off and wither away, but the tree continues its life. Some Israelites may depart from their people, but the main trunk remains unimpaired.

11. Jewish Fellowship

A man once complained to the Kobriner that when he was the only Jew in his town he had prospered. Ever since others had settled there, his trade had dwindled. The Rabbi interpreted for him the verse:[1] "Many are the sorrows of the wicked." "Many," namely, the fact that there are so many Jews, is the sorrow of the wicked. "But he that trusteth in the Lord" considers "his being encom-

[1] Psalm 32: 10, paraphrased.

passed" by other Jews "as a kindness." He rejoices to live among Jews.

O. Y., p. 98.

12. When Left Alone

The Kozmirer Rabbi said to a Hasid who had halted his frequent visits to him: "A Jew is like the dough of the Matzah. When it is kneaded and rolled, it is fit for unleavened bread, but as soon as it is left alone, it becomes Hametz."

O. S., p. 60e.

13. Uniting at the Center

Said the Koretzer: "Let us be like the lines leading to the central point of the circle: all come to one point and unite there. But let us not be like the parallel lines which are always separate."

Nof. Tz., p. 49.

14. Unity and Peace

The Bershider loved peace and unity in Israel. If one spoke evil of another Jew, he would rebuke him and beg him to cease. He was told that a man by the name of Samuel spoke slightingly of him. The Bershider commented: "Why make a disagreement between Samuel and myself?"

He used to say: "When thou seest that thy fellow-man dislikes thee, show him thy love the more. Any disagreement between Jews causes a breach to appear in the Throne of Holiness through which unholy spirits enter. Hence it is the duty of every Jew to love and to befriend anyone who has disagreed with him, and thereby to repair the breach. When Israelites are united, they become the very Throne of Holiness, the Shekinah dwells in them, and all holiness descends upon them."

In his last year, he said: "Put aside all Mitzwoth and labor to unite Jewish hearts."

M. P., pp. 43-44.

188. THE UNLEARNED AND THE IGNORANT

1. The Power of an Earnest Word

There lived in Kotzk a water-carrier, who, though illiterate, possessed deep religious feeling. Once in synagogue he heard the word "Tameh" (unclean), and it remained fixed in his memory. Unable to remember the customary prayers, he used the word "Tameh" as his prayer, repeating it with great vehemence hundreds of times. He became the butt of the townspeople's jests and was nicknamed "Tameh." The pious water-carrier ignored his mockers and continued to pour out his heart to the Creator in his own fashion.

It happened that the Kotzker Rabbi overheard his prayer. He appreciated the impossibility of teaching the untutored laborer the correct prayers, but wished him at least to substitute the word "Tahor" (clean) for "Tameh" (unclean). The water-carrier repeated "Tahor" many times, but soon became confused, and said "Tamor." He became aware that it was unlike either the first or the second word. He ran to the Rabbi and tearfully begged to be allowed his "own" word, inasmuch as he could not pray with the "Rabbi's word." The Kotzker complied with his request. To this day, the water-carrier may be heard, ardently praying: "Tameh, Tameh, Tameh."

Kotzker Maasioth, p. 1.

2. The Real Scholar

A committee from a small town asked Rabbi Mendel Libavitzer to recommend to them as their Rabbi a worthy man of learning. A short time later, it came to the ears of the Libavitzer that the Rabbi whom he had recommended as a great Zaddik and as a man of scholarship was being outrageously treated by the community. The Libavitzer sighed and said: "This is a lesson to me not to recommend an excellent man to a community before I investigate the community's reputation. But, it may be asked: 'Why did they require an exceptional Zaddik and an outstanding scholar if they did not intend to obey and respect him?' This may be explained by the Talmudical story: when Rabbi Akiba was still an ignorant person, he hated a scholar as do all unlearned folk. He used to boast: 'Who will give me a scholar that I may bite him as if I were an ass!' [1] Why did he require some one to give him a scholar? Because, being ignorant, he could not recognize the real scholar, and it was required that a discerning person give him a scholar, so that he might know he would be mistreating a man of real learning.

"It is now apparent that the committee wished me to recommend them a genuine scholar, since they were unable to perceive one, and feared lest they might abuse one who was not a man of real learning."

F. U. A. O., ii, 94.

[1] Pesachim 49.

3. The Rule of Servants

Said the Savraner: "It is written: 'Servants rule over us; no one can deliver us out of their hand' (Lamentations 5:8). 'The heart of a king is in God's hands, and He turns it according to His will.' [1] But if servants rule over us, there is no deliverance."

E. Tz., p. 55.

[1] Proverbs 21:1.

4. The Self-Delusion of the Ignorant

Said the Koretzer: "Only the ignorant may think of himself as a man of perfection. Remember the Lord's injunctions: 'And thou shalt talk of them,'[1] namely of the words of the Torah, not of words of worldly affairs. And again: 'Thou shalt meditate thereon day and

[1] Deut. 6:7.

night'; [2] on it, and not on other affairs. And who but the ignorant may think himself righteous even though he has failed fully to perform God's commands? Do you not know that you have transgressed in word and thought innumerable times?"

Nof. Tz., p. 57.

[2] Joshua 1:8.

5. *The Peddler's Worship*

The Rimanover said: "When the poor, ignorant village peddler returns to town shortly before dark, and, ignoring his fatigue and hunger, hastens to the House of Prayer to recite the afternoon and evening services, then the Seraphim and Ophanim tremble before his worship, for it splits the very Heavens."

Em. L., p. 49.

6. *The Unlearned Beadle*

Rabbi Abraham Joshua Heshel Apter observed several young Hasidim studying a profound book of the Kabbalah, while an old man, the beadle, was setting in order the Beth ha-Midrash. He went over to them and said: "No doubt you consider yourselves much better Jews than this untutored beadle. Let me inform you, however, that you will find it necessary to labor earnestly before you can attain the position of this old man as a simple-hearted, unsophisticated Jew."

D. D., p. 230.

7. *The Generous Tavern-Keeper*

The Premislaner told the following tale: "I went up to Heaven in a dream and stood at the Gates of Paradise in order to observe the procedure of the Heavenly Tribunal. A learned Rabbi approached and wished to enter. 'Day and night,' he said, 'I studied the Holy Torah.' 'Wait,' said the Angel. 'We will investigate whether your study was for its own sake or whether it was as a matter of profession or for the sake of honors.'

"A Zaddik next approached. 'I fasted much,' he said. 'I underwent many ablutions; I studied the Zohar.' 'Wait,' said the Angel, 'until we have completed our investigation to learn whether your motives were pure.'

"Then a tavern-keeper drew near. 'I kept an open door and fed without charge every poor man who came to my inn,' he said.

"The Heavenly Portals were opened to him. No investigation was required.

"I said to myself: If charity opens the Gates of Paradise, whether it be practiced for its own sake or for honors, I vow to become a collector of funds for charity."

D. D., p. 266.

189. UNSELFISHNESS (ALTRUISM)

1. Unselfish Prayer

A storekeeper complained to the Kobriner that his business was meager, whereas his neighbor, likewise a merchant, was flourishing. The Kobriner replied:

"I shall pray for you on condition that you give thanks to the Lord, and say: 'Blessed be the Lord who sends His abundance to a fellow-Israelite.' At first you will utter these words without the acquiescence of your whole heart; later, however, you will sincerely mean them. Does not the Torah command us 'to do right with our lips and with our heart?' (Deut. 30: 14)."

O. Y., p. 54.

2. Service from Fear and Love

The Berditschever said: "The difference between fear and love in the service of the Lord is this: he who serves from fear never forgets his own existence, but fears the Mightier One. On the other hand, he who serves from love forgets about himself entirely."

Horodetzky, book ii, p. 87.

190. WANDERING

1. Voluntary Galuth

Said the Komarner: "He who voluntarily leaves his home and wanders about as a beggar, living a life of discomfort, but trusting always in the Lord, becomes a partner in the 'Exile of the Shekinah.' His sins are forgiven and he understands the secrets of the Torah. Happy is the lot of those who go into 'exile.' " [1]

M. Hat., p. 72.

[1] Not only Hasidic Rabbis but also their predecessors and opponents engaged in the painful life of wandering about as beggars. The famous Gaon of Wilna did this. It seemed to serve as a corrective of too regular and agreeable a life, and gave the wanderers an opportunity to gain an insight into the life of many types of people. During their wanderings, the travelers were enabled to think out problems of philosophy, theology and morality. Yoshe Kalb in I. J. Singer's novel travels about as a wanderer to do penance for his sin. Dr. Chaim Zhitlowsky in "A Note On Chassidism" in the English translation of "The Dybbuk" declares (pp. 14-15): "A few chosen spirits, filled with sorrow and pity for their people, often spent their whole lives in fasting and other ascetic practices, flagellation and 'Golus abrichten,' i.e., wearing a hair shirt and wandering through the world as beggars. Through their own sufferings they hoped to lighten the load of sin which rested upon the whole of Israel."

191. WEALTH AND THE WEALTHY

1. *"Temporal Goods"*

The Kotzker Rabbi met one day on the highroad a boyhood friend who, as he became wealthy, became less and less devout. The rich man invited the Rabbi to step into his splendid carriage. While seated, the Rabbi gazed at the signs of his friend's great affluence, and said: "Pray, tell me, where are your 'temporal goods'?"

The wealthy Jew answered: "Does not this costly equipage indicate clearly that I possess a goodly store of valuables?"

"Nay," exclaimed the Rabbi. "These are your 'eternal reward' which you will miss in the 'World-to-Come.' What I desire to know is: 'Where is your share in this 'temporal world'?"

The wealthy host meditated upon the Rabbi's words, and his heart became humble.

S. S. K., ii, 19.

2. *The Purpose of Wealth*

Said the Besht: "The wealth of the entire world exists merely because sometimes the Zaddik may find comfort through it. There was once a great palace which required years to build. One day in a storm a Zaddik found refuge in the palace. When the rain halted and the Zaddik had taken his departure, the palace crumbled to the earth. It had served its purpose."

M. R. T., p. 108.

3. *Reversing Positions*

Once the Belzer learned from the Jews of Brody that a number of persons in the city who had formerly been wealthy had grown so poor they were compelled to seek menial employment. At the same time, other Jews who had formerly been their hirelings, had become rich employers of many workmen.

The Belzer remarked: "Doubtless the men of wealth were punished for exploiting and oppressing their laborers. Therefore the Lord has reversed their positions."

D. S., p. 142.

4. *Meyer Anselm Rothschild*

Rabbi David Moses Tzartkover declared that he found in the Community Record-Book of Tzartkov the following story:

Meyer Anselm was a Warden for the Tzartkover Rav, Rabbi Hirsch Hurwitz. Once a sum of money, deposited with the Rav, was missing. Suspicion rested upon the Warden, and the Rav ordered him to take an oath to the effect that he neither had taken the money himself or knew who had done so. Rather than take an oath, even truthfully, Meyer Anselm made good the loss by gradual payments, for which he was compelled to sell everything he owned.

In the meantime, however, a drunken peasant, while in his cups, boasted to an innkeeper that he had stolen the money from the Rav. The money was recovered and given to Meyer Anselm. The Rav asked his pardon for believing evil of him, and pronounced a blessing over him that he might become a man of vast wealth.

Meyer Anselm later settled in Frankfort and adopted the name of Rothschild. Once he passed on the street the well-known Hakham Zevi. He stopped him and offered him a donation of money. The Hakham Zevi refused, though he had lost his position because of his battle against the followers of Sabbatai Zevi, and was in pecuniary distress. Rothschild thereupon dropped a purse to the ground, and pronounced it "Hefker," namely, "anybody's." The Hakham picked up the purse, and blessed Rothschild, petitioning great success for him.

The blessings of the two Rabbis were the cause, it is said, of the phenomenal wealth of the Rothschild family.

D. S., p. 68.

5. Devote to the Lord Your Wealth

Commenting on the text in Genesis 27:11, the Lizensker said: "It was Isaac's intention to bless Esau with material riches and Jacob with spiritual wealth only. But the Divine Love, the mother of Jacob, desired to give Jacob also a share in this world, and she used persuasion on Jacob's behalf. But Jacob feared that material riches would incline him away from the Lord. And he said: 'My brother Esau is indifferent to holiness and yearns for earthly pleasures; I am innocent, however, of such longings. Perhaps my material wealth will cause defects in my devotion, and my Father in Heaven will search me out and declare me a deceiver; perhaps I may bring down upon myself a curse rather than a blessing.'

"And the Shekinah answered: 'Upon Me be thy curse, My son. I shall guide thee in thy prosperity, that thou mayest hold to thy way; only obey My voice, and devote thy worldly abundance unto Me; make use of it to perform deeds of clemency and to fulfill My commandments.'"[1]

Noam E., p. 21.

[1] The Shekinah speaks through Rebeccah.

6. Does God Love the Rich?

Rabbi Nahum of Tzernobil was accustomed to befriend poverty-stricken Hasidim but was abrupt with wealthy ones. A rich Hasid asked him: "Rabbi, does not the Talmud teach that the Shekinah rests upon him who is wise, strong and rich?[1] Does not this prove that God loves the rich?"

The Rabbi smiled and said: "Do you truly believe that God cares for that which is external to a man? The wise, strong and rich man on whom the Shekinah rests, is the one described in 'Pirkei Avoth' (4:1): 'Who is wise? He who learns from all men. Who is mighty?

[1] Sabbath 92.

He who subdues his passions. Who is rich? He who rejoices in his portion.' " [2]

F. R. H.-M., p. 39.

[2] Singer, p. 195.

7. The Influence of Riches

Rabbi Yerachmiel said: "When thou attainest riches and honors, be not unduly pleased: they may have been given thee in reward for thy good deeds so that thou mayest have no claim left in the World-to-Come. Examine thyself to discover whether thou hast not become less worthy than thou wast before receiving riches and honors. If thou hast not descended in thy goodness, perchance thou art deserving and may truly rejoice therein."

Tif. B., p. 13.

8. Noblesse Oblige

A Maggid rebuked a miserly rich man by quoting from Genesis 27:28-9: "So God give thee . . . plenty of corn and wine. . . . Be lord over thy brethren." He commented: "If God gave you riches, conduct yourself like a nobleman over your brothers, not like a stingy knave."

L. H. F., p. 102.

9. Wealth, Poverty and the Torah

Said the Kozmirer: "We read: 'Whoso fulfills the Torah in the midst of poverty, shall in the end fulfill it in the midst of wealth; and whoso neglects the Torah in the midst of wealth shall in the end neglect it in the midst of poverty' (Ethics 4:11).[1] Shall we say that the Tanna curses a man by the punishment of poverty? Not so. The Tanna prays for both men and says: he who fulfills the Torah while he is poor may safely be entrusted with riches. And he who does not fulfill it while he is rich would surely neglect the Torah even more in poverty. Therefore, may he remain wealthy, and fulfill at least a few precepts which he finds easy."

V. S., pp. 44-5.

[1] Singer, p. 196.

192. SAYINGS OF WISDOM

1. Wisdom by the Koretzer

A.

Said the Koretzer:

"1. The Satan is inconsistent. He persuades a man not to go to synagogue on a cold morning; yet when the man does go, he follows him into it.

2. Between a Hasid and a clever man, the Hasid is superior. Between a clever Hasid and a kind man, the kind man is superior.

3. Thirteen years I taught my tongue not to tell falsehoods. For another thirteen years I taught it to tell the truth.

4. It is better for a man that his soul should depart from him than that he should utter a lie.

5. I conquered my anger and placed it in my pocket. When I have need of it, I draw it forth."

M. D., p. 214 and M. P., p. 52.

B.

"1. Dreams are the waste of the brain.

2. Sciences, though they may seem to be the waste of the Torah, in truth serve to clarify it.

3. Many a man's brain would be benefited, if it could absorb the waste of the Sage's brain.

4. A man must labor hard his entire life to rid himself of pride.

5. Intellect is a man's guard. Without it, he would be as an infant requiring constant care.

6. Holy thoughts guard a man's brain, but when the subject of his thinking is evil, they depart from him.

7. If your intellect is clouded, disperse the clouds through the spirit of fervent prayer.

8. Be not satisfied with merely appealing to a sinner to repent; help him to repent.

9. I love to pray at sunrise, before the world becomes filled with hatred and vanity.

10. He who is careful not to utter lies will not be compelled to lie in bed by reason of illness.

11. Palestine represents the inwardness of the world.

12. A man is higher than the knowledge he acquires; hence a Disciple of the Sages is called the 'Lord of the Torah.'

13. It is important that we implore God's blessing over the fruits and grains. Through them the Shekinah ascends on high.

14. Silence through humility in the sight of an evil deed is preferable to reproof.

15. God esteems highly the good deeds of men that are known only to those who perform them and their Maker.

16. The child who begins to talk early will be a wise man.

17. He whose mind is occupied with thoughts of improvement for himself and his dependents has only good thoughts.

18. When a man goes to sleep in joyful mood, his dreams will be pleasant.

19. He who truly loves another can read his thoughts, whether good or evil.

20. When a man of wickedness enters a synagogue, a sense of discomfort pervades the shrine, since the holiness within it strives to escape.

21. The truth of the Torah is said to be very deep; hence the haughty man, who holds his head high, is very far from it.

22. The Shekinah does not abide in a place of melancholy.
23. The Soul of man shall teach him, if he but heeds it."

Nof. Tz., pp. 3-24.

C.

"1. God is everywhere, even in evil thoughts.
2. When telling a lie will be regarded as a serious crime, then the Messiah will come.
3. We read: 'Ye are the children of the Lord your God' (Deut. 14:1). Ye are the children of the Lord, when you show by your actions that He is your God.
4. It is true that God is able to do whatsoever He wills. But man has the similar power, by virtue of his free will."

Nof. Tz., pp. 50-2.

2. Wisdom by the Bershider

Said the Bershider:

"1. Work for peace within thine own household, then in thy street, and then in thy town.
2. See not evil in another and good in thyself, but see good in another, and evil in thyself.
3. Measure not thy conduct with exactitude: this is a sign of pride.
4. Criticize not another's conduct, but only thine own."

M. P., p. 44.

3. Wisdom by the Besht

Said the Besht:

"1. Think not that you are superior in your devotion to your fellow-man. If he is not endowed with as fine an intellect as yours, he is equal to you when he serves God to the best of his ability. A worm may be as important as you in the eyes of the Creator, since it serves Him with all the strength granted to it.
2. Brood not upon your sin, for this leads to melancholy and prevents sincere service to God.

Express contrition in your heart for your wrongdoing; resolve not to repeat it, and serve God with joy. Make no response to one who ridicules your devotions. If he retorts in anger, your devotions will thus lead to quarrelsomeness and thereby become worthless.
3. Let it make no difference to you how your necessities have been vouchsafed to you. It may be God's will that your wishes be fulfilled in a manner contrary to your hopes.
4. Accustom yourself to keep constantly in mind the knowledge that whatever gives you pleasure derives its ability to please from God. Every pleasure will then become an act of praise to the Lord for endowing everything with His Spirit.
5. A beggar tearfully asked the king for aid; he received a small donation. A smiling nobleman came to the king, praised him for a recent act, and asked a favor; this was granted him. The nobleman's favor was worth many times that which the tearful suppliant re-

ceived. Likewise, pray with a joyful heart, and you will attain much more than one who prays in melancholy.

6. A man is where his thought resides at the moment. God is even in transgression: without His grant or power to move or to think, no wrongdoing is possible. Nehemiah teaches this in the words: 'Thou givest life to everything' (Nehemiah 9:6).

7. True worship is such that the worshiper should deem it a miracle that his soul has not departed from him, when it was so closely attached to its Maker.

8. A religious work is inspired during its inception. After it is published, it becomes holy Torah and may be interpreted like Torah.

9. He who has placed himself on a way that is not good, will surely not despise evil (A Paraphrase of Psalm 36:5)."

Kahana, pp. 91-9.

193. WOMAN

1. Beauty in Woman

The Besht once said: "When you admire beauty in a woman, remember that her beauty is but a reflection of the Supreme Source of Beauty—the Lord. Why be attracted by the reflection? Attach yourself rather to the Source of Beauty itself?"

S. Dubnow, H. of H., p. 54.

2. Tears Are Bribes

A widow was sued for rent before the Sachatzover Rabbi. She began to weep copiously. The Rabbi refused to hear the case on the ground that he had learned from the Kotzker that tears are a form of bribery.

S. S. K., ii, 21.

3. The Strong and the Stronger

To the Apter once came a matron of evil repute to take his counsel. The Apter chided her, saying: "Woman, after sinning in secret, how dare you soil my lodgings with your breath?"

The matron made an unabashed reply: "The Lord knoweth more of my sin than you do, yet He hasteneth not to present His reckoning, nor does He reveal my secret or turn His face from me. Yet the Rabbi of Apt, sitting in judgment, thinks it no wrong to discover what the Lord hath veiled."

The Apter was wont to say: "No one ever overcame me in argument, save once a woman."[1]

B., p. 501b.

[1] The Talmud ascribes to Rabbi Joshua ben Hananya these very words. (Derekh Eretz Rabba, chapter 6.)

4. *Angels Created by Women*

The Berditschever before Passover walked through the town and watched the Jewish women, scrubbing, cleaning, rubbing and making "Kasher" the household utensils and furniture. He said: "We find in the Order for the blowing of the Shofar on Rosh ha-Shanah in the Machzor, a semi-mystical prayer which reads: 'May it be Thy will that the Angels that emerge from "Crusak" shall speak good on our behalf, so that our sins may be forgiven.' I explain it as follows: May it be Thy will that the angels that emerge from the women's 'Cleaning, Rubbing, Scrubbing And Kashering for the sake of obedience to Thy command speak good on our behalf so that our sins may be forgiven.' " [1]

D. Z., p. 55.

[1] In the Machzor "Crusak" is made up of the initial letters of the names of the Shofar sounds. The word in the Machzor is somewhat different, but this combination is used to avoid the pronouncing of an Angel's name, not found in the Bible, which the Kabbalists prohibit.

194. WORDS AND THEIR POWER

1. *Speaking Beautifully*

A learned man who partook of the Sabbath meal at the home of Rabbi Baruch Medzibozer, the grandson of the Baal Shem Tov, said to his host:

"Let us now hear you talk of your doctrine; you speak so beautifully!"

"May I be struck dumb ere I speak beautifully!" was Rabbi Baruch's reply; and he said nothing more.

Spiegel, p. 156.

2. *Unhewn Stones*

The Riziner cited this passage from the Bible: "An altar of earth thou shalt make unto me . . . and if thou wilt make me an altar of stone, thou shalt not build it of hewn stone; for if thou lift up thy tool upon it, thou hast polluted it" (Exodus 20:24-5).

The altar of earth Rabbi Israel interpreted as the altar of silence, which is more pleasing to God than aught else; but if the altar be constructed of words these must be unhewn.

Spiegel, p. 156.

3. *The Power of Talk*

The Riziner read the verse (Amos 4:13): "He that formeth the mountains and createth the wind, and declareth unto man what is his talk."[1] He said: "One who praises another usually commences with a less important matter, and follows it up with the mention of more and more important deeds of might. He emphasizes that not only is

[1] "Sicho" means "his talk." J. T. translates "his thought."

the other person able to perform them, but can achieve an even more difficult accomplishment. This is a logical procedure, for should he relate the more difficult matters first, there would be no need to mention the easier deeds. Therefore, it follows that the creation of the wind is a mightier deed than the formation of mountains. Why? Because the wind frequently levels the hills. It also follows that talk is mightier than wind. In what respect? In that talk oftentimes causes greater tribulations than a tempestuous wind. Therefore, we are not permitted to say: 'I did no harm with my hands; I merely expressed an opinion.' "

N. I., p. 40.

4. The Stammerer

The Moscower Rabbi was a stammerer. Once he rendered a decision against an unmannerly person who had a case in court before him. The loser became angry and began to call the Rabbi: "Liar, swindler, lover of bribes, unlearned, etc."

The Rabbi replied: "And you are a stam—me—rer!"

"I, a stammerer?" asked the litigant.

"Surely," answered the Rabbi. "If you call me what you are, I may call you what I am."

The man left in shame.[1]

M. D., p. 298.

[1] The story is non-Hasidic in origin but Hasidic in spirit.

5. The Bratzlaver on "Talk" (Dibbur)

"1. Poverty overtakes him who speaks worthless and malicious words.

2. Words regarding matters of Torah become a veritable lamp which lights up dark places within him who stands in need of repentance.

3. Speech that is unheard and unheeded is worthless.

4. Talk is the vessel through which God's abundance is received. Hence prayer must be expressed in words, and not merely in thought.

5. Evil talk creates a contentious spirit which brings evil to the speaker and continually harasses him.

6. How can you say: 'It was mere talk; no harm was done by me'? Were this true, your words of prayer and kindness would be a waste of breath.

7. A corrective for evil talk is the study of the Torah with enthusiasm, the worship of God from the heart, and the speaking of truth. One brings the other in its train.

8. Loose talk by the wicked poisons the very air and induces wickedness in the listener.

9. Unholy words strengthen the hands of the religions of falsehood; they lengthen the Exile; tl.ey thrust one further away from the holiness of Palestine; they conceal truth; they raise up quarrels, and cause the Shekinah to be separated from Israel.

10. Through his evil tongue a man loses his understanding; he loses his love of God, and he gains instead a love of base desires. His memory becomes faulty and his forgetfulness is frequent. His heart dies within him, and he remembers not the Life of Eternity, the only true and valid life.

11. Evil words are wings for impiety and unbelief.

12. A man should serve the Lord with every drop of his blood. Quarrels and contentions feed upon those drops of blood which have not been used in the service of the Lord.

13. Holy talk is allied to the Shekinah, the Divine Appearance, the Soul of the Messiah, the Holy Spirit, Immortal Life, and the Unity of God.

14. Holy talk need never be absent from a man, though he fall into the lowest depths. It is like a mother who remains with her child at all times to shield him. Call upon the Lord, and He will raise you up.

15. The command of our Sages (Ethics of the Fathers 2:5): 'Judge not thy neighbor until thou art come into his place' means that we must never talk against our fellow-men, since no mortal can possibly know when he will stand in another's position. Only God can know this.[1]

16. The study of Torah lightens up the pathways of truth. The unlearned cannot know what the truth is.

17. The word is all-powerful, particularly in mediation between man and his Creator. One who meditates frequently on his Maker enjoys both worlds."[2]

L. E. H., pp. 27-29.

[1] Singer, p. 187.
[2] See Rubric 73: "Holy Meditation in Solitude."

6. The Power of Speech

Said the Besht: "If thou speakest, bear in mind that thy power of speech comes from thy soul which is part of God.

"When thou hearest bear in mind that thy power of hearing comes from thy soul.

"Thus thou wilt be able to unite thy soul with the Shekinah.

"Bear, also, in mind that thy profane words are composed of the same letters of the alphabet as thy sacred words. Therefore, in the former, too, there is holiness. Bring them to their Source."

K. S. T., p. 31a.

7. Recognizing Evil Words

A Hasid complained to the Tzartkover that he was distressed when in a multitude he listened to evil gossip. "You should rather rejoice, my dear man," replied the Rabbi. "Do you not learn in this fashion the nature of evil words? How would you know how to avoid gossip if you knew not how to recognize abhorrent talk?"

V. S., p. 41.

8. Satan's Assistant

Said the Koretzer: "When you speak evil of another man, the Satan will compel you to be his witness against the object of your words. Would you become the Satan's assistant? Blame the fault, not the man."

Nof. Tz., p. 49.

9. The Wise and the Wicked

Said the Medzibozer: "As for the wise, what he is, he says; as for the wicked, what he says, he is." [1]

Butz. D., p. 30.

[1] In the paragraph concerning the Four Sons, the Haggadah says: "Hakham mah hu omer?" (The wise one; what does he say?) The Rabbi utilizes the meaning of each word when it stands by itself.

10. Controlling Our Words

Said the Koretzer: "We read in the Zohar the explanation of the verse: 'And shalt talk of them' (Deut. 6:7). Think you that we are only enjoined to say the words? Nay, the word 'Dabar' has also another meaning, namely 'to control.' We are commanded to control the words of our mouth, not to speak them in anger, falsehood or flattery."

And the Master added: "How can one hope to improve another through angry words when anger is impurity of the highest degree? He causes the other to add to his sin."

He also read to his Disciples the words of Rabbi Hayyim Kossover: "We find in the Talmud: 'The angry man receives nothing but anger.' At night a man's soul ascends to Heaven and inscribes his record of the day's deeds. But if one of his deeds was anger, he is not permitted to write anything else. This is the worst offense and cancels everything else."

M. P., pp. 53-4.

195. WORK AND EFFORT

1. Without Hard Labor

Rabbi Berish of Biala was asked to explain the following: "The Talmud teaches that if a man boasts he became proficient in a subject of learning without effort, he cannot be believed.[1] But why disbelieve him, when he may be able to convince us by passing a test in the subject?"

The Rabbi answered: "The Talmud does not mean that he cannot be believed that he acquired knowledge. What the Talmud does say is that his boast of acquiring knowledge without hard labor and study cannot be credited."

S. S. K., p. 87.

[1] Megillah 6.

2. A Knock at the Door

Before the Besht became renowned, it chanced that once he lacked money for the Sabbath. At sunrise on Friday, he went to the house of a stranger, knocked at the door, and then took his departure. The man, awakened, dressed hurriedly and ran after the Besht. When he approached the Besht, and observed his poor raiment, he asked: "If you came to me to obtain aid, why did you go away?"

The Besht replied: "When a man is born, his sustenance is born with him. It is merely his imperfections that cause his livelihood to await the persuasion of his efforts before it comes to him. Since each man's imperfections are different in scale, the amount of effort required is also different. I believed that my life, removed from worldliness, entitled me to gain my needs with but little effort; hence I knocked at your door. After I had made this effort, I felt confident that God would aid me, and it makes no difference to me whether help will come through you or through another person."

M. R. T., ii, 32.

3. The Two Princes

Said the Mezeritzer: "A king sent two sons to a foreign country to acquire a knowledge of its culture and its finance. On the way they were shipwrecked and lost all their possessions. On reaching their destination they found the new country to be rich in resources and opportunities, but the cost of living was high. They obtained employment, yet their wages sufficed only for a comfortable livelihood, leaving nothing to save. One of the princes was wise, however, and deprived himself by strict economy of everything except his necessities; hence he succeeded in accumulating a sizable sum with which to begin business. On occasion he made profits, and oftentimes lost. After several efforts, he felt he had gained a modicum of knowledge, and returned to his father with gifts. The other son grew weary of working for his upkeep and returned, little improved in knowledge and empty-handed; the father declined to receive him.

"The soul is the prince, sent down to the world to acquire understanding and good deeds. The wise man does not spend all his efforts on profitless living in this world, and he returns to God bearing gifts. The foolish man returns empty-handed, and is refused entrance to the Lord's Seat of Glory."

T. M. M., pp. 238-9.

196. WORLD AND SPIRIT (WORLDLINESS)

1. The Mirage

Rabbi Nachman Bratzlav said: "When the rays of the sun enter a house through a dusty window, they form illumined pillars. But if one tries to feel them, he discovers there is nothing there. Worldly desires are comparable to these seeming pillars fashioned by the sun."

Dubnow, T. H., p. 303.

2. Light Through Diminishing

Said the Gerer Rabbi: "We see that a candle, a wick and oil give forth light through diminishing. Likewise, the man who limits his material wants to a minimum, may give out spiritual light." [1]

S. S. K., i, 85.

[1] A suggestion is given in the word: "Nefesh," a human soul. It contains the initials of "Ner," a candle; "Pethilah," a wick; and "Shemen," oil.

3. The Outsider

A Hasid asked the Kotzker Rabbi: "Since you separate yourself from worldly affairs, how are you able to advise in such affairs?"

The Rabbi replied: "Some times an outsider sees more clearly than the one who is inside."

S. S. K., i, 70.

4. The All-Embracing Soul

Said the Koretzer: "Our Sages declare: 'This world is like a wedding hall.' [1] Just as the wedding hall is the scene of preparation for the joint life of a young pair, so is this world merely the scene where we should prepare ourselves for a life in union with the All-Embracing Soul in the World-to-Come."

M. U. S., p. 15.

[1] Erubin 54.

5. Observing the World

Said the Medzibozer: "The world is exquisite when we do not take part in its pleasures, but observe it from the outside. But if we enter into its worldliness, the world becomes tiresome to us."

Butz. D., p. 31.

6. The Material Curtain

Said the Besht: "When a man prays solely for material benefits, his prayer of supplication is wasted. It forms a material curtain between God and himself, because he has brought matter into the domain of spirit. He receives no answer whatsoever."

K. S. T., p. 13a.

7. Profit and Enjoyment

Said the Besht: "The man who anticipates the gain of a large profit finds little enjoyment in his food. Likewise one who appreciates spiritual riches will find no pleasures in worldliness."

K. S. T., p. 17b.

8. The Diver

Said the Besht: "When a diver lowers himself into the sea in quest of pearls, he must conserve his breath and concentrate solely upon the finding of the pearls. Likewise when we dive into the sea of worldliness in quest of Torah and Mitzwoth, we must take care not to lose our holiness and be turned aside by material pleasures. Otherwise their force will crush our spiritual life, even as the force of the water may crush the careless diver."

M. R. T., ii, 60.

9. Hindrances to Study

When Rabbi Meir Weil accepted a call to become Rabbi in Berlin, he halted on his journey, in order to visit Rabbi Eliezer Tarnigrader who was then Rabbi of Frankfurt-on-the-Oder. The Tarnigrader said to him: "Let me give you counsel from my own experience. Do not disclose in public your sagacity in worldly affairs, otherwise you will be overwhelmed with all manner of cases involving civil arbitration, and you will have no time remaining for the continuance of your own studies. When I was a student in Berlin at Daniel Jaffee's synagogue, people came to me for arbitration. I was careless enough to allow myself to be drawn into the settlement of their disputes. I was soon flooded with similar requests and had no time for my literary work. I then began to ask the disputants to repeat their arguments several times, and informed them I could not comprehend affairs of commerce. This was effective, and I was soon enabled to complete my books."

Ohel N., p. 9.

10. Without Worldly Desires

Said Rabbi Yerachmiel: "We read: 'At a hundred it is as if he were already dead and had passed away from the world' (Ethics 5:24).[1] What ethical message does this statement give us? The message is this: the truly good man should be, with reference to worldly desires, like the man of a hundred years: as if he were already dead, and had passed away from the world."

Tif. B., p. 12.

[1] Singer, p. 204.

11. Smallness and Greatness

Said the Koretzer: "In everything there must be first smallness and then greatness. In grain, the straws first come out; then the ears. Among the nations there first came the peoples small in spirit; then came Israel. In Torah, first came the doubt; then came the knowledge. In Israel, first came the idolaters, then the believers in Divine Unity. A generation in which there is no improvement of ideals must perish."

M. P., p. 37.

197. WORRY AND ANXIETY

1. The Sin of Worry

Said the Lekhivitzer: "To worry is a sin. Only one sort of worry is permissible; to worry because one worries."

O. Y., p. 9.

2. The Unpreventable

Said Rabbi Yerachmiel: "Why shouldst thou worry concerning that which thou art unable to prevent? Better follow my counsel, and seek faith. Even though thou mayest not find true faith, thou wilt have thy sins forgiven. Thus saith the Lord: 'If ye can find a man . . . that seeketh faith (truth), and I will pardon' (Jeremiah 5:1)."

Tif. B., p. 12.

198. YOM KIPPUR: CHARITABLE DEEDS

1. Charity Plates

The community leaders of Medziboz, the Besht's home town, decided to abolish the custom of placing charity plates at the entrance of the synagogue on the day before Yom Kippur. The noise caused by this almsgiving interfered with the decorum of the Services.

The Besht opposed the decision, saying: "The sound of audible almsgiving dispels all unholy thoughts."

M. R. T., p. 47.

2. In the Wrong Division

Rabbi Joseph Dov Ber of Brisk noticed that a wealthy money-lender remained in the synagogue after Yom Kippur Services, and recited Psalms. He went over to him and said: "In an army there are different divisions: infantry, cavalry, artillery, and so forth. If a soldier dislikes his division and joins another without permission, he is punished as severely as if he had deserted. The practice of reciting Psalms was adopted for the benefit of the poor; it is their division. You, as a wealthy money-lender, must demonstrate your repentance by investigating closely the circumstances of your debtors, and by restoring their pledges to those who are in need of them. Now, however, you should return to your home and sleep, as others in your division are doing."

S. ha-Tov, p. 140.

3. A Controllable Thirst

The Tzanzer Rabbi was informed on Yom Kippur that a man was fainting from thirst. He ordered that a spoonful of water be given him. The man then approached the Rabbi and begged for permission to drink more. "You may do so," answered the Rabbi. "But I must establish one condition, namely that you donate to charity a sum of money for every drink you take." Nothing further was heard from the thirsty worshiper.

O. I. H., p. 19.

4. The Yom Kippur Jew

In his sermon on Yom Kippur, Rabbi Mendel of Rimanov used as a text the verse (Exodus 21:21): "Notwithstanding, if he continue a day or two, he shall not be punished; for he is his money."[1] He said: "If one stands up with a sincere heart, full of regret, and in the mood of repentance—one day on Yom Kippur, or even two days, on the two days of Rosh ha-Shanah—but during the remainder of the year gives no attention to observing the commandments of the Torah, then the favorable verdict he has earned by his sincere service of the Lord on these few days shall be nullified. It is evident that his sincerity arose not out of his love of God, but because of his love for money and prosperity."

O. Y., p. 132.

[1] The text is translated by the Rimanover: "Nevertheless if he stands up a day or two, the verdict shall not be put into execution, for it is his money."

5. The Voice Is a Surety

The Kobriner on Yom Kippur took as the text of his sermon the words in the Prayer "Unethanneh Tokef" [1] which read: "But fasting for the purpose of uninterrupted repentance, the voice of sincere prayer, and the money donated for charity serve to nullify the unfavorable verdict." Said the Rabbi: "Some of us are too weak physically to abstain from food. Some have no money to donate to charity. But every one of us can offer sincere prayer from the heart. Hence, no excuse can be presented for neglecting this requirement as a means of influencing the verdict in our favor. Moreover, when the voice of prayer is not from the heart, a man's other excuses regarding physical weakness and lack of money do not prevail. If he does not perform what he can, it is obvious that were he strong in body and possessed the means to give charity, he would in all likelihood have avoided deeds essential to change the verdict. A suggestion is given in the Song of Songs (2:14): 'For thy voice is a surety' for the other two conditions." [2]

O. Y., p. 164.

[1] See note to 202:5.
[2] "Arev" means either "sweet" or a "surety."

6. The Count and His Dog

The Koznitzer told on Yom Kippur the following story: "A poor Jew had a marriageable daughter, but no money for her dowry. His wife insisted he endeavor to collect the amount, but since he was exceedingly shy, he secured only a small sum. The Jew could endure it no longer, and he resolved to return. On the road he encountered a Polish Count in his carriage. The Count, noting his distress, elicited his story, and gave him an amount sufficient for the dowry.

"When Judgment was to be rendered on New Year's Day, the Prosecuting Angel brought forth the accusation that the Jews had failed to assist the poor man in his need, and had surrendered to a non-Jew the great Mitzwah of aiding a poor girl to marry. As the charge seemed well-founded, the Defending Angel had little to say in behalf of the Jewish community.

"But after Rosh Ha-Shanah the Count saw a handsome dog and purchased him for an amount twice as large as the sum he had given the Jew for his daughter's dowry. When the nobleman went to the kennel to feed him, the dog jumped up and tore the meat out of his hand. The Count in anger drove the dog away from his estate.

"From this incident, the Defending Angel secured the evidence necessary to demonstrate that the Count had not aided the poor Jew from a sense of sincere charity, but had acted only upon a passing whim, inasmuch as the sum he had given the Jew had little value in his eyes.

"Thereupon the case against the Jews was considerably weakened before the Heavenly Tribunal."

N. H. K., p. 32.

7. The Three Drinks

The Strelisker saw his Jewish servant arise from bed on Yom Kippur night and drink a portion of water. The Rabbi did not indicate that he had witnessed this, fearing that the servant might desist from quenching his thirst, and thereby become ill. A second time this occurred, and the Rabbi still remained silent. When the servant arose a third time, the Rabbi called out to him: "It is Yom Kippur, and since you have taken two drinks within a short time, you may now desist without fear of harmful results to your health."

E. Tz., p. 77.

199. YOM KIPPUR: CONFESSION

1. Even Before Selichoth

The Berditschever chanced to pass the night at a wayside inn. He heard a thief in the next room relating to his comrade the story of his work the night before.

"What a holy people is Israel!" exclaimed the Rabbi. "It is still a long time to Selichoth,[1] yet the man has already begun to confess his sins."

M. D., p. 216.

[1] Prayers for forgiveness recited after midnight, commencing a week before Rosh Ha-Shanah and ending on Yom Kippur Eve.

2. *Truth in the Confessional*

The Berditschever opened his discourse: "A world turned topsy-turvy I see before my eyes. In years gone by, the Jews spoke the truth in the streets and in the market-places, but in the House of Prayer they told a lie. It is the other way now: on the streets and in the market-places they all speak falsehood, but in the House of Prayer they tell the truth. A riddle? Here then is the explanation: honesty and good faith were the torches lighting their path in the olden days. And so they made good the Scripture word of a righteous Aye and Naye, and all their trading was done in good faith. But when they came into the House of Prayer, they would beat their breasts and say: 'We have defrauded, we have robbed.' That was, then, a lie, for they had been true to God and to their fellow-men. To-day it is the reverse: in their trading they lie and defraud, and in their confessional prayer, they speak the truth." [1]

[1] Fuchs, *J. T.*, p. 5. See also Joseph Margoshes, *Jewish Morning Journal*, Sept. 4, 1931.

3. *Imperfect Confession*

Said Rabbi Bunam: "We find that when David, following his offense with Bathsheba entreated God and said but once: 'I have sinned against God,' Nathan answered that he was forgiven (II Samuel 12:13). On the other hand we say many times on Yom Kippur: 'We have sinned,' and we receive no knowledge whether we are forgiven. This is because David meant: 'I have sinned, and Thou mayest do with me what Thou wishest, as I deserve no clemency.' But we say: 'We have sinned, and we expect Thee to forgive us.' Therefore our confession is imperfect."

S. I., p. 77.

4. *The Tell-Tale*

A man was reciting the Confession on Yom Kippur behind the future Ropshitzer Rabbi, and he leaned his Machzor on the Rabbi's back. The Rabbi turned and said to him: "You have sinned, and you tell on me."

E. Tz., p. 93.

200. YOM KIPPUR: THE FAITH OF THE IGNORANT

1. *"Bless the Women"*

The Ropshitzer told the following tale: "One year in Poland, many mothers died in childbirth. The Rimanover Rabbi ordered an ignorant villager to read the afternoon service on Yom Kippur Eve. The untutored yokel stumbled through the Amidah, making many errors because of his inability to read Hebrew correctly. When he came to the prayer commencing with the words: 'Bless for us, O Lord our God, this year,'[1] he read in place of 'Bless our year (Shnotheinu) like the good years' (Ke-Shanim ha-Tovoth), 'Bless our women (Nshotheinu) like the good women' (Ka-Nashim ha-Tovoth), and he finished the prayer: 'Blessed art Thou, O Lord, who blesseth the women' instead of 'the years.' The Lord regarded his error as a simple-hearted plea of genuine sincerity, and accepted it on High. Henceforth, the death of mothers in childbirth was halted."

O. N., p. 25.

[1] Singer, p. 47.

2. The Entire Prayer Book

There is a beautiful legend of the little farmer boy who, having been left an orphan at an early age, was unable to read, but who had inherited a large, heavy prayer book from his parents. On the Day of Atonement, he brought it into the synagogue, laid it on the stand, and, weeping, cried out: "Lord of Creation! I do not know how to pray; I do not. know what to say—I give Thee the entire prayer book."[1]

Spiegel, p. 148.

[1] See No. 4 of this Rubric for a longer version.

3. The Whistle

The story goes that one Day of Atonement when the Jews were gathered in the synagogue, and all the Rabbis were there, among them the Besht, one ignorant farmer brought his son with him to the Services. The son, who could not read a word of the ritual, had with him a whistle which he used ordinarily when watching the cattle. He was exceedingly fond of this whistle which he used frequently at home. During the Neilah prayer, which marks the climax of the Holyday, the boy took out his whistle and blew it. The Besht jumped up and congratulated the Jews: God had opened the gates; the Rabbis, with all their prayers and their learning, could not prevail with God, as had the young herdsman in his ignorance, by his simple desire to serve God.[1]

Kahana, p. 49.

[1] Zeitlin, S., "Chassidism: A Revolt of the Masses," *Jewish Tribune,* Aug. 1, 1930, p. 14; see also Spiegel; and others.

4. The Entire Prayer Book

Rabbi Zevi Elimelech Dinover was seen to go over to the Reader's stand in his synagogue, open up a Prayer Book with the Secrets of the Kabbalah, according to Rabbi Isaac Luria, and begin to pray. The watching people were surprised to notice that the Dinover did not turn any page in the Prayer Book. He was asked why he had opened it if he did not intend to read the prayers therein. He replied with this story:

"In the time of the Besht there died in a village both parents of a Jewish male child. There was no one to claim the orphan, and the village-owner took pity on him, and reared him. He did not conceal from the boy the fact of his Jewish birth, and the lad became interested in Jews and their customs. Once he saw passing through the village a company of Jews with their families, traveling towards the city. He was told that it was near the Judgment Day, and they were going to pray for a good year. Since he felt no lack of anything, this made no impression on him. When, however, he saw the Jews again pass through the village a week later, and they told him that it was near the Day of Forgiveness when every Jew's status for life or for death was sealed, the lad bethought himself of his non-Jewish life, and he knew instinctively that he had committed grave sins against God.

"The boy unpacked the few belongings that he had inherited from his deceased parents, and found among them a thick prayer-book. This he took with him, begged for a ride, and arrived in the city. In the synagogue he heard every one praying tearfully. He was the only person who knew not how to pray. The lad's sorrowful face caught the attention of the Besht. Knowing something of the lad's story, the Besht appreciated his plight, and he prayed to the Lord that the lad might receive an inspiration how to act, so that he might not return to his non-Jewish way of life. The lad took the heavy prayer-book in his hand, placed it on the worshiper's stand, and cried out: 'Oh, my Father in Heaven! I know not what to say. But, see, I bring to you the entire Prayer Book!' He thereupon bent his head on the stand over the book and wept copiously. His penitence was accepted, and the Besht began to recite the 'Borekhu' with a joyful countenance."

"With respect to this Kabbalist Prayer Book, I am like the lad in the story," said the Dinover. "I open the book and say: 'May it be Thy will that my prayer be as acceptable as if it were recited with all the holy thoughts found in the book itself.' "[1]

E. Tz., p. 112.

[1] See Spiegel, p. 148; and Lucy Cohen, *Jewish Mysticism,* pp. 84-8; see above No. 2 of this Rubric.

201. YOM KIPPUR: FORGIVENESS

1. *"I Pardon"*

Once in the fervor of the Atonement Prayer, the Berditschever reached the words: "He spoke: 'I pardon.' " He broke off, exclaiming: "Lord of the Universe, we have no more the power to say: 'He spoke.' Speak for Thyself and proclaim the pardon."

L. I. B., p. 65; (B., p. 455m).

2. *The Prince and the Tutor*

Rabbi Schmelke on Yom Kippur related the following parable: "A king appointed a tutor to take constant care of his son's conduct.

The son refused to heed the preceptor's instruction and indulged in many transgressions. The tutor, indignant at his pupil, informed the king, who thereby became estranged from his son. In contrition, the prince sought many times to gain his father's love, but the tutor would remind the king of his son's grave misconduct, and the king would not relent. Once during the tutor's absence, the prince ran to the king, imploring his father's forgiveness and favor. The father's heart melted within him, and he embraced the lad with gladness.

"The Satan," said Rabbi Schmelke, "is like the tutor in the parable. He opposes our reconciliation with our Father in Heaven. But on Yom Kippur the Satan is absent; all our impulses are holy, and we are granted an opportunity to implore God with a broken heart to extend forgiveness to us."

S. ha-Tov, p. 46.

3. Dismissing Our Iniquities

Rabbi Itzikel Kalisher said: "In the Yom Kippur Amidah we say: 'Blessed art Thou O Lord, who dismisseth our grievous offenses every year.' But how can we be sure that God dismisses our iniquities? May this not be a vain blessing which takes the name of the Lord in vain? We may compare this to a young student who received a cake from his mother and refused to share it with his playmate. One boy, desiring a piece of the sweetmeat, loudly pronounced the blessing for cake, whereupon the owner of it felt impelled to give him a part of it, in order to save him from the offense of having recited a blessing in vain. It is the same with ourselves. We believe that the Lord will feel bound to forgive our transgression, in order to save us from breaking the Third Commandment on this holiest of days."

S. S. K., iii, 100.

4. Eating with Trust

Said the Koretzer: "Our eating on the day before Yom Kippur is of more value than our fasting on Yom Kippur. By eating, we demonstrate our trust that God will forgive our sins."

Nof. Tz., p. 28.

5. The Scarlet Thread

Said the Koretzer: "We read: 'Like the scarlet thread are thy lips' (Song of Songs 4:3). As the scarlet thread hung at the Temple on Yom Kippur showed by its miraculous change into white the forgiveness of sins,[1] thy sins now will be forgiven if thou art able to change thy everyday prayers and study, mixed as they are with foreign thoughts, into pure worship and concentrated study."

Nof. Tz., p. 20.

[1] Mishnah Yoma, vi.

6. God's Name

Said the Koretzer: "The day after Yom Kippur used to be called: 'The Day of God's Name.' In the Penitential Period we say in the

'Amidah': 'The Holy King' [1] which is only an attribute of God. On this day we begin to say again: 'The Holy God.' We give to the Lord His Name."

[1] Singer, p. 45.

Nof. Tz., p. 14.

202. YOM KIPPUR: PRAYERS

1. Our Wants Are Many

Said the Gerer Rabbi: "We read in the Neilah Services of Yom Kippur the following phrase: 'Many are the wants of Thy people and their knowledge is short.' This means: 'Because their knowledge is short, their wants are therefore many.'"

S. S. K., i, 86.

2. Remembering Israel's Welfare

The Sadigurer Rabbi explained that the High Priest on leaving the Holy of Holies on Yom Kippur was able to offer only a brief prayer for Israel's welfare, as is recorded in the Machzor. This was due to the fact that in the presence of the Holy of Holies, he completely forgot about material needs, and thought only of spiritual wants. Only on leaving was he able also to remember the less important necessities of the world.

N. I., p. 64.

3. No Need for Comparison

Reading the High Priest's Yom Kippur prayer: "Grant Israel all their needs, that they may not be compelled to make a livelihood, one from the other, and the Jew from the non-Jew," the Berditschever said:

"Why should the High Priest pray that we make no living from the non-Jew? Perhaps it can be explained thus: When a Jew is judged in Heaven and it is seen that he is sinful, the Lord, in His compassion, orders a greater sinner to be summoned. In comparison, the lesser sinner seems to be a good man. Should the majority of Israel be found wanting, the Lord brings forth an erring non-Jewish nation, in comparison with whose iniquities those of Israel diminish. But the High Priest prays that Israel may be possessed of sufficient goodness to have no need for comparison."

N. B. L., p. 24.

4. Warming Up the Prayers

Two brothers came to the Lubliner for the Penitential Days. On Yom Kippur one became grievously ill, and his brother was forced to nurse him. In the evening the Lubliner visited him to inquire regarding the patient. The Hasid expressed regret that he could not attend the Services on Yom Kippur, and that he had been compelled to desecrate the most Holy Day of the year by warming up the medicine.

"Now I understand," remarked the Rabbi, "why we prayed so fervently to-day. You warmed up our prayers."

N. H. L., p. 56.

5. Earth to Earth

A Hasid wept loudly while he recited the words of the "Unethan-neh Tokef" [1] prayer: "From earth man originates, and at the end to earth he will return." Another Hasid whispered to him: "Why shouldest Thou weep? Were thy origin gold and thy end earth, thou wouldest have occasion to lament. But since thou merely returnest to the place of thy origin, and in the meantime enjoy seventy years of life, what hast thou lost by the transaction?"

Ch. Ch., p. 119.

[1] "And let us chant the might," said at the Musaph Services of Rosh Ha-Shanah and Yom Kippur.

6. The Frightened Fox

Said the Besht: "The lion became enraged at his subjects, the animals of the forest. They asked the fox to placate the King of Beasts by relating to him an appropriate fable. The fox replied, however, that fear had caused him to forget his fables. Hence the beasts were compelled to wait on the lion themselves.

"In the same fashion, on the Awesome Days, the people of the congregation should not depend upon their Rabbi to pray on their behalf. Each one should do so by and for himself."

K. S. T., p. 4a.

7. Like a Statue

Rabbi Nathan Khelmer was standing all day Yom Kippur in the Lizensker's synagogue, and he moved neither his head nor his limbs. He stood as if made of stone. The Lizensker remarked: "It is fear of the Lord that has nearly paralyzed his body."

Hith. Z., p. 34.

203. YOM KIPPUR: PURIFICATION OF THE SOUL

1. Wash Away Uncleanness

Said the Belzer: "At the end of the Yom Kippur Amidah we say: 'I stand before Thee as a vessel full of shame and confusion.' [1] We implore thereby that the Lord may wash away our shame and impurity as easily as one may cleanse a vessel full of unclean substances."

D. S., p. 106.

[1] Singer, p. 263.

2. How to Purify Ourselves

On Yom Kippur Eve, Rabbi Schmelke said: "We are taught by the Baraitha: 'Grains that have become unclean and are planted, become clean.'[1] Thus when the grain which came out of the ground is reunited with mother earth, its source, it becomes Levitically clean.

"Our souls come from God, and when they become unclean and impure, we may cleanse and purify them by returning them to their Source. Our souls must cleave entirely to the Fountain of Holiness. Then we may hope that the promise of the Lord may be fulfilled (Deut. 4:4): 'But ye that did cleave unto the Lord, your God, are alive every one of you this day.'"

S. ha-Tov, p. 47.

[1] Sifra 10:11, to Levit. 11:37.

3. *Purified Through Fire*

Said the Koretzer: "Gold and silver become purified through fire. If you feel no sense of improvement after your prayer, you are either made of base metal, or your prayer was cold."

Nof. Tz., p. 49.

4. *Foreign Substance*

Said the Besht: "When it is desired to solder a piece of silver to a silver vessel, the edge of the piece must be cleaned so that no foreign substance may intervene. Likewise when a man wishes to cleave to God, he must purify himself of every foreign thought beforehand."

M. R. T., ii, 58.

5. *A Good Fast*

At the conclusion of Yom Kippur, Rabbi Meir Shalom Porissover once said: "To-day I fasted well. In the beginning I felt neither hunger nor thirst, and I prayed to God to enable me to feel the prescribed affliction of the soul. I then commenced to suffer from hunger and felt the affliction."

D. Z., p. 36.

6. *The Gerer's Yom Kippur Sermon*

"'If I am not for myself, who will be for me? And if not now, when?' (Ethics of the Fathers 1:14; Singer, p. 186).

"If I do not perform my service to the Lord, who will perform it for me? And if not now, at the present moment, when? When will the present moment, in which I have not served God, come back to me? The present moment, which was never here before, will never be here again. Before, there was a different moment; later, there will be a different moment. And every moment has a different service to perform in it.

"Therefore let us labor in the Torah. The Torah is the property of all Israel, and the laborer in it associates himself with all Israel. Let us work for the whole of Israel, and the whole of Israel will work for us. Some one in Israel has served God in the moment that we have wasted. By being associated with Israel, we have an association with the service done at that moment by one of Israel. But if we are for ourselves, what are we? If we are not associated with Israel, how can we atone for the wasted present moment? The next moment cannot atone for this moment.

"If any one has committed a serious sin, let him beware thinking of it. For where our thoughts are, there we also are with our soul. Let not your soul sink into the mire of sin; it may not be able to extricate itself and repent.

"And even if a man has committed a minor offense, why should he think of it? Why should he place his soul in the mire? Turn mire hither and thither, and it remains mire. What good can come to Heaven from disturbing your sin in your mind? During the time thus consumed you may perform a good deed which will truly be like presenting God with a pearl.

"Turn away from evil; hold it not in remembrance; do good. If you have sinned much, balance it by doing much good. Resolve to-day from the depth of your heart and in a joyful mood, to abstain from sin and to do good. Hurry over the prayer: 'For the Sin,' [1] and meditate preferably on the prayer: 'And Thou, O Lord, shalt reign.' " [2]

D. Z., p. 65.

[1] Singer, p. 259.
[2] Singer, p. 240.

7. *The Scapegoat*

Said Rabbi Lazerov: "We read in Leviticus, chapter sixteen (verse 8), that the Lord commanded one he-goat to be sent into the wilderness for Azazel, the demon, and one to be brought forth as an offering unto God. What reason is there for sending a he-goat to the Devil? God teaches us this lesson: If we must be extravagant in our concern for luxuries, let us at least devote an equal sum for charity, for the synagogue and for our religious duties. Let us treat God at least as well as we treat the Devil." [1]

E. J. W., p. 40.

[1] Non-Hasidic in origin, but Hasidic in spirit.

204. YOUTH

1. *Guiding the Youth*

Rabbi Leib Pistiner said: "When a child is taught to walk, his parent holds his hand at first; then he allows him to walk alone, but stands near by; then he goes further and further away from him, until at last the child becomes accustomed to walk steadily on his own feet. In the same fashion, the erstwhile Bar Mitzwah should have his religious teacher's close attention at first; then he should be permitted to lead himself more and more. Too often the rabbis give their sole attention to the adults, while the adolescents receive only scant attention. This is taught by the verse (Psalms 48:15): 'He shall guide us as in our youth.' [1] It is further taught by the history of our people. At its inception, God provided the new nation of Israel with every necessity under the uninterrupted guidance of Moses. Then from time to time he sent Judges to raise up Israel when he stumbled. Later He sent the Prophets and Rabbis to lead Israel, without granting to them any powers of rulership. God believed the time had come for Israel to have attained maturity. The people now understood the benefit of obeying leaders who instructed them not by the might of their hand, but by the influence of their spirit."

O. Y., p. 102.

[1] Another translation is: "He will guide us eternally." "Almuth" may be derived from "Elem," "youth," or from "Olam," "world, forever."

2. The Two Roads

The Apter Rabbi told the following parable: "Two men came to the crossroads; one chose an uneven road, the other a straight even road, to reach his destination. The first encountered many obstacles but at last arrived in the city. The second had smooth journeying at first, but near the end of the road, he found no further passage-way, and was forced to return, wasting much time and strength.

The first traveler is the good man: he must devote great energy to journey on the path of the upright but he can continue to his last day.

The second traveler is the man of evil. He reveres wealth and pleasure, and derives great enjoyment from them. But the day comes when he no longer takes delight in the larger accumulations of gold or in the heightened pleasures, and he knows not how to continue. To his dismay he discovers that the distance is too great for him to return to the high principles he cherished in his youth."

E. O., p. 123.

3. Different Grades

Using as a text (Genesis 6:16): "With lower, second and third stories shalt thou make it," the Lizensker said: "We may interpret these words in two ways. There are three types of persons: the perfect, the moderately good, and the wicked. All should be cared for by the leader.

"A second meaning is permissible. There are three periods in a man's life. While he is young he is most susceptible to transgressions. In his middle age, he is too engrossed with the labors of livelihood to sin. In his old age, he is able to work for the improvement of his soul, and to repair the injuries inflicted upon it before. It is for this reason that the wording: 'thou shalt make it' comes near 'the third stories.'"

Noam E., p. 7.

4. Indigestible Food

Said the Koretzer: "In the same way that a little child cannot digest meat and must subsist on milk, a youth cannot understand

Kabbalah and should study other subjects. Mysticism is indigestible food for a young man."

M. P., p. 15.

5. *The Sweetness of the Mitzwoth*

Said the Besht: "Before a lad becomes thirteen years of age, he is vouchsafed some of the pleasures derived from the performance of Mitzwoth; he is not forced to battle against his inclinations in doing them, so that he may gain the desire for the performance of Mitzwoth later. It is like a man who enters a confectionery store and is offered a free sample of a new confectionery. If he finds it sweet and wishes more of it, he is asked to pay. The adult may taste the sweetness of the Mitzwoth only after he has triumphed over his inclinations."

M. R. T., ii, 44.

6. *Fire and Ice*

The Trisker Maggid, Rabbi Abraham, son of Rabbi Mordecai Tzernobiler, halted one cold winter day at an inn. In the tavern-room stood an iron stove which burned wood. When the stove would be filled with wood, a great heat came forth. But after the wood was consumed, it required only a few moments before the room was cold as ice. The Maggid remarked: "The youthful Hasid is like this stove. For a moment he burns like fire with Hasidic ecstasy, and then he grows cold as ice."

D. D., p. 305.

205. THE ZADDIK AND HIS PROBLEMS

1. *Men Made Perfect*

Zaddikim are just men made perfect by perceiving God's power in all earthly things, the smallest and the vastest alike, of which power some portion enters thereby their soul. Of such it is written in Job 22:28, that fulfillment attends upon their word, a verse expounded by our Sages in this manner: if it were the will of the perfect, they might create a world. (Sanhedrin, f. 65b.) "The perfect directs and God pays heed."[1] Also: "God's doom, when decreed, is averted by the perfect."

Cf. Bl., Pr., p. 37 ff.

[1] Based on Job 22:25. A popular Hasidic phrase.

2. *That His Son May Live*

"We read in the Talmud," said the Lubliner, "that one who gives charity so that his son may live is a perfect Zaddik.[1] The question arises: Is not one who gives without mentioning a reward, a greater Zaddik? The answer is: That man is a perfect Zaddik, when he

[1] Pesachim 8.

wishes his son to live, so that he may serve the Lord whole-heartedly, and accomplish good deeds."

N. H. L., p. 35.

3. The Greatest Zaddik

Said Rabbi Hirsch Rimanover: "Some Zaddikim serve the Lord in the old way: they walk on the state road. Others at times adopt a new way: they walk on the side road. Still others pursue a way of their own choosing: they walk on the path. The last reach their destination first."

M. T., p. 20.

4. Influencing Others

Said the Belzer: "By recounting the greatness of the Creator, the Zaddik influences others to praise the Lord, as it is written (Psalm 145:6): 'And Thy wondrous works will I rehearse, and men shall speak of the might of Thy tremendous acts.'"

D. S., p. 104.

5. Subduing Other Needs

Rabbi Enzel of Stry, a noted adversary of the Hasidim, once tried to confuse Rabbi Judah Zevi of Rozdol. He said:

"Rozdoler, I am of the belief that the spiritual essence of a Zaddik is an impulsion like other natural needs of man."

The Zaddik replied: "True, but before it can manifest itself, it must have subdued all other natural needs." [1]

Bl., Gem., p. 76.

[1] For another version see: "The Rebbe and Mortal Desires"; 145:2.

6. City Folk and Villagers

Said the Pulnoer: "Two persons inherited an identical amount of money. One lived in a village and looked upon his fellow-townsmen with contempt. The other lived in a large city, and with humility looked up to those more important than himself. The ordinary Jew, far from the Lord's presence, oftentimes looks down upon people he believes are on a lower level.

"The Zaddik, however, who is near to God, looks up with humility towards the Heavens."

Kahana, p. 133.

7. Prayers for All

The Ropshitzer used to say: "The Zaddikim expect those who are in trouble to come to them with a request that prayers be recited in their behalf. I, however, arise in the morning, and pray that all who are in trouble may be relieved. I do not wish them to come to me and say afterwards that the Ropshitzer helped them by his prayers for them in particular."

E. Tz., p. 88.

8. The Zaddik's Miracles

A Hasid asked the Tzanzer: "Are the miracles ascribed to the Zaddikim in books such as the 'Stories of the Zaddikim' true?" "I cannot vouch for them as written down," replied the Tzanzer. "But I am convinced that a real Zaddik can accomplish whatever he desires, provided it is not against the will of the Lord."

E. Tz., p. 133.

9. Speech Without Words

Said the Medzibozer: "We read: 'Then they that feared the Lord spoke one with another' (Malachi 3:16).[1] When two Zaddikim come together, this coming together is in itself speech, even though they utter no word."

[1] Literally "were spoken": "Nidberu."

Butz. D., p. 16.

10. The Shield of Sufferings

A Zaddik became very ill, and the Besht was asked by his Disciples to pray for the Zaddik's recovery, but he refused. A few days later a band of brigands who planned to raid the town were surprised by the police and captured. The Zaddik's malady left him the same day. The Besht explained that the Zaddik's pains had served to delay the raid on the town until the police could discover the brigands. "The sufferings of a Zaddik act as a shield."

K. S. T., p. 30a.

11. The Sediment of Evil Inclinations

Said the Besht: "When a man squeezes winegrapes into a vessel, he must first use a sieve with large holes to strain it; later he uses a cheese cloth. But no matter how many times he will strain it, some sediment will still remain. It is the same with the Zaddik. He must rid himself of his evil inclinations and continue to do so his entire life. But there are always a few dregs left over."

M. R. T., ii, 111.

12. Unconscious Counsel

Said the Koretzer: "The true Zaddik is always able to see without his eyes and to hear without his ears. A man comes to ask my counsel, and I hear that he himself is telling me, unknowingly, what I should advise him."

M. P., p. 6.

13. The Unfulfilled Prayer

Said Rabbi Jacob Zevi Porissover: "When the Lord does not wish to fulfill a Zaddik's prayer, He raises the Zaddik higher in holiness, and permits him to see that it is not good for his wish to be fulfilled. When Moses begged to enter Palestine, God told him to go to higher ground [1] and behold that he need not cross the Jordan. It would not be to his advantage."

D. Z., p. 51.

[1] Deut. 3:27.

14. The Zaddik's Grief

Said the Koretzer: "We find that ten generations passed from the time of Adam to the Flood, who were not punished for their sins. Ten generations passed from the Flood until the destruction of Sodom, during which Sodom was spared. Why? Because God is All-Merciful, and cares not how much the people sin against Him. But when a Zaddik comes into the world and feels aggrieved at the contempt in which the people hold God, then the Lord feels compelled to restrain His mercy and to punish the wicked. The coming of Noah brought the Flood; Abraham brought the destruction of Sodom; Moses, the drowning of the Egyptians. It is for this reason that the Zaddikim feel compelled to offer prayers for the wicked."

M. P., p. 16.

15. Two Kinds of Zaddikim

Said the Lizensker: "There are two kinds of Zaddikim. One is a true saint, but he knows it, and believes he need not repent since he does not sin. Such a Zaddik cannot influence others to repent, because he does not himself adhere to repentance.

"The other Zaddik is likewise a true saint, but of a higher type. He constantly passes judgment upon his own actions, to discover whether they were performed from holy motives only and for the sake of pleasing the Lord, rather than for the sake of his own soul's benefit. If he discovers an impure motive in his conduct, he repents of it with fervor. Such a Zaddik is able to influence others to repent, for he himself cleaves to repentance. This is the meaning of the Talmudical saying: 'Greater are the penitents than the perfect Zaddikim.' " [1]

O. E., p. 5.

[1] Berakhoth 34, in a longer form.

16. Why "Good Jew"?

Rabbi Bunam was asked: "Why call a Zaddik 'Good Jew'? If he prays well, he should be called a 'good worshiper'; if he learns well, a 'good learner.' " The Rabbi replied: "The good Jew thinks goodness, eats, sleeps and intends goodness; he is altogether good."

S. S. K., iv, 101.

BIBLIOGRAPHY OF BOOKS USED

A. H.   1.

Atereth ha-Zaddikim, published by A. Kahan, Warsaw, 1924; Yiddish.

B.   2.

Die Chassidischen Buecher, by Martin Buber, Hellerau, 1928; German.

B. D.   3.

Butzina De-Nehorah, by Rabbi Baruch of Medziboz, Grandson of the Besht; amplified by letters of the Besht, of Rabbi Baruch, of the Rabbi of Schepetovka, of the Savraner and of the Tschernobiler. Published in 1880 in Lemberg; second edition at Piotrkov, 1889 (56 pages). In an accompanying statement by the editor, Nachman Jacob of Baer, it is affirmed that the selections were made from the addresses of Rabbi Baruch of Medziboz, by an adherent of the Zaddik, an assertion which only a faithful believer would credit. At the same time the collection contains a kernel of historical truth, particularly in the narratives of the collector concerning the Medzibozer and his contemporaries, as well as the Letters of the Zaddikim published in the volume. See Dubnow, i, 295. We have made use of the edition at Bilguray, 1926; Hebrew.

Beoh. H.   4.

Be-Ohelei Habad, by M. Indritz, published at Chicago, 1927; Yiddish.

Bl., *Gem.*   5.

Gemeinde der Chassidim, by Chaim Bloch, Vienna, 1920; German.

Bl., *Pr.*   6.

Priester der Liebe, by Chaim Bloch, Vienna, 1930; German.

B. N.   7.

Beth Nahum, published by A. Kahan; Warsaw, 1927; Yiddish.

B. P.   8.

Beth Pinchas, by P. Shapiro; Bilguray, 1926; Hebrew.

B. S.   9.

Beth Shelomoh, published by A. Kahan; Warsaw, 1929; Yiddish.

B. Z.   10.

Beth Zaddik, published by A. Kahan; Warsaw, 1927; Yiddish.

Ch. Ch. 11.
Hokhmah und Harifuth, by M. A. Wiesseon; Vienna, 1927; Yiddish.

D. O. 12.
Dor Deah, by Y. A. Kamelhar, Bilguray, 1933; Hebrew.

D. E. M. R. 13.
Derekh Emunah U-Maaseh Rav, by J. S. Cohen; Warsaw, 1898; Hebrew. Narratives concerning the Disciples of the Besht and their Moral Opinions, assembled by J. Gutman of Gora Kalvarya. 114 pages.

D. S. 14.
Dover Shalom, by A. S. B. Michelson; Prezemysl, 1910; Hebrew.

D. Z. 15.
Derekh Zaddikim, by A. Yellin; Warsaw, 1912; Hebrew.

E. A. 16.
Esser Ataroth, by Israel Berger, Rabbi in Bucharest; Warsaw, and Piotrkov, 1910; Hebrew. The collection deals with Moses Zevi of Savran, and others.

E. J. W. 17.
Encyclopedia of Jewish Wit, by J. L. Lazerov; New York, 1928; Yiddish.

E. K. 18.
Esser Kedushoth, by I. Berger; Warsaw, 1925; Hebrew. The collection deals with Zevi Hirsch of Zydaczov, and other Galician Zaddikim.

Em. K. 19.
Emeth Keneh, published by A. Rosengarten; Piotrkov, 1907; Hebrew.

Em. L. 20.
Em Labinah, by Y. A. Kamelhar; Lemberg, 1909; Hebrew.

E. O. 21.
Esser Oroth, by I. Berger; Warsaw, 1913; Hebrew. The collection deals with the Maggid of Mezeritz, Pinchas of Koretz, Levi Isaac of Berditschev, the Maggid of Koznitz, Jacob Isaac of Lublin, Heshel of Opatov, Israel of Rizin, and others.

E. Tz. 22.
Esser Tzachtzochoth, by I. Berger; Piotrkov, 1910; Hebrew. This collection deals with Elimelech of Lizensk, Moses Leib of Sassov, and others.

E. Z.   23.

Emunath Zaddikim, published by A. Kahan; Warsaw, 1924; Yiddish.

F. R. H.-E.   24.

Fun Rebe's Hauf, by I. Ewen; New York, 1922; Yiddish.

F. R. H.-M.   25.

Fun Rebin's Hauf, by D. L. Mekler; New York, 1931; Yiddish.

F. U. A. O.   26.

Fun Unzer Alten Otzar, by B. Jeuszsohn; Warsaw, 1932; Yiddish.

G. H.   27.

Gevurath ha-Zaddikim, published by A. Kahan; Warsaw, 1924; Yiddish.

G. ha-A.   28.

Geulath ha-Aretz, by M. Ashkenazi; Warsaw, 1904; Hebrew.

G. I.   29.

Gevurath Israel, published by A. Kahan; Warsaw, 1924; Yiddish.

Ha-B.   30.

Ha-Beer, published by R. Friedling; Bilguray; 1932; Hebrew; periodical.

H. G.   31.

Hemdah Genuzah, published by J. H. Bigeleisen, Vienna, —; Hebrew.

H. H.   32.

Hithgadluth ha-Zaddikim, published by A. Kahan; Warsaw, 1928; Yiddish.

Hith. Z.   33.

Hithgadluth ha-Zaddikim, by S. G. Rosenthal; Warsaw, —; Hebrew.

H. v. H.   34.

ha-Hasiduth ve-ha-Hasidim, by S. A. Horodetzky; Berlin, 1923; Hebrew. See Dubnow, i, 308.

J. M. J.   35.

Jewish Morning Journal, a New York Yiddish Newspaper. Quotations are made in this Anthology from the Yiddish versions of Hasidic tales made by Joseph Margoshes.

K. E. 36.
Kedushath Eliezer, published by A. Kahan; Warsaw, 1930; Yiddish.

K. L. M. 37.
Kitzur Likkutei Maharan, by Rabbi Nachman Bratzlaver; Wilna, —; Hebrew. Published originally by Rabbi Nathan of Nemirov, Mohilev, 1811.

K. M. 38.
Kotzker Maasiyoth, by E. Bergman; Warsaw, 1924; Yiddish.

K. S. T. 39.
Kether Shem Tov, by Aaron of Apt (Opatov); Slavuta, —; Hebrew. This volume makes use of material from the Besht, the Pulnoer, and others, as well as from the *Likkutei Amarim* and the *Yekarim.* Other editions appeared in Zolkiev, 1784 and 1798; Koretz, 1797; Lemberg, 1849, 1858 and 1865.

L. E. H. 40.
Likkutei Etzoth ha-Shalem, by Rabbi Nachman Bratzlaver; Warsaw, 1913; Hebrew. For further information, see note 27 of Introduction.

L. H. F. 41.
Lustiger Hauz Freind, by I. Izbitz; St. Louis, 1919; Yiddish.

L. I. B. 42.
Levi Isaac Berditzever, by J. Zevi; Lodz, 1929; Yiddish.

L. S. 43.
Lev Sameach, published by S. Freund; Prezemysl, 1925; Yiddish.

M. D. 44.
Midor Dor, by M. Lipson; Tel Aviv, 1929; Hebrew.

M. E. H. 45.
Meir Einei ha-Golah, by Abram Alter; i, Piotrkov, 1928; Warsaw, 1931; Hebrew.

M. G. 46.
Meoroth ha-Gedolim, published by A. Zeilingold, Bilguray, —; Hebrew.

M. Ged. 47.
Meoroth ha-Gedolim, published by A. Zeilingold; Warsaw, 1927; Yiddish.

M. Hat. 48.

Menorah ha-Tehorah, by J. A. Frankel; Prezemysl, 1911; Hebrew.

M. H. H. 49.

Maasiyoth ha-Gedolim Hadash, by M. Z. Sladovnik; Warsaw, 1925; Hebrew.

Mif. H. 50.

Mifaloth ha-Zaddikim, published by B. Munk; Warsaw, —; Hebrew.

M. M. 51.

Maasiyoth me-ha-Gedolim, by A. N. Halevi; Warsaw, 1924; Hebrew.

M. N. 52.

Maasiyoth Noraim, by M. A. Bergman; Piotrkov, 1914; Yiddish.

M. P. 53.

Midrash Pinchas, by Pinchas of Koretz; Warsaw, 1876; Hebrew; 60 pages. The redactor says that he chanced to secure a part of the Holy Writ of the Koretzer which his Disciples had written down, and he determined to publish these as well as the words of his Disciple, Rabbi Raphael of Bershid (the Bershider). See also the *Ner Yisrael,* commentaries on passages from Hai Gaon and Joseph Gikatilla, included with a collection of the sayings of the Koretzer, Zitomir, 1846(?) Some of these are in Yiddish.

M. P. S. 54.

Midrash Pinchas Sheni, by Pinchas of Koretz; Warsaw, 1899; Hebrew.

M. R. T. 55.

Midrash Ribesh Tov, by L. Abraham; Kecskemet, 1927; Hebrew.

M. S. Hag. 56.

Mazkereth Shem ha-Gedolim, by M. S. Kleinman; Piotrkov, 1908; Hebrew.

M. T. 57.

Mevasher Tov, by Y. A. Kamelhar; Rzeszov, 1931; Hebrew.

N. Besht 58.

Niflaoth Besht, published by A. Kahan; Warsaw, 1924; Yiddish.

N. B. L. 59.
Niflaoth Beth Levi, published by A. J. Kleiman; Piotrkov, 1911;
Yiddish.

N. E. 60.
Niflaoth Elimelech, published by A. J. Kleiman; Piotrkov, 1910;
Yiddish.

N. G. 61.
Niflaoth Gedoloth, published by A. Zeilingold; Bilguray, 1911;
Yiddish.

N. H. 62.
Niflaoth ha-Yehudi, published by A. J. Kleiman; Warsaw, 1925;
Yiddish.

N. H. K. 63.
Niflaoth ha-Maggid Koznitz, published by A. J. Kleiman;
Piotrkov, 1911; Yiddish.

N. H. L. 64.
Niflaoth ha-Hozeh Lublin, published by A. J. Kleiman; Piotrkov, 1911; Yiddish.

N. Ha-G. 65.
Niflaoth ha-Geonim, published by A. Kahan; Warsaw, 1924;
Yiddish.

N. Ha-S. 66.
Niflaoth ha-Shem, published by A. Kahan; Warsaw, 1924;
Yiddish.

N. Ha-Zad. 67.
Niflaoth ha-Zaddikim, published by A. J. Kleiman; Piotrkov,
1911; Hebrew.

Nif. Ha-Z. 68.
Niflaoth ha-Zaddikim, published by A. Kahan; Warsaw, 1927;
Yiddish.

N. I. 69.
Niflaoth Israel, published by A. J. Kleiman; Warsaw, 1930;
Yiddish.

Nif. Yeh. 70.
Niflaoth ha-Yehudi, by J. K. K. Rokotz; Warsaw, 1908;
Hebrew.

N. K. L. 71.
Niflaoth Kedushath Levi, published by A. Zeilingold; Bilguray, 1911; Yiddish.

Noam E. 72.
Noam Elimelech, by the Lizensker; Warsaw, 1881 (?); 176 pages. Dubnow, i, 287; originally published at Lemberg, 1788; Zolkiev, and elsewhere.

Nof. Tz. 73.
Nofeth Tzufim, by Pinchas of Koretz; Warsaw, 1929; Hebrew.

N. R. B. 74.
Niflaoth Rabbi Bunam, published by A. J. Kleiman; Warsaw, 1926; Yiddish.

N. T. S. 75.
Niflaoth Tifereth Shelomoh, published by A. Kahan; Warsaw, 1928; Yiddish.

O. E. 76.
Ohel Elimelech, by A. S. B. Michelson; Prezemysl, 1910; Hebrew.

O. H. 77.
Or ha-Meir, published by R. Margulies; Lemberg, 1926; Hebrew. A small pamphlet on the Premislaner.

Ohel N. 78.
Ohel Naftali, by A. S. B. Michelson; Warsaw, 1911; Hebrew.

O. I. 79.
Ohel Isaac, by M. Walden, Piotrkov, 1914; Hebrew.

O. I. H. 80.
Otzroth Idisher Humor, by I. Ashkenazy; New York (?); 1929; Yiddish.

O. N. 81.
Ohel Naftali, published by Zeidman and Ausnit; Lemberg, 1912; Yiddish.

O. O. 82.
Or Olam, published by A. Kahan; Warsaw, 1928; Yiddish.

O. S. 83.
Ohel Shelomoh, by I. M. Rabinowitz; Piotrkov, 1924; Hebrew.

O. Y. 84.
Or Yesharim, by M. S. Kleinman; Piotrkov, 1924; Hebrew.

O. Z. 85.

Or Zaddikim, by Hersenhorn and Strassberg; Lublin, 1927; Yiddish.

P. I. 86.

Peer Israel, published by S. Freund; Prezemysl; 1925; Yiddish.

P. v. K. 87.

Peer ve-Khavod, by B. Ehrman; Muncats, 1912; Hebrew.

R. T. 88.

Ramathaim Tzofim, by S. Shinaver; Warsaw (?); Hebrew. This is a commentary on the Midrash: *Tanna debei Eliyahu,* on the basis of the teachings of his Masters: Jacob Isaac of Lublin, Yehudi of Parsischa; Solomon Yehudah Loeb of Lenczno, Rabbi Isaac of Neskhis, R. Menachem Mendel of Kotzk and Rabbi Isaac Meir of Ger, composed by the Zaddik Rabbi Samuel of Shinav and Nashelsk; Warsaw, 1881.

S. B. 89.

Sippurei Besht, published by A. J. Kleiman; Piotrkov, 1911; Yiddish.

S. B. R. 90.

Sha'ar Bath Rabim, by C. Yedvobner; Bialystok, 1914; Hebrew.

S. Ch. 91.

Sichoth Hayyim, published by A. J. Kleiman; Warsaw, 1927; Yiddish.

S. H. 92.

Sippurei ha-Gedolim, by M. Z. Slodovnik; Warsaw, 1925; Yiddish.

Sef. Ham. 93.

Sefer ha-Middoth, by Rabbi Nachman Bratzlaver; Warsaw, 1912; Hebrew; see Introduction, p. lxxvii.

S. Hat. 94.

Shemen ha-Tov, by A. S. B. Michelson; Piotrkov, 1905; Hebrew.

S. H. H. 95.

Seder ha-Doroth he-Hadash, published by E. I. Stand; Lemberg, 1865; Hebrew.

S. ha-Has. 96.

Sefer ha-Hasiduth, by A. Kahana, Warsaw, 1922; Hebrew. See Dubnow, i, 306-7. Mentioned as Kahana, below.

S. ha-B. 97.
Shivchei ha-Besht, published by S. A. Horodetzky; Berlin, 1922;
see Introduction, p. lxix.

S. Hay. 98.
Sichoth Hayyim, by S. Z. Breitstein; Piotrkov, —; Hebrew.

S. I. 99.
Simchath Israel, by I. Berger; Piotrkov, 1910; Hebrew.

Sh. Z. 100.
Shivchei Zaddikim, by M. Tzitrin; Warsaw, —; Hebrew.

Sif. Z. 101.
Sifthei Zaddikim, by P. Dinovitzer; Bilguray, 1928; Hebrew;
see also editions of 1862; Josefov, 1894.

S. K. 102.
Sifthei Kodesh, by J. K. K. Rokotz; Lodz, 1929; Hebrew.

S. M. 103.
Shivchei Meir, published by M. Babad; Lemberg, —; Yiddish.

S. N. 104.
Shivchei Naftali, by Hersenhorn and Strassberg; Lublin, 1927;
Yiddish.

S. S. K. 105.
Siach Sarfei Kodesh, by J. K. K. Rokotz; Lodz, 1929; Hebrew;
5 volumes.

S. Zad. 106.
Sifthei Zaddikim, published by Armkraut and Freund; Prezemysl, 1920; Yiddish.

T. H. 107.
Tifereth ha-Zaddikim, published by A. Kahan; Warsaw, 1924;
Yiddish.

T. H. A. 108.
Tifereth ha-Achim, published by A. Kahan; Warsaw, 1924;
Yiddish.

T. ha-Has. 109.
Toledoth ha-Hasiduth, by Simon Dubnow; Tel Aviv, 1930;
Hebrew. Translated into German, *Geschichte des Chassidismus,*
2 volumes, Berlin, 1931. Mentioned as Dubnow, below.

Tif. B. 110.
Tifereth Banim, by J. K. K. Rokotz; Warsaw, 1911; Hebrew.

Tif. Yeh. 111.
Tifereth ha-Yehudi, by J. K. K. Rokotz; Warsaw, 1911; Hebrew.

Tif. Z. 112.
Tifereth ha-Zaddikim, by S. G. Rosenthal; Piotrkov; 1928; Hebrew.

T. M. 113.
Tifereth Menachem, published by A. Kahan; Warsaw, 1924; Yiddish.

T. Mah. 114.
Tifereth Maharal, by J. Rosenberg; Warsaw, —; Yiddish. Narratives of Aryeh Loeb of Spola, assembled by Judah Rosenberg, Lodz, 1912.

T. M. M. 115.
Torath ha-Maggid Mezeritz we-Sichothav, by S. A. Horodetzky; Berlin, 1923; Hebrew. The material assembled is based upon excerpts from the older works *Maggid Devarav, Or Torah,* and the *Or ha-Emeth* (first published at Zitomir, in 1900, and concerning the authenticity of which there is much doubt). Dubnow, i, 309, 297, 296, and 288.

T. T. 116.
Tel Talpioth, by M. Nomberg; Warsaw, 1912; Hebrew.

Tz. H. 117.
Tzidkath ha-Zaddikim, published by A. Kahan; Warsaw, 1924; Yiddish.

V. S. 118.
Vayakhel Shelomoh, by S. Rapaport; Piotrkov, 1908; Hebrew.

Y. I. 119.
Yeshuath Israel, tales of Rabbi Israel of Rizin and Sadigura; Hersenhorn and Strassberg; Lublin, 1926; Yiddish.

Z. H. 120.
Zikhron ha-Zaddikim, published by A. Kahan; Warsaw, 1927; Yiddish.

Z. Z. 121.
Zikhron Zaddik, by S. E. Stamm; Wilna, 1908; Hebrew.

BIBLICAL VERSES

INDEX OF HASIDIC RABBIS

S = Son.   D = Disciple.   C = Contemporary.